Adapted Physical Education and Recreation

Claudine Sherrill
Texas Woman's University

Adapted Physical Education and Recreation

A Multidisciplinary Approach

Wm. C. Brown Company Publishers
Dubuque, Iowa

wcb

Consulting Editor

Aileene Lockhart
Texas Woman's University

Copyright © 1976 by Wm. C. Brown Company Publishers

Library of Congress Catalog Card Number: 75-29554

ISBN 0—697—07130—8

Printed in the United States of America

Dedicated to
my parents, Ivalene and Robert Sherrill
of Logansport, Indiana

Contents

Part 1

A Multidisciplinary Approach

Part 2

Diagnosis, Appraisal, and Prescriptive Teaching

Part 3

Adapted Physical Education for Special Populations

Foreword

Those who dare to teach and lead can never cease to learn! But learn and change each of us must if he is to continue to grow, progress, and remain current. However, time marches on more rapidly and surely than most of us care to admit. Therefore, to meet needs, satisfy interests, and challenge abilities of every individual each of us is dedicated to serve, teachers and leaders must march to the tune of today's drummer while listening for tomorrow's beat and keeping an eye on past, present, and future happenings.

Each of us must be weary and leary of old wine placed in new bottles— the tried and true couched in new and pseudoscientific terms that are difficult to understand. Confusion results when the obvious is clouded and the simple made complex. Oversimplified approaches that only stress *what* and *how* leave much to be desired; oversophisticated discussions of theory with little regard for sound practice and what goes on in the real world are hollow and inadequate. It is important to know and communicate *why* a particular method or specific technique is used in a given situation with a particular individual. This requires getting back to basics—fundamentals of the physical, biological, and behavioral sciences comprise the bedrock foundation in this process.

Theory and practice, the old and the new, research evidence and personal experience, the simple and the complex, the innovative and the traditional, the obvious and the subtle are all integral parts of understanding individuals as persons of worth and dignity and in meeting the specific needs of each one. This publication on *adapted and developmental physical education and recreation* tells it like it is and has it all—it is the most complete and current book written on this topic to date and is the Cadillac of publications in this area.

A great deal of lip service is continually given current concepts and present day trends such as noncategorical approaches, behavioral objectives, performance goals, mainstreaming, interdisciplinary cooperation, and multiagency teamwork. In this publication these concepts are not only talked about and presented; they are discussed in terms of practical suggestions, realistic approaches, and functional ways for implementation. Each activity and procedure is important and presented as part of a truly interdisciplinary approach for regular and special physical education, recreation, and related programs for those with various handicapping conditions. This publication blends theory and practice and presents the author's great and varied experience in the field. Claudine Sherrill's thorough treatment of all aspects of these programs enhances each reader's understanding of the field; vision and perspective are projected so that movement with students can be forward and onward.

Discussion and realistic presentations of similarities and differences among specific modalities accentuate the basic team concept. Relationships and interrelationships among different educational, therapeutic, recreational, habilitative, and rehabilitative approaches provide a basis for better service to individuals in school, community, and special programs. Ways to utilize fully the unique contributions of each specialization so as to reduce undesirable overlap further the inter-disciplinary/multiagency concept in action.

The title of this publication—*Adapted Physical Education and Recreation: A Multidisciplinary Approach*—reflects its comprehensive and current nature. In addition to being an excellent textbook for courses in physical education/adapted physical education, recreation/therapeutic recreation, and special education, it is a valuable resource for many other areas—education, occupational therapy, physical therapy, dance therapy, administration, and psychology. *Everyone* working in the field should have a copy as a ready resource for background information in all involved disciplines, practical suggestions in terms of methods and activities, and easily understood discussions of virtually all handicapping conditions. Many examples and per-

sonal anecdotes throughout the publication anchor discussions and give added meaning to written and pictorial materials.

Strengths of this publication—there are many—include: (1) documentation and visualization with many pictures and other graphic materials throughout each chapter that will be especially appealing to practitioners, students, parents, and volunteers—the book is an excellent resource for these groups; (2) Various charts and forms that present information in concise, easy to understand, practical, and functional ways; (3) selected references and key resources that are listed at the end of each chapter are beneficial and current; (4) practical suggestions for implementing programs and activities that are provided and discussed throughout the book; (5) emphasis on *why* as well as *what* and *how* of programming in these areas; (6) research bases for statements and points that are made along with identification of needed research and voids in many areas; (7) scientific foundations in various areas that are designed to assist in understanding *whys* and *wherefores* of these programs and activities; (8) strong emphasis on each person, regardless of type or severity of handicapping condition, as individual of worth, dignity, and value; (9) stress on exploratory approaches so that each individual can attain success in terms of his own interests, needs, and abilities; (10) treatment and discussion of controversial issues rather than ignoring them; (11) emphasis on developmental sequences and functional abilities rather than particular ages at which certain milestones are reached or when specific skills should be developed; (12) relationships between classroom activities and those in physical edcucation, recreation, and related programs—interrelationships among psychomotor, cognitive, and affective domains; (13) thorough and complete treatment of each individual area and specific topic as well as the entire field.

As motor development, physical proficiency, perceptual-motor function, movement, physical fitness, constructive use of leisure, and lifetime sports continue to receive more emphasis in total function and life-style of everyone, including persons with various handicapping conditions, this publication is like an oasis on a desert. Litigation and legislation require *education for all* to be more than words; zero-reject principles mandate schools to meet needs of *all* students regardless of type or severity of handicapping conditions. *Right to treatment* interpretations of laws have implications for physical education, recreation, and related activity areas. *Right to recreation* is implied or directly stipulated through equality of opportunity requirements for all activities in which the nonhandicapped participate. These have all been punctuated by requests of personnel in the field who continue to demand assistance in these areas.

This publication helps to meet these demands and needs. It will be helpful to the neophyte initiating or becoming involved in a program for the first time. It will be valuable to the veteran enriching or expanding an ongoing program. Regardless of an individual's background, experience, training, or field of specialization, there is much of value in these pages for him. Contents help teachers and leaders provide programs and activities based on the individuality of each participant as he strives for maximum degrees of independence.

Recognition of this type of individuality leads to programs, activities, and approaches based on *participant* abilities, interests, and needs. Ultimately we are helping each to succeed, progress, and achieve so that he can stand erect with head high and say—

Give me pride;
Give me substance;
Give me a life of my own
And I'll stop feeding off yours.

Julian Stein

Preface

The title *Adapted Physical Education and Recreation* reflects the belief that the major purpose of physical education instruction is to develop leisure time competencies for richer and fuller living. It is based on the concept that school physical education and community recreation personnel will work more closely together in future decades to insure carry-over values from class instruction into optimal use of community recreation facilities. The reality that persons with handicapping conditions have a greater abundance of leisure time than others further reinforces the need for multi-disciplinary approaches to the education of the whole child. While it is recognized that the role of the community recreation and the therapeutic recreation specialist encompasses art, music, drama, and numerous other widely diversified program areas, this book focuses upon *physical recreation* and *adapted and developmental education* leading to such recreation.

Part I is based upon an interdisciplinary concept of education which presupposes that the physical educator will be an integral part of a team which studies all aspects of a pupil's behavior in an effort to identify the multiple causes of failure and which utilizes the diagnostic findings of many disciplines in the modification of the learning environment to assure success. It essentially negates the traditional categories of *handicapped* and *normal* and reaffirms belief in the whole child and the broad spectrum of similarities and differences which comprise human behavior.

Unlike traditional textbooks, which accept the 1952 definition of adapted physical education as

> a diversified program. . . for students with disabilities who may not safely or successfully engage in unrestricted participation in the vigorous activities of the general physical education program,

this book proposes a new definition and explores innovative noncategorical approaches aimed toward optimal integration of all persons into mainstream physical education and recreation.

Adapted physical education is defined as *the science of identifying problems within the psychomotor domain and developing instruc-*

tional strategies for remediating these problems and preserving ego strength. That we all have handicaps and/or disabilities is accepted as is the premise that each human being desires involvement in play activities regardless of his level of skill and fitness.

The general physical education program is conceived as that part of the curriculum which teaches an understanding of the body (and the self) in motion *and at rest.* It is not limited to vigorous activities but includes instruction in relaxation, opportunities for creative expression, practice in social interaction, and guidance for finding and developing one's leisure self. The role of the adapted physical education specialist is to ascertain that *all* children and youth reap the benefits of a broad, comprehensive program; that play experiences are positive and ego-enforcing and that physical education activities are coordinated with the overall diagnosis, appraisal, and educational prescription for the student.

Unlike other textbooks, no attempt is made to differentiate between the many terms pertaining to physical education and recreation for persons with handicapping conditions. *Adapted, developmental, special, therapeutic, rehabilitative, and corrective* are all viewed as synonyms. It is believed that the particular term used in each community will reflect state legislation, preferences of local leaders, and to some extent tradition.

Likewise no attempt is made to differentiate between such adjectives as *handicapped, disabled, impaired, special, and exceptional.* Such terms all imply individual differences and are accorded equal valence and positive connotation. The descriptor *handicapped* is used with greater frequency than the others because of its widespread acceptance in legislative and grant writing circles.

Part II of this book offers a generic approach to the development of competencies in educational diagnosis, prescription, implementation, and evaluation. Content from the learning disabilities literature is interwoven with physical education.

Part III focuses upon the characteristics of special populations and summarizes research findings related to particular instructional techniques and adaptations. In-depth treatment of medical terminology is designed to help the educator understand the whole child and to function as an intelligent listener and synthesizer in multidisciplinary staffings. In keeping with the philosophy of mainstreaming, specific physical activities are not recommended for each different population. It is hoped that the information presented will enable the reader to implement the *normalization process* through individualized program planning and leisure counseling.

This book is performance-based. Specific behavioral objectives are listed for each chapter. Readings should be used in conjunction with many and varied practicum experiences, since the author believes strongly that no course in adapted physical education and recreation should be taught without opportunities for translating theory into practice.

After reading this book and becoming involved in its suggested practicum experiences, the reader should be able to perform the following tasks:

I. *Appraisal of Psychomotor Functioning* (*Diagnosis*)
This task includes the identification, analysis, and evaluation of conditions which impede the accomplishment of educationally relevant behaviors related to physical education.

    a. Input or sensory reception
    b. Central processing dysfunctions
    c. Maladaptive behavior
    d. Output, with emphasis upon psychomotor functions

II. *Design of Instructional Intervention* (*Prescription*)
The following subtasks are included in this category of functioning:

a. Identification of physical education activities in which learner can succeed
b. Arrangement of environmental conditions for optimal learning
c. Selection of teaching style
d. Determination of motivational devices
e. Determination of sequence in which activities should be presented, amount of time to be spent on each, and duration of intervals between instruction
f. Consideration of appropriate teacher response to success (reinforcement) and to failure (extinction)
g. Collaboration with physician and/or neurologist in adapting learning conditions to drug therapy, diet control, or other noneducational prescriptions which may affect motor learning and perceptual-motor performance.

III. *Program Implementation and Evaluation*
The following subtasks are included in this category of functioning:
a. The translation of classroom theory and research into action
b. Demonstration of ability to teach physical education activities to individuals and small groups of exceptional children
c. Demonstration of ability to integrate special children into the mainstream
d. Demonstration of ability to evaluate learner gains in achievement and/or socialization-normalization
e. Demonstration of continuous evaluation of program and the implementation of needed changes

IV. *Professional Leadership in School and Community*
The following subtasks are included in this category of functioning:
a. Demonstration of advocacy for rights of the handicapped and favorable legislation
b. Skill in cooperative staffings in the multidisciplinary setting
c. Understanding of roles of others on the multidisciplinary team
d. Active participation in organizations and parent-professional groups pertaining to the handicapped
e. Knowledge of human and documentary resources and skill in locating and disseminating new data

Acknowledgments

To the many individuals and agencies who shared in this adventure, a heartfelt thank you. Special recognition is extended to *Wynelle Delaney, DTR,* who co-authored the chapter on Dance Therapy and Adapted Dance; *Jane Spragens,* who contributed case studies on the orthopedically handicapped; *Barbara Ross* and *Marsha Ramey* who assisted with the chapter on mental retardation; *Charles Buell* who reviewed the chapter on blindness and visual impairment; *Miriam Kojis, RN,* who developed the section on thermal injuries; *Joel Rosentswieg,* who critiqued several chapters; *Julian Stein* who reviewed the entire manuscript and offered many valuable suggestions.

For their creative talent, patience, and perseverance, I am deeply indebted to *Mary Jane Cardenas* who provided the original line drawings of children; *C. David Mathis,* who did the medical illustrations; and *Rae Allen* who assumed responsibility for most of the photography. Grateful acknowledgment is given also to Marilyn Hinson, Fonda Johnstone, Tim Branaman, Paul Patterson, and George Ross for their excellent photographs.

Special appreciation to *Mary Ridgway* who took care of copyright clearances and a million other details, and to my several typists: Ricki Henry, Marsha Ramey, Ebb Pack, and Carole Normile. I wish to thank all of the graduate students who critiqued chapters and offered moral support, but especially Joanne Rowe, who shared my work; Lucy Ruda, who shared her laughter; and Kathy Hoffman, who shared her special children and kept the faith.

Without the cooperation of parents, teachers, and administrators from several school districts, much of this book would have been impossible. I am particularly grateful to Superintendent Edwin A. Killian, Muriel Hanson, Jacqueline Phillips, Richard Ness, and Richard Smith at the *Denton State School;* Jack Litty, Tim Branaman, and Marie Huie of the *Carrolton-Farmers Branch Public Schools in Texas;* and Norma Baker and Gail Cox of the *William Henry Burkhart Elementary School in Perry Township, Indianapolis.*

For their assistance in reviewing particular sections of the manuscript and/or supplying information and photographs, thank you to The Joseph P. Kennedy, Jr. Foundation; Robert Shelton, National Camps for Blind Children, Lincoln, Nebraska; Harold C. Algyer, American Diabetes Association; Marion Gardner, National Academy of Sciences in Washington, D. C.; Keith Roberts, The National Easter Seal Society for Crippled Children and Adults; Jules Saltman, American Lung Association; John Conwell, M.D., Dallas neurologist; Howard Hull, J. A. Preston Corportion; Adam Crane, Biofeedback Research Institute; William Hillman, Bureau of Education for the Handicapped; and Grace J. Warfield, the Council for Exceptional Children.

Acknowledgments can be complete only if they extend backward into time to those persons who sparked the initial enthusiasm in teaching and writing: to Dr. Harry A. Scott of Teachers College, Columbia University, who spoke of competency based teaching in the early 1950s; to Dr. Josephine Rathbone, also of Teachers College, who instilled in me a deep concern for the right of all persons to efficient and beautiful bodies, and to Dean Anne Schley Duggan, Texas Woman's University, who taught me to hear the different drummer and to keep step to the music—however measured or far away.

Claudine Sherrill

Part 1
A Multidisciplinary Approach

Behavioral Objectives

After studying Chapter 1 and becoming involved in its suggested practicum experiences, the reader should be able to:
1. Define adapted physical education and describe its role in the curriculum.
2. Discuss several variables which contribute to failure in physical education and recommend solutions.
3. Cite instructional innovations, technological advances, and other factors which are shaping modern adapted physical education.

After studying Chapter 2 and becoming involved in its suggested practicum experiences, the reader should be able to:
1. Discuss current implications of each of the following emphases important in the history of adapted physical education: medical gymnastics, corrective physical education, body mechanics and physical conditioning, physical rehabilitation, adapted physical education, developmental physical education, special physical education.
2. Name at least one pioneer associated with each of the terms just listed, discuss the changes each introduced, and the extent to which these ideas and practices still endure.
3. Summarize the history of special education and therapeutic recreation and discuss their relationship to physical education.
4. Demonstrate competence in use of ERIC, IRUC, and TRIC in gathering materials for a term paper.

After studying Chapter 3 and becoming involved in its suggested practicum experiences, the reader should be able to:

1. List several objectives of physical education, state the rationale for each, and rank them in order of priority in accordance with personal beliefs.

2. Describe four different instructional approaches in regular physical education with respect to the following variables: (a) learning environment; (b) starting and stopping routine; (c) presentation of new learning activities including type of formation, quantity of new material, and mode of communication; (d) execution or practice of activities; (e) role of the teacher; (f) role of the student; (g) type of evaluation; (h) characteristics of students.

3. Define the following terms: intramurals, extramurals, interscholastic and intercollegiate athletics, wheelchair athletics, and Special Olympics. Name one national or state association, excluding the AAHPER, which can serve as a source of further information for each.

4. Discuss readiness for competition in terms of child growth and development. State beliefs with respect to elementary school competition. Cite several authorities with whom you concur and several with whom you disagree.

5. State the similarities and differences between adapted physical education and therapeutic recreation.

After studying Chapter 4 and becoming involved in the suggested practicum experiences, the reader should be able to:

1. Describe the activities which may comprise a broad, comprehensive physical education program for different age groups.

2. Compare the percentages of time devoted to specific activities in the regular and adapted programs. Cite reasons for differences in the allocation of time.

3. Describe seven developmental stages in play. Cite the stage at which the trainable mentally retarded child is probably frozen and discuss the implications of program planning.

4. Summarize the similarities and differences between the handicapped and nonhandicapped with respect to the use of leisure time at different ages.

5. Describe the developmental stages in competition. Discuss implications for planning physical education activities for the trainable, the educable, and the nonretarded.

6. Discuss the pros and cons of eight instructional patterns in physical education.

7. Describe the instructional patterns in special education and the physical education practices associated with each.

Recommended Activities Are Listed At The End Of Each Chapter.

1 What Is Adapted Physical Education?

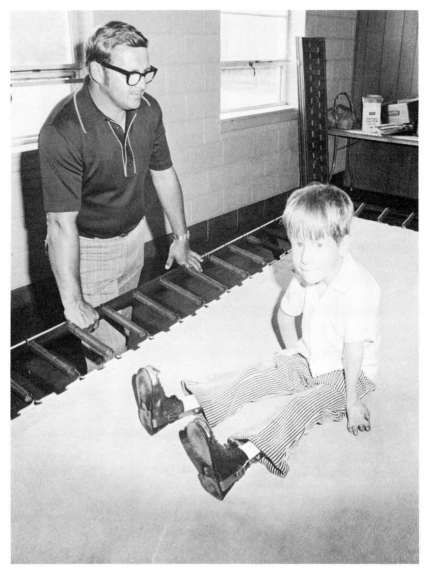

Figure 1.0. Boy with arthrogyposis on trampoline.

In physical education all children fail at one time or another: coming in last on the relay team, missing the basket or field goal which would have tied the game, choking and struggling in the swimming pool. How often must a child fail in order to be labeled clumsy, awkward, uncoordinated, a motor moron? How long does a label, once internalized, endure? What effect does it have on his growth and development? Most especially how does failure affect body image and self-concept?

Adapted physical education is concerned primarily with children who fail. It is the science of analyzing movement, identifying problems within the psychomotor domain, and developing instructional strategies for remediating problems and preserving ego strength. [1] The adapted physical educator attempts to design a learning environment which will insure success for children who normally fail. Many individuals believe that improved self-concept which results from a carefully planned progression of successful play activities is the greatest contribution which physical education can offer to the educational process. It is appropriate, therefore, for the teacher of adapted physical education to study failure, its causes, and prevention.

Many physical education settings are antithetical to learning. Such practices as choosing up sides, playing elimination games, and expecting all children to engage in the same activities contribute to failure. Consider the following incidents which occur frequently in classes comprised of normal children.

I

"What shall we play today?" asks the teacher. "Kickball" is the unanimous choice of the third grade class. Wishing to be democratic and to encourage the development of leadership as well as the ability to follow, Mr. A poses the expected question: "Who wants to be leader?" Nearly everyone's arm raises, and some children chime "I," "I," "I."

"Billy, you be the leader for team one. Jerry, you can be the leader for team two. Now

Figure 1.1. Kangaroo jump: an activity in which awkward children find success.

let's choose up sides quickly." One by one the children are chosen—first Billy's and Jerry's best friends, then their friend's best friends. The well-skilled children are always among the first to be chosen, and there is much laughter and enthusiasm. Clearly the needs of the majority of the class are being met.

Now only Jimmy and Darol are left. Skinny or obese, it doesn't really matter—they are different from the others, a little less coordinated, a little slower maturing. Does anyone remember that they were the last boys to be chosen yesterday and the day before that? Mr. A was an outstanding athlete in college and a varsity player on several teams. Never in his life has he been chosen last. How could he possibly understand what it feels like?

Jimmy and Darol stand there, waiting, hoping, trying to smile, acting like they don't

1. Psychomotor domain and similar terms used in this book all refer to an integrated perceptual-cognitive-motor approach.

care, wanting to cry, just wishing it was over with. Everyone staring—or do they even notice? "Oh, well," shrugs Jimmy, "this way I won't have to come up to bat."

II

Circle dodgeball—the children's favorite. Dodge, twist, jump! At all costs, avoid the ball. Try harder than last time. Won't help. The other kids always try to hit me first. They know I'm easy to put out. And so, I join the circle—eliminated again.

Jump rope—got to run in without the rope touching me. Got to concentrate. Got it. 1-2-3-4 I can jump until I miss. Leah and Amy and all my friends make it to 100. 6-7-8 Ooops, miss. And so I go to the end of the file again to wait my turn. 97-98-99-100. . . and on and on—I'm glad my friends are so good—they've tried to help me—but P.E. is just a time when I wait a lot for a turn that never lasts very long.

D-O-N-K-E-Y. Another elimination game. Part of the tradition of sports. Each time the kid in front of me makes a basket and I don't, I get a letter on me. I'm not very good. Usually I get eliminated first. If no one's watching, I can sneak around the fence and have a smoke.

III

Ann has made an A on every *written* test in physical education she's ever taken. When she hits a ball in tennis class and it fails, as usual, to go where she intended, she knows before the teacher ever tells her that her elbow was bent, the racket face was closed, or that she swung too soon. In fact, Ann knows a lot about tennis —on the verbal level. It's just that her body won't do what her mind says—it never has.

IV

This year Peter's parents sent a note from their physician to have their son excused from physical education. They are sensitive persons, concerned about their action, worried about the values he'll never derive from guided motor activities—but every day for six years Peter's physical education has started the same way—two laps around the football field. Peter is five feet tall, 160 pounds of rounded, squat-

ted body, undeniably obese. He can't run, and each day he dies a little when subjected to the ridicule of his classmates. In the beginning his learning disability was his obesity. Now, more and more it is his attitude.

V

Mike tries—he really does—every muscle in his body reveals effort—he's tense, anxious, eager to please. In the agility race he hits his head on the beam he is trying to duck under, trips over the rope he must jump, twists his neck as he tries the required forward roll, and then gamely runs toward the finishing line. The other teams finished seconds ago. The cheering is over. It's quiet. The team tolerates him, hoping they won't have him next time. What is his learning disability—space perception, poor coordination, just plain awkwardness?

And what does the physical educator say? "Good! All the teams ready? Let's do that relay again! Mike, you exchange places with John." John was on the winning team, and it is only fair to Mike's team to give them a fair chance to win. Does the teacher hear the barely audible slurs? The "Ugh, do we have to have him?" as Mike reluctantly joins the new group.

The teams are evened up now! Ready—set—go! Kids love relays. They are an integral part of physical education, and everyone must participate—abide by the rules—run the same distance.

These anecdotes describe normal children. They were abstracted from statements of university students asked to recall the physical education experiences from childhood which most influenced their adult attitudes. In contrast, let's focus upon good physical education in the elementary schools.

A Model Physical Education Program

Children are taught physical education in classes not greater than 25-30 pupils in size. Individual needs and interests are identified, and instruction is adapted accordingly. Even within a homogenous class, pupils may be divided into smaller ability groupings on the basis of fitness or motor skill. Their teacher views teaching, guidance, and counseling as inseparable processes, and each child is helped to develop interest and skill in activities in which he can experience success. Dance and such individual sports as bowling, tennis, and golf are introduced early in the elementary grades to meet the needs of children who shy away from team activities. Warm-up exercises are individualized. Each child, for instance, aspires to a different number of bent knee sit-ups depending upon his abdominal strength. Children with low strength execute their sit-ups with hands on their thighs while the more athletically inclined undertake the traditional sit-up with hands clasped behind the neck. In learning racket games, the awkward children use shorter rackets while the coordinated begin with rackets of regulation length.

Children are not expected to conform to the regulation rules of such games as volleyball and softball. They were never meant for children nor for uncoordinated adults. In classes based upon the principle of success, all pupils are not required to stand behind the baseline when they serve a volleyball. Each stands at a point on the court where he knows he can get the ball over. The well-coordinated children accept the regulation rule of hitting the ball one time while the less athletic may volley it multiple times. In softball, innings are played by time rather than by three outs, thereby deemphasizing the pressures inherent in striking out and assuring equal turns at bat and optimal skill development. The well-skilled athlete can learn and practice regulation rules in after school athletic programs or in league play. The instructional period is a time when games are modified in accordance with individual differences. Each child is accepted for what he is—awkward, uncoordinated, obese, skinny, or gifted. There is no doubt in his mind which is more important to

Figure 1.2. Preschooler experiments with racquet sports.

his teacher—he or the game, the subject matter or the child.

But these are the fortunate children! When learning is based upon the concept of individual differences, children seldom fail. No matter how sound are the educational principles of the teacher, how strong his integrity, and how persevering his nature, the physical educator in the 1970's seldom finds himself in an ideal situation.

Problems Confronting the Physical Educator

Let us analyze some of the problems which confront us today and make failure almost inevitable for some students. Some administrators consider physical education of less importance than other academic subjects. The hierarchy of values inherited from the Greeks that some human activities by their nature are intellectually and spiritually more valuable than others still persists. Vestiges of Puritan thought linger to make education for play seem less significant than training for work.

Evaluative practices are good indicators of the hierarchy of values which dominate a school system. Should letter grades be given in physical education? Or should we use pass or fail? If letter grades are awarded, should these be figured in the overall grade average? Should a low grade in physical education keep a child off the honor roll? Should failure to complete the four required semesters of physical education in college prevent the senior from graduating?

Conscious or unconscious subscription to a hierarchy of values which recognizes some subjects as intrinsically more valuable than others dictates administrative practices unfavorable to physical education. Some of these practices follow.

1. Scheduling a child into all of his *academic* subjects first and then assigning him to physical education in whatever period remains free. It is not uncommon in some schools for teachers to have children from several grade levels at one time on the playground. The less homogeneous the group the more difficult it is, of course, to adapt activities to individual needs.

2. Allowing physical education classes to have a greater number of students than other classes. The size of a class often determines whether a physical educator teaches children or games!

3. Punishing children by requiring them to stay in the classroom during physical education. Whoever heard of punishing a student by withholding the privilege of participating in a reading or arithmetic activity?

4. Expecting the physical educator to use his class period to set up chairs in the auditorium, clean up the lawn, perform other tasks unrelated to instructional objectives, or excusing a child so that he can make up a test in another academic subject.

5. Providing inadequate facilities and equipment. A community reveals its commitment to good instruction through the amount of space allocated to playfields and indoor instructional areas, the budgetary appropriations, and the sports equipment made available.

Other Variables Contributing to Failure

Children sometimes fail physical education because of established traditions, customs, and practices which are no longer sound. The lag between what is taught in teacher preparation institutions and the implementation of new ideas in public schools is unjustifiably long. Few institutions in our society are more conservative than schools. Stereotyped notions of physical education impede good teaching. For instance, many schools still cling to the concept of recess as a time of fun and games, which has as its main purpose *letting off steam.* Physical educators, ill-prepared to teach dance, aquatics, and individual sports, perpetuate this myth by offering only low organized games, team sports, and warm-up exercises.

Changes in attitudes toward physical education have been fostered to a great extent by the works of persons outside of our field:

Newell C. Kephart, in educational psychology, in *The Slow Learner in the Classroom,* Columbus: Charles E. Merrill, 1962.

Gerald Getman, an optometrist, in *How to Develop Your Child's Intelligence,* Minneapolis: By author, 1962.

Ray H. Barsch, a special educator, in *Enriching Perception and Cognition,* Volume 2, Seattle, Washington: Special Child Publications, 1968.

Marianne Frostig, a clinical psychologist, in *Movement Education,* Chicago: Follett Educational Corporation, 1970. Also in the Move-Grow-Learn Card File, 1969.

Special educators are often more convinced of the values of physical education than are the the specialists themselves who are too busy responding to the pressures of interscholastic basketball and pee wee football to reappraise their work and reassign priorities. The impetus for Special Olympics and the inclusion of retarded children in play activities did not emanate from physical education circles, but rather from The Joseph P. Kennedy, Jr. Foundation, federal and state grants, and community agencies.

The practice of requiring all physical educators to administer standardized fitness or skill tests also leads to failure. No student should be subjected to a test when both he and the teacher can predict subaverage performance beforehand. The fetish to have scores recorded for each child, even when statistical treatment of such data strengthens the rationale for additional staff and increased budget, is not justifiable in terms of the influence of failure on self-esteem. Nor is the administration of a battery of diagnostic tests desirable when the child fails more often than he succeeds. Testing, like other aspects of physical education, must be individualized!

The domination of public school physical education by team sports and the compulsion to give all children opportunities to compete are other reasons for failure. Masculinity is often equated with successful sports participation, and few little boys in our culture admit to not liking team sports. Most coaches are superb teachers. What other faculty member must demonstrate the results of his teaching each Friday night before hundreds of spectators? The pressure to coach is not being criticized here but rather the lack of concern for, or perhaps the feeling of futility with respect to the many clumsy, uncoordinated

children who could be given alternative physical activities in which they might succeed. Why must all children be subjected to football, basketball, and volleyball and so few be introduced to aquatics, dance, camping, and the individual sports? The following poem speaks eloquently for the recognition of individual differences and the provision of well rounded programs of physical education.

I Knew This Kid

I knew this skinny little kid
   Who never wanted to play tackle football at all
But thought he'd better if he wanted
   His daddy to love him and to prove his courage
And things like that.
   I remember him holding his breath
And closing his eyes
   And throwing a block into a guy twice his size.
Proving he was brave enough to be loved, and crying softly
   Because his tailbone hurt
And his shoes were so big they made him stumble.
I knew this skinny little kid
   With sky-blue eyes and soft brown hair
Who liked cattails and pussy willows,
   Sumac huts and sassafras,
Who liked chestnuts, and pine cones and oily walnuts,
   Lurking foxes and rabbits munching lilies,
Secret caves and moss around the roots of oaks,
   Beavers and muskrats and gawking herons,
And I wonder what he would have been
   If someone had loved him for
Just following the fawns and building waterfalls,
   And watching the white rats have babies.
I wonder what he would have been
   If he hadn't played tackle football at all. [2]

Children may fail because of the expectations of adults. John Holt in one of his many books criticizing American education states:

Children fail because they are afraid, bored, and confused. They are afraid, above all else, of failing, of disappointing or displeasing the many anxious adults around them. . . . Even in the kindest and gentlest of schools, children are afraid, many of

2. James Kavanaugh, *Will You Be My Friend?* (Los Angeles: Nash Publishing Co., 1971), p. 3.

them a great deal of the time, some of them almost all the time. This is a hard fact of life to deal with. What can we do about it? [3]

What practices commonly employed in physical education provoke fear? Teacher-imposed objectives guarantee failure for some children while insuring success for others. Whenever instruction is so structured that all children must attempt the same motor task on the same day and progress at a uniform rate of speed, individual differences are disregarded. The common practice of demonstrating a new skill and then observing each student as he takes his turn creates excessive tension in youngsters who fear ridicule from their peers and criticism from their teacher.

Coping With Failure

Responses to failure are as varied as the individual differences which contributed to nonsuccess. Are our schools failure-oriented as so many critics suggest? Is physical education failure-oriented? How can we prevent failure?

Glasser believes that there are only two kinds of failure: failure to love and failure to achieve self-worth.[4] These two abilities are so closely related that it is artificial to separate them. To experience success the child must feel that *someone* cares about his performance. In the school context, love may be thought of as social responsibility—caring for others, wishing them success, helping them achieve. Physical education, perhaps more than any area of the curriculum, offers opportunities for experiencing social responsibility, i.e., the capacity for love.

No child who has ever run a relay can doubt that his teammates care. The fielder running to catch a fly ball knows that the other players care. Even in the simple dodging and chasing games of early childhood there are ample opportunities for recognition, particularly when a sensitive teacher insures that everyone has a chance to be *it*. Positive feelings achieved through play are believed to carry over into the

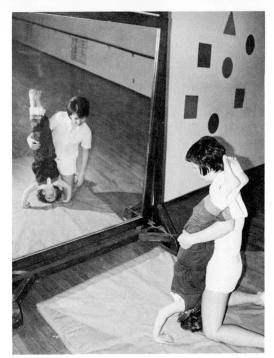

Figure 1.3. Seeing oneself in the mirror reinforces success.

classroom setting. Success breeds success. As long as the learning environment is structured so that each receives some praise and individual attention, physical education seems conducive to teaching social responsibility and developing self-esteem. The greater the child's feeling of worth, the better he can tolerate some of the rejection which may occur as he passes through later developmental stages—seeks new friends, runs for office, tries out for the team, and interviews for jobs.

It is imperative that educators structure the initial years of learning so that the child experiences more successes than failures. Glasser states in this regard:

A child who has functioned satisfactorily for five years is confident that he will continue to do

3. John Holt, *How Children Fail* (New York: Pitman Publishing Co., 1964), p. xiii, 39.
4. William Glasser, *Schools Without Failure* (New York: Harper & Row, 1969).

so. . . . this confidence may wane but will still remain effective for about five more years, regardless of how inadequate his school experience is. If, however, the child experiences failure in school during these five years (from ages five to ten), by the age of ten his confidence will be shattered, his motivation will be destroyed, and he will have begun to identify with failure. . . . He will abandon the pathways of love and self-worth and grope blindly toward what seems to him to be the only paths left open, those of delinquency and withdrawal. Although success in school is still possible, with each succeeding year it becomes more difficult and more unlikely.[5]

Good teaching implies adapting the curriculum to individual needs. In a sense *all good physical education is adapted physical education.* The regular classroom teacher engages in adapted physical education each time he plans special activities for those pupils who might not succeed in the undertakings of the class as a whole. The specialist in adapted physical education, however, differs from the regular teacher. The adapted physical educator is concerned primarily with children who fail. These children may be essentially *normal* or they may have been assigned such labels as mentally retarded, orthopedically handicapped, or emotionally disturbed. Not all children with labels belong in adapted physical education. Nor do all children without visible disabilities belong in regular physical education. Many mentally retarded children have proven to be excellent athletes and deserve opportunities to participate in regular physical education. An individual in leg braces may be able, without adaptations, to engage successfully in swimming, gymnastics, or archery. A pupil with a congenital amputation of the arm may be a star soccer player; some have excelled in baseball, basketball, and football!

Educational Accountability

The current emphasis on educational accountability is forcing educators to reevaluate the role of the school and the services it renders. Leon M. Lessinger, former U. S. Associate Commissioner of Education, says:

If one airplane in every four crashed between takeoff and landing, airline customers would be in a lynching mood; if one automobile in every four went out of control, Detroit would be closed down tomorrow. Yet our schools, which are more important than airplanes or automobiles, somehow fail one youngster in four. . . while doing 30 billion dollars of (bad) business annually. To get the results which parents, taxpayers and students are rightly demanding, we must learn the management of change: the efficiency of modern corporations can provide the key to making every kid a winner.[6]

Physical educators must be among the first to learn the management of change and all that it implies. Research indicates that the normal child will learn those things which he wishes to learn whether he receives classroom instruction or not. Certainly the majority of young children learn to run, jump, skip, and throw without the benefit of a physical education teacher. Given an environment conducive to movement exploration, they discover new ways to use space, time, force, and flow. Hopscotch, sandlot football, and the ever favorite baseball are learned from the peer group if perceptual-cognitive-motor problems do not interfere with mastery of the desired skills.

How much time do physical educators spend teaching and/or reviewing activities which children already know? If a student does not demonstrate the minimum level of achievement, does he receive carefully planned individualized instruction or is he subjected to continued group instruction? In the average public school setting today, on whom does the physical educator place his emphasis: the awkward, the average, or the gifted performer? With whom does he work, often with no remuneration, after school and on weekends?

5. William Glasser, *Schools Without Failure* (New York: Harper & Row, 1969), pp. 26-27.
6. Leon Lessinger, *Every Kid a Winner— Accountability in Education* (New York: Simon and Schuster, 1970), from book's cover.

Role of the Adapted Physical Educator

Adapted physical education, conceived as the diagnosis, evaluation, and remediation of perceptual-cognitive-motor problems, is gaining increasing recognition. In some communities the adapted physical education specialist is designated as a learning resource teacher who travels from school to school working closely with the educational diagnostician and/or other members of interdisciplinary teams in planning and implementing individualized instruction. In other instances, he is employed primarily to teach children in special education classes and to serve as a consultant to the teacher in the self-contained classroom. In the growing number of school systems embracing the concepts of diagnostic, clinical, or prescriptive teaching, the adapted physical educator is designing instructional strategies to ameliorate such problems as obesity, low fitness, and apraxia which interfere with success.

The specific role of each adapted physical education teacher depends upon the philosophy embraced by the school system in which he is employed and the degree to which it accepts the challenge of innovation. Change comes slowly in some cities. The newly employed adapted physical education teacher should not be unduly surprised if he finds himself assigned to a roomful of stall bars, pulleys, dumbbells, and plinths and expected to work primarily on posture correction and strength development.

In order to understand fully the present status of adapted physical education and to help shape the future, it is necessary to look at the past. Persons tend to cling tenaciously to the ideas and practices introduced to them during their period of formal professional preparation. A knowledge and appreciation of the nature and scope of adapted physical education in previous decades leads to improved communication among educators of varying ages.

Recommended Activities

1. Write an autobiography or make a tape recording, assessing your experiences with persons who are ill, disabled, or handicapped. How do you feel about working with them? Why?
2. Make a list of residential facilities for special populations within a two-hour driving distance. Visit several, following correct procedures for gaining admission. Write or make a tape recording of your observations concerning their physical education and recreation programs.
3. Select a handicapping condition that you know very little about. Find one or more persons with this condition, and volunteer to work with them in physical education activities for a set number of periods.

2 History: A Prophet with Its Face Turned Backward

Figure 2.0. Rope swing over horse reveals change from traditional use of apparatus.

It has been said that history is a prophet with its face turned backward. What implications does the past hold for the present and the future? How did the ideas of the great pioneers gain acceptance and contribute to the exciting future that now confronts us?

Origin in Swedish Gymnastics

Adapted physical education in the United States, like regular physical education, had its origins in Sweden and Germany. Per Henrik Ling —(1776-1839) is usually recognized as the *father of adapted physical education*. A teacher at the Central Institute of Gymnastics at Stockholm, Sweden, Ling developed the system of medical gymnastics which was the forerunner of modern day physical education for persons with handicapping conditions. Many physicians studied under Ling, and ambitious professionals began to produce books under the title of *Medical Gymnastics*. Illustrative of these are books published by the French physician Charles Londe in 1821 and by Anders Wide in London in 1899.

The Ling system of medical gymnastics was introduced into the United States before the Civil War by George H. Taylor, Medical Director of the Remedial Hygienic Institute of New York City. Physicians in the United States remained partial to the Ling system throughout the 1800s. Concurrent with the development of Swedish gymnastics was the widespread practice of the German system of gymnastics devised primarily by Jahn (1778-1852) and brought to America in 1825 by Dr. Charles Beck, teacher at the Round Hill School in Northampton, Massachusetts.

Compulsory Public School Physical Education

The early history of adapted physical education in the United States parallels the development of the public schools and the ac-ceptance of the concept of compulsory school attendance. Until the Civil War, public schools were practically nonexistent. The number of high schools in this country increased 500 percent from 1870 through 1890. The first state to require that physical education be taught in the public schools was California in 1866; however, the law did not endure, and Ohio, in 1892, is usually recognized as the first state to require physical education. Wisconsin followed in 1897 and North Dakota in 1899. Physical education, in every instance, was comprised primarily of that which we know today as gymnastics, calisthenics, and body mechanics.

Early Professional Preparation

The early leaders of American physical education were physicians. The first college programs and subsequently the public schools stressed exercise for the purpose of maintaining good health and preventing physical deformities. Particular emphasis was placed on correction of posture defects through exercise. Foremost among the early physician-physical educators were Edward Hitchcock of Amherst College, Dudley Allen Sargent of Harvard University, William G. Anderson of Yale University, Thomas D. Wood of Stanford and Columbia, Clark W. Hetherington of the University of Missouri, Fred E. Leonard of Oberlin College, Wilbur P. Bowen of Michigan State Normal School, James H. McCurdy of Springfield College, and George L. Meylan of Columbia. Virtually all physical education in the nineteenth century was medically oriented and corrective or adapted in nature.

Changes During the Nineteenth Century

Many of the sports which now comprise our physical education programs were not yet invented in the early nineteenth century. The few colleges and universities professed great seriousness of purpose, and athletics were not accepted as worthy educational experiences. Neither were women a part of the higher education scene until Oberlin College became coeducational in 1833. Gymnasia did not exist until the late 1850s, when the impending war between the states brought a vigorous revival of interest in physical education.

Sports which originated and/or were introduced in the United States during the nineteenth century include: fencing, 1814; baseball, 1839; intercollegiate track, around 1868; intercollegiate football, 1869; competitive swimming, 1875; tennis, 1881; basketball, 1891; golf, 1894; and volleyball, 1895. The Olympic Games were not revived until 1896, a lapse of over 1500 years since their origin in Greece. Women were not admitted to Olympic competition, however, until 1912.

The origin of sports during the nineteenth century and the subsequent enthusiasm of students for intercollegiate athletics offered new alternatives in the use of gymnasia and led, indirectly, to the fragmentation of physical education into regular and corrective or adapted activities. The new physical education was based upon a thorough medical examination by a physician who assumed responsibility for assigning each student either to *regular* physical education or to *corrective* physical education.

Trend Away from Medical Training for Physical Educators

Until the late 1920s, however, it was difficult to distinguish between leaders of regular and corrective physical education since most physical educators continued to earn medical degrees. Not until 1926 do statistics show a definite trend away from medical training for physical educators. This trend undoubtedly affected the professional preparation of men more than of women since the latter were not welcomed in the medical schools during the nineteenth century. The gradual transition from medically oriented physical training to sports centered physical education was completed in the 1920s when Columbia University, New York University, Stanford University, and the University of Pittsburg conferred the first doctoral degrees in physical education.

Corrective Physical Education

Although references to *corrective exercise* can be found in several sources,[1,2] it was not until 1928 that the term *corrective physical education* appeared in the title of a book. Two such books were published in 1928:

1. Stafford, George T. *Preventive and Corrective Physical Education.* New York: A. S. Barnes and Company, 1928.
2. Lowman, Charles; Colestock, Claire; and Cooper, Hazel. *Corrective Physical Education for Groups.* New York: A. S. Barnes and Company, 1928.

In 1934, Josephine Rathbone of Teachers College, Columbia University, published her classic textbook *Corrective Physical Education.* Rathbone, as well as Stafford, became interested in corrective physical education through involvement in physical therapy[3] in the Boston area. Stafford was in private practice in physical therapy in Boston from 1919 until 1923, when he accepted a position as Supervisor of Corrective Physical Education at the University of Illinois at Urbana, where he remained until his retirement. Rathbone, a student at Wellesley College, was influenced by Mary McMillan, the first president of the

1. Hartvig Nissen, *Practice of Massage and Corrective Exercise* (Philadelphia: F. A. Davis Company, 1916).
2. Jesse Feiring Williams, *The Organization and Administration of Physical Education* (New York: The Macmillan Co., 1922), p. 24.
3. Physical therapy was known as physiotherapy at that time.

American Physiotherapy Association (1921-1923) and by physician Frank B. Granger, at the Boston City Hospital, who was both her teacher and coworker. Granger[4] is recognized as *father* of physiotherapy. Rathbone taught at the Normal School in New Britain, Connecticut, and at Wellesley College before accepting a position at Teachers College, Columbia University, in the late 1920s. There she influenced more teachers in the areas of corrective physical education, massage, and relaxation than perhaps anyone else in this country.

Lowman, Colestock, and Cooper all resided in California at the time of the publication of their book. Lowman was founder and first chief of staff of Orthopedic Hospital in Los Angeles; later he became Medical Director of the School of Physical Therapy at the University of Southern California, a position he still holds. Colestock and Cooper were physical educators.

The term *corrective physical education* endured from the 1920s through the 1950s. Rathbone's textbook underwent a number of revisions. Ellen Kelly, then chairman of the department of the University of Oklahoma, wrote *Preventive and Corrective Physical Education*, published in 1950 and revised in 1958. These editions were coauthored with George Stafford. *Corrective Therapy for the Handicapped Child*, coauthored by Eleanor B. Stone and John W. Deyton, appeared in 1951.

Physical education, both regular and corrective, was strengthened by the increased demands for fitness required by the two world wars. The appalling number of rejections for military service in World War I resulted in widespread legislation requiring physical education in the public schools. In 1919, only eighteen states required physical education. The number increased to twenty-seven in 1921; thirty-two in 1923; and thirty-eight in 1935. Regular physical education utilized sports, dance, and aquatics as a means of developing the "whole child" while corrective or remedial physical education emphasized change or improvement in function or structure by means of selected exercises. Early professional preparation courses in *correctives* were concerned primarily with the evaluation of postures and fitness and the use of specific exercises to correct or ameliorate defects.

Emphasis Upon Body Mechanics

In the mid-1930s, the emphasis in corrective physical education changed from therapeutic, remedial, and postural exercises to body mechanics and physical conditioning. In 1934, Joel E. Goldthwait, a physician, pioneered in this movement with the publication *Body Mechanics in Health and Disease*. In 1936 Ivaclare Sprow Howland followed with *The Teaching of Body Mechanics in Elementary and Secondary Schools*. Numerous other books followed.

World War II sparked a renewal of interest in physical fitness and provided impetus for more physical education legislation so that by 1949 forty-four states, embracing more than 90 percent of the population of the United States, had enacted laws requiring public school physical education.

Rehabilitation and Corrective Therapy

The terms *reconditioning* and *rehabilitation* gained widespread acceptance as the United States Armed Forces began to provide convalescent services for its veterans. Dr. Howard Rusk, who inaugurated a Convalescent-Rehabilitation Program for the Army Air Force in 1943, pioneered in the development of physical rehabilitation programs first for veterans and later at Bellevue Hospital in New York. Corrective therapy, formally organized as a profession in 1946, grew out of

4. Ida May Hazenhyer, "A History of the American Physiotherapy Association," *The Physiotherapy Review* Vol. 16, No. 1 (January-February, 1946), p. 4.

the rehabilitation movement and provided employment in Veteran's Administration Hospitals for many service men with training in corrective physical education.

Sports for the Handicapped

The inevitable use of sports, dance, and aquatics in hospitals as part of the total rehabilitation of veterans led to a whole new concept of public school physical education for the handicapped. Legislative provisions for special education began to appear also in the 1940s. George T. Stafford's classic book *Sports for the Handicapped,* published in 1939 and again in 1947, attracted attention to the innovative use of sports and other recreational activities in the total rehabilitation of students at the University of Illinois, which even today is well known for its leadership in the education of persons with handicapping conditions.

Adapted Physical Education

Increased interest in the needs of all students with respect to physical education and recreation led to the appointment of a national committee in 1946 to consider alternative ways of serving the handicapped in the public schools. The committee, led by Arthur S. Daniels, of Indiana University, was appointed by the chairman of the Therapeutics Section of the American Association for Health, Physical Education, and Recreation, the logical body within our profession to assume such responsibility.

The efforts of this ad hoc committee resulted in the publication of a document entitled *Guiding Principles for Adapted Physical Education in Elementary and Secondary Schools and Colleges* which was approved by the Board of Directors of AAHPER and endorsed by the Joint Committee on Health Problems in Education of the American Medical Association and the National Education Association.

The following definition of adapted physical education was part of this document.

Adapted physical education is a diversified program of developmental activities, games, sports, and rhythms suited to the interests, capacities, and limitations of students with disabilities who may not safely or successfully engage in unrestricted participation in the vigorous activities of the general physical education program. [5]

This definition seems to emphasize *disabilities* rather than *individual differences.*

Textbooks Entitled Adapted Physical Education

In 1954, Arthur S. Daniels published the first textbook which incorporated the term *adapted physical education* into its title: *Adapted Physical Education: Principles and Practices of Physical Education for Exceptional Students.* Radically different from previous publications, it included chapters on body mechanics problems, amputations, rheumatic fever, cardiac conditions, cerebral palsy, epilepsy, poliomyelitis, visual and auditory handicaps, and other conditions requiring special services.

Numerous other authors followed his example. In 1960 Hollis Fait, of the University of Connecticut, published his first edition of *Adapted Physical Education.* H. Harrison Clarke, at the University of Oregon, and his son David Clarke, then at the University of California at Berkeley, published *Developmental and Adapted Physical Education* in 1963. This textbook emphasized the role of measurement and evaluation in adapted physical education and introduced the reader to the case study approach. In 1964 Gene Logan, then at Southwest Missouri State College, published *Adaptations of Muscular Activity* (second edition under the title *Adapted*

5. Committee on Adapted Physical Education, "Guiding Principles for Adapted Physical Education," *Journal of the National Association for Health, Physical Education, Recreation* Vol. 23, No. 4 (April, 1952), p. 15.

Physical Education in 1972), an innovative blend of kinesiology, exercise physiology, and body mechanics which focused in large part upon the remediation of postural problems. In 1965 Ellen Kelly's third edition of her 1950 textbook bore the title *Adapted and Corrective Physical Education.*

Only Josephine Rathbone, then retired and residing in Springfield, Massachusetts, remained steadfast in her retention of the term *Corrective Physical Education* as the title of her seventh edition (1965) of the classic textbook first published in 1934. In this book Miss Rathbone states:

"Correctives" is not a narrow field. The scope of the work is much greater than most people envision. It is not just a few exercises for strengthening specific muscles, or a method of training a person to stand in perfect balance. It includes consideration of the health problems of the weak child, to help him develop as normally as possible; it involves consideration of the athlete, to protect him from injury and strain, and bring him back to normal functioning again if he is hurt. It even includes helping the ill-formed and otherwise physically handicapped person to get as much joy out of living as possible. The scope of "correctives" involves consideration of the individual at different stages in development, and includes every known physiological and psychological aid to bring a person to a higher level of accomplishment.[6]

Textbooks by Other Titles

The explosion of knowledge in the succeeding decades resulted in the publication of several other textbooks with varying titles. Among these were the following:

1962—*The Science of Physical Education for Handicapped Children,* Harper and Brothers, written by Donald K. Mathews, physical educator at Ohio State University; Robert Kruse, Director of the School of Physical Therapy, Cleveland Clinic; and Virginia Shaw, physical educator at Washington State University.

1966—*A Practical Program of Remedial Physical Education,* by Grover Mueller, executive director of the American College of Sports Medicine and former director of the Division of Physical and Health Education of the Philadelphia Public Schools, and Josephine Christaldi, Supervisor of Remedial Physical Education of the Philadelphia Public Schools.

1966—*Special Physical Education,* by Hollis F. Fait, of the University of Connecticut at Storrs. Revised edition, 1972.

1969—*Physical Education for the Handicapped,* by Agnes Hooley, Bowling Green University in Ohio, and Ruth Wheeler, Ohio State University at Columbus. Second edition, 1976.

1969—*Principles and Methods of Adapted Physical Education,* by David Auxter of Slippery Rock State College in Pennsylvania, and Daniel Arnheim and Walter Crowe, both of California State College at Long Beach. Revised edition, 1973.

1972—*Games, Sports and Exercises for the Physically Handicapped,* by Ronald C. Adams, Director of Therapeutic Recreation and Adapted Physical Education at the Children's Rehabilitation Center, University of Virginia Hospital at Charlottesville; Alfred Daniel, physical therapist in the Cherry Hill Public Schools of New Jersey; and Lee Rullman, consultant in Therapeutic Recreation, Province of Ontario, Canada. Second edition, 1975.

1972—*Developmental Activities for Children in Special Education,* by Cynthia Hirst and Elaine Michaelis, both of Brigham Young University in Provo, Utah.

1973—*Individualized Physical Education for the Handicapped Child,* by Thomas M. Vodola of Ocean School District, Oakhurst, New Jersey.

6. Josephine Rathbone and Valerie V. Hunt, *Corrective Physical Education* 7th ed. (Philadelphia: W. B. Saunders, 1965), pp. 2-3.

1973—*Handbook of Adapted Physical Education Equipment and Its Use,* by Michael Sosne, of the Battle Creek Public Schools in Michigan.

1974—*Movement Experiences for the Mentally Retarded or Emotionally Disturbed Child,* by Joan Moran, of the Texas Woman's University and Leonard Kalakian of Mankato State College.

1974—*Physical Activities for Individuals with Handicapping Conditions,* by Dolores Geddes then of the AAHPER Staff in Washington, D.C.

Emphasis Upon Physical Fitness and Developmental Activities

Much of the progress in our field since World War II is rooted in the philosophy of physical fitness as a reflection of the strength of a democratic society. The emphasis in many programs, in spite of the titles of textbooks, is primarily upon developmental activities rather than upon adapted physical education.

The widely reported research findings of Kraus and Hirschland (1955) concerning the inferior performance of American children on the six-item Kraus-Weber Test of Minimum Muscular Fitness shocked the American public and subsequently resulted in pressure to identify physically underdeveloped pupils in the public schools and to give such children special attention. Responding to the almost universal concern of citizens, President Eisenhower in 1956 established the President's Council on Youth Fitness and a President's Citizens' Advisory Committee. A vast public relations program was launched. The various communication media were moderately successful in convincing Americans that high level fitness was a desirable outcome of physical education.

Under the leadership of Charles B. Wilkinson (Bud) as Kennedy's Special Consultant on Youth Fitness, the President's Council on Youth Fitness was reorganized in 1963 as the President's Council on Physical Fitness. It ex-

tended its activities into the areas of adult fitness, community recreation, and related fields and emphasized that its major concern was physical activity rather than fitness *per se.* Wilkinson served in this capacity from 1961-1964; Stan Musial was the President's Consultant on Physical Fitness from 1964-1967; Captain James A. Lovell, Jr., USN, the well known NASA astronaut, succeeded Musial in 1967.

In 1968 the Council was renamed the President's Council on Physical Fitness and Sports. The program now continues under the chairmanship of Captain Lovell.

The AAHPER Fitness Test

In 1957 a special committee of the Research Council of the American Association for Health, Physical Education, and Recreation, headed by Paul A. Hunsicker of the University of Michigan, developed the original AAHPER Youth Fitness Test. This was the first attempt by our profession to establish national norms for fitness. *The AAHPER Fitness Test Manual* was not published until 1965. The original test was comprised of seven items: (1) pull-ups for boys and flexed-arm hang for girls; (2) sit-ups; (3) shuttle-run; (4) standing long jump; (5) fifty yard dash; (6) softball throw for distance; and (7) the 600-yard run-walk.

In 1974 a revised edition of the *AAHPER Youth Fitness Test Manual* was made available. The three basic changes were (1) elimination of the softball throw for distance; (2) replacing of straight leg sit-up with the bent knee sit-up done for one minute; and (3) acceptance of optional runs for the 600-yard run-walk. These options are the mile or 9-minute run for ages 10-12 or the 1 1/2 mile or 12-minute run for ages 13 and older.

The AAHPER Unit on Programs for the Handicapped

Concern for the handicapped has increased steadily since 1965, when the Project on Recreation and Fitness for the Mentally Retarded was launched by the AAHPER with a grant from the Joseph P. Kennedy, Jr. Foundation. This project was the forerunner of the present Unit on Programs for the Handicapped which was established in 1968. Events of historical importance include:

March, 1965—Mrs. Eunice Shriver was keynote speaker at the Recreation Division Luncheon of the AAHPER Conference in Dallas, Texas. At this time she issued a formal challenge to our profession to serve the mentally retarded.

April, 1965—The Recreation Division commissioned the Task Force on Programs for the Mentally Retarded, now the Task Force on Programs for the Handicapped. The original members of this task force were Julian Stein, Chairman, Laura Mae Brown, Hollis Fait, Belle Mead Holm, John McGuinn, James A. Mello, Cecil Morgan, Wayne Nichols, Janet Pomeroy, Lawrence Rarick, Lola Sadlo, Thomas A. Stein, and George T. Wilson. Serving in ex-officio capacities were Robert Holland, Project Director; Jackson M. Anderson, AAHPER Staff; and Edwin J. Staley, Vice-President of Recreation Division. This task force, with some changes in membership, still meets regularly.

July, 1965—The Recreation Division submitted the proposal for the Project on Recreation for the Handicapped to the AAHPER Board of Directors. This was approved on July 1 and funded for a three year period. The Task Force on Programs for the Mentally Retarded was enpowered to act as the advisory committee for the Project. Robert L. Holland, on leave of absence from the Ohio State Department of Education, served as Director of the Project during its first year.

July, 1966—The present Unit Director, Dr. Julian Stein, assumed leadership for the project.

October, 1966—National Conference on Recreation and Fitness for the Mentally Retarded, Washington, D. C.

April, 1968—AAHPER established the Unit on Programs for the Handicapped at the national conference in St. Louis. The Unit was charged to expand the interests of the Project from the mentally retarded to all special populations and to continue its search for outside funds. At that time also the application for membership to AAHPER began to list Programs for the Handicapped as a special interest area. In the years which followed approximately 10 percent of the total AAHPER membership checked Programs for the Handicapped as one of their two or three interest areas on the membership application.

One of the greatest contributions of the Unit on Programs for the Handicapped has been its widespread dissemination of resource materials and its prompt service in answering letters requesting help in planning and conducting activities for the handicapped. In December, 1965, the first issue of *Challenge*, a newsletter on programming for the retarded, was published. Originally it was distributed free to anyone who requested it. Now a nominal subscription fee is charged for this bimonthly publication. Julian Stein and his program assistant, Wanda Burnette, have served as editors of *Challenge* since its inception. Since October, 1968, the *Journal of Health, Physical Education, Recreation* (JOHPER) has included in each issue a feature on the programs for the handicapped.

The Present—In the reorganization of AAHPER into several autonomous societies, the Unit on Programs for the Handicapped was not assigned to any of the new structures. Its continued existence was assured, at least temporarily, through federal funding in 1972 of an *Information and Research Utilization Center in Physical Education and Recreation for the Handicapped* (IRUC) with Dr. Stein as Director.

As a demonstration project, this center collects, analyzes, categorizes, and disseminates materials about adapted physical education, therapeutic recreation, and related programs to such resource centers as Clearinghouse on Exceptional Children in the Educational

Resources Information Center (ERIC) program; the national center in the Special Education Instructional Materials Center/ Regional Media Center, Area Learning Center (IM/RMC/ALC) Network; and selected colleges and universities. IRUC does not send materials directly to individuals as did the original AAHPER Unit on Programs for the Handicapped. It does, however, refer individuals to the resource centers in their own geographic area.

IRUC and the Unit on Programs for the Handicapped are now merged into one office in AAHPER headquarters which is located in the NEA Building. To insure the continuation of services, AAHPER members are urged when indicating affiliations for the Alliance to designate the *Association for Research, Administration, and Professional Councils* (formerly General Division) as one of their two choices. When this Association is selected, the substructure, *Therapeutic Council*, should be designated.

Multidisciplinary Emphasis

The education of special children is becoming increasingly multidisciplinary. Many schools have developed ARD (admission, referral, dismissal) committees which assume responsibility for deciding which children should be admitted to special education, how long they should receive special services, and when they should be dismissed and referred back to the regular program or to an alternate educational plan. These decisions are based upon a thorough study of the child by representatives of many different disciplines: medicine, special education, physical education, psychology, nutrition, social work, optometry, physical therapy, and vocational guidance and counseling. After each specialist has evaluated the pupil, the group meets together to listen to one another's reports, exchange ideas, and ultimately to arrive at an educational diagnosis and a comprehensive

plan for remediation. The terms *diagnostic teaching, prescriptive teaching,* and *educational therapy* have all evolved from the multidisciplinary exploration of children's needs. Whereas the terms *diagnosis* and *prescription* were once limited to medical circles, the modern physical educator is expected to write a diagnosis based upon observation and appraisal of educationally relevant behaviors as opposed to the medically oriented behaviors studied by the physician. Prescriptive teaching, within the psychomotor domain, is simply adapted physical education.

This practice represents a trend away from grouping all children together who are mentally retarded and giving them a special kind of physical education simply because they are retarded. The emphasis instead is upon the observation of behaviors, the diagnosis of problems, and the prescription of the type of physical education needed: individual, small group, or regular size. The prescription also includes the characteristics of the learning environment, instructional methodology, specific activities, and frequency and duration of class sessions. The child who is weak in several school subjects may have an educational prescription for each one. He will not, of course, need prescriptions for subjects in which achievement is average or above. The multidisciplinary approach assures that all persons concerned with the total education of the exceptional child are designing and implementing learning activities that complement each other.

In the 1970s the trend in special education has swung in pendulum fashion away from labels toward decategorization and mainstreaming. Several reports [7,8,9] funded by the Bureau of Education for the Handicapped

7. Louis Schwartz, Andrew Oseroff, Howard Drucker, and Rhea Schwartz, *Innovative Non-Categorical Interrelated Projects in the Education of the Handicapped* (Washington, D. C.: U.S. Office of Education, 1972).
8. Francis P. Connor, Joan R. Wald, and Michael J. Cohen, *Professional Preparation of Educators for Crippled*

describe innovative educational approaches in which pupils are no longer categorized, classified, or programmed according to specific physical, mental, emotional, or social conditions. The philosophy underlying this change is the belief that *all* children share essentially common desired behaviors. The time honored aspiration of individualizing instruction requires fundamentally *generic* competencies of observation, diagnosis, appraisal, remediation, and evaluation rather than specialized skills for working with the retarded, the crippled, the normal, and the gifted. New *generic* teacher preparation models have evolved as alternatives to separate certification programs for teachers of children in different disability categories.

Mainstreaming is the newly coined term for the practice of integrating handicapped children with their nonhandicapped peers, i.e., for getting them back into the mainstream of education. Texas was among the first states to pass legislation requiring the mainstreaming of all handicapped children. This legislation, known as *Plan A,* is under study by educators throughout the country. Implementation of the mainstreaming concept calls for fewer separate self-contained classrooms and greater flexibility of scheduling. Children with learning problems in one or more subjects travel back and forth between the regular classroom and the resource room where they receive individualized or small group instruction for varying amounts of time each day.

The individual who teaches physical education to exceptional children must keep abreast of developments in both special education and physical education. It is recommended that he become a member of both the American Alliance (formerly Association) for Health, Physical Education, and Recreation (AAHPER) and the Council for Exceptional Children (CEC). A brief history of special education provides background for understanding current practices in working with the handicapped.

Origin of Special Education

The use of the term *special education* in the United States probably dates not earlier than 1884. At that time persons who worked with handicapped children were employed by residential institutions since public education for *the crippled* did not begin until 1899.

First Residential Schools in the United States

Deaf

The first schools for the deaf were the American School for the Deaf in Hartford, Connecticut, and the New York School for the Deaf in White Plains, New York, founded in 1817 and 1818 respectively. Thomas Hopkins Gallaudet is credited with founding the school in Connecticut.

In 1856 the institution now known as Gallaudet College evolved through the efforts of philanthropist Amos Kendall. Initially named the Columbia Institution for the Instruction of the Deaf and Dumb and Blind, it limited its educational resources to the deaf and dumb in 1865. Edward Minier Gallaudet, the son of Thomas Hopkins Gallaudet, served as the institution's first president from 1864-1910. In 1894, the collegiate division was renamed Gallaudet College in honor of the founder of the first school for the deaf. The lower school division retained the name of Kendall School. Gallaudet College, located in Washington, D.C., is currently the only liberal arts college for the deaf in the world.

Blind

The first schools for the blind were founded between 1830 and 1833 in Boston, New York, and Philadelphia. Only one of the early

Children (New York: Teachers College, Columbia University Press, 1970).

9. AAHPER, *Guidelines for Professional Preparation Programs for Personnel Involved in Physical Education and Recreation for the Handicapped* (Washington, D. C.: AAHPER, 1973).

residential facilities, the Perkins Institution in Boston, provided physical education for its students. The director of Perkins Institution, Dr. Samuel Gridley Howe, a physician, is credited with establishing the first compulsory physical education program for the blind.

Mentally Retarded

The first institution for the mentally retarded in the United States was organized in Massachusetts in 1848. Because of the high incidence of deaths at birth and in early childhood among the severely retarded, admission to such institutions originally included a larger proportion of educable than trainable children. In most institutions today, the greater proportion of residents are profoundly and severely retarded.

Crippled

The earliest residential facilities for the crippled in the United States bore such names as Hospital of the New York Society for the Relief of the Ruptured and Crippled (1863), the Children's House of the Home for Incurables in Philadelphia (1877), and the Home of the Merciful Saviour for Crippled Children in Philadelphia (1882). The James Lawrence Kernan Hospital and Industrial School of Maryland for Crippled Children was established in Maryland in 1895.

In the twentieth century, the newly organized institutions were called schools or hospital-schools rather than hospitals. Illustrative of these are the Widener Memorial School for Crippled Children in Philadelphia (1906), the Massachusetts Hospital-School in Canton (1907), and the Van Vevren Browne Hospital School in Detroit (1907).

First Public Schools for the Handicapped

The first public school for crippled children in the United States opened in Chicago in 1900. Similar classes opened in New York in 1906, in Detroit and Cleveland in 1910, and in Philadelphia and Baltimore in 1913. Historically, the term *crippled* has been used by federal and state agencies to denote orthopedic handicaps. The trend toward providing public education for individuals with handicapping conditions other than orthopedic defects occurred much later. Most of the impetus for public schooling for the exceptional seems to have come after World War II.

Establishment of First Special Education Department

The proceedings of the annual conference of the National Education Association (NEA) in 1898 reveals that the educators of the deaf were the first to institute an official drive for a Department of Special Education within the NEA. In his closing address to this group, Dr. Alexander G. Bell made the following plea for special education:

. . . Now, all that I have said in relation to the deaf would be equally advantageous to the blind and to the feeble-minded. We have in the public-school system a large body of ordinary children in the same community. We have there children who cannot hear sufficiently well to profit by instruction in the public schools, and we have children who are undoubtedly backward in their mental development. Why should not these children form an annex to the public school system, receiving special instruction from special teachers, who shall be able to give instruction to little children who are either deaf, blind, or mentally deficient without sending them away from their homes or from the ordinary companions with whom they are associated. [10]

Primarily through the efforts of Dr. Bell and his associates a Department of Special Education was created within the NEA in 1902.

---

10. *National Education Association Proceedings* (37th Annual Meeting, Washington, D. C., July, 1898), pp. 1031-33.

Council for Exceptional Children

Current Status

The organization to which special educators belong which is comparable to the AAHPER is The Council for Exceptional Children, 1920 Association Drive, Reston, Virginia 22091. The official journal of CEC is *Exceptional Children*. Prior to 1958, this journal was published under the name of *Journal of Exceptional Children*.

Persons who can provide further information about the CEC are the Executive Director, William C. Geer, and the editor of *Exceptional Children*, Grace J. Warfield. Almost every college or university which confers a degree in special education has a student chapter which is an affiliate of the *SCEC*, the Student Council for Exceptional Children, which was founded in 1965. An amendment to the CEC bylaws in 1972 permits high school students to be associate members of the CEC. At present, the CEC has approximately 60,000 members distributed over more than 900 chapters throughout the United States. Student members representing over 300 college and university chapters comprise about one-fourth of the membership.

History

The history of the CEC can be traced back to 1922, when a small group of teachers and administrators in attendance at summer school joined their faculty members at Teachers College, Columbia University, in the formation of the International Council for the Education of Exceptional Children. The first president, Elizabeth E. Farrell, served four terms. The twelve founding members represented eight states, Canada, and India.

In 1941, the ICEC merged with the Department of Special Education of the NEA. The name of the organization was changed officially to The Council for Exceptional Children (CEC) in 1958.

Divisions of the CEC

Many members of CEC are also members of one or more of the eleven divisions within the parent organization. Each division has its own membership dues, publications, and convention programs. The following list of these divisions with the year that each was formed offers insight into the expanding educational services made available to exceptional children during the past two decades.

1953—*CASE* Council of Administrators of Special Education

1953—*TED* Teacher Education Division

1954—*DVH* Division for the Visually Handicapped, Partially Seeing and Blind

1958—*TAG* The Association for the Gifted

1958—*DOPHHH* Division on the Physically Handicapped, Homebound and Hospitalized

1962—*CCBD* Council for Children with Behavioral Disorders

1964—*CECMR* Division on Mental Retardation

1963—*DCCD* Division for Children with Communication Disorders

1968—*DCLD* Division for Children with Learning Disabilities

1973—*DEC* The Division for Early Childhood

1974—*CEDS* Council for Educational Diagnostic Services

Teacher Certification and State Legislation

Since the education of children is legally the responsibility of the state, the types of service rendered in the different states vary. State legislation, budgetary appropriations, and teacher certification all help to determine the quality of public school education. In 1931 only eleven states had certification requirements in one or more areas of special education. By 1954, such standards had been established by thirty-two states and the District of Columbia.

In few states, however, is a course in adapted physical education specified as a certification requirement for special education teachers. Nor is the practice of requiring physical education majors to enroll in a survey course on exceptional children widely implemented although it has been given much lip service.

Not until 1956 had all states established educational provisions for exceptional children through legislative action. The discrepancy between state, local, and actual practices is widely known. It is estimated that only 40 percent of the children who need special education services are receiving them at the present time.

Therapeutic Recreation Service

Paralleling the contributions of education, recreation has emerged during the twentieth century as a viable force in rehabilitation. In 1967 federal legislation making available funds for research and demonstration projects for the handicapped linked together the two separate disciplines of physical education and recreation. Now, more than ever before, it is imperative that the adapted physical educator understand the nature and scope of therapeutic recreation and the significant milestones in its evolution.

Therapeutic recreation is defined as a process which utilizes recreation services for purpositive intervention in some physical, emotional, and/or social behavior to bring about a desired change in that behavior and to promote the growth and development of the individual. The therapeutic recreation specialist is competent in the therapeutic use of such widely diversified program areas as music, dance, art, drama, horticulture, camping, and sports. He is skilled also in leisure counseling and assists persons in making the transition from institutional to community recreation.

National Therapeutic Recreation Society

Current Status

The organization to which therapeutic recreation specialists belong is the National Therapeutic Recreation Society (NTRS). This is a branch of the powerful National Recreation and Park Association (NRPA) which is located at 1601 North Kent Street, Arlington, Virginia 22209. Official publications of NTRS are the *Therapeutic Recreation Journal* which is published quarterly, and the *Therapeutic Recreation Annual,* previously called *Recreation in Treatment Centers.* Further information about NTRS can be obtained through the executive secretary, David C. Park, at the headquarters address.

History

The contributions of play to mental and physical health have been recognized since the time of ancient Greece. It was not until the twentieth century, however, that the possibilities of recreation as purposive intervention were explored. Early impetus for the profession evolved from two sources: (1) mental institutions, particularly state hospitals, and (2) Red Cross activities during and following World War I. In 1929, the Illinois State Hospital and Colony was one of the first residential facilities to create a Department of Recreation. Its early contributions are preserved in the classic report of Schlotter and Svendsen.[11] In the ensuing decades, nearly all residential facilities in the United States employed personnel to conduct recreational activities. The philosophy of recreation as therapy varied widely, however, with some institutions adhering to medically prescribed activities and others regarding play itself as therapeutic. The Red Cross and later (1931) the Veterans Administration (VA) were re-

11. Bertha E. Schlotter and Margaret Svendsen, *An Experiment in Recreation with the Mentally Retarded* (1932 Revised ed., 1951, 1956, 1959).

sponsible for the initiation and acceptance of recreation in military and veterans hospitals. The purpose of hospital recreation as a part of the VA's Physical Medicine and Rehabilitation Services in the 1960s was

to provide, as an integral phase of the total medical program, a comprehensive, well-balanced, and professionally executed range of recreation activities to meet the needs, interests, and capabilities of all patients. All activities offered by the recreation program require medical approval. [12]

From World War I until the middle 1950s, the term *hospital recreation* prevailed. During this time both the American Recreation Society (1948) and the American Association for Health, Physical Education, and Recreation (1952) created sections to serve persons in this new profession. Terminology changed from *hospital recreation* to *recreation therapy* in the 1950s and then to *therapeutic recreation* in the 1960s. New organizations which contributed to changes in terminology and professional philosophy were The National Association of Recreational Therapists, Inc. (NART) in 1953; the Council for the Advancement of Hospital Recreation, also in 1953; and finally the National Therapeutic Recreation Society (NTRS) in 1966. [13] This latter organization, which was formed by the merger of all existing groups, now has approximately 2000 members.

In the 1960s the populations receiving therapeutic recreation services expanded from the ill, disabled, and handicapped to include the aged, the very young, the criminal offender, and others in need of leisure counseling and special programming. Emphasis shifted also away from hospitals and institutions to community based programs designed to implement the *principle of normalization*. In essence, normalization became a process for making the patterns and conditions of everyday life as close as possible to the patterns and norms of the mainstream of society. The thera-

peutic recreation specialist thus became closely aligned with the social sciences as he began to identify more with community recreation.

Professional Literature

The maturation of therapeutic recreation as a profession is reflected in the many new publications which appeared in the 1970s. Among these are

1970—*Recreation and Leisure Service for the Disadvantaged*, edited by John A. Nesbitt, Paul D. Brown, and James F. Murphy.

1972—*Therapeutic Recreation: Its Theory, Philosophy, and Practice*, by Virginia Frye and Martha Peters.

1973—*Therapeutic Recreation Service: Principles and Practices*, by Richard Kraus.

1974—*Recreation and Special Populations*, edited by Thomas A. Stein and H. Douglas Sessoms.

1974—*Therapeutic Recreation Service: An Applied Behavioral Science Approach*, by Elliott Avedon.

1975—*Therapeutic Recreation: A Helping Profession*, by Gerald S. O'Morrow.

1975—*Therapeutic and Adapted Recreational Services*, by Jay Shivers and Hollis Fait.

In 1971, the Therapeutic Recreation Information Center (TRIC) was originated by Fred W. Martin. TRIC is a computer based information acquisition, storage, retrieval, and dissemination center similar to IRUC, discussed on page 17, and ERIC (Educational Resources Information Center). TRIC is designed to provide comprehensive annotated bibliographic reference materials on all aspects of

12. Special Services Pamphlet 6-3 (Veterans Administration, Recreation Services, Washington, D. C.: United States Government Printing Office, n.d.)

13. William A. Hillman, Jr., "Therapeutic Recreation as a Profession: A Status Report," *Therapeutic Recreation Annual* Vol. VII, (1970), pp. 1-7.

therapeutic recreation. Persons interested in this service should contact Fred W. Martin at the University of Oregon, Department of Recreation and Park Management and Project EXTEND-ED at Eugene, Oregon 97403.

Other Important Events in the History of the Handicapped

1912—Establishment of Children's Bureau in Washington, D. C. to promote the welfare of children and to prevent their exploitation in industry. The current address is Children's Bureau, Department of Health, Education and Welfare, Washington, D. C. 20025.

1917—Origin of the National Society for the Promotion of Occupational Therapy, the forerunner of the American Occupational Therapy Association (1921).

1919—National Society for Crippled Children and Adults founded. Easter Seals. Current address is 2023 W. Ogden Avenue, Chicago, Illinois 60612.

1920—The National Civilian Vocational Rehabilitation Act, a forerunner of the Social Security Act.

1921—Origin of forerunner of American Physical Therapy Association. Current address is 1156 15th Street, N. W., Washington, D. C. 20005.

1930—Historic White House Conference on Child Health and Protection. The Committee on the Physically and Mentally Handicapped wrote the often quoted Bill of Rights for Handicapped Children.

1935—Social Security Act passed.

1938—National Foundation for Infantile Paralysis founded by Franklin Delano Roosevelt; the memorable March of Dimes Campaigns. (See 1958 also.)

1939—Social Security Act, Title V, Part 2, as amended, authorized a program of services for every state for:

1. Locating all crippled children.
2. Providing skilled diagnostic services by qualified surgeons and physicians at state clinics located in permanent centers, or held periodically in other centers so as to be accessible to all parts of the state.
3. Maintaining a state register of all crippled children.
4. Selecting properly equipped hospitals, convalescent homes, and foster homes throughout the state and providing for the care of crippled children at such hospitals and homes.
5. Providing skilled medical, surgical, nursing, medical-social, and physical-therapy services for children in hospitals, convalescent homes, and foster homes.

1943—The Vocational Rehabilitation Act. The amended Vocational Rehabilitation Act (Public Law 113—78th Congress) provided federal aid to enable State Boards of Vocational Education and State Agencies for the Blind to furnish disabled persons, aged sixteen and over, with all services necessary to render them employable.

1944, 1952, also 1915-17. Major epidemics of poliomyelitis which left thousands of persons paralyzed. In 1952 alone, there were 57,628 cases of polio reported.

1946—Association for Physical and Mental Rehabilitation (APMR) established, the forerunner of American Corrective Therapy Association (ACTA).

1950—The National Association for Music Therapy, Inc. (NAMT) was formed. Current address is Box 610, Lawrence, Kansas 66044.

1950—The National Association for Retarded Citizens (NARC) founded. Current address is 2709 Avenue E, Arlington, Texas 76010.

1955—Salk vaccine recognized as 80-90 percent effective against paralytic polio.

1958—National Foundation for Infantile Paralysis became National Foundation and turned attention to birth defects and genetic counseling. Current address is 800 Second Avenue, New York, New York 10017.

1961—Kennedy appointed the first President's Panel on Mental Retardation.

1964—Association for Children with Learning Disabilities (ACLD) formed.

1965—Elementary and Secondary Education Act (ESEA) passed.
Included Titles I-V.

1965—Teens Aid the Retarded (TARS) originated under auspices of Dallas Association for Retarded Children.

1966—American Dance Therapy Association, Inc., (ADTA) founded in New York City.

1967—National Therapeutic Recreation Society (NTRS) created as a branch of the National Recreation and Park Association, 1601 North Kent St., Arlington, Virginia 22209.

1967—Bureau of Education for the Handicapped (BEH) created. This new bureau is the principal agency of the Office of Education which administers and carries out programs and projects related to Physical Education and Recreation for the Handicapped.

1967—ESEA amended under Public Law 90-170, Title V, Sec. 502, to support research and demonstration projects specifically in physical education and recreation for the handicapped. This was part of the Mental Retardation Amendments originally supported by Senator Edward Kennedy and signed by President Lyndon B. Johnson.

1968—AAHPER Unit on Programs for the Handicapped approved. This replaced Project on Recreation and Fitness for the Mentally Retarded.

1968—First Special Olympics held; AAHPER—Kennedy Foundation Special Fitness Awards were established.

1970—Title VI, Public Law 91-230, Education of the Handicapped Act, passed.

1970—Developmental Disabilities Services and Construction Act passed. Funds not available until the fiscal year of 1971.

1970—Series of institutes sponsored by BEH held on the Development of Guidelines for Professional Preparation Programs for Personnel involved in Physical Education and Recreation for the Handicapped. Report published in 1973.

1972—Information and Research Utilization Center (IRUC) in Physical Education and Recreation for the Handicapped funded by BEH and established in conjunction with AAHPER Unit on Programs for the Handicapped.

1972—National Center on Educational Media and Materials for the Handicapped (NCEMMH) established at the Ohio State University at Columbus. This center serves as a network coordinating office for thirteen *Area Learning Resource Centers* (ALRC) located strategically throughout the United States.

1972—AC/FMR (Accreditation Council for Facilities for the Mentally Retarded) issued standards, including recreation services, which all residential facilities must implement in order to receive accreditation. They are available through the Joint Commission on Accreditation of Hospitals (JCAH), 875 North Michigan Avenue, Chicago, Illinois 60611.

1973—Rehabilitation Amendments (PL 93-112) completely recodified the old Vocational Rehabilitation Act and placed emphasis upon expanding services to more severely handicapped clients. The *Nondiscrimination Clause* which specified that no qualified handicapped person shall be excluded from federally assisted programs or activities is in PL 93-112.

1973—Leisure Information Service Created. This center publishes a bi-weekly review of public and private assistance in the leisure field. For further information, contact Donald E. Hawkins, 729 Delaware Ave., S.W., Washington, D.C. 20024.

1973—National Advisory Committee on the Handicapped (NACH) was created. *Janet Wessel* of Michigan State University in East Lansing was the first physical educator to be appointed to NACH (1975).

1973—National Ad Hoc Committee on Physical Education and Recreation for the Handicapped formed by BEH Project Directors at Minneapolis (AAHPER) Conference.

1974—At the annual conference in Anaheim, California, the AAHPER was reorganized as the *American Alliance for Health, Physical Education, and Recreation* with seven independent associations. Three of these included programs for the handicapped: ARAPCS (Association for Research, Administration, Professional Councils and Societies); NASPE (National Association for Sport and Physical Education); and AALR (American Association for Leisure and Recreation).

1975—National Consortium on Physical Education and Recreation for the Handicapped (NCPERH) evolved from National Ad Hoc Committee. First president was Leon Johnson, University of Missouri.

1976—Public Law 94-142 enacted. Called the "Education for All Handicapped Children Act," it states specifically that *instruction in physical education* shall be provided for all handicapped children.

Recommended Activities

1. Look up the addresses of your local and state chapters of such organizations as:
   AAHPER—American Alliance for Health, Physical Education, and Recreation
   NTRS—National Therapeutic Recreation Society
   ADTA—American Dance Therapy Association
   CEC—Council for Exceptional Children
   NARC—National Association for Retarded Citizens
   ACLD—Association for Children with Learning Disabilities

2. Join two or more professional organizations and attend several meetings of the local chapter.

3. Make a calendar of the dates and geographical locations of state and national conventions of several professional organizations. Attend at least one state convention, and keep a list of the names of professional leaders whom you meet.

4. Go to the library and look up the professional journals of at least five national organizations which relate either to the handicapped or to adapted physical education.

3 Basic Concepts: The Framework for Innovation

Figure 3.0. Discus thrower on long leg braces typical of those worn by child with spina bifida.

Figure 3.1. Integration of handicapped and nonhandicapped carries over into social recreation (Julian Stein).

The integration of handicapped children into as many of the *mainstream* activities of the school as possible is a current trend. Physical education, art, and music are often the areas of the curriculum in which such integration occurs first. The success of integration depends, in large part, upon the quality of the regular physical education program and the extent to which it meets individual differences.

The recent emphasis upon educational accountability leads to a study of regular physical education: what it is and what it is not. A sound understanding of the potential of regular physical education and related programs contributes to the innovation of effective, comprehensive curricular models for the handicapped, the ill, and the disabled.

What Is Physical Education?

Physical education is an *academic subject* similar to reading, arithmetic, and social studies. It is *instructional* and should offer a planned sequence of *new* material each day. Participation should be *required* as it is in other subjects or make-ups should be scheduled. The teacher is responsible for lesson plans which include clear statements of behavioral objectives, learning activities, motivational techniques, and evaluation procedures. Physical condition is not play nor is it recess.

It encompasses any activity which teaches an understanding and appreciation of the human body and its capacity for movement. Older definitions stress *learning through the physical,* but inasmuch as this phrase tends to perpetuate the myth of mind, body, and soul as separate entities, it is rejected. Most learning in physical education does occur through using the body in one way or another, but the resulting changes in behavior are totally interrelated: cognitive-perceptual-psychomotor-affective. Table 1 presents the broad spectrum of behaviors for which the physical educator is responsible. Many of the behaviors listed in columns one and two develop in most children as a result of normal growth and maturation. Therefore, they often have not been listed among the objectives for physical education. With the current emphasis upon meeting the needs of special populations and the extension of public education to preschool age groups, it is important to broaden traditional definitions of physical education to encompass motor development, perceptual-motor integration, and the development of related language skills.

Objectives

In 1971, *PEPI,* the Physical Education Public Information Project, was launched by the AAHPER in an effort to clarify the objectives of a good physical education program for the American public. The media of television, radio, and press were used to bombard voters and taxpayers with five simply stated concepts which underlie physical education.

TABLE 1 *Spectrum of Behaviors for Which the Physical Educator Is Responsible*

Motor Development	Perceptual-Motor Integration and Language Development	Perceptual-Motor-Cognitive Integration	Application-Analysis-Synthesis-Evaluation
1. Gross movement patterns requisite to body control and safe locomotion	5. Body image, concept, cathexis	11. Wide variety of play interests	15. Sufficient weekly exercise for optimal health and fitness
2. Fine motor coordinations requisite to self-help skills and daily living activities	6. Fine motor coordinations requisite to academic and/or vocational success	12. Sufficient physical recreational skills, knowledges, and understandings for group acceptance and self-actualization	16. Knowledges and understandings requisite to enjoyment of sports, dance, and aquatics as a spectator, a consumer of television, radio, and other media, and as a participant in discussions
3. Gross motor patterns requisite to play activities	7. Personal attractiveness requisite to social acceptance	13. Relaxation and release of neuromuscular tensions	17. Knowledges and understandings requisite to optimal use of community recreation resources and to intelligent decision-making as a voter, citizen, consumer, and parent
4. Perceptual-motor skills related to motor learning and motor performance	8. Physical fitness	14. Motor skills, knowledges and understanding requisite to success in one or more physical activities with carry over values	
	9. Positive attitudes toward body, self, others, movement, play, and competition		
	10. Creativity in exploring use of time, space, and energy		

The Infant

The Preschool Child

The Elementary School Child

The Middle School Student

The Secondary School Pupil

1. A physically educated person is one who has knowledge and skill concerning his body and how it works.
2. Physical education is health insurance.
3. Physical education can contribute to academic achievement.
4. A sound physical education program contributes to development of a positive self-concept.
5. A sound physical education program helps an individual attain social skills. [1]

Instructional Approaches

The priorities assigned to specific objectives are reflected in instructional approaches. When physical education is taught through an *explanation-demonstration* approach, it is often defined as a well rounded program of sports, dance, and aquatics in middle and secondary school and as a program of games, dance, and self-testing activities in elementary school. When taught through a *guided discovery or exploration* approach, it is frequently defined as movement education. Both approaches have merit, and both types of programs, when properly conducted, meet the criteria of physical education as an academic subject.

The Explanation-Demonstration Approach

The explanation-demonstration approach presented in Table 2 is analogous to the command teaching style. For decades it has been recognized as an efficient way of teaching motor skills, particularly in large classes. Success is based upon *observing* a demonstration, *listening* to the explanation, and *emulating* the performance of the teacher. The student is essentially a passive recipient in the teaching-learning process.

In the 1970s, regular physical education appears to be moving toward increased freedom for the student. It is assumed that freedom will foster creativity, cognition, self-discipline, and a greater sense of responsibility for self-actualization.

Many children, however, are not ready to cope with freedom. Some, like the severely and profoundly mentally retarded, have limitations which prevent cognitive growth and require a stimulus-response type of teaching. Emotionally disturbed children may need structure in order to feel secure and to learn to relate to others. Structure is considered of prime importance in the education of a child with learning disabilities, brain damage, and/or neurological impairment.

The adapted physical educator, regardless of his preference of teaching style, must understand *structure* within the special education framework and be willing to manipulate the variables of the learning environment in order to provide the same degree of structure on the playground that is maintained in the classroom.

Implementation of the principle of structure demands that specific activities be initiated at exactly the same time each day. Nothing is left to chance. Learning activities follow a rigid sequential order, and the child is not permitted to discontinue his work until the task is completed correctly. In many special education classrooms, even space is structured with high partitioned carrels which block out distracting stimuli. Only when the child functions with success in most of his activities does the teacher gradually lessen the structure. The child is then presented with opportunities to make choices between two activities, then three, and so on until he can cope with total freedom. With certain kinds of children, this process may require years. Some persons require high degrees of structure all of their lives.

In a lighter vein, Angie Nall, Director of a remedial clinic in Beaumont, Texas, empha-

1. Fay Biles, "The Physical Education Public Information Project is Ready to Move," *JOHPER*, Vol. 42 (September 1971), pp. 53-55.

sizes the importance of structure for certain children in all aspects of living.

It is the dangling-in-the-air feeling that is so common to these children that makes them so hard to live with. They cannot make choices. Choices of too big a scope only frustrate them. Not knowing their limits frustrates them. This is the reason for Structured Living. This goes into all areas of a child's life: structured tasks, structured discipline, structured play. Just remember the house you live in with its plan, its wall which makes its limits, and its dependability. So structure your child's life. The results are worth the effort. [2]

Adapted physical education is *prescriptive education*. The prescription agreed upon by the diagnostic and evaluation team must be carried out. At the present time the highly structured environment for children with learning disorders is endorsed by such noted authorities as Laura Lehtinen, William M. Cruickshank, Hortense Barry, Helmer R. Myklebust, and Edith Fitzgerald.

The explanation-demonstration approach, as outlined in Table 2, is recommended especially for children with: (1) mental retardation, particularly at the lower levels and/or whenever the pupil has difficulty understanding and following verbal directions; (2) emotional disturbance; (3) hyperactivity; and (4) learning disorders. The explanation-demonstration approach is modified into a demonstration or follow the leader style for children who cannot understand verbal directions.

The Movement Exploration Approach

The movement exploration approach, outlined in Table 3, is recommended for most children, particularly at the elementary school level. It is more difficult to implement than the explanation-demonstration teaching style, possibly because many children, as well as adults, are so oriented to following directions that they lack sufficient readiness to cope with problem solving. The empathic teacher may move slow-

ly from the explanation-demonstration style to the movement exploration approach, gradually reducing structure and increasing freedom in accordance with the students' needs.

The movement exploration approach is analogous to guided discovery and problem solving styles in that the physical educator uses the processes of cognitive dissonance, inquiry, and discovery in helping the child to better understand himself, his body, and his capacity for movement. *Cognitive dissonance*, a term originally proposed by Festinger, [3] is evoked through the use of carefully planned questions which produce an irritation or disturbance in the students which can be resolved in the physical education setting only through such integrated cognitive-perceptive-psychomotor abilities as: (1) inquiring; (2) comparing; (3) drawing conclusions based on the comparison; (4) making decisions; (5) using different strategies in approaching a problem; (6) inventing; (7) discovering; and (8) reflecting. In movement exploration the teacher neither demonstrates nor gives answers; she perpetuates cognitive dissonance by asking one question after another. Cognitive dissonance is caused also by the teacher's failure to praise and/or to criticize; the child must determine for himself whether his cognitive-perceptual-psychomotor efforts are productive and self-actualizing; he must find his own movement style and establish his own standards of excellence. What is more frustrating in a school setting than not knowing what the teacher wants? This is cognitive dissonance. What is more unsettling than not knowing what oneself wants? This too is cognitive dissonance—mental dissatisfaction.

The process of inquiry or exploration begins with seeking answers to others' ques-

2. Angie Nall, "What is Structured?" (Pamphlet printed by Ontario Association for Children with Learning Disabilities, no date), p. 3.

3. Leon Festinger, *The Theory of Cognitive Dissonance* (Evanston, Illinois: Row, Peterson, 1957).

Table 2 *Explanation-Demonstration Style*

Command Approach		**Traditional Skills Approach**	

Learning Environment

Small space
Clearly defined boundaries
Floor spots
Circles and lines painted on floor
Equipment always set up in same location
External stimuli reduced
Activity stations partitioned off from one another
Cubicles available

Learning Environment

Space increased to normal play area
Clearly defined boundaries
No floor spots
Regulation sports markings painted on floor
Equipment in different locations
External stimuli increased
No partitions

Cubicles available

Starting and Stopping Routine

Goes to assigned floor spots and sits until teacher starts class	Goes to assigned space and/or piece of equipment and performs prescribed exercises until teacher starts class	
Assigned starting place is same all semester	Assigned space and/or equipment is rotated so student starts in different place every month or so	

Starting and Stopping Routine

Student finds own space and sits until teacher starts class	Student goes to space or equipment of her own choice and warms up
Warm-ups may be prescribed as a set routine for each piece of equipment	Warm-ups may be created or chosen freely by student

Participates in Warm-Ups

On assigned spot as directed	In locomotor activities as directed

Participates in Warm-Ups

In one space chosen by student	In locomotor activities in specified formations and directions	In locomotor activities using space any way she desires

Table 2 *Explanation-Demonstration Style—Continued*

Command Approach	Traditional Skills Approach
Presentation of New Learning Activities	*Presentation of New Learning Activities*
Teacher states behavioral objectives	Teacher states behavioral objectives
Teacher designates student leaders or teacher aides	Students choose own leaders
Teacher puts students into formation	Teacher puts students into formation
Teacher gives directions	Teacher gives directions
One task presented at a time	Several tasks presented at a time

<table>
<tr><td></td><td>Teacher prescribes sequences in which they must be practiced</td><td>Students free to choose sequence in which tasks are practiced</td></tr>
</table>

Command Approach	Traditional Skills Approach
In form of sentences accompanied by demonstrations involving as many students as possible	In form of sentences accompanied by demonstrations
Practice (Execution)	*Practice (Execution)*
Student	*Student*
Practices in formation prescribed by teacher	Chooses own space or formation for practice
Waits turn and follows set routine for going to end of file	Waits turn but chooses own space and own activity while waiting
Starts on signal	Chooses own time to start
Moves in unison with peers to verbal cues, drum, or music	Moves in own rhythm
Stops on signal	Chooses own time to stop
Rotates or changes activity	Rotates or changes activity
On signal	When she chooses
In same direction (CCW)	In same direction (CCW)
Teacher	*Teacher*
Moves about room	Moves about room
Offers individual praise	Offers individual praise
Identifies and corrects movement errors	Identifies and corrects movement errors
By sentences and references to mechanical principles	By questions which evoke answers from students

Table 3 *Movement Exploration Style*

Guided Discovery	Motor Creativity
Learning Environment	*Learning Environment*
Space varies Boundaries clearly defined, but space limitations change with each problem Imaginary floor spots Imaginary floor markings Equipment varies and location changes in accordance with problem No partitions Cubicles available	Determined by student within the limits imposed by school rules and regulations about use of space and equipment
Starting and Stopping Routine	*Starting and Stopping Routine*

Same as traditional skills approach except that
    Student assumes responsibility for own warm-ups
    Explores alternative ways of warming up
    Discovers best warm-ups for self
	Determined by student within the limits imposed by school rules and regulations about use of time, i.e., scheduling

Presentation of New Learning Activities	*Presentation of New Learning Activities*

Teacher states behavioral objectives
Teacher establishes structure
    In form of questions
    Designed to elicit
    Increased body ↗↘ Exploration of time,
    awareness   space, force, and flow in relation to movement
Teacher offers *no* demonstration
Teacher emphasizes that there is no one correct answer and reassures students that no one can fail
Teacher provides each student with ball, rope, or prop needed
Student assumes responsibility for his own props or equipment
	Student states behavioral objectives
	Student establishes own structure
	    In form of original questions and/or hypotheses
	    Designed to elicit perceptual-cognitive-motor exploration of the domains of
	        Artistic originality—self-expression
	        Scientific discovery—search for explanations
	        Comic inspiration—invention

Table 3 *Movement Exploration Style—Continued*

Guided Discovery	Motor Creativity
Execution (Practice)	*Execution (Practice)*
Student	*Student*

<table>
<tr><td>

Finds own space
Chooses own time to start
Moves in own rhythm
Creates answers in the form of movement
  responses
    Considers all movement alternatives
    Discovers movement patterns most
      efficient for her
  Chooses own time to stop
  Changes activity when teacher poses
    new question

</td><td>

Finds own space
Chooses own time to start
Moves in own rhythm

    Attempts to find movement responses to
      own questions through such productive-
      divergent processes as-
        flexible thinking
        original thinking
        elaborative thinking
        willingness to take risks
        preference for complexity
        curiosity

</td></tr>
</table>

Teacher	*Teacher*

<table>
<tr><td>

Moves about room
Offers words and phrases of acceptance
  (*No Praise and No Corrections*)
Poses additional questions to individual
  students
Helps with language development by acquainting
  student with names of their movement
  discoveries

</td><td>

Moves about room
Offers words and phrases of acceptance

Mostly observes

</td></tr>
</table>

tions and progresses toward formulating and investigating one's own problems and questions. The total process of movement exploration is analogous to research. Both can be defined as seeking answers to questions. Both can use the following procedures: (1) identification of a problem; (2) formulation of hypotheses; (3) collection and interpretation of data; (4) drawing of conclusions; (5) verification or rejection of hypotheses.

In the early stages of movement exploration the teacher may guide the children in testing only one hypothesis or possible answer to a question. Later he will help the students to identify and explore all of the possible answers. These answers will vary for each child in accordance with differences in body build, absence of limbs, restrictions of movement, levels of fitness and coordination, and presence of posture deviations.

Discovery is the end process of movement exploration. Mosston proposes that students may discover the following things:

1. Facts (in any subject matter)
2. Ideas, concepts
3. Relationships (similarities, differences)
4. Principles (governing rules)
5. Order or system
6. A particular physical activity—a movement
7. How?
8. Why?
9. Limits (the dimension of "how much," "how fast," etc.)
10. How to discover
11. Other elements: Can you suggest any? [4]

Discoveries may be shared verbally or nonverbally but all entail integrated cognitive-perceptual-psychomotor learning. The physical educator should encourage nonverbal answers in the form of various movements. Ultimately movement exploration should lead to creativity. Like intelligence, creativity is not a single entity. It can be broken down into many behaviors, some of which students may score high in and others they may seem to lack. Most authorities agree that creativity, both in thought and movement, is comprised of the behaviors defined in Table 4. Considerable controversy exists in educational circles as to whether or not creativity can be taught. Few physical educators have attempted to measure motor creativity and/or to study behavioral change with respect to creativity. Almost all agree, however, that creativity is a desirable outcome of education.

The movement exploration approach, outlined in Table 3, may be prescribed for children with: (1) poor coordination; (2) low fitness; (3) physical and/or orthopedic handicaps; and (4) health conditions as asthma, sickle cell anemia, and cardiac defects which impose limitations with respect to duration and intensity of exercise. This approach leads to the individualization of instruction and enables physical educators to help children assume responsibility for understanding their own needs and for adapting sports, dance, and aquatic activities to meet these needs. Through experiences in movement exploration, the physically handicapped person may discover new ways of using his body, wheelchair, prostheses, braces, and crutches undreamed of by a nonhandicapped instructor. Numerous textbooks concerning movement education discuss problem solving with balls, hoops, and wands, but the challenge to apply the movement exploration approach to the physically handicapped remains largely unmet.

Two other approaches are sometimes used in public school physical education programs: (1) the fitness approach and (2) the perceptual-motor training approach. These are not included in this chapter because individuals deficient in fitness and/or perceptual-motor skills should receive specific

4. Muska Mosston, *Teaching Physical Education—From Command to Discovery* (Columbus, Ohio: Charles E. Merrill Books, Inc., 1966), p. 145.

Table 4 *Pupil Behaviors in the Creative Process**

Behavior	Meaning
Cognitive	
1. *Fluent Thinking* To think of the *most*	Generation of a quantity, flow of thought, number of relevant responses
2. *Flexible Thinking* To take different approaches	Variety of kinds of ideas, ability to shift categories, detours in direction of thought
3. *Original Thinking* To think in *novel* or unique ways—	Unusual responses, clever ideas, production away from the obvious
4. *Elaborative Thinking* To *add* on to—	Embellishing upon an idea, embroidering upon a simple idea or response to make it more elegant, stretching or expanding upon things or ideas
Affective	
1. *Risk Taking* To be *challenged* to—	Expose oneself to failure or criticisms, take a guess, function under conditions devoid of structure, defend own ideas
2. *Complexity* To have courage to—	Seek many alternatives, see gaps between how things are and how they could be, bring order out of chaos, delve into intricate problems or ideas
3. *Curiosity* To be *willing* to	Be inquisitive and wonder, toy with an idea, be open to puzzling situations, ponder the mystery of things, to follow a particular hunch just to see what will happen
4. *Imagination* To have the *power* to—	Visualize and build mental images, dream about things that have never happened, feel intuitively, reach beyond sensual or real boundaries

*From the *Total Creativity Program* by permission of the author Frank E. Williams. This program, comprised of several volumes, packets, and tape cassettes, is distributed by Educational Technology Publications, 140 Sylvan Avenue, Englewood Cliffs, New Jersey 97632.

guidance in these areas in addition to experiencing their regular physical education program.

Widespread confusion exists in many communities concerning such terms as athletics, free play, recess, recreation, recreation education, and therapeutic recreation. None of these words are synonyms for physical education although some refer to programs conducted by individuals with identical or similar professional preparation as the physical educator.

What Is Not Physical Education?
Athletics

Athletics are an outgrowth of the physical education program which are engaged in voluntarily before or after school hours, during the noon hour, and on weekends. The emphasis is upon *competition* and *winning* although the competition may be against oneself, another person, or a team. The same activity, usually a sport (defined broadly to include not only individual and team sports but also swimming, track, and gymnastics) is practiced over and over again in order to *perfect* skills. Athletics may be conducted as intramurals, extramurals, interscholastic programs, and intercollegiate programs. The *intramural program* includes sports competition in which all participants come from one school. An intramural program is *recreational* in that participation is voluntary. Ideally, an intramural program should be organized with A, B, C, D *ad infinitim* leagues, thereby providing an opportunity for every student—regardless of his level of skill—to compete with students of like abilities. Handicapped students should be integrated into an intramural program which is organized in accordance with this "ideal."

The *extramural program* may be defined as sports competition, including playdays and sportsdays, in which participants from two or more schools participate. The once popular playdays and sportsdays which formed the core of this program appear to have faded into the past. The term *extramural athletics* now seems to be used synonymously with the interscholastic and intercollegiate athletic programs. Invitational tournaments and meets of one or two days duration are also designated as extramurals.

Interscholastic and *intercollegiate* athletics essentially refer to the same kind of competition, the former being conducted in elementary, middle, and secondary schools, and the latter being conducted in colleges and universities. Competition at this level is generally highly organized, with tryouts to make the team, regularly scheduled practices, training rules to be followed, and a schedule of games to be played which is established months in advance. *Extramural* competition, including interscholastic and intercollegiate athletics, is associated with the *gifted* athlete. Handicapped students have not generally been integrated into extramural athletics.

Wheelchair athletics were originated in the 1940s when paraplegics, amputees, and thousands of other disabled veterans returned home from World War II. It is now estimated that over 10,000 athletes engage in organized wheelchair competition throughout the United States. These individuals, like their nonhandicapped counterparts, are gifted athletes with desire and stamina to adhere to a rigid training program in which the goal is excellence.

Since 1960 wheelchair games have been held in connection with the Olympic Games. The Paralympics, Olympics for paraplegics, are held annually. Every fourth year the Paralympics immediately follow the Olympic Games in the Olympic's host city.

The events included in Paralympics are: archery—F.I.T.A. round, Columbia round, St. Nicholas round (novice); dartchery—combination of darts and archery; basketball; fencing—sabre, epee, foil (novice); field events—discus, javelin, club throw, shotput; lawn bowling; pentathlon—javelin, shotput, 60-yard dash, swimming, archery; precision javelin; snooker; swimming—front freestyle,

Figure 3.2. Wheelchair athletics: a fifty-yard dash in Tinley Park. (Staff photo by Rich Faverty.)

Figure 3.3. Wheelchair basketball in New York City.

back freestyle, breaststroke, team relay; table tennis—singles, doubles; track events—40-yard dash, 60-yard dash, 100-yard dash, 220-yard dash, 440-yard dash, 880-yard run, one-mile run, slalom, relays; and weight lifting.

Both wheelchair athletics and regular intercollegiate and interscholastic competition meet the needs of the gifted athlete. Traditionally no provisions have been made for the poorly coordinated or *unathletic* individual to compete with individuals from other schools. Pleasure derived from competition in a sport in front of a crowd of spectators has been equated with a high degree of skill.

Special Olympics

In 1968, the first Special Olympics for the Retarded, an international event sponsored by The Joseph P. Kennedy Junior Foundation, was held at Soldier Field, Chicago. One thousand mentally retarded youngsters from all over the United States and Canada participated in a competitive program of track and field and swimming events. Despite the fact that many physical educators were uncertain as to the effects of competition on the retarded, the games were an acknowledged success, opening up new vistas for the mentally

retarded, of whom only 25 percent were receiving as much as one hour per week of physical education in schools and institutions.

Since 1968, the Special Olympics movement has swept the country, modifying attitudes towards athletic competition for the retarded, enlarging perceptions as to their capabilities in the development of motor skills, the learning of rules, and the participation in team sports, and structuring opportunities for thousands of children to compete against peers of comparable ability in front of responsive spectators, including parents, relatives, teachers, coaches and, increasingly, the public media.

More than 300,000 children, representing both educable and trainable retarded, were involved in the Special Olympics within the program's first five years. From a single one-time track meet, Special Olympics has developed into a year-round training program, culminating in a series of more than two thousand state and local meets in every state, the District of Columbia, France, Canada, Puerto Rico, and several other foreign countries.

The Special Olympics program consists of training and competition in nine official sports events, including track and field, swimming,

Figure 3.4. Special Olympics shot-put champions with Dave Hale of the Chicago Bears.

volleyball, basketball, bowling, floor hockey, gymnastics, diving, and ice skating. Special Olympics has received the endorsement of every major official amateur sports organization.

A very significant part of the Special Olympics program is the creation of a cadre of more than 100,000 volunteers who work with the mentally retarded youngsters, conduct year-round training, assist in running the state and local games and give vital community support to the Special Olympics and other programs for the mentally retarded.

The basic philosophy of the Special Olympics games is summarized in the following paragraph.

No matter what the degree of disability or level of skills, there's a place for every mentally retarded child in the Special Olympics games. The children are categorized by performance as well as age so they compete with others of the same proficiency as they. And so, at the national Special Olympics, a little girl from Iowa won a Silver Medal, even though

it took her 10 seconds to run 50 yards. And a boy from Massachusetts won a Silver Medal for the 300-yard run, though it took him more than a minute to complete the course. No matter what their speed or strength, they tried. [5]

The future plans of the Kennedy Foundation for the Special Olympics are optimistic. The Foundation projects that by 1976, more than one million mentally retarded children will be involved in the year-round Special Olympics program. This would mean a significant gain in outreach in over one-third of the universe of need. More than 400,000 volunteers will be required to accommodate such growth, and the Foundation anticipates that Special Olympics will have become an integral part of almost every public school system offering education and training to the mentally retarded.

Of the many contributions made by the Special Olympics movement, perhaps the greatest is the recognition of a wide range of individual differences in athletic ability among the mentally retarded, and the general improvement in intellectual, social, motor and behavioral skills produced by regular participation in physical education and training programs.

As the trend towards integration of the handicapped with the nonhandicapped accelerates, an increasing number of students who are classified in their verbal studies as *mentally retarded* or *learning disabled* are becoming members of varsity interscholastic teams. Already proponents of Special Olympics are involved in policy discussions regarding eligibility rules. Once a mentally retarded child has demonstrated his ability to compete successfully with the nonretarded, must he continue to be segregated in athletics?

The Special Olympics program encourages the normalization process of the mentally

5. Special Olympics, Inc., "A New Kind of Joy," (Pamphlet printed by The Joseph P. Kennedy, Jr. Foundation, no date), p. 5.

Figure 3.5. Dashing along the fifty yard track. (Staff photo by Rich Faverty.)

retarded in every aspect of their lives. Mrs. Eunice Kennedy Shriver, Executive Director of the Foundation and President of Special Olympics, Inc., has expressed the hope that some day there will be a regular progression from Special Olympics to regular sports programs and even to the Olympic Games themselves. Increasingly, the Special Olympics program is attracting participants with severe mental and physical disabilities, including multihandicaps. Although at this writing the essential criterion for eligibility remains a diagnosis of mental retardation, perhaps in the future similar programs will be extended to all poorly skilled individuals, who cannot qualify for regular athletic programs. Further information about the Special Olympics can be obtained by writing to Special Olympics, Inc., 1701 K Street N W, Suite 205, Washington, D. C. 20006.

Recreation

Recreation may be unorganized or organized, occurs during leisure time, and is engaged in voluntarily. When unorganized and spontaneous, it is synonymous with free play. *Recess* in most public schools is a time for recreation, fun and games, and letting off steam. It is inherently satisfying. When organized, recreation may be a planned program of activities conducted by a recreation leader or a specialist whose professional preparation may vary considerably from that of the physical educator. Recreation is not instructional, and the child may play the same games or engage in the same activities over and over, simply because they are fun, enjoyable, pleasurable, amusing, fulfilling, or relaxing. Administratively, an organized recreation program may be conducted by a school, church, community center, residential facility, agency, organization, or even a business or industry which provides recreational facilities for its employees.

Recreation, whether unorganized or organized, encompasses all of the activities in which an individual engages during his leisure time, excluding those needed for sustenance like eating and sleeping, those selected for remuneration to supplement one's regular salary, and those related to homework and job preparation. Work can, however, be recreation if the individual voluntarily devotes more time to it than is required. On the other hand, work engaged in voluntarily during leisure hours may serve as an antidote to emptiness, loneliness, and alienation. Recreation then may be defined as any activity engaged in during leisure time, voluntarily, which is inherently satisfying, healthful, and socially acceptable.

Recreation encompasses many program areas including:

1. *Fine Arts*—Drama, literature, architecture, painting, music, sculpture, and dance
2. *Folk Arts*—Cooking, sewing, needlework, crafts, gardening, music, dance, interior decoration, conversation, home entertainment
3. *Outdoor Activities*—Walking, hiking, camping, picnicking, nature study, ecological study, sunbathing
4. *Sports, Games, Athletics*—Individual, dual, and team sports; aquatics; track; gymnastics; fishing; boating; table games; cards
5. *Pets, Plants, and Children*—Growing and/or raising things
6. *Passive Entertainment*—Sitting, listening, watching, small talking, riding about in automobile, window shopping
7. *Travel or Tourism*—Long or short trips away from home, visiting sites of historical, cultural, or natural interest
8. *Voluntary Service*—Being a board member, leader, gray lady, coach, officer of a club
9. *Hobbies, Collections*—Photography, stamps, coins, recipes, poetry
10. *Educational Activities*—Enrolling in courses for fun; sensitivity training; attending lectures; participating in group discussions

Therapeutic Recreation

Therapeutic recreation refers specifically to a program conducted for the ill, the disabled, the handicapped, the disadvantaged, the aged, the delinquent or criminal, or anyone in a residential facility or hospital who may be scheduled for *recreation* and expected to participate whether he wishes to or not. As an integral part of the total rehabilitation program, therapeutic recreation may be prescribed in the same manner as physical therapy, occupational therapy, and the other adjunctive therapies.

Nugent, like many professional recreators who are reluctant to accept mandatory activities even in a clinical setting as meeting the criteria of recreation, discusses the difference between nudging and pushing, encouraging and requiring. He states:

Recreation, and please I want to emphasize this point, to the individual must be ultimately voluntary. But that does not mean that you are not going to have to nudge a person whose life has been devoid of normal social growth experiences and activities and whose concept of self is inappropriate, one who is fearful and apprehensive, to get him into the world of activity, whatever the activity may be at that time. There is a big difference between nudging a person and pushing him, particularly in the reaction you get. All of us have, at one time or another, had demands made of us and we were ultimately grateful for this. We have been nudged (and sometimes pushed) to find out what we really can do and that we can enjoy doing it. Why begin from a different perspective or use a different approach just because a person has a disability? [6]

6. Timothy J. Nugent, "Recreation as a Therapeutic Tool in Rehabilitation," in *Therapeutic Recreation and Adapted Physical Education Within Rehabilitation,* ed. Thomas R. Collingwood (Hot Springs, Arkansas: Arkansas Rehabilitation Research and Training Center, 1971), pp. 20-21.

Alternative Concepts of Leisure

Other authorities, in analyzing the definition of recreation as it applies to the therapeutic setting, have pointed out that the concept of *leisure time* is different for the institutionalized and/or the unemployed than for the ordinary person. The retarded, for instance, have to be taught leisure. For them, it may become a form of work. For individuals whose opportunities for full-time employment are limited, leisure time services (therapeutic recreation) might well replace vocational training. Perhaps if leisure is obligatory and so abundant that it becomes empty and boring, as is the case with many of our aged, ill and handicapped, then work—or any change in the routine—does become recreation. In most institutions jobs, whether they bring financial remuneration or not, are coveted and contribute to increased esteem from others less fortunate.

Therapeutic recreation, when first prescribed for a patient, may be neither voluntary nor a leisure activity. Moreover, it may not even be enjoyable if the recipient is in a state of deep depression or, for some reason, prefers to be left alone. The skilled therapeutic recreation specialist moves from great structure to little structure and from mandatory activities to voluntary ones, so that ultimately the patient engages voluntarily in the recreation program.

Activity Therapy Services

In some institutions therapeutic recreation services may be designated as part of a program of activity therapy services, rehabilitation services, adjunctive therapies, or ancillary services. In such instances, the therapeutic recreation specialist may be known as an activity therapist, the setting will be interdisciplinary, and specialists in therapeutic recreation, occupational therapy, art therapy, music therapy, dance therapy, volunteer services, and related areas will be found working closely together within a single administrative unit headed by an Activity Therapies Coordinator.

Similarities and Differences

The therapeutic recreation specialist is more like the adapted physical educator than unlike him. Both are expected to perform the functions of diagnosis, purposive intervention, and evaluation on an independent basis, as a coequal on a rehabilitation team. Both work with the ill, the disabled, the handicapped, the disadvantaged and others with individual differences so great that they cannot benefit from participation in regular programs.

Traditionally the adapted physical educator has been associated with a school or educational setting whereas the therapeutic recreation specialist has been associated with a hospital setting or residential facility. The roles of both types of specialists are expanding rapidly. The therapeutic recreation specialist not only works with an individual during his period of confinement in a hospital or residential facility but provides *follow up* services in the halfway house setting and in the community.

The therapeutic recreation specialist must be knowledgeable therefore about community as well as institutional recreation. Whereas in the past, the therapeutic recreation specialist was employed most often in residential facilities for the mentally ill and the mentally retarded, he more recently is expected to have competences to work with the aged, the alcoholic, the drug addict, the delinquent and criminal, and others who may need recreation and leisure counseling of a long term nature.

The greatest difference between the adapted physical educator and the therapeutic recreation specialist lies in the scope of the program each is qualified to conduct. The adapted physical educator is responsible only for physical activities which lead to increased understanding and appreciation of the body. The therapeutic recreation specialist is responsible for ten or more widely diversified pro-

Figure 3.6. Horseback riding is one of many lifetime sports which the blind can enjoy with the sighted. (Christian Record Braille Foundation. Photo by Robert L. Sheldon.)

gram areas which lead to enriched use of leisure time. Each finds satisfaction in the encouragement of carry-over values and in follow up procedures to ascertain that the child is using community resources. Leisure time counseling is performed by both specialists, but the adapted physical educator generally limits his guidance to sports, dance, and aquatics whereas the therapeutic recreation specialist's guidance can be as diversified, broad, and extensive as his capabilities permit.

Recreation or Leisure Education

In some schools *recreation education* is an academic subject similar to reading, arithmetic, and social studies. In such instances the sessions are *instructional* and focus upon the development of skills in different program areas which may later *carry over* to voluntary use during *leisure time. Leisure education* is a synonym for recreation education.

The greater the child's handicapping condition, the more likely he is to have an overabundance of leisure time. Perhaps no part of his education is as important as the development of recreational skills. For the ill, the handicapped, and the disabled instruction in recreational skills is encompassed by the broad field of therapeutic recreation; for others this type of program is called recreation education.

Physical education, athletics, recreation,

therapeutic recreation, and recreation all contribute to self-actualization and to that elusive quality of happiness which man ever seeks. Handicapped individuals must feel a sense of mastery and productivity to realize happiness.

Jay B. Nash, in his beautiful book *Philosophy of Recreation and Leisure*, describes the happy man as follows:

The happy man, the healthy man, the normal man, and the busy man are one, busy but not cramped, active but with sufficient guide for recuperation. The happy man will be the one who has accomplished and is still advancing. The rung of a ladder was never meant to rest upon but merely a vantage place from which to take the next step.

Who is the happy man? He painted a picture; he sang a song; he modeled in clay; he danced to a call; he watched for the birds; he studied the stars; he sought a rare stamp; he sank a long putt; he landed a bass; he built a cabin; he cooked outdoors; he read a good book; he saw a great play; he worked on a lathe; he raised pigeons; he made a rock garden; he canned peaches; he climbed into caves; he dug in the desert; he went down to Rio; he went to Iran; he visited friends; he learned with his son; he romped with his grandchild; he taught youth to shoot straight; he taught them to tell the truth; he read the Koran; he learned from Confucius; he practiced the teachings of Jesus; he dreamed of northern lights, sagebrush, rushing rivers and snow-capped peaks; he was a trooper; he had a hundred things yet to do when the last call came.[7]

7. Jay B. Nash, *Philosophy of Recreation and Leisure* (St. Louis: The C. V. Mosby Company, 1953), p. 217 (out of print). Republished by the Wm. C. Brown Company, Publishers, 1960.

Recommended Activities

1. Develop a lesson plan and teach a miniclass which demonstrates your understanding of the following teaching styles: (a) Command; (b) Traditional Skills; (c) Guided Discovery; and (d) Motor Creativity.
2. Develop lists of criteria for use in evaluating your effectiveness in implementing each teaching style.
3. Read a book or several articles on the creative process. Make a list of teacher behaviors which might facilitate the development of fluency, flexibility, originality, and elaboration in students in the adapted physical education setting.
4. Observe some athletic event for the handicapped like a Special Olympics meet or a wheelchair basketball game.
5. Invite a specialist in community recreation to speak to your class. Find out the nature and scope of recreation activities made available to the handicapped in your community.
6. Visit a residential or day care center for the ill and handicapped and observe the therapeutic recreation program in action.

4

Similarities and Differences in Regular and Adapted Programs

Figure 4.0. Movement exploration with a medicine ball, which weighs nine pounds, helps children understand and accept individual differences with respect to force production and absorption.

. . . But meanwhile he had grown horribly sensitive. He never ran if he could help it, because he knew it made his limp more conspicuous, and he adopted a peculiar walk. He stood as much as he could, with his club-foot behind the other, so that it should not attract notice, and he was constantly on the lookout for any reference to it. Because he could not join in the games which other boys played, their life remained strange to him; he only interested himself from the outside in their doings; and it seemed to him that there was a barrier between them and him. Sometimes they seemed to think that it was his fault if he could not play football, and he was unable to make them understand. He was left a good deal to himself. He had been inclined to talkativeness, but gradually he became silent. He began to think of the difference between himself and others.[1]

In order to adapt the physical education and recreation program to the interests, capabilities, and limitations of a handicapped child, one must understand the developmental characteristics of boys and girls of different age groups. Provision of success-oriented activities for the one or two *different* children in the group depends upon the number of games, sports, aquatic, and rhythmic activities which one knows and his skill in manipulating the variables which affect their degree of difficulty. The purpose of this chapter is to describe the widely diversified activities which comprise a comprehensive physical education program.

Traditionally the physical educator has sought to develop skills in sports, dance, and aquatics which may enrich the present as well as carry over into adult life. The teaching style utilized most often in the upper grades entails explanation and demonstration of the activity, individual and group practice, analysis and correction of movement errors, and eventual application of the newly acquired skills, knowledges, and understandings in the game setting. Activities which comprise the middle and secondary school program include: (1) sports, which are subdivided into team, dual, and individual; (2) aquatics; (3) dance; and (4) body mechanics and conditioning activities.

Activities comprising the modern day elementary school program depend, to a large extent, upon the teaching style. The explanation-demonstration approach, often called the *games or skills approach,* and the problem-solving approach, which sometimes stresses perceptual-motor learning, were described in the last chapter. Both approaches include some of the same activities, but differ greatly with respect to the percentage of time spent on each, the manner of presentation, and the type of practice or execution. Simply stated, the two approaches encompass the activities in Table 5.

Kirchner recommends the following percentages of time to be spent on each activity comprising the regular physical education program (Table 6). Other proponents of the problem-solving approach recommend that a greater amount of time be devoted to movement exploration and self-testing, while traditionalists continue to fill the curriculum with games and dance.

Program planning is a cooperative endeavor. Teachers from several grade levels should develop a curriculum guide which reflects the unique needs and interests of children in their particular community and/or school. Weather conditions, the availability of facilities and equipment, the professional preparation of the teachers, the ethnic and socioeconomic backgrounds of the students and the administrative philosophy concerning amount of structure and appropriate teaching styles all influence the percentage of time to be spent on each activity.

In adapted physical education the percentage of time to be spent on each activity will vary with the handicapping conditions of the students. For most youngsters, especially during the primary years, the emphasis should be

1. W. Somerset Maugham, *Of Human Bondage* (New York: Double Day & Company, Inc., 1915), p. 36.

Table 5 *Activities Comprising Elementary School Physical Education*

Explanation-Demonstration Approach	Problem-Solving Approach
1. Body mechanics, calisthenics, posture education, fitness activities	1. Introduction or warm-up activities, developmental activities, movement education
2. Self-testing, stunts and tumbling, some apparatus activities	2. Self-testing Stunts, tumbling, and small apparatus activities, large apparatus activities, educational gymnastics
3. Games	3. Games
4. Rhythmical activities with emphasis in K-3 Singing Games 4-6 Folk, square, and ballroom dance	4. Creative Dance with some attention to other forms of dance
5. Ball Handling-Drills Hand-eye coordinations Foot-eye coordinations	5. Ball Handling-Movement exploration and self-testing Hand-eye coordinations Foot-eye coordinations

Table 6 *Percentages of Time for Activities in Regular Physical Education**

Type of Activity	Percentage of time per level		
	Preschool	1-3	4-6
Self-testing Including Movement Exploration Educational Gymnastics Et cetera	60	40-50	30
Games	20	30-40	50
Dance	20	20	20

*Glen Kirchner, *Physical Education for Elementary School Children.* Dubuque, Iowa: Wm. C. Brown Company Publishers, 1970, p. 55.

Table 7 *Percentages of Time for Activities in Adapted Physical Education*

Type of Activity	Percentage of time per level		
	Preschool	1-3	4-6

Movement Exploration
   Including
   Self-testing
   Gymnastics
   Track
   Ball Handling
   Water Play and/or
      Swimming
   Rhythmical Activities
	90	70	50

Games
   Low organized
   Lead-up
   Relays
   Lifetime Sports
	5	15	25

Dance
   Singing Games
   Creative
   Folk
   Square
   Ballroom
	5	15	25

upon refining the basic motor skills and movement patterns, increasing body awareness, encouraging understanding and acceptance of movement potential, and preserving ego strength. Dance also is perhaps more important to the handicapped child than the nonhandicapped. Indeed, only a very thin line exists between dance therapy and dance education.

Table 7 presents the percentages of time which have been found to be optimal in working with children who have learning disabilities and/or who are especially clumsy and uncoordinated. Some perceptual-motor training is included under movement exploration but it is recommended that perceptual-motor train-ing should be scheduled in addition to the daily period of physical education instruction.

The more severely handicapped a child, the greater percentage of time which should be spent in movement exploration. Whereas games and dance are mostly group activities, movement exploration is *I* centered. Success in movement exploration is described in terms of improving one's own performance. For handicapped children, this often implies the courage to try something for the first time. Movement exploration, in Table 7, encompasses all of the activities which can be taught through a *Can You?* approach. With the mentally retarded, learning disabled, and possibly the deaf, movement exploration may be more

Figure 4.1. Creative dance offers opportunities for refining motor skills and increasing body awareness.

Figure 4.2. More emphasis is given to movement exploration with the severely handicapped than with the normal.

follow-the-leader than responding to verbal challenges. Some children must have visual stimuli to follow in order to learn. It should not be assumed that guided discovery and problem-solving can be taught only through the auditory sense modality.

Developmental Stages in Play Patterns

Children progress through clearly observable developmental stages which, in turn, determine their readiness for particular physical activities. Since some children in the elementary school setting have mental ages comparable to that of the two- or three-year-old, the following description of developmental stages (Table 8) begins with the preacademic child. Emotionally disturbed and mentally retarded children frequently display immature play patterns.

It is possible that many mentally retarded children of elementary and secondary school age whose mental ages remain frozen at the preacademic level can experience greater success in a program of individual sports which stresses competition against the self than through group activities for which they may never achieve readiness. Severely retarded children should not be taught relays nor expected to participate in games which require standing in a set formation. A good measure of readiness is whether the child understands the concept of a circle or line well enough to get into formation without assistance from the teacher. Of course, by continuous drill a child can be trained to stand in a circle but it is doubtful that he will understand the objective of the game. There are many other physical education activities which offer greater potential value to the trainable child than low organized games.

Often handicapped children are so protected by their parents, siblings, and teachers that they have never engaged in group games. Illustrative of this problem is the following quotation from an adapted physical education specialist.

For several years I had been working with a group of educable mentally retarded children who were segregated from their normal peers on the playground, in the lunchroom, and in nearly all school activities. To offset this, we took the children to the gymnasium of a local university twice a week where they received individual instruction in swimming; trampoline, balance beam, mat, and sidehorse activities; and movement exploration. Many of them became beautiful athletes, and I knew their motor skills were way beyond those of the

TABLE 8 *Developmental Stages in Play*

Chronological Age	Developmental Stages in Play
18 mos-2 yrs	Solitary or parallel play observable. Child plays with toys alone or in room with another child, but each is so absorbed in his own activity that no interaction takes place.
2-4 yrs	Solitary and parallel play continues. Child is extremely possessive of toys and conflict arises when one tries to "borrow" possessions of the other. Not yet ready for organized games. Can benefit from creative dance and movement exploration. Enjoys exploring apparatus, but not ready for instruction. Ideal time to begin instruction in swimming.
4-5 yrs	Cooperative play begins, usually of a "let's make believe" nature and taking turns on apparatus. He plays hide and seek and tag and tries to imitate older peers, but is not yet ready for circle games led by an adult. Can benefit from creative dance, movement exploration, and self-testing with balls, hoops, etc. Ready for small group instruction.
5-6 yrs	Cooperative or shared play with 2-5 in a group. May participate in simple circle games but too energetic to remain in a set formation for a long duration. Is beginning to understand concept of standing in file and waiting for turn; may begin tumbling activities. Still benefits from creative dance, movement exploration, self-testing, and apparatus play.
6-8 yrs	Participation in increasingly complex low organized games, beginning with the circle formation and progressing to more difficult formations. Wants to be "it" all the time but gradually learns to take turns. Not yet ready for team activities in which the group wins rather than the individual. May begin instruction in ballet, tap, and acrobatic dance but creative dance is still most beneficial educationally.
8-10 yrs	Participation in lead-up sports and relays with gradual understanding of the concept of team competition. May begin folk, square, and ballroom dance. Ready for "couple" activities in dance and tumbling.
10 yrs on	Participation in regulation sports with adult rules adapted to needs, all forms of dance, and all forms of aquatic activities.

Figure 4.3. Group games, like cageball, demand social readiness and self-confidence.

"normal" children who had received no gymnastics instruction.

Four boys in particular were so good that I decided to confront the school administration with the idea of integrating them into the regular third grade physical education class. After considerable difficulty, I obtained permission. Since I was the teacher of the "normal" third graders as well as the ungraded retarded children, I anticipated no problems. The four boys felt secure with me and eagerly awaited their extra physical education periods.

First day. Brownies and Fairies. The children were all lined up waiting for the call: "The Brownies are coming." I gave it, and as always the children began running, dodging, tagging, and shouting in joyous manner. I looked out and there in the middle of the confusion was Billy, my best athlete, who could turn flips on the trampoline, outrun, or outthrow any of the "normal" children. He stood frozen, hands over face as if to protect himself, in a stooped posture of fear, eyes closed, teeth clenched, and muscles rigid.

It was only then that I realized that Billy had never been in a game with more than ten children; had never been chased, pursued by a group; had never been exposed to the high intensity of noise that we take for granted in the gymnasium.

It is obvious that a high degree of motor skill is not the only criterion for integrating handicapped children into normal physical education. Special education classes are small, limited in enrollment to less than fifteen students in most states, and generally ungraded. Many children in special education have not been exposed to large group games and hence skip important developmental stages in play. Before they can be integrated into the regular physical education activities of their peers, they must be taken through these developmental stages. After completing such orientation and being integrated, they may still need the support, ego reinforcement, and counseling of the adapted physical educator in much the same way that a student teacher needs the guidance of the cooperating and supervising teachers.

In analyzing the needs of each individual child in special education, it is important that the physical educator ask these questions.

1. What is his mental age? Is he frozen at a particular developmental stage in play?

   If he is, accept him as he is. Do not try to force him into activities for which he may never be ready. Not all children need group games and relays for self-actualization.

2. In which developmental stage is he?
   (a) Ages 18 mos.-4 years. Solitary or parallel play.
   (b) Ages 4-5 years. Cooperative or shared play, no structured formation.
   (c) Ages 5-6 years. Small group (2-5) play in simple structured formations.
   (d) Ages 6-8 years. Large group (normal class size) play in structured formations.
   (e) Ages 8-10 years. Lead-up games, relays, dance in couple formations.
   (f) Ages 10 and up. Regulation sports, dance, and aquatics.

3. Has he skipped any developmental stages? Does his handicap permit his being taken back through the developmental stages missed?

4. If he is frozen at one of the early stages because of mental and/or physical limitations, how can the activities be

adapted so as not to insult his social intelligence?

5. To what extent will his condition affect the speed with which he can master activities? Does he have time, within the span of his childhood and adolescence, to progress through all of these developmental stages? If not, which ones should be omitted?

6. Are you teaching him activities with carry-over value for the abundance of leisure time which he is likely to have?

7. Are you acquainting him with community recreation facilities and resources as part of his physical education program?

8. Are you providing group therapy and/or instruction for family members which will reinforce the child's newly developing leisure patterns and enable him to gain support (transportation, companionship, expenses) in the use of community resources?

Perhaps the major difference between the nonhandicapped and the exceptional individual which has implications for adapted physical education is the amount of leisure each has in childhood as compared with that which he will have in adulthood. Often the exceptional children, particularly those with physical conditions and learning disabilities, are enrolled in all kinds of training activities during their early years. They may tire easily and require more sleep and supervised rest than their peers. When the disability has not been diagnosed to the parent's satisfaction, the child may be taken from clinic to clinic and required to adapt to a variety of anxiety-filled testing situations and energy-taxing remediation programs. In childhood, for many reasons, the handicapped may have less leisure time for mastering recreational skills than his friends and siblings.

The handicapped person has increasingly greater blocks of leisure time as he grows older. He watches his peers fall in love, marry,

Figure 4.4. Acquainting the handicapped with community resources is part of adapted physical education.

rear families, and find security and fulfillment in job satisfactions—time consuming endeavors, all or part of which may be denied the handicapped. The following words of a college educated mother concerning her nine-year-old son with learning disabilities illustrates the point.

We don't want to put Dave in special education so we are doing all we can to help him keep up with the others. He's making mostly D's, but I think he'll do better on the next report card. He was just trying to do too much so I took him out of his swimming lessons at the Y. I'm not letting him play football either, and he can wait another year or two before rejoining the Scouts. I'm real fortunate to have employed a special education teacher to tutor him after school on writing and spelling. It's costing $5.00 an hour every day, but it sure is worth it.

Later the same mother told me:

> I just don't know what we're going to do with Dave. The other kids won't accept him; every afternoon he gets in a fight on the school bus. I guess I'm going to have to accept the fact that he will never be popular. But I could cry; he is so lonely and he keeps asking "Why do those kids hate me so much?"

If a handicapped child must skip some developmental stages in play, the ones least valuable to him are probably those which are game-centered or team sport oriented. The younger he is when lifetime sports are introduced, the more years he has to acquire the skills which will enable him to participate in activities and use community facilities with the nonhandicapped. The awkward child particularly should be given instruction in swimming, dance, and individual sports at an earlier age than normal children so that he can get a "head start" and thereby compete equitably or even excel in some leisure activities. Such instruction serves as insurance against loneliness, boredom, and less desirable compensatory behaviors.

Developmental Stages in Competition

Children progress through clearly identifiable developmental stages with respect to readiness for competition. The following stages, with the exception of numbers five and six, are those cited in the *Special Olympics Instructional Manual.* No age groups are associated with the developmental stages since these vary widely and reflect individual differences in personality and temperament as much as maturation.

1. Competes with himself to improve his own performance as he tries to do more sit-ups or push-ups, jump rope longer, or throw a ball higher into the air and catch it.
2. Competes with himself against his own best performances as he tries to run the 50-yard dash or swim the 25-yard freestyle faster, jump higher or further, or throw a softball further.
3. Tries to attain specific goals to receive a medal, certificate, patch, ribbon, points, other recognition, or the personal satisfaction that comes from success.
4. Cooperates with others to achieve a mutual goal such as winning a relay, simple game, or lead-up activity.
5. Competes with a partner or one opponent in individual sports like bowling, golf, and tennis. Competes against others also in trying to make the best score in fitness, track, and self-testing activities.
6. Competes in dual sports like *doubles* in tennis, badminton, and table tennis. Cooperates with his partner in doubles tennis, with his team in bowling, and in other situations demanding a limited number of interactions.
7. Competes with others to win a position on a team or a place in a group in which only a certain number can participate and/or compete against other teams or groups.

Summarized, the developmental stages in competition are (1) competition against self; (2) individual and dual competition; and (3) team competition. Although the success of very young children in little league baseball and peewee football has resulted in considerable controversy concerning the age at which one is ready to compete with others, many educators concur that team competition, including relays, should not be introduced until the third grade. It is doubtful that some handicapped children, particularly the severely retarded, ever acquire the mental and social readiness for team competition.

The rationale for not introducing team competition until the third grade is based primarily upon the social characteristics of children rather than their level of motor skill or their ability to grasp rules and strategy. Each of us has seen beautifully skilled seven- and eight-year-old athletes, already specialized in pitching, catching, or fielding. We have also seen many children sitting on a bench—waiting—and hoping.

Parents who really understand the objectives of physical education and the nature and scope of a well rounded, comprehensive program of activities will not want their children to specialize in team sports at so early an age. Aquatics, dance, individual and dual sports including gymnastics and track, movement exploration, and self-testing activities are every child's educational right to a well rounded and enriching life. Too much time spent on any one sport deprives an individual of the vital experiences needed to understand and appreciate his body and its capacity for an infinite variety of movements.

Instructional Patterns in Physical Education

Eight widely used instructional patterns in physical education follow:

Integration Practices (Mainstreaming)
1. Participation in regular physical education.
2. Observation of regular physical education with occasional involvement through keeping score, officiating, and assisting the teacher.
3. Partial participation in regular physical education with special help given during the class and/or during assigned extra periods by a resource teacher, teacher aide, honor student, or tutor of some kind.

Segregation Practices
4. Participation in a regularly scheduled group physical education program designed specifically for the handicapped.

5. Participation in a regularly scheduled tutorial program of adapted physical education in which instruction is conducted on a one-to-one basis.
6. Participation in an *honors program* in adapted physical education in which the student assumes responsibility for a designated number of hours of activity—synonymous with *contract teaching* in that the student does most of the work on his own and periodically reports his progress to the teacher.

Substitution Practices
7. Waiving of the physical education requirement for the entire year. Assignment to study hall or classroom during the physical education period.
8. Substituting band, office duty, athletics, or pep squads for physical education requirement.

Most state legislatures require physical education but students may be excused from the requirement upon the recommendation of a physician. Two states, which have laws prohibiting such excuses, are Pennsylvania and California. These states require participation in alternative instructional programs, the most common of which are the three segregated practices.

Instructional Patterns in Special Education

Special education offers widely diversified instructional patterns for educating the student. The type of special education to which a child is assigned will determine the nature and scope of the physical education experiences available to him.

The instructional patterns used most often in special education are

1. *Special Schools.* These may be either public or private residential or day schools, among which are special

Figure 4.5. Lifetime sports skills, like boating, are included in a physical education program for the blind. (Christian Record Braille Foundation. Photo by Robert L. Sheldon.)

facilities for the blind, the deaf, and the mentally retarded.

> *Physical Education.* Any of the eight instructional patterns in physical education may be employed since the range of individual differences, even within a homogeneous group, is great. Ideally every special school should employ specialists in both regular and adapted physical education.

2. *Special Education Classes Within a Public School.* This pattern is probably most common in the majority of states. The special education class is a self-contained classroom with one teacher expected to conduct all learning experiences, sometimes with the assistance of teacher aides or specialists in art, music, and physical education.

> *Physical Education.* Any of the eight instructional patterns may be employed. Most often, however,

children in special education are segregated from the "normal" children on playgrounds as well as in classrooms. Thus the term *special physical education* has come into widespread use. If the handicaps of the children are mild, as in the case of moderately retarded children, the special physical education program may be identical to the regular physical education program. When the competences of the children are similar, there is a trend toward integrating exceptional children into regular physical education programs.

3. *Modifications of the Special Class*
   (a) *Partially Integrated Classes.* The child is carried on the roll of the special education teacher and ultimately is her responsibility; however, he spends part of each week or day in the regular classroom with *normal* children. This pattern is more applicable to middle and secondary school than to elementary school.

   > *Physical Education.* Physical education, art, and music are often the first subjects in which the child participates with his peers. Unfortunately this placement frequently reflects a belief that the primary objective of these *frill* subjects is socialization rather than careful individual assignment to regular, adapted, or special instruction based upon diagnosis and evaluation.

   (b) *Resource Room.* The child is carried on the roll of the regular teacher who is responsible for his progress. He is assigned to the resource room for special help in a particular subject as difficulty arises. These assignments are often of short duration. The resource room is used widely also as a means of providing special help for the blind and deaf as well as those with only partial sensory impairments.

Physical Education. Any of the eight instructional patterns may be employed. The availability of a resource teacher in physical education is a decided asset in meeting individual differences.

(c) *Itinerant Special Education Teacher or Consultant.* Same as above except that the availability of the resource teacher's services is limited.

4. *Hospital Instruction.* Hospitals may have special classes established with a full-time teacher. Instruction is usually ungraded. Or the itinerant teacher may visit and give individual instruction.

Physical Education. This may be provided on an individual basis by an itinerant adapted physical educator. In most hospitals it will be supplemented with therapeutic recreation, dance therapy, physical therapy, and/or other adjunctive therapies.

5. *Home Instruction.* Same as above. Often the instruction is provided primarily by the parents who follow the directions of the itinerant teacher.

Physical Education. Same as above. Physical education often takes the form of rehabilitative exercises, conditioning, or perceptual-motor training. Interpreted broadly, the patterning prescribed by Doman-Delacato theorists for brain-injured children and executed by parents might fall here.

Recommended Activities

1. Visit the American Red Cross office in your community and become acquainted with the staff. Ask about their courses on teaching swimming to the handicapped.
2. Visit a local YMCA, YWCA, or other agency which may provide swimming for the handicapped. Contrast their swimming certificates with those of the Red Cross.
3. Observe children of several different ages at play in the neighborhood or park setting. Ask several children what their favorite games are.
4. Invite the special education coordinator in your community to speak to your class. Learn how exceptional children in your community are grouped for education. Solicit permission to visit special education classes.
5. Identify private day or residential facilities for the handicapped within a fifty mile radius. Arrange a field trip for the purpose of observing handicapped children at play.
6. Evaluate your background in the sports, dance and aquatic activities which should be included in a physical education curriculum for the handicapped. If you are unfamiliar with any activity listed in this chapter, arrange to observe classes where that activity is being taught.

Part 2
Diagnosis, Appraisal, and Prescriptive Teaching

Behavioral Objectives

After reading Chapters 5-13 and testing the activities with small groups of children, it is anticipated that the reader will be able to:

1. Implement the concepts of educational diagnosis and prescriptive teaching in an adapted physical education or recreation setting.

2. Develop a program designed specifically to slow a pupil down or to speed him up, compatible with his drug therapy.

Recommended Activities are listed at the end of each chapter.

5 Educational Diagnosis and Prescriptive Teaching in Physical Education

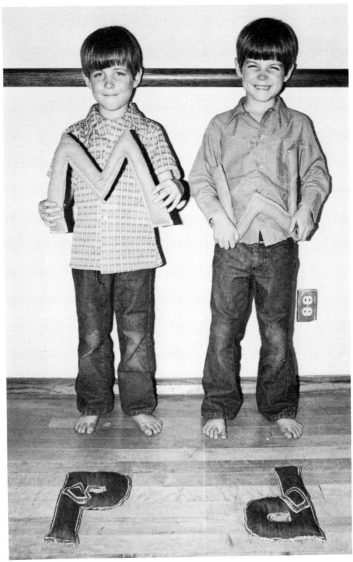

Figure 5.0. First-graders improve laterality through problem-solving motor activities with beanbags shaped like reversible letters. Boy on left stands in front of *d* while making *m*. Boy on right stands in front of *p* while making *w*.

Educational diagnosis in physical education implies the analysis, synthesis, and organization of all of the data about a pupil which might affect his motor performance and/or success in physical education activities.

The adapted physical educator does not collect all of the data but relies upon the other specialists comprising the multidisciplinary team. He must, however, be able to recognize the variables which affect motor performance and to interpret the findings pertaining to them. Ideally this interpretation is a team endeavor and occurs in a staffing. Often, however, the staffing focuses exclusively upon the academic needs of a pupil, and the physical educator is left to his own resources in reviewing individual files, learning relevant information, and writing an educational diagnosis pertaining specifically to physical attributes and perceptual-motor performance.

Appraisal of a child's strengths and weaknesses does not end with the writing of the educational diagnosis. It is a continuous process which includes the design of individualized instructional intervention, implementation through prescriptive teaching, and periodic reassessment. This chapter includes a number of checklists designed to draw together the content to be presented in chapters 6-10 and to provide a guide for writing the educational diagnosis.

Summary Diagnostic Form Based on Observations

What do you consider to be his or her major health problem or handicapping condition?

1. _____

2. _____

What is the average number of school absences in a semester?

0-3	4-7	8-15	over 15

Which seems to be his physical education preference and/or strength?

| Dance | Developmental Exercise | Individual Sports |
| Aquatics | Gymnastics, Stunts | Team Sports |

In which developmental stage of play should he be classified?

Solitary or parallel	Games and dance with "I" emphasis
Cooperative or shared	Activities emphasizing team or group goals
Small group (6 or less)	Regulation sports, dance, aquatics

In which developmental stage of competition should he be classified?

Competes with self against his own best performance
Tries to attain specific individual goals
Cooperates with others in achievement of a team goal
Competes against one other
Cooperates with partner in competition against 2 opponents
Cooperates with team members in competition against a team

At which level of game complexity should he be classified?

1. Everyone does same thing in same direction as in Follow the Leader, Musical Chairs, Hot Potato, Red Light-Green Light, Catch My Tail, or Teacher Ball.
2. Everyone runs from one base to another on the same cue to escape an "it;" this "it" remains the same throughout the game as in Midnight and Old Mother Witch.
3. Same as 2, but with a different "it" for each exchange of bases.
4. Some children remain stationary whereas others run, chase, or flee in response to a cue number or word. All movement is in the same direction as Fire Engine, Mickey Mouse, Circle Call Ball, and Steal the Bacon. The more children who remain stationary, the easier the game.
5. The same as 4 except that the direction varies as in Squirrels in the Trees and Two Deep.
6. Some children play an offense role while others play defense as Dodgeball, Brownies and Fairies, and Trades.
7. Role changes frequently, direction of movement varies, and penalties are enforced when fouls or violations are made like Keep Away.
8. Same as 7, except score keeper must keep track of number of points earned by each team as in Kick Ball.

Can participate in games based upon the following locomotor activities and/or motor skills;

walk	dodge	bounce
run	squat	dribble
leap	throw	catch
jump	kick	volley
hop	strike	pivot
tag	bat	

Can participate in rhythmic or dance activities based upon the following locomotor movements and/or basic skills:

walk	gallop	waltz
run	slide	two-step
leap	skip	polka
jump	step-hop	bleking
hop	schottische	draw

Which is his level of rhythmic performance and/or temporal perception?

| No evidence of understanding concept nor ability to move in time to stimulus. | Can move in time to metronome or drum beat. | Can move in time to verbal stimulus Up-2-3, Down-2-3. | Can move to music with well defined beats and accents. | Can move to any kind of music without problems. |

Which of the following visual problems does the pupil exhibit?

accommodation	double vision	ocular muscle imbalance
nearsightedness	suppression of one eye	convergence insufficiency
farsightedness	squint (cross-eye)	horizontal tracking
astigmatism	binocular coordination	vertical tracking

What correction or training is the pupil receiving for his visual problems?

none	prescribed eye exercises
corrective glasses	prescribed gross motor activities
patch over one eye	prescribed tracking activities

Which problems of visual perception does the pupil exhibit?

form discrimination	object constancy
color discrimination	phi phenomenon
figure-background	retinal inhibition
depth perception	form constancy
directional constancy	

Which problems of auditory perception does the pupil exhibit?

pitch discrimination	figure-background
intensity discrimination	directionality of sound
tonal quality discrimination	temporal perception

Which problems of proprioception does the pupil exhibit?

duplication of specific joint positions	static balance
imitation of movements	dynamic balance
directional accuracy in moving objects	spatial orientation
distance accuracy in moving objects	size estimation
weight discrimination	force production

Which two sense modalities appear to be the strongest?

visual   tactile   kinesthetic
auditory   vestibular   olfactory
gustatory

Which stimulus is most effective as an attention getting device and a starting and stopping signal?

voice   bell   raised arm
whistle   flicker of lights   flag raised or thrown in air
drum   hand clapping   other _____

Observe the pupil in his attemps to learn a gross motor skill. At which level does his learning appear to break down?

Perception	*Formulation of the Motor Plan Central Processing*	*Motor Output*
sensory input	visual memory and sequencing	readiness (set)
mental awareness	auditory memory and sequenc-	perceptual-motor matching
discrimination	ing	imitation of movements
organization (parts into wholes)	haptic memory and sequencing	duplication of joint positions
cue selection (figure-back-	mental practice (motor plan-	perceptual-motor sequencing
ground)	ning)	motor feedback
	mental creativity	total assembly
		automatic response (relaxa-
		tion)
		fixation (consistency under
		stable conditions)
		diversification (consistency
		under changing conditions)

In comparison with the average of other children in his group, which behaviors does this child exhibit to a greater degree than the others?

motor awkwardness   distractibility
poor spatial orientation   perseveration
immature body image   social imperception
negative self-concept   low frustration tolerance
hyperactivity   crying
loneliness   aggression toward others
self-destructive acts

Which of the following conditions which may affect balance are evidenced?

hydrocephalus
amputation
taller than average height
extremely long legs
excessively large busts
small or defective feet
absence of big toe
poor postural alignment
lack of body part symmetry
inconsistent opposition of limbs
unequal length of legs
takes medications which may affect balance

visual deficits
chronic ear infections
history of meningitis
semicircular canal impairment
cerebellar ataxia
gait abnormalities
spasticity
athetosis
imbalance of muscular strength
poor kinesthesis
fear of heights

Put an x in the proper box to denote special strengths and weaknesses. Every box should not have an x.

Component	Strengths to Be Built Upon	Weaknesses to Be Remediated or Compensated for
Static (extent) flexibility		
Dynamic flexibility		
Speed in changing direction		
Running: explosive strength		
Explosive arm strength (throwing)		
Explosive leg strength (jumping)		
Static strength		
Dynamic arm strength		
Dynamic leg strength		
Hanging strength		
Abdominal strength		
Upper back strength		
Lower back strength		
Circulo-respiratory endurance		

Summary Evaluation of Postures

Educational Diagnostician _____ Date _____

Name _____ Age _____

Height (inches) _____ Weight (lbs.) _____ Sex _____

Body Type

Endomorph	Mesomorph	Ectomorph
1 2 3 4 5 6 7	1 2 3 4 5 6 7	1 2 3 4 5 6 7

Height-Weight Status

| Overweight
Very Short | Slender
Short | Normal
Average | Stocky
Tall | Overweight
Very Tall | Obese |

Body Alignment

Forward Head, Neck	0 1 2 3	Paste rear and side posture pictures in this column.
Round Shoulders	0 1 2 3	
Winged Scapulae	0 1 2 3	
Chest	Hollow Funnel 0 1 2 3 Barrel Pigeon	Paste foot print on the back of this form.
High Shoulder	0 RH 1 2 3 LH 1 2 3	
High Hip	0 RH 1 2 3 LH 1 2 3	
Scoliosis	L dorsal L lumbar L total R dorsal R lumbar R total	
Lordosis	0 1 2 3	
Other Spinal Column Deviations	Flat Back Kyphosis	
Protruding Abdomen	0 1 2 3	
Bowlegs	Femur 0 1 2 3 (Coxa valga) Tibia 0 1 2 3 (Genu valgum)	
Knock-knees	Femur 0 1 2 3 (Coxa vara) Tibia 0 1 2 3 (Genu valgum)	
Back Knees	0 1 2 3	
Pronation	0 1 2 3	
Flatfoot (Pes planus)	0 1 2 3	
Toeing (direction)	In 0 1 2 3 Out 0 1 2 3	
Tight Achilles Tendon	0 1 2 3	
Other (foot)		
Toes		

Symbols are 0, 1, 2, 3 with 1 meaning mild and 3 meaning severe. Write in N to indicate *normal for age* but deviation if present at different age.

Crippling Conditions

On a separate page describe congenital anomalies or other problems which may help explain postures. Describe gait if deviant.

1. Circle answers which best describe ball handling behaviors.

Task	Throwing			Kicking		
	Yes		**No**	**Yes**		**No**
Uses same limb consistently	Right Left			Right Left		
Uses other limbs in opposition	Always	Usually	Seldom	Always	Usually	Seldom
Transfers weight	Always	Usually	Seldom	Always	Usually	Seldom
Aims accurately	Always	Usually	Seldom	Always	Usually	Seldom
When aim is inaccurate, it usually goes too far in which directions?	Right Left High Low Inconsistent			Right Left High Low Inconsistent		

2. In comparison with the average of other pupils of his same age and sex, this child's ball handling skills can be described best by which adjectives?

Motor Skill	Superior	Average	Inferior
Throwing			
Catching			
Batting			
Pitching			
Bunting			
Place kicking			
Shooting baskets			
Volleying			
Other			

In comparison with the average of other children in his group this pupil can be described best in the physical education setting by which phrases? Circle only one under each heading.

Attention	*Memory*	*Imitation*
attentive	remembers well and retains	imitates easily and well
average	remembers fairly well	imitates fairly well
nonattentive	forgets easily	average
distracted	never remembers	imitates little and with difficulty
confused		can do things only his own way
not there		
scatterbrained		

Initiative	*Understanding of Instructions or Explanations*	*Mental Flexibility*
a self-starter	grasps instructions	receptive to new ideas
has considerable initiative	understands after asking ques-	average
average	tions	prefers the old and familiar
responds to prodding	average	resents change
relies entirely on others	confused, but knows he	perseverates
	doesn't understand	
	thinks he understands, but	
	really doesn't	
	confused and helpless	

In which area is the pupil stronger?

receptive language
expressive language

Which phrases best describe the pupil's language functioning?

no problem	expressive language deficit
inner language deficit	gesture and/or sign language
receptive language deficit	no usable language

Which extrinsic award and/or social incentive works best as a motivator?

verbal praise	coins or tokens
hug	stars on wall chart
food (specify kind)	point system
hand clapping	other _____

Prescriptive Teaching

An educational prescription includes the pupil's classification and/or placement, a delineation of the environmental conditions and teaching style under which he is most likely to experience success, and suggestions for remediating or compensating for weaknesses and/or deficits. Activities should be stated also which are contraindicated because of particular postural deviations, health problems, or handicapping conditions. The criteria for classifying children into regular or adapted physical education can be summarized as follows:

1. Regular physical education
   Child needs no adaptations, or he can make his own and still score within —1 and +1 standard deviations of the mean or better.

2. Adapted physical education substituted for some of the regular class sessions with the percentage of time to be devoted to regular and adapted physical education specified. Under this plan a paraplegic might participate in regular physical education during such units as archery, fly casting, and bowling and attend adapted physical education sessions when his peers practice team sports and other

activities from which he cannot derive optimum benefit.

3. Regular physical education supplemented by a specified number of extra sessions per week during which individualized or small group assistance is given. This plan is ideal if the child's condition is such that extra instruction and practice may enable him to catch up with the group. It is recommended also for children whose conditions restrict them to individual sports not included in the regular class. This classification recognizes the importance of socialization with normal peers, i.e., helping with score keeping and officiating in regular physical education, while learning alternate motor skills in adapted physical education which permit optimum use of leisure time and community resources.

4. Adapted physical education

Separate instruction should be provided for children who fail more often than they succeed in motor activities. This assignment may be made also in school systems where the regular physical education classes are so large that there is insufficient time or space for individual attention. In general, a class of more than 35-40 pupils does not allow for adapting activities to the needs of the handicapped.

The physical education classification depends, in large part, on the degree to which the pupil can function in a group and the flexibiltiy of scheduling within the regular program. Basic questions to be answered are

1. Under which conditions can the pupil best learn and practice physical education skills?

   a. individual instruction
   b. small group—less than 6 pupils
   c. small class—7-20 pupils
   d. regular class—21-40 pupils
   e. large class—over 40 pupils

2. Is the regular physical education teacher flexible enough to allow the pupil with a handicapping condition to attend occasionally? Are there some units, like archery, which he can attend regularly? When he attends, to what extent will he be actively involved? How often must he attend to gain peer group acceptance and make friends which will carry over outside of the physical education setting?

3. If the child's need for socialization is greater than the accomplishment of other possible physical education objectives, which kind of assignment will best facilitate the making of friends? Will involvement in the regular program really contribute toward this end? What conditions must be present?

The educational prescription states the number of times per week the pupil should have physical education and the duration of each period. It also indicates whether he will learn specific skills most efficiently under conditions of massed or distributed practice.

Massed, or concentrated, schedules are those which have little or no rest or alternate activity between the beginning and end of a practice of one activity.

Distributed, or spaced, schedules are those in which practice periods are spread out or separated by either rest or some activity which is different from the one being learned.

The adapted physical educator will need to learn more about this subject from textbooks [1, 2] or courses in motor learning. Little research is available concerning the efficacy of massed versus distributed practice for persons with specific mental or physical handicapping conditions. In general, distributed practices seem to be better for learning new motor skills than massed ones. The more skilled, confident, and interested a person is, the longer practice period he can tolerate. The awkward

1. Joseph B. Oxendine, *Psychology of Motor Learning* (New York: Appleton-Century-Crofts, 1968), pp. 205-221.
2. Robert N. Singer, *Motor Learning and Human Performance* (New York: The Macmillan Co., 1968), pp. 190-205.

Figure 5.1. Partner-tug-of-war with towels should be tried before team-tug-of-war.

less motivation from a set time period than from a set number of trials or repetitions. When he knows he has just five trials before going on to another activity, for instance, he is likely to exert maximum effort on each one. Some research indicates that the number of trials should be large in the early stages of learning and then progressively decreased as skill improves. Hunt[3] among others, however, recommends that a practice session for a cerebral palsied person end soon after he experiences his first success. In this way positive attitudes are developed toward both the self and the activity. It seems highly possible that the response to massed and distributed practice varies with each specific skill, self-concept, and temperament. Much research on this topic is needed in adapted physical education.

The educational prescription should recommend the percentage of time during the semester to be devoted to the achievement of each of these and other objectives:

Body Awareness, Basic Movements, and Language Skills

Perceptual-Motor Remediation

Fitness Activities

Relaxation Activities

Game, Dance, and Aquatics aimed toward peer group interaction and acceptance, cooperation, sharing, taking turns, and sportsmanship

Leisure Education—skills and interests to fill empty hours, reduce loneliness, increase use of community resources, and facilitate social contacts with individuals and small groups.

The adapted physical educator may wish to ask both the pupil and his parents to rank these objectives in order of importance before writing his prescription. After assigning percentages of time to broad areas, he will need to break each objective down into measurable tasks and suggest the amount of time or number of trials for the accomplishment of each task.

The following questions concerning special environmental adaptations should be answered.

1. Should the class be conducted outdoors or indoors? What are the criteria for determining days too windy, cold, or damp for outdoor play?
2. Is a pollen or dust free environment needed? Should mats and other equipment be of non-allergic composition?
3. Are ramps required or special equipment for persons with prostheses, crutches, or wheelchairs?
4. Are mirrors, videotapes, or films needed for optimum achievement of goals?
5. What adaptations should be made in temperature, lighting, acoustics, and other variables?
6. What should be the space (dimensions) of the instructional area?

Some environmental conditions, like the reduction of space, characterize certain teaching styles. These were described in conjunction with four distinct instructional approaches in Chapter 3. Among the environmental variables which should be consciously manipulated for the good of the child are size of space, definition of boundaries, and starting position and routine. The options are as follows on page 74.

3. Valerie Hunt, *Recreation for the Handicapped* (New York: Prentice-Hall, Inc., 1955), p. 141.

Environmental Options to Be Prescribed

Most restrictive   *Least restrictive*

Size of Space

Cubicle	Reduced	Normal Play Area

Boundaries

Clearly defined by partitions, fences, or hedges	Defined by painted lines, ropes, mats, textural surface of ground or floor	Defined verbally using land-marks and/or imaginary lines

Starting Position and Routine

Floor or wall spots. Pupil goes directly to spot and sits or stands until teacher gives instructions.	Assigned space like a specific one-fourth of room or piece of apparatus. Pupil may do warm-ups or play before class officially begins as long as he remains in this space.	No assigned space. Pupil may move and play as he wishes before class officially begins.

The overall teaching climate can be designed to speed a child up or slow him down. Traditionally, physical education has strived to develop speed, reaction time, and circulorespiratory endurance. If a pupil tends to be hyperactive, particularly if he is taking medication to control this problem, the teaching climate must be modified to emphasize deceleration, relaxation, and self-control. Chapters 11 and 12 focus upon such objectives.

The teaching prescription may recommend the implementation of certain principles in the organization and conduct of adapted physical education. Illustrative of such principles in checklist form are the following:

1. Maintenance of high degree of structure
2. Reduction of environmental space
3. Provision of additional time and special quiet place for calming down and making transition from physical activity back to the sedentary demands of the classroom
4. Elimination of irrelevant auditory stimuli
5. Elimination of irrelevant visual stimuli
6. Enhancement of stimulus value of instructional apparatus or equipment.
   If color is to be used, which color?
7. Reliance upon special social incentives and/or extrinsic awards (behavior modification)
8. Application of shaping or operant conditioning techniques (breaking lesson into minute tasks with reward for each tiny success)
9. Special attention to whole-part-whole methodology
10. Balancing of team or group composition so that behavioral extremes neutralize each other. Specifically, should this pupil be placed with mostly active or passive children?

Cushion Activities in which the pupil feels secure and is confident of success are important in working with these pupils. The teaching prescription should list such activities so that the adapted physical educator can capitalize on each pupil's strengths. These cushion activities may also be used as a reward after the child has exerted optimum effort toward the mastery of a new skill.

Remediation and/or compensation activities should be listed which will assist in ameliorating weaknesses. It is recommended that the problem be listed in one column and directly opposite it, a listing of specific activities. An example follows in Table 9.

Table 9 *Illustrative Physical Education Prescription*

Problem	Remediation and/or Compensation
1. Static Balance	a. Instruction on principles of balance with special emphasis on use of wide base and lowering center of gravity
	b. Provision of barre or rope to hold onto during exercises performed on one foot
	c. Five trials daily of each of the following: Stork stand, eyes open; Bass stick test; Alternate leg swings to music (32 counts); Static squat with arm circles (20 seconds); Pliés to music; Balancing on boxes or blocks of varying dimensions
2. Round Shoulders	a. Body awareness training in front of full-length mirror 3 times daily, 5 minutes each time
	b. Option of two of these activities daily: (1) back crawl in swimming pool or in supine lying position on narrow bench (2) crab walk—lengths or equivalent time in games like crab walk soccer or tag (3) isometric presses on doorway (4) exercises stated on p. 101.

Recommended Activities

1. Read Chapters 6-13 before attempting to use the illustrative checklists and questions in this chapter.
2. Write a case study on a child whom you have observed for several weeks. In this case study, answer the questions and fill in the checklists contained herein.
3. Select several persons who appear to need help in the regular physical education setting. Identify one or more specific problems of each and write prescriptions suggesting compensatory and/or remediation activities.

American Alliance for Health, Physical Education, Recreation. *Testing for Impaired, Disabled, and Handicapped Individuals.* Washington, D.C.: AAHPER, 1975.

American College of Sports Medicine, ed. *Guidelines for Graded Exercise Testing and Exercise Prescription.* Philadelphia: Lea & Febiger, 1975.

Benton, Sheila. *Intensive Programming for Slow Learners.* Columbus, Ohio: Charles E. Merrill Publishing Co., 1968.

Carter, Darrell B., ed. *Interdisciplinary Approaches to Learning Disorders.* Philadelphia: Chilton Book Company, 1970.

Geddes, Dolores. *Physical Activities for Individuals with Handicapping Conditions.* St. Louis: The C. V. Mosby Co., 1974.

Morris, P. R., and Whiting, H. T. A. *Motor Impairment and Compensatory Education.* Philadelphia: Lea & Febiger, 1971.

Overs, Robert; O'Connor, Elizabeth; and DeMarco, Barbara. *Avocational Activities for the Handicapped: A Handbook for Avocational Counseling.* Springfield, Illinois: Charles C. Thomas, 1974.

Peter, Laurence J. *Prescriptive Teaching.* New York: McGraw-Hill Book Co., 1965.

Rarick, G. Lawrence; Dobbins, D. Alan; and Broadhead, Geoffrey D. *The Motor Domain and Its Correlates In Educationally Handicapped Children.* Englewood Cliffs, New Jersey: Prentice-Hall, Inc., 1976.

Vodola, Thomas M. *Individualized Physical Education Program for the Handicapped Child.* Englewood Cliffs, New Jersey: Prentice-Hall, Inc., 1973.

Wessell, Janet. *I Can: Individualized Physical Education Curriculum Materials.* East Lansing: Michigan State University, 1975.

6 Postures

Figure 6.0. Instructor requests student to select the body type picture which most closely resembles his own as part of posture counseling. See Rowe and Caldwell Somatic Apperception Test reference on page 84.

The expression of the face balks account,
But the expression of a well-made man appears not only in his face,
It is in his limbs and joints also, it is curiously in the joints of
    his hips and wrists,
It is in his walk, the carriage of his neck, the flex of his waist and
    knees, dress does not hide him,
The strong sweet quality he has strikes through the cotton and broadcloth,
To see him pass conveys as much as the best poem, perhaps more,
You linger to see his back, and the back of his neck and shoulder side.

Walt Whitman
from Children of Adam, part 2
of I Sing the Body Electric [1]

Each man's postures are expressions of his thoughts, feelings, and moods. Physical education is the only subject in the curriculum which focuses upon the body as an instrument of expression. Through the appraisal of the postures of school children and the subsequent amelioration of problems of body alignment, the physical educator makes a unique contribution to personality development, peer acceptance, and vocational success.

Each person possesses not one but many postures. Any position is a posture, and one individual asssumes thousands of static and dynamic postures each day—standing, walking, running, sitting, sleeping, stooping, climbing, and ad infinitum. The appraisal of body alignment is based, therefore, upon careful observation of many postures.

Group Screening

Screening for postural deviations should be completed early in the semester. Whenever possible, students should be kept unaware that they are being so screened. Instead, they may think they are practicing selected locomotor skills or engaging in movement exploration. Ideally, they are moving in a circle and responding to changes in direction while the

Figure 6.1. Mirror work to increase body awareness.

teacher observes from the center of the circle. Their movements should be natural, spontaneous, and relaxed. Prior to beginning the circular activity it is desirable to group the students informally according to body build. To facilitate this process, four or five students representing different body types are selected as leaders. The students are then requested to stand behind the person with the body type most similar to his own. The resulting files are structured into a circle, and screening begins.

One of the most efficient procedures is to group the students into quartiles. First identify the 25 percent of the class which has the best postures and the 25 percent which has the worst postures. Then place the remaining students in the upper and lower middle quartiles.

1. Harold Chapnick, ed., *The Illustrated Leaves of Grass* (New York: Grosset and Dunlap, Inc., 1969), p. 74.

Approximately one week later, without reviewing your notes, repeat the screening procedures. Compare the names of the students assigned to each quartile with those assigned previously. Schedule individual posture examinations for those students who fell into the lowest quartile during both screening sessions.

Identical procedures may be used in the classroom when the students are unaware that their sitting postures are being evaluated. The way a student sits at a desk, the tilt of his head, the distance of his eyes from the paper, and whether or not his feet touch the floor all have significance in determining postural fitness. Postures, like movement patterns, are unique to the individual. Family similarities appear in postures as well as in faces. Genetic predispositions toward body build, weight, height, and level of energy have as great an influence on postures as do environmental factors.

Individual Examination

Students identified as needing special guidance and counseling with respect to postures are scheduled for an individual examination which may last as long as an hour. The actual evaluation is not time consuming, but once again it is important to consider the whole child, his anxiety about being singled out as different, and his thoughts and feelings about his physical self. The general procedures used in posture counseling parallel those described under fitness counseling in Chapter 10. Unless the teacher plans to schedule relatively frequent follow-up conferences, the individual examination should not be conducted.

Figure 6.3 presents one of the many forms which can be filled out during the examination. It is available through Reedco Incorporated, 5 Easterly Avenue, Auburn, New York 13021. The Reedco form is identical to that used in the New York Posture Test[2] with

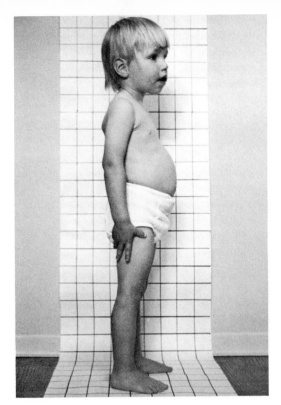

Figure 6.2. Two-year-old stands in front of posture grid. His posture is normal for his age.

the exception of three omissions: feet, side view of shoulders, and side view of chest.

Posture Grid

The room in which the posture examination is administered should have a grid comprised of two-inch squares on the wall. The vertical lines are at right angles to the horizontal lines and extend all of the way to the floor. These lines provide reference points for ascertaining the correct alignment of body parts. Footprints should be painted on the floor in front of the grid to facilitate correct standing positions.

2. The New York State Fitness Test, which includes the Posture Test, can be obtained by writing to the State Education Department, Division of Health, Physical Education, and Recreation, Albany, New York 12224.

Table 10 *Anatomical Reference Points Crossed By the Plumb Line*

Back View	Side View	Front View
1. Center of head	1. Earlobe	1. Center of forehead
2. Center of spinous processes	2. Tip of shoulder (acromion process)	2. Center of nose
3. Cleft between buttocks	3. Greater trochanter of femur (center of hip)	3. Center of chin
4. Center between knees	4. Posterior to patella	4. Center of linea alba
5. Center between ankles, i.e., an equal distance between the two medial malleoli	5. About 1 1/2 inches in front of lateral malleolus	5. Center of umbilicus
		6. Center of symphysis pubis
		7. Center between knees
		8. Center between ankles, i.e., an equal distance between the two medial malleoli

Some individuals prefer a posture screen comprised of vertical and horizontal strings hooked onto a frame so as to make two, four, or six-inch squares which serve as reference points. The student stands behind the screen and is viewed through it.

Plumb Line

A plumb line is a long string which is suspended from the ceiling. A weight is attached to the lower end of the string to assure that it hangs straight. It is used as a vertical reference point to check the alignment of body parts. When used in the evaluation of posterior and anterior views, the plumb line can be considered the midline or line of gravity for the body. Table 10 states the anatomical land points which the plumb line should crossect in a well balanced body. Abnormally large busts or buttocks may change these landmarks as do amputations and other orthopedic deviations.

Posture Photographs

Photographs of students whose postural fitness warrants individual examination are recommended for the following reasons:

(1) To enable the student to see himself as others see him and to serve as a motivational device toward positive change.
(2) To orient parents and the general public to the broad objectives of physical education.
(3) To serve as a criterion measure against which postural change can be estimated.
(4) To supplement school files, thereby improving the permanent record of the whole child.

These procedures are recommended in photographing postures:

1. Two students standing in front of the grid can be photographed simulta-

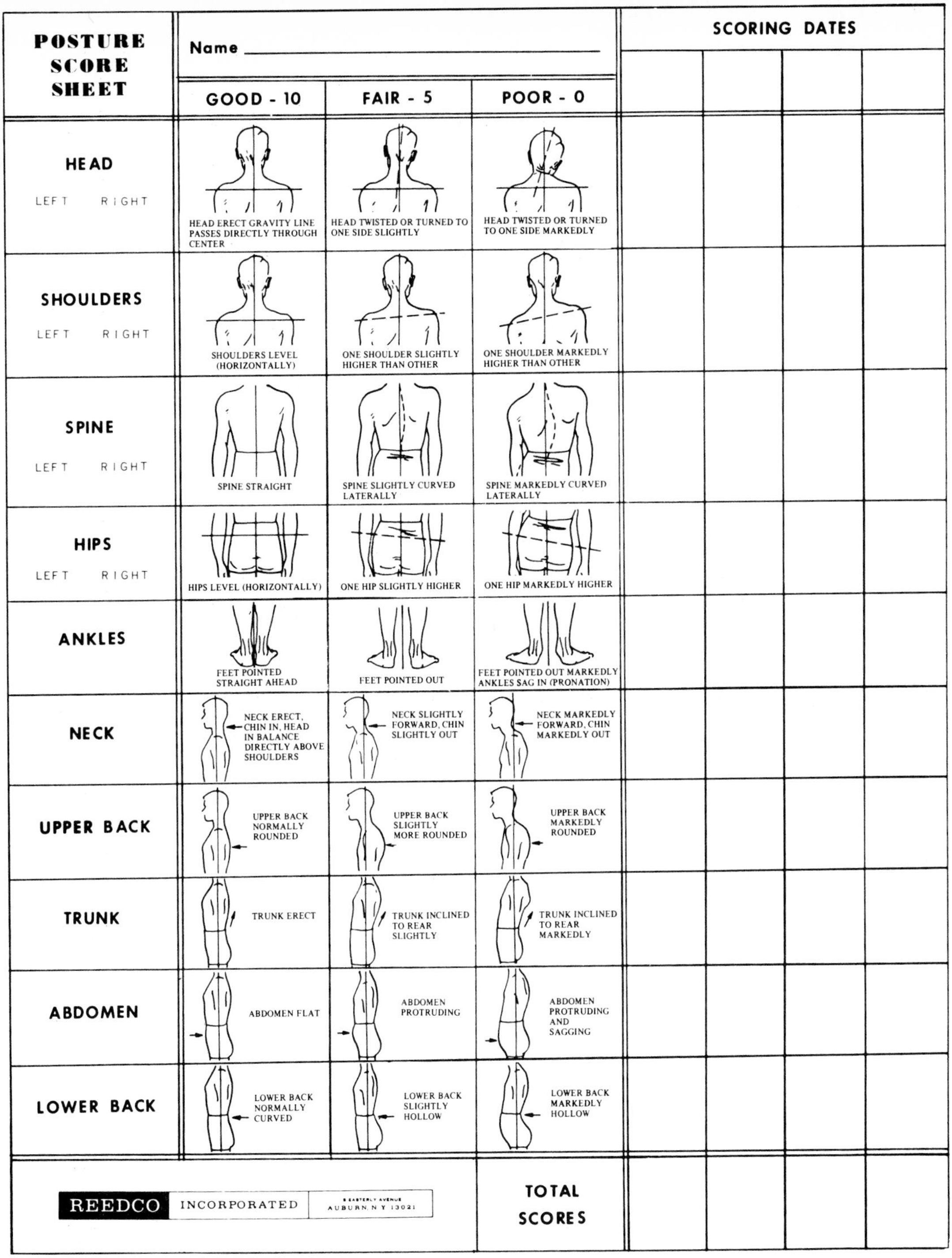

POSTURE SCORE SHEET	Name _____			SCORING DATES					
	GOOD - 10	**FAIR - 5**	**POOR - 0**						
HEAD LEFT RIGHT	HEAD ERECT GRAVITY LINE PASSES DIRECTLY THROUGH CENTER	HEAD TWISTED OR TURNED TO ONE SIDE SLIGHTLY	HEAD TWISTED OR TURNED TO ONE SIDE MARKEDLY						
SHOULDERS LEFT RIGHT	SHOULDERS LEVEL (HORIZONTALLY)	ONE SHOULDER SLIGHTLY HIGHER THAN OTHER	ONE SHOULDER MARKEDLY HIGHER THAN OTHER						
SPINE LEFT RIGHT	SPINE STRAIGHT	SPINE SLIGHTLY CURVED LATERALLY	SPINE MARKEDLY CURVED LATERALLY						
HIPS LEFT RIGHT	HIPS LEVEL (HORIZONTALLY)	ONE HIP SLIGHTLY HIGHER	ONE HIP MARKEDLY HIGHER						
ANKLES	FEET POINTED STRAIGHT AHEAD	FEET POINTED OUT	FEET POINTED OUT MARKEDLY ANKLES SAG IN (PRONATION)						
NECK	NECK ERECT, CHIN IN, HEAD IN BALANCE DIRECTLY ABOVE SHOULDERS	NECK SLIGHTLY FORWARD, CHIN SLIGHTLY OUT	NECK MARKEDLY FORWARD, CHIN MARKEDLY OUT						
UPPER BACK	UPPER BACK NORMALLY ROUNDED	UPPER BACK SLIGHTLY MORE ROUNDED	UPPER BACK MARKEDLY ROUNDED						
TRUNK	TRUNK ERECT	TRUNK INCLINED TO REAR SLIGHTLY	TRUNK INCLINED TO REAR MARKEDLY						
ABDOMEN	ABDOMEN FLAT	ABDOMEN PROTRUDING	ABDOMEN PROTRUDING AND SAGGING						
LOWER BACK	LOWER BACK NORMALLY CURVED	LOWER BACK SLIGHTLY HOLLOW	LOWER BACK MARKEDLY HOLLOW						
REEDCO INCORPORATED 8 EASTERLY AVENUE AUBURN N Y 13021			**TOTAL SCORES**						

Figure 6.3. Posture score sheet. Reprinted by permission of Reedco Incorporated.

neously and the resulting snapshot divided.

2. Only back and side views of the student are essential.

3. The students should be barefoot. Swimming trunks or shorts are recommended for boys. Pants and bra or a two-piece swimming suit are recommended for girls. Long hair should be pinned up so that the spinous processes of the cervical vertebrae are visible.

4. The back should be bare with a black dot placed on each spinous process. An ordinary magic marker makes the dot.

5. Polaroid cameras have the advantage of instantaneous film development. If the snapshot is not good, a second one can be taken immediately.

6. Students must be assured that pictures will be held in confidence. Often it is more valuable to give the pictures to the student for further study than to file them.

The remainder of this chapter describes body typing and various postures which may be identified during the individual examination. The severity of the postural deviation is marked as 1, 2, or 3 with 3 being the most severe. Exercises to ameliorate postural problems are suggested also.

Body Typing

Posture evaluation begins with the classification of each student with respect to body type or build. This procedure, called *somatotyping*, enables the physical educator to determine the student's limitations in sports, dance, and aquatics and thus to offer scientific guidance in assisting him in the development of lifetime leisure skills.

William H. Sheldon is accredited with refining somatotype techniques.[3] He identified three basic body types and photographed 4,000 men, classifying them in accordance with the characteristics of each body type. This research showed that no one meets the qualifications for any one body type but that each individual is comprised of components of all three types.

A somatotype classification is comprised of three numbers as 236 or 171. Each digit ranges from 1 to 7, with 1 representing the lowest amount of a characteristic.

The first number in the series indicates the degree that characteristics of the *endomorph* body build are present. These characteristics are (1) roundness and softness of the body, (2) breasts and buttocks well developed, (3) high square shoulders and short neck, and (4) predominance of abdomen over thorax.

The second number indicates the degree that characteristics of the *mesomorph* body build are present. These characteristics are (1) solid, well developed musculature, (2) bones usually large and covered with thick muscle, (3) forearm thickness and relative largeness of wrist, hand, and fingers, (4) large thorax and relatively slender waist, (5) broad shoulders and well developed trapezius and deltoid, (6) buttocks exhibit muscular dimpling, and (7) abdominal muscles prominent and thick.

The third number indicates the degree that characteristics of the *ectomorph* body build are present. These characteristics are (1) small bones and thin muscles, (2) linearity, fragility, and delicacy of body, (3) limbs relatively long, trunk short, and shoulders narrow, (4) shoulders droop and predisposed toward winged scapulae (5) abdomen and lumbar curve flat, (6) thoracic curve relatively sharp and elevated, and (7) no bulging of muscle at any point.

A predominantly endomorphic person commonly has a somatotype of 721, 731, or 631. For such persons, physical education

3. William H. Sheldon, *Atlas of Man: A Guide for Somatotyping of Adult Males At All Ages* (New York: Harper & Row), 1954.

should emphasize the management of obesity. Strenuous activities such as contact sports, weight lifting, and pyramid building are contraindicated, particularly during periods of rapid growth. Their joints are more subject to trauma than those of other pupils, either from cumulative daily gravitational stresses or sudden traumas. Almost always, during childhood and adolescence, physiological age is not commensurate with chronological age. The endomorph is predisposed to such postural deviations as knock-knees, pronated feet, flat feet, sagging abdomen, round shoulders, and round back. Physical education for obese youngsters is discussed in Chapter 18.

A predominantly mesomorphic person commonly has a somatotype of 171, 172, 272, or even 372. For success in contact sports, the pupil requires a certain amount of cushioning by fat. A 2, 3, or 4 rating in endomorphy is therefore desirable for athletes. Football players typically have somatotypes of 273, 371, or 471; baseball players tend to have 262, 263, or 462; while tennis players and long distance runners may be classified as 153 or 154. Mesomorphs are better adapted structurally, organically, and neurologically to meet stress than other body types. They seldom exhibit severe posture deviations. Their major prob-

lem seems to be a substantial gain in weight after age thirty.

A predominantly ectomorphic person commonly has a somatotype of 217, 227, or 236. The 217 extreme seldom succeeds in athletic endeavors; he is characterized by muscle flaccidity, a floppiness of movement, and looseness at joints which predisposes him to many postural problems which do not respond to exercise. He simply lacks potential to persist in movement long enough for the principle of overload to be operative; he fatigues easily and is sometimes described as having *asthenia*. He can be helped best by a "slowing down" program of physical education which provides instruction in relaxation and supervised rest. Less extreme ectomorph types often excel in activities like cross country running in which they set their own pace. They tend to have too little body padding to engage safely in contact sports. Likewise, they chill easily and require shorter swimming periods and outdoor play sessions than their peers.

Several body image tests have been designed to determine the extent to which persons recognize their own body types. In most of these the pupil is presented with seven pictures, each differing from the other quantitatively on somatotype dimensions. The pic-

| 1 | 2 | 3 | 4 | 5 | 6 | 7 |

Most ectomorphic

Most endomorphic

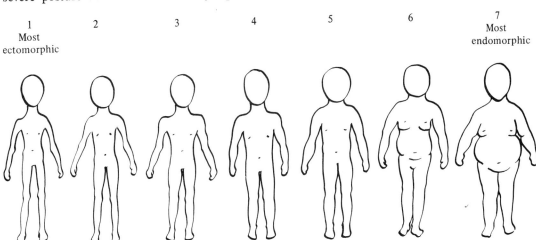

Figure 6.4. Seven body types differing on somatotype dimensions.

tures are presented in random order, and the child is requested to select the one which most resembles himself.[4, 5] In other instances, he is asked "Which drawing is most like you?" and "Which drawing would you rather be like?"[6] Regardless of the approach used, instruction geared toward understanding and appreciating body types is valuable.

The Spinal Column

Normal Development

At birth the entire spinal column of the infant is flexed in a single C curve. Only when the extensor muscles of the neck and back are sufficiently strengthened by random kicking and wiggling do the cervical and lumbar curves begin to appear. The cervical curve develops at about four to five months of age while the lumbar curve begins to develop sometime after the child learns to walk. Toddlers and young children with disabilities which prevent upright locomotion characteristically have *flat backs*. This condition is normal during the months when the child is gaining confidence in walking and running activities. If flat back persists beyond the toddler stage, it is considered a postural deviation.

The normal preschool child tends to develop an exaggerated lumbar curve which may persist throughout grade school. This condition is caused by the imbalance in the strength of the abdominal muscles and the hip flexors. It is normal for the abdominal musculature of the preschool child to be too weak to maintain the pelvis in a neutral position.

The resulting lordosis characterizes the young child's postures until sufficient abdominal strength is developed to counteract the downward pull of the hip flexors. Lordosis, therefore, is normal in a young child and should not be labeled as a posture deviation until adolescence. The degree of lumbar curvature should, however, lessen from year to year.

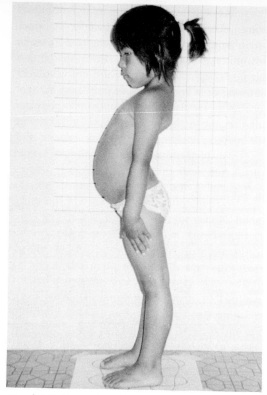

Figure 6.5. Protruding abdomen and lordosis are normal for the preschool child.

In the adult, four curves are readily discernible in the spinal column. Viewed from the back, these are
(1) Concave—Cervical spine comprised of seven vertebrae
(2) Convex—Thoracic spine comprised of twelve vertebrae
(3) Concave—Lumbar spine comprised of five vertebrae

4. Allen S. Rowe and Willard E. Caldwell, "The Somatic Apperception Test," *The Journal of General Psychology* Vol. 68 (January, 1963), pp. 59-69.

5. Eleanor G. Gottesman and Willard E. Caldwell, "The Body-Image Identification Test: A Quantitative Projective Technique to Study An Aspect of Body-Image," *The Journal of Genetic Psychology* Vol. 108 (March, 1966), pp. 19-33.

6. Ellington Darden, "A Comparison of Body-Image and Self-Concept Variables Among Sport Groups," *Research Quarterly* Vol. 43 (March, 1972), pp. 7-15.

(4) Convex—Sacral spine comprised of five sacral vertebrae fused in adulthood and called the sacrum.

Erect, extended carriage results when the thoracic and sacral flexion curves are in balance with the cervical and lumbar hyperextension curves. Whenever one curve increases, the other curves tend to increase also to compensate for the imbalance.

In adulthood the flexor muscles of the trunk and abdomen should be equal in strength to the extensor muscles of the back. Each exerts a pull on the spinal column in a kind of tug-of-war. As long as neither side wins, *anteroposterior* stability is said to be good and no posture deviations exist. When a posture problem becomes evident, it is important to analyze the imbalance of the muscle groups by considering these questions.

(1) Muscles on which surface are too tight, i.e., stronger than their antagonists? Which stretching exercises are indicated?

(2) Muscles on which surface are too loose, i.e., weaker than their antagonists? Which strengthening exercises are indicated?

Usually strength exercises are chosen for amelioration of posture problems. The principle of *reciprocal innervation* should be remembered: when muscles on one surface are being strengthened, muscles on the antagonistic surface are being stretched simultaneously. Regardless of the type of exercise selected, both surfaces are affected.

Deviations of the Spinal Column

The most common deviations of the spinal column are (1) forward head and neck; (2) lordosis; (3) kyphosis; (4) flat back; and (5) scoliosis.

Forward Head and Neck

Normally the head is balanced above the cervical vertebrae in such a way that minimal muscle effort is required to resist the pull of gravity. When the earlobe is no longer in alignment with the tip of the shoulder (acromion process), forward head and neck is diagnosed.

Mild Degree

In its mildest form, the head tends to droop forward for two reasons: (1) when any segment of the body is out of alignment, greater muscle effort is required to resist the pull of gravity and (2) the neck extensors are not sufficiently strong to counteract the pull of gravity. The normal posterior concavity of the cervical spine increases so slowly that most persons are unaware that forward head and neck is developing. In the mild stage the best ameliorative exercise is practice in discriminating between good and poor alignment. Balancing and carrying relatively heavy weights on the head while performing locomotor movements increase proprioceptive awareness as does movement exploration in front of the mirror.

Severe Degree (See Figure 6.7)

In more severe cases, usually accompanied by dorsal kyphosis, the cervical spine hyperextends to whatever degree is necessary to compensate for the forward droop of the head and the increasing dorsal convexity of the thoracic spine. The natural compensation of the body to maintain the balance of the head and the other spinal curves results in adaptive shortening and tightening of the cervical extensors, mainly the upper trapezius and splenius capitis and cervicis. This tightness is accentuated in the area of the seventh cervical vertebrae where a layer of fat tends to accumulate. The combined prominence of the seventh cervical vertebra and excess adipose tissue is called a *dowager's hump*. The neck flexors tend to stretch, sag, and become functionally worthless. This hyperextension of the neck is sometimes called cervical lordosis.

In mild forms both the neck flexors and extensors are weak. Gravity, rather than an im-

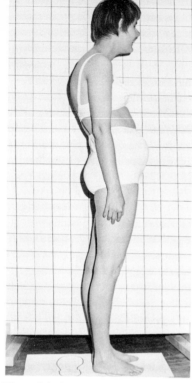

Figure 6.6. Severe degree of forward head and neck causes compensatory dorsal and lumbar curves (Denton State School).

balance of muscular strength, is primarily responsible for the forward position. In the severe form the flexors and extensors are still weak, but the neck extensors have adaptively shortened and tightened, giving the false impression of strength. In mild forward head and neck, the extensors primarily need strengthening exercises. Flexibility is not a problem. As the condition becomes progressively severe, the muscles may feel stiff, tense, and sore. The emphasis in exercise shifts to flexibility, particularly stretching the cervical extensors.

Disorders which often accompany forward head and neck are kyphosis and/or round shoulders. The student whose head tends to droop forward may be forced to elevate his chin and lift his head to maintain his eyes on a level plane; this, in turn, exaggerates the hyperextension of the neck.

Forward head and neck may eventually become normal carriage in our sedentary American life where emphasis is placed upon early book learning and a large proportion of the population holds desk jobs. It is estimated that 70 percent of all American school children have some degree of forward head and neck.

Ameliorative Exercises

1. *Chin to shoulder touch.* Attempt to align head and neck with other segments of the body. Rotate slowly to the left until chin touches shoulder. Repeat to opposite side.
2. *Lateral flex with ear touch.* Attempt to align head and neck with other segments of the body. Laterally flex to the left until ear touches shoulder. Repeat to opposite side.

Excessive Head Tilt

If the top of the head is tilted toward the right, the deviation of right tilt (RT) is recorded. The symbol LT is used for the opposite condition. A head habitually held in a tilted position is often symptomatic of vision or hearing impairments. Almost always the individual is unaware of the tilt and needs exercises for improving proprioception.

Over a long duration of time the head tilt causes an adaptive shortening and tightening of the neck muscles on the side of the tilt. Tight muscles on the right side may be stretched by lateral flexion exercises to the left and vice versa. A slow static stretch and hold is more effective than rhythmic exercises.

Torticollis

Torticollis, or wry neck, results from a shortening of one of the sternocleidomastoids. This causes a rotation of the head to the op-

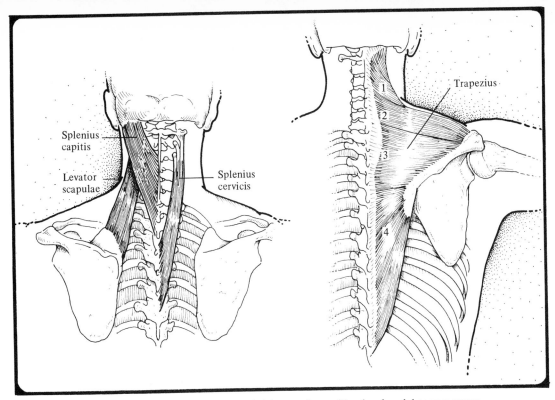

Figure 6.7. Cervical extensors adaptively shorten and tighten as forward head and neck becomes severe.

posite side and a lateral flexion to the same side. The condition may be acquired or congenital. When acquired, stretching exercises are recommended in combination with remediation of the visual or auditory loss which precipitated the curvature. When congenital, the condition may be corrected at an early age by surgery and/or bracing.

Torticollis is often accompanied by a raised shoulder. The lateral spinal curvature in the cervical region may eventually provoke a compensatory lateral curvature in the thoracic region.

Kyphosis

Translated literally *kyphos* means a sharp angulation. Increasing backward convexity in the thoracic region results in the condition commonly known as humpback, hunchback, Pott's curvature, or round upper back. Increased backward convexity in the lumbar region results in the condition known as flat back or lumbar kyphosis. For the purposes of this book, use of the term kyphosis is limited to the postural deviation of round upper back. The condition is rarely found among normal children in the public school setting.

True kyphosis is associated with disease of the intervertebral disks or of the epiphyseal area of the vertebrae. The intervertebral disk is the fibrocartilage padding between vertebral bodies. The disk is comprised of two parts: (1) the outer annulus fibrosus known for its strength and elasticity and (2) the inner nucleus pulposus which contains fluid which absorbs shock in locomotor movements and maintains the separation of the vertebral

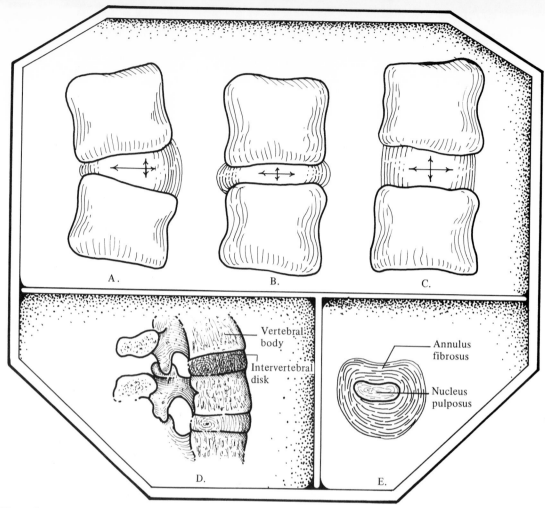

Figure 6.8. The intervertebral disk. (A) flexion of the spine permitted by shift of fluid. (B) compression of the disk occurs when noncompressible fluid of nucleus expands the elastic annulus. (C) normal extended position with annulus fibers held taut; internal pressure is indicated by arrows. (D) section of vertebrae. (E) cross section of intervertebral disk.

bodies. The nucleus pulposus has all of the characteristics of a hydraulic system.

Any degenerative disease of the intervertebral disk is characterized by changes in pressure which cause pain. In old age, the fluid content of the nucleus pulposus decreases and the annulus fibrosus becomes progressively less elastic; these changes limit motion of the back. Any prolonged inactivity seems to contribute to degeneration of the intervertebral disks. Severely and profoundly retarded individuals whose mobility is limited often exhibit kyphosis at a young age.

Pott's Disease, or tuberculosis of the spine, also causes kyphosis. This inflammation of the vertebral bodies occurs most often in children and young adults. The word *tuberculosis* means "a little swelling," and Pott's Disease is characterized by the formation of little tubercles on the vertebral bodies. Destruction and compression of the vertebral bodies affects the spinal cord and adjacent nerves to the extent that movement becomes extremely painful. The characteristic kyphotic curvature is called a *gibbus*, meaning hump. The condition of having a humpback is *gibbosity*. A medical synonym for Pott's Disease is *tuberculous spondylitis.*

Juvenile kyphosis, or *Scheurmann's Disease,* is a disturbance in normal vertebral growth. It results from *epiphysitis,* inflammation of an epiphysis,[7] and/or *osteochondritis,* inflammation of cartilage, either of which may cause fragmentation of vertebral bodies. One or several vertebrae are involved. The etiology is generally unknown, and the condition has been likened to Perthes' Disease in that it seems to have an active phase during which exercise, particularly forward flexion, is contraindicated. The child should be protected from all flexion movements by a hyperextension brace which places the weight on the neural arches rather than the defective vertebral bodies. Although the child experiences some discomfort, the pain is not great enough to impose limitation of natural movement; sometimes the condition is pain-free. In such instances it may be difficult to prevent the child from engaging in physical activity. Unfortunately if bracing and nonactivity are not enforced, the resulting kyphotic hump may be both severe and persistent. When X rays reveal the coalescence of fragmented areas, the child may participate in physical education classes with no restrictions. Occasionally he will continue to wear a back brace, body jacket, or cast for a number of months after the disease is arrested.

The following characteristics may be observed in kyphosis:

(1) Upper back extensors and lower trapezius are weak.
(2) Anterior intercostals and pectorals are excessively tight.
(3) Sternum is depressed.
(4) Rib cage is lowered and attachments of the diaphragm around its circumference are lowered which causes malposition of internal organs.
(5) Flexibility of the rib cage and/or the shoulder joint may be limited.
(6) A compensatory curve may develop in the lumbar region.

Kyphosis is usually, but not always, accompanied by round shoulders, hollow chest, and forward head and neck.

Ameliorative Exercises for Strengthening Back Extensors and Trapezius III and IV

1. Prone lying on a table with head and trunk hanging downward, head supported on a chair.
   In this position, with hands clasped behind the neck, raise the trunk slowly to a horizontal position.
2. Prone lying, hands on hips. Raise head and shoulders only approximately two inches off of floor.
3. Prone lying on a table with arms in overhead position: do breaststroke.

Ameliorative Exercises for Stretching Anterior Intercostals and Pectorals

1. Hanging, facing outward, from stall bars or a horizontal bar.
2. Sitting in chair; top of chair at about midthoracic level: hands behind head. Lean trunk backward as you adduct scapula and pull arms backward. Do not hyperextend lumbar spine.

Note that none of these exercises permits forward bending. It should be remembered that forward bending is contraindicated in kyphosis.

Lordosis

Lordosis, also called sway or hollow back, is an exaggeration of the normal posterior con-

7. Epiphysis is defined as a juvenile piece of bone separated from a parent bone in early life by cartilage, but later becoming a part of the parent bone; a center for ossification at each extremity of long bones.

cave curve in the lumbar region. It not only affects the five lumbar vertebrae, but also throws the pelvis out of correct alignment.

Lordosis has many possible causes: (1) genetic predisposition; (2) weak abdominal muscles which allow the pelvis to tilt downward anteriorly; (3) weak gluteal muscles and hamstrings which cannot counteract this anterior tilt; (4) overly tight lumbar extensors which contribute to an anterior tilt; (5) overdeveloped hip flexors which cause anterior tilt; and (6) on rare occasions occupations like professional dance. Before recommending ameliorative exercises for lordosis, it is necessary to administer flexibility tests to determine specifically which muscles are tight. Illustrative tests follow.

Flexibility of Hip Flexors

Can you lie on table with one knee clasped to chest and the other leg straight and hanging completely over the end of table? If you have normal flexibility, you can keep one knee flexed to the chest and waistline flat on table while simultaneously lowering other leg to a 180° continuum with the trunk.

Flexibility of Spinal Extensors

1. Can you lie on the floor relaxed with legs extended and flatten your waistline to the floor? How long can you keep it there?
2. Can you stand against the wall, with heels no more than 1-2 inches from the wall, and flatten waistline against the wall? It is a failure to bend the knees or to round the upper back.
3. Can you stand and touch toes without bending your knees? (Observe whether spine has smooth, continous contour.)
4. Can you paint the rainbow?
5. Can you assume a wide stride long sitting position on the floor? To what extent can you touch chest to thighs while in this position?

In true lordosis the following characteristics will probably be present.

Figure 6.9. Paint the rainbow can be used as a test of lumbar flexibility and as an exercise to ameliorate lordosis.

1. Anterior tilt of pelvis.
2. Tight lower back muscles, tight lumbodorsal fascia, tight hip flexors, tight iliofemoral (Y) ligaments, weak abdominals, weak hamstrings, and weak gluteals.
3. Knees may be hyperextended.
4. Compensatory kyphosis may develop to balance the increased concavity; if so, the pectorals and anterior intercostals may be tight also.
5. Upper body tends to shift backward as a compensatory measure. This shifts the weight of the body from the vertebral bodies onto the neural arches, bringing the spinous processes closer together than normal and sometimes pinching nerves.
6. Lower back pain.
7. Faulty functioning of internal organs, including those of digestion, elimination, and reproduction.
8. Predisposition toward dysmenorrhea, menstrual pain.
9. Increased incidence of back strain and back injuries.

Correction of lordosis, at least in the early stages, is largely a matter of increasing proprioceptive awareness so that the student can feel the difference between an anterior and a posterior tilt. Alternate anterior and posterior pelvic tilts should be practiced while supine lying, kneeling, sitting, standing, and perform-

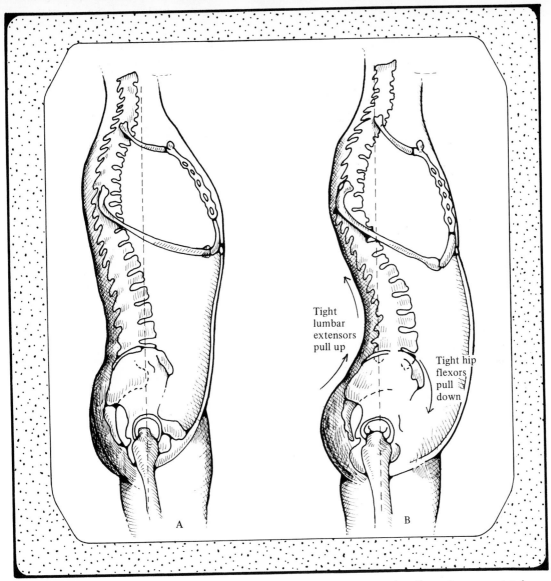

Tight
lumbar
extensors
pull up

Tight hip
flexors
pull
down

A

B

Figure 6.10. Pelvic tilts. (A) normal pelvic tilt (neutral position) in good posture. The buttocks are tucked in. Anterior and posterior muscles are equal in strength. (B) anterior pelvic tilt causes lordosis and protruding abdomen. The anterior iliac spines are rotated downward by tight hip flexors. The posterior sacrum is rotated upward by tight lumbar extensors.

ing various locomotor activities. Activities like the backbend which emphasize hyperextension of the lumbar spine are contraindicated.

Weak abdominals almost universally accompany lordosis. For this reason strength exercises for the abdominals should be undertaken along with stretching exercises for the tight lumbar extensors. This dual purpose is accomplished to some extent without special effort in accordance with the principle of reciprocal innervation.

Figure 6.11. Rounded back in angry cat exercise ameliorates lordosis.

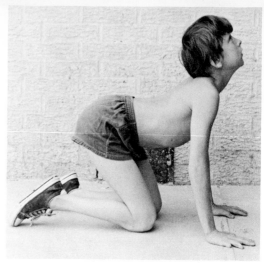

Figure 6.12. Flattened lower back in angry cat exercise.

Ameliorative Exercises

1. Bicycling motion of legs while lying supine with back flattened to maintain contact with the floor.
2. Paint the rainbow. From a supine lying position, flex hips until feet are vertically overhead and twelve to eighteen inches from it.
3. Angry cat exercise. From a hands and knees creeping position, alternate rounding the back like an angry cat with flattening the back.
4. Cross sitting forward bend. From a cross sitting position with hands clasped behind neck, bend forward so that head approaches floor without lifting buttocks. Maintain a slow stretch for several seconds.

In all exercises and activities, whether for posture correction or not, avoid arching the back. Particularly watch the tendency to hyperextend the lumbar spine when performing abdominal exercises and other movements from a supine lying position.

Spondylolisthesis

Spondylolisthesis is a deformity in which the body of the fifth lumbar vertebra and a portion of the spinal column above it slip forward over the base of the sacrum. This problem may be precipitated by lordosis. It limits motion in forward bending and often is very painful because of nerve involvement.

Flat Back

Flat back is a decrease or absence of the normal anteroposterior curves. It is the opposite condition from lordosis. The posterior concavity of the lumbar curve is descreased, i.e., the normal posterior concavity is gradually changing toward convexity.

Characteristics of flat back include:

1. The pelvic inclination is less than normal with the pelvis held in a more-or-less continuous posterior tilt.
2. Back appears too flat with little or no protrusion of the buttocks.

3. Lower back muscles are weak.
4. Hip flexors, especially the psoas major, are weak and elongated.

Flat back is associated with the debutante slouch seen so often in fashion magazines in which young women pose languidly with hips thrust forward and upper back rounded. Such models are usually flat chested and so thin that the abdomen cannot protrude. It is sad that the fashion world chooses to present this image to the American public rather than one of good body alignment with normal busts, hips, and buttocks in gracefully curved balance. Flat back is also characteristic of the body build of young toddlers who have not been walking long enough to develop the lumbar curve.

Ameliorative Exercises
1. Alternate anterior and posterior pelvic tilts from a hook lying position to increase proprioceptive awareness.
2. Hyperextension of the lumbar spine to strengthen back muscles.
3. Prone lying trunk lifts and hold.
4. Prone lying leg lifts and hold.

Scoliosis

Scoliosis is a lateral curvature of the spine. Although the condition begins with a single curve, it usually consists of a primary curve and a compensatory curve in the opposite direction. Usually appearing in early childhood, scoliosis may arrest itself without treatment. Often, however, it becomes progressively debilitating. It is more serious than any of the other common posture deviations and should be referred to a physician.

Lateral curves are described in their early stages as C curvatures and in their later stages as S curvatures. They are classified also as functional, transitional, and structural curves. The structural curve is a permanent one which can be corrected only by surgery; it is usually an S curve. The functional curve is one in which the bony tissues are still pliable and the involved muscles are still flexible. When certain *keynote positions* are assumed, the functional curve straightens out for the duration the position is held. A functional curve can be ameliorated by therapeutic exercise, and most physicians choose to combine prescribed exercises with bracing and/or surgery.

Keynote positions may be used as diagnostic devices or as corrective exercise. Among

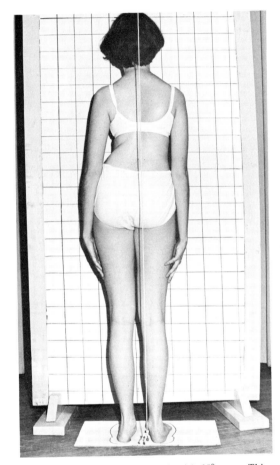

Figure 6.13. Right dorsal scoliosis with 65° curve. This eighteen-year-old has worn a Milwaukee brace and had Harrington instrumentation and spinal fusion. Further correction is not feasible.

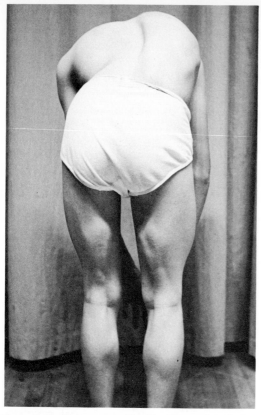

Figure 6.14. Sixteen-year-old with right total scoliosis in Adam's Position. If the curve were not structural, it would disappear in this keynote position.

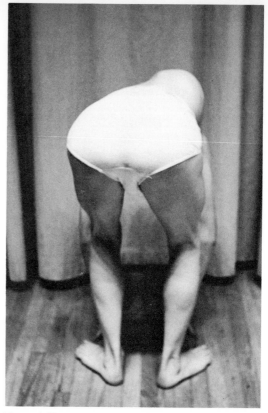

Figure 6.15. Permanent sciliotic hump prominent in Adam's Position. Boy lacks lumbar flexibility to touch toes without bending knees.

the most common keynote positions are the following:

1. Adam's position—relaxed forward bending held for several seconds from a standing posture. The knees are straight so that the flexion occurs from the hips and spinal column.
2. Hanging with both arms from a horizontal bar.
3. Symmetrical arm raise from a standing position. The individual with a total left curve flexes the right arm at the shoulder joint to whatever height is necessary to straighten the spine. The other arm is maintained in a position of abduction. In some cases, raising both

arms and/or raising one leg sideways may help the curve to disappear.

If the lateral curve is not temporarily obliterated by any of these positions, it can be assumed that scoliosis is in a transitional or structural stage. In such instances the physical educator should insist that the child be examined by a physician. No corrective exercises should be undertaken without a permission slip from the parents and a medical clearance from the physician who hopefully will prescribe specific exercises to be practiced under the supervision of adapted physical education personnel.

Lateral curves are named in terms of the direction of their convexity. Among right

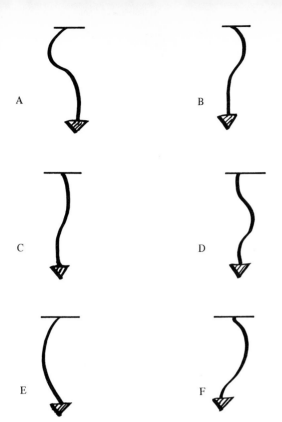

Figure 6.16. Six possible C curves. (A) left dorsal; (B) right dorsal; (C) left lumbar; (D) right lumbar; (E) left total, including dorsal and lumbar spines; (F) right total, including dorsal and lumbar spines.

handed persons, the most common type of scoliosis is the *total left curve*. The six possible C curves are depicted in Figure 6.16.

Explanation of Rotation in Normal and Lateral Curvatures

Kinesiologically, rotation of the trunk is defined in the direction which the anterior vertebral bodies move. If the trunk rotates to the right, the vertebral bodies are turned to the right. Normally any rotation of the trunk to the right is accompanied by a slight amount of lateral flexion to the right. In scoliosis the rule with respect to the normal rotation of vertebral bodies reverses itself. Thus scoliosis is a condi-

tion in which the vertebral bodies rotate toward the convexity of the curve and the spinous processes toward the concavity. This occurs partly because the bodies are less firmly bound together by strong ligaments than the spinous processes.

In the total left curve to the convex side, the following characteristics may be observed.

1. Spinous processes deviate from midline, rotating toward the concavity of the curve.
2. Left shoulder is higher than the other shoulder. Left shoulder may also be carried forward. In appraisal of the asymmetry of the shoulders, check the inferior angles of the scapula to see if one is carried lower than the other, abducted further away from the spinal column, or winged away from the rib cage. Also check the angle between the neck and the shoulder on both sides of the body.
3. The head may be tilted to one side.
4. There is a lateral displacement of the trunk toward the side of convexity since the thorax is no longer balanced directly over the pelvis.
5. Posteriorly, the ribs usually bulge out on the convex side of the curve; rib cage tends to lose its flexibility.
6. Right hip is usually higher than the other and the right iliac crest more prominent. Said in another way, when there is a lateral pelvic tilt, the convexity of the spine is toward the lower hip.
7. Contour of the waistline is affected with the notch on the concave side greater than that on the convex.
8. Right leg may be longer than left. In other words, a long leg will push the hip to a higher level and contribute to curvature on the opposite side.
9. Side bending tends to be freer to the right (concave side) than the left.
10. Forward flexibility of the spine may be

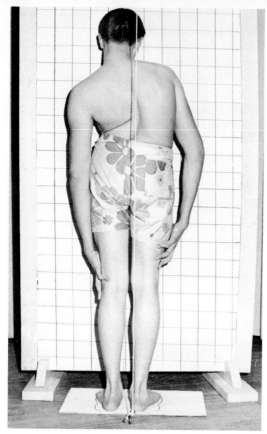

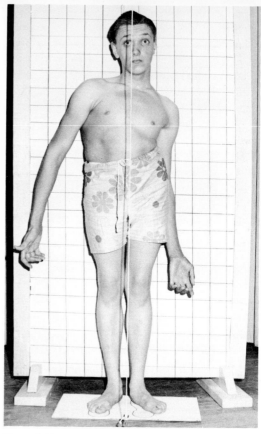

Figure 6.17. Right total scoliosis with 80° curve in sixteen-year-old. Curve was first noticed at age six.

Figure 6.18. In right total scoliosis, the right shoulder is high and carried forward.

limited as a natural protective mechanism of the body against further deformity.

11. Muscles on the concave side become increasingly tight while those on the convex side are stretched and weakened.

Principles for planning ameliorative exercises for a child with functional scoliosis include:

1. Work on improvement of body alignment in front of a mirror before undertaking specific exercises for scoliosis.

2. Use keynote positions (with exception of Adam's position) as corrective exer-

cises. When a position is identified in which the curve is temporarily obliterated, spend as many seconds as comfortable in it; rest and repeat.

3. Emphasize swimming and other activities which encourage development of the trunk without placing the strain of weight bearing on the spine.

4. Avoid forward flexibility of spine unless prescribed by a physician.

5. Use breathing and chest expansion exercises to maintain flexibility of chest and prevent further distortion of thorax.

6. If you tend to be conservative and wish

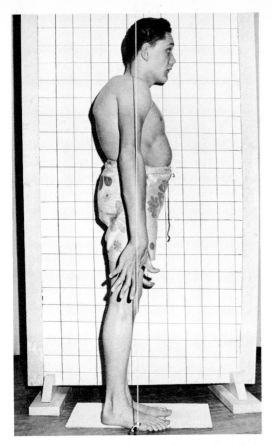

Figure 6.19. Right (convex) side of right total scoliosis shows back hump and bulging rib cage. Muscles on this side require strengthening.

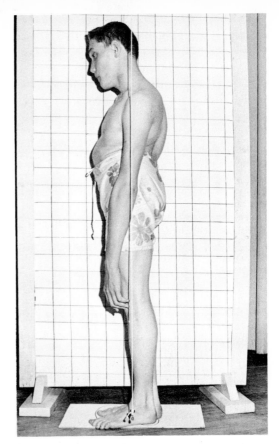

Figure 6.20. Left (concave) side of right total scoliosis reveals muscles which need stretching.

to avoid controversial practices, use only symmetrical exercises which develop left and right sides equally. Exercises for strengthening the back extensors are recommended.

7. If you are willing to use activities that authorities are about equally divided on, try such *asymmetrical* exercises as:
   a. Hang facing outward from stall bars and swing legs in.
   b. Hang from stall bars with right hand only (for left total curve.) Right side is to the stall bars and left hand is used whenever needed for balance.

c. Kneel on right knee, with leg extended to side, right arm curved above head. Laterally flex trunk several times to the left.

   The purpose of most asymmetrical exercise is to stretch muscles on the concave side and/or to strengthen muscles on the convex side. Generally exercises prescribed by physicians are asymmetrical in nature.

8. Encourage the student with scoliosis to participate in regular physical education classes and athletic competition.

Scoliosis is more prevalent in girls and among ectomorphic body types, but it is not confined to either. About 75 percent of the known cases are idiopathic. About 12.5 percent are congenital anomalies while the other 12.5 percent result from paralysis or paresis of muscles on one side of the spinal column. Many victims of poliomyelitis suffer from scoliosis.

Severity of Scoliosis

Many individuals seem to have mild lateral curvatures and other asymmetries of idiopathic origin which do not affect their health, happiness, or productivity. Street clothes ordinarily hide such deviations, and it is always a surprise when a scoliosis is revealed in a swimming class, posture examination, or the informality of the dressing room. When scoliosis is not identified as such until the early adult years, the condition has probably arrested itself and should not be a matter for undue concern.

Factors to be considered in referring individuals to their physician are as follows.

1. Age of child—The younger the child, the more serious the condition since he has more years of growth ahead of him.
2. Degree of asymmetry—If curve does not disappear when individual is lying down, in Adam's position, or hanging from a horizontal bar, the child should be referred immediately. The condition is usually structural.

Physicians classify the severity in terms of the number of degrees which the major or primary curve deviates from normal. A mild scoliosis is 15 to 35 degrees; moderate is 35 to 75 degrees; and severe is 75 to 150 degrees. Among the kinds of treatments used are the Milwaukee brace, Risser localizer cast, turnbuckle cast, spinal fusion, and spine instrumentation. The following brief case study is illustrative of the kinds of problems brought to adapted physical educators.

Case Study

Our son is seven years old and in the regular second grade. He has scoliosis; a right dorsal, left lumbar S curve.

This was discovered when he was five years old and needed treatment for a lung infection. Our regular physician was out of town, so a new one was called who noticed a protrusion of the rib cage and suggested that X-rays be taken.

The boy has been wearing the brace one year now, and the curve is almost straightened. The orthopedist has suggested that spinal fusion be planned for about three years from now to eliminate further need for a brace. Such fusion permanently eliminates movement in the affected area of the spine, and we are hoping that some alternative measures can be found.

Our son is presently doing exercises for abdominal and trunk strength and breathing exercises for chest flexibility. Is there anything else we, as parents, should be doing?

Other Asymmetries

Shoulder Height

When the two shoulders are of unequal height, the higher one is recorded as LH (left high) or RH (right high). To ascertain the unevenness of shoulders, it is best to use a horizontal line on the wall behind the student. Other techniques which may be used include:

1. If the head is not tilted, the distance between the shoulders and ear lobes on the right and left side may be sighted and compared.
2. The level of the inferior angles of the scapulae may be compared. The inferior angles are at about the level of the seventh thoracic spinous process.
3. The level of the two clavicles may be compared.

Whenever a high shoulder is recorded, a lateral spinal curve convex on the same side should be suspected. Innumerable adults, however, seem to have shoulders of uneven heights without evidence of scoliosis. It is

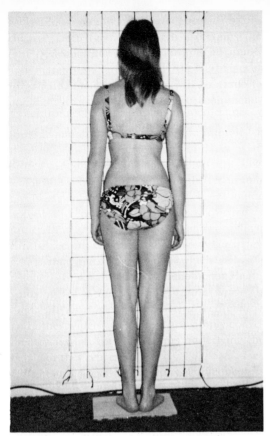

Figure 6.21. Left shoulder high and some evidence of a beginning left scoliotic curve. Note uneveness of waistline notches.

hypothesized that unequal muscle development may cause one shoulder to appear higher than the other.

Hip Height

When two hips are of unequal height, the higher one is recorded as LH or RH. Traditionally the anterior superior iliac spines serve as the anatomical landmarks for judging asymmetry. A string may be stretched between these two points.

Differences in hip height may be caused by scoliosis, uneven leg length, or the habit of standing on one leg for long periods of time.

To determine leg lengths, the student is placed in a supine lying position. The length of each leg is recorded as the distance from the anterior superior iliac spine to the medial malleolus.

Round Shoulders

Round shoulders is a forward deviation of the shoulder girdle in which the scapulae are abducted with a slight lateral tilt. This brings the acromion processes (shoulder tips) in front of the normal gravitational line. Round shoulders should not be confused with round back (kyphosis). They are distinctly different problems.

Synonyms for round shoulders are abducted scapulae, forward deviation of the shoulder girdle, protraction of scapulae, and separation of scapulae. Kinesiologically, the condition results when the strength of the abductors (pectoralis minor and serratus anterior) becomes greater than that of the adductors (rhomboids and trapezius III). To determine the extent of the forward deviation, the distance between the vertebral borders of the scapulae is measured. In the adult the normal spread is four to five inches depending upon the breadth of the shoulders.

The incidence of round shoulders is high among persons who work at desk jobs and hence spend much of their time with the shoulders abducted. Athletes often exhibit round shoulders because of overdevelopment of the anterior arm, shoulder, and chest muscles resulting from sports and aquatics activities which stress forward movements of the arms. This tendency may be counteracted by engaging in an exercise program designed specifically to keep the posterior muscles equal in strength to their antagonists. Perhaps the easiest way to do this is swimming a few laps of the back crawl each day. Certainly the well rounded athlete who enjoys many different ac-

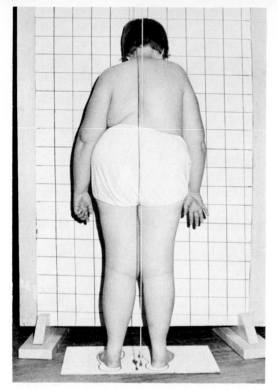

Figure 6.22. Round shoulders can be detected from a rear view by the palms of the hands. This child also has mild scoliosis, knock knees, and pronated feet.

tivities is less likely to develop round shoulders than one who specializes almost exclusively in tennis, basketball, or volleyball.

Round shoulders is associated also with poor health and general body weakness. If muscles on both the anterior and posterior surfaces are weak, gravity becomes the predominant force in pulling the scapulae forward and down. The rhomboids and trapezius III must have minimal strength to offset the natural effects of gravitational pull. The following segmental analysis demonstrates the compensatory changes in alignment of body parts which result from round shoulders.

Head and Neck: Forward.

Thoracic spine: Increasing convexity which tends to negate the effectiveness of the upward pull of the sternocleidmastoid and scaleni muscles which normally maintain the upper ribs and sternum in a high position. The weak back muscles are elongated by the increased convexity of the spine.

Chest: Lowered position. Whereas persons with good postures lead with the chest, this individual leads with the shoulders. The failure of the anterior muscles to exert their usual effect on the sternum and ribs results in a lowered position of the diaphragm which, in turn, affects breathing.

Shoulder joint: Increased inward rotation of the humeral head.

Arms: Arms are carried more forward than usual with palms facing toward the rear whereas normally only the little finger of the hand can be seen from the rear. The elbows may be held out close to the body. These changes in arm position are caused primarily by the inward rotation of the humeral head which in turn affects the origin and insertion of the pectoralis major, which no longer exerts its usual tension on the rib cage.

Lumbar spine: Lordosis may develop to compensate for increased convexity of thoracic spine.

Knees: Knees may hyperextend to compensate for the change in the lumbar curve. With the alignment of almost all of the body segments altered, the entire body slumps, creating the impression of general fatigue. This posture is assumed temporarily in times of extreme mental depression or bereavement, revealing the unity of mind and body. Mentally ill persons who have been institutionalized several years often assume the round shouldered postures of defeat.

Ameliorative Exercises

Exercises for round shoulders should simultaneously stretch the tightened anterior muscles and strengthen trapezius III and the rhomboids. So many exercises for round shoulders are recommended in textbooks that it is difficult to evaluate their respective effectiveness in accomplishing these goals. Scott and Rosentswieg[8] subjected the twelve exercises listed most often to electromyographical analysis. The four which appeared to be most effective, in rank order from best to good, are

1. Pull Resistance. Sit on chair facing the wall with pulleys, with the arms extended sideward at shoulder height and the hands grasping the handles. Slowly move the arms backward, keeping them at shoulder height.
2. Prone Lateral Raise of Weights. Assume a prone position on a bench. The hands grasp dumbbells on the floor to each side of the body. The weights are lifted toward the ceiling as far as possible, keeping the arms straight. Hold. (Chin should remain on the bench.)
3. Push Against Wall. Sit cross-legged with the head and back flat against the wall. The arms are bent at shoulder height with the palms facing the chest, fingertips touching and the elbows against the wall. Keeping the head and spine against the wall, press the elbows back with as much force as possible.
4. Head Resistance. Lie on back, arms out to side, palms down, knees flexed, and feet spread. Raise hips and arch back so that shoulders are off mat, supporting weight on feet, hands and back of head in a modified wrestler's bridge.

Winged Scapulae

Also called projected scapulae, winged scapulae refers to a prominence of the inferior angles of the scapulae. The scapulae are pulled away from the rib cage and the vertebral borders are lifted. Since the serratus anterior is the muscle which normally holds the inferior angle of the scapula close to the rib cage, it is believed to be weak when winging occurs.

Winged scapulae are normal in preschool and elementary school children since the ser-

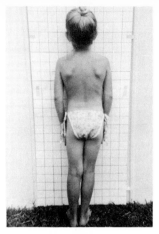

Figure 6.23. Winged scapulae is normal in preschool child. Atrophied right leg has not yet affected shoulder height.

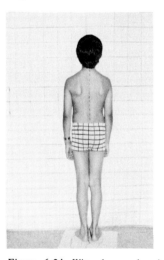

Figure 6.24. Winged scapulae in predominantly ectomorphic preadolescent.

ratus is slower in developing than its antagonists. Since the serratus anterior is a prime mover for upward rotation and abduction, it is strengthened by hanging, climbing, and other activities executed above the head.

8. Charlotte Scott. "A Quantitative Electromyographic Study of the Trapezius During Selected Exercises Designed to Ameliorate the Postural Deviation Designated as Round Shoulders" (Unpublished Ph.D. dissertation, The Texas Woman's University, 1969), directed by Joel Rosentswieg.

Many girls in our society do not outgrow winged scapulae as do boys. This postural deviation is often a part of the debutante slouch described earlier. Winged scapulae often accompany round shoulders. They are associated also with congenital anomalies and postural conditions in which the ribs protrude.

Sprengel's Deformity

Giving the appearance of a hunchback, Sprengel's deformity is really a congenitally elevated scapula. The entire shoulder appears to be displaced forward, and the arm is restricted in abduction. Some rotation accompanies the elevation so that the inferior angle is brought closer than normal to the spinal column.

Deviations of the Chest

Asthma, other chronic upper respiratory disorders, and rickets may cause changes in the rib cage with resulting limitations in chest flexibility and improper breathing practices. These changes are designated as functional, transitional, and structural depending upon their degree of severity. Congenital anomalies, of course, do account for some chest deviations.

Hollow Chest

The most common of the chest deviations, this term denotes the relaxation and depression of the anterior thorax which normally accompanies round shoulders and/or kyphosis. Specific characteristics of hollow chest are (1) concave or flattened appearance of anterior thoracic wall; (2) depressed (lowered) ribs; (3) low sternum; (4) tight intercostal and pectoral muscles; (5) limited chest flexibility; and (6) habitually lowered diaphragm which limits its movement in breathing.

Hollow chest can be traced to the failure of the sternocleidomastoid, scaleni, and pectoral muscles to exert their usual lifting effect on the ribs and sternum. The sternocleidomastoid and scaleni are elongated and weak. The pectoral muscles are excessively tight and strong.

Barrel Chest

The barrel chest is characteristic of persons with severe chronic asthma who become hyperventilated because of their inability to exhale properly. Over a period of years the excess air retained in the lungs tends to expand the anteroposterior dimensions of the thorax so that it takes on a rounded appearance similar to that of full inspiration.

Specific characteristics of barrel chest are

1. Thoracic spine extends.
2. Sternum is pushed forward and upward.
3. Upper ribs (second through the seventh) are elevated and everted. Eversion of the ribs is defined as the inner surfaces rotating to face downward. This occurs when the lower border of the rib turns forward.
4. Costal cartilages tend to straighten out when the ribs elevate.
5. Lower ribs (eighth through the tenth) move laterally, thus opening the chest and widening the subcostal angle.
6. Floating ribs are depressed and spread.
7. Diaphragm is habitually depressed which in turn displaces the internal organs in the direction of the abdominal wall.
8. Abdomen protrudes in response to organs pressed against the weakened abdominal wall.

Barrel chest is normal for infants and preschool children. The lateral widening of the thorax from side to side so that it no longer resembles a barrel occurs normally as a result of the vigorous play activities of young children. Severely handicapped persons who cannot engage in physical activities often have chests which remain infantile and underdeveloped.

Funnel Chest

The opposite of barrel chest, this condition is an abnormal increase in the lateral diameter of the chest with a marked depression of the sternum and anterior thorax. The sternum and adjacent costal cartilages appear to have been sucked inward.

Funnel chest, also called *pectus excavatum*, is usually a congenital anomaly. It appears in many severely retarded persons. It may be caused also by rickets or severe nasal obstruction, i.e., enlarged adenoids.

Pigeon Chest

Also called chicken breast or *pectus carinatum,* this condition takes its name from the abnormal prominence of the sternum. The anteroposterior diameter of the thorax is increased as a result of the forward displacement of the sternum. The deviation is rare, caused by rickets during the early growth period. It may also be congenital in nature.

Harrison's Groove

Harrison's Groove, another rare condition, is a horizontal groove across the lower anterior region of the thorax. The etiology is uncertain. The diaphragm appears to pull inward on the thoracic wall, causing the ribs below the groove to flare outward. Some paraplegics exhibit a Harrison's Groove. The top part of the chest above the groove is usually sunken.

Abdominal Relaxation

The degree of abdominal weakness is classified as mild, moderate, or severe or first, second, and third degree respectively. Abdominal protrusion is normal in the young child and usually accompanied by lordosis. Participation in the vigorous activities of the elementary school years should result in a flat, taut abdomen in adolescence and early adulthood. The lower part of the abdomen contracts reflexly whenever the body is in complete extension as in most locomotor activities. The emphasis upon extension in modern dance and ballet contributes particularly to abdominal strength as does swimming the front crawl and other strokes executed from an extended position. The upper part of the abdomen works in conjunction with the diaphragm, gaining strength each time breathlessness in endurance type activities forces the diaphragm to contract vigorously in inhalation. Abdominal exercises in a physical education class are a poor substitute for natural play activities. They are not recommended as long as the child derives pleasure from running, jumping, climbing, hanging, and skipping.

When a life-style changes from active to sedentary, regardless of the reason, abdominal exercises should become part of the daily routine. In middle and old age, the upper abdominal wall may become slightly rounded but the musculature below the umbilicus should remain flat and taut.

The anterior abdominal wall is comprised of four muscles: (1) rectus abdominis, (2) external obliques, (3) internal obliques, and (4) transversus abdominis. Three muscles run more-or-less in the same directions as the threads comprising a well-made girdle. The most superficial muscle, the external obliques, forms a regular V on the abdominal wall, extending from the lateral aspects of the lower eight ribs to the iliac crest and pubis. The rectus abdominis and internal obliques are on the second layer. The rectus abdominis, which runs longitudinally from the costal cartilages to the pubis, has been compared to a bowstring for it helps to control lumbar curvature. It is the only longitudinal anterior muscle which controls lordosis. The internal obliques form an inverted V (Λ) on the abdominal wall, extending from the iliac crests to the costal cartilages. Although the abdominal muscles are prime movers for trunk flexion, their major purpose is to hold in the abdominal viscera. The deepest abdominal muscle, the transversus abdominis, which crosses the abdomen horizontally, is involved mainly in respiration.

The posterior abdominal wall is formed by the quadratus lumborum and psoas major, very deep muscles which attach, in part, to the transverse processes of the vertebrae. The internal organs are in front of the quadratus lumborum and the psoas major. The quadratus lumborum is a prime mover for lateral flexion of the trunk. The psoas major causes flexion at the hip joint. When the anterior abdominal wall is weak, the psoas reverses its usual function and causes hyperextension of the lumbar spine. This explains the tendency of the back to arch during so many abdominal exercises. *No student should be allowed to engage in abdominal exercises which hyperextend the spine.* Should this problem occur, the level of difficulty of the exercise should be decreased.

Of the anterior muscles comprising the abdominal wall, the external and internal obliques are usually the weakest. They derive strength primarily from twisting movements of the trunk. Because of its location, the external oblique muscle is most important in flattening the abdomen.

Because the abdominal wall of the child normally protrudes, it is important to evaluate strength upon the basis of performance tests rather than upon appearance alone.

Principles to be followed in teaching abdominal exercises.

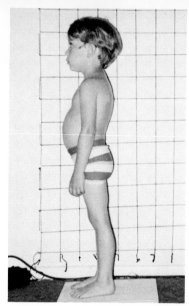

Figure 6.25. Good posture for a normal preschooler includes a protruding abdomen.

1. Teach abdominal exercises which will simultaneously stretch the tight lumbar extensors and hip flexors.
2. Use the supine hook lying rather than straight leg lying position to eliminate the action of the strong hip flexors.
3. Avoid hyperextension of the spine.
4. Avoid prone-lying exercises like the swan and the rocking chair.
5. Eliminate the possibility of breath holding during exercise by requesting the students to count, sing, whistle, or hum. Incorrect breathing tends to build up intra-abdominal pressure which may result in a hernia.
6. Include lots of twisting movements of the trunk.
7. Gradually build tolerance for endurance type exercises which cause vigorous breathing which in turn strengthen the upper abdominal wall.
8. Use locomotor activities which em-

phasize extension of the spine. Skipping and swimming are especially good.

9. Take advantage of the extensor reflex elicited in the creeping position.
10. Use the upside-down positions in yoga for training the extensor muscles. The neck stand is preferred to the head stand.

Ameliorative Exercises in the Creeping Position

1. Crosslateral creeping. As the right arm moves forward, the left knee should move forward.
2. Crosslateral creeping combined with blowing a ping pong ball across the floor.
3. Crosslateral creeping combined with pushing an object like a bottle cap or toy automobile with the nose.
4. Angry Cat. Alternate (1) humping the back and letting the head hang down with (2) extending the spine with the head held high.
5. In static creeping position, move the hips from side to side.

Ideally creeping exercises are performed in front of the mirror in order to improve proprioceptive awareness and ascertain that the spine is not hyperextended. *It is important also to use knee pads when creeping exercises are undertaken.*

Figure 6.26. Crosslateral creeping is an excellent abdominal exercise.

Ameliorative Exercises in the Supine Hook Lying Position

1. Abdominal pumping (Mosher exercise). Arms in reverse T.[9] Retract abdominal wall strongly, pulling the anterior pelvis upward and depressing the thorax.
2. Curl down or reverse trunk curl. Knees and hips are flexed and knees are drawn toward chest, so curl commences at the lower spinal levels. Obliques are more active in reverse curls than in regular trunk curls. First 1/3 of curl is most valuable.
3. Sit-up with trunk twist for maximal activity of oblique abdominals. Feet should not be held down because holding them activates the unwanted hip flexors.
4. Double leg raise and hold. Then lower legs slowly to starting position. Watch for arching of back just before the feet touch the floor. May also be done with *soles of feet together and knees apart:* this lessens pull of psoas even more.
5. Paint the rainbow type activity. Head touching wall, bring legs up to touch wall with knees.
6. Double knee raise and patticake.
7. Alternate ballet legs. From bent knee position, raise knees to chest and then lift legs alternately as done in the synchronized swimming stunt by the same name. To make this more difficult legs can be adducted and abducted in this position.
8. Double knee circling. Keep heels close to thighs. Arms in reverse T. Flex the hips until the thighs are vertical. Keeping the shoulders flat, make circles with the knees.

9. The *reverse T arm position* is used to prevent lumbar hyperextension. Arms are abducted and elbows bent at a right angle. Hands reach upward above the head.

More difficult variation: Flex knees toward the chest, straighten legs to vertical and make circles with both feet. Keep the shoulders flat and the heels together.

9. Alternate leg circling. Retract the abdominal wall and flex both knees to chest. Extend one leg and then the other in reciprocal leg circling or bicycle motion. Return the flexed legs to the chest and then lower to the floor.

   Vary the difficulty by changing the size of the circles, the number completed before resting, and the speed of the performance. Most difficult is making small circles at slow speed just above the floor. Right foot makes clockwise circles while left foot makes counterclockwise circles. Both legs make clockwise circles. Both legs make counterclockwise circles. Describe figure eight with one foot or both together.

10. Drumming. Feet are used like drum sticks, alternately beating the floor.

11. Alternate knee and elbow touch in opposition. Hands behind neck. Each time try to reach farther with the elbow and less far with the opposite knee.

12. Supine bent knee lower trunk twist. Arms in reverse T. Raise both knees until the thighs are vertical. Keep shoulders flat and lower knees toward the mat on one side, return to a vertical position. Repeat to other side and return. Legs should not be allowed to fall; must be controlled throughout the movement.

Regardless of type, abdominal exercises should accomplish the following purposes:

1. Relieve congestion in the abdominal or pelvic cavities; this includes expelling gas and improving local circulation.
2. Retrain the upper abdominal wall to increase its efficiency in respiration.
3. Retrain the lower abdominal wall to improve its efficiency with respect to holding the viscera in place.

The exercises cited on the previous pages are helpful in relieving menstrual pain. They may also lessen the discomfort of constipation and/or the accumulation of gas (flatus) in the digestive tract.

Visceroptosis

Ptosis is a Greek word which means "a dropping." In adults, when an abdominal protrusion is severe, it can be assumed that the viscera (internal organs) have actually dropped down into a new position. The stomach, liver, spleen, kidneys, and intestines may all be displaced, resulting in adverse effects upon their various functions.

Beevor Sign

The umbilicus is pulled out of alignment to the stronger side if there is an imbalance of strength in the abdominal muscles on the right and left sides. This phenomenon is called the Beevor Sign.

Deviations of the Thighs and Lower Legs

A quick screening device to judge the overall alignment of the legs is the game known as "Four Coins." The challenge is "Can you put a coin between your thighs, your knees, your calves, and your ankles and simultaneously hold all of the coins in place?" If the body parts are well proportioned and correctly aligned, this task should present no problem. When the student stands with feet together and parallel, the medial aspects of the knees and the medial malleoli should be touching their opposites.

Individual differences in the alignment of the legs and in locomotor patterns are largely dependent upon the structure of the hip joint. Students who toe inward or outward in their

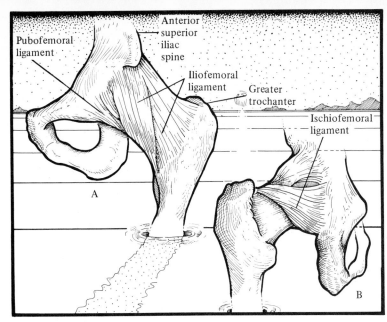

Figure 6.27. Ligaments of the hip joint. (A) anterior view. Iliofemoral ligament checks extension and inward and outward rotation; pubofemoral ligament checks outward rotation and abduction; (B) posterior view. Ischiofemoral ligament checks inward rotation and adduction in the flexed position.

normal walking gait, for instance, usually have nothing wrong with their feet. The origin of the problem can be traced instead to an imbalance of strength in the muscles which rotate the femur at the hip joint. Likewise *tibial torsion,* a condition in which the anterior aspect of the knee faces inward or outward, may be more a problem of femoral alignment than that of the patella.

Normal Structure of the Hip Joint

The hip joint is formed by the articulation of the femoral head with the acetabulum of the pelvis. The acetabulum is a cup-shaped hollow socket which is formed medially by the pubis, above by the ilium, and laterally and behind by the ischium. Around the circumference of the hip socket is a fibrocartilaginous ring which serves to deepen the socket and assure a more stable articulation between the femoral head and the acetabulum. The joint is reinforced by the iliofemoral, pubofemoral, and ischiofemoral ligaments. Of these ligaments the iliofemoral (Y ligaments) are most often injured. Located on the anterior surface of the hip joint and nicknamed for its inverted Y shape, this band of fibers serves to check both inward and outward rotation and extension. The student who is unable to turn the legs fully outward in ballet exercises or who cannot do the splits may trace his movement limitations to the tightness of the hip ligaments, particularly the iliofemoral ligaments.

When the iliofemoral ligaments and iliopsoas are both tight, they combine their tension with that of the lumbar extensors to cause hyperextension of the lower back. The iliofemoral ligament is stretched in supine long lying and wide stride long sitting. It is relaxed in hook lying and sitting.

Inside the acetabulum the femoral head normally faces slightly upward, medially, and forward so that the mechanical axis of the femur passes through the center of the patella. This is nature's way of keeping the weight-bearing joints aligned directly under one another.

Individual Differences in Hips and Thighs

Individual differences in the obliquity of the femoral shafts, the collodiaphysical angles, and the widths of pelvic girdles explain variations in appearance and mechanical efficiency.

The angle of obliquity is determined when both femoral condyles rest on a flat surface. From the intercondyloid space one line is drawn vertically upward and the other line is drawn through the shaft of the femur. Figure 6.28 depicts the upper and lower limits of normal obliquity.

The width of the pelvic girdle affects the obliquity of the shaft which in turn affects mechanical efficiency in athletic events. During puberty the width of the female pelvis tends to widen in preparation for its function as a birth canal. This widening increases the obliquity of the shafts of the femurs which increases running time. This fact helps to explain why girls tend to compete equally with boys in locomotor events until puberty after which girls having typical "feminine hips" seldom win over the opposite sex. It also forms a rationale for classifying students, regardless of sex, according to the pelvic widths and organizing races so that narrow-hipped students compete against one another and the less mechanically efficient wide-hipped persons run against each other. Of course, other factors which affect running speed like length of legs, body weight, and muscular strength need to be considered also.

The collodiaphysical angle is formed by the long axis of the shaft and the long axis of the neck. Figure 6.29 depicts the upper and lower

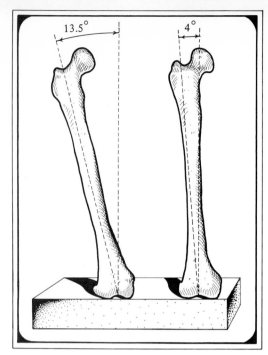

Figure 6.28. Obliquity of femoral shafts. The greater the obliquity of the femoral shafts, the less the mechanical efficiency.

limits of normal angulation. The angulation of the neck of the femur can cause either knock knees or bowlegs. Normal angulation ranges between 120°-130°.

Coxa Valga

When the angle formed by the long axis of the shaft and the long axis of the neck increases beyond 120°, the deviation is considered a deformity and labeled *coxa valga*. The word *coxa*, which means hip or hip joint, may be somewhat misleading since it is the angulation of the femoral head which is at fault.

The exaggerated angulation may result in a bow-legged effect. The affected leg is longer, and both inward and outward rotation are limited. This condition is almost always congenital.

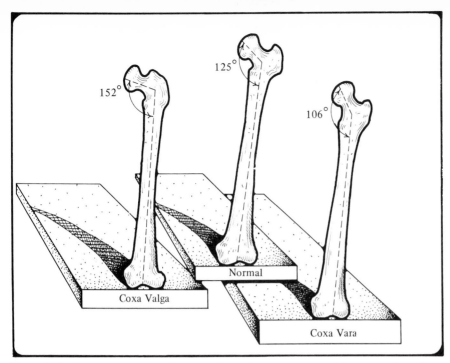

Figure 6.29. Collodiaphysical angulation of the neck of the femur explains coxa valga and vara.

Coxa Vara

When the angle formed by the long axis of the shaft and the long axis of the neck decreases greatly below 120°, the deviation is considered a deformity and labelled *coxa vara*. The decreased angulation may result in a knock-kneed effect. The affected leg usually is shorter. Outward rotation and abduction are limited. In severe cases the child cannot spread his legs apart.

The incidence of coxa vara is more frequent than that of coxa valga. The cause is either congenital or acquired. The acquired type, which occurs most frequently in boys ages ten through sixteen, is most common.

Adolescent coxa vara may result from a hip fracture, a dislocation, or a gradual displacement. Symptoms are (1) pain on weight bearing, (2) fatigue, (3) limited range of movement, and (4) progressive stiffness. Adolescents most vulnerable to coxa vara are those who are obese and structurally immature or their exact opposite, ectomorphic boys in a rapid growth phase.

Treatment generally involves several weeks of crutch walking during which it is essential that no weight be borne on the affected leg. Bracing and corrective surgery are sometimes indicated.

Individual Differences in Hip Rotation

The normal femur is thought to be capable of rotating either inwardly or outwardly 90°. The five basic positions of the feet in ballet comprise an excellent test of the flexibility of the hip joint. Individuals unable to imitate these positions may have *femoral torsion*.

Femoral torsion, also called *anteversion*, is

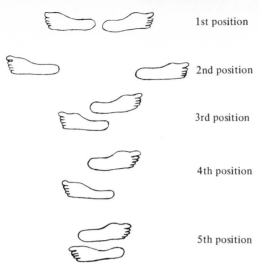

1st position

2nd position

3rd position

4th position

5th position

Figure 6.30. Ability to imitate the five basic foot positions in ballet shows hip joint flexibility.

a twisting or bending forward of the femur. Perhaps because of the fetal position, femoral torsion is much greater in infancy than adulthood. It generally disappears of its own accord. Young children with femoral torsion find it easy to assume a frog sitting position, i.e., with knees closed and the lower legs spread out to the sides. Individuals who habitually toe outward are capable of 60-80 degrees of outward rotation but limited to less than 20 degrees of inward rotation. Individuals who habitually toe inward are capable of 60-80 degrees of inward rotation but limited to less than 20 degrees of outward rotation.

Toeing Inward

Toeing inward (pigeon toes) is usually caused by an imbalance in the strength of the muscles which serve as prime movers for hip rotation. When the inward rotators, gluteus minimus and gluteus medius, are stronger than the outward rotators, the student toes inward.

Ameliorative Exercises

1. Develop proprioceptive awareness of the different foot positions through movement exploration on all kinds of surfaces.
2. Stretch the tight inward rotators by doing activities which emphasize outward rotation. Ballet techniques are especially effective.
3. Strengthen the weak outward rotators by doing activities which emphasize outward rotation.
4. Avoid inward rotation movements.

Toeing Outward

Toeing outward occurs when the posterior group of muscles on the sacrum called "the six outward rotators" (See Fig. 6.32) is stronger than the prime movers for inward rotation. Since toeing outward is a way of widening the stance and improving the balance, it may be observed in toddlers just learning to walk, the aged, the blind, and others who are unsure of their footing.

Ameliorative Exercises

1. Develop proprioceptive awareness of the different foot positions through movement exploration on all kinds of surfaces.
2. Stretch the tight outward rotators by doing activities which emphasize inward rotation.
3. Strengthen the weak inward rotators by doing activities which stress inward rotation.
4. Avoid outward rotation movements.

Hyperextended Knees

Also called back knees or *genu recurvatum,* hyperextended knees is a deviation in which the knees are pulled backward beyond their normal position. This posture problem can be identified best from a side view.

Hyperextension of the knees tends to tilt the pelvis forward and contribute to lordosis, thereby throwing all of the body segments out of alignment. It occurs more often in children than adults and in ectomorphs than in other

Figure 6.31. Right knee in hyperextension after knee surgery following an automobile accident. Malalignment of legs contributes to lordosis.

body types. In young children hyperextended knees may be symptomatic of anxiety and tension. It is observed frequently when a new motor skill is being attempted. When a child poses for posture pictures, he may thrust his knees backward as he "freezes" for the camera. In most instances, hyperextended knees is not a habitual posture but one which appears now and then.

When the backward curvature of the legs is complicated by inward rotation (tibial torsion) of the knees, the popliteus muscle and posterior ligaments of the knee joint are put on the stretch. This increases vulnerability to knee injury. Touching the toes from a standing position, the bear walk, and similar activities are contraindicated for they encourage the stretch-

ing of the already lax hamstring muscles. Exercises for amelioration of hyperextended knees should emphasize knee flexion, thereby strengthening the hamstrings. Ideally the exercises should entail simultaneous hip extension and knee flexion.

Bowlegs (Genu Varum)

Although the Latin term *genu* meaning "knee" emphasizes the capacity for knees and ankles to touch simultaneously, bowing can occur in the shaft of the femur as well as the tibia. *Varum* refers to inward bowing. One or both legs may be affected. The long sitting position is a better posture than standing to ascertain the presence of bowlegs. The amount of space between the femoral condyles determines the degree of severity as follows: first degree, 1-3 inches apart; second degree, 3-5 inches; and third degree, 5 inches or more.

The legs of infants are often bowed. The natural pull of the peroneal muscles on the shaft of the tibia during the first months of walking tends to straighten out the bow. In this instance an imbalance in strength between two muscle groups works to the toddler's advantage. By the age of two or so the tibials have gained sufficient strength to offset the pull of the peroneals and any bowing which remains may become structural. Persistent bowing should be referred to an orthopedist while the bones are still malleable enough to be straightened by braces.

In adulthood, bowing is structural and exercises are not beneficial. Many individuals with bowlegs have strong muscles and are not impaired noticeably by this deviation. Bowlegs tends to shift the weight toward the lateral border of the foot and to maintain the foot in a supinated position.

Individuals who simultaneously hyperextend the knees and inwardly rotate the thighs are often diagnosed incorrectly as having bowlegs. If the patellae face inward, it is likely that the apparent bowlegs is a functional adaptation which can be eliminated by strength-

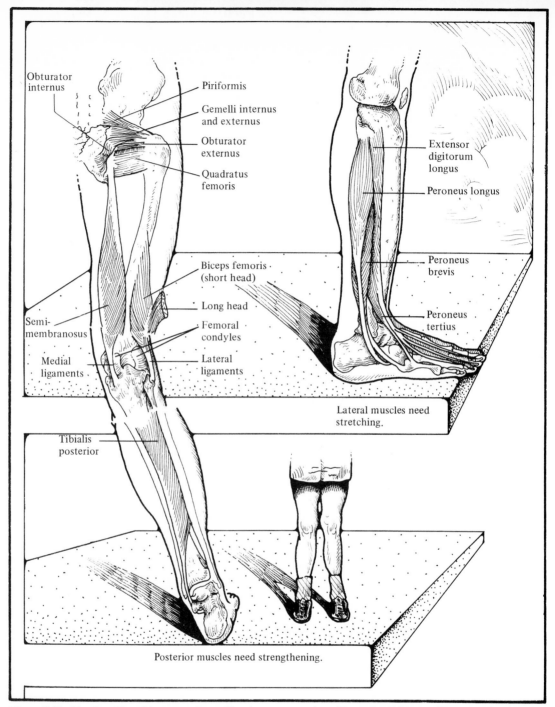

Obturator
internus

Piriformis

Gemelli internus
and externus

Obturator
externus

Quadratus
femoris

Extensor
digitorum
longus

Peroneus longus

Biceps femoris
(short head)

Long head

Femoral
condyles

Peroneus
brevis

Semi-
membranosus

Medial
ligaments

Lateral
ligaments

Peroneus
tertius

Lateral muscles need
stretching.

Tibialis
posterior

Posterior muscles need strengthening.

Figure 6.32. Muscles affected in genu valgum. Knock knees elongates tendons of insertion on medial side and tightens tendons of insertion on lateral side. Lateral muscles of lower leg tighten, pulling outer border of foot upward and forcing weight onto inner border. Medial hamstring is semimembranosus.

ening the outward rotators of the hips and relaxing the knees so that correct leg and thigh alignment is possible.

Knock-Knees (Genua Valga)

The Latin word *valgum* can mean either knock-knees or bowlegs but is used in most adapted physical education references as knock-knees, referring specifically to the bending outward of the lower legs so that the knees touch but the ankles do not. The long sitting position is recommended for determining the severity of the condition.

Knock-knees occurs almost universally in obese persons. In the standing position, the gravitational line passes lateral to to the center of the knee rather than directly through the patella as is normal. This deviation in the weight bearing line subjects the lateral meniscus to increased stress and puts the tibial collateral ligament (medial aspect of knee) under increased tension, thereby predisposing the knee joint to injury. Knock-knees is usually accompanied by weakness in the longitudinal arch and pronation of the feet. (See Fig. 6.32)

Ameliorative Exercises

1. Stretching the muscles on the lateral aspect of leg (peroneal group).
2. Strengthening the medial ligaments of the knee and such hip joint muscles as the sartorius and medial hamstrings which pass over the knee joint to insert on the tibia.
3. Strengthening the tibials.
4. Strengthening the outward rotators of the hip joint.

Tibial Torsion

Tibial Torsion may be caused by inward rotation of the tibia or of the entire leg; in either case the tibia is twisted and the weight bearing line is shifted to the medial aspect of the foot. The deviation is often more marked in one leg than the other, with the affected foot toeing inward and pronating.

The normal tibia can rotate inwardly only when the knee is flexed and not bearing weight. An orthopedic condition in early childhood which prevents weight bearing may cause excessive tightness in the muscles which pull the tibia inward: semimembranosus, semitendinosus, sartorius, gracilis, and popliteus. This, in turn, may result in a structural twisting of the tibia. It is extremely important therefore that a student on crutches or in a wheelchair be assisted in keeping the leg in correct alignment. The person with one leg shorter than the other who puts his weight on the longer limb and maintains the shorter one in relaxed flexion while standing also contributes to twisting of the nonweight bearing tibia.

Congenital anomalies of the foot may be accompanied by twisting of the lower end of the tibia. When the foot is carried abnormally

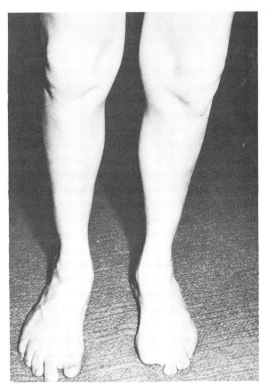

Figure 6.33. Medial torsion of left tibia in young adolescent with surgically corrected club foot.

inward in relation to the leg, the talus may be rotated over the medial malleolus, resulting in stretching of the lateral ligaments and abnormal tightness in the medial ligaments of the joints of the foot. Congenital tibial torsion is usually corrected in infancy by plaster casts, braces, splints, and/or surgery.

Tibial torsion should be suspected in knock knees, pronation of the feet, and flat feet. Exercises should stress amelioration of pronation and strengthening and stretching whichever hip, thigh, and lower leg muscles are needed to bear weight in correct position.

Deviations of the Feet

Poor alignment in any part of the body affects the weight bearing function of the feet. Obesity increases the stress on the muscles. No part of the body is abused as badly as the feet. Consequently complaints of aching feet are common. Examination of the feet should begin with questions concerning pain or discomfort in the following "pain centers" of the foot: (1) sole of foot under metatarsal-phalangeal joints; (2) sole of foot close to the heel where the plantar ligaments attach to the calcaneus; (3) under surface of navicular; (4) middorsum where shoelaces tie; and (5) outer surface of sole of foot where most of weight is borne. These areas should be inspected closely for thicknesses and other abnormalities.

Structure of the Foot

Contrary to what many lay persons think, most movements of the foot do *not* occur at the ankle joint. Limited only to plantar flexion and dorsal flexion, the ankle joint (articulation between tibia and talus) does not figure in most deviations of the foot.

The two joints of the foot where most of the movements occur, and subsequently the deviations, are the *talonavicular* and *talocalcaneal* joints. In the former the talus is transferring the weight of the body to the forward part of the foot, and in the latter it is transferring the weight to the back part of the foot. How this weight is transferred determines the presence or absence of foot problems.

Normally the weight of the body in locomotor activities is taken on the outer border of the foot and then transferred via the metatarsal area to the big toe which provides the push-off force for forward movement. When this sequence occurs, the foot is maintained in slight supination which is considered the "strong position" of the foot. All locomotor activities should be performed in this slightly supinated position which forces the weight of the body to be taken on the outer border of the foot.

Kinesiologically, supination is a combination of adduction and inversion (turning the soles of the feet inward). The same muscles which act as prime movers for inversion (supination) are responsible for maintenance of a strong longitudinal arch. They are the tibialis anterior and the tibialis posterior. Almost all foot exercises involve strengthening and tightening of these two muscles of the lower leg.

Two Arches of the Foot

The longitudinal arch extends from the calcaneus to the distal end of the first metatarsal. The inner component has great flexibility and is adapted to shock absorption. The height of longitudinal arches appears to be determined genetically and bears little relationship to strength. A low arch can be as strong or stronger than the high arch which tends to be vulnerable to injury. The outer component of the longitudinal arch is nearly flat in contour, lacks mobility, and is suited to the function of support.

The longitudinal arch is held in place primarily by the three "bowstring" ligaments. They are (1) the long plantar ligament; (2) the plantar calcaneo-cuboid ligament; and (3) the spring ligament (also called plantar calcaneonavicular ligament). These ligaments are named for the two bones to which they attach.

The transverse arch, sometimes called the metatarsal arch, is a side to side concavity on the underside of the foot which is formed by the five metatarsals. This arch is not apparent in the weight bearing position, and some authorities dispute its existence.

Fallen Arches

Fallen or broken arches, in the layman's language, are sprains of the ligaments which normally provide support for the longitudinal arch. These sprains are classified as traumatic or static.[10]

A *traumatic arch sprain* is caused by violent stretching of one or more ligaments. This occurs when the intertarsal joints are forced through a greater range of movement than they are accustomed. The traumatic sprain may be *acute* or *chronic* depending upon how many times it has occurred previously. The chronic arch sprain is extremely resistant to treatment. The acute arch sprain, like any other sprain, is characterized by pain, swelling, and discoloration. It is treated like other sprains with local injections into the hematoma, compression, ice followed by local heat, adequate strapping, and avoidance of weight bearing. A medial or lateral heel wedge to relieve tension is often prescribed when weight bearing is resumed. Once an arch sprain occurs, the foot should be strapped prior to physical education activity for several months.

Static sprain is the term given to arches which are more-or-less permanently lowered because the ligaments are too elongated to maintain the tarsals and metatarsals in their respective positions. The condition cannot be traced to a particular injury. Instead it is the result of continuous stress on the longitudinal arch. Obesity, the superimposed weight of equipment and uniform, violent exercises without sufficient conditioning, and long hours on the feet all contribute to the gradual stretching of the bowstring ligaments. The first symptom is generally pain in the long plantar ligament which extends from the calcaneus to the metatarsal heads. This pain is relieved only when weight is taken off the foot.

Static arch sprain does not respond well to the ordinary treatment for sprains. It is recommended therefore that it be handled like the condition of flat foot although static sprains do not always result in "broken arches" or flat feet. Arch supports and adequate strapping should be prerequisities for participation in physical education. In addition, the student should practice prescribed foot exercises daily for strengthening the tibials and improving alignment of the foot.

Flat Foot (Pes Planus)

Flat foot may be congenital or postural. The black race is predisposed to congenital flat foot, obviously not a handicap with respect to athletic achievement. If the muscles of the legs and feet are strong and flexible and the body is in good alignment, the congenital flatfoot is not considered a postural deviation.

Infants are born with varying degrees of flat feet. Strong arches develop as the natural consequence of vigorous kicking and strenuous locomotor activities. Faulty body mechanics and improper alignment of the foot and leg may create an imbalance in muscle strength which in turn prevents maintenance of the longitudinal arch in the correct position. Almost always the same poor posture practices which cause flat foot result also in pronation and toeing outward. Tibial torsion and/or knock knees frequently accompany flat foot also.

To evaluate the degree of severity of flat foot, the *Feiss line* method is used. This entails drawing an imaginary line from the medial malleolus to the metatarsophalangeal joint of

10. Don H. O'Donoghue, *Treatment of Injuries to Athletes* (Philadelphia: W. B. Saunders, 1962), pp. 592-595.

the big toe. The distance which the navicular (scaphoid) is from the Feiss line determines whether the condition is first, second, or third degree as follows:

First degree—navicular one inch below line
Second degree—navicular two inches below line
Third degree—navicular three inches below line

The *Helbing's Sign* may also be used to evaluate the severity of flat foot. It is defined as a medial turning inward of the Achilles tendon as viewed from behind.

Ameliorative Exercises

1. Strengthen the tibials.
2. Strengthen and tighten other muscles, ligaments, and tendons on the medial aspect of the foot by inversion exercises.
3. Stretch the tight muscles, ligaments, and tendons on the lateral aspect of the foot.

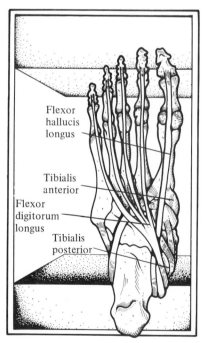

Flexor hallucis longus

Tibialis anterior

Flexor digitorum longus

Tibialis posterior

Figure 6.34. Tendons on plantar surface.

Pronation

Of all of the postural foot defects, pronation is the most common and the most debilitating. It is defined variously as taking the weight of the body on the inner border of the foot, rolling inward on the ankles, and combined eversion and abduction. Eversion, which is the kinesiological term for turning the sole of the foot outward, occurs when the lateral muscles of the lower leg (peroneals) are tighter than the tibials. This deviation occurs mainly in the talonavicular and talocalcaneal joints.

The inward rotation of the tarsal bones often causes a stretching of the bowstring ligaments and the subsequent dropping of the tarsals so that flat foot or static arch sprain are related disorders. The student tends to toe outward and to complain of pain in the longitudinal arch and in the calf muscles (gastrocnemius and soleus). The Feiss line and the Helbing's Sign previously described under flat foot are used also for diagnosis of pronation.

Pronation may occur in early childhood as well as other growth periods. In affluent areas well over 10-20 percent of the children may wear corrective shoes designed to ameliorate the condition of pronation. In these shoes the medial border is built up in such a way as to force the weight of the body to be taken on the outer border of the foot. The shoes are prescribed by physicians. Children who wear corrective shoes should not change to tennis shoes for physical education activity nor should they go barefooted without the permission of their orthopedist.

Ameliorative Exercises

1. Begin with nonweight bearing exercises and do not add weight bearing exercises until indicated by orthopedist.
2. Emphasize toe curling exercises to strengthen the flexors of the toes.
3. Emphasize plantar flexion and inversion.

4. Avoid dorsiflexion exercises and maintainence of foot in dorsiflexion for long periods of time.
5. Avoid eversion movements.
6. In picking up marbles and other objects with the toes, stress a position of inversion as
   a. Pick up marbles with right foot.
   b. Deposit into box across the midline which forces the foot into inversion.
7. In relay activities for correction of pronation, make sure objects held by toes of right foot are passed to the left to assure inversion.

Hollow Foot (Pes Cavus)

Hollow foot, a congenital defect, is the exact opposite of flat foot. The longitudinal arch of the foot is abnormally high and the forefoot is less flexible than normal. *Pes cavus* is often complicated by a congenital deformity in the midtarsal area which is the club foot condition of *talipes equinus,* so called because it makes the human foot resemble that of a horse.

Ameliorative exercises are not recommended for pes cavus. The Achilles tendon and bowstring ligaments may be stretched gently as part of daily foot care to prevent a worsening of the condition.

Club Foot (Talipes Equinus)

The Latin word *talipes* stems from *talus,* meaning heel, and *pes,* meaning foot. *Equinus* comes from *equus,* meaning horse. A malposition of the foot which probably results from the fetal position, *talipes equinus* accounts for 75 percent of all congenital foot defects.

Casts, braces, and surgery in infancy correct the condition to a large extent, but the child's gait may be slightly affected. Talipes equinus is discussed more fully in the chapter 18, "Crippled and Other Health Impaired," starting on page 370.

Deviations of the Metatarsal Area

Deviations of the metatarsal area include the following: (1) plantar neuroma, (2) metatarsalgia, (3) calluses, (4) papillomas, and (5) dermatitis. Any of these conditions may affect postures and gaits.

Plantar Neuroma (Morton's Toe)

A neuroma is a tumor along the course of a nerve or at the end of a nerve. In the case of Morton's Toe, the tumor is of the plantar nerve in the area between the third and fourth metatarsophalangeal joints. When compressed between the metatarsal heads, the tumor results in excruciating, intermittent pain.

This condition is relatively common among athletes although it is sometimes misdiagnosed as a sprain of the metatarsal arch. The treatment is surgical excision after which physical activity is contraindicated for a period of four to six weeks.

Metatarsalgia

Metatarsalgia is a severe pain or cramp in the metatarsal area. The ending of the word stems from the Greek *algos,* meaning pain, and can be related to the condition of *neuralgia,* defined as a severe pain along the course of a nerve. Metatarsalgia is thought to be caused by wearing improper shoes or engaging in physical activities for long periods of time which place excessive stress on the ball of the foot.

Physical education should consist of exercises for increasing the flexibility of the foot and various nonweight bearing activities until the pain disappears. The physician often recommends that arch supports be worn thereafter. Jumping and sprinting may be contraindicated for several months.

Calluses

A callus is a thickening of the skin which results from undue pressure, friction, or irritation usually caused by poorly fitted shoes.

Calluses become painful when the underlying tissues or periosteum is bruised. They may occur anywhere on the body, but the most frequent source of pain is under the metatarsal heads.

The pain of calluses is relieved by inserting pads in the shoe which shift the weight of the body to another part of the foot. Calluses may be softened with lanolin and buffed down by any emory board, but the best treatment is prevention through wearing only properly fitted shoes.

Papillomas

The term *papilloma* refers to any benign skin tumor. On the sole of the foot the most common type is the *plantar wart* which tends to grow inward. Surgical excision, chemotherapy, and X-rays are the most common treatments. Weight-bearing activities are painful during the weeks following the removal of a plantar wart, but with proper padding highly motivated students will wish to continue participating in physical education.

Dermatitis

Dermatitis in the metatarsal area is usually a fungus infection such as athlete's foot. The use of talcum powder and lamb's wool between the toes tends to relieve itching and pain.

Deviations of the Toes

Deviations of the toes may be congenital or postural. If congenital, they are often hereditary. If postural, they are almost invariably caused by poorly fitted footwear.

Syndactylism

Extra toes, the absence of toes, or the webbing of toes all affect mechanical efficiency in locomotor activities but a child with good coordination can learn to compensate well enough to achieve recognition as an outstanding athlete. Illustrative of this is Tom Dempsey, stellar kicker for the Philadelphia Eagles

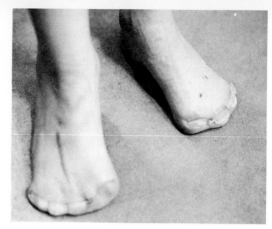

Figure 6.35. Absence of big toe affects balance and locomotor efficiency.

of the National Football Conference, who has part of his kicking foot missing.

Webbing of toes is usually corrected surgically and extra toes may be removed to facilitate purchase of shoes. The most debilitating defect is absence of the big toe which plays a major role in static balance and in the push-off phase of locomotor activities.

Hallux Valgus

Hallux is the Latin word for big toe, and *valgus* is a descriptive adjective meaning bent outward. Hence *hallux valgus* is a marked deviation of the big toe toward the four lesser toes. This adduction at the first metatarsophalangeal joint causes shoes to exert undue pressure against the medial aspect of the head of the first metatarsal, where a bursa (sac of synovial fluid) is present in the joint. Several changes in this bursa may occur as a result of the pressure exerted by the shoe. If the bursa enlarges, it is called a *bunion,* the Greek word for turnip. This phenomenon happens so often that the terms *bunion* and *hallux valgus* are used as synonyms. If the bursa becomes inflammed, it is called *bursitis.* If the irritation results in a deposit of additional calcium on the first metatarsal head, this new growth is called an *exostosis.*

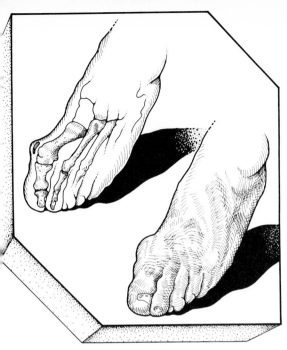

Figure 6.36. Bunion limits flexion of big toe.

Overlapping Toes

Any of the toes may overlap each other but the most common deviation is that of the fourth toe overlapping the fifth toe. Ill fitting shoes cause this divergency.

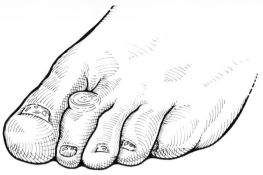

Figure 6.37. Hammer toes.

Hammer Toes

Normally the metatarsophalangeal, the proximal interphalangeal, and the distal interphalangeal joints are all in extension in the weight bearing position. If any toe is unable to maintain its extended position because of shifting of the bones of the foot, the result is usually a *hammer toe*. Characteristics are (1) the proximal phalanx is hyperextended; (2) the middle phalanx is flexed; (3) the distal phalanx is either flexed or extended; and (4) the extensor tendon of the proximal phalanx is made prominent by the hyperextension. A callus on the plantar surface of the metatarsal head of the affected toe may compound the problem.

Recommended Activities

1. Photograph the back and side views of the postures of selected persons in the following age ranges: (a) under 6; (b) ages 6-11; (c) ages 12-16; (d) ages 17-30; (e) ages 31-59; and (f) over 60. Note the postural characteristics of each age group and suggest, where appropriate, specific activities for improvement of postures.

2. Have someone photograph or videotape some of your postures. Analyze each segment of your body in terms of good alignment, and write a report describing your posture deviations and recommended activities.

3. Visit a nursing home or center for the aged and observe the postural characteristics of its residents.

4. Develop a collection of slides or "close-up" photographs of feet which depict deviations.

5. Using ink or poster paint, make footprints of persons of different ages, beginning with a toddler. Note the developmental changes in the longitudinal arch.

6. Develop a ten point scale for judging body mechanics and use it in a group screening situation to assign the pupils to quartiles. If other raters are assisting, compare your ratings with theirs. Discuss similarities and differences.

7. Teach and/or lead your class in several exercises for each posture deviation.

Recommended Reading

Drury, Blanche J. *Posture and Figure Control Through Physical Education.* Palo Alto, California: The National Press, 1961.

Lindsey, Ruth; Jones, Billie J.; and Whitley, Ada Van. *Body Mechanics—Posture, Figure, Fitness.* Dubuque, Iowa: Wm. C. Brown Company Publishers, 1974.

Logan, Gene A. *Adapted Physical Education.* Dubuque, Iowa: Wm. C. Brown Company Publishers, 1972.

Lowman, Charles Leroy, and Young, Carl Haven. *Postural Fitness.* Philadelphia: Lea & Febiger, 1960.

Mueller, Grover W., and Christaldi, Josephine. *A Practical Program of Remedial Physical Education.* Philadelphia: Lea & Febiger, 1966.

Rathbone, Josephine, and Hunt, Valerie V. *Corrective Physical Education.* Philadelphia: W. B. Saunders, 1965.

Wells, Katharine F. *Posture Exercise Handbook.* New York: The Ronald Press Company, 1963.

Williams, Marian, and Worthington, Catherine. *Therapeutic Exercise for Body Alignment and Function.* Philadelphia: W. B. Saunders, 1961.

7 Locomotor Movement Patterns and Related Skills

Figure 7.0. Dive forward and roll over three.

Closely related to the evaluation of postures is the appraisal of movement patterns and fundamental skills. Careful observation of the ways in which a child moves is the first step in planning a program of remediation. What the child can do should be recorded as well as what he cannot do so that his physical education prescription can be based upon strengths rather than weaknesses. The appraisal of postures, basic movements, movement patterns, and fundamental skills should be completed before evaluation of fitness through standardized tests is undertaken.

Several terms must be clarified before screening procedures are developed. Definitions of these terms evolved out of the movement education approach to physical education which gained widespread acceptance in the United States in the 1950s. This approach deemphasizes uniform criteria for "good form" toward which all students must aspire and stresses instead problem solving as a means of helping each child to discover his unique movement capabilities and to adapt performance to his own weight, body type, congenital defects, and other individual characteristics.

A *basic movement* is a change in position by any part of the body. The term is synonymous with *muscle action* and *prime movement* as used in kinesiology.

A *movement pattern* is a combination of basic movements used in daily living activities or in the performance of physical education skills. The acts of walking and running, for instance, can be analyzed as alternate flexion and extension at the hip, knee, and ankle joints. Changing from a standing to a sitting position requires flexion at the hip, knee, and ankle joints while returning to an upright stance involves extension at the same joints. Warm-up exercises can also be thought of as combinations of basic movements. Thus jumping jacks require alternate abduction and adduction at the hip joints; touching the toes is

alternate flexion and extension of the spinal column; and trunk circling involves lateral flexion to the right, hyperextension, lateral flexion to the left, and flexion.

The ability of the teacher to break each pattern into its basic movements enables him to determine which groups of muscles need strengthening and stretching. It also awakens him to the similarities between certain patterns and challenges him to build teaching progressions based upon those movements the child can do best.

Movement patterns are either *locomotor* or *nonlocomotor* depending upon whether the objective is to move through space or to keep the base of support stationary. Whereas the locomotor patterns of the nonhandicapped are primarily walking, running, and jumping, those of persons with orthopedic problems may include maneuvering a wheelchair, pedaling a tricycle, or propelling a scooter board. Thus locomotor movement patterns can be subdivided into *ambulatory* and *nonambulatory* depending upon whether or not the person can walk unassisted.

Nonlocomotor movement patterns are those in which at least one part of the body remains stationary, serving as the base of support. Parts of the body may move through space but the body as a whole remains in the same place. The joints comprising the human body are called axes; hence movements of body segments around an axis are *axial* in nature. Illustrative of these are arm swings with the shoulder joint serving as the axis and head circling with the intercervical joints serving as axes. Physical education for nonambulatory persons consists mainly of nonlocomotor movement patterns.

Movement patterns are described as *bilateral, unilateral,* and *crosslateral* depending upon how the limbs are used. This system of classification is used widely in special education (Getman, Kephart, Doman-Delacato) and in the therapies (Fay and Ayres).

In the bilateral movement pattern both limbs move simultaneously as in the arm movements of the breaststroke and the leg movements of the squeeze or frog kick in swimming. Developmentally, bilateral movements of the arms and legs are the first to occur. They are particularly obvious as the infant stretches out both arms to reach for an object held at his midline. Children and adults with poor coordination often involuntarily reach out simultaneously with the nondominant limb when the dominant hand is called into action in such instances as (1) receiving a cup and saucer from the hostess; (2) unexpectedly having to catch a set of car keys just tossed; or (3) protecting the body from a flying object. In such cases the adult is said to be "frozen at the bilateral level." A synonym for bilaterality is the *homologous* movement pattern.

In the unilateral movement pattern the right arm and right leg move simultaneously or vice versa. In some instances only one of the four limbs moves. The immature creeping pattern in which the right arm and right leg are moved at the same time after which the left extremities move simultaneously is considered unilateral. The adult who steps forward with his right foot as he throws a ball with his right hand is unilateral as is the individual who maintains his feet rigidly in a stationary position. A synonym for unilaterality is *homolateral* movement pattern.

In the crosslateral or crossdiagonal movement pattern, the right arm and left leg move simultaneously and vice versa. This is the mature movement pattern in creeping, walking, running, throwing, kicking, and most sports activities. For well coordinated children, crosslateral movement patterns come naturally. Crosslaterality is based upon the principle of opposition, i.e., the limbs work together in opposition as nature's way of improving balance in the execution of daily living activities.

Movement patterns are dependent upon perceptual-motor functioning, body size and relative proportions of body segments, center of gravity, fitness, and other factors which vary from age to age. Many movement patterns exhibited by young children are normal for their age but do not remotely resemble the refined patterns characteristic of adults. Thus movement patterns are classified as (1) developmental, (2) mature, or (3) immature.

Developmental patterns are those which are normal for a particular age group but which will not be acceptable in later years. Wickstrom[1] has written a comprehensive book on developmental motor patterns in the preschool and elementary school years. Many of his excellent line drawings on running, jumping, throwing, catching, kicking, and striking are based upon cinematographical research.

Mature movement patterns are those which are mechanically efficient. Usually they conform more or less to "good form" for adults. It should be remembered, however, that "good form" encompasses many individual differences. Little is known about "good form" for an amputee, a paraplegic, or a dwarf. Obviously the movement patterns of adults with structural divergencies cannot be judged by the same criteria as athletes.

Immature patterns are those which fail to meet the criteria of mechanical efficiency and economy of energy. In other words, the movement pattern does not produce the end result expected of a performer of a certain age with a certain amount of instruction. His scores are consistently below the norms. Mechanical efficiency is closely related to optimal perceptual-motor functioning and total fitness.

Each time a teacher identifies a motor pattern as immature, he has an obligation to analyze *why* so that specific remediation can be built into the educational prescription. It is recommended that the following list of terms

1. Ralph L. Wickstrom, *Fundamental Motor Patterns* (Philadelphia: Lea & Febiger, 1970).

be used as a checklist in conjunction with the analysis of immature motor patterns.

1. *Inconsistency.* Exhibition of greater trial-to-trial inconsistency than their more proficient peers. Variation from trial to trial in preferred hand or foot, balance, force, rhythm, and other motor characteristics.

2. *Perseveration.* Inability to stop at the appropriate time and/or to perform a prescribed number of movements without overflow. For example, when dribbling a ball, the child may continue the dribbling action of the hand after the ball is no longer within reach.

3. *Mirroring.* Evidenced when child is imitating the movement of someone facing him. Inability to transpose right-left visual cues to his own body; failure to separate own directional movements from those of a leader.

4. *Asymmetry.* Deficit in bilateral coordination evidenced when two limbs are supposed to contribute equally to force production or balance.

5. *Loss of Dynamic Balance.* Inability to maintain postural control of the body in relation to gravity. Evidenced by bumping into objects as well as frequent shifts of position.

6. *Falling After Performance.* An idiosyncracy exhibited after completion of a specified motor task. May be a compensatory measure to control perseveration or reduce loss of balance.

7. *Extraneous Motions.* Excessive and/or irrelevent motions that tend to disrupt the temporal organization of a skill. The movement of the limbs may exceed the normal ranges for efficiency, they may be held in unusual positions, or additional movements may be added to the skill sequence.

8. *Inability to Maintain Rhythm or Pattern.* Tendency to progressively accelerate or diminish the pace to the extent that child's movements do not match those of the leader. Or inability to maintain self-imposed rhythm of a task such as hopping or jumping in a repetitive manner.

9. *Ability to Control Force.* Inability to generate the correct amount of force to execute a motor task. Usually pertains to distance or height. Child throws, kicks, strikes, or jumps with too much force or too little. Relates to problems of balance and maintenance of rhythm.

10. *Inappropriate Motor Planning.* A catch-all category for problems of sequencing related to the interaction of rhythm and force in complex tasks. The delay or prematurity of a motor response as in swinging too late or too early; the misapplication of force as in failure to strike the center of the ball or to apply the right amount of force at the right time. [2]

On the pages which follow, each locomotor pattern is analyzed in detail and checklists are provided for identifying the aspects of each movement pattern which are mature rather than developmental or immature. Although the focus is upon assessment, these checklists can be used also as step-by-step guides in helping students to refine their natural movement patterns. Most children learn best by problem solving. Given a gymnasium or playground with apparatus and an assortment of other children to play with, observe, challenge, and imitate, the average child will try an infinite variety of motor activities. It is in this kind of setting that the teacher appraises the motor behavior of individuals. His role is primarily that of observer, and he must be prepared to analyze widely diverse skills ranging from easy through difficult.

Sports and dance skills related to the basic locomotor patterns presented in this chapter

2. Items 1-10 were taken from this source: John L. Haubenstricker and Vern Seefeldt, "Sequential Progression in Fundamental Motor Skills of Children with Learning Disabilities," (Speech given at the International Conference of the Association for Children with Learning Disabilities, Houston, Texas, March 1, 1974).

are analyzed also. If a child can jump, for instance, to what extent can he transfer his knowledge and skill to track and field events? Can he perform a long jump, a high jump, or a triple jump? Which of his natural movement patterns, when refined, offer the greatest potential for success among his peers? *The specialist in adapted physical education looks first at the strengths of the child.* He assumes that the pupil knows a great deal already. Not until he has fully appraised the child's present movement capabilities does his role change from observation, diagnosis, and appraisal to guidance, counseling, and teaching.

Rolling

Developmentally the first locomotor movement pattern which appears is rolling, or the ability to turn the body from side to side. This motor achievement resembles the log roll. It evolves during infancy as follows:

Two months old—roll from side to back
Four months old—roll from back to side
Six months old—roll from back to back or abdomen to abdomen by means of partial turns with rest periods between them.

In executing these turns, the infant turns his head first, then his shoulders, then his pelvis, and last his legs. The muscles of the abdomen and posterior trunk are prime movers for this rotatory action. A person with severe motor involvement may be unable to perform any locomotor movements other than variations of the log roll.

Early Purposive Patterns

The first purposive locomotor movement patterns to appear are hitching, crawling, and creeping. Hitching is a form of backward locomotion in a sitting position. The infant uses one leg to scoot himself along the floor and keeps the other leg doubled under him or extended to help maintain his balance. Hitch-

ing is the predominant mode of travel for such a short time that it is generally excluded from lists of locomotor movements.

The terms *crawling* and *creeping* are sometimes used interchangeably, but child growth and development theorists make a definite distinction between the two patterns. Crawling is primarily an arm action which pulls the body along the floor while the abdomen and legs drag along behind. This pattern appears between the fourth and ninth months but may be skipped altogether. Creeping is a locomotor pattern in which the weight of the body is distributed equally to the hands and knees. Most authorities believe that the evaluation of crawling and creeping should be based primarily upon the presence of opposition, i.e., a crosslateral pattern.

Physical educators have long recognized the value of creeping in the development of trunk muscles and arm and shoulder strength. Rathbone was stressing the importance of creeping exercises in the early 1930s, introducing thousands of teachers to the Klapp Creeping System from Germany. In the Klapp system, opposition of limbs was expected along with lateral flexion and rotation of the head and neck toward the side of the forward knee. Criteria recommended by Rathbone for the evaluation of creeping are

(1) the spine should appear loose (flexible) throughout
(2) the shoulders should be on the same level as the hips
(3) the knees should point straight ahead or slightly outward
(4) the pelvis should not swing strongly from side to side
(5) the feet should remain in contact with the floor
(6) the head should bend and twist away from the forward moving arm [3]

3. Josephine Rathbone, *Corrective Physical Education* (Philadelphia: W. B. Saunders, 1959), p. 266.

Figure 7.1. Thirteen-year-old mentally retarded boy finds creeping through a tunnel a real challenge.

Some children skip the creeping stage, often appearing precocious by their early walking. Rathbone suggests that such children have missed a valuable developmental stage which normally contributes to postural fitness and strong trunk muscles. Getman notes that retarded children often miss the "all fours" creeping stage and that many normal children who become crosseyed at about the age of three have by-passed the creeping stages. [4]

Prior to suggesting criteria for the evaluation of other locomotor movement patterns, it is important to review the approximate ages at which certain kinds of motor performance appear. Table 11 is recommended as a diagnostic rating scale for preschool children and others who may be performing motorically at the 1-5 age level. The age given for each task is a statistical average or norm which must be interpreted as encompassing individual differences. Thus children who perform a task three or four months earlier or later than the norm are still classified as average. The primary purpose of Table 11 as a rating scale is discovery of where a child is *now* and the subsequent development of an educational prescription based upon the sequence of tasks not yet mastered. In accordance with the philosophy of this text, the rater checks performance as either *immature* or *developmental,* meaning mature for the child's age. The concepts of pass-fail and right-wrong should not be used in this rating scale nor any of the others in this chapter.

Walking

The art of walking is not perfected until approximately three years after the child has taken his first step, i.e., some time after age four in the normal child. Walking patterns reveal many individual differences with each person tending to assume a gait which is efficient for his particular body structure. Developmental changes in head, trunk, and limb proportions contribute, in large part, to the transition from immature to mature walking. The proportionately large head and high center of gravity in the toddler, for instance, help to explain his wide base of support. Other factors which may affect the walking pattern include disorders in bilateral integration, such common structural anomalies as uneven length of legs, and deficits in strength and flexibility.

Gait, a term for walking which includes carriage, rhythm, and speed, also reflects personality or temperament. It evolves as the total self interacts with the environment. Thus

4. G. N. Getman, *How to Develop Your Child's Intelligence* (Luverne, Minn.: G. N. Getman, 1952), p. 40.

children tend to emulate the walking gaits of those around them. Institutionalized mentally retarded children, for instance, may exhibit certain walking patterns simply because of inadequate exposure to other gaits. Ordinarily walking is broken down into periods of double and single support depending upon whether one or both feet are in contact with the floor. In slow walking, as is characteristic of many persons with handicapping conditions, both feet may be on the floor as much as 30 percent of the time. If the period of double support exceeds this, the person is described as having a shuffling gait. The seriousness of this problem can be determined by observing him in attempts to step over bamboo poles, rungs of a ladder, or other low obstacles placed 12 to 18 inches apart on the floor. In some cases shuffling is due to laziness or poor concept formation rather than inadequate muscle tonus to lift the foot off of the floor. If the latter is believed the cause, exercises should be administered to strengthen the flexors of the hip, knee, and ankle which contract to facilitate the swinging phase.

Further observation should ascertain that the heel strikes the ground first after which the body weight is transferred sequentially along the outer border of the foot to the metatarsal area and the toes. The step ends with a push off or thrust of the flexor muscles of the big toe. The person unable to demonstrate this heel-ball-toe action may require physical therapy and/or concentrated exercises aimed at strengthening or stretching particular muscles. Simplified tap dance or games requiring the child to tap different parts of the foot to the floor are recommended. If the main difficulty is the push off, running in sand and other toe curling exercises like picking up marbles are helpful.

The symmetry or rhythm of a gait is judged on the basis of the amount of time spent in each phase of walking. Research shows that this is remarkably similar from person to person: 10-20 percent to heel strike, 30-35 percent to transfer of weight along outer border; 10 percent to metatarsal phase; 30 percent to toes; and 3-10 percent to the actual push off. A gait is considered symmetrical if the same amount of time, space, and force are used by the right and left sides of the body in each phase of walking. A good test of symmetry which encompasses rhythm and speed involves challenging the child to carry a potato balanced on a teaspoon or a full cup of liquid. An alternate test is to walk with an object balanced on his head. These tests can be executed on a balance beam as well as the floor. Auditory awareness can be heightened by blindfolding the children and encouraging them to listen to footsteps and guess the name of a person on the basis of the distinctive sounds of his gait. It is often necessary to focus a child's attention on sounds of heaviness, shuffling, or scraping which may characterize his gait and to practice walking in opposite ways: heavy, light; fast, slow; shuffle, lift; flat foot, heel-ball-toe.

A forward lean rather than good body alignment often characterizes the walk. To heighten proprioceptive awareness, students should practice body leans of different degress and learn which is appropriate for walking and other locomotor activities. *Forward lean*, a term used also in teaching running, is the line between foot contact of the extended rear leg and the center of gravity. The lean should be from the ground so that the whole body, not just the hips and waist, is involved. Forward lean can be discussed in terms of the hands of a clock. Thus in walking, the body should be in 12 o'clock position. In the mile run the lean is about 10 degrees, about one-third of the way between 12 and 1 o'clock. In middle distance runs, the lean increases to between 15 and 18 degrees, or halfway between 12 and one. In sprinting the lean is greatest, about 25-30

Table 11 *Approximate Ages At Which Children First Perform Locomotor Tasks*
(A Diagnostic Rating Scale)

Age	Locomotor Task	Rating	
		Immature	Developmental
Between ages 1-2, the child learns to:			
13 mo	Climb up stairs (creeping fashion)		
14 mo	Stand alone		
15 mo	Walk alone (flat-footed gait)		
16.5 mo	Walk sideways		
16.9 mo	Walk backwards—several steps		
18-20 mo	Ascend stairs in upright position, with help		
18 mo	Run with flat-footed gait, without period of non-support		
24 mo	Step down from a low height (8-inch elevation)		
24 mo	Transfer weight during walking from heel to toe		
24 mo	Handle tricycle; demonstrate ability to steer, back, and manage sharp turns		
Between ages 2-3, the child learns to:			
27 mo	Ascend short flight of stairs, leading with same foot and marking time on each rung		
27.6 mo	Walk with one foot on low balance beam and other foot on floor. Beam 2.5 meters long, 6 cm wide and 10 cm high		
28 mo	Descend short flight of stairs, leading with same foot and marking time on each rung		
	Jump off floor with two foot take off and two foot landing		
29 mo	Maintain static balance on one foot for 3 seconds		
	Ascend short flight of stairs, using alternate feet, with support		
30 mo	Walk on tiptoes		
31 mo	Stand on balance beam with both feet		
	Ascend short flight of stairs, alternate feet, without support		
31.3 mo	Walk a straight line in given directions		
32 mo	Maintain balance and take a few steps on low balance beam		
32.1 mo	Jump down from chair—10-12 inches high		
36 mo	Demonstrate some ability in management of two-wheeled scooters		

Table 11 *Approximate Ages at Which Children First Perform Locomotor Tasks—Continued*

Age	Locomotor Task	Rating	
		Immature	Developmental
Between ages 3-4, the child learns to:			
37 mo	Walk a line one inch wide for distance of ten feet without stepping off		
37.3 mo	Distance jump—1-3 feet		
38 mo	Alternate feet part way on balance beam		
	Execute 1-3 consecutive jumps		
	Jump over a rope 6 inches high		
42 mo	Execute 10 or more consecutive jumps		
43 mo	Execute 1-3 consecutive hops		
	Perform early skipping movements with skip on one foot and walk on other foot (shuffle-skips)		
45 mo	Walk a circular path 21 1/2 feet without any step offs		
48 mo	Descend short flight of stairs with alternate feet, with support		
	Gallop (43 percent can imitate this task)		
	Propel and manipulate wagon with one knee on wagon floor and other foot on ground		
Between ages 4-5, the child learns to:			
49 mo	Descend short flight of stairs, alternate feet, without support		
48-60 mo	Demonstrate control over starts, stops, and turns in running		
56 mo	Walk, alternating feet, the full-length on balance beam		
59.5 mo	Walk length of balance beam in 6-9 seconds		
60 mo	Execute 10 or more consecutive hops		
	Gallop (78 percent can imitate this task; success in gallop usually occurs before skip)		
	Alternate feet in mature skipping pattern		

degrees, or at 1 o'clock. Only by practicing walks and runs does the pupil learn to discriminate between good and poor postural alignment.

Criteria for the evaluation of walking are summarized in Table 12. On this and on subsequent tables in this chapter, the teacher should check the items which characterize the pupil's movement pattern. Observations should include walking on several different terrains and/or surfaces, and the evaluation should offer a comparison of the pupil's success on even versus uneven terrains as well as uphill, downhill, and level walking.

Abnormal Gaits

Several gaits characteristic of specific diseases and/or neurological involvement can be identified.

(1) *Scissors Gait.* Characteristic of spastic cerebral palsy, the legs are flexed and adducted at the hip joint, causing them to cross alternately in front of each other with the knees scraping together. The knees may be flexed to a greater degree than normal, and the weight of the body may be taken primarily on the toes.

(2) *Shuffling Gait.* Associated with severe mental retardation. Inadequate muscle tonus to lift the foot off of the ground during the normal swinging phase of walking.

(3) *Staggering Gait.* May result from alcoholism, drug poisoning, brain tumors, multiple sclerosis, or general paresis.

(4) *Cerebellar Gait.* Characteristic of ataxic cerebral palsy. Irregularity of steps, unsteadiness, tendency to reel to one side. Individual seems to experience difficulty in judging how high to lift legs when climbing stairs. Problems are increased when the ground is uneven.

(5) *Tabetic Gait.* Also associated with ataxia, but caused by disease of dorsal column of spinal cord which results in loss of proprioceptive sense in the lower extrem-

Figure 7.2. Child with spastic cerebral palsy exhibits scissors gait.

ities. Individual uses wide base, shuffles or slaps feet, and tends to watch the ground. Problem is increased in the dark or with the eyes closed.

(6) *Steppage Gait.* Also called foot-drop gait and characterized by flopping of the foot on the floor. Knee action is higher than normal, but toes still tend to drag on floor. Caused by paralysis or weakness in the anterior tibial muscles.

(7) *Trendelenburg Gait.* Limp caused by paralysis or weakness of gluteus medius. Pelvis is lower on nonaffected side, i.e., if right gluteus is affected, left hip is lower when standing with weight of body on right leg. In walking each time the weight is transferred to the right foot, the body leans slightly to the left (the nonaffected side).

Table 12 *Checklist for Evaluation of Walking*

Developmental or Immature Walking	Mature Walking

1. Forward lean
    a. from ground
    b. from waist and hips
	1. Good body alignment

2. Wide base of support with heels 5-8 inches from line of progression	2. Narrower base of support with heels 2-3 inches from line of progression
3. Toes and knees pointed outward	3. Toes and knees pointed straight ahead
4. Flat-footed gait	4. Heel-ball-toe transfer of weight
5. Excessive flexion at knee and hip joints	5. Strong push-off from toes
6. Uneven, jerky steps*	6. Smooth and rhythmical shift of body weight with minimal up-and-down movement of body
7. Little or no pelvic rotation until second or third year. Body sways from side to side	7. Minimal rotatory action of pelvis (short persons will have more than tall ones)
8. Rigidity of upper torso	8. Compensatory rotatory action of torso and shoulders inversely related to pelvic rotation
9. Outstretched arms	9. Arms swing freely and in opposition with legs
10. Relatively short stride. In preschool children, the distance from heel to heel is 11-18 inches	10. Greater length of stride dependent upon length of leg. In the average adult man, the distance from heel to heel is 25-26 inches
11. Rate of walking stabilizes at about 170 steps per minute	11. Rate of walking decreases to about 115-145 steps per minute

*Jerkiness may be caused by a flat-footed or shuffle gait or by excessive stride length.

(8) *Waddling Gait.* Child rolls from side to side as he walks. Can be caused by paralysis of both gluteus medius muscles, dislocated hips, or muscular dystrophies with weakness of the hips.

(9) *Hemiplegic Gait.* Both arm and leg on the same side are involved. Also tends to occur with any disorder producing an immobile hip or knee. Affected leg is rigid and swung from the hip joint in a semicircle by muscle action of the trunk. Individual leans to his affected side, and arm on that side is held in a rigid, semiflexed position.

(10) *Propulsion or Festination Gait.* Characteristic of Parkinson's Disease, also called *paralysis agitans.* Individual walks with a forward leaning posture and short shuffling steps which begin slowly and become progressively more rapid.

Running

Running demands more balance than walking because the weight of the entire body is supported on one foot at a time. Unlike walking, there is no period of double support. Running also differs from walking by having a nonsupport phase, a time when the body is actually in flight or "sailing through the air."

The physical educator should be able to evaluate the different kinds of runs: (1) jogging; (2) sprinting; (3) middle distance runs—880 yards and up; and (4) long distance runs—mile and over for children. The 440-yard dash can be classified as either a sprint or a middle distance run depending upon the circulorespiratory endurance of the students. Table 13 shows that each type of run varies with respect to foot plant, knee action, forward body lean, and arm action. These four components are generally the ones on which pupils need the most practice.

To understand the mechanics of running, children should be taught the meanings of such words as forward lean, driving leg, recovery leg, center of gravity, and striding. *Forward lean* is the line between foot contact and center of gravity. Forward lean is greatest early in the sprint when the runner is accelerating rapidly and levels off after the point of maximum speed is reached. Many coaches believe that forward lean cannot be taught. It is a direct result of forward acceleration and, to some degree, of air resistance. The *driving leg* is the one which extends and pushes against the ground. The *recovery leg* is the one in which the high knee lift is important. The *center of gravity* is the point in the pelvis below which the recovery foot should try to land. The rate of striding is dependent upon four factors: (1) speed of extension of driving leg; (2) speed with which recovery leg is brought through; (3) length of time body is in air; and (4) landing position of the recovery foot in relation to the center of gravity.

Severely and profoundly retarded children who lack the concept of running should be introduced to it by walks down hills steep enough to quicken the pace to a run. In early stages of learning they may have a rope around the waist and be pulled into a running gait. Patient teaching is required also to convey the concepts of starting, stopping, and staying in a lane.

Less involved children will need special instruction related to running on the balls of the feet, lifting the knees, and swinging the arms. To facilitate running on the balls of the feet, practice can be up short, steep hills or steps. Jumping and hopping activities also tend to emphasize staying on the balls of the feet. Possible solutions to inadequate knee lift include riding a bicycle, particularly uphill; running up steep hills or steps; and running in place with knee action exaggerated to touch the outstretched palms of hands. Correction for swinging arms across the body or without

Table 13 *Comparison of Three Types of Runs*

Characteristics	Sprint	Middle Distance Run	Long Distance Run
Foot Plant	Land high on ball of foot; heel does not touch.	Land lower on ball of foot than in 50-yard dash; heel does not touch.	Land low on ball of foot, drop to heel.
Knee Action	Lift knee high and straight forward.	Lift knee less high than in 50-yard dash.	Lift knee slightly as compared to other runs.
	Thigh should be more-or-less horizontal to ground at end of knee lift.	Thigh should be less horizontal, about 70°-80° at end of knee lift.	Thigh is less horizontal at end of knee lift than in other runs.
	Less rear kick than in other kinds of runs.	More rear kick than in sprint.	More rear kick than other runs.
Forward Body Lean	Lean between 25 and 30 degrees—about 1 o'clock.	Lean between 15 and 18 degrees—about halfway between 12 and 1 o'clock.	Lean about 10 degrees —about one-third of way between 12 and 1 o'clock.
Arm Action	Pump arms vigorously with hands reaching chin level or higher.	Use slightly less vigorous arm action.	Swing arms naturally at about shoulder level.

vigor include practice in front of a mirror and running with a baton or small weight bar.

Observation of the running pattern during a short sprint is probably the best single screening device for predicting overall success in traditional physical education activities. Because of its extreme importance, a detailed analysis of sprinting is presented in Table 14. The left-hand column describes the normal running pattern for a preschool child. The right-hand column describes the mature pattern of a successful sprinter. The rater should place a checkmark in front of those phrases which best describe the pupil's run.

Ascending and Descending Stairs

The infant's exploration of space includes stairsteps if they are available. Even before he begins to walk, he may be ascending stairs using a pattern strikingly similar to his creeping movements on a level surface. The criteria used in the evaluation of creeping apply to this early method of ascending the stairs.

Upright stair and ladder climbing progresses through two stages, each of which is performed first with help and later independently.

Stage 1—Leading with one foot and mark-

Table 14 *Checklist for Evaluation of Sprinting*

Developmental Running	Mature Running
1. Short running stride	1. Increased length of stride

2. Exaggerated leg and foot movements
   (a) Toeing out of foot of recovery leg
   (b) Outward rotatory movement of recovery knee especially obvious from back view
   (c) Foot of recovery leg crosses midline in back just before it swings forward
	2. Minimal rotatory leg movements
	   (a) Toes point straight ahead
	   (b) Knees point straight ahead

3. Knee not lifted high in the air in forward swing	3. Knee of recovery leg swung forward higher and faster. Thigh should be more-or-less horizontal to ground at end of knee lift
4. Low heel kick-up as leg is swung forward (as viewed from rear)	4. Heel brought closer to the buttock on knee lift
5. Mechanically inefficient push-off—less extension in rear leg	5. Increase in extension and velocity of driving leg, i.e., rear leg when it pushes off
6. Support phase relatively long—this is because driving leg moves slower	6. Decrease in amount of time spent in ground contact—only 1/60 to 3/60-second
7. Forward foot contacts ground at point ahead of the body's center of gravity	7. Forward foot contacts ground at point directly under the body's center of gravity; knee bends slightly immediately after foot touches ground
8. Little forward lean early in sprint	8. Forward lean between 25 and 30 degrees early in sprint; less later
9. Excessive up-and-down movement of body	9. Minimal amount of body rise
10. Limited range of arm movement	10. Hand swings as high as chin on forward swing; elbow reaches as high as shoulder on backswing
11. Excessive bending and rigidity in arm movement at elbows	11. Elbows maintained in 90-degree angle with tendency to straighten on downward part of backswing and to bend on forward swing
12. Arms tend to swing across trunk toward the the midline	12. Minimal shoulder rotation
13. Arms not working in true opposition to legs	13. Arms working in opposition to legs

Figure 7.3. Thirteen-year-old child with Down's Syndrome descends stairs in immature fashion.

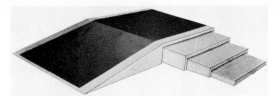

Figure 7.4. A gradual inclined ramp from 1/2 to 8 inches in height. Steps are 2, 4, and 6 inches high respectively. Reprinted by permission © J. A. Preston Corporation, 1971.

Figure 7.5. Rails with three steps on one side and two on the other. Reprinted by permission © J. A. Preston Corporation, 1971.

Figure 7.6. Interlocking climbing stools, each four inches high. Reprinted by permission © J. A. Preston Corporation, 1971.

ing time until the trailing foot is on the same step or rung in a period of double support. The lead foot is generally the preferred or dominant foot.

Stage 2—Mature foot-over-foot pattern, supporting the weight on the alternate foot on each step.

Descending stairs and ladders follows the same developmental pattern but occurs several months later. Sinclair reports that 89 percent of her three-year-old subjects could ascend stairs using a foot-over-foot pattern but only 12 percent could use the mature pattern in descending. Almost a year later, at age four, most of the children exhibited a foot-over-foot pattern in descending.

Since contemporary architecture seems to provide fewer and fewer steps for practice of ascending and descending skills, it may be desirable to purchase or construct staircases, ramps, and ladders scaled down to the small child's leg and foot size. Commercially available staircases provide steps which are 2, 4, 6, and 8 inches high with 4 inches being the recommended height. The practice steps also vary in width with the following dimensions commonly used: (1) 32 X 32 X 2; (2) 36 X-36 X 4; and (3) 40 X 40 X 6.

Characteristics of the mature ascending pattern are

1. Slight forward lean from ankle joints, not the hips.
2. Center of gravity balanced directly above forward foot.
3. Placement of entire foot on each step.
4. Reliance upon knee extension rather than plantar flexion at ankle joint for most of power.
5. Handrails not used.
6. Eyes straight ahead rather than looking down.

Characteristics of the mature descending pattern are:

1. No forward or backward lean.
2. Center of gravity balanced approximately over center of base of support.
3. Handrails not used.
4. Eyes straight ahead rather than looking down.

Leaping

The earliest form of a jump is really a leap for it involves a one-foot take-off and a transfer of weight to the opposite foot. Leaping, however, is generally associated with dance and movement exploration. It is usually characterized by a forward-backward stride, a one-foot take-off, a period of flight or nonsupport, elevation during the flight, and a transfer of body weight in the air so that the child takes off on one foot and lands on the other. Sideward leaps are used in tests of dynamic balance and agility and in some dances.

The child usually attempts his first leaps at about age two. These may be called "step-down jumps" since they almost always involve stepping down from a height. Thus an excellent screening technique is placing the child on a 12- to 18-inch height and instructing him to jump off. His responses, from least

Figure 7.7. Ten-year-old displays excessive neuromuscular tension as she concentrates on leaps.

mature to most mature, may be any of the following:

(1) Refuses to jump—just stands—cries.
(2) Sits down and scoots off of the height.
(3) Squats or stoops and then jumps down.
(4) Steps down from an upright position.
(5) Jumps down using a two-foot take-off and a two-foot landing.

Hurdles

Illustrative of a basic locomotor movement pattern which becomes a sports skill is the popular event in track and field called hurdling. The movement pattern in the hurdle is essentially a leap with the lead-leg extended forward and the trail-leg bent backward as the body clears a bar.

The recommended height of the hurdles is 18 to 24 inches for young children. For older boys and girls a height of 30 to 36 inches is recommended. For elementary and middle school children six to eight hurdles are recommended spaced out over 60 yards or 87 1/2 yards (80 meters). The placement of six hurdles over 60 yards is as follows on page 137.

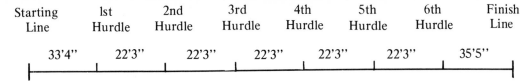

Placement of Six Hurdles

Starting Line	1st Hurdle	2nd Hurdle	3rd Hurdle	4th Hurdle	5th Hurdle	6th Hurdle	Finish Line
	33'4"	22'3"	22'3"	22'3"	22'3"	22'3"	35'5"

Since the child sprints the distances between the hurdles, the hurdling event might be described as six leaps interspersed between sprints. He learns the pattern of run-run-leap by negotiating very low obstacles in the beginning. The height of these obstacles is raised gradually. It is best to let the child discover his own pattern by challenging, "How fast can you run and leap over each of the hurdles?"

Before formal instruction can be given, the child must be taught the following terms: (1) lead-leg, (2) trail-leg, (3) take-off, (4) flight, (5) land, (6) body lean, (7) stride, and (8) hurdle. The take-off is mechanically most efficient when executed from five to seven feet from the hurdle. Ideally three strides are taken between hurdles. The pattern is land on lead-foot, step, step, take-off on trail-foot, clear the bar, land on lead-foot, and repeat.

Jumping

Considerable confusion exists in the literature with respect to the definitions of jump, hop, and leap. Kephart's indiscriminate use of the word jump in the Purdue Perceptual-Motor Survey is particularly misleading. Table 15 clarifies the three terms.

The following list of motor skills shows the natural developmental progression from a leap to a jump to a hop. The observer should check the developmental stage at which the child is presently functioning.

(1) Step-down from height.
(2) Vertical jump (two-foot take-off and two-foot landing).
(3) Jump-down from height with two-foot landing.
(4) Modified running long jump (really a

Table 15 *Comparison of Leap, Jump, and Hop*

	Leap	Jump	Hop
Take-off	Always a one-foot take-off	May be either two-foot or one-foot take-off	Always a one-foot take-off
Flight	Weight always transferred from one foot to the other	Weight always transferred to two feet	Weight never transferred
Landing	Always a one-foot landing	Always a two-foot landing	Always a one-foot landing on same foot

Figure 7.8. *Above* Three-year-old improves kinesthetic awareness of up and down as a lead up to jumping.

Figure 7.9. *Right* Jumping on top of and in and out of tires is a lead up to trampoline skills.

Figure 7.10. Children exhibit varied jumping patterns as bamboo poles are rhythmically brought together and separated.

leap) with a one-foot take-off, transfer of weight in air, and one-foot landing.

(5) Regulation standing long jump with two-foot take-off.

(6) Jump down with one-foot take-off and two-foot landing.

(7) Modified running long jump with a one-foot take-off and a two-foot landing.

(8) Jump over an object with a two-foot take-off and a two-foot landing.

(9) Hop.

(10) Regulation running long jump with a one-foot take-off and two-foot landing.

The best test of jumping skill is to observe which pattern comes naturally rather than to demonstrate a particular kind of jump which is then imitated by the child. The child should be tested first while standing on a bench 12 to 18 inches high and later while standing on a level surface. The challenge posed may be: How many different ways can you make your body cross over this line on the floor? Children with known neurological problems like cerebral palsy may need a horizontal bar or rope to hold onto for balance while attempting jumping tasks.

Well-coordinated children can perform the regulation standing long jump with the two-foot take-off and two-foot landing at about age three. No significant differences appear in the long jumping abilities of boys and girls until about age eight at which time boys begin to excel.

Standing Long Jump

Since the standing long jump is included in almost all tests of fitness as a measure of leg power, the characteristics of the immature versus the mature movement patterns are listed in Table 16.

Running Long Jump

The running long jump is a jump for distance at the end of a sprint. The world record for adult women is over twenty-two feet and for men is over twenty-nine feet. At the recent Texas Special Olympics the best distances for mentally retarded boys and girls respectively in the thirteen to fifteen age division were 16'7'' and 14'10.''

A special area of the playground with a jumping pit filled with fine sand must be designed if the running long jump is to be learned safely. The dimensions for such an area are depicted below.

The beginner in long jumping must first identify the *take-off foot*. To do this, he may kick at an imaginary ball. The supporting foot during the kick should be the take-off foot for the long jump. Early movement exploration should involve a short running approach, a stamp on the preferred foot, and an attempt to jump upward and forward. Later, during the flight phase, the pupil strives to run in the air by alternately bringing the knees forward. This running in the air is sometimes called a hitch kick. Table 17 presents a simple analysis of the mature running long jump pattern.

Dismount

The term *dismount* used in gymnastics is a jump from a piece of apparatus down to the floor. Dismounts are used to end routines on the balance beam, the even parallel bars, the

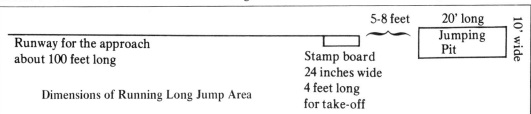

Dimensions of Running Long Jump Area

Table 16 *Checklist for Evaluation of Standing Long Jump*

	Developmental or Immature	Mature
Preliminary Crouch	1. Little or no crouch	1. Assume preparatory crouch with hips, knees, and ankles in deep flexion
	2. Trunk not parallel to ground	2. Trunk is almost parallel to ground
	3. No backward-upward swing of arms	3. Weight moves forward as arms swing backward-upward
	4. No return movement of arms	4. Weight continues to move forward as arms swing forward-downward
	5. Insufficient shoulder joint flexion—arms not lifted high enough	5. Crouch phase ends when arms are in line with trunk
Take-off	6. Take-off begins with *simultaneous* extension at hip, knee, and ankle joints	6. Take-off begins with *successive* initiation of extension at hip, knee, and ankle joints
	7. Take-off angle is more than 45°	7. Take-off angle is approximately 45°
	8. Arm swing not coordinated with leg movements	8. Arms swing forward-upward as heels are lifted
Flight Upward	9. Incomplete body extension at take-off	9. Body is in full extension at beginning of flight
	10. Arms never fully flexed overhead to form single long lever with trunk	10. Arms are flexed at shoulder joint and elbows extended. Arms are in line with trunk to form single long lever
	11. Knee and hip flexion occur simultaneously	11. Lower legs flex first during flight
Flight Downward	12. Incomplete hip flexion during flight	12. Hip joint flexion begins when knee flexion reaches 90°
	13. Forward arm action not coordinated well with knee and hip extension	13. As knees come forward and knee joint extends, arms and trunk reach forward
	14. Incomplete knee extension at end of flight	14. Knees are fully extended at end of flight

Table 16 *Checklist for Evaluation of Standing Long Jump —Continued*

	Developmental or Immature	Mature
Landing	15. Toes or ball of foot contacts ground first	15. Heels touch ground before toes
	16. Incomplete spinal and hip flexion at moment of contact	16. Trunk and thighs are almost touching at moment of contact
	17. Center of gravity too far backward at moment of contact resulting in unsteady landing	17. Instantaneous flexion of knees when heels contact ground
	18. Hands touch the floor	18. Arms reach forward-upward to help maintain balance

Table 17 *Checklist for Evaluation of Running Long Jump—Mature Pattern*

Approach	Sprints 120-130 feet
Take-off	1. Strikes take-off board with a flat foot
	2. Keeps center of gravity directly above the slightly flexed take-off leg
	3. Brings other leg and its opposing arm forward and upward with vigorous knee action as take-off foot pushes off
Flight	1. The knee of free leg is already in the air
	2. Next the take-off leg is brought forward and free leg shifts slightly back
	3. Finally the free leg comes forward again to join take-off leg just before landing
	4. Arms are forward-upward throughout flight and move in opposition to legs
Landing	1. Land on heels first
	2. Arms swing up over head and back simultaneously with heel contact
	3. Arms continue forward to touch sand in landing pit

uneven parallel bars, the horse, and the buck. Judged for their aesthetic appearance and mechanical efficiency, dismounts may involve difficult movements such as handsprings and cartwheels or simple jumps downward using a two-foot take-off and land.

No knowledge is more important to a child than how to get off of a piece of gymnastic apparatus or play equipment safely. The first skill that should be taught on a balance beam is the *jump-off dismount*. Once a child feels secure about his jumping ability he will no longer fear falling. Only then should locomotor movements (walks, runs, skips) on the balance beam be introduced.

Figure 7.11. A first attempt at vaulting with good spotters on either side.

Vault

Jumping becomes a sports skill when it is used in gymnastics as a means of getting over a piece of apparatus. How many different kinds of apparatus can the student *vault* over? (1) a low beam about thigh or hip high; (2) a tumbling bench; (3) a vaulting box; (4) a horse; or (5) a buck.

Instead of demonstrating regulation vaults and expecting the student to imitate, the teacher should observe the different movement approaches explored by the student in his attempts to get over the apparatus. Which of the following movement patterns offer him the most success?

(1) *Squat Vault*—Weight taken equally on both arms, knees are pulled upward, tucked to chest, and then continue forward. Body passes over box in a squat position.

(2) *Straddle Vault*—Weight taken equally on both arms and legs are abducted in wide stride semi-sitting position. Hands are on inside and legs on the outside. Body passes over box in this straddle position.

(3) *Flank Vault*—Initially done with both arms on the box. Regulation flank vault is performed with one arm. While arms support weight of body, both legs are lifted

simultaneously over the box. The side of the body passes over the box. Sometimes called a side vault.

(4) *Front Vault*—Same as flank vault except the front of the body passes over the box.

The beginning vault is often a combined side-front vault with both hands on the box and the knees bent as the legs pass over. Most elementary school textbooks recommend that the squat vault be taught first. The law of individual differences rules that *all* children should not be introduced to the same progression of vaults nor tested on a single movement pattern selected by the teacher. When allowed to discover their own way of getting over, first grade children can succeed at vaulting. A beatboard or springboard is necessary to attain the height necessary for propulsion of the body over the box.

Jumping on a Springboard, Beatboard, or Minitramp

The movement patterns used on the springboard, beatboard, minitramp, and diving board are similar. For better transfer of learning the child should have experience on all four pieces of apparatus. If the budget allows the purchase of only one, the beatboard is recommended.

Figure 7.12. Clapping hands diverts attention from tuck position.

Figure 7.13. Assuming a straddle position in the air.

The following questions serve as guides for observation and evaluation of the natural movement pattern of the child when challenged to run up the board, jump once on the end of the board, and then land on the mat.

(1) Does he run slowly with hesitancy or at an appropriate speed?

(2) How long is his approach, i.e., how many steps does he take prior to reaching the beatboard?

(3) Does he run flat-footed or on the balls of his feet?

(4) Does he slow down or stop before he executes the jump on the end of the board?

(5) Does he use a two-foot take-off from the board?

(6) Which foot is the last to push off before the two-foot take-off is initiated?

(7) Does he gain maximum height in his jump?

(8) Is the amount of forward lean mechanically efficient so he falls neither forward or backward?

(9) Does he bend at hip, knee, and ankle joints upon landing in order to absorb the shock?

(10) Does he have trouble maintaining his balance upon landing?

Specific tasks which the child can be asked to perform as he jumps are

(1) Clap hands overhead, behind back, in front of body

(2) Land beyond a certain line or marker on the mat

(3) Assume a tuck position in the air

(4) Assume a pike position in the air

(5) Assume a straddle position in the air

(6) Assume a hurdle position in the air

(7) Assume a laterally flexed position in the air

(8) Make a turn in the air

(9) Land with feet together, feet apart, one foot in front of the other

(10) Land with arms in various positions

(11) Land and immediately perform a forward roll

Figure 7.15. Crotch seat mount is performed by twelve-year-old with surgically corrected bilateral club foot condition.

Figure 7.16. Observation of arm movements in trampoline jump is an excellent diagnostic technique.

Mount

The term *mount* used in gymnastics is a jump from a beatboard, springboard, or minitramp up onto a piece of apparatus. Mounts are used to begin routines on the balance beam, the even parallel bars, the uneven parallel bars, the horse, and the buck.

Some of the easiest mounts which can be practiced on various pieces of apparatus are

(1) Straight Arm Support Mount
  a. Short approach
  b. Double-leg take-off
  c. Both hands on top of beam or bar
  d. Jump to push-up position with both arms straight
  e. Thighs supported against beam
  f. Head high
  g. Back arched
  h. Toes pointed

(2) Crotch Seat Mount
  a. Perform straight arm support mount
  b. Swing one leg sideward (abduction)
  c. Continue swing until body straddles beam
  d. Hands grip beam behind
  e. Toes pointed
  f. Good body alignment

(3) Squat Mount
  a. Perform straight arm support mount
  b. Simultaneously tuck knees to chest
  c. End squatting with arms on outside
  d. Head up

Children need practice jumping up onto things as well as jumping down. If no apparatus can be improvised, they may jump (two-foot take-off) *up* the stairs, *up* on automobile tires, *up* on street curbs, *up* on rocks, and so on.

Jumping on a Trampoline

The trampoline is used so widely with exceptional children that it seems appropriate to include a checklist for evaluating the basic jump. This does not mean, however, that the joy of bouncing up and down in one's natural style should be destroyed by a well-meaning teacher who wishes all of his charges to use "correct form." Kephart, Getman, Cratty,

Figure 7.16. Observation of arm movements in trampoline jump is an excellent diagnostic technique.

The problems which the child exhibits on the trampoline are the same as those he has overcome and/or learned to compensate for when on the ground. Table 18 is a checklist for evaluation of trampoline jump.

It is hypothesized that the tonic neck reflex and other abnormal postural reflexes are evidenced in the immature jumping patterns of preschool children with learning disabilities. Cinematographical research is underway to examine this hypothesis. Observations of young children, particularly those suspected of some degree of cerebral palsy, seem to bear out the presence of the typical ipsilateral flexion pattern with semiextension and abduction of the limbs on the opposite side. The head turns slightly toward the extended arm. Abnormal reflexes will be discussed more fully in the chapter on cerebral palsy. Using the trampoline as a diagnostic aid, physical educators often recognize deviations in basic movement patterns before the parents and pediatrician.

and others have recommended the trampoline as one of the best means of improving laterality, i.e., the kinesthetic awareness of right and left requisite to the maintenance of balance and good body alignment. This objective can be achieved only if the child is subjected to extensive problem solving and challenged to transfer what he knows about locomotor and nonlocomotor movements to the enigmatic surface of the trampoline.

Emphasis should not be on the learning of such traditional skills as the seat drop during early lessons but rather upon motor fluency and originality. The child may attempt rolls, animal walks, rope jumping, turns in the air, and other stunts. The teacher who is capable of maintaining silence, accepting the child as he is, and observing closely will find the trampoline an extremely valuable diagnostic aid.

High Jumping

High jumping, a popular track and field event included in the Special Olympics, is another refinement of this basic movement pattern. It involves a running approach and a lift of the entire body up and over a horizontal bar which is raised after each successful performance. At the recent Texas Special Olympics mentally retarded boys and girls in the ten-to-twelve bracket high jumped 4'4" and 3'6" respectively. In the thirteen-to-fifteen age group boys jumped 5' and girls jumped 4'3".

Four methods of high jumping are recognized: (1) scissors, (2) western roll, (3) straddle roll, and (4) Fosbury flop. All begin with a running approach, usually five to seven steps so that the last stride brings the student down on the heel of his take-off foot.

The same procedures apply in evaluating the high jump as in the vault. No attempt is made to teach correct form until the child

Table 18 *Checklist for Evaluation of Trampoline Jump*

Developmental or Immature Pattern	Mature Pattern
1. Does not land consistently on same spot	1. Lands consistently on the same spot
2. Looks at feet or trampoline	2. Focuses eyes on one spot at end of trampoline
3. Exhibits poor body alignment which demands constant postural adjustments Consistent forward lean Consistent backward lean Consistent lean to R Consistent lean to L	3. Exhibits good body alignment with body segments each balanced above the other
4. Lands with feet together	4. Lands with feet approximately shoulder width apart
5. Points toes outward or inward	5. Keeps toes pointed straight ahead
6. Lands in forward-backward stride	6. Lands with both feet parallel
7. Lands on toes or balls of feet	7. Lands flat-footed
8. Lands with more weight on one foot than the other	8. Lands with weight equally distributed on both feet
9. Has trouble stopping	9. Can stop instantaneously
10. Take-off characterized by incomplete extension at hip, knee, or ankle joints	10. Take-off characterized by extension at hip, knee, and ankle joints
11. Bending at waist; flexion of neck	11. Complete extension of spinal column
12. Legs apart in flight	12. Legs together in flight
13. Rotation of some body part	13. No rotation of pelvis, trunk, or head
14. Little height achieved in bounces	14. Flight characterized by optimum height
15. Rigidity of both arms, little or no movement Rigidity of one arm Incomplete upward movement of arms Arms abducted instead of flexed Arm movement not coordinated with lift and descent of body	15. Arms move upward to form a single lever with the trunk as body ascends; arms move downward as body descends
16. Arms not moving simultaneously and identically R or L hand higher R or L hand clenched in fist R or L elbow flexed R or L knee flexed R or L arm abducted R or L forearm pronated	16. Good bilateral coordination of arms—both making identical movements
17. Legs not moving simultaneously and identically R or L knee bent R or L hip rotated inward R or L hip rotated outward	17. Good bilateral coordination of legs

Figure 7.17. A winning high jump by a mentally retarded adolescent at national Special Olympics.

engages in a period of problem solving and movement exploration designed to find his natural movement pattern. The teacher simply observes, recording the techniques which the child uses, and later structures learning by modifying and refining the jumping style most natural to each individual.

Questions which the teacher attempts to answer through observation are as follows:

1. Does the child approach the bar from the right or left side?
2. How many steps comprise his running approach?
3. What is the angle of the approach in degrees?
4. How close to the bar is the child when he takes off? This is estimated in inches.
5. Which foot does he begin his run on?
6. Which foot does he end his run on? This is the take-off foot.
7. Which leg is the kick-up leg? The kick-up leg determines whether the child is designated as a right-footed jumper or a left-footed jumper. Thus a child who

kicks up with his right leg is a right-footed jumper.

8. Which of the two basic styles of kicking up does he use?
   (a) The inside leg is the kick-up leg. The approach is from the right when the right foot is the kick-up leg. This is called the *scissors jump*.
   (b) The outside leg is the kick-up leg. The approach is from the left when the right foot is the kick-up leg. This style is used in the *western roll, straddle roll,* and "Fosbury Flop." In elementary school literature it is sometimes called the *barrel or straddle roll.*
9. What is the relationship of his body to the bar at the time of clearance? The answer to this question determines the name of the jump.
   (a) Vertical or semivertical position—this is scissors jump providing inside foot was kicked up.
   (b) Layout position
       (1) Side to the bar—western roll

(2) Face to the bar—straddle roll
(3) Back to the bar—"Fosbury Flop"
In all of these the outside foot is kicked up.

10. On what part of the body does he land? Kick-up foot? right shoulder? back?

It is not presumed that the special educator will teach high jumping nor many of the other skills presented in this chapter. Specialized training is needed to learn techniques for refining the natural movement patterns of children and to ensure success in sports events. The special educator should, however, be a skilled observer of movement, responsible for recording answers to these questions on each child's individual record form and willing to provide the physical education specialist with such information before the formal instructional unit is begun. Moreover the special educator should be present as an observer who makes written notes on each pupil's motor performance during the physical education period. If the physical educator is not aware of his colleague's potential contributions, the special educator should acquaint him with the checklist being used and take the initiative in establishing a cooperative teaching relationship.

For optimum learning to occur the special educator must also assume responsibility for correlating reading, writing, spelling, and arithmetic activities with the vocabulary of movement and body image. Words and phrases which children must master to derive benefit from instruction in the many kinds of jumping include:

lead-foot	pike
trail-foot	straddle
take-off foot	layout
kick-up foot	approach
inside leg	angle
outside leg	angle of approach
vertical	crossbar clearance
horizontal	stamping foot
tuck	driving leg

take-off	take-off point
landing	landing point
two-foot take-off	roll
one-foot take-off	arm action
lifting force	counterbalance
leg swing	inward rotation
strides	peak of jump
springing upward	height of jump
foot plant	center of gravity

It is reasonable to believe that diagnosis and appraisal with respect to motor performance should include the evaluation of word comprehension and verbal concepts. Assessment of body image should go beyond the identification of body parts and the discrimination between right and left. It must encompass knowledge about the body in space—approaching, taking off, flying, and landing. For what child has not dreamed of flying? Leaping and jumping are the legacy of every teachable child who is not orthopedically handicapped.

Hopping

Hopping is the most difficult of the basic locomotor skills. Sinclair reported that only 28 percent of her three-year-old subjects could hop; 71 percent of the four-year-old children could hop; and 96 percent of the five-year-old children could hop. Not until age five could the children hop equally well on the preferred and nonpreferred foot. Sinclair's subjects had no known perceptual-motor problems. [5]

Children with neurological deficits which affect balance may never learn to hop. Cratty reports that only one-fourth of the children with Down's Syndrome (Mongolism) he tested could hop in square or circular patterns. The moderate mental retardation could hop on one foot in succession, and only 5 percent of them could hop in square or circular patterns. The performance of mildly mentally retarded

5. Caroline B. Sinclair, *Movement of the Young Child* (Columbus, Ohio: Charles E. Merrill Co., 1973).

children approached that of normal children although games such as hopscotch were decidedly difficult for almost half of them.[6]

Before challenging a child to perform a task which may be unrealistic for his capabilities, the teacher should test him on static balance. Can he stand motionless with all of his weight on one leg? For how many seconds? On which leg is this task the easier? If he fails the test of static balance, what are the reasons? Inadequate leg strength, poor body alignment, faulty proprioception, or deficits in the vestibular system?

Cratty reported that approximately 75 percent of children with Down's Syndrome he tested in Los Angeles could not maintain their balance on one foot for more than a few seconds. Most of these children found it almost impossible to balance on one foot with eyes closed. Only two-thirds of the moderately mentally retarded children could maintain their balance on one foot for more than five seconds without vision. Approximately 70 percent of the mildly mentally retarded children could maintain their balance on one foot with arms folded across their chests, and about one half of them could maintain the balance position on one foot with their eyes closed. Mildly mentally retarded children seem to improve most significantly in their ability to balance between the chronological ages of eight and fourteen years of age.

Few tests of hopping are standardized and yield numerical scores. The best known is that included by Kephart in the Purdue Perceptual Motor Survey. The following items comprise the test.

Hop 1/1. The child is asked to stand with his feet together, he is then asked to hop on the right foot, lifting the left. Next he is asked to alternate, hopping first on the right and then on the left.

Hop 2/2. This task is the same as the foregoing except that the child hops twice on the right foot, twice on the left, etc.

Hop 2/1. This item requires the child to hop twice on the right foot, once on the left, twice on the right, etc.

Hop 1/2. This item asked the child to hop once on the right foot, twice on the left, etc.[7]

Performance on these tasks is evaluated in accordance with the following four point scale:

4—The child performs all tasks easily.
3—The child can alter sides symmetrically.
2—The child can hop on either foot at will, can alternate but cannot maintain a rhythm.
1—The child can only perform symmetrically.

Applying Kephart's concept of hopping alternately from one foot to another without breaking the rhythm, Keogh and Pedigo established the norms in Table 19 for boys on three hopping patterns.

6. Bryant J. Cratty, *Developmental Sequences of Perceptual Motor Tasks* (Freeport, Long Island, New York: Educational Activities, Inc., 1967), p. 5.

7. Newell C. Kephart, *Slow Learner in the Classroom* (Columbus, Ohio: Charles E. Merrill Books, Inc., 1960), pp. 128-129.

Table 19 *Percentage of Boys Able To Hop Three Patterns*[8]

Age	3L,3R	2L,2R	3L,2R
6 1/2	23%	16%	7%
7	35%	19%	10%
7 1/2	48%	38%	18%
8	63%	53%	31%

8. Jack F. Keogh and P. Pedigo, "An Evaluation of Performance on Rhythmic Hopping Patterns" Sponsored by the National Institute on Child Health and Human Development (Grant HD09059-03), UCLA, 1967 (Unpublished).

Rhythmic Two Part Motion

Developmentally the average child does not learn how to combine basic locomotor movements until about age three. The gallop is the first combination to be mastered. Sinclair reported that 76 percent of her three-year-olds and 92 percent of her four-year-olds could gallop. Most of her children succeeded in galloping before they could hop.

Since the gallop is a combination of the walk and the leap, it seems reasonable to introduce the skill at the time the child refines his leap. This may be the first skill learned in a forward-backward stride position with the same foot leading throughout. The teacher who is concerned with the establishment of dominance should observe which foot is the lead one and whether the same foot is used consistently in this role. Sinclair observed that most children learned to lead with their non-preferred foot much later than with their preferred foot.

The slide is identical to the gallop except that it is executed sideward rather than forward and hence requires a better defined sense of laterality. Approximately 34 percent of Sinclair's three-year-olds and 77 percent of her four-year-olds could slide. In the early years children seem to have a preferred side in sliding. There is a tendency for beginners to cheat by rotating the head, trunk, pelvis, or hip in the direction of the slide rather than truly leading with the shoulder. The importance of moving sideward as a means of improving balance and laterality was emphasized by Kephart who noted that this is one of the few skills which teach lateral transfer of weight rather than forward-backward transfer.

Preschool children need special help with words which have several definitions. *Slide* is such a word. As well as being a fundamental dance skill, it is a piece of playground apparatus, a picture flashed on the screen by a projector, and a verb meaning to glide over a slippery surface.

Figure 7.18. Age differences are reflected in skipping. The older girl associates skipping with her dance class and tries to stylize her movement into "something pretty."

In elementary school folk dances executed in a circle, the slide is one of the easiest and most popular steps. The pattern traditionally used is seven slides to the right with a transfer of weight to the opposite foot on the eighth count followed by seven slides to the left and a transfer of weight. This sequence should be practiced early.

Skipping is a combination of a walk and a hop in an uneven rhythm. It is learned after the leap, jump, and hop are mastered. Approximately half of the four-year-olds can skip but by the first grade almost all children can skip. Boys generally experience more difficulty than girls. Mastery seems to progress through two or three stages: (1) a type of shuffle on one foot alternated with a walk on the other; (2) a skip on one foot alternated with a walk on the other; and finally (3) a skip alternately performed by both feet. As in all locomotor patterns, the arms work in opposition to the legs.

Rathbone lists skipping along with hanging by the arms and balancing as the three forms of physical activity which are especially important in childhood. She states: "Skipping will help to lift the body high, to extend it. It will also set a pattern of joyousness, which, in itself, encourages elevation. The adult who discourages a child from skipping and hopping about is harming his body as much as his spirit."[9]

Splinter Skills

Whereas physical educators express concern about transfer of learning and the carryover values of a particular movement pattern into other sports activities, special education teachers talk of *splinter skills* and the problem of *splintering*. A splinter skill is one which can be done well in one setting but is not carried over into related activities. Examples follow:

(1) A child walks the low balance beam in the classroom with confidence. He refuses to traverse a railroad tie, a fence rail, and a log fallen across a stream. Or, if he does attempt the challenge, performance is poorer than expected.

(2) A child has learned the gallop, the slide, and the skip to particular music on the teacher's tape recorder. When different music is played, it appears that he has never performed these dance skills before.

(3) A student preparing for an examination memorizes a list of facts in a particular order and can recite them perfectly. The examination asks the facts in a different order, and the student cannot record what he "knows" he knows.

In the appraisal of motor performance, the teacher should suspect splintering if the child can perform a particular skill better than all others; if he cannot modify or adapt a skill to a new activity or setting; or if he cannot stop in the middle and then resume where he left off rather than having to return to the beginning.

Splintering usually occurs when a skill has been mastered through drill rather than problem solving. Children with learning disabilities are thought to be particularly susceptible to splintering. It is important, therefore, when observing performance for the purpose of identifying motor dysfunctions that the teacher sees each movement pattern adapted to different environmental stimuli.

The checklist which follows summarizes modifications of some of the locomotor movement patterns as they appear in track and field and gymnastics. The left-hand column states the age in years at which the average child demonstrates fairly mature movement patterns. This is also the optimal age for introducing the pupil to the new skill if he has not learned it already from the older children in the neighborhood.

Both track and field and gymnastics are individual sports which emphasize competition against self rather than competition against

9. Josephine Rathbone, *Corrective Physical Education* (Philadelphia: W. B. Saunders, 1954), p. 5.

others. They are both included in Special Olympics events throughout the world. Because they are based upon the natural movements of childhood and do not involve the manipulation of balls, track and field and gymnastics are recommended elementary school activities for children with handicapping conditions.

Table 20 *Checklist on Track and Field and Gymnastics Skills*

App. Age	Track and Field Skills	No Attempt	Attempted but Failed	Immature Pattern	Mature Pattern
5	Sprinting				
5	Standing long jump				
6	High jump scissor style				
7	Running long jump				
8	Running relays				
9	Hurdles				
9	Middle distance runs				
9	High jump straddle style				
10	Long distance runs				
10	Triple jump				
	Gymnastic Skills				
3	Consecutive jumps on trampoline				
4	Jump-off dismount from balance beam				
4	Forward walk on beam				
5	Backward walk on beam				
5	Sideward walk on beam				
6	Approach and jump off of springboard				
7	Front support arm mount				
7	Squat vault				
7	Straddle vault				
8	Front vault				
8	Flank vault				
5	Combinations of locomotor movements on trampoline				
5	Combinations of locomotor movements on balance beam				

Recommended Activities

1. Interview several mothers concerning the ages at which their children first performed the locomotor tasks listed in Table 11.
2. Observe normal and handicapped preschool children at play. What differences, if any, are evident in their motor performance?
3. Observe one child at play in a gymnasium or on a playground for thirty minutes. Record the number of different locomotor and nonlocomotor movement patterns he uses. Record the number of times he changes level and/or direction. Compare your tabulations with those of others in your class. Using this information, participate in a discussion on motor creativity with emphasis on fluency.
4. Use the checklists in this chapter to practice the evaluation of locomotor movement patterns and related skills: walking, running, ascending and descending stairs, leaping, standing long jump, running long jump, vertical jump, trampoline jump, and hop.
5. Observe children vaulting over various pieces of apparatus. Which movement patterns offer them the most success: squat vault, straddle vault, flank vault, front vault? Teach one of these vaults to a group of beginners, and make a list of the movement problems or errors exhibited in their first several attempts.
6. Observe several pupils in their first attempts at learning to high jump. Answer the questions on page 145.

Recommended Reading

American Alliance for Health, Physical Education, and Recreation. *Special Olympics Instructional Manual.* Washington, D. C.: AAHPER and The Joseph P. Kennedy, Jr. Foundation, 1972.

Cratty, Bryant J. *Developmental Sequences of Perceptual Motor Tasks.* Freeport, Long Island, New York: Educational Activities, Inc., 1967.

Ducroquet, Robert. *Walking and Limping: A Study of Normal and Pathological Walking.* Philadelphia: J. B. Lippincott Company, 1968.

Geddes, Dolores. *Physical Activities for Individuals with Handicapping Conditions.* St. Louis: C. V. Mosby Co., 1974.

Godfrey, Barbara B., and Kephart, Newell C. *Movement Patterns and Motor Education.* New York: Appleton-Century-Crofts, 1969.

Kirchner, Glenn. *Physical Education for Elementary School Children.* Dubuque, Iowa: Wm. C. Brown Company Publishers, 1974.

Moran, Joan, and Kalakian, Leonard. *Movement Experiences for the Mentally Retarded or Emotionally Disturbed Child.* Minneapolis: Burgess Publishing Co., 1974.

Sinclair, Caroline B. *Movement of the Young Child.* Columbus, Ohio: Charles E. Merrill Co., 1973.

Wickstrom, Ralph L. *Fundamental Motor Patterns.* Philadelphia: Lea & Febiger, 1970.

Wilt, Fred, and Ecker, Tom, ed. *International Track and Field Coaching Encyclopedia.* West Nyack, New York: Parker Publishing Company, Inc., 1970

8 Perceptual-Motor Strengths and Weaknesses

Figure 8.0. Movement exploration uses kinesthetic, vestibular, and visual sensory input to increase body awareness. (Creative Playground by Sharon Schmidt.)

Systematic efforts to unravel the mysteries of how patterned motion is accomplished are seen in studies which go by different names: motor learning, sensory-motor learning (sensori-motor, sensori neuromotor); psycho-motor learning (psychomotor); menti-motor learning (ideo-motor); neuro-muscular learning (neuro-motor); perceptual-motor learning (perceptuo-motor, visuo-motor, tactual-motor). What do all of these terms imply? Definitions, when given at all, are usually so diverse, contradictory and imbricated as to render them confusing. . . . What's in a name? Regardless of the one chosen, those who would understand learning of any sort must remember that so far as is presently known *the ingredients of learning are intricate, multi-dimensional, delicately integrated and basically inseparable.*

Aileene Lockhart [1]

The practice of formally assessing perceptual-motor strengths and weaknesses has a relatively short history beset with controversy, misunderstanding, and competition. From the 1940s onward, several disciplines endeavored to develop techniques for assessing perceptual-motor development and identifying associated dysfunctions. Leaders in the fields of medicine, optometry, clinical psychology, physical therapy, and occupational therapy all contributed substantially to the evolution of evaluation techniques in the perceptual-motor domain before most physical educators became interested in the movement. Today physical educators, with their sophisticated backgrounds in kinesiology, neurophysiology, and experimental research, are often critical of existing tests of perceptual-motor functioning and of the terms which pervade the field: *laterality, directionality, mixed dominance, bilateral coordination,* and so on. One of the purposes of this chapter is to acquaint physical educators with the language of their colleagues in other fields and to encourage interdisciplinary approaches to the assessment of perceptual-motor dysfunctions. The physical educator who is naive and/or negative with respect to the work of Kephart, Getman, Frostig, and others will more than likely be excluded from the diagnostic and evaluation team which makes important decisions concerning all aspects of the child's curriculum. When no physical educator is a part of this team, perceptual-motor dysfunctions may be either ignored or interpreted narrowly as problems of ocular control and hand-eye coordination which interfere with normal progress in learning to read and write. Without a physical educator on the team, it is doubtful that the *whole* child will be appraised. Nor will the resulting program of remediation include a comprehensive, well-rounded program of physical education.

It is essential that physical education specialists become increasingly involved in the refinement of existing techniques as well as the development of new valid and reliable tests of perceptual-motor functioning. This chapter is divided into three parts. The first presents background information on perception. The second presents items which purport to measure aspects of perceptual-motor functioning. The third part of the chapter describes perceptual-motor training in the physical education setting.

Perception

Perception is defined in many ways. Some definitions combine it with sensation, and others delimit the process of perceiving to the translation of the neural impulse into a sensation, i.e., the mental awareness of conditions which prevail within or outside of the body. In order for a state of mental awareness to exist, four prerequisites are necessary.

1. A stimulus capable of initiating a response from some part of the nervous system.
2. A sensory receptor or sense organ which can react to the stimulus.

1. Aileene Lockhart, "What's In A Name?" *Quest,* Vol. 2 (April 1964), pp. 9-13.

3. An ascending pathway (tract) for conducting the impulse arising in the sensory receptor to the brain.
4. A region within the brain capable of translating impulses into sensations. The four regions primarily responsible for translating electrical impulses into sensations are (a) cerebral cortex; (b) thalamus; (c) hypothalamus; and (d) cerebellum.

Perception seems to encompass both sensory reception and central processing. The translation of electrical impulses into sensations must be considered central processing since it occurs within the brain. At present, there is no way of determining whether motor awkwardness is caused primarily by dysfunctions of perception or central processing. Except in theoretical learning models, the two neurological processes are not clearly separable.

For the purposes of this book, perception is defined as the basic, immediate discriminatory behavior that relates the individual to his surroundings. The process of perception usually includes *awareness, discrimination, organization,* and *cue selection. Awareness* is neurological feedback that something is happening. *Discrimination* is the ability to differentiate between stimuli, including the acuity with which the child can discriminate between sounds, tempos, colors, forms, joint positions, or degrees of muscular tension. *Organization* refers to the capacity to organize stimuli into a meaningful whole. *Cue selection* refers to the ability to attend to relevant cues and to block out irrelevant stimuli. Special educators often refer to perception as *decoding*, the ability to obtain meaning from sensory stimuli, i.e., receptive understanding of words, pictures, gestures, joint position, and muscle tension. Problems of perception can then be categorized as dysfunctions of auditory, visual, and proprioceptive decoding.

Perception can be stimulated by ten different sense modalities, each of which neurologically is distinctly different in structure and function. Each has a special type of end organ (sensory receptor) which is sensitive only to certain stimuli and each has a separate pathway from the sensory receptor up the spinal cord to the brain. These sense modalities are (1) vision; (2) audition; (3) taste; (4) smell; (5) touch and pressure; (6) kinesthesis; (7) vestibular sense; (8) temperature; (9) pain; and (10) common chemical sense.

Visual Perception

Visual perception has been broken down also into such discrete attributes as discrimination, figure-background phenomena, depth perception, object constancy, phi phenomenon, and retinal inhibition. A child will not have disturbances of all of the attributes. *Discrimination* refers to the ability to discriminate visually between different forms, sizes, weights, heights, colors, textures, distances, speeds, and rhythms. Young children tend to rely first upon color and later upon forms or shapes of objects for identification and classification. Other discriminative abilities normally develop sequentially with increasing maturity. *Visual figure-background phenomena* refers to the ability to identify and focus attention upon a single object or figure in a cluttered and/or complex background. Children who become so confused during a tag game that they cannot locate *it* and individuals who cannot follow the serial path of a golf ball or baseball are illustrative of persons with figure-background problems. The ability to differentiate visually between a selected object and a complex background develops slowly and does not reach peak performance until adolescence. *Depth perception* refers to the ability to judge distances and to discriminate between the spatial dimensions of near and far. It is also called *stereopsis*. Children who exhibit unreasonable fear of walking a high beam or jumping into a swimming pool may have problems of stereopsis. *Object constancy* refers to the ability to identify an object regardless of the direction it points, the shape it assumes, and the hue it is colored. A chair, for instance, must be perceived as a chair whether it is big or little, wooden or upholstered, red or green, rightside up or upside down. *Phi phenomenon*, sometimes called autokinetic movement, refers to the erroneous perception of movement when an object is actually stationary. This phenomenon may occur when the child focuses upon the same object, like the page of a book, for a prolonged period of time; in such instances, the words seem to float about. *Retinal inhibition* occurs when a person appears to be looking directly at an object and gives no evidence of seeing it. Difficulties in attending to visual cues fall into this category.

Auditory Perception

Auditory perception also can be broken down into several different factors. *Auditory discrimination* refers to the ability to distinguish between different frequencies (pitches), intensities, and tonal qualities (timbre) of sounds. *Auditory figure-background phenomenon* implies the ability to distinguish relevant sounds (usually words) from background of noise and confusion. *Directionality of sound* refers to the ability to determine the direction from which auditory stimuli are emanating. *Temporal perception* refers to the ability to discriminate between fast and slow, even and uneven, accented and unaccented as well as to recognize variations in rhythm such as 4/4, 3/4, or 6/8.

Haptic Perception

Haptic perception encompasses kinesthetic, vestibular, and tactile input. The haptic receptors are located throughout the body in (1) skin and deeper underlying tissue; (2) muscles and tendons which attach muscles to bone; (3) skeletal joints and connecting ligaments between all moveable bones; (4) blood vessels; and (5) hair cells located in the semicircular canals, utricle, saccule, and cochlea of the inner ear. The simultaneous input of these receptors is integrated in the parietal area of the brain into information about the body, its environment, and their interrelationships. Specifically, the haptic system provides two major kinds of information. In the first category, the *touch-pressure sense modality* gives information about the environment as: (1) surface texture; (2) surface area or size, shapes, borders, angles, and openings; (3) qualities of consistency such as hard, soft, resilient, or viscous; (4) temperature; (5) pressure; and (6) pain. In the second category, the *kinesthetic and vestibular sense modalities* provide information about the body itself as: (1) dynamic movement patterns of the trunk, arms, legs, mandible, and tongue; (2) static limb positions or postures; (3) linear and rotatory directions of movement of the skull, limbs, and body as a whole; (4) the location of the body in relation to external objects; (5) weight of resistance to gravity; (6) the relative weights of external objects which are being pushed, pulled, lifted, or lowered; and (7) the relationship of the body to gravitational pull.

The term *haptic perception* was originated by Viktor Lowenfeld, a professor of art education at the Pennsylvania State University, in the late 1930s in conjunction with a study of psychological changes in childhood and adolescence as related to imagination. He noted that children's drawings tended to be *haptic* in that the child's creative expression is

. . . mainly connected with such subjective experiences as bodily feelings, muscle sensations, and touch impressions. It also is obvious that the child's way of perceiving space is determined by his subjective relationship to it, since the child's perception is derived from bodily, not from visual, experiences. . . . that is why it can be assumed that *the child's world of imagination is mainly bound up with* the self, with subjective feelings, and subjective relationships toward surroundings.[2]

2. Viktor Lowenfeld, *Creative and Mental Growth* (New York: The Macmillan Company, 1952), p. 228.

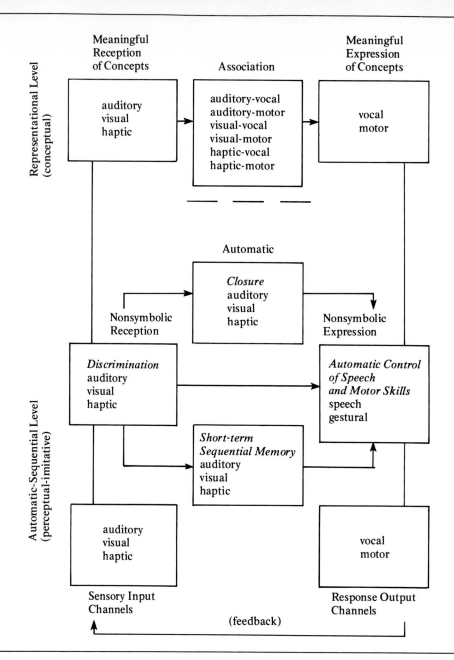

Figure 8.1. Clinical model of the communication process depicting terms used in the Illinois Test of Psycholinguistic Ability (ITPA). This model led to the use of the term *haptic* among special educators. Reprinted by permission.[3]

3. Samuel A. Kirk and Winifred D. Kirk, *Psycholinguistic Learning Disabilities: Diagnosis and Remediation* (Chicago: The University of Illinois Press, 1971), p. 100.

It was not until the last decade, however, that the term *haptic perception* came into common usage. It was popularized by Samuel A. Kirk and his colleagues in special education at the University of Illinois in Urbana in their clinical model of the communication process underlying the development of the Illinois' Test of Psycholinguistic Ability (ITPA). In 1969, an entire chapter entitled "Haptic Processing" in a NINDS * research monograph served to increase the frequency with which the term is used in special education. 4

Tactile Perception

Dysfunctions of the touch-pressure sense modalities include failure to: (1) identify the presence of pressure on the skin; (2) locate the exact point on the skin where touch is made; (3) differentiate two or more stimuli which are applied simultaneously; (4) indicate the direction of an object moving over the skin; and (5) register sensitivity to pain and temperature. Most tests of tactile perception involve the fingers. Finger localization, the ability to identify without vision which finger is touched by the examiner, is considered a valid measure of body image as well as a perceptual ability. The ability to recognize objects by touch and to distinguish shapes, letters, or numbers drawn on the skin requires the integration of sensations from a series of points on the skin's surface. To test discrimination of surface textures, it is generally best to allow the child to rub or pull the stimulus object through the fingers. Little information about subtle differences in textures can be obtained merely by touching. Often it is difficult to distinguish between language deficits and poor tactile discrimination. Before the latter is tested, it is important to ascertain that the child knows the meaning of such adjectives as thick, thin, smooth, rough, wet, and dry.

Proprioception

The kinesthetic and vestibular sense receptors can be grouped together as propriocep-

Figure 8.2. Martian canals for sand and water play help to improve tactile awareness. (Playground Corporation of America.)

tors. Proprioception includes sensations pertaining to balance, position, and movement. The vestibular apparatus in the inner ear registers stops, starts, and changes in direction related to static and dynamic balance. The kinesthetic receptors in the joints are believed most vital to the perception of space and movement. These joint receptors discharge at a given rate for a given angle of a joint. It has been found that subjects can detect the bending of a single joint as little as a fraction of 1 degree. In this regard, Gibson states: "We

* *NINDS* refers to National Institute of Neurological Diseases and Stroke.
4. James C. Chalfant and Margaret A. Scheffelin, *Central Processing Dysfunctions in Children: A Review of Research* (NINDS Monograph, No. 9, Bethesda, Maryland: U. S. Department of HEW, 1969).

detect the angles of our joints, not the length of our muscles." [5]

Awareness of position and movement of the joints seems to depend solely upon joint receptors. The amount of information which is obtained from muscles and tendons is limited. Specifically muscle receptors register stretch, and tendon receptors register strain. Receptors in joints, muscles, tendons, ligaments and skin all contribute to perception of muscular effort required to resist and/or overcome gravity and to impart force to an external object. Kinesthetic perception is not a general ability. It is comprised of many different factors, each of which must be taught and measured separately. Among the tasks which are included on most tests of kinesthesis are

(1) Positioning of body segments
    (a) Duplication of specific positions as measured by the angle made by two limbs at a joint
    (b) Imitation of movements
(2) Positioning of entire body or spatial orientation
    (a) Duplication of specific positions
    (b) Imitation of movements
(3) Accuracy and precision in moving objects
    (a) Direction, as related to accuracy in aiming: right, left, clockwise, counterclockwise, up, down, forward, backward, sideward, upright, tilted, horizontal, vertical, diagonal. This relates also to alignment of body parts as in feeling good and poor postures.
    (b) Distance, involving appropriate force production to send objects of certain weights prescribed distances
(4) Duplication of muscular tension of known amount
    (a) As measured in microvolts by electromyographical apparatus
    (b) By jumping, hopping, or leaping a given distance or height
    (c) By exerting force against some measurable resistance

(5) Maintenance of balance with and without vision
    (a) Static
    (b) Dynamic
(6) Size discrimination—Ability to move between wide and narrow spaces, to duck under, to step or jump over. Ability to estimate dimensions of height, breadth, and depth on self and in relation to self. Accurate estimation of self as big or little, fat or thin, of body measurements.
(7) Weight discrimination—Ability to discriminate between light and heavy when holding objects, to feel center of gravity, to estimate stability. Ability to determine whether an external object can bear one's weight.

The sensitivity of the vestibular and kinesthetic proprioceptors to stimuli is one of the most important factors in motor coordination. The description of a child as poorly coordinated, awkward, or clumsy refers specifically to the speed and accuracy with which the nervous system coordinates the activities of perception, central processing, and motor response. If the problem is primarily perception, it is difficult to determine which sense modality is malfunctioning: vision, kinesthesis, or the vestibular sense.

Programs of perceptual-motor training frequently stress visual, auditory, and tactile perception and omit kinesthetic and vestibular perception. When activities for the improvement of kinesthesis are included, they often are not labeled as such. For instance, Kephart's theoretical constructs of laterality and directionality are components of proprioception. *Laterality* is the proprioceptive awareness of right and left which is developed within the child's own body through trial and error in movement experiences. Since upright posture demands an internal awareness of right and left in order to maintain balance

5. J. J. Gibson, *The Senses Considered As Perceptual Systems* (Boston: Houghton Mifflin Co., 1966), p. 109.

against the pull of gravity, it can be assumed that children develop some degree of laterality before they can walk. The proprioceptive awareness of right and left is best measured by activities entailing balance and by observing the frequency with which a child loses balance or falls. *Directionality* is the proprioceptive awareness of the body in space and includes sensory perception of up, down, forward, backward, and sideward, and other directional aspects.

Kinesthetic learnings occur through movement experiences which increase awareness of changes in joint positions and of how muscles feel when they develop tension within themselves and when they relax. Thus a well-coordinated person masters a new motor pattern with relative ease because he is able to replicate the same positions and movements over and over again, each time making corrections for too little or too much muscular tension and thereby progressively approximating the good form exhibited by the teacher. In motor learning theory, this is known as *progressive approximation.* In contrast the child with poor kinesthesis may lack the ability to feel the extent to which each trial approximates another and to judge the efficiency of his movements. The process of *trial and error* may be a complexity of random efforts with repetitions of the same errors in spite of his ability to understand mechanical principles and to visualize the correct movement. His body simply refuses to do what the mind wills, and the child becomes increasingly discouraged by discrepencies between intended versus actual movements. Illustrative of this problem are the individuals who know they should not bend their elbows as they stroke in tennis but who do so anyway, who know they should tuck their heads during forward rolls but fail to do so, who can visualize precisely the right moment to contact the ball with the bat but who cannot do so. Such individuals often demonstrate great insight in the verbal analysis of the motor task undertaken, in the identification of their movement errors, and in the suggestion of corrections.

Every physical educator has been confronted with the challenge of improving a child's kinesthesis. Verbal reminders seldom help. Nor does additional practice since the child with poor kinesthesis, unlike the normal child, fails to profit measurably from trial and error. Oxendine states in this regard:

The possibility of improving the kinesthetic sense has been of considerable interest to physical educators. However, the probability of improving a basic sensory capacity through practice seems remote. There is no convincing evidence that kinesthesis can in fact be improved. What *can* be improved is a particular position or movement response. [6]

Is it really true that one must have superior skills to enjoy an activity? How can we develop good attitudes toward sports participation in persons with below average kinesthetic abilities?

Appraisal of Perceptual-Motor Functioning

There is no general perceptual-motor ability. Tests which purport to measure general abilities are comprised of many items, each of which is designed to measure a separate specific factor. Unfortunately, however, researchers do not yet agree on the factors which should comprise perceptual-motor tests. Nor do representatives of different disciplines agree.

Table 21 summarizes the factors which widely used classroom tests purport to measure. Although all of the tests reportedly discriminate between normal and neurologically impaired populations and some of them are believed to discriminate between

6. Joseph Oxendine, *Psychology of Motor Learning* (New York: Copyright© 1968 Meredith Corporation. Reprinted by permission of Appleton-Century-Crofts, Educational Div. Meredith Corporation), p. 296.

Frostig Developmental Test of Visual Perception (1963)	Kephart-Roach Purdue Perceptual-Motor Survey (1966)	Ayres Southern California Perceptual-Motor Tests (1965-69)
1. Eye-Motor Coordination a. Keeping pencil between two horizontal or curved lines b. Connecting dots or figures	1. Balance and Posture a. Walking board b. Hopping and jumping	1. Imitation of Postures Reproduction of 12 arm and hand movements
2. Figure-Ground a. Overlapping outlines b. Embedded figures	2. Body Image and R-L Discrimination a. Identification of body parts b. Imitation of movement c. Obstacle course d. Kraus-Weber e. Angels-in-the-snow	2. Crossing Midline of Body Using right or left hand to touch designated ear or eye
3. Form Constancy Overlapping and Embedded Forms	3. Perceptual-Motor Match a. Chalkboard activities b. Rhythmic writing	3. Bilateral Motor Coordination Rhythmic tapping using palms of hands on thighs
4. Position in Space Figures like stars, chairs, ladders in different positions in space	4. Ocular Control Ocular pursuits	4. Right-Left Discrimination Identification of right and left dimensions of various objects
5. Spatial Relations Reproducing designs or figures by connecting dots appropriately	5. Form Reproduction Drawing simple geometric figures on blank paper	5. Standing Balance Eyes open
		6. Standing Balance Eyes closed

good and poor readers, the evidence is not conclusive. Until further research ascertains the exact nature of perceptual-motor attributes and better tests are devised, the verbiage of Frostig, Kephart, and Ayres will continue to dominate special education. It is recommended that the adapted physical educator be fully acquainted with and able to administer the tests of Frostig, Kephart, and Ayres in order to communicate optimally with colleagues in other fields. Some of the terms and phrases popularly used in perceptual-motor appraisal represent hypothetical *constructs* rather than specific aspects of behavior which can be seen or measured directly. A *construct* is an imaginary mechanism which helps a teacher think about the phenomenon he is studying. Thus *bilateral integration, apraxia, tactile defensiveness, laterality, directionality,* and other widely used terms are simply convenient ways to express concepts underlying the behavior they represent.

The tests evolved by physical educators purport to measure such dimensions as motor educability, motor ability, psychomotor ability, motor proficiency, motor performance, and motor coordination. Historically each of these terms has a slightly different meaning. Some of the terms are now outdated. It is hypothesized that the tests published under these titles all measure perceptual-motor efficiency. As test originators become more sophisticated with respect to perception, they will recognize that the separation of motor proficiency from perceptual efficiency is difficult if not impossible. Visual, tactual, kinesthetic, and vestibular input are extremely important in the imitation of stunts and/or motor tasks required in most so called tests of motor ability.

Table 22 summarizes selected tests in physical education which purport to measure motor proficiency or psychomotor abilities. Brace's Test (1927) which is included in this

chapter as a recommended measure of imitation of postures does not delineate specific factors as do the newer tests. At the time of its development, educators were not as concerned with specific factors as we are now. It is obvious, however, that most of his items measure balance and different kinds of agility.

It is interesting to note that most special education and rehabilitation literature does not use the term *agility.* Its equivalent seems to be *postural* and/or *bilateral integration,* a term which seems to encompass balance and speed in changing position and/or direction in space. In several recent factor analyses, agility has not emerged as a separate factor. Fleishman found that agility, defined as speed of change of direction, was accounted for by the explosive strength factor in the shuttle run.[7] Cratty, although he uses the term agility in his Six-Category Gross-Motor Test, could not statistically isolate it as a separate factor from balance.[8] Special educators look for cross lateral or opposition movements under the broad heading of postural and bilateral integration. We would all concur that dynamic balance and speed in changing positions are affected by the smoothness and ease with which the limbs are moved in opposition.

Ayres distinguishes between bilateral integration and bilateral coordination.[9] *Bilateral integration,* the smooth working together of the two sides of the body, implies maturity of postural reflexes and equilibrium reactions in gross motor activities. *Bilateral*

7. Edwin A. Fleishman, *The Structure and Measurement of Physical Fitness* (Englewood Cliffs, New Jersey: Prentice-Hall, Inc., 1964), p. 99.

8. Bryant J. Cratty and Sister Margaret Mary Martin, *Perceptual-Efficiency in Children* (Philadelphia: Lea & Febiger, 1969), p. 193.

9. A. Jean Ayres, "Disorder in Postural and Bilateral Integration," *Sensory Integration and Learning Disorders* (Los Angeles: Western Psychological Services, 1972), p. 135.

Table 22 *Factors that Widely Used Motor Proficiency Tests Purport To Measure*

Lincoln-Oseretsky Motor Development Scale (1955)	Fleishman (1964)	Cratty Six-Category Gross Motor Test (1969)
1. Static Coordination	1. Control Precision	1. Body Perception
2. Dynamic Manual Coordination	2. Multilimb Coordination	2. Gross Agility
3. General Motor	3. Response Orientation	3. Balance
4. Motor Speed	4. Reaction Time	4. Locomotor Agility
5. Simultaneous Movements	5. Speed of Arm	5. Throwing
6. Asynkinesia	6. Rate Control	6. Tracking
	7. Manual Dexterity	
	8. Finger Dexterity	
	9. Arm-Hand Steadiness	
	10. Wrist-Finger Speed	
	11. Aiming	

coordination refers to fine motor activities, specifically the use of the palms of the hands to tap out rhythmic patterns on the thighs. Frostig also confines the use of the term *coordination* to fine motor activities, specifically pencil-paper tasks.

The average public school teacher continues to use the term *coordination* in many contexts. Yet factor analytical studies have repeatedly failed to identify such a motor attribute separate from other abilities. There apparently is no such thing as general coordination; there are instead thousands of specific abilities which can be measured by performance tests in which points are given for accuracy, speed, or balance.

The appraisal of perceptual-motor abilities of children cannot wait for researchers in different disciplines to reach agreement about the names of factors and the best techniques for assessing strengths and weaknesses. The best way for the public school teacher to measure perceptual-motor functioning is to develop precise behavioral objectives.

Behavioral Objectives as Test Items

Ten sets of behavioral objectives follow. They should be used as check lists in determining specific strengths and weaknesses in identification of body parts, right-left discriminations, changing positions in space, crossing the midline, imitation of movements, moving objects in space, visual tracking, static balance, dynamic balance, and lateral dominance. Success (motor output) in these tasks depends on the integrity of proprioceptive tactual input and central processing. Some children fail to make adequate motor responses because of auditory and/or visual deficits in understanding and remembering test instructions. To identify such children, the instructions for implementing the following behavioral objectives are either auditory or visual.

I. Major Task: Identification of Body Parts
   Other Tasks: Auditory Discrimination, Memory, and Sequencing
   A. Given opportunities to touch body

parts and surfaces after the teacher has called their names, the student can:

1. Touch body parts one by one in response to such one-word directions as elbow; wrist; chin; waist.
2. Touch two body parts simultaneously.
3. Touch five body parts in the same sequence as they were named by the teacher.
4. Do all of the above with his eyes closed.

II. Major Tasks: Identification of Body Parts; Right-Left Discriminations

Other Tasks: Auditory Discrimination, Memory, and Sequencing

A. Given opportunities to touch body parts and surfaces after the teacher has called out the instructions, the student can:
1. Use the right hand to touch parts named on his right side.
2. Use the right hand to touch parts named on his left side (this involves crossing the midline and should be more difficult than item 1).
3. Use the left hand to touch parts named on the left side.
4. Use the left hand to touch parts named on the right side.

B. Given opportunities to position a beanbag shaped like a *b*, the student can make a *p*; a *q*; a *b*; and a *d*.

C. Given opportunities to touch body parts of a partner who is facing him, the student can follow verbal instructions without demonstrations. He can:
1. Use his right hand to touch body parts on the right side of the partner.
2. Use his right hand to touch body parts on the left side of the partner.

III. Major Tasks: Changing Positions in Space; Right-Left Discriminations; Other Directional Discriminations; and Shape (Form) Discriminations

Other Tasks: Auditory Discrimination, Memory, and Sequencing

A. Given opportunities to identify the position of his body in relation to fixed objects, the student can:
1. Stand in front of, in back of, to the right of, and to the left of his chair or of a softball base.
2. Run to first base on a softball diamond.
3. Demonstrate where the right fielder, the left fielder, and the center fielder stand on a softball diamond.
4. Put specified body parts on top of diamonds, squares, circles, and other shapes on the floor.
5. Climb over a rope or horizontal bar or duck under it.

B. Given opportunities to follow verbal directions in warm-ups without the benefit of demonstration, the student can:
1. Assume the following basic exercise positions: supine long lying and hook lying, prone lying, long sitting, hook sitting, cross legged sitting, kneel, half kneel, squat, half squat.
2. Demonstrate different foot positions in response to the following commands: wide base, narrow base, forward-backward stance, square stance, closed stance, open stance.
3. Perform a specific exercise seven times, use the eighth count to return to starting position, and stop precisely on the stop signal.

IV. Major Task: Crossing the Midline; Chalkboard Skills; and Ball Handling Skills

Other Tasks: Auditory Discrimination, Memory, and Sequencing

A. Giving the opportunities to move the right arm across the midline in response to verbal instructions with no demonstration, the student can:
   1. Draw lines from left to right and from right to left on the chalkboard.
   2. Draw geometrical shapes or write numbers or letters on the far upper or lower left hand corners of the chalkboard.
   3. Throw a ball diagonally to a target on his far left.
   4. Field a ball on the ground which is approaching his left foot.
   5. Perform a backhand drive in tennis.
   6. Catch a ball which rebounds off the wall to his left.
   7. Toss a tennis ball vertically upward in front of left shoulder.

V. Major Task: Imitation of Movements
Other Tasks: Visual Discrimination, Memory, and Sequencing

A. Given opportunities to imitate the arm and leg movements of the teacher in an Angel in the Snow sequence, he can:
   1. Imitate bilateral movements.
      a. Move both arms apart and together while legs remain stationary.
      b. Move both legs apart and together while arms remain stationary.
      c. Move all four limbs apart and together simultaneously.
      d. Move any three limbs apart and together simultaneously while the fourth limb remains stationary.
   2. Imitate unilateral movements.
      a. Move the right arm and right leg apart and together simul-

taneously while the left limbs remain stationary.
      b. Move the left arm and left leg apart and together simultaneously while the right limbs remain stationary.
   3. Imitate cross lateral movements.
      a. Move the right arm and left leg apart and together simultaneously while the other limbs remain stationary.
      b. Move the left arm and right leg apart and together simultaneously while the other limbs remain stationary.

B. Given opportunities to imitate the arm movements of the teacher as depicted in Figure 8.3, without verbal instruction, the student will not mirror movements. He can:
   1. Start and stop both arms simultaneously.
   2. Correctly imitate six out of nine arm movements.

C. Given opportunities to imitate the arm movements of the teacher who is holding a racquet, he can: correctly imitate, while holding a racquet, six out of nine arm movements in Figure 8.3.

VI. Major Tasks: Imitation of Ball Movements; Reproduction of Aim and Force
Other Tasks: Visual Discrimination, Memory, and Sequencing

A. Given opportunities to imitate the movements of the teacher, without verbal instructions, the student with a tennis ball can:
   1. Imitate the teacher's movements precisely, using his right arm when the teacher is using his.
   2. Toss the ball into the air to exactly the same height the teacher tosses his.
   3. Bounce the ball so it lands on the floor in precisely the same place as

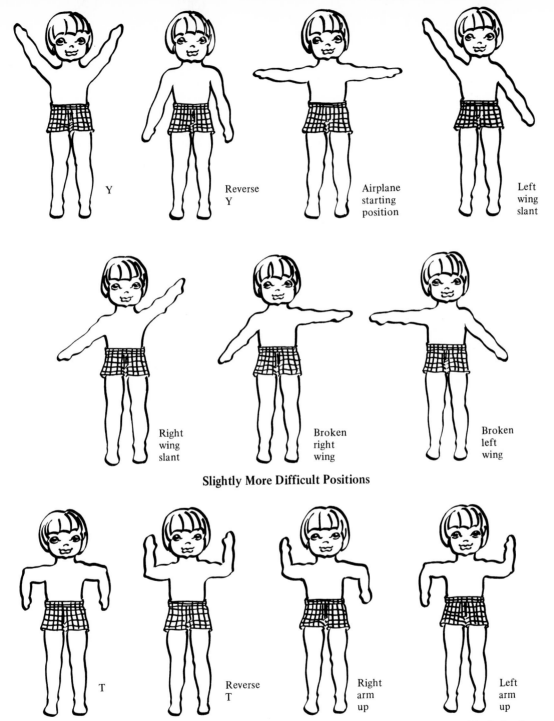

Figure 8.3. Arm positions which children should be able to imitate. The top seven positions are used in the Purdue Perceptual Motor Survey.

does the teacher's (in front of right foot, to the left side of left foot, and so on).

4. Bounce the ball so that it rises to the same height as the teacher's before it is caught.

5. Throw the ball so that it touches a wall target in relation to him precisely the same place as did the teacher's throw.

VII. Major Tasks: Horizontal Tracking; Vertical Tracking; and Ball (Beanbag) Handling Skills

Other Tasks: Visual Discrimination, Memory, and Sequencing

A. Given opportunities to track with both eyes a small hand mirror which the teacher is moving about 20-24 inches from his face, the student can:

1. Track the mirror from left to right.

2. Track the mirror as it circles in a clockwise direction, then in a counter-clockwise direction.

3. Track the mirror as it moves in a large figure eight.

B. Given opportunities to track flying beanbags (easier than flying balls), the student can:

1. Run or move his body so that the beanbag hits some part of him as it falls.

2. Run or move his body so that he catches seven out of ten beanbags before they fall.

3. Run or move his body so that he strikes the beanbag with some kind of a racquet, paddle, or bat before it falls.

C. Given opportunities to track ground balls being rolled toward him, the student can:

1. Stop those balls coming to his right.

2. Stop those balls coming to his midline.

3. Stop those balls coming to his left.

Figure 8.4. The Russian bear squatting position serves as a test of static balance.

VIII. Major Task: Static Balance

Other Tasks: Visual or Auditory

Given opportunities to explore static balance, the student can:

1. Balance on one foot with eyes open for twenty seconds.

2. Balance on tiptoes with eyes open for twenty seconds.

3. Balance on a stick, a rock, or a log with one foot.

4. Perform a knee scale.

5. Balance while maintaining a squatting position.

6. Assume a tripod balance or head stand.

7. Repeat each of the above with eyes closed.

IX. Major Tasks: Dynamic Balance; Locomotor Agility; and Changing Positions

Other Tasks: Visual or Auditory

Given opportunities to explore dynamic balance, the student can:

1. Walk a straight line in heel-to-toe fashion.

2. Jump backwards five times and stop without losing balance.

3. Walk a balance beam while holding a ten pound weight in one arm.

4. Alternate walking and squatting on a balance beam.

5. Turn completely around three times as he walks a beam.
6. Do six kangaroo jumps with a rubber playground ball held securely between the legs.

X. Major Tasks: Lateral Dominance; Ball (Beanbag) Handling Skills; and Tracing, Drawing, Writing Skills
Other Tasks: Visual or Auditory
Given opportunities to explore movement possibilities with beanbags, balls, ropes, bats, pencils, and other implements he can:

1. Demonstrate more skill with his preferred hand than his nonpreferred hand.
2. Exhibit a consistent preference for one hand over the other.

The behavioral objective approach to perceptual-motor appraisal results in a concrete list of things the student can and cannot do which should serve as the basis for developing long term educational prescriptions. It is important that the physical educator identify the sense modality through which the child seems to learn best: visual, auditory, or haptic (tactile and proprioceptive input). Deficits should be noted also since they are sometimes as handicapping as real blindness or deafness.

Testing as Teaching

Visual, auditory, or haptic deficits complicate the valid appraisal of motor abilities, but the child needs continuous exposure and repeated practice on specific perceptual-motor tasks. Tests which can be used for the purpose and which are fun are: Brace Test of Imitation of Stunts, Lincoln-Oseretsky Motor Development Scale, SMH Test of Motor Impairment, Stork Stand, Bass Stick Test, Heath Rail-Walking Test, Modified Bass Leap Test, Modified Scott Sideward Leap Test, and Tests of Lateral Dominance, Fleishman's hypothesized structure of psychomotor abilities is reviewed

also although their measurement requires apparatus not usually available in the public schools.

Brace Test of Imitation of Stunts

Previously called the Brace or Iowa-Brace Test of Motor Educability, this compilation of twenty-one stunts which students must imitate does discriminate between awkward and well-coordinated children.[10] Anyone familiar with the content of the chapters on self-testing, stunts, and tumbling in elementary school physical education methods books will recognize the stunts in the Brace test as everyday activities. The items can be taught on a one-a-day basis by the classroom teacher as a means of enriching the movement experiences of the children.

Test 1. One Foot-Touch Head or Needle Scale. Stand on left foot. Bend forward and place both hands on the floor. Raise the right leg and stretch it back. Touch the head to the floor and regain the standing position without losing balance. It is a failure: (1) not to touch head to the floor; (2) losing the balance and having to touch the right foot down or step about; and (3) not to keep left leg straight.

Figure 8.5. One foot-touch head or needle scale.

Test 2. Side Leaning Rest. Sit down on the floor, legs straight out and feet together. Put the right hand on the floor behind you. Turn to

10. David K. Brace, *Measuring Motor Ability* (New York: A. S. Barnes and Co., 1927).

the right and take a side leaning-rest position, resting on the right hand and the right foot. Raise the left arm and keep this position for five counts. It is a failure: (1) not to take the proper position; and (2) not to hold the position for five counts.

Figure 8.6. Side leaning rest.

Test 3. Grapevine. Stand with both heels tight together and the feet flat on the floor. Bend down, extend both arms down between the knees, around behind the ankles, and hold the fingers together in front of the ankles without losing the balance. Hold this position for five seconds. It is a failure: (1) to fall over; (2) not to touch and hold the fingers of both hands together; (3) not to hold the position for five seconds; and (4) to lift the heels.

Figure 8.7. Grapevine.

Test 4. One-Knee Balance or Knee Scale. Face to the right. Kneel down on the knee with the other leg raised from the floor and arms stretched out at the side. Hold your balance for five counts. It is a failure: (1) to touch the floor with any other part of the body than the one leg and knee; and (2) to fall over.

Figure 8.8. One-knee balance or knee scale.

Test 5. Stork Stand. Stand on the left foot. Hold the bottom of the right foot against the inside of the left knee. Place the hands on the hips. Shut both eyes and hold the position for ten seconds without shifting the left foot about on the floor. It is a failure: (1) to lose the balance; (2) to take the right foot down; and (3) to open the eyes or remove the hands from the hips.

Figure 8.9. Stork stand.

Test 6. Double Heel Click. Jump into the air and clap the feet together twice and land with the feet apart (any distance). It is a failure: (1) not to clap the feet together twice; and (2) to land with the feet touching each other.

Figure 8.10. Double heel click.

Test 7. Cross-Leg Squat or Turk Stand. Fold the arms across the chest. Cross the feet and sit down cross-legged. Get up without unfolding the arms or having to move the feet about to regain the balance. It is a failure: (1) to unfold the arms; (2) to lose the balance; and (3) to be unable to get up.

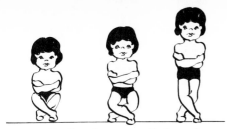

Figure 8.11. Cross-leg squat or Turk stand.

Test 8. Full Left Turn or Top or Full Pirouette in Air. Stand with the feet together. Jump into the air and make a full turn to the left, landing on the same spot. Do not lose the balance or move the feet after they strike the floor. It is a failure: (1) not to turn all the way around; and (2) to move the feet after they strike the floor.

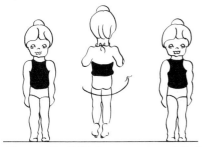

Figure 8.12. Full left turn or top or full pirouette in air.

Test 9. One-Knee-Head to Floor or Fish Hawk Dive. Kneel on one knee with the other leg stretched out behind, not touching the floor, the arms out at side parallel to the floor; and bend. It is a failure: (1) to touch the floor with the raised leg or with any other part of the body before completing the stunt; (2) not to touch the head to the floor; and (3) to drop the hand.

Figure 8.13. One knee-head to floor or fish hawk dive.

Test 10. Hop Backward. Stand on either foot. Close the eyes and take five hops backward. Maintain your balance for five seconds after the fifth hop. It is a failure: (1) to open the eyes; and (2) to drop the other foot.

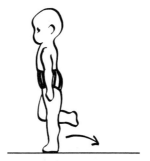

Figure 8.14. Hop backward.

Test 11. Forward Hand Kick. Jump upward, swinging the legs forward, bend forward and touch the toes with both hands before landing. Keep the knees as straight as possible. It is a failure: (1) not to touch both feet while in the air; and (2) to bend the knees more than 45 degrees.

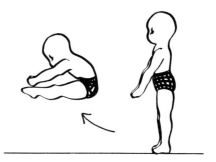

Figure 8.15. Forward hand kick.

Test 12. Full Squat-Arm Circles. Take a full squat position with arms out sidewise. Wave the arms so that the hands made a circle about 12 inches across, and jiggle up and down at the same time for ten counts. It is a failure: (1) to move the feet about the floor; and (2) to lose the balance and fall.

Figure 8.16. Full squat-arm circles.

Test 13. Half-Turn Hop-Left Foot or Half Pirouette in Air. Stand on the left foot and hop one-half turn to the left, keep the balance. It is a failure: (1) to lose the balance; (2) to fail to complete the half-turn; and (3) to touch the floor with the other foot.

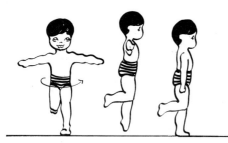

Figure 8.17. Half-turn hop-left foot or half pirouette in air.

Test 14. Three Dips or Push-ups. Take a front leaning-rest position, i.e., place the hands on the floor, with arms straight, extend the feet back along the floor until the body is straight (in an inclined position to the floor). Bend the arms, touching the chest to the floor, and push up again until the arms are straight. Do this three times in succession. Do not touch the floor with the legs or waist. It is a failure: (1) not to push up three times; (2) not to touch the chest to the floor at any time; and (3) to rest the knees, thighs, or waist on the floor at any time.

Figure 8.18. Three dips or push-ups.

Test 15. Side Kick or the Bell. Throw the left foot sideways to the left, jumping upward from the right foot; strike the feet together in the air and land with the feet apart. The feet should strike outside the left shoulder line. It is a failure: (1) not to swing the feet enough to the side; (2) not to strike the feet together in the air; and (3) not to land with the feet a shoulder-width apart.

Figure 8.19. Side kick or the bell.

Test 16. Flea Hop or Kneel, Jump to Feet or the Upswing. Kneel on both knees. Extend the toes of both feet out flat behind. Swing the arms and jump to the feet without rocking back on the toes or losing the balance. It is a failure: (1) to have the toes curled under and rock on them; and (2) not to execute the jump, and not to stand still on both feet.

Figure 8.20. Flea hop or kneel, jump to feet or the upswing.

Test 17. Russian Dance or Frog Dance or Bear Dance. Squat as far down as possible; stretch one leg forward; do a Russian dance step by hopping to this position with first one leg extended, then the other; do this twice with each leg. The heel of the forward foot may touch the floor. It is a failure: (1) to lose the balance; (2) not to do the stunt twice with each leg; and (3) to keep leg extended.

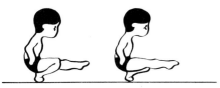

Figure 8.21. Russian dance or frog dance or bear dance.

Test 18. Full Right Turn or Top or Pirouette in the Air. Stand with both feet together. Swing the arms and jump up in the air, making a full turn to the right. Land on the same spot and do not lose the balance, that is, do not move the feet after they first strike the floor. It is a failure: (1) not to make a full turn and to land facing in the same direction as at the start; and (2) to lose the balance and have to step about to keep from falling.

Figure 8.22. Full right turn or top or pirouette in air.

Test 19. Human Ball or Egg Roll. Sit down; put the arms between the legs and under and behind the knees; grasp the ankles; roll rapidly around to the right with the weight first over the right knee, then right shoulder, then on the back, then on the left shoulder, then left knee; then sit up facing in the opposite direction from that in which you started. Repeat

from this position and finish facing in the same direction from which you started. It is a failure: (1) to let go of the ankles; and (2) not to complete the circle.

Figure 8.23. Human ball or egg roll.

Test 20. Single Squat Balance. Squat as far down as possible on either foot. Stretch the other leg forward off the floor, hands on hips. Hold this position for five counts. It is a failure: (1) to remove the hands from the hips; (2) to touch the floor with the extended foot; and (3) to lose the balance.

Figure 8.24. Single squat balance.

Test 21. Jump Foot. Hold the toes of either foot in the opposite hand. Jump up and jump the free foot over the foot that is held, without letting go. It is a failure: (1) to let go of the foot that is held; and (2) not to jump through the loop made by holding the foot.

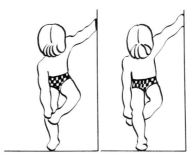

Figure 8.25. Jump foot.

SCORE SHEET FOR BRACE TEST

Name of Student _____ Name of Teacher _____
Age _____
Grade _____
Sex _____ Total Score _____

Scoring Brace Test. The pupil is given two points for the successful completion of each stunt on the first trial, one point for success on the second trial, and zero points if he fails to pass the test in two attempts.

Stunt	Trial 1	Trial 2
1. Needle scale	0	0
2. Side leaning rest	2	
3. Grapevine	2	
4. Knee scale	2	
5. Stork stand	0	0
6. Double heel kick	0	1
7. Turk stand	2	
8. Full left turn	2	
9. Fish hawk dive	0	0
10. Hop backward	2	
11. Forward hand kick	0	0
12. Full squat arm circles	2	
13. Half turn hop, left foot	0	1
14. Three dips	0	0
15. Side kick	2	
16. Kneel, jump to feet (flea hop)	0	0
17. Russian dance	0	0
18. Full right turn	2	0
19. Single squat balance	0	0
20. Human ball	0	0
21. Jump foot	0	0

The Lincoln—Oseretsky Motor Development Scale [11]

The test of motor proficiency used most often in research is the Lincoln-Oseretsky Motor Development Scale which purports to measure: (1) static coordination; (2) dynamic manual coordination; (3) general motor coordination; (4) motor speed; (5) simultaneous movements; and (6) asynkinesia or undesired associated movements. Originally developed by a Russian and revised by Sloan who was employed at the Lincoln State School for the Retarded in Illinois, the test has reliability coefficients ranging from .59 to .93 for each sex and for ages six through fourteen. The odd-even split halves reliability coefficient for the total battery is .96 for males and .97 for females.

The Lincoln-Oseretsky Test is comprised of thirty-six items arranged in order of difficulty. A perfect score is 159 points. The following brief description of items suggests motor tasks which can be practiced as part of a comprehensive program of perceptual-motor training.

1. *Walking backwards* in a heel-toe fashion on a line six feet in length.
2. *Crouching on tiptoe,* timed for ten seconds.
3. *Stork stand,* eyes open, timed for ten seconds.
4. *Touching the nose* alternately with right and left index finger. Three trials with eyes open and three trials with eyes closed.
5. *Touching fingertips* with thumb beginning with little finger of dominant hand and then returning in reverse order. Repeat with nondominant hand.
6. *Tapping rhythmically with feet and index fingers.* Sitting in chair, student simultaneously taps both index fingers and both feet without breaking rhythm for ten seconds.
7. *Jumping over a rope* sixteen inches high with two-foot take-off and land.
8. *Describing arcs,* beginning with left index

finger on right thumb and alternating this action with right index finger on left thumb. Timed for ten seconds with eyes open and ten seconds with eyes closed.
9. *Standing heel to toe,* with eyes closed, timed for fifteen seconds.
10. *Closing and opening hands* alternately with arms pronated in outstretched position, timed for ten seconds.
11. *Making dots* with pencil in each hand, timed for fifteen seconds. The number of dots made by each hand should be approximately equal.
'12. *Catching tennis ball* with one hand when thrown from a distance of ten feet. Five trials for each hand.
13. *Making a ball* by wadding up cigarette paper with thumb and fingers. Two trials for each hand. Number of seconds required to make ball is recorded.
14. *Winding thread* 6 1/2 feet long onto an empty spool. One trial for each hand. Number of seconds is recorded.
15. *Balancing a rod crosswise* on index finger for ten seconds. The rod is eighteen inches long. Two trials for each hand.
16. *Describing circles in the air* with both index fingers simultaneously for ten seconds. Arms and wrists must remain motionless; arms are abducted to 90 degree angle with hands clenched except for the index fingers.
17. *Tapping with each hand* independently for ten seconds. Score is the number of dots made by each hand.
18. *Placing coins and matchsticks in a box.* Pennies are placed by left hand while matchsticks are placed by right hand. Score is the number of seconds required.
19. Jumping and making one-half turn in the air. Must land on balls of the feet and hold for three seconds.
20. *Putting matchsticks in a box* with right and left hands simultaneously picking up

11. William Sloan, *The Lincoln-Oseretsky Motor Development Scale* (Chicago: C. H. Stoelting Company, 1955).

matchsticks and placing them in a line one inch apart on their respective sides of the box. There are ten matchsticks for each hand.

21. *Winding thread* around index finger while walking. Trial with each hand. Number of seconds required is recorded.

22. *Throwing a tennis ball* from a distance of eight feet at a target which is ten inches square. Five trials with each hand, starting with ball in front of shoulder like a shot put.

23. *Sorting forty matchsticks* by putting them into four equal piles located in each corner of a box. Score is number of seconds required for each hand.

24. *Drawing horizontal lines* between two specified horizontal lines. Score is number of lines made by dominant hand in fifteen seconds and by nondominant hand in twenty seconds.

25. *Cutting out circle* with scissors. Score is number of seconds for each hand.

26. *Putting coins in two boxes,* one at a time, ten in each box. Score is number of seconds required for each hand.

27. *Tracing maze with each hand.* Score is number of seconds required for each hand.

28. *Balancing on tiptoes* with eyes closed. Score is number of seconds.

29. *Tapping with feet and fingers* simultaneously, alternating right and left sides. Right foot and right index finger tap simultaneously followed by tap of left foot without finger.

30. *Jump, touch heels* with two-foot take off and land without losing balance.

31. *Tap feet and describe circles* with index fingers. Pattern R, L, R, L tap of feet while index fingers simultaneously describe circles.

32. *Stand on one foot* with the eyes open for ten seconds. Repeat on other foot.

33. *Jumping and clapping* the hands three times before landing.

34. *Balancing on tiptoe,* one foot at a time, with eyes open, for ten seconds.

35. *Opening and closing hands* for ten seconds while sitting with forearms supinated and arms flexed to a 90 degree angle at the shoulder joint. Thumb is straight up in the fist position.

36. *Balancing a rod vertically* on index finger for five seconds while sitting in a chair. The rod is eighteen inches long. Three trials for each index finger.

Pearman, in 1968, revised the Lincoln-Oseretsky test by reducing the thirty-six items to a seven item battery on which he obtained a reliability coefficient of .88.[12] The seven items are: 5, 13, 14, 16, 17, 18, and 31.

In 1972, a motor development scale for moderately and severely retarded children comprised of fifty-one items, most of which were taken directly from the Lincoln-Oseretsky test, was published.[13] Although the authors report that the individual items have been administered since 1968 to children with Down's Syndrome, no reliability and validity coefficients are reported, no norms have been developed, and no information is included about mean scores on performance. The major value of the book lies in its excellent illustration of each test item, thus facilitating the administration of the test.

The SMH Test of Motor Impairment [14]

The Stott, Moyes, and Henderson (SMH) Test of Motor Impairment, which evolved after

12. Roger A. Pearman, "An Analysis of the Lincoln-Oseretsky Motor Development Scale with an Emphasis on the Reduction of Total Test Items," Unpublished M. A. thesis, College of Education, Western Kentucky University, Bowling Green, Kentucky, August, 1968.

13. H. D. Bud Fredricks, Victor L. Baldwin, Philip Doughty, and L. James Walter , *The Teaching Research Motor-Development Scale for Moderately and Severely Retarded Children,* Springfield, Illinois: Charles C. Thomas, 1972.

14. D. H. Stott, F. A. Moyes, and S. E. Henderson, *Test of Motor Impairment* (Ontario: Brook Educational Publishing Limited, 1972).

years of experimentation with the thirty-six Oseretsky items, appears to offer real promise. Nine sets of test items, one for each age group between sub-five years through thirteen plus years, are presented. A set includes only five items arranged to measure the same areas of function evaluated by the Oseretsky test: (1) control and balance of the body while immobile; (2) control and coordination of the upper limbs; (3) control and coordination of the body while in motion; (4) manual dexterity with the emphasis on speed; and (5) tasks which emphasize simultaneous movement and precision. Oseretsky's sixth category, that of asynkinesis, was eliminated after research showed that such associated movements occurred in nearly 75 percent of mentally normal children, ages eight to ten.

In the SMH Test of Motor Impairment, the child begins with the five items for his chronological age. For example, a six-year-old would be tested on the following: (1) one leg balance; (2) bouncing one-hand catch; (3) hopping forward; (4) threading beads; and (5) tracing three circles. If he fails one or more items, he is tested at the age level below. If he passes all items, he is given the progressively more difficult items in each successive age group until a failure does occur.

Considerable research has showed the test to be reliable and valid. The test-retest reliabilities for each age group range from .91 to .98. Keogh, in a test-retest on twenty of the tasks using six- to eight-year-old children obtained a correlation of .71. [15] Validating studies have resulted in tetrachoric correlations around .85.

Tests of Balance

The *Stork Test* is among the most widely used measures of static balance. The test is performed first with the eyes open. If the stance is maintained for several seconds, it is then made more difficult by closing the eyes.

The student maintains his weight on the preferred foot while the sole of the other foot is positioned along the medial surface of the supporting knee. The hands are placed on the hips. Three trials are given. The score is the highest number of seconds in any one trial that balance is maintained.

Heath Rail-Walking Test [16]

Equipment: Three wooden rails. Rails 1 and 2 are nine feet long, and Rail 3 is six feet long. The rails are 4, 2, and 1 inches wide respectively.

Instructions:
Three trials are required on each beam. A trial ends when a step-off occurs. The number of feet walked during the three trials is recorded as a sub-score. The perfect sub-score for Rails 1, 2, and 3 are 27, 27, and 18 feet respectively. A sub-score of nine is required on each beam before progressing to a narrower width. Because of difference in degree of difficulty, the three sub-scores are empirically weighed in a 1-2-4 ratio. Thus a perfect score for the entire test is 153.

The Modified Bass Leap Test

Ten leaps are executed from a starting point as illustrated in Figure 8.26. The student earns five points for each successful landing on the ball of the foot. After landing, he attempts to balance on one foot for five seconds before undertaking the next leap. During this phase, he earns one point for each second he remains balanced on the ball of the foot. Thus a perfect score for the test is 100 points. Penalties are assessed for landing errors and balance errors. Five points are subtracted if the student commits any of the following errors on a landing: (1) fails to stop; (2) touches any part of the

15. Jack F. Keogh, *Analysis of Individual Tasks in the Stott Test of Motor Impairment* (Los Angeles: University of California, 1968).

16. S. Roy Heath, "Rail-Walking Performance as Related to Mental Age and Etiological Type Among the Mentally Retarded," *American Journal of Psychology* Vol. 55 (April, 1942), pp. 240-247.

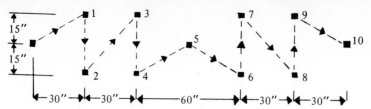

Figure 8.26. Floor plan for the Modified Bass Leap Test. The masking tape markers are 1 inch by 3/4 inch.

body to the floor other than the ball of one foot; and (3) fails to cover the masking tape marker with his foot. During the five seconds which the student balances in place, he sacrifices one point per second for each of the following errors: (1) touches any part of the body to the floor other than the ball of one foot and (2) moves the supporting foot. At the end of each five second period or when the balance is lost, the student leaps to the next marker.

The Modified Scott Sideward Leap Test [17]

The starting point for this test is A as depicted in Figure 8.27. The distance between points A and B is variable, depending upon the length of each student's leg. To begin the test, the number of inches from the hip joint to floor is measured after which the student puts his left foot on the appropriate line with toes facing the arrow. The test is comprised of four trials, two to the left and two to the right. Each trial consists of three tasks, each worth five points, so that a perfect score for the test as a whole is sixty points. The following sequence of tasks comprise each trial:

Task 1—Leap sideward from A to B, landing on ball of foot. Foot must cover spot B completely.

Task 2—Immediately bend forward and downward and use hand to push a small object off of spot C or D, depending upon which direction is faced.

Task 3—Maintain balance on ball of foot five seconds, beginning with the moment the foot

landed on spot B in task 1. One point is scored for each second the balance is maintained.

A = Variable starting point
B = Point of first landing
C and D = Points where small objects lie.

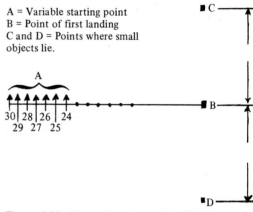

Figure 8.27. Floor plan for the Modified Scott Sideward Leap Test.

Tests of Lateral Dominance

Lateral dominance refers to the side of the body which leads. It is generally determined upon the basis of eye, hand, and foot preference. Several groups within special education feel strongly about lateral dominance, and it behooves the physical educator to appraise this aspect of behavior if he is associated closely with persons who think it is important.

Lateral dominance is a natural outgrowth of unilaterality, the developmental stage through which children pass in the preschool

17. M. Gladys Scott and Esther French, *Measurement and Evaluation in Physical Education* (Dubuque, Iowa: Wm. C. Brown Company Publishers, 1959), p. 320.

or early elementary school years. Certainly every parent is concerned about whether his child will be right-handed or left-handed. For the most part, this concern does not extend beyond handedness.

With the growing interest in children with learning disabilities in the 1960s, it was observed that large numbers of them did not evidence preference of one hand over the other even in adolescence. One day they wrote with the right hand, the next day with the left. On throwing tests with several trials, they used the hands interchangeably. Or they might write with the right hand, but do almost everything else with the left. They seemed equally awkward regardless of the hand employed. Hence, the perceptual-motor dysfunction of *mixed or crossed dominance* evolved.

Elaborate neurological theories were hypothesized to explain causes of mixed dominance, and numerous research studies were undertaken concerning the relationship between cerebral dominance and reading ability or academic achievement. At about the same time, the theory was proposed that the eye, hand, and foot on the same side of the body should be dominant. If a child was left-eyed, right-handed, and left-footed, he was said to have *mixed dominance*. Remediation procedures aimed at forcing the child into homolateral dominance by *putting one arm in a sling or wearing a patch over the dominant eye.* Less severe measures involved allowing the child to participate only in unilateral activities using the dominant side. The practice of having a child stand with his right foot forward while throwing with his right hand is distressing to anyone knowledgeable about body mechanics. In such settings physical educators either learned to compromise or lost the child altogether. The proponents of lateral dominance were unyielding.

The emphasis upon lateral dominance seems to have lessened over the years. The greater concern today seems to be the opposite problem, the individual who is so one-sided that he cannot use a house key with his nonpreferred hand nor perform fine motor tasks. Either extreme is a problem which the physical educator should note as part of the appraisal of perceptual-motor functioning.

Several terms have been developed to describe the conditions which exist in lateral dominance.

The predominant use of the right hand for unilateral skills is referred to as *dexterity*. When the left hand is used for such tasks, this is called *sinistrality*. *Ambidexterity* refers to a condition in which the two hands exhibit approximately equal skill and are used to perform similar tasks. *Homolaterality* refers to the situation in which the hand, eye, and foot on the same side are dominant. *Contralaterality* is used to denote *mixed dominance* in which the individual has some dominant characteristics on each side, such as being right-handed and left-eyed. The term *ambisinistrality* has been used recently in reference to a condition in which neither hand has been developed to an adequate level of efficiency and, therefore, no dominance is present. This is contrasted with ambidexterity in which a relatively high level of skill has been developed in both hands. [18]

Hildreth cites the following interesting facts about handedness, which is one aspect of lateral dominance.

Left-Handedness decreases sharply from infancy to adulthood; young children show an inconsistency in handedness; more boys than girls are left-handed; the percentage of left-handedness has increased during the past decade because of growing acceptance of the lefthander; mentally retarded children have a higher ratio of left-handers than does the normal population; the skills most definitely right-handed are those which are specifically taught; and skills which have been performed previously with the right hand can be learned with the left if the need arises. [19]

18. Joseph Oxendine, *Psychology of Motor Learning* (New York: Copyright © 1968 Meredith Corporation. Reprinted by permission of Appleton-Century-Crofts, Educational Div. Meredith Corporation), p. 306.

19. Gladys Hildreth, "The Development and Training of Hand Dominance: I. Characteristics of Handedness," *Journal of Genetic Psychology*, Vol. 75 (December, 1949), pp. 197-220.

The percentages of lateral dominance of one type or another seem to vary. In the United States 10-15 percent of the population is estimated to be left handed; however, the range in research reports varies from about three to twelve percent. Denhoff makes the following statement about mixed lateral dominance.

. . . We found that mixed dominance and laterality occurred in over 25 percent of normal six- to seven-year-old children. This often persisted until ages 8 to 12, while gross motor skills, fine patterned movements, visual-perceptual-motor skills, and language skills matured before 7 1/2 years. . . It is true that a large number of clumsy children who fail in school have mixed dominance and laterality. I find that in my clinical practice, however, it is also true that a high number of nonclumsy, nonschool failure population also have mixed dominance and laterality. [20]

Two standardized tests of lateral dominance are

1. The Harris Tests of Lateral Dominance which can be ordered from The Psychological Corporation, 304 East 45th Street, New York, New York 10017. This test was copyrighted by Albert J. Harris in 1947. Several research studies are based upon its use.
2. The D-K Scale of Lateral Dominance which can be ordered from the Foundation for Research in Mental Development, Box 1483, Wilmington, Delaware 19899. This test was developed in 1969 by Russell A. Dusewicz and Keith M. Kershner.

Fleishman's Hypothesized Structure of Psycho-Motor Abilities [21]

In physical education there is a definite trend toward the use of precise laboratory apparatus in the measurement of psychomotor abilities. The following list of abilities was based upon the administration of over 200 different motor tasks to thousands of subjects.

1. Control Precision—the ability of the hands or feet to perform fine, highly controlled movements as in a rotary pursuit test.
2. Multilimb Coordination—the ability to coordinate a number of limbs simultaneously as in bilateral and cross-lateral movements.
3. Response Orientation—the ability to move in the correct direction when given a stimulus, especially under highly speeded conditions. Combination of the ability to *select* the correct response for a given stimulus and then to *perform* it with controlled precision.
4. Reaction Time—the ability to respond quickly to a stimulus when it appears. Ability may depend upon whether the stimulus is visual or auditory. May also depend upon type of response required. In finger reaction time test, it is better to keep finger on key than to have to move finger through space to key.
5. Speed of Arm Movement—the ability to make gross, discrete arm movements with speed when accuracy is not required. Can be measured by alternate tapping.
6. Rate Control—the ability to make continuous motor adjustments in relation to changes in the direction and speed of a continuously moving target or object. Entails ocular pursuit as well as movements of limb or body.
7. Manual Dexterity—the ability to use the hand skillfully under speed conditions to manipulate fairly large objects such as winding thread on spool, wrapping package, manipulating tools.
8. Finger Dexterity—the ability to use

20. Eric Denhoff, "Motor Development as a Function of Perception," *Perceptual-Motor Foundations: A Multidisciplinary Concern* (Washington, D. C.: AAHPER, 1969), pp. 55-56.

21. Edwin A. Fleishman, *The Structure and Measurement of Physical Fitness* (Englewood Cliffs, New Jersey: Prentice-Hall, Inc., 1964), pp. 16-26.

fingers skillfully under speed conditions to manipulate tiny objects such as pegs on Purdue Pegboard test, small parts assembly tasks, wiring electric circuits, repairing watches.

9. Arm-Hand Steadiness—the ability to perform precise positioning movements as in threading a needle when speed and strength are minimized.

10. Wrist-Finger Speed—the ability to make rapid tapping movements which are not dependent upon visual alignment and control.

11. Aiming—also called hand-eye coordination—the ability to aim under speeded conditions. In the experimental setting, it generally entails going from one circle to another, placing one dot in each circle as rapidly as possible.

Summary Checklist for Use in Screening

Children with deficits in perceptual-motor functioning often fail to receive needed help because of weaknesses in diagnostic and referral procedures. The tests reviewed in this chapter, for instance, are generally administered after a child is referred to the adapted physical educator. Who is responsible for initial identification? Upon what basis is referral made? In most school systems, the assignment to adapted physical education is made by the special education coordinator or school principal. In some states assignment comes from a committee which reviews recommendations made by the classroom teacher. Seldom is the adapted physical educator expected to screen all pupils in a school system nor does he have sufficient time for in-depth observation of all children. It is important, therefore, that he assume initiative in preparing materials which will help his colleagues identify children who may benefit from perceptual-motor training. The following checklist developed specifically for use by classroom teachers may help to meet

this need. It lists characteristics commonly exhibited by children with learning disabilities and/or mild neurological damage and has proven successful as a screening device for identifying perceptual-motor awkwardness. It is recommended that this checklist be filled out for each child early in the year. Pupils with more than ten items checked should be subjected to thorough study and quite possibly assigned to adapted physical education.

Characteristics of Students Who Need Perceptual-Motor Training

Name_____Age____Sex____Date_____
School _____Teacher_____

This checklist is to be completed by the classroom teacher, speech therapist, or physical education instructor. The observations should be made during regular class periods without the knowledge of the student being observed. The observation should be over a period of time sufficient for an objective view of the student.

1. Fails to show opposition of limbs in walking, sitting, throwing.
2. Sits or stands with poor posture.
3. Does not transfer weight from one foot to the other when throwing.
4. Cannot name body parts or move them on command.
5. Has poor muscle tone (tense or flaccid).
6. Uses one extremity much more often than the other.
7. Cannot use arm without "overflow" movements from other body parts.
8. Cannot jump rope.
9. Cannot clap out a rhythm with both hands or stamp rhythm with feet.
10. Has trouble crossing the midline of the body at chalkboard or in ball handling.
11. Often confuses right and left sides.
12. Confuses vertical, horizontal, up, down directions.

13. Cannot hop or maintain balance in squatting.
14. Has trouble getting in and out of seat.
15. Approaches new tasks with excessive clumsiness.
16. Fails to plan movements before initiating task.
17. Walks or runs with awkward gait.
18. Cannot tie shoes, use scissors, manipulate small objects.
19. Cannot identify fingers as they are touched without vision.
20. Has messy handwriting.
21. Experiences difficulty tracing over line or staying between lines.
22. Cannot discriminate tactually between different coins or fabrics.
23. Cannot imitate body postures and movements.
24. Demonstrates poor ocular control, unable to maintain eye contact with moving objects, loses place while reading.
25. Lacks body awareness; bumps into things; spills and drops objects.
26. Appears excessively tense and anxious; cries or angers easily.
27. Responds negatively to physical contact; avoids touch.
28. Craves to be touched or held.
29. Overreacts to high frequency noise, bright lights, odors.
30. Exhibits difficulty in concentrating.
31. Shows tendency to fight when standing in line or in crowds.
32. Avoids group games and activities; spends most of time alone.
33. Complains of clothes irritating skin; avoids wearing coat.
34. Does not stay in assigned place; moves about excessively.
35. Uses either hand in motor activities.
36. Avoids using the left side of body.
37. Cannot walk sideward to either direction on balance beam.
38. Holds one shoulder lower than the other.
39. Cannot hold a paper in place with one hand while writing with the other.
40. Avoids turning to the left whenever possible.
41. Cannot assemble puzzles which offer no difficulty to peers.
42. Cannot match basic geometric shapes to each other visually.
43. Cannot recognize letters and numbers.
44. Cannot differentiate background from foreground in a picture.
45. Cannot identify hidden figures in a picture.
46. Cannot catch balls.
47. Cannot relate the body to environmental space. Is unable to move between or through objects guided by vision and an awareness of body dimensions.
48. Seems "lost in space," confuses North, South, East, and West.

Relationship Between Perceptual-Motor Training and Physical Education

Perceptual-motor training is *not* synonymous with physical education and should not be substituted for instruction in leisure time activities and the development of fitness. It is believed, however, that perceptual-motor training is an integral *part* of *adapted physical education.* Just as the school provides remedial reading specialists, it has an obligation to employ some physical educators with a specialization in the diagnosis, evaluation, and remediation of perceptual-motor problems. Perceptual-motor training should not be substituted for a well-rounded program of sports, dance, and aquatics. It should be provided for awkward children as a *supplement* to the regular program.

Perceptual-Motor Training

Perceptual-motor training in adapted physical education should not duplicate that in the

Figure 8.28. Making shapes with stretch rope is part of perceptual-motor training in physical education.

following instructions, and studying the similarities between shapes made in the classroom and formations used on the playground. Young children should achieve success in small groups (four to eight pupils) before challenged to become part of a larger circle or line. Several variations of each formation should be explored so that a group in a circle, for instance, can respond easily to such commands as facing in or out, facing clockwise (CW) or counterclockwise, (CCW), facing a partner, standing behind a partner, or standing side-by-side with a partner. Formations may be painted on the floor or temporarily marked by rope or cord to help severely involved children in their early efforts at conceptualizing shapes, getting in the correct position, and staying there.

Before games and dances are introduced, shape (form) perception should be stressed through small group circle and line activities which do not require a partner. The class should be broken down into several groups with four to eight children in each for the following shape perception activities.

1. Follow the verbal instruction of the teacher: Single circle, facing in, facing out, facing in, facing CCW, facing in, facing CW, facing CCW.
2. When the groups can respond successfully to one instruction at a time, give a sequence to be remembered and carried out.
   Example A:
   Single circle, facing CCW
   Walk eight steps forward
   Then do four jumps backward
   Repeat the sequence, facing CW
   Example B:
   Single circle, facing in
   Walk four steps forward
   Single circle, facing out
   Walk four steps forward
   Single circle, facing in
   Eight slides CCW

classroom. The objectives may be identical, but the activities differ. In the classroom the child usually sits at his desk or stands in a designated place. He traces, draws, connects dots, or uses scissors to make shapes. The emphasis is upon eye, hand, or eye-hand movements to teach concepts about space. In the physical education setting the child practices purposeful movement of the entire body; he learns that shapes can be dynamic or static. The emphasis is upon making shapes with his own body and working together with a group to make the shapes or formations requisite for playing games or performing dances.

If the educational prescription for a child calls for a great amount of structure, limited space, and the reduction of external stimuli, then activities using the traditional circle and line formations are ideal. The principle of structure is implemented by an understanding of formations, the ability to move smoothly from one formation to another, and skill in maintaining proper spatial relationships within the formation. Several sessions can be devoted to learning the names of formations,

Single circle, facing out
Eight slides CW

3. When a sequence of locomotor activities using different formations is mastered, add to it tasks using a ball, rope, hoop, or scarf.

Example A:

Single circle, facing in

Stand in place, bouncing ball to self four times

Single circle, facing CCW

Walk forward, dribbling ball four times

Single circle, facing out

Stand in place, tossing ball into air and catching it four times

Single circle, facing CCW

Do something original with the ball four times

Example B:

Single circle, facing in, with colorful scarf in each hand

Touch toes and stretch arms upward four times

Single circle, facing out, arms up

Single circle, facing in, arms down

Repeat three times

Single circle, facing CCW

Walk forward eight steps while performing large arm circles

4. Each group is seated with a deck of specially made cards. Each card depicts a different formation. The leader shuffles the deck, someone draws, and the group jumps up and makes designated formation. The shuffling and drawing continue until all cards are used.

5. Formations or shapes are projected onto the wall using an opaque or slide projector. The group makes the formation which appears on the wall. Words can be projected rather than diagrams and pictures.

6. Teacher holds up artificial fruit or vegetable as apple, orange, grape, banana, ear of corn, or hot red pepper. Group forms large or small circle or rectangle in keeping with shape of object being shown.

7. Each child has one hand holding a long, continuous stretch rope shared by the group. When the name of a formation is called, the rope is stretched into the correct shape.

8. Each group has a list or diagram of four or five shapes which have duplicates hidden about the play area. The rules of a scavenger hunt are followed. When all of the duplicate cards are found, the group carries them to the teacher and demonstrates ability to get into each formation.

9. Each group has a long and a short bamboo pole representing the hands of a clock. On command, the poles are moved to show different times of day. Bodies lying on the floor can be substituted for the hands of a clock or made into the arrow on a compass.

Table 23 which follows on pages 186 and 187 enumerates the play formations with which children should become familiar. Circles, lines, and scattered formations are most appropriate for the primary grades. Files, shuttles, longways sets, and squares are introduced in the intermediate grades. The illustrative games and dances cited for each formation offer a high degree of structure with emphasis upon the skills of listening and following instructions. Unless an educational prescription calls for the explanation-demonstration instructional approach, most physical educators prefer the freedom of the scattered formation in which children can develop motor creativity through problem solving.

Most children with learning disabilities, however, seem to need repeated drills in order to approach normalcy with respect to spatial awareness, right-left discriminations, and directional understandings. Drills, or perceptual-motor training, should be a means, not an end. The classroom teacher uses them as one way of improving reading and writing skills. The physical educator views them as the lead up activities requisite to success in games and dance. It is believed that success in play builds self-confidence which, in turn, carries over into the classroom and contributes to academic achievement.

Developmental Stages in Understanding Formations and Directions of Movement

Learning formations and directions of movement, whether through the explanation-demonstration approach or the problem-solving approach, should parallel the developmental stages in reproducing such forms on paper, blackboards, walls, floors, sand, air, or water. The ability of young children to get into a formation is related to the degree to which they have grasped the *concept* of the formation requested. If the ability to draw a shape can be used as a measure of the child's grasp of the concept, it is important to note the following developmental stages in drawing:

1. Looks at writing implements, may hold them, and watches others make marks with them.
2. Crude scribbling seemingly at random, without producing any coherent design;
3. Rudimentary space perception evidenced by coloring within the general outlines of a figure;
4. Ability to stay within a design, and accurate drawing of figures;
5. The reproduction of more complex designs, and drawing pictures of objects.
6. Prints numbers and letters;
7. Acquires handwriting skills, with decreasing amounts of visual monitoring of movements needed, i.e., can write without the need of constantly watching his moving hand. [22]

Children begin scribbling sometime after the twelfth month, initially producing randomized dots and lines. No conclusive evidence is available as to whether horizontal, vertical, or lateral lines are produced first. The first shape which a child learns to reproduce is a circle; this is also the formation in which the child plays his earliest games.

The ability to draw a circle appears at about age three. The ages at which a child can reproduce different forms while looking at sample drawings follow:

Age 4—Can draw circles and squares fairly accurately but may not close the circles. Unable to draw rectangles, triangles, or diamonds.

Age 5—Can draw closed circles, squares, and rectangles fairly well.

Age 6—Can draw previously learned shapes with greater accuracy but still has not mastered triangles and diamonds.

Age 7—Can draw triangles and diamonds with reasonable accuracy.

Counterclockwise Direction Predominates

The direction in which the child draws a circle is important to note also. Preschoolers generally begin a circle on the upper right hand portion of the paper and proceed clockwise, the direction of rotation least often used in dance and sport activities. From age six upward, most children draw circles in a *counterclockwise* direction, the traditional direction of movement in folk dancing, in jogging, and in rotating from station to station in the gymnasium. The counterclockwise direction is used more often than the clockwise in drawing squares, rectangles, and triangles among individuals with mature movement patterns. Elementary school physical education should provide many opportunities for exploring different shapes or forms which the body can assume and for experimenting with counterclockwise and clockwise locomotor movements and nonlocomotor movements of the limbs, head, and trunk.

While much research has been conducted

22. Bryant J. Cratty and Sister Margaret Mary Martin, *Perceptual-Motor Efficiency in Children* (Philadelphia: Lea & Febiger, 1969), p. 67.

Table 23 *Basic Game and Dance Formations*

Formation	Drills or Movement Exploration	Games	Dances
1. Single circle	Facing in Facing out Facing counterclockwise (CCW) Facing clockwise (CW) With "it" in the middle With "it" as part of the circle When part of the circle, "it" may be described as assuming a 1 o'clock, 3 o'clock, 6 o'clock position	Parachute activities Hot Potato Cat and Rat Duck, Duck, Goose Mickey Mouse (Spaceman) *With "it" in Middle* Circle Call Ball Catch the Cane	Farmer in the Dell Hokey-Pokey Loopty Loo Did You Ever See A Lassie? Go In And Out The Windows Captain Jinks Cshebogar
2. Double circle When boys and girls are partners, the girl is traditionally on the boy's right X O Boy Girl	Both facing in (also called "Two Deep") Both facing out Facing partner Facing in, side by side Facing out, side by side Facing CCW, side by side Facing CW, side by side Boy rotates CCW, girl remains stationary Girl rotates CCW, boy remains stationary Grand right and left, girl rotates CCW while boy rotates CW	Two Deep Caboose Dodgeball Run for your Supper	How D'Ye Do, My Partner Seven Steps Hot Cross Buns Pop Goes the Weasel Skip to My Lou Bleking American Schottische Patticake Polka
3. Single line or row X X X X X Usually has teacher or "it" in front, sometimes called teacher ball formation	Side by side Straight versus crooked Curved Staggered	Mother, May I? Red Light, Green Light Fire Engine (Beef Steak) Midnight Old Mother Witch Chinese Wall Pom-Pom-Pull Away Teacher Ball	Technique classes in modern dance, ballet, tapdance
4. Double line X X X X X X X X X X	Side by side Two deep, all facing front Two deep, all facing back Two deep, facing partner, no space between Two deep, with both lines having backs to other, with space between	Brownies and Fairies Crows and Cranes Steal the Bacon Line Dodgeball Volleyball Newcomb	*Running Set* Crested Hen (3 pupils) I See You (Any No.) Troika (3 Pupils)

Table 23 *Basic Game and Dance Formations—Continued*

Formation	Drills or Movement Exploration	Games	Dances
5. Scattered or random formation within set boundaries	Within walls of room Within rectangular area Within circular area Within triangular area Within alleys or lanes	Squirrel in the Tree Hide and Seek Huckleberry Beanstalk Keep Away Tag	Social or fad dancing Creative dance
6. Single file or column X X X X X	Each child behind the other Straight versus crooked "It" in front of file Everyone in file facing forward Everyone in file facing backward Everyone in file facing alternately forward and backward Everyone in file facing diagonally right or left	Basketball Shooting Games H—O—R—S—E Twenty-One Over and Under Relay Running Relays Ball Handling Relays	
7. Double file or longways set X X X X X X X X X X	Each child and his partner behind the leading couple Girl traditionally on the right of the boy Lead or head couple Last or rear couple All couples facing forward All couples facing backward All partners facing each other, same as zigzag line	Three-Legged Relay Partner Relay Tandem Relays	A Hunting We Will Go London Bridge Bumps-a-Daisy Paw Paw Patch Virginia Reel
8. Shuttle formation Drill and relays. Object is shuttled back and forth from file to file	Two files, facing one another X X X X X X X X X X Two files, diagonally facing same goal like a basket O X X X X	Can shuttle object and go to end of own file OR Shuttle object and go to end of the other file	Good use of space in continuous practice of locomotor skills
9. Square or Quadrille, comprised of four couples OX X O O X XO First Couple Second Couple	Girl on right of boy, standing side by side facing your partner Facing your opposite First couple out to the right (CCW) Circle all Swing your partner Swing your opposite		Most square dances as Arkansas Traveler Texas Star Dive for the Oyster Red River Valley Take A Little Peek

on the ability of young children to reproduce shapes with a pencil or crayon, little information is available concerning developmental stages in moving the entire body or parts of the body in one direction or another. The difficulty so often experienced in teaching an allemande left followed by a grand right and left reveals the need for more problem solving with respect to directions.

If the selection of physical education formations is made upon the basis of a child's readiness and/or the criterion of probable success, many questions must be asked. Which direction of movement is easier for a child: counterclockwise or clockwise? Is preference for direction similar to right- and left-handedness? If so, we should accept a child's continued preference for clockwise directions and, when possible, place him where he is using his preferred direction.

Directions in Singing Games and Dance

In singing games and folk dance, it is worth noting the traditional direction of moving when boys and girls are directed to change partners, which entails rotating in different directions. The girls, who traditionally are on the outside, rotate counterclockwise while the boys rotate clockwise. Some dances, like the American Schottische, call for the two partners to each step hop in an individual circular or diamond floor pattern and then return to one another. In such instances the girl step hops in a clockwise pattern and the boy step hops in a counterclockwise pattern.

In many folk dances, performing a waltz step, two step, or polka with a partner requires that the couple move about the circle in a counterclockwise direction and less often in a clockwise direction. Although the direction of the circle is counterclockwise, the couple is making clockwise turns.

Anyone who has taught folk dance knows that instructions concerning direction of movement are more often misunderstood than any other aspect of the lesson. One reason for this is frequent incorrect use of the terms *right* and *left* in lieu of clockwise and counterclockwise. It should be remembered that whenever partners facing each other in a closed position perform in synchrony that the boy is moving with his left foot while the girl is moving with her right or vice versa. When standing in a double circle, facing partners, boys must move to their left as girls move to their right in order to perform together a series of steps, like eight slides, in a counterclockwise direction. It is obvious that the teacher who persists in telling her students to move to the *left* or *right* will eventually be confronted with bedlam. *Instructions pertaining to floor patterns, i.e., moving in circular, triangular, or rectangular paths, must be given in terms of counterclockwise and clockwise.*

Directions in Volleyball: Visual Pursuit and Rotation

The lead up games to volleyball which are begun at about the third-grade level can be used to reinforce right-left discriminations and to provide practice in visual pursuit and/or tracking. For most children, these lead up games represent their initial experience in tracking large objects which move through a predictable low-high-low arc and in catching and/or striking balls which *descend* rather than ascend (like a bouncing ball) or approach horizontally (like a thrown ball).

Newcomb, the best known lead up game to volleyball, substitutes throwing and catching various objects over a net for volleying. It is based upon the assumption that tracking and catching a descending ball are prerequisites to tracking and striking (volleying); certainly catching and throwing are more familiar skills than volleying and serving. *Visual tracking* is an important contribution of volleyball at the elementary-grade level. Children should not be rushed into the mastery of the relatively difficult skills of volleying and serving. Nor should individual differences be ignored and all children forced to use the same skills in a game setting. When a volleyball approaches, each child should have options: to catch the ball and return it across the net with a throw or to volley it across. Likewise, when it is his turn to serve, the child may choose to put the ball into play with a throw from behind the baseline or a serve from any place on the right hand side of the court. Thus, in the early stages of learning the serve, some children may be only three giant steps behind the net while others have the coordination and arm and shoulder strength to achieve success from behind the baseline.

Badminton, tennis, and deck tennis also emphasize visual pursuit skills; they should be introduced at the same time as other net games. Any kind of racquet can be used; the shorter the handle, the better for beginning players. *Large* yarn balls can be substituted for shuttlecocks.

Team games teach spatial awareness through *position play.* Playing a particular position on the court and rotating from position to position reinforces the concepts of right, center, and left and of front and back. Below is a progression for teaching right-left discriminations as they relate to volleyball, newcomb, group badminton, tennis, and deck tennis. Starting with a small number of children on a team and gradually increasing the number of team members is educationally sound, whereas assigning eight to ten elementary school children to a team is not. Socially, children must learn to relate to and work with one or two friends before being thrown into larger impersonal game settings. The average class needs a net for every six beginning players; this is not a budgetary problem for the creative teacher who uses strings with crepe paper (or rag) streamers as substitutes.

Thus it can be seen that rotation in

Progression One: Three on a Team

Three players
1. *Right back [RB]*
2. *Left back [LB]*
3. *Center front [CF]*
Rotation: Clockwise
Serve: By RB

```
RB                    LB
          CF
XXXXXXXXXXXXXXX          Net
          CF
LB                    RB
```

Progression Two: Four on a Team

Four players
1. Right back (RB)
2. Center back (CB)
3. Left back (LB)
4. Center front (CF)
Rotation: Clockwise
Serve: By RB

```
RB        CB        LB
          CF
XXXXXXXXXXXXXXX          Net
          CF
LB        CB        RB
```

Progression Three: The Regulation Game

Six players
1. Right back (RB)
2. Center back (CB)
3. Left back (LB)
4. Left front (LF)
5. Center front (CF)
6. Right front (RF)
Rotation: Clockwise
Serve: By RB

```
RB                    LB
          CB
RF        CF        LF
XXXXXXXXXXXXXXX          Net
LF        CF        RF
          CB
LB                    RB
```

volleyball depends upon the child's ability to make right-left discriminations, his ability to walk or move sideward, backward, and forward, and his comprehension of clockwise as a direction. The teacher who cares about transfer of learning and wishes to save children with directional deficits embarrassment on the playground will use the concept of rotation in the classroom, having the child sitting in the *RB* chair, stand, recite, and then allowing everyone to rotate in a clockwise position so a new child is *RB* and preparing to recite.

Directions in Softball

A child's success or lack of success in softball, kickball, and baseball may be an excellent indicator of his perceptual-motor efficiency, especially with respect to right-left discriminations, crossing the midline, and visual pursuits. No other physical activity offers richer opportunities for perceptual-motor training.

First, the understanding of the diamond and the positions of the players on the field requires the ability to make right-left discriminations. The concept of infield versus outfield offers a new dimension of spatial awareness. The expectation that each player *covers* a particular area of the field and *backs up* other players is based upon spatial awareness. Bases are run in a *counterclockwise* direction. Pitches are described as inside, outside, high, low, and curved to the right or left. A batter who misses the ball is told that he swung too early or too late. Decision making by a fielder as to where to throw the ball is based upon visual memory of sequences. Is there a player on third base? On first and third? On all of the bases? Where should the ball be thrown first? The batter must make decisions with respect to directions also. If there is a runner on third base, where should he bat the ball? If there are runners on first and second base, where should he hit the ball? And *ad infinitum*.

Figures 8.29 to 8.37 offer suggestions for teaching children three sets of terms which are applicable to any sport which entails use of a bat or racquet. The different types of stances are seen in golf also. Opportunities for practicing each of the situations depicted should be provided within the structure of the classroom where distractions are minimal. Knowledges gained in the classroom can be applied later in problem solving during a game situation. For instance, when the ball goes to the right instead of over the net in a tennis game, can the child reason why? When the golf ball goes to the left into a sandtrap instead of straight down the fairway, does the student know what caused the directional deviation?

Variations in Batting Which Should Be Practiced in the Classroom with a Yarn or Paper Ball

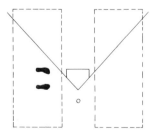 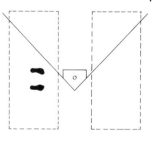 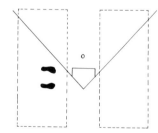

Figure 8.29. Swinging too early. Ball has not yet passed over the plate. If hit, it will probably go to the left.

Figure 8.30. Correct timing of swing. Ball is directly over plate. When hit, it will probably go toward the shortstop.

Figure 8.31. Swinging too late. Ball has already passed over the plate. If hit, it will probably go to the right.

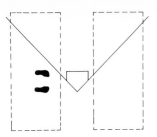

Figure 8.32. Square stance. Best for beginners.

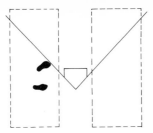

Figure 8.33. Open stance. If hit, the ball will probably go to the left.

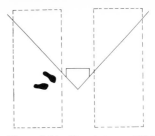

Figure 8.34. Closed stance. If hit, the ball will probably go to the right.

Batting Positions for Left-Hander

Figure 8.35. Shoulder to pitcher.

Figure 8.36. Bat must be parallel to ground when it hits the ball.

Figure 8.37. The follow through requires crossing the midline.

Recommended Activities

1. Develop a file of perceptual-motor tests.
2. Administer each of the tests described in this chapter to at least one pupil, preferably the same child. Write a report presenting the findings of the tests and make an educational diagnosis in the form of several conclusions about specific perceptual-motor strengths and weaknesses.
3. Invite the special education coordinator in your community to the class to describe the specific perceptual-motor tests and evaluation procedures currently being used in the public schools.
4. Observe an educational diagnostician or other specialist in the collection of data for a child's files.
5. Refer to the bibliography of films with perceptual-motor implications on pp. 138-139 of the AAHPER Publication, *Foundations and Practices in Perceptual-Motor Learning—A Quest for Understanding,* and/or to similar bibliographies. Order and view some of the films.

Sources of Tests

1. Brooks Educational Publishing Limited, Box 1171 , Guelph, Ontario.

2. C. H. Stoelting Company, 1350 South Kostner Avenue, Chicago, Illinois 60623.

Sources of Games and Dances
Recommended Reading

AAHPER. *Foundations and Practices in Perceptual-Motor Learning.* Washington, D. C.: AAHPER, 1971.

Ayres, Jean. *Sensory Integration and Learning Disorders.* Los Angeles: Western Psychological Services, 1972.

Benton, Arthur L. *Right-Left Discrimination and Finger Localization.* New York: Paul B. Hoeber, Inc., 1969.

Brown, Jason W. *Aphasia, Apraxia, and Agnosia.* Springfield, Illinois: Charles C. Thomas, 1972.

Cratty, Bryant J. *Perceptual and Motor Development in Infants and Children.* New York: The Macmillan Company, 1970.

McCulloch, Lovell. *A Handbook for Developing Perceptual-Motor and Sensory Skills Through Body Movement.* Austin: Austin Writers Group, 1973.

O'Donnell, Patrick A. *Motor and Haptic Learning.* San Rafael, California: Dimensions Publishing Co., 1969.

Roach, Eugene G., and Kephart, Newell C. *The Purdue Perceptual-Motor Survey .* Columbus, Ohio: Charles E. Merrill, 1966.

Shontz, Franklin C. *Perceptual and Cognitive Aspects of Body Experience.* New York: Academic Press, 1969.

9 Developmental Vision Problems

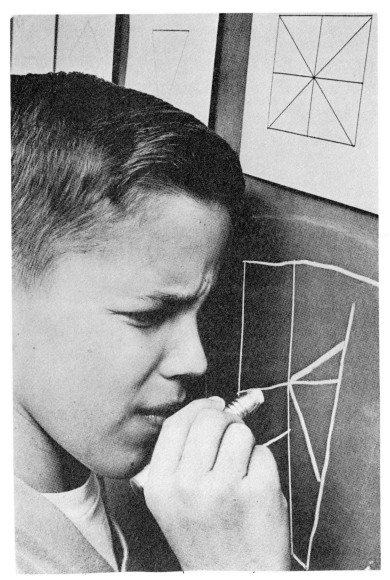

Figure 9.0. Developmental vision problems are revealed in chalkboard drawings. (The American Corrective Therapy Journal.)

Many pupils have visual problems which interfere with success in physical education and other academic subjects. The Snellen Chart measures only distance vision. Problems in near vision, as may be experienced in reading and writing, are more difficult to appraise.

In the multidisciplinary approach to educational diagnosis, an ophthalmologist, optometrist, and/or a developmental vision specialist appraises performance on *ocular-motor tasks*, which are responsible for the reception of visual stimuli, and *visual processing tasks*, which require the analysis and synthesis of visual information. Moreover a number of perceptual-motor surveys such as that of Kephart which are administered by classroom teachers and physical educators include tasks of *ocular fixation and pursuit*. As a result, ocular or visual tracking activities are included in many perceptual-motor programs. Getman, among others, differentiates between the processes of sight and vision and between ocular and visual tracking. [1] *Sight* is defined as the ability to distinguish light from no light and to see fine detail; it is acuity. *Vision* is a much broader term which encompasses both the reception of light and the central processing by which visual information acquires meaning. *Ocular tracking* is eye movement following a moving target such as a *Marsden Ball*, a sponge ball suspended from the ceiling by a string. In early progressions, the child lies on his back while tracking the pendulum movements of the ball and attempting to identify letters or forms pasted on it. Later he practices tracking from a sitting or standing position. Ocular tracking is purely muscular and does not presume acquisition of meaning from what one sees. *Visual tracking*, on the other hand, refers to the total ability to move the eyes in the proper direction and speed to derive meaning as quickly, correctly, and effectively as possible from visual stimuli.

Tracking and other visuo-motor activities are used widely in training programs for children with learning disabilities. Unfortunately little research evidence is available to show the effectiveness of such procedures in improving the processing of visual stimuli. There appears to be considerable disagreement among optometrists and ophthalmologists with the former taking the lead in perceptual-motor training and the latter assuming a conservative role. The following document is illustrative of ophthalmological thinking.

The Ophthalmologist's Role in Dyslexis

Position Statement

This statement is reprinted from the report of an international dyslexia seminar held in Indianapolis, Indiana sponsored by IDEA, the Institute for Development of Educational Activities, Inc., (an affiliate of the Charles F. Kettering Foundation). Copies of the complete report are available from the National Society for the Prevention of Blindness, Inc.:

1. Not enough objective scientific evidence yet exists to prove that perceptual motor training of the visual system can significantly influence reading disability.

2. In coping with dyslexia, ophthalmologists should be involved in an interdisciplinary approach, which ideally consists of an educator, ophthalmologist, pediatrician, and psychologist with available consultation from a neurologist, psychiatrist, reading specialist, audiologist, and social worker.

3. Eye care should never be treated in isolation when the patient has been referred with a reading problem.

1. G. N. Getman, "Concerns of the Optometrist for Motor Development," in *Foundations and Practices in Perceptual Motor Learning* (Washington, D. C.: AAHPER, 1971), p. 26.

4. The belief that eye dominance can be at the root of so profound and broad a human problem as reading and learning disability is both naive, simplistic, and unsupported by scientific data.

5. Latent strabismus may be associated with a reading disability in certain individuals. This may be treated according to the doctor's own ophthalmological principles, but it is significant to the learning problem only in improving reading "comfort or efficiency."

6. Eye glasses, including bifocals, prescribed specifically for the treatment of dyslexia have not proven effective.

7. Just how children with reading disabilities should be taught is a technical problem in educational science, which lies outside the competency of the medical profession.

8. Educational research is needed in the correction and prevention of reading disabilities.

9. Children with reading disabilities, once diagnosed, should be removed from the milieu where accepted methods of teaching are practiced, in order to give them special instruction along totally different lines.

10. The percentage of dyslexics within the community has been overestimated by some writers. Others have underestimated the magnitude of the problem. Regardless of the actual figure, reading disabilities among children are grave enough and sufficiently important to justify official recognition.

11. A national commission should be established to review presently available and identify specific areas for further work in the scientific as well as the educational area.[2]

Several optometrists and/or vision therapy specialists [3], [4], [5] have written books describing procedures for visual training and improvement of hand-eye coordination. These books have gained widespread use by teachers and parents of children with learning disabilities and/or developmental vision problems. Optometrists believe that the words *vision, intelligence, understanding, judgment,* and *comprehension* overlap in meaning. They envision their services as encompassing all of the processes relating to visual perception rather than just the improvement of sight through corrective lenses.

Optometry is the profession of vision care. It is concerned with *seeing* as applied to clarity of eye sight, clarity of thinking and clarity of learning. Optometry achieves its purpose sometimes through the skilled prescription of glasses alone; sometimes through visual training procedures; and sometimes by both.

Lenses affect the focus of the eyes. But, optometry also recognizes that this is a direct adjustment of only one step in the intricate cycle and delicate balance of vision. This adjustment may affect, indirectly, many other bodily functions as well.

Optometric research has resulted in visual training procedures which, through the eyes, can rearrange balancing and matching processes in the brain—to make information reliable, experience accurate, learning easier and intelligence greater.[6]

In optometric vision therapy, specially designed instruments, lenses, and prisms are used. For example, Kirshner describes his successes with the Oculo-Rotor, a device that consists of a revolving mirror that can be varied in rotation rate, which is used in conjunction with a slide or movie projector. The picture is reflected from the mirror onto a large screen, and the child visually tracks the revolving picture. The optometrist measures the child's eye movement skill by determining the fastest rotation rate at which he can see a target (picture) which requires 50 percent

2. "The Ophthalmologist's Role in Dyslexia-Position Statement," *Sight Saving Review* (Fall, 1969).

3. Frank A. Belgau, *A Motor Perceptual Developmental Handbook of Activities* (LaPorte, Texas: Perception Development Research Associates, 1967).

4. G. N. Getman, *How To Develop Your Child's Intelligence* (Luverne, Minnesota: Research Publication, 1962).

5. A. J. Kirshner, *Training That Makes Sense* (San Rafael, California: Academic Therapy Publications, 1972).

6. Optometric Extension Program Foundation, Inc., Duncan, Oklahoma, a statement reprinted in "Seesickness Easily Missed—but not by Experts," by Evelyn Loewendahl, *The American Corrective Therapy Journal,* Vol. 27, No. 6 (November-December, 1973), p. 170.

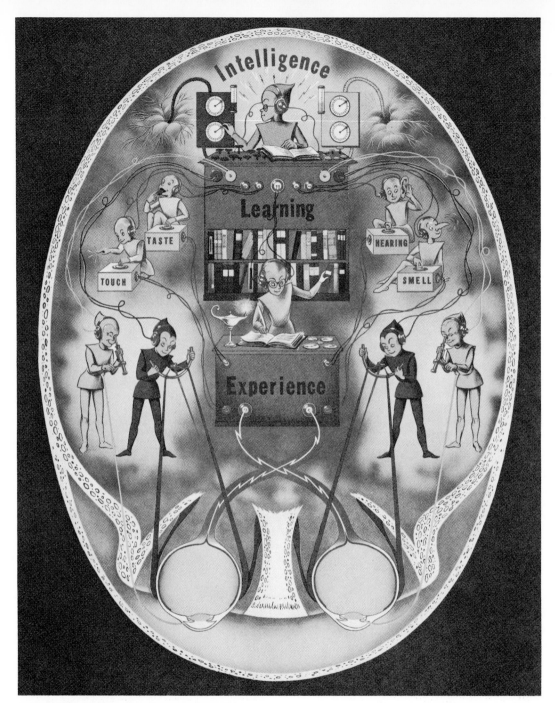

Figure 9.1. A diagrammatic interpretation of vision.
Reprinted by permission of the Optometric Extension
Program Foundation, Inc. ©1958.

(20/40) vision. The average six-year-old can view a target at 40 rpm through an angle of 21 degrees. This angle occurs when the target rotates through a diameter of four feet which is viewed from a distance of ten feet. The Kirshner Oculo-Rotor is also used for testing and training quick fixation. Using it in conjunction with two projectors, alternate targets are flashed on the wall ten feet apart every one-half to three seconds. The child stands ten feet from the wall so that the viewing angle is approximately 60 degrees. His rapid identification of the alternating targets requires horizontal, vertical, and diagonal eye movements.

If a child exhibits problems in identifying targets flashed every one-half to three seconds, it follows that many physical education tasks will result in excessive tension and failure. Among the velocities of balls projected by the overarm and underarm patterns in sports are the following:

1. Individual velocities of several male varsity baseball pitchers ranged for fast balls from 86-122 feet per second.
2. Mean velocities for boys and girls on the overarm softball throw were girls, Grade I, 28 and Grade VIII, 54 feet per second; boys, Grade I, 35 and Grade VIII, 75 feet per second.
3. Velocity of ball on tennis serve, over 80 feet per second in order to clear the net when struck at point eight feet above the ground.
4. Velocities of underarm softball pitch ranged from 108-109 feet per second for skilled males.

Small wonder that the young baseball player at the batter's plate cannot keep his eye on the ball. The older a child is when he first learns to bat or return a tennis ball, the greater the velocity he must cope with, assuming that he plays with peers. Little research has been conducted concerning the mean age at which children can visually follow balls moving at various velocities. Nor is much known about what a young child actually sees in the demonstration of a motor skill which lasts only a second or two. For instance, in learning to play golf, the beginner observes and attempts to imitate the swing of his teacher. Film measures of such swings reveal that the average swing time with a no. 5 iron is 1.41 seconds; a no. 9 iron, 1.34 seconds; a drive from the tee, about .85 second. Does failure to imitate accurately a golf swing then reflect poor kinesthesis or the inability to track visually the club head through the backswing, downswing, and follow-through?

In order to teach children with learning problems, the physical educator must become as knowledgeable about vision as proprioception. He should be aware of the visuo-motor training techniques that his pupils may be exposed to in the classroom and at home. Moreover, he may work with a developmental vision specialist in devising visuo-motor perceptual-training applicable to the physical education setting. *For such training to be effective, it is believed that it must be specific to the ball handling skills required in each sport.* This chapter therefore presents basic information about the oculo-motor tasks of accommodation, refraction, and binocular coordination. The cognitive tasks involved in the processing of visual stimuli at the higher cortical levels are reviewed also.

In order to see, the eyes must be focused for the correct distance and pointed in the correct direction. These two adjustments are made by different sets of muscles and controlled by the involuntary and voluntary nervous systems respectively. *Focusing,* the combined processes of *accommodation* and *refraction,* is involuntary, done unconsciously. The pointing, or steering tasks known as *binocular coordination,* are directed by six external muscles of each eyeball which receive nerve impulses from the voluntary nervous system like other muscles of the body. In addition to the voluntary movements of the eye muscles, there are constant or automatic movements which resemble extremely small tremors. Called *saccadic movements*, these frequent eye jumps continuously alter the position of the image on the retina, preventing fatigue by stimulating new receptors. These saccadic movements are essential to vision since an image falling upon a single immobile point of the retina for more than two or three seconds is no longer perceived. At this time, the relationship of the reflex saccadic movements to visual fixation and tracking is not well understood.

Ocular-motor tasks described in this chapter are accommodation, refraction, binocular fusion, binocular coordination, and scanning or tracking.

Oculo-Motor Tasks

Keep your eye on the ball is an admonition used perhaps too frequently by physical educators. What does it mean? Will reminding a pupil to keep his eye on the ball actually help? What is involved in focusing upon a moving object? Are the processes similar in tracking an object from left to right as from far to near?

Accommodation

Accommodation is the technical term for the ability to focus alternately on far and near objects and/or to track an object from far to near. It is the mechanism whereby the lens system adapts to the varying natures of entering light rays. Specifically, the *lens system* includes the biconvex lens of the eye and the smooth convex anterior surface of the cornea.

Figure 9.2A shows how parallel rays of light (those from a distance of twenty feet) are brought to a focus on the retina in the normal or *emmetrophic eye*. The lens is its normal resting shape, and the ciliary muscle which

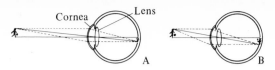

Figure 9.2. The mechanism of accommodation. (A) In the normal eye, the image of a distant object falls on the retina; (B) In near vision, or when an object approaches the eye, the lens changes shape to maintain the focus of the image on the retina.

controls the curvature of the lens is relaxed. No accommodation is needed by the normal eye for far vision.

Figure 9.2B depicts the mechanism of accommodation which occurs reflexly in response to the need to maintain a clear retinal image of an object moving toward the body. The ciliary muscle, which is innervated by cranial nerve III, has contracted. Contraction of the ciliary muscles results in a relaxation of the ligament surrounding the lens, thus causing the lens to thicken or increase its curvature. The increased thickness of the lens refracts the light to a greater degree, thus allowing near objects to be brought into sharper focus. The closer the object comes, the more the lens must increase its curvature in order to maintain eye focus. This accommodation is accompanied by pupillary constriction and by a medial movement of each eye.

It should be emphasized that keeping the eye on the ball requires more accommodative effort on the part of some children than others. Although the stimulus for accommodation is reflex in nature, visual acuity for close objects is influenced also by the coordination and strength of the ocular muscles.

Normally the ability of the eye lens to accommodate is greatest in childhood and diminishes with age. The term given to diminished power of accommodation caused by normal aging is *presbyopia*. The need of persons from about age forty-five and over to switch glasses for near and far vision is characteristic of presbyopia. With increasing age the lens of the eye simply becomes less able to respond to the efforts of the ciliary muscles to change its curvature.

Refraction

Refraction, simply defined, is the bending of light rays. The most common refractive errors are farsightedness, nearsightedness, and astigmatism. Almost all glasses are designed to correct one or more of these refractive errors. It is imperative that educators know that farsightedness is practically universal in infants and becomes gradually less as age increases. This fact helps to explain individual differences in reading readiness and awkwardness in fine motor tasks. Boys particularly show characteristics of farsightedness in the primary grades. Since it is considered normal for their age group, young children generally are not fitted with glasses to correct their farsightedness.

Refractive errors which have been corrected by glasses are normally of little concern to the physical educator. Generally corrective glasses make a child's vision almost normal. No student should be allowed to engage in physical education without his glasses unless a statement to this effect is received from an ophthalmologist or optometrist. The practice of removing glasses before swimming, trampoline work, and tumbling is unjustifiable in most cases. If teachers who encourage the removal of glasses could see as little as their pupils, they would be horrified by the handicap imposed upon their charges. It is recommended, however, that school systems request parents to fit children with plastic unbreakable or case hardened lenses or to provide safety guards. The incidence of eye injuries caused by breaking corrective lenses is extremely low. It is unfortunate that the overcaution of parents and teachers in the form of the constant reminder *Don't break your glasses* does tend to influence attitudes toward physical education activities.

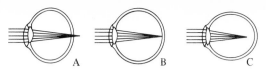

Figure 9.3. Refraction. (A) Farsightedness: parallel rays of light come to focus behind the retina; (B) Normal vision; parallel rays of light come to focus on the retina; (C) Nearsightedness: parallel rays of light come to focus in front of the retina.

Should a child not wear his glasses to school, the physical educator should know how refractive errors can influence physical performance. He should also have sufficient knowledge of these visual defects to help identify children who need referral.

Figure 9.3 depicts the point at which rays of light from an object in the distance are brought to focus when the accommodating mechanism is relaxed. In farsightedness, parallel rays of light come to focus behind the retina, contributing to good *distance vision*. In the normal eye, both distance and near vision are good. In nearsightedness, the parallel rays of light come to focus in front of the retina, contributing to good *near vision*.

Farsightedness

Also called *hyperopia* or *hypermetropia*, farsightedness is the most common refractive error. If the degree of hyperopia is slight, it is compensated for by the power of accommodation, i.e., the ciliary muscle contracts, the lens thickens, and the refractive power is increased so as to bring the lens forward on the retina. In more severe cases, the continuous accommodative efforts give rise to headache, nausea, dizziness, fatigue, and complaints about close work. Farsightedness is generally corrected by glasses only when such symptoms are recognized.

The normal farsightedness of infants and young children is caused by the fact that, at birth, the eyeball is only three-fourths of its adult length and too short for its focusing mechanism. As the eyeball grows in length, the problem of farsightedness subsides. In adulthood, the eyeball is about an inch in diameter and somewhat longer from front to back than side to side. Individual differences in the length of the eyeball, as well as the balance between the focal length of the refracting media and length of eye, explain hyperopia in adulthood.

Nearsightedness

Also called *myopia,* this condition is a more serious disadvantage than farsightedness because clear vision at a distance cannot be obtained through the accommodative mechanism. In fact, any increase in the refractive power of the lens results in blurring.

Myopia, in large part, appears to be determined genetically. If one parent is myopic, 60 percent of the offspring will probably have the same problem. Myopia can be subdivided into two types: (1) simple myopia, which is relatively common and can be corrected by glasses, and (2) progressive or degenerative myopia which can lead to blindness. The etiology of each is obscure. Anatomically, however, the physical length of the eyeball is longer than normal and the focusing mechanism is not long enough.

Considerable controversy rages as to whether students with severe myopia should be allowed to engage in contact sports. Most older references and some new ones state that myopes are particularly prone to detachment of the retina.[7] Myopes are cautioned to avoid tag games, falls, and diving from high boards because of the great danger of separation of the retina from the eye. In contrast, Cornell athletes with corrected myopia are permitted to participate in football, basketball, wrestling.[8] Physician Alexius Rachun calls the view that myopes should avoid contact sports "a carry-over from the days when the false belief was held that traumatic retinal detachment occurred in sports." Rachun does concur that the "rare student with extreme, progressive myopia" should not participate in contact sports.

Barraga[9] points out that the young myopic child misses a great deal of incidental learning and tends to have trouble with spatial relationships throughout life. The world beyond twenty feet is generally an unknown void which myopes may ignore. They may learn to read early, excel in academic studies, and give no evidence of visual impairment since their activities typically are restricted to a small space.

Often physical education is the first school subject with which the myope experiences difficulty. Unless he wears corrective lenses, he cannot see thrown or batted balls until they reach a proximity of twenty feet or closer. Sometimes he cannot even see teammates. Once the condition is diagnosed and glasses fitted, the myope can usually participate without restrictions. Fear of being hit by a ball and poor attitudes toward physical education may persist for many years.

Astigmatism

The third and last refractive error usually results from unevenness in the surface of the cornea. Instead of converging at one point on the retina, the rays of light are refracted unevenly at different planes causing images to blur. *Astigmatism* is generally not recognized until the early school years when problems occur in reading.

7. C. R. S. Jackson, *The Eye in General Practice*, Sixth Edition (Baltimore: The Williams and Wilkins Company, 1972), p. 93.

8. Alexius Rachun, "Athletes With Ocular Defects Need Careful Handling," *Medicine In Sports*, Vol. 9, No. 2, (March, 1969), p. 1.

9. Natalie C. Barraga, "Utilization of Sensory-Perceptual Abilities," *The Visually Handicapped Child in School*, ed. by Berthold Lowenfeld (New York: The John Day Company, 1973), p. 128.

Binocular Fusion

Binocular fusion refers to the integration of nerve impulses from the two eyes into a single set of information. The occipital cortex appears to be responsible for the analysis and synthesis of visual stimuli. Screening tests for binocular fusion include the Keystone Telebinocular, the Ortho-Rater, and the Massachusetts Vision Test. Poor binocular fusion is a medical problem and should be diagnosed and treated by the medical profession.

Poor binocular fusion is manifested in double vision (*diplogia*) and/or the suppression of one eye and the eventual development of functional blindness in one eye (*amblyopia*). These conditions may be caused by central nervous system deficits in processing, unequal refractive conditions, faulty focusing, or low convergence reserve. If the external muscles of the eyeball are not sufficiently coordinated or strong to align the two eyes on the same target, binocular fusion is affected.

Binocular Coordination

The coordinated movements of the eyes necessary for focusing an image on the retina are dependent upon the ability of the twelve ocular muscles to make conjugate or paired movements. The pairs of muscles which work together are depicted in Figure 9.4. Three pairs of cranial nerves innervate the twelve muscles, influencing the ability to perform the six cardinal directions of gaze.

Fine muscle coordinations performed at close range require two oculo-motor conditions. First is the ability to *converge* both eyes so that they both aim in exactly the same place. This requires a high degree of precision because the eyes must converge at a line whose thickness is that of the letter "i." The second condition is that the eyes must make small, precise movements (saccadic fixations) on the stimulus object. In reading, inefficient saccadic fixations result in loss of place, skipping of lines, omissions, and poor comprehension. In activities which require a change of focus, as in drawing a geometric form from a model, binocular coordination is further complicated by the relationship between convergence and accommodation.

Commonly identified problems of binocular coordination are (1) muscle imbalance, (2) convergence or divergence insufficiency, and (3) squint or *strabismus*. The term *muscle imbalance* implies weakness or paralysis of one or more of the six extrinsic muscles of each eye. Table 24 states the deviations caused when an ocular muscle is paralyzed or weak.

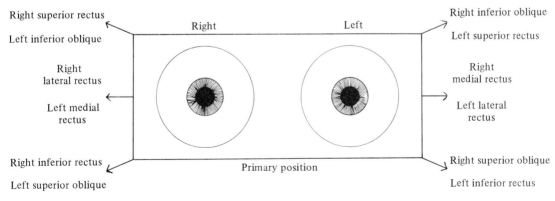

Figure 9.4. The six cardinal directions of gaze.

Table 24 *Extrinsic Muscles of the Eye*

Name of Muscle	Normal Action	Deviation Caused When Muscle is Paralyzed or Weak	Cranial Nerve Innervation
Lateral (external) rectus muscle	Moves eye outward toward temple	Inward squint	VI Abducens
Inferior oblique	Moves eye up and out; also rotates it outward	Downward and outward	III Oculo-motor
Inferior rectus	Moves eye down	Upward and outward	III Oculo-motor
Superior oblique	Moves eye down and out; also rotates it inward	Upward and outward	IV Trochlear
Superior rectus	Moves eye up	Downward and outward	III Oculo-motor
Medial (internal) rectus	Moves eye inward toward nose	Outward squint	III Oculo-motor

Convergence and divergence, both aspects of accommodation, refer respectively to the ability of the eyes to turn inward to maintain focus with an approaching object and to turn outward to maintain focus with an object which is moving away. A convergence insufficiency manifests itself primarily in a blurring of print while reading, a running together of words, and a sensation of eyestrain.

Squint, strabismus, and cross-eyes are more-or-less synonyms. Approximately 4 million persons are estimated to have strabismus which is usually present at birth or appears within the first five years. Among brain-injured and mentally retarded residents of state institutions, over 50 percent are affected.

Squints are classified as (1) nonparalytic, (2) paralytic, or (3) latent. In the nonparalytic or concomitant squint, which is the most common of the three types, the angle of the squint does not vary with the direction of the gaze. It usually stems from failure of the binocular reflexes to become firmly established as a result of normal growth and development although it may be caused also by ocular disease.

Farsighted children develop squints more often than other children because the accommodative effort of the ciliary muscle is out of proportion with that being exerted by the medial rectus muscles in the act of convergence. When overconvergence occurs, one eye turns inward. In the beginning, such squints are intermittent, occurring most often when the child is ill, tired, or upset. When one of the eyes turns in, out, up, or down to the extent that fusion of the two visual images is difficult or impossible, the results is double vision or *diplogia.*

The child may cope with this double vision by using each eye alternately or by consistently suppressing the image of the poorer eye. In the latter, disuse of the squinting eye eventually leads to *amblyopia* or lazy eye. In amblyopia the sensitivity in the receptor cells in the unused retina is diminished. If this condition is allowed to persist, functional blindness in the one eye occurs.

Squint, particularly in the young child, can be corrected by several techniques: (1) refraction, (2) occlusion, (3) orthoptic training, and (4) surgery. *Refraction* is the use of corrective glasses; it is especially important that children with squint wear prescribed glasses during all aspects of physical education. *Occlusion* refers to wearing a patch over one eye. *Orthoptic training* consists of eye exercises prescribed by a specialist in orthoptics. *Surgery* is a last result, when the squint does not respond to other types of treatment.

Convergent squints (one eye turned inward) are about ten times more common than divergent squints (one eye turned outward). The divergent squint is usually intermittent, appears only in distance vision, and is more obvious under conditions of bright illumination. It generally requires surgery whereas the convergent squint responds well to other kinds of treatment.

The paralytic and latent squints will not be discussed here because of their low incidence among school children. They generally occur in later life as a result of head injuries, intracranial vascular accidents, aneurysms, and tumors.

Little is known about the relationship between participation in physical education and the amelioration of squint. Belgau states that a convergent squint (cross-eyes) tends to straighten out during hanging exercises.

Kirshner recommends the use of the Brock String Test as a screening test for binocular coordination. [10] A twenty-two inch white shoe string with a red bead at one end is used. The opposite end is placed on the forehead, and the pupil focuses both eyes on the bead and then points to the picture in Figure 9.5 which resembles what he sees. Next the bead is slipped upward to a point four inches from the end of the string which is farthest from his forehead. The pupil again points to the picture in Figure 9.5 which resembles what he sees.

Scanning or Tracking

There are three kinds of scanning tasks in which the eye scans the surface and briefly fix-

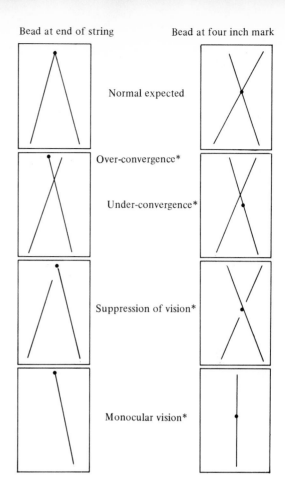

Bead at end of string — Bead at four inch mark

Normal expected

Over-convergence*

Under-convergence*

Suppression of vision*

Monocular vision*

*Shows abnormal function. Refer to specialist.

Figure 9.5. Brock String Test.

ates the image upon the retina: (1) the natural zig-zag scanning that occurs when a child looks around the room; (2) the pursuit or tracking of a moving object; and (3) the learned systematic scanning required for reading. In most tests of scanning the child is allowed to explore visually an object or picture while his eyes and head movements are observed. Research suggests that frontal lobe damage interferes with the ability to actively search, scan, or examine objects, particularly the ability to perceive fast moving objects.

10. A. J. Kirshner, *Training That Makes Sense* (San Rafael, California: Academic Therapy Publications, 1972), p. 46.

Four main variables or tasks are manipulated in assessing a pupil's ability to track a moving object: (1) the amount of head and/or body movement permitted or required; (2) the angle through which the target is moved; (3) the speed of movement of the target; and (4) the response required. Horizontal tracking is believed to be easier than vertical tracking and near-to-far and far-to-near tracking. Left-to-right horizontal tracking is emphasized in most school programs since it is the direction of reading and writing in our society.

The popular Purdue Perceptual-Motor Survey includes a section on ocular pursuit and convergence.[11] The child is instructed to watch a pen light which is moved along the arc of a circle with a radius of about twenty inches, having its center at a point between the child's eyes. The pen light is moved approximately eighteen inches in each of the cardinal directions of gaze: left, right, up, down, diagonally up and left, up and right, down and left, and down and right. The ocular pursuits of both eyes, the right eye only, and the left eye only are assessed. Convergence is tested by observing the smoothness and speed with which the child can alternately focus on a target four inches in front of his face and one twenty inches away.

Kephart, Getman, and others have emphasized the importance of eye focus and ocular tracking in perceptual-motor training. Current practice dictates that the movements of the eyes be evaluated in the execution of motor tasks.

The following questions may serve as a guide in this procedure.

1. Do both eyes focus simultaneously on a stationary target? Is the attention span sufficient to maintain this focus a set number of seconds? What type of stationary target holds the attention the longest? Does size, shape, color, or location of the target make a difference in the ability to focus?
2. Can the child maintain eye focus on a stationary target as he moves toward it? Away from it? To its left? To its right? Is success influenced by speed or other characteristics of the movement?
3. Can the child maintain eye focus on a moving target? Does he move his head rather than his eyes? When he loses the target, can he regain it again quickly? Are the ocular pursuit movements smooth as the eyes follow the target across midline?
4. Do both eyes move together? Does one eye remain stationary while the other follows the target? Or does one eye seem to lead and the other to move more slowly?

Central Processing of Visual Stimuli

The processing of visual stimuli by the cerebral cortex involves: (1) visual analysis, the separation of the whole into its component parts; (2) visual integration, the coordination of mental processes; and (3) visual synthesis, the incorporation or combination of elements into a recognizable whole. While these processes are interrelated and little understood, they are believed to give meaning to what man sees. It is estimated that 90 percent of man's information about his environment comes from the central processing of visual data. Deficits in visual discriminations, spatial awareness, and object recognition (*visual agnosia*) can be traced to central processing tasks.

Tests of visual discrimination require the pupil to describe one or more dimensions of a presentation: (1) number of visual stimuli which are presented; (2) rate of presentation; (3) duration of presentation; (4) color-hue; (5) brightness; (6) contrast; (7) size; (8) shape; (9) sequential order; and (10) motion. Discrimination tests are made more difficult by increasing the number of visual stimuli presented simultaneously, increasing the

11. Eugene G. Roach and Newell C. Kephart, *The Purdue Perceptual-Motor Survey* (Columbus, Ohio: Charles E. Merrill Publishing Co., 1966), p. 60.

number of unfamiliar stimuli, or by decreasing the number of seconds the pupil is allowed to view the stimulus. Intervals shorter than one half second decrease success because of the amount of time needed for the human eye to fixate on more than one point to gain sufficient visual information.

Tests of spatial awareness require estimates of distance, height, weight, texture, and other properties by vision alone. Questions often used as measures of visual input and central processing are as follows.

(1) How many of your average size steps will walking from Point A to Point B require?

(2) How narrow can you make the width of this door by pulling together the curtains and still be able to squeeze your body through the space?

(3) How many beans are in this quart jar?

(4) What are the dimensions of this room? Will a certain piece of furniture fit in that space?

(5) Which direction are you facing?

(6) Is the fudge batter thick enough to pour it out to cool?

(7) Is the fur of a certain animal smooth or rough?

(8) How large should you cut the slices of this pie in order to serve eight persons?

Tests of object recognition involve naming or labeling objects. Numerous clinical cases exist in which persons are unable to name objects despite the fact that they can see them, describe their parts, and reproduce pictures of them. This phenomenon, historically called *visual agnosia* or *central blindness*, has been linked with lesions of the occipital and parietal cortex. The underlying disorder seems to be one in which visual processing is incomplete because the child lacks the ability to synthesize visual stimuli and integrate them into a unified whole. Instead he focuses upon one dominant visual stimulus like color or form and guesses. Attempts to integrate two or more visual stimuli are usually unsuccessful.

Tests of Visuo-Motor Perception

Several tests which purport to measure visuo-motor perception such as the Bender Visual-Motor Gestalt Test (1938), the Frostig Developmental Test of Visual Perception (1963), and the Purdue Perceptual Motor Survey (1966) actually are measures of visual processing operations. When children are required to copy designs from a pattern, to duplicate dot patterns by linking dots with a line, or to draw lines stopping and starting on a target, it is difficult, if not impossible, to separate visual processing from motor performance. Other tasks commonly included on tests of visual perception include measures of *figure-ground* (find a hidden figure or one of several intersecting figures); *form constancy* (find all of the squares on a page regardless of color, background, size, tilt); *directional or rotational constancy* (differentiate between b, d, p, q); and *object constancy* (differentiate between a football, a cageball, a medicine ball, a playground ball, and a tennis ball). Most tests of visuo-motor perception, at this time, are paper-pencil measures. A few physical educators have experimented with projections of geometric forms on the gymnasium wall with instructions to walk out the form or shape you see. Others have projected mazes and diagrams with hidden figures which demanded large muscle responses. Much research is needed to devise measures of visuo-motor perceptual tasks requisite to success in specific physical education activities.

Recommended Activities

1. Develop a file of tests which purport to measure visual perception and/or visuo-motor perception. Fully document the source where each test was found.

2. Administer one of the following tests to several children: Bender Gestalt Visual-Motor Test; Frostig Test of Developmental Vision; Purdue Perceptual Motor Survey.
3. Invite an optometrist or ophthalmologist to speak to your class concerning the sequential and orderly development of vision from infancy through old age.
4. Invite a reading specialist to speak to your class concerning the relationships between vision and reading abilities.
5. Observe a lecture-demonstration on the use of such screening devices as the Keystone Telebinocular, the Ortho-Rater, the Massachusetts Vision Test, and the Snellen Test. Discuss the significance of such screening in relation to the physical education setting.
6. Devise physical education activities for strengthening understandings of figure-ground, form constancy, directional or rotational constancy, and object constancy.

Recommended Reading

Benton, Curtis D. "Vision and Learning Disabilities" in *The Child With Learning Disabilities: His Right to Learn.* San Rafael, California: ACLD, 1971.

Bruner, Jerome. *Eye, Hand, and Mind: Studies in Cognitive Development.* London: Oxford University Press, 1969.

Gesell, A., et al. *Vision: Its Development in Infant and Child.* New York: Paul B. Hoeber, 1949.

Getman, G. N., et al. *Developing Learning Readiness.* New York: McGraw-Hill Book Company, 1966.

Kirshner, A. J. *Training That Makes Sense.* San Rafael, California: Academic Therapy Publications, 1972.

Koppitz, Elizabeth. *The Bender Gestalt Test for Young Children.* New York: Grune and Stratton, Inc., 1964.

Money, John. "The Laws of Constancy and Learning to Read" in *International Approach to Learning Disabilities of Children and Youth.* San Rafael, California: ACLD, 1967.

Wagman, Irving H. *Oculomotor Systems.* New York: Harper and Row, 1964.

Fitness for Fully Living

Figure 10.0. A developmental physical education
laboratory in action.

We must take immediate steps to ensure that every American child be given the opportunity to make and keep himself physically fit . . . fit to learn, fit to understand, to grow in grace and stature, to fully live.

John F. Kennedy

Fitness in the physical education setting too often has been interpreted narrowly as fitness to play, to excel in athletics, and to score in certain percentiles on tests of strength and endurance. Physical fitness must encompass fitness for sitting as well as for running, for reading and writing as well as for playing, for white collar jobs as well as those which are more physically demanding. Neuromuscular relaxation is as important a part of physical fitness as is cardiovascular endurance.

Screening for Fitness

The screening test which appears to be used most widely throughout the nation is that recommended by the President's Council on Physical Fitness and Sports. The test includes:

1. *Regulation Pull-ups for Boys* (and girls who wish to try)
   Grasp bar with palms facing forward; hang with arms and legs fully extended. Feet must be free of floor. Can you pull your body up with the arms until the chin is placed over the bar? Good. Now lower your body until the elbows are fully extended. How many times can you do this? One complete pull-up is scored each time the pupil places his chin over the bar.

   To Pass:
   Boys, ages 10-13, one pull-up
          14-15, two pull-ups
          16-17, three pull-ups

   Modified Pull-ups for Girls (and boys of low fitness)
   Adjust height of bar to chest level. Grasp bar with palms facing forward. Extend arms under bar, keeping body and knees straight. Heels are on the floor and are braced to prevent slipping. Can you pull the body up with the arms until the *chest* touches the bar? Now lower body until arms are fully extended. How many times can you do this? One pull-up is counted each time the chest touches the bar.

   To Pass:
   Ages 10-17, eight modified pull-ups

2. *Straight Leg Sit-ups with Trunk Twist*
   Lie on back with feet about one foot apart. Partner holds down feet. Hands are grasped behind head. Can you sit up, twist trunk to left, and touch right elbow to left knee? Good. Return to starting position. Now can you sit up, twist trunk to right, and touch left elbow to right knee? How many times can you do this? One sit-up is scored each time you return to starting position.

   To Pass:
   Boys, ages 90-17, 14 sit-ups
   Girls, ages 10-17, 10 sit-ups

3. *Squat Thrust*
   Four counts. Bend forward to squatting position and put hands on floor. Thrust legs behind you to assume regulation pushup position. Return to squat position. Return to erect standing position. How many squat thrusts can you do in ten seconds?

   To Pass:
   Girls, ages 10-17, 3 squat thrusts in 10 seconds
   Boys, ages 10-17, 4 squat thrusts in 10 seconds [1]

The following checklist may be administered to all students at the beginning of the school year. The use of the word *fitness* is avoided in the checklist because of its negative connotations to some persons.

1. President's Council on Physical Fitness and Sports, *The Blue Book* (Washington, D. C.: Superintendent of Documents, 1968).

Checklist Pertaining to Energy Level

Check the characteristics which best describe you during an average school day. Indicate if you would like help or if you prefer to work the problem out by yourself.

Characteristics	Yes	No	Check if you would like help
1. Drowsiness during the day—a dull, sluggish feeling.			
2. Difficulty in concentrating on class work—general lack of motivation.			
3. Frequent yawning.			
4. Difficulty in staying awake after meals—desire for short naps.			
5. Breathlessness after running short distance or climbing stairs.			
6. Persistent feeling of tension—inability to relax.			
7. Tendency toward irritability—wish you could be left alone.			
8. Willingness to take a pill to make you feel better—or to try anything.			
9. Feeling that there is nothing to look forward to after school—nothing in particular planned.			
10. Too tired to go out at night.			

Answer yes or no to the following questions in terms of your level of energy and amount of free time after school.

1. If a chance to earn money were available, could you take on an after school job of 2-3 hours twice a week?   **Yes**   **No**

2. Do you have to get eight hours of sleep to feel good the next day?   **Yes**   **No**

Numerous factors contribute to low fitness: (1) obesity; (2) underweight; (3) asthma and other chronic respiratory problems; (4) susceptibility to infectious diseases including the common cold; (5) poor nutrition; (6) inadequate sleep; (7) a life-style which does not encompass physical exercise; (8) a repugnance toward perspiration, dirt, wind, and other environmental factors surrounding physical activity; (9) fear of failure and/or embarrassment; and (10) a genetic predisposition toward low fitness. Persons who are mentally ill, emotionally disturbed, or who use alcohol, drugs, and other mood modifiers excessively are generally characterized by low physical fitness since mind and body contribute equally to a state of well-being.

No child should be compelled to engage in a program of fitness conditioning which has no *personal* meaning, nor should he be subjected to fitness tests which he is destined to fail. One of the great tragedies of the physical fitness emphases of the 1950s and 1960s was the universal testing and evaluation of all children, using identical fitness tasks and norms as though individual differences had ceased to exist in the public schools. It is hoped that teachers will adapt fitness tests to the needs of individual pupils.

Fitness Counseling

The individual with subminimal fitness needs a special kind of physical education program designed to change his attitudes toward exercise, to support him in attempts to increase pain tolerance, and to raise his level of fitness as quickly as possible. These objectives can be accomplished best when implemented in groups of not more than ten students. Low physical fitness deserves a guidance and counseling approach as much as does low mental and emotional fitness. For this reason, the school psychologist or a specialist trained in group therapy techniques should work closely with the physical educator in shaping attitudes and modifying behavior. Time should be allocated for individual conferences and small group therapy sessions during which the reasons for low fitness are explored and alternative methods of developing strength and circulo-respiratory endurance are analyzed.

The adapted physical educator should have some academic background in guidance and counseling. In addition to theoretical knowledge, he must be a careful listener and a good observer. The most important attribute of a would-be counselor is belief in the worth and dignity of every human being. Questions which teachers should consider before extending their role to fitness counseling are as follows:

How do we look upon others?

Do we see each person as having worth and dignity in his own right?

Do we treat individuals as persons of worth, or do we subtly devaluate them by our attitudes and behavior?

Is our philosophy one in which respect for the individual is uppermost?

Do we respect his capacity and his right to self-direction, or do we basically believe that his life would be best guided by us?

To what extent do we have a need and a desire to dominate others?

Are we willing for the individual to select and choose his own values, or are our actions guided by the conviction (usually unspoken) that he would be happiest if he permitted us to select for him his values, standards, and goals?

The primary purpose of fitness counseling is to change attitudes toward the body and its capacity for strength, flexibility, and circulo-respiratory endurance. When attitudes are changed, new habits of exercise result. The fact that so large a proportion of the American public remains unfit demonstrates that physical educators in the past have been relatively unsuccessful in shaping and changing attitudes.

The attitudes which exist in the teacher, rather than his knowledge, his theories, and his techniques, are the most important determinants of attitude change and behavior modification on the part of the student. Students cannot cope with problems of obesity, awkwardness, and low fitness until they can objectively analyze the causal factors and resultant consequences. In many instances they lack faith in their ability to change themselves and suffer from poor self-concepts. They may feel defeated, hostile, or misunderstood; they seldom feel good about themselves. It is necessary, therefore, to change the attitude toward self before modifying attitudes toward exercise and fitness.

Some of the roles which a physical educator may play in fitness counseling include:

(1) Listener

This role is essentially passive with the teacher's comments limited to "Hmm," "Yes," "Uh-huh." It may be beneficial to a student in desperate need of emotional catharsis but contributes neither to improved self-concept nor attitude change. Nevertheless, we have all seen students who were so angry, wound up, or upset that they required only a sympathetic listener until they calmed down sufficiently to relate to another person.

(2) Interpreter

In this role the teacher attempts to clarify and objectify the student's feelings by restating his words in a different way, i.e., more clearly and objectively.

Example:

Student: I know the students are always laughing at me because I am so clumsy and awkward. No one wants me on his team. I don't have many friends.

Teacher: You resent the fact that your classmates seem to judge you upon the basis of your athletic ability and not for what you are.

(3) Reflector

The teacher responds with reflective statements which convey an understanding and acceptance of the student's attitudes and feelings. This involves learning to perceive the world as the student sees it and to perceive the student himself as he is seen by himself. This role may be conceived as empathy or adopting the student's frame of reference.

During a counseling session the teacher's attitude and responses should make it easier for a student to listen to himself. When the student perceives that the teacher thinks he is worth listening to, his self-respect is heightened. When another self (the teacher) can look upon his obesity or awkwardness or lack of fitness without shame or emotion, the child grows in his own capacity to look at himself objectively. Realization that whatever attitude he expresses is understood and accepted leads to a feeling of safety and the subsequent courage to test new ideas and try different methods of improving fitness.

Fitness counseling may encompass several stages: (1) initial collection of data; (2) establishing rapport; (3) listening with appropriate responses; (4) providing support and reinforcement in the exercise setting; and (5) continuous evaluation and follow-up. Facts about the student's fitness are gathered through observations, interviews, and various tests. The greater the data accumulated about an individual, the more insight the teacher has. When the team approach to fitness counseling is implemented, the physical educator may have access to achievement scores in other areas, indices of self-concept, intelligence quotient, psychological evaluations, and information about family background. There appears to be a trend toward faculty from many different disciplines sitting down together to share perceptions about a particular child and to recommend remediation. The individual with low fitness frequently has multiple problems. The team approach assures that he will be treated as a *whole* child rather than by bits and pieces.

To understand fitness problems in their true perspective, the teacher needs information about the student's life experiences, his values, and his perception of what is meaningful in life. Requesting the student to prepare an autobiography may meet this need. The tendency to write only about fitness and athletic ability in an autobiography for the physical education teacher can be counteracted by suggesting that such questions as these be answered.

1. What makes you unique and different from every other human being?
2. What have been the most meaningful events in your life?
3. Which human beings have touched your life significantly?
4. What things in your life have happened that you would change if you could?
5. What do you intend to be doing ten years from now?
6. What will you be like when you are middle aged?

In some instances, negative feelings about the self and/or fitness may be too embarrassing, intimate, or difficult for the student to approach in a face-to-face situation. Writing out responses to such questions as these facilitates communication.

1. How do you feel about your fitness? (or weight or failing a test or whatever)
2. How do you think others feel about your fitness?
3. How do you think others think you feel about your fitness?
4. How do you think others should feel about your fitness?

It is important to note whether the student interprets *others* as peers, parents, teachers, or a combination. His responses tend to present an accurate picture of the *significant others* who may covertly or overtly be shaping his attitudes.

Rapport between two persons begins at the moment of face-to-face contact. It is essential, therefore, that the very first conference with a student conveys feelings of acceptance and understanding and a belief in his self-actualizing potential. Counseling sessions should be held in a quiet setting in which the teacher is free from interruption. All sessions should be conducted in private with assurance that information will be kept in confidence.

Briggs emphasizes that two feelings are necessary on the part of the child for optimal growth and positive change: (1) I exist; therefore I am lovable and (2) I am competent.[2] Early conferences may be devoted to getting acquainted, finding common interests and values, and sharing ideas. An invitation to go fishing, take a walk, or eat out may contribute to the establishment of rapport more readily than formal interviews or conferences. Only when the child feels he is lovable and competent is he ready for preplanned regular counseling sessions.

Every word spoken by a teacher in a counseling setting carries some meaning to the student. Likewise shifts in postures, hand gestures, slight inflections in tones, pauses, and silences convey acceptance or nonacceptance. It is recommended that over 50 percent of the teacher's responses in a counseling session fall into the reflection category. The teacher sets the limits on how long a session may last, but the student may determine how short it can be. In other words, a student should feel free to terminate a session whenever he wishes.

2. Dorothy Corkille Briggs, *Your Child's Self Esteem: The Key to His Life* (New York: Doubleday and Co., Inc., 1970).

Concurrent with the fitness counseling sessions, the student should be provided with adapted physical education, either of an individual or small group nature. In some respects, fitness counseling is similar to dance or play therapy in that movement experiences frequently provide the basis for discussion. Sometimes an adapted physical education lesson will turn into a counseling session and vice versa.

Successes and failures in the gymnasium are accepted with equanimity. Neither praise nor blame is offered. The teacher uses words primarily to reflect what the student is feeling in a manner similar to that employed in the counseling session. On some occasions the teacher may imitate the movement of the student, using this technique to reflect how he looks to another and to reinforce his belief that others can accept him and his movement as the best of which he is capable at the moment. Imitation of movements, performed without words, shows willingness to suffer what the student is suffering, to feel as he feels, to perform through his body, and to walk in his shoes.

Success in counseling is dependent upon the skill of the teacher in the following functions: (1) seeing the student as a co-worker on a common problem; (2) treating the student as an equal; (3) understanding the student's feelings; (4) following the student's line of thought; (5) commenting in line with what the student is trying to convey; and (6) participating completely in the student's communication. The teacher's tone of voice is extremely important in conveying willingness and ability to share a student's feelings.

As fitness counseling proceeds, the student should grow in self-acceptance. The following criteria may serve as one basis for evaluation: (1) the student perceives himself as a person of worth, worthy of respect rather than criticism; (2) the student perceives his abilities and characteristics with more objectivity and greater comfort; (3) the student perceives himself as more independent and more able to cope with problems; (4) the student perceives himself as more able to be spontaneous and genuine; and (5) the student perceives himself as more integrated, less divided. Self-acceptance implies the desire and ability to change what can be changed, to accept what cannot be changed, and the wisdom to know the difference. Fitness counseling will not be 100 percent successful; some students will remain obese, many will continue in life-styles devoid of exercise, but the physical educator will have the experience of viewing fitness through others' eyes and experiencing what others feel as they attempt to cope with movement problems. The insights which result may well lead to the creation of new and more effective techniques for building physical fitness.

Teaching for Fitness

A common misconception is that physical education activities automatically develop muscular strength and endurance. Thus, two laps around the field at the close of each class period or three minutes of calisthenics at the beginning seldom have the effect anticipated. The same amount of exercise executed faithfully each day will contribute to the maintenance of whatever level of strength and circulo-respiratory endurance already exists but it will *not improve* fitness. In order to increase existing levels of fitness, the *principle of overload* must be applied.

This principle states that increases in muscular strength and circulo-respiratory endurance result from an increase in the intensity of work performed in a given unit of time. The intensity of work can be progressively increased in the following ways:

1. Increase the number of pounds being lifted, pushed, or pulled. This results in

progressive resistance exercises.

2. Increase the number of repetitions, sets, or type of exercise performed.
3. Increase the distance covered.
4. Increase the speed with which the exercise is executed.
5. Increase the number of minutes of continuous all-out effort.
6. Decrease rest interval between active sessions.
7. Increase intensity/type of activity during rest/relaxation phases.
8. Use any combination of the above.

In each instance, the intensity of work should represent all-out effort, taxing the student to the limits of his physiological capacity. The overload principle forces the student to compete against himself, each day bettering his previous performance.

The greatest problem in teaching for fitness is motivation. All-out effort may result in pain, muscular soreness, and oxygen deficit. Only a superb teacher can induce the average youth to increase his level of pain tolerance. Yet this goal must be accomplished if a student classified as having subliminal fitness is to progress to minimal fitness and beyond. Rasch and Burke state in this regard:

If an individual desires to increase his muscular strength, hypertrophy, and endurance he must be willing regularly to subject his body to the stress of repeated all-out efforts. In the case of a patient in a physical medicine and rehabilitation clinic this may be at a relatively low level of accomplishment on an absolute scale, but the important thing is achieved only when the person concerned is motivated by some powerful psychological drive. [3]

In the pages which follow, techniques are presented which apply the overload principle.

Progressive Resistance Exercises

The technique of progressive resistance exercises (PRE) is used widely in rehabilitative settings as well as athletics. The relatively high incidence of knee injuries among athletes and the subsequent surgery and rehabilitation have served to acquaint many persons with progressive resistance exercises. The postoperative patient is encouraged to undertake a regimen of knee extension exercises as soon after surgery as pain tolerance allows. Designated as quadriceps femoris progressive resistance exercises, extension of the leg at the knee joint is first executed without external weights. As the strength of the muscle group increases, progressively heavy weights are strapped to the foot.

The PRE technique, based upon knowledge of the individual's pain tolerance, entails the following three procedures:

1. Determine maximal resistance that can be lifted *ten* times (10 RM).
2. Then plan four exercise sessions weekly comprised of thirty repetitions executed as follows:
   Ten repetitions at 1/2 10 RM (half the maximal resistance determined in procedure one)
   Ten repetitions at 3/4 10 RM (three-fourths the maximal resistance determined in procedure one)
   Ten repetitions at 10 RM (the maximal resistance determined in procedure one)
3. Increase the 10 RM (maximum resistance that can be lifted ten times) each week.

The 10-20 Repetitions Sequence

Another weight training technique uses the heaviest weight that can be lifted ten times (10RM). The number of repetitions increases over a ten-day period in accordance with the following plan.

3. Philip J. Rasch and Roger K. Burke, *Kinesiology and Applied Anatomy* 4th ed. (Philadelphia: Lea & Febiger, 1971), p. 504.

	1st 3 days	4th day	5th day	6th day	7th day	Last 3 days
First Progression	10	12	14	16	18	20
Second Progression	Same as above, but with a heavier weight.					

accomplished

advice advise

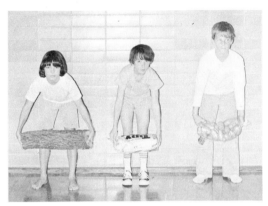

Figure 10.1. Use of logs, cat sand, and ten pound bag of potatoes in a weight lifting program.

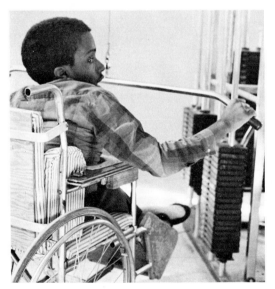

Figure 10.2. The universal gym can be used by the severely multihandicapped.

For individuals with less strength, a 5-10 repetitions sequence can be patterned after the 10-20 series. This technique can be applied to any kind of weight lifting program. Among the kinds of weights successfully used with exceptional children are

1. Teddy bears and other stuffed animals filled with seven, ten, and fifteen pounds respectively of aquarium sand
2. Fireplace logs
3. Sacks of potatoes, cat sand, dry dog food, or flour found in grocery stores—one, five, ten, twenty-five, fifty, and 100 pound bags are usually available
4. Plastic bottles filled with sand
5. Back packs such as those used on hiking and camping trips
6. Dumb bells
7. Universal gym
8. Homemade weights from tin cans, cement, and wooden dowels or broomsticks

Interval Training

Developed originally to condition long distance runners and swimmers, interval training can be adapted to any physical activity. It is especially beneficial for children with asthma and/or low fitness. The basic objective is to exercise for short periods of time with a rest interval between exercise periods in order to develop greater energy potential for a particular motor activity.

The interval training prescription (ITP) should be planned for each student individually or for small homogeneous groups rather than for the class as a whole. A typical ITP for one day might resemble that at the bottom of the page.

Mathews and Fox report that after the first two weeks training only twice weekly will result in significant gains in circulo-respiratory endurance.[4]

In order to plan the ITP, the following terms must be understood.

1. *Set*—Term which encompasses both the work interval and the rest interval. An ITP may have any number of sets.
2. *Work Interval*—Also called a bout. A prescribed number of repetitions of the same activity under identical conditions. Traditionally the work has been walking, running, or swimming a prescribed number of yards at optimum or near optimum speed *in an effort to raise the heart rate to 180 beats per minute.* If the heart rate does not reach this level after two or three work intervals, the student should be encouraged to run faster. For variety work intervals may entail performing an optimum number of squat thrusts, sit-ups, or push-ups within a prescribed number of seconds.
3. *Rest interval*—The number of seconds or minutes between work intervals during

which the student catches his breath and prepares for the next repetition. During the rest period the student should walk rather than sit, lie, or assume a stationary position. Prescribing a light activity like walking, arm circles, or toe touches may be psychologically beneficial in that it keeps the mind off of the impending exhaustion and provides structure. The number of seconds comprising the rest interval depends on individual heart recovery rate. *The next repetition should not be begun until the heart rate drops to 120 beats per minute.* If the heart rate does not recover within the rest interval, the student should be excluded from further interval training for the remainder of the day.

If taking the pulse rate is not feasible, the time of the rest interval should initially be approximately twice the amount of time consumed by the work interval.

4. *Repetitions*—The number of times the work interval is repeated under identical conditions. The amount of effort exerted in each repetition should be kept more or less constant.
5. *Target time*—The best score that a student can make on the prescribed activi-

4. Donald K. Mathews and Edward L. Fox, *The Physiological Basis of Physical Education and Athletics* (Philadelphia: W. B. Saunders, 1971), p. 86.

ITP for Running

Day 1	Repetitions	Distance each work interval	Amount of time each rest interval	Total Distance per set
Set 1	4	220 yds.	Depends on heart recovery rate	1/2 mile
Set 2	8	110 yds.	Depends on heart recovery rate	1/2 mile

ty. Target times are usually determined for the 110-, 220-, and 440-yard dashes and/or any other activities to be included in the ITP. Target times are generally not determined until the first two weeks of training are completed. The target time is then used as a motivational device to encourage all-out performance.

6. *Level of aspiration*—A statement made by the student of the score he thinks he can attain in a particular activity. This is also a motivational device.

All-out effort is often motivated after the first few weeks by prescribing the speed of the sprint as follows:

one repetition of 660 yards in 2:03
six repetitions of 220 yards in 0:33
six repetitions of 110 yards in 0:15

Older children may be guided in developing individualized exercise sessions comprised of sets which reflect their own levels of aspiration. Presumably, if the child states the number of seconds in which he can run 110 yards six times consecutively he will be more motivated to accomplish the goal (level of aspiration) established by himself than one imposed by an adult.

In keeping with the overload principle, the exercise sessions become increasingly more demanding each week. Early in the semester many of the work intervals may be relatively slow runs continued for long distances. As the semester progresses the long runs are gradually replaced with shorter, faster sprints. *For adolescents and adults a total workout distance of over 1.5 miles must eventually be achieved for maximum circulo-respiratory benefits.* Research is needed to provide comparable information about elementary school children, particularly those with asthma and other respiratory problems.

The following list of procedures may help the adapted physical education specialist in planning each ITP.

1. Test each student individually to determine his maximum running time for 110-, 220-, and 440 yards. If a track is not available, adjust these distances in accordance with the space available on your playground.

2. Upon the basis of these preliminary scores, organize the students into small homogeneous groups. If the class is small, each child may work with a single partner of like ability.

3. Develop specific behavioral objectives for each small group. Whenever possible, let the group participate in the development of objectives. Give each child a written copy of the objectives.

4. Explain the principle of interval training to the group and establish a cardfile where the students may pick up their individualized ITPs at the beginning of each physical education period. This procedure serves as a substitute for roll call and enables the students to begin exercise immediately upon entering the room.

5. An ITP card for three children of similar ability appears on the next page.
   On the right-hand side of the card, the students check whether each set was easy, medium, or difficult after its completion. These checks help the teacher to determine the extent to which the degree of difficulty (strenuousness) should be changed on the next ITP. On the back of the card the students may record their individual scores or write comments.

6. Apply the principle of overload in developing new cards for each session. Older students can develop their own ITPs.

7. Retest periodically to determine if behavioral goals are being met and to regroup students if necessary.

Day 5	Repetitions	Activity	Rest Interval	Evaluation		Ruda Rowe Stokes
Set 1	4 reps	Run 220 yards	Walk for 60 seconds between sprints	Easy	Medium	Hard
Set 2	6 reps	Squat thrusts for 10 seconds	Head circling for 20 seconds between bouts			
Set 3	4 reps	Crab walk for 10 seconds	Movement of choice for 20 seconds between bouts			
Set 4	8 reps	Run 110 yards	Walk for 30 seconds between sprints			

Circuit Training

Circuit training develops selected aspects of fitness as the student moves from station to station, performing a different fitness task at each station, and completes the circuit a prescribed number of times. Ideally the task performed at each station uses different groups of muscles, thereby developing different aspects of fitness. The circuit on page 219 is based upon Fleishman's factor analysis of physical fitness. With the exception of horizontal bars for Station 2 and floor and wall markings for Station 5, no equipment is needed.

For adolescents and adults, from six to ten stations are recommended depending upon available space and equipment. For elementary school children, from two to six stations may be attempted.

The amount of time at each station varies but initially is relatively brief. Thirty seconds at each station, with ten seconds for rotation, has been found satisfactory. Thus a circuit can be completed in approximately 2 1/2 minutes. As the semester progresses the amount of time at each station can be extended or the number of completed circuits increased. The intensity of the work demanded should be increased gradually in keeping with the overload principle.

Planning and Implementation of Circuit Training

Procedures to be followed in teaching and preparing students for circuit training are

1. Ascertain that the students know how to perform the fitness tasks.
2. Divide the class into squads, preferably homogeneous groupings, and assign each squad to a different starting point on the circuit.

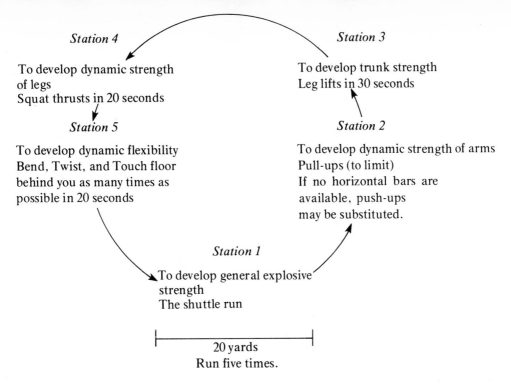

Station 4

To develop dynamic strength
of legs
Squat thrusts in 20 seconds

Station 5

To develop dynamic flexibility
Bend, Twist, and Touch floor
behind you as many times as
possible in 20 seconds

Station 3

To develop trunk strength
Leg lifts in 30 seconds

Station 2

To develop dynamic strength of arms
Pull-ups (to limit)
If no horizontal bars are
available, push-ups
may be substituted.

Station 1

To develop general explosive
strength
The shuttle run

20 yards
Run five times.

3. Practice the mechanics of rotating in a counterclockwise direction from station to station.

4. Develop an individualized circuit training plan for each student. Among the many ways individualized circuits can be developed Methods Plans A and B.

Method A for Adolescents and Adults

Decreasing Discrepency Between Actual Time and Target Time

This method is the least structured in that each student rotates from station to station at his own rate of speed and finishes the circuit training portion of the class at a different time. Specific directions should be given with respect to where to go and what to do when the circuit is completed. This method is not recommended for young children, nor for individuals who need structure.

Procedures in Method A are as follows:

1. Test every student, giving him several trials at each station. Each trial should be for a set time period as 30 seconds during which the fitness task is performed as many times as possible. Record the student's best score at each station as illustrated in the chart on the next page.

2. Base each student's individualized circuit upon one-half of his best test performance at each station. To illustrate, one circuit for Litty will consist of four runs, each twenty yards long; three pull-ups; fourteen leg lifts; nine squat thrusts; and ten bend, twist, and touch tasks.

3. Determine the number of seconds required for Litty to go through the prescribed circuit three times.

4. Establish the *target time* as two-thirds of the actual time required to complete three circuits.

5. In the exercise sessions which follow encourage Litty to bring his circuit time

Score Sheet for Circuit on Page 219

	Shuttle Run		Pull-ups		Leg-lifts		Squat Thrusts		Bend, Twist, and Touch		Actual Time to Complete Circuit at 1/2 Max	Target Time 2/3 of Actual Time
	Max Score	1/2 Max	Max Score	1/2 Max	Max Score	1/2 Max	Max Score	1/2 Max	Max Score	1/2 Max		
Litty	5.8	11.6*	6	3	28	14	18	9	20	10		
Ross	6		4		12		12		12			
Garcia	5		2		2		8		6			

*To decrease running speed by half, the number of seconds must be multiplied by two.

down to his target time. When this goal is accomplished, the number of circuits may be increased, the number of seconds at each station increased, or an entirely new circuit comprised of different fitness tasks begun. If the goal is not achieved in several weeks, the target time may be reset or a new circuit begun.

Method B for Children

Competing Against Own Best Score

This method is structured so that all students begin and end the circuit at the same time. Rotation occurs only on signal, and students give an all-out performance at each station until the signal to stop sounds. The objective is to compete against oneself, making a higher score than the previous turn at the station. This method is recommended for elementary school children and individuals who need structure.

Procedures for Method B are as follows:

1. Assign each student a home station, where his score card is kept. Prior to starting the circuit he may check his previous scores. At the completion of the circuit he records his new scores.

   To assist in fast, efficient recording, a shoe bag can be attached to the wall with each child's card in a different compartment. Ideally each card is a different color or in some way made easily identifiable.

2. Determine the number of seconds required for the group to change stations and keep this factor constant by calling, "Rotate -1-2-3-4-5-6-7-8-9-10." On your last count all students should be ready to begin the next fitness task.

3. For young students or those who have problems with handwriting, a recorder may work at each station. Immediately upon completion of the circuits the child tells the recorder his scores. It is important that this be done quietly, keeping each child's score in confidence. At no time should circuit training become competition with others. Or for students who cannot remember all of their scores until home station is reached, score cards can be carried with them from station to station. Sometimes instead of recording a numerical score, the process is simplified by writing a + if he improved his score and a 0 if he did not.

Aerobics

Aerobics is a progressive physical conditioning program which stimulates circulo-respiratory activity for a time period sufficiently long to produce beneficial changes in the body. The originator of the now widely used aerobics exercise program is Kenneth H. Cooper, a physician and major in the United States Air Force Medical Corps, who currently directs The Aerobics Center at 12100 Preston Road in Dallas, Texas. Based upon a longitudinal study of the circulo-respiratory fitness of over 5,000 adult male subjects, Cooper's first book, published in 1968, stressed two underlying principles: (1) if the exercise is vigorous enough to provide a sustained heart rate of 150 beats per minute or more, the training effect benefits begin about five minutes after the exercise starts and continue as long as the exercise is performed; and (2) if the exercise is not vigorous enough to produce or sustain a heart rate of 150 beats per minute, but is still demanding oxygen, the exercise must be continued considerably longer than five minutes, the total period of time depending on the oxygen consumed. [5]

The aerobics exercise program can be divided into three phases: (1) evaluation of circulo-respiratory fitness by means of the twelve minute run test; (2) a period of progressive conditioning which extends over several weeks; and (3) maintenance of optimal fitness by earning a specific number of points for exercise each week. The points are based upon the amount of oxygen consumption per minute during the exercise as illustrated in Table 25.

Evaluation of Aerobic Fitness

Prior to undertaking an aerobics training program, individuals who are unaccustomed to

Table 25 *Points Awarded on the Basis of Time and Oxygen Requirements for the One Mile Run*

Time in Minutes	Points	Oxygen (ml's/kg/min)
20:00 to 14:30	1	7
14:30 to 12:00	2	14
12:00 to 10:00	3	21
10:00 to 8:00	4	28
8:00 to 6:30	5	35
6:30 or less	6	42

exercise and who may already have circulo-respiratory problems should be examined by a physician. After a medical examination, fitness for aerobic training is evaluated by the distance covered in a twelve minute run-walk. Students are classified into five categories of fitness as depicted in Table 26.

Progressive Aerobic Conditioning

The fitness classification of the student determines the number of weeks of conditioning which will be required in order to work up to the maintenance phase of thirty points per week. The following guidelines can be used in this regard: (1) very poor category—16 weeks; (2) poor category—13 weeks; and (3) fair category—10 weeks. For students in these three categories, conditioning begins with the accumulation of ten points a week during the first two to three weeks after which an additional three to five points are required each week until the sum of thirty is reached. Stu-

5. Kenneth Cooper, *Aerobics* (New York: M. Evans and Company, 1968).

Table 26 *Fitness Categories Based upon Distance Covered in 12 Minute Run-Walk*

Fitness Category	Distance Covered	Oxygen Consumption
I Very Poor	less than 1.0 mile	28.0 ml's or less
II Poor	1.0 to 1.24 miles	28.1 to 34 ml's
III Fair	1.25 to 1.49 miles	34.1 to 42 ml's
IV Good	1.50 to 1.74 miles	42.1 to 52 ml's
V Excellent	1.75 miles or more	52.1 ml's or more

dents who score in the good and excellent fitness categories do not participate in the program of progressive conditioning. They go directly to the maintenance phase, earning thirty points each week.

Maintenance of Optimal Aerobic Fitness

The most efficient way to earn thirty points is to jog 1 1/2 miles in twelve minutes four times a week. For covering 1 1/2 miles in twelve minutes 7 1/2 points are awarded. The following activities, each worth five points, create a basis for developing an individualized maintenance program:

Bicycling 5 miles in less than 20 minutes
Running 1 mile in less than 8 minutes
Swimming 600 yards in less than 15 minutes
Handball played for a total of 35 minutes
Stationary running for a total of 12 1/2 minutes

For individual sports enthusiasts one set of singles tennis games earns 1 1/2 points; nine holes of golf earn 1 1/2 points; water or snow skiing for 30 minutes earns 3 points; and ice or roller skating for 15 minutes earns 1 point. For

the bicycle rider who enjoys leisurely pedaling, at least thirty minutes of cycling is required to earn one point.

Jogging and Hiking

Jogging, hiking, and performing walk-runs using the concept of the scout's pace all contribute to fitness if the principle of overload is applied from day to day. These activities are particularly successful when correlated with social studies and/or related to a trip across the state, the United States, or another continent. Individual mileage sheets, superimposed upon maps, can be kept by the students. Merit badges or certificates for achievement may be awarded for the completion of every fifty mile distance.

Hiking is one of the few activities in which a severely handicapped student can participate. It can be done in braces, on crutches, or in a wheelchair. The rehabilitation of most individuals with cardiovascular disease includes daily walks of increasingly long duration and at progressively faster speeds. The exercise plan presented in Table 27 has been

Table 27   *A Fourteen Week Run-Walk Program*

Week	Distance in Miles	Time Goal Minutes	Points for Aerobics Fitness Plan
1	1	20:00	
2	1	18:00	5
3	1	16:00	5
4	1	15:00	5
5	1 1/2	27:00	7 1/2
6	1 1/2	26:00	7 1/2
7	1 1/2	25:00	7 1/2
8	1	14:25	10
9	2	33:00	10
10	2	32:00	10
11	1 1/2	21:40	15
12	2	28:50	20
13	2	28:30	20
14	2 1/2	36:00	25

successful with secondary school youths whose level of fitness initially was too low to enjoy other forms of physical education.

Jogging, or cross-country track, is becoming increasingly popular with all age groups. When motivated by an adult who will run with them, many first and second grade children can jog a mile or further with less discomfort than the adult who accompanies them. Every child, no matter how poor is his motor coordination, can find pleasure in leisurely running. The *scout's pace* can be used in early stages of training as follows: jog 110 yards, walk 55 yards, jog 110 yards, walk 55 yards, ad infinitum. The scout's pace can also be interpreted as meaning run as far as you can, then walk until breath is restored, after which running is resumed.

Continuity Exercises Based Upon Rope Jumping

Procedures in developing a continuity exercise program which utilizes the interval approach include:

1. Make a tape recording which establishes a cadence of 80 jumps per minute, i.e., one every 3/4 second.
2. Test the students to determine how long they can jump without a rest interval.
3. Upon the basis of individual scores, assign the students to homogeneous groups, each of which has a leader.
4. Develop a sequence of continuity exercises for each group, giving the leaders the written instructions.
5. Assuming the class can be divided according to exercise capabilities into three groups, easy, medium, and difficult, illustrative sequences appear at the bottom of this page.
6. Each group has approximately one-third of the floor space with its leader in front. All groups exercise simultaneously to the tape recording or to a piece of music but each group is doing its own thing based upon its abilities. The groups which finish first go to preestablished stations where students work on skills.
7. The principle of overload is applied in changing the sequence from week to week. Whenever possible, use contemporary music, i.e., the top ten songs of the day. Integrating popular music with exercise encourages students to perform the routines outside of the school day since certain tunes are heard repeatedly over radio and television.
8. When push-ups, sit-ups, and other exercises are being performed, encourage optimum class involvement by asking the students to call out the cadence count in military fashion.

Astronaut Drills

The drills traditionally used in football practices can be adapted to meet the fitness needs of children as well as to reinforce concepts pertaining to body positions and body parts. Many football teams employ only three signals or verbal cues in their grass drills: *Go, Front,* and *Back.* The correct response to each cue follows on page 224.

ILLUSTRATIVE SEQUENCES INDIVIDUALIZED TO MEET CAPABILITIES

Easy Sequence	Medium Sequence	Difficult Sequence
1. Rope Jump 1 minute	1. Rope Jump 3 minutes	1. Rope Jump 4 minutes
2. Rest 60 seconds	2. Rest 30 seconds	2. Rest 20 seconds
3. Rope Jump 30 seconds	3. Rope Jump 1 1/2 minutes	3. Rope Jump 2 minutes

1. *Go*—run in place with vigorous high knee action. Maintain top speed.
2. *Front*—drop to prone lying position and assume a ready position to ensure quick response to the next cue.
3. *Back*—drop to supine lying position and assume a ready position to ensure quick response to the next cue.

These cues are given in various orders, challenging the student to persist in continuous motion. The principle of overload is applied through progressively increasing the duration of time spent in the *Go* position. After students have mastered these cues, others might be added: Right side lie, Left side lie, Squat, Long Sit, and so on.

Obstacle Courses

Perhaps no activity is as popular with elementary school pupils as following a leader through an obstacle course. Apparatus for these courses can be purchased commercially or constructed by teachers and parents.[6] Homemade obstacle courses are often built around a theme. Assigning pieces of equipment novel names creates the mood for

Figure 10.3. A homemade obstacle course offers fun and challenge (Austin State School).

themes built around space travel, a jungle trek, a western outpost, or an Indian village.

Seldom is a class small enough that all students can move through an obstacle course simultaneously. Congestion and confusion should be prevented by assigning not more than two students to each piece of apparatus and by having them stand at their assigned apparatus while awaiting the signal *Go* rather than all standing in a file behind the leader. Thus only fourteen students can move efficiently through a seven piece obstacle course at any given time. The flexible teacher will post a time schedule listing each student's name and stating the time at which he is excused from regular class activities to go through the obstacle course.

Warm-Up Exercises

A *warm-up* is a preparatory activity engaged in immediately before a game, fitness test, or all-out performance of any kind for the purpose of improving performance and preventing injury by increasing muscular temperature, circulation, range of joint mobility, and producing a condition of readiness. The physiological basis for warm-ups lies primarily in the fact that the effectiveness of muscular contractions depends upon temperature. The internal body temperature at rest is 37° C or 98.6° F. During exercise of high intensity and long duration, deep muscle temperature rises 1-2° C. This increase usually occurs during the first thirty minutes of exercise and then plateaus. An increase in body temperature does not occur easily, however, because the temperature control system of the human body is highly effective.

Most coaches, athletes, and dancers believe that warming-up decreases the incidence of injuries. Little research has been conducted on the relationship between warm-ups and injury,

6. Portable obstacle course can be purchased from J. A. Preston Corporation, 71 Fifth Avenue, New York, New York 10003.

but few high level performers are willing to chance the risk. Until it is proven that the incidence of injuries is not decreased by warm-ups, it seems prudent to encourage students to engage in the kinds of warm-ups which best meet their needs. It is reasonable to believe that some persons need extensive warm-ups while others need little or none.

Karpovich cites the conflicting findings of several studies pertaining to warm-ups and emphasizes the strong influence of psychological factors on the effects of warm-ups. He states:

It stands to reason that some honest subjects may be afraid to go all-out without warming up, and therefore their performance will be adversely affected. This is probably the main reason for warming up for all physical activities except those requiring a definite element of skill, such as gymnastics, tennis, billiards, or pitching a baseball.[7]

Warm-ups may be classified as active or passive and as specific or general. Active warm-ups entail exercise of some kind while passive warm-ups encompass hot showers, diathermy, and massage. Specific warm-ups are those in which the movements imitate the ensuing activity. General warm-ups are those which utilize several major groups which are not necessarily the ones which will be exercised in ensuing activities. Specific warm-ups are recommended over general warm-ups. Rasch and Burke emphasize that activities involving hand-eye and foot-eye coordination are especially susceptible to warm-ups. They state:

The beneficial results may be explained in terms of (a) learning, (b) neural facilitation, or the tendency for synaptic threshholds to be reduced after the passage of the first few adequate stimuli, and (c) the opportunity to review sensory cues immediately before performing complex coordinations.[8]

Specific warm-ups, which generally employ a forward-backward stride, are used to *stretch* muscles which will be used later in the physical education period. Perhaps jogging is the best specific warm-up since success in most motor activities depends upon running speed and agility in executing quick stops, starts, turns, and dodges. For a throwing and catching game the best warm-ups are throwing and catching, gradually increasing the speed and force of the throw.

General warm-ups, so often conducted as calisthenics at the beginning of a class period, offer little or no contribution to the objectives of physical education. The image of mass drill in jumping jacks, side stretches, and toe touches has indeed hurt our profession.

It has become increasingly evident over the years that physical fitness can be increased only through application of the overload principle. Not all children need to engage in programs for building strength, circulo-respiratory endurance, and flexibility. The activities in this chapter are recommended primarily for individuals with subminimal fitness. Children with adequate fitness should engage in maintenance programs and concentrate on development of leisure skills.

7. Peter V. Karpovich and Wayne Sinning, *Physiology of Muscular Activity* (Philadelphia: W. B. Saunders Company, 1971), p. 31.
8. Philip J. Rasch and Roger K. Burke, *Kinesiology and Applied Anatomy* 4th ed. (Philadelphia: Lea & Febiger, 1971), p. 519-520.

Recommended Activities

1. Develop a slide presentation, flannel board talk, videotape, or film designed to instruct the lay person on the specific components of fitness. Use it with at least one group.
2. Make a tape recording or write a paper elaborating upon the meaning of "Fitness for What?" as it pertains to you personally.
3. Experiment with the concept of level of aspiration by recording the scores you think you will make on several fitness

tests, taking the tests and recording your actual scores, and subtracting to obtain your discrepency scores. Read some research studies on level of aspiration, particularly as it relates to self-concept.

4. Make a decision concerning which is your favorite test for each of the following components of fitness: (a) static or extent flexibility; (b) dynamic flexibility; (c) explosive strength; (d) static strength; (e) dynamic strength; (f) strength of trunk muscles; (g) work capacity or circulo-respiratory endurance. State the criteria which served as the basis for your decision making.

5. Learn to take pulse rate and blood pressure. Practice recording these parameters before and after various kinds of exercises.

6. Administer each of the tests described in this chapter to at least five persons. Combine their scores with those collected by your classmates for the same age range and sex. Compute the mean, median, and standard deviation.

7. Select a person with low fitness and write an exercise prescription of several weeks duration to meet his special needs.

8. Conduct a mini-lesson demonstrating your understanding of three of the training techniques described in this chapter.

Recommended Reading

American Association for Health, Physical Education, and Recreation. *Special Olympics Instructional Manual*. Washington, D.C.: The Association, 1972.

American College of Sports Medicine, ed. *Guidelines for Graded Exercise Testing and Exercise Prescription*. Philadelphia: Lea & Febiger, 1975.

Cooper, Kenneth, and Brown, Kevin. *The New Aerobics*. Philadelphia: Lippincott, 1970.

Fleishman, Edwin A. *The Structure and Measurement of Physical Fitness*. Englewood Cliffs, New Jersey: Prentice-Hall, Inc., 1964.

Hockey, Robert V. *Physical Fitness*. St. Louis: The C. V. Mosby Company, 1973.

Neilson, N. P., and Jensen, Clayne R. *Measurement and Statistics in Physical Education*. Belmont, California: Wadsworth Publishing Co., 1972.

Sorani, Robert. *Circuit Training*. Dubuque, Iowa: Wm C. Brown Company Publishers, 1966.

11 Relaxation and Reduction of Hyperactivity

Figure 11.0. Concentrating on body parts.

Instruction and practice in relaxation are integral parts of a comprehensive adapted physical education program. Relaxation, defined physiologically, is a neuromuscular accomplishment that results in a reduction of muscular tension. Tension is the amount of electrical activity present in a muscle. The shortening of muscle fibers is attended by an increase of electrical voltage. Shortening, contracting, and tightening are synonyms in the sense that each implies increased muscle tension. The release of tension within a muscle is attended by a decrease of electrical voltage which is expressed in microvolts or millivolts. Complete muscle relaxation is characterized by electrical silence, i.e., zero action potentials.

Neuromuscular tension is a positive attribute. No movement can occur without the development of tension in the appropriate muscle groups. Unfortunately, however, many persons maintain more muscles in a state of tension than is necessary for the accomplishment of motor tasks. Such excessive neuromuscular tension is known as *hypertension*, not to be confused with arterial hypertension. The purpose of relaxation training is to prevent or reduce hypertension.

Not all persons need relaxation training. Individual differences in tension should be assessed, and only students who exhibit abnormal signs should be assigned to relaxation and slowing down activities in lieu of the vigorous activities which traditionally comprise the program.

Signs of Hypertension

Excessive neuromuscular hypertension is identified by the presence of certain signs.

Hyperactivity: Inability to remain motionless for set period of time; wriggles in chair; shifts arm or leg; plays with hair; scratches, rubs or picks at skin; makes noises with feet; drums fingers on desk top or doodles with pen; chews gum, pencil, or fingernails; fails to keep place in line or any set formation.

Facial Expression: Lines in face seldom disappear; eyes frequently shift focus; lips quiver or seem abnormally tight; cheek muscles show tension; immobile expression as frozen smile or incessant frown; eye tic.

Breathing: Unconscious breath holding; shallow, irregular breaths; hyperventilation.

Skin: Nervous perspiration; irritations caused by picking; hives, eczema.

Voice: Two extreme opposite patterns, the most common of which is talking too much, louder than usual, faster than usual, and with higher pitch; deep sighs indicating excessive respiratory tension; crying.

These signs are characteristic of persons on the verge of emotional breakdowns but they also appear in times of great stress as final examination period, death or severe illness in family, impending divorce of parents and/or incessant bickering among family members. Certain prescribed drugs, as diet pills, as well as those consumed illegally, result in overt signs of hyperactivity. Constant physical pain or discomfort is sometimes evidenced in signs of hypertension.

When the problems causing hypertension are not resolved over long periods of time, the sufferer slips into a stage of *chronic fatigue.* He often experiences insomnia. When he does not sleep, he typically awakes unrested. Symptoms of chronic fatigue are (1) increase of tendon reflexes; (2) increase of muscle excitability; (3) spastic condition of smooth muscles exhibited in diarrhea and stomach upsets; (4) abnormal excitability of heart and respiratory apparatus; (5) tremors; (6) restlessness; and (7) irritibility. In this stage many persons seek the help of a physician; generally they complain of feeling tired all of the time. They know they are not really sick but neither do they feel well.

Hypertension in Children

In the past, hypertension has been associated more with adults than children. It is now recognized that many hyperactive youngsters, especially those with learning disabilities, exhibit signs of neuromuscular hypertension which can be ameliorated through relaxation training. Likewise many essentially *normal* persons are simply high-strung just as others are slow moving and easy going. Levels of hypertension seem to be largely determined by heredity and reinforced by the environment.

The pupil who needs training in tension reduction may feel guilty about his hypertension, particularly if he has been led to believe that he is different from others in the household. Many children deny that they feel tense. Others, accustomed to hypertension, do not realize that conditions of less tension exist.

Testing for Excess Tension

Awareness of residual hypertension can be developed by instructing the pupil to lie on his back and release all tensions. The teacher lifts one body part at a time and then lets go. The degree of hypertonus present is recorded as *negative, slight, medium,* or *marked* on the right and left sides for the muscles of the wrist, elbow, shoulder, ankle, knee, hip, and neck. Hypertonus is detected by such *unconscious* muscular responses as:

1. Assistance: student assists teacher in lifting the body part.
2. Posturing or set: student resists gravity when teacher removes support.
3. Resistance: student tenses or resists the action of the teacher in lifting the body part.
4. Perseveration: student continues a movement after the teacher starts it.

The presence of residual hypertension can be assessed also through electromyography. Among the increasing number of commercial instruments which monitor electromyographical (EMG) response is the Electromyometer,[1] which costs less than $400, and is now being used in several programs of relaxation therapy for learning disabilities children. The Electromyometer, like any electromyographical apparatus, records the amount of electrical activity present in the muscle fibers. Biofeedback in the form of sound and a digital read out reinforces attempts to reduce tension, making the apparatus effective both as a teaching and evaluation device.

Teaching Relaxation

Techniques of teaching relaxation vary with the age group, the nature of the handicapping condition, and the number of class sessions to be spent. Each of the techniques described in this section aims at lowering the tension, i.e., the electrical activity of skeletal muscles. With the exception of the Jacobson techniques, few have been subjected to scientific research. Although their effectiveness may not be substantiated statistically, the various techniques each have strong proponents and seem worthy of exploration. Imagery, deep body awareness, the Jacobson techniques, static stretching exercises, yoga, and Tai Chi are considered. Breathing exercises, also important in relaxation training, are presented in Chapter 17.

Imagery

The *imagery* or ideational approach is well received in the primary grades. Andrews recommends poems and short stories designed to help children become rag dolls flopping, ice cream melting, merry-go-rounds stopping, balloons slowly deflating, icicles melting, faucets dripping, salt pouring from a shaker, bubbles getting smaller, and snowflakes drifting downward.[2] For greatest effectiveness the children must be drawn into discussions of

1. Information about the Toomin Electromyometer can be obtained from Biofeedback Research Institute, Inc., 41 West 71st Street, New York, New York 10023.
2. Gladys Andrews, *Creative Rhythmic Movement for Children,* (Englewood Cliffs, N.J.: Prentice-Hall, Inc., 1954), pp. 152-155.

what relaxes them and encouraged to make up their own stories and poems. It is also enlightening to ask children to develop lists of their favorite *quiet* things and *slow* activities. Focus may be directed toward enacting things that start out fast, gradually decrease in speed, and eventually become motionless.

Illustrative of some ideational approaches used to elicit relaxed movements follow:

You are a soft calico kitten lying in front of the warm fire place. The fire is warm. You feel so-o-o good. First you stretch your right arm—oh, that feels good. Then you stretch your left arm. Then you stretch both legs. Now you are relaxed all over. The fire is so warm and your body feels so relaxed. This must be the best place in the whole world—your own little blanket in front of your own fire. You are so-o-o relaxed that you could fall asleep right now. You are getting sleepy now—maybe you will fall asleep now.

You are the tail of a kite that is sailing gently high, oh so-o-o high in the light blue sky. The kite goes higher and so do you—very slowly and very gently in the soft breeze. Now you are going to the right. Oh the breeze is warm and ooh so soft—it is blowing so gently that you can feel it only if you think real hard. Can you feel the soft, warm breeze blowing you to the left? It is so-o-o gentle and so-o-o soft.

You are becoming a puppet. The change starts in your feet. Slowly each part of your body becomes lifeless and is completely relaxed, as if it were detached from you.

Let's make believe we are a bowl full of jello! Someone has left us out of the refrigerator and we begin to dissolve slowly away. Our arms float down and our body sinks slowly into the bowl.

Older children, no longer able to assume magically the feeling-tone of an animal or object, continue to find relaxation in the mood of certain poems and stories read aloud. They may lie in comfortable positions in a semi-darkened room while listening and attempt to capture the essence of the words through consciously releasing tensions. Instrumental music may be substituted for reading if the group desires.

Deep Body Awareness

To facilitate deep body awareness, the teacher begins the class with everyone in a comfortable supine lying position. He then directs their attention to specific parts of the body, asking the pupils to analyze and verbalize the sensations they are experiencing. If pupils seem reluctant to share aloud their feelings, the teacher may offer such additional guidance as:

1. Which parts of your arm are touching the floor? Is the floor warm or cool, smooth or rough, clean or dirty?
2. How long is your arm from the tip of the middle finger to shoulder joint? From tip of the middle finger to elbow? From tip of the middle finger to wrist crease? How heavy is your arm? How heavy are each of its parts?
3. Can you feel the muscles loosening? If you measured the circumference of your upper arm, how many inches would you get?
4. Can you feel the blood pulsating in veins and arteries?
5. Can you feel the hairs on your arm? The creases in your wrist? The finger nails? The cuticles? Any scars?
6. What other words come to mind when you think about arm?

The underlying premise in deep body awareness is that a pupil must increase kinesthetic sensitivity before he can consciously control it. He must differentiate between parts of a whole and be able to describe these parts accurately. As deep body awareness is developed, each pupil discovers which thoughts and methods of releasing tension work best for him personally.

Jacobson Techniques

Most widely known of the techniques of neuromuscular relaxation are those of Edmund Jacobson, a physician and physiologist, who began his research in tension control at Harvard University in 1918. His first two books, *Progressive Relaxation* and *You Must Relax*, were published in 1920 and 1934. Since 1936, Dr. Jacobson has served as Director of the Laboratory for Clinical Physiology, 55 East Washington Street, Chicago, Illinois 60602. He has continued to conduct research and publish new books, some of which are listed in the bibliography.

Jacobson's techniques, known originally as a system of *progressive conscious neuromuscular relaxation*, are referred to as *self-operations control* in his later books. The progression of activities is essentially the same. He suggests three steps for learning to recognize the sensations of *doing* and *not doing* in any specific muscle group: (1) tension followed by relaxation against an outside resistance such as the teacher pushing downward on a limb which the student is trying to lift; (2) tension within the muscle group when no outside resistance is offered followed by release of the tension; and (3) release of tension in a resting muscle group which has not been contracted.

Jacobson recommends that relaxation training begin in a supine position with arms at the sides, palms facing downward. The mastery of *differential control* of one muscle group at a time begins with hyperextension at the wrist joint only. All other joints in the body remain relaxed while the pupil concentrates on bending the hand backward. The resulting tension is felt in the back upper part of the forearm.

Self-operations control, as outlined by Jacobson, is a slow procedure. Each class session is one hour in length. During that time a particular tension, like hypertension of the wrist, is practiced only three times. The tension (also called the control sensation) is held one to two minutes after which the pupil is told to *go negative* or completely relax for three to four minutes. After the completion of three of these tension and relaxation sequences, the pupil lies quietly with eyes closed for the remainder of the hour. Session two follows the same pattern except that the tension practiced is bending the wrist forward so as to tense the anterior muscles of the forearm. Every third session is called a zero period in that no tension is practiced. The entire body is relaxed the whole time.

In all, seven sessions are recommended for learning to relax the left arm. During the fourth session the tension created by bending the elbow about 35° is practiced. During the fifth session the tension created in the back part of the upper arm when the palm presses downward against a stack of books is practiced. The sixth session is a zero period. The seventh session calls for progressive tension and relaxation of the whole.

Detailed instructions are given for proceeding from one muscle group to the next. The completion of an entire course in relaxation in the supine lying position, requires the following amount of time: left arm, 7 days; right arm, 7 days; left leg, 10 days; right leg, 10 days; trunk, 10 days; neck, 6 days; eye-region, 12 days; visualization, 9 days; and speech region, 19 days. Then the same order and same duration of practices are followed in the sitting position. While Jacobson indicates that the course can be speeded up, he emphasizes that less thoroughness results in reduced ability to recognize tension signals and turn them off.

Static Stretching Exercises

To illustrate the efficacy of static stretching, try these experiments, holding each position for 60 or more seconds.

1. Let the head drop forward as far as it will go. Hold this position and feel the stretch on the neck extensors.

2. Let the body bend at the waist as in touching the toes. When the fingertips touch the floor, hold, and feel the stretch in the back extensors and hamstrings.
3. Do a side bend to the left and hold.
4. Lie supine on a narrow bench and let your head hang over the edge.
5. Lie on a narrow bench and let the arms hang down motionless in space. They should not be able to touch the ground.

When the pupil learns to release tension in these static positions, relaxation is achieved. Yoga, because it is based upon such static stretching, is often included in instructional units on relaxation.

Yoga

Yoga is a system of physical, mental, and spiritual development which comes from India where it dates back several centuries before Christ. The word *yoga* is derived from the Sanskrit root *yuji* which means to join or bind together. Scholars recognize several branches of yoga, but in the United States the term is used popularly to refer to a system of exercises built upon held positions or postures and breath control. More correctly, we should say *Hatha yoga* rather than yoga when teaching aspects of this system to our students. In the word Hatha the *ha* represents the sun (expression of energy) and the *tha* represents the moon (conservation of energy). In yoga exercises, these two are always interacting.

Hatha Yoga offers exercises particularly effective in teaching relaxation and slowing down the hyperactive child. The emphasis upon correct breathing in Hatha Yoga makes it especially valuable in the reconditioning of persons with asthma and other respiratory problems. Moreover, the nature of Hatha Yoga is such that it appeals to the middle aged and to individuals whose health status prohibits participation in vigorous, strenuous physical activities.

Hatha Yoga, hereafter referred to as yoga, can be subdivided into two types of exercises: *asanas* and *pranayanas*. Asanas are held positions or postures like the lotus, the locust, and cobra poses. Pranayanas are breathing exercises. In actuality asanas and pranayanas are interrelated since correct breathing is emphasized throughout the assumption of a particular pose. Several of the asanas are identical or similar to stunts taught in elementary school physical education. The yoga bent bow is the same as the human rocker. The cobra is similar to the swan and/or the trunk lift from a prone position to test back strength. The plough pose resembles the paint the rainbow stunt.

Differences between yoga and physical exercise as it is ordinarily taught are

1. Exercise sessions traditionally emphasize movement. *Yoga is exercise without movement.*

2. Exercises usually involve several bounces or stretches with emphasis upon how many can be done. Yoga stresses a *single slow* contraction of certain muscles followed by a general relaxation. Generally an asana is not repeated. At the very most, it might be attempted two or three times.

3. Exercises usually entail some pain and discomfort since the teaching progression conforms to the overload principle. In yoga, the number of repetitions is not increased. The duration of time for which the asana is held increases in accordance with ease of performance.

4. Exercises ordinarily stress the development of strength, flexibility, and endurance. Yoga stresses relaxation, balance, and self-control.

In summary,

The gymnast's object is to make his body strong and healthy, with well-developed muscles, a broad chest, and powerful arms. The yogi will get more or less the same results; but they are not what he is looking for.

He is looking for calm, peace, the remedy for fatigue; or, better still, a certain immunity to fatigue.

He wants to quiet some inclination or other of his, his tendency to anger, or impatience—signs of disturbance in his organic or psychical life. He wants a full life, a more abundant life, but a life of which he is the master. [3]

Tai Chi

Tai Chi Chuan, pronounced *Tie Jee Chwahn* and called Tai Chi for short, is one of the many slowing-down activities found to be successful with hyperactive children. An ancient Chinese system of exercise, it is practiced by an increasing number of adults in the United States. In large metropolitan areas on the east and west coasts, instruction from masters, usually listed in the telephone directory, is available. Tai Chi is used by many dance therapists.

Tai Chi is a series of 108 specific learned patterns of movements called *forms* which provide exercise for every part of the body. The forms have colorful names which tend to captivate children: Grasp Bird's Tail Right, Stork Spreads Wings, Carry Tiger to Mountain, Step Back and Repulse Monkey, Needle at Sea Bottom, High Pat on Horse, Parting with Wild Horse's Mane Right. The 108 forms are based upon thirty-seven basic movements; thus, there is much repetition in the execution of a series of forms.

Tai Chi is characterized by extreme slowness, a concentrated awareness of what one is doing, and absolute continuity of movement from one form to another. The same tempo is maintained throughout, but no musical accompaniment is provided. All movements contain circles, reinforcing the concepts of uninterrupted flow and quiet continuity. All body parts are gently curved or bent, allowing the body to give into gravity rather than working against it as is the usual practice in western culture. No posture or pose is ever held. As each form is approximately completed, its movement begins to melt and blend into the next form. This has been likened to the cycle of seasons when summer blends into autumn and autumn into winter.

Although instruction by a master is desirable, Tai Chi is simple enough that it can be learned from a pictorial text. Maisel recommends that the movements be memorized by repeatedly performing forms one through twenty in the same order without interruption. [4] One form should never be practiced in isolation from others. Later, forms twenty-one through fifty-seven are learned as a unity as well as forms fifty-eight through 108. This approach is especially beneficial for children who need practice in visual perception, matching, and sequencing. Its greatest strength, however, lies in the principle of slowness. Each time the sequence of forms is done, day after day, year after year, the goal is to perform it more slowly than before.

For persons who feel disinclined to memorize and teach preestablished forms, the essence of Tai Chi can be captured by restructuring class calisthenics as a follow-the-leader experience in which flowing, circular movements are reproduced as slowly as possible without breaking the continuity of the sequence. For real relaxation to occur, the same sequence must be repeated daily.

Suggestions for Reducing Hyperactivity

The etiology of hyperactivity is generally unknown. An accepted behavioral characteristic of many brain-injured children, it is manifested also by many children with no known handicaps. One has only to observe a

3. J. M. Dechanet, *Yoga in Ten Lessons* (New York: Cornerstone Library, 1965), p. 18.
4. Edward Maisel, *Tai Chi for Health* (New York: Holt, Rinehart and Winston, 1972), p. 68.

new litter of kittens or puppies to note substantial differences in levels of activity, energy, and aggressiveness. What keeps children keyed up? How can hyperactivity be channeled into productivity? How can hyperactivity be reduced?

A common misconception is the belief that regular physical education provides an outlet for releasing excessive nervous tensions and letting off steam. This may be true on some days for a few of the better coordinated youngsters who find satisfaction in large motor activities. It is not a valid supposition when physical education is an instructional setting in which pupils are introduced daily to new learning activities. Hyperactive children have just as much trouble listening to the physical educator and conforming to the structure of the play setting as they experience in the classroom. The mastery of a new motor skill, or even the practice of an old one, is no more relaxing than reading or learning to play the piano.

Once a skill is refined and is performed without conscious thought, it can become a channel for releasing tensions. Simple repetitive activities like jogging and swimming laps may serve this purpose for some individuals just as knitting, gardening, or playing the piano is soothing to others. A good physical education program, however, devotes little of its time allotment to such repetitive activities. *Letting off steam* simply is not an objective of the regular physical education program.

The hyperactive child needs vigorous physical activity as do all pupils. Whereas normal children typically make the transition from play to classroom work without special help, the hyperactive child requires a longer period of time and assistance in making the adjustment. *This is not a reason for excusing him from physical education.* It does call for recognition of individual differences and the availability of a quiet, semidark area where children can lie down before returning to the classroom and practice the relaxation tech-

niques they have been taught. Large cardboard boxes which children can crawl into and hide are recommended for the primary grades. When a place free from noise cannot be found, earphones with music or a soothing voice giving relaxation instruction can be used to block out distractions. The use of this quiet space should not be limited to a particular time of day nor to certain children. All persons, at one time or another, need a retreat where they can go of their own accord, relax, and regain self-control.

If several children appear to be especially hyperactive during a physical education period, the teacher should end the vigorous activity early and devote the last ten minutes or so to relaxation training. Changes of weather, particularly the onset of rain, seem to heighten neuromuscular tensions. Examinations, special events, and crises carried by the news media may have pupils so keyed up that the best physical education for the entire class is rest and relaxation. Certainly the physical educator should ask himself at the beginning of each period: "Do the pupils need slowing down or speeding up? Is any one child especially keyed up? Which activity can he be guided into before a discipline problem occurs?"

Hyperactivity can be reduced only if the causes are eliminated. The following adaptations seem to help the hyperactive child retain self-control in the activity setting.

1. Decrease the space. If outdoors, rope off boundaries. If indoors, use partitions.
2. Decrease the noise by arranging for smaller classes and using yarn balls and beanbags rather than rubber ones. Use verbal stop and start signals instead of a whistle. Do not tell the children to be quiet; inhibiting their natural inclination to shout, run, jump, and throw only raises tension levels.
3. Structure the activities so that the children do not have to wait in lines and take turns. Good physical education im-

plies maximal involvement of all the children all of the time. Each pupil should have his own ball, rope, or piece of apparatus.

4. Designate certain spaces as learning stations and use the same direction of rotation each period. If necessary, rope or partition off these stations to minimize distractions.
5. Deemphasize speed by stressing accuracy and self-control.
6. Avoid speed tests. This approach necessitates a whole new look at measurement and evaluation in physical education. On a paper-pencil test, do not count questions which are not answered as wrong. Instead send the child home with a similar test and instructions to repeatedly practice taking it until they can answer all questions accurately within a set time limit. This may require ten trials for some

children and fifty for others. Learning to cope with speed tests, however, should take place in a nonthreatening situation.
7. Avoid relays based upon the team or individual which can finish the fastest. Instead, experiment with different concepts: Who can go the slowest? Who can use the most interesting movement pattern? Who can be the most graceful? Who can be the most original? Who can create the funniest movement pattern?
8. Build in success. Even a hyperactive child will remain motionless to hear himself praised. Much of the residual neuromuscular tension which characterizes certain children stems from failure and fear of failure. After success in a new motor skill has been achieved, stop the pupil while he feels positive about his efforts and direct his attention to something new.

Recommended Activities

1. Observe several children in classroom and physical education settings, and compare signs of hypertension present in each.
2. Visit a day care center or residential facility for the mentally ill and observe signs of hypertension in the patients. If relaxation training or dance therapy is provid-

ed for the patients, arrange to observe sessions.
3. Conduct at least two mini-lessons in which you demonstrate your competence in teaching such relaxation techniques as imagery, deep body awareness, Jacobson self-operations control.

Recommended Reading

General Relaxation

Arnheim, Daniel D.; Auxter, David; and Crowe, Walter. "Tension Reduction" in *Principles and Methods of Adapted Physical Education.* 2nd edition. Saint Louis: The C. V. Mosby Company, 1973, pp. 149-162.

Cratty, Bryant J. "Intellectual Activity, Activation, and Self-Control," *Physical Expressions of Intelligence.* Englewood Cliffs, New Jersey: Prentice-Hall, Inc., 1972, pp. 169-189.

Jacobson, Edmond. *Anxiety and Tension Control—A Physiologic Approach.* Philadelphia: J. B. Lippincott Company, 1964.

Jacobson, Edmond. *You Must Relax.* 4th edition. New York: McGraw-Hill Book Company, Inc., 1957.

Rathbone, Josephine, and Hunt, Valerie. "Tension Techniques in Relaxation," *Corrective Physical Education.* 7th edition. Philadelphia: W. B. Saunders, 1965, pp. 216-236.

Steinhaus, Arthur. "Facts and Theories of Neuromuscular Relaxation." *Quest* Monograph III (December, 1964), pp. 3-14.

Yoga

Dechanet, J. M. *Yoga in Ten Lessons.* New York: Cornerstone Library Publications, 1965.

Hittleman, Richard. *Introduction to Yoga.* New York: Bantam Books, 1969.

Tai Chi

Maisel, Edward. *Tai Chi for Health.* New York: Holt, Rinehart, and Winston, 1972.

Tegner, Bruce. *Kung Fu and Tai Chi: Chinese Karate.* Ventura, California: Thor Publishing Co., 1973.

Related Readings

Kavanaugh, James. *Celebrate the Sun.* Los Angeles: Nash Publishing, 1973.

Link, Mark. *In the Stillness is the Dancing.* Niles, Illinois: Argus Communications, 1972.

Organizations

1. National Foundation for Progressive Relaxation, 55 East Washington Street, Chicago, Illinois 60602.

2. American Association for the Advancement of Tension Control, P. O. Box 7512, Roanoke, Virginia 24019.

12 Dance Therapy and Adapted Dance

With Co-author Wynelle Delaney, DTR

Figure 12.0. Creative dance with crepe paper streamers.

One of the wonders of human movement, and specifically of the dance experience, is its changing, amorphous, and quicksilver nature. It is process, not permanent fixed product. The same is true of the child, a human changeling hung between his beginning and his becoming, suspended in his being for a very brief and special time. It is beautifully apparent that dance and the child are natural companions. If, as Merleau Ponty suggests, our bodies are our way of having a world, the child is busily at home in his own body forming and shaping his own world, its inner and outer hemispheres. He is making himself up as he goes along. [1]

Nancy W. Smith

Perhaps no part of the physical education curriculum is as important to the handicapped child as creative rhythmic movement boldly and imaginatively taught. It can be enjoyed by the nonambulatory in beds and wheelchairs, by the crippled and other health impaired who need mild range-of-motion exercise, and by the thousands of youngsters who find greater fulfillment in individual and dual activities than in team sports. Whereas much of physical education focuses upon cooperation, competition, and leadership-followership, creative dance offers opportunities for self-discovery and self-expression. It is axiomatic that a child must understand and appreciate his body and its capacity for movement before he can cope with the external demands of the world. The additional barriers to self-understanding and self-acceptance imposed by a handicapping condition intensify the need for carefully guided, nonthreatening movement experiences designed to preserve ego strength, increase trust, and encourage positive human relationships. Gesture, pantomime, dance, and dance-drama can substitute for verbal communication when the child lacks or mistrusts words to express his feelings.

Dance is an integral part of physical education. As such, it must be given the same amount of time and emphasis in the curriculum as other program areas. Table 28 presents Guidelines for Children's Dance.

The emphasis, at least for normal children, is clearly upon guided discovery and motor creativity. Most handicapped children can benefit from the same kinds of dance experiences as their peers. The exception is the pupil whose educational prescription indicates that he cannot yet cope with freedom in a group setting or that he lacks the mentality and/or readiness for problem solving. Children whose understanding of language is too inadequate to comprehend the verbal challenges of movement exploration fare best in simple, repetitive activities.

Inherent in the nature of singing games, folk and square dance, ballet, and tap dance is perceptual-motor training. The teaching style used is drill, i.e., demonstration-explanation-imitation. Success is largely dependent upon visual and auditory perception, memory for steps and sequences of steps, and the ability of the body to do what the mind wills. The elements of time, space, force, and flow are established by the instructions. Structure is reinforced by the tempo of the music, the formation in which the dancers stand, and the spatial relationships between couples. The emphasis is upon correct imitation rather than creative discovery. The pupil knows exactly what is expected of him and finds security in performing the same steps as everyone else. The competent teacher assures success by breaking the parts of a dance down to a level commensurate with the students' skills. A dance for moderately and severely retarded children might involve nothing more than following the leader in the execution of simple rhythmic activities in an AB or ABA form. The nature of the dance experiences provided a child should depend upon his educational prescription. Whenever possible, all of the activities in Table 28 should be included.

Creative Dance is a term used primarily in

1. Nancy W. Smith, "Prologue," in *Children's Dance* edited by Gladys Andrews Fleming (Washington, D. C.: AAHPER, 1973), p.v.

Table 28 *Guidelines for Children's Dance*[2]

Movement-Centered Dance Activities

The following movement-centered activities are basic to children's dance development and, when adapted to age level, should form the major part of the dance curriculum from early through middle childhood and beyond. It is upon the success of these experiences, especially the first four, that satisfactory and satisfying dance learnings will depend.

Experiences evolving from the use of the movement elements of space, time, force, and the development of an awareness of sequential changes in body shape.

Movement exploration, improvisation, investigation, and invention, using dance ideas such as those evolving from experiences with movement elements, from imaginary and literary sources, from properties of various kinds, or from music and other types of sound accompaniment.

Experiences with movement which help to synchronize it with musical structure, such as pulse, accent, phrasing; the development of sensitivity to the quality of musical sounds and the ability to relate to them in many different ways.

Experiences with basic locomotor and nonlocomotor movements; making combinations of these movements; discovering and learning traditional dance steps.

The organizing of movement into dances of various complexities.

The relating of dance movement to other curriculum experiences, such as art, music, science, social studies, and language arts—wherever and whenever appropriate.

Of the many kinds of "learned" dances, certain ones help to motivate movement in early childhood. Some of these are known as action or movement songs, others as singing games or song dances. These should be included in a comprehensive dance curriculum.

Traditional folk dance patterns are best left for the middle childhood years, where they will be learned quickly and danced with satisfaction if based upon earlier learnings. Further experiences which might be included in the dance program for the middle childhood years are the following.

Experiences with movement, arrived at through exploration, which can be used to increase body strength, flexibility, and precision.

Experiences in ethnic and popular "fad" dance patterns.

Opportunities for performing dances for schoolmates other than regular classmates and possibly for outsiders, such as parents.

Sharing and reacting to other children's dances.

2. Task Force on Children's Dance, "Guidelines for Children's Dance," *JOHPER*, Vol. 42, No. 6 (June, 1971), p. 22.

TABLE 28 *Guidelines for Children's Dance—Continued*

Audience-Centered Dance Activities

The following audience-centered experiences should expose the child to dance as a performing art, helping him to understand and appreciate its ramifications. Children of all ages can participate as an audience to their aesthetic and artistic advantage.

Seeing pictures and slides of dance.

Seeing films of concert dance artists.

Seeing and discussing lecture-demonstrations by professional and semiprofessional dancers, with active participation when possible.

Seeing concert or theatre dance programs appropriate to age level and experience.

Participating in other enriching experiences, such as dramatic performances, music concerts, museum exhibits, or book and science fairs.

early childhood education and the elementary schools. It implies a movement exploration approach to self-discovery, creativity, and nonverbal communication. The instructional environment is one of problem solving; there is no demonstration and no imitation. The content is a variety of movement experiences through which the child learns to manipulate the elements of force, space, time, and flow. Since dance is independent of other art forms, these movement experiences do not necessarily involve music nor accompaniment to sounds. The concept of *rhythmic movement* in creative dance relates to the natural rhythm of the body and the universe and not to the ability to keep time with externally imposed accompaniment.

Creative dance is the first form of dance to which children should be exposed. It is probably more valuable in the curriculum of children with handicapping conditions than any other form. Like sports, creative dance can be individual, dual, or group depending upon readiness to interact, trust, and share with others. Just as games are considered lead-up activities to regulation sports, creative dance

can serve as the foundation for modern or contemporary dance.

Modern Dance, also called contemporary dance, is one of the fine arts. It presupposes an understanding and appreciation of the body as a tool for self-expression and the ability to manipulate force, space, time, and flow in movement. Beginning courses in modern dance are replications of the content and experiences of *creative dance.* Once this background is gained, instruction in modern dance generally focuses upon the improvement of technique (movement skills) and/or choreography (creativity skills). Just as some persons engage in sports for the joy of moving, some pupils dance because it is inherently satisfying. Others, like highly skilled athletes, seek excellence in public performance.

Movement Elements

Both creative and modern dance focus upon the movement elements. *The element of space* can be broken down into several factors:

1. Direction of body movement: right, left, forward, backward, sideward, up, down, in, out, over, under.

2. Level of movement: high, low, medium or of body position: lie, sit, squat, kneel, stand.

3. Dimension of movement: large, small, wide, narrow, tall, short.

4. Path of movement: direct (straight) or indirect (curved, zigzag, twisted, crooked).

5. Focus of eyes: constant, wandering, near, far, up, down, inward, outward.

The element of shape pertains to the different shapes which the body can assume. Dance therapists using the concepts of effort-shape devised by Rudolph Laban and Warren Lamb refer frequently to *shaping*. Developmentally children are said to demonstrate *horizontal shaping* at ages 4-5; *vertical shaping* at ages 5-6; *sagittal shaping* at ages 6-7; two shaping combinations at ages 8-12; and three shaping combinations in adolescence and maturity.

1. *Horizontal shaping* is the ability to shape in the horizontal plane with widening and narrowing (spreading and enclosing) movements. The horizontal plane includes all rotatory movements, i.e., turning toward or away from a stimulus.

2. *Vertical shaping* is the ability to shape in the vertical plane with rising and sinking (ascending and descending) movements.

3. *Sagittal shaping* is the ability to shape in the sagittal plane with forward and backward (advancing and retreating) movements.

The element of time can be broken down into several factors:

1. Tempo or rate of speed of movement: fast, slow, accelerating, decelerating.

2. Rhythm: even or uneven referring to regularly or irregularly timed movements.

The element of force (effort). Dance educators seem to prefer the term *force* to denote such qualities of movement as heavy, light, tensed, relaxed, strong, weak. Laban used the term *weight* defined as the measurable degree of strength used in the action. Dance therapists who adhere to effort-shape concepts prefer the term *effort* which is defined as the way in which kinetic energy is expended in space force, and time.

The element of flow is sometimes separated from force to describe free versus bound movement. *Flow* also refers to the ease with which transitions are made from one movement sequence to another. The element of *flow* may be especially important in working with hyperactive, labile, or emotionally disturbed children since it can be associated with precise feeling states which lend insight into problems of self-control. Flow can be judged on a seven point continuum ranging from hyperactive, uncontrolled, free, abandoned, exaggerated, and fluent at one extreme to inhibited, restrained, bound, repressed, tied-up, and overcautious at the other extreme.

In creative dance, activities are designed to give experience in the manipulation of these movement elements and their inherent factors. The term *creative dance* is somewhat of a misnomer if creativity is defined as fluency, flexibility, originality, and elaboration. Dance experiences may be shaped to contribute to self-discovery, nonverbal communication, or creativity. It is important that the educator emphasize one of these at a time rather than attempting to accomplish all objectives simultaneously. Table 29 depicts the vast differences in the movement problems to be solved under each objective.

Table 29 *Questions to Elicit Specific Behavioral Traits through a Study of the Element of Space*

Self-Discovery	Nonverbal Communication	Creativity

Can you define space?
  a) Own
    inner, out boundaries,
    top, bottom boundaries
  b) Others
  c) Shared
Do you understand spatial factors
  as they relate to movement?
  a) Direction—Can you make
    your body go up, down, for-
    ward, backward, sideward?
  b) Level—Can you move
    through space on a low,
    medium or high level?
  c) Dimension—How large a
    movement can you make
    with your arms?
  d) Path—Can you walk in a
    direct pathway? an indi-
    rect pathway?
  e) Focus—Can you maintain
    continous focus with a
    moving object?
Can you execute movements for
  traversing space?
Direction
What locomotor movements enable
  the body to go up and down?
  a) jump
  b) hop
  c) leap
What locomotor movements
  can be used to go forward
  and backward?
  a) animal walks
  b) human walk
  c) run
  d) jump
  e) hop
  f) gallop, skip
  g) leap
  h) schottische, polka, etc.
	How can movement be used to
	  show possession of space or
	  of objects in space?
	Can you guess what space be-
	  longs to another by his move-
	  ments?
	Can he guess the boundaries of
	  your space?
	How might you show possession
	  of space if you were
	  a) male or female lion with a
	    litter of cubs
	  b) softball player sharing
	    the field with other players
	  c) dog guarding a bone
	  d) automobile driver on a busy
	    freeway
	  e) standing in line at a cafe-
	    teria
	What kind of communication move-
	  ments can you make when
	  a) someone invades your space
	  b) you wish to share your
	    space with a friend
	  c) you wish to share the space
	    of a stranger
	  d) you are frightened to ex-
	    plore a new space
	  e) you are depressed or lonely
	    in your space
	How does the color (hue) and
	  lightness or darkness of a space
	  affect your movements?
	How does the size of a space
	  affect your feeling-tone and
	  your movements?
	How does sound (noise or quiet)
	  in a space affect your move-
	  ments?
	How do you move if you are lost
	  in space versus confident of
	  your directions?
		Fluency
		  How many different ways
		  can you move in space?
		Flexibility
		  Is your fluency all in one
		  category or do you shift
		  easily using all possible
		  categories: direction,
		  level, dimension, path,
		  focus. Do you use differ-
		  ent categories of locomo-
		  tor movements as body
		  upside down versus right
		  side up; body weight on
		  one limb versus two, three,
		  or four limbs; et cetera.
		Originality
		  How many of your move-
		  ments are novel in the
		  sense that no one else
		  thinks of them?
		Elaboration
		  Do you experiment with
		  variations of locomotor
		  movements as performing
		  them with toes pointed in
		  versus toes pointed out?
		  Do you embellish your
		  movements with extra
		  identifiable details?
		Risk Taking
		  Do you have the courage
		  to risk using your body in
		  new ways in space?
		Complexity
		  Are you challenged to
		  group movements to-
		  gether in new sequences,
		  to experiment with various
		  forms, to create an orderly
		  composition out of chaos?

Table 29 *Questions to Elicit Specific Behavioral Traits—Continued*

Self-Discovery	Nonverbal Communication	Creativity

Other Spatial Factors
  Locomotor and nonlocomotor factors applied to each of spatial factors
Can you execute movements in each of the planes: horizontal, vertical, sagittal?
Are you aware of specific joints and body parts in space?
		Curiosity
		  Are you willing to devote time and energy to exploring all possible movement alternatives?
		Imagination
		  Do you have the power to visualize movement sequences beyond the limits of your performing ability?

Self-discovery aims at developing an understanding and appreciation of the body and its capabilities. The acquisition of information about movement elements, the development of language skills, and improved motor coordination are all implied as the pupil is guided toward the correct answer to each question. The emphasis, however, should be on the joy of movement and discovery of what the body can do, not on the acquisition of skills which can be measured and graded. It seems best to avoid grading children's early attempts at movement. The physical educator must remain ever aware that some handicapped children, particularly those with brain damage, have special problems in the perception and subsequent manipulation of space and time factors.

A child may understand and appreciate his body and derive great satisfaction from his exploration of space but still be unable to use movement to convey his needs, wishes, feelings, and moods to others. In contrast, some severely handicapped persons like Helen Keller and Christy Brown have become quite adept at nonverbal communication with only limited movement capabilities. The mastery of sign language and pantomime broadly interpreted can be dance education. The use of gesture as expressive movement can be traced back to Dalcroze, but dance specialists have not typically focused upon the communicative aspects of dance in education. In the last two decades, the increasing incidence of emotionally disturbed persons and the evolution of dance therapy as a new profession have led to a reexamination of dance as a means of helping individuals relate to one another and to communicate meaningfully without words.

The traits which researchers claim comprise creativity have little to do with communication, skill in movement, or understanding of self. Ideally dance experiences leading to self-discovery and increased skill in communication will foster fluency, flexibility, originality, and elaboration but the number of outstanding dance performers who lack creativity cannot be denied. Clearly the traits of creativity must receive special attention in early childhood. The learning disabled pupil may appear more creative than his peers because perceptual deficits force him to see the world in a different perspective. Perhaps this is a strength which can be built upon. The crippled child confined to a wheelchair may have a beautiful creative mind capable of choreography if his imaginative powers are sharpened by many and varied opportunities to view dance and study movement elements.

Rhythm Skills

Dance is an independent art form. It can exist without music, accompaniment, costumes, scenery, or props. Traditionally, however, a major objective in dance education has been to teach children to relate movement effectively to accompanying sounds and to music. Too often this objective has been implemented by encouraging children to listen to a piece of music, a song, or a poem and then to develop movement sequences which fit the accompaniment. This approach tends to *turn off* those pupils with problems of auditory perception and timing. Many handicapped children do not respond naturally to pulse beats nor to the time intervals between the beats. With such children, it is advisable to separate instruction in dance from that in music until success is achieved in one or the other.

King, as well as several other authorities, recommends that sound rhythms initially should follow the tempos of the children, not vice versa as is traditionally the practice.[3] Ernie Davis, outstanding in his work with mentally retarded children, concurs that the teacher should beat the drum to the tempo established by the child, thereby ascertaining that his first attempts to move with accompaniment are successful. Every effort should be made to determine the natural rhythm of the child—whether he favors fast, slow, or medium tempos; 4/4 or 3/4 phrases; the rhythmic pattern or the underlying beat; whether he responds to accents; and whether he makes transitions from one tempo to another. During this period of observation the

child should be encouraged to make up his own accompaniment: a song, a nursery rhyme, a verse, hand clapping, foot stamping, or use of a tambourine, drum, or jingle bells. Only when the child gives evidence of moving in time to his own accompaniment should the next progression be introduced, that of conforming to an externally imposed rhythm.

Elements of Rhythm

Rhythmic structure in dance has four aspects: *pulse beats, accents, rhythmic patterns,* and *musical phrasing.*

1. *Pulse beat,* the underlying beat of all rhythmic structure, can be taught as the sounds of walk or run; the ticking of a clock, watch, or metronome; the tapping of a finger; the clapping of hands; or the stamping of feet. The beats can occur in fast, medium, or slow tempos and in constant or changing rates of speed.
2. *Accent* is an emphasis, i.e., an extra loud sound or extra hard movement. Syllables of words are accented, and beats of measures are accented.
3. *Rhythmic* pattern is a short series of sounds or movements which is superimposed on the underlying beat and described as even or uneven. Illustrative of *even* rhythmic patterns are the walk, run, hop, jump, leap, step-hop, schottische, and waltz. Illustrative of *uneven* rhythmic patterns are the gallop, slide, skip, two-step, polka, and bleking. In rhythmic patterns the duration of time between beats varies. The simplest patterns for children are as follows:
   (a) *Uneven* long short patterns as in the gallop, skip, and slide in 6/8 tempo

3. Bruce King, *Creative Dance.* (New York: Bruce King Studio, 1970), p. 24.

(b) *Even* twice as fast or twice as slow walking patterns in 4/4 tempo

Walk ♩ ♩ ♩ ♩   4 steps to a measure

Run ♫ ♫ ♫ ♫   8 steps to a measure

Slow walk ♩ ♩   2 steps to a measure

4. *Musical phrasing* is the natural grouping of measures to give a temporary feeling of completion. A phrase must be at least two measures long. It is the expression of a complete thought or idea in music. Phrasing may help to determine the *form* of a modern dance composition, and children should be guided in the recognition of identical phrases within a piece of music. One movement sequence is created for each musical phrase; identical phrases may suggest identical movement sequences.

Some children require no special help in movement to music. They do not need adapted dance. Others who have grown up in homes without music or who have central nervous system deficits affecting temporal perception must be provided a carefully designed progression of experiences broken down into parts so small that success is assured. A succession of units might include:

(1) creative movement without accompaniment in which an idea, feeling, or mood is expressed

(2) creative movement with the child encouraged to add sound effects

(3) creative movement interspersed with discovery activities in which the child can beat a drum, clash cymbals, or use other rhythmic instruments as part of his dance-making process. No instructions are given on how to use the instruments; they are simply made available along with the freedom to incorporate sounds as he wishes

(4) creative movement accompanied by the teacher or another pupil using a variety of interesting sounds which fit the child's dance-making

(5) discussions concerning what kind of accompaniment best supports the theme or idea of different movement sequences; through problem-solving the child tells the teacher what kind of accompaniment he wants; the idea is tried, after which the child evaluates whether it worked or not

(6) introduction of the concept that a dance can be repeated over and over again; it has some kind of *form*—at least a beginning and an end—and both movements and accompaniment must be remembered so that they can be reproduced.

At this point the pupils learn the difference between dancing, i.e., moving for pleasure, and making a dance. They are helped to see their creation as an art product which may endure like a painting or a musical composition. They take pride in organizing their movement sequences into an integrated whole and comparing their dance-making process and product with those of dance artists on the various films which can be rented for this purpose. Since handicapped children typically become adults with an abundance of leisure, it is extremely important that spectator appreciation of modern dance and ballet be developed concurrently with their first attempts at dance making. Perhaps a performing group from a local high school or college can be invited in to demonstrate dance compositions. It is futile to expect children to retain excitement about dance making (choreography) unless they are exposed to the art products of others and led to believe that dance is a significant part of the cultural-entertainment world.

Only when dance experiences in which movement is primary and accompaniment is secondary prove successful should the study of rhythmic skills be introduced to children known to be weak in temporal perception. These pupils typically will be off the beat as often as on it; they are likely to accent the wrong beat of a measure; and they may find the recognition of musical phrases hopelessly frustrating. Dance researchers have not yet designed studies to investigate the learning problems of these pupils. There seems to be some feeling among dance educators that any pupil can keep in time with the music if he tries hard enough. Such is not the case! Just as reading specialists are seeking alternative approaches to teaching their subject, dance educators must devise ways in which the rhythmically disabled and retarded pupil can find success. Murray, even in the early 1950s, stressed that calling attention to inaccurate response and creating tensions through continuous drill do not solve the problem.[4] Nothing is sadder than a child concentrating so hard on tempo that the joy of movement is lost. If he does not keep time to the music, then truly he may be hearing a different drum beat.

Both the dance educator and the dance therapist rely heavily upon the medium of creative dance to accomplish certain objectives. Dance education can be therapeutic just as dance therapy can be educational. Certainly the adapted physical educator who uses creative dance as a means of helping handicapped children to understand and appreciate their bodies and their movement capabilities is engaged in a therapeutic endeavor. He does not, however, consider his work to be dance therapy anymore than he would claim to be doing physical therapy or occupational therapy. Since the incorporation of the American Dance Therapy Association, Inc., in May of 1966, dance therapy has gained increasing recognition as an independent profession.

Dance educators, therapists, and artists may use similar approaches in working with handicapped persons. The unique professional preparation of each of these specialists, however, enables them to accomplish different objectives. The dance therapist, with a strong background in psychology, may label his activities as rhythmic body action, spontaneous dance, dramatic play, fantasy action, movement exploration, improvisation, or relaxation. He generally avoids the word *teach* since therapy implies affective rather than cognitive behavioral changes.

Dance can be an art form, an educational experience, or a therapeutic tool. It is readily adaptable to widely diversified needs, ages, and objectives.

The places where dance lives—space, time, energy, motion, are so broad and general that it has a spectrum which will stretch to enormous distances to encompass feeling and emotion. At one end is dance as an art form and at the other end is dance in the classroom as an exercise in learning experience.[5]

Bella Lewitzky
California Institute of the Arts at Valencia

Figure 12.1 attempts to depict dance activities which comprise the spectrum of feeling and emotion. Dance therapy forms the base of the spectrum, for it emphasizes rhythmic, expressive movement as a means of establishing initial contact with human beings who have lost the capacity to relate effectively to others. It aims to provide safe, nonjudgmental experiences in body action which lead to increased trust and improved communication. At the top of the theoretical model is dance as an art form, the vision of most dance educators as they guide their pupils toward creativity, motor skill, and communication.

Rhythmic body action, a term used more in

4. Ruth Lovell Murray, *Dance in Elementary Education* (New York: Harper and Row, 1953), p. 167.
5. Bennett Schiff, *Artists in Schools* (Washington, D. C.: National Endowment for the Arts, n.d.), p. 124.

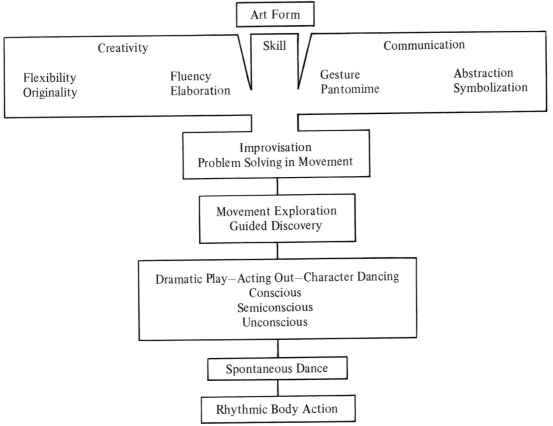

Figure 12.1. A theoretical model of dance in the spectrum of feeling and emotion.

dance therapy than in education, was coined by Marian Chace in her classic definition of dance therapy as

. . . a specific use of rhythmic body action employed as a tool in the rehabilitation of patients in present-day institutions. [6]

Rhythmic body action may be nothing more than rocking back and forth, clapping, or stamping. It may involve the entire body or only parts. Broadly defined, the term rhythmic body action can encompass all authenic dance experiences. In therapy with deeply disturbed, withdrawn, depressed, or catatonic patients, rhythmic body action in a circle is often a first step toward socialization. The movements in

the initial stages of dance therapy are similar to the warm up techniques used in dance education—arm and leg swings, stretches, and eventually total body involvement through locomotor activities. The purpose is different, however, since the therapist uses this approach to help the patient to relate to the group, to assay his loneliness through moving in unison with others, rather than to increase muscle flexibility and prevent injury. Rosen summarizes the desired outcomes of rhythmic body action.

6. Marian Chace, "Dance Alone is Not Enough. . ." from mimeographed materials distributed by St. Elizabeth's Hospital and Chestnut Lodge in Washington, D. C.

In a group, the patient learns that his individualized ways of moving are acceptable, and he learns to accept others and their individualized patterns; he learns to move in harmony and unison with others, to follow and to lead; and as he participates in all the varied movement experiences of the group, he becomes more and more capable of functioning as a part of it. If he is permitted he will dance out spontaneously the compelling impulses of his life and he will feel gratification and pleasure in the experience of being able to express them so vividly, with his body. [7]

Spontaneous dance, a term given to therapeutic connotations by Bender and Boas [8] in their work with disturbed children at Bellevue Hospital in New York, refers to locomotor and nonlocomotor activities initiated by the children themselves in a play setting. The inhibitions and resistance of patients may be overcome by encouraging them to execute cartwheels, somersaults, runs, leaps, and skips. Movement seems to stimulate children into expressing deeply buried fantasies and personal conflicts. Bender and Boas noted that the children talked through and explained their fantasies while engaged in movement and unaware that they were providing data for the psychologists and therapist. Spontaneous dance is seen also as a natural response to a jukebox or other music source. Even severely retarded children seem to derive great benefits from spontaneous dance.

The therapist may use spontaneous dance as a setting for evaluating the needs of a child. Persons trained in effort-shape record the characteristics of a patient's movements in signs which appear as follows:

The sign for space

The sign for weight

The sign for time

The sign for flow

North describes the use of these signs and their many variations in the assessment of personality as it is revealed through spontaneous movement behavior. [9] Excellent quantified rating scales appear in her book for separated appraisal of the patient's use of space, weight, time, flow, and selected combinations of these movement elements.

Dramatic play and character dancing provide opportunities for emotional catharsis. The acting out and/or living through old (or someone else's) real-life situations gives a sense of how it feels to fit within such situations. Children can also attempt to become that which they fear or admire, or do not understand. They can experience living the character in a story or a life-plot in a nonthreatening environment.

Characterization of stories provides opportunities for older children to regress in a socially acceptable manner and to receive help in distinguishing between real and make-believe worlds. Bunzel, who employed the technique of inventing stories which patients interpreted through movements, noted the frequency that roles were requested which seemed to fulfill wish-dreams. To illustrate, Bunzel states:

. . . the pretty daughter of a beautiful mother asked to play Cinderella in a story which she helped to develop. Surprisingly enough other members of the group agreed and after the performance, for the rest of the year, this girl was brought more and more into the foreground, where she found recognition and firm support. [10]

7. Elizabeth Rosen, *Dance in Psychotherapy* (New York: Bureau of Publications, Teachers College, Columbia University, 1957), p. 61.

8. Loretta Bender and Franziska Boas, "Creative Dance in Therapy," *American Journal of Orthopsychiatry* Vol. 2, No. 2 (April, 1941), pp. 235-245.

9. Marion North, *Personality Assessment Through Movement* (London: MacDonald and Evans Ltd., 1972).

10. Gertrude Bunzel, "Psychokinetics and Dance Therapy," *Journal of Health, Physical Education, and Recreation* Vol. 19, No. 3 (March, 1948), p. 180.

Character dancing, as used in dance therapy, entails the assumption of the role of an imaginary character like, for instance, a giant. The main objective of character dancing is to provide socially acceptable outlets for controlled regression and sublimation of aggressive and erotic drives. Patients are given an opportunity to project aggressive and hostile feelings onto a make-believe character and to practice shifting from one behavior to another as in portraying such opposites as *a mean giant* and *a nice giant*.

Courtney uses the term *fantasy-action* as a special kind of dramatic play which enables children to identify with fantasied objects in order to work experimentally toward mastering the future.[11] Through the fantasy-action, children attempt within an imaginary world to solve real-life experiences with which they have not yet learned to cope.

Movement exploration is used similarly by the dance therapist and the dance educator. It is guided discovery in helping the child to find himself and test his movement effectiveness against reality. The child must exhibit readiness for understanding and accepting himself as he is and must be helped to realize that he is loved for what he is, not for what he can do.

Free exploration, invention, and improvisation are used interchangeably in children's

Figure 12.3. Watching a wadded plastic bag "grow" provides impetus for improvisation.

Figure 12.4. Moving like the expanding plastic bag.

dance. This technique allows children to create without regard for a plot or story line; it implies spontaneous, intuitive problem solving—movement and thought inseparable in the evolution process. Murray explains the process this way:

Even when a child is given complete freedom to move as he wishes, there usually must be a reason, a purpose, a catalyst to evoke such movement. It may be a problem which allows for a variety of solutions. It may be a piece of music of a certain quality to which movement is improvised. It may be a scarf or crepe paper streamers to wave about as he moves with them or makes them move. It may be any one of thousands of images he has chosen to interpret in

Figure 12.2. Fantasizing in the creative dance setting.

11. Richard Courtney, *Play, Drama, and Thought: The Intellectual Background to Dramatic Education* (London: Cassell and Co., Ltd., 1968), p. 88.

movement. It may merely be that he is "it" in Follow the Leader and must invent a sequence of movements for the group to follow. [12]

In dance therapy improvisations are used primarily in order to provide opportunities to fantasize in a socially acceptable manner and to release aggressive, hostile, or erotic feelings in a safe, nonjudgmental environment. In dance education practice in improvisation is thought to develop skills in choreography (dance making).

Pantomime and mimetic dance activities in the therapeutic setting help patients to establish contact with reality and provide practice in the selection of appropriate movements for expressing specific emotions or feelings. Mimetic dance activities also serve as an effective way of motivating patients to act out or talk about ideas and experiences associated with the past. Greater personal involvement is necessary in pantomime than in the other dance therapy activities.

Dance therapists focus primarily upon the development of communication and socialization skills whereas dance educators seek simultaneously to perfect motor skills, to elicit creativity in choreography, and to increase the communicative quality of dance as an art form. The adapted physical educator may identify more easily with the dance therapist than the dance teacher. Associate membership is open to him in the American Dance Therapy Association, Inc., and an increasing number of workshops are available for learning about therapeutic relationships and the dance.

The following pages written by a registered dance therapist offer specific ideas which the adapted physical educator can test in the school setting. In those parts of the country where dance therapists are available, they may be employed to work cooperatively with the adapted physical educator or to provide consultant services. It should be remembered that a person who uses dance therapeutically is not a dance therapist unless he has received the special extensive training which qualifies him to meet the registry standards of the American Dance Therapy Association, Inc.

Through the therapeutic use of rhythmic and expressive movements children gain better perspective about themselves, their own ideas, and their feelings. They come to know their bodies better. They gain skill and control as they move through space. They find ways to use body action constructively; insight is gained into the meanings implied in their body action; and a more accepting self-body-image is developed.

Therapeutic dance encourages and fosters children's faith in their own ideas and in their own ways of expressing these ideas. A sense of personal worth begins to emerge. Children begin to like themselves better as they come to believe in their own ideas and begin to realize that their ideas do count, are worth listening to and watching, and can be shared. Positive group relationships develop through sharing and experimenting with ideas. Opportunities begin to occur for gaining appreciative understanding of other persons' ideas and their ways of expressing them.

Working with the expression of feelings is interwoven in various ways into dance, both indirectly in body action at the nonverbal level and directly with words and action at a conscious level. It is usually characteristic of dance therapy techniques that emotional tensions are worked with indirectly by centering attention on how the muscles can be used—such as hard or fast, or slow or easy ways—rather than speaking directly to the children's feeling-states. When children express their tensions in forceful moving-out behavior, activities are centered around aggressive-moving circle *dances* or controlled slow-motion-aggressive-pantomime. At other times, fast running, challenging ways of jumping-falling-rolling-pushing-spinning, or tug-of-war facilitate the reduction of tensions. When tensions seem high, and forceful moving-out ac-

12. Ruth Lovell Murray, *Dance in Elementary Education* (New York: Harper and Row), 1963, p. 48.

Figure 12.5. Five-year-old moves in response to "What Does Ugly Look Like?"

tion seems contraindicated because the children's behaviors are expressed in depressed turned-in movements, the action moves into gently-paced rocking, swaying, swinging, controlled slow rolling, or tension-relaxation muscle isolation movements. On other occasions, when the children's tension levels are not high, activities focus on feelings directly at a conscious level. Only then do the children experiment with the different ways that feelings can be expressed through movement.

Activities Used With Children in Dance Therapy

Some of the activities used in helping children become aware of their bodies and how their muscles work include the following:

1. Stretches, contractions, relaxations: Individually, with partners, and in moving circle-dance action.

2. Opposites movements: Experimenting with such movements as tall-short, wide-narrow, fast-slow, stiff-floppy, open-closed, heavy-light, high-low.

3. Feeling the floor different ways with bodies: By rolling across the floor stretched out full length at varying speeds and levels of muscle tension; rolling around in tight curled-up balls; doing front and back somersaults; crumpling body movements to effect collapsing to the floor; free falls sideward-forward-backward.

4. Exploring movement through space: Making different shapes and patterns; creating geometric patterns; *writing* imaginary letters and numbers with their bodies stationary and/or traveling.

5. Using different traveling styles across the floor: Running, jumping, walking, and creeping; variations within each style; working individually, with partners, and with groups of different sizes.

6. Muscle isolation: Using specific parts of the body in movement patterns while the rest of the body remains immobile; or following the action of the specific set of muscles leading a movement pattern; immobilization of body parts by playing *freeze* and *statue* games which stop movement in midaction; continuing on in movement retaining the *frozen* or *statue* position; having partners arrange each other's bodies into shapes or *statues*.

7. Reflection movement patterns of others: Moving in synchrony with a partner's movements as though looking in a mirror; moving on phrase-pattern behind a partner as though echoing his movements; moving in opposite patterns to partner's; reflecting similar or complementary movement patterns, yet different.

Figure 12.6. Reflecting the movement patterns of others.

Children's ideas can be encouraged to emerge in a variety of ways. At times emphasis is upon verbalization of abstract, conceptual ideas and at other times the focus is on body movement expression. Many times verbal and physical expression are combined. The following activities are some of the experiments and experiences which children seem to enjoy.

1. Single word or object stimulus

   e.g., "How many different ideas can the word 'beach' remind you to think about?" "What kinds of ideas come to you when you hear the word 'beach'?"

   e.g., "How many different ways can you pretend to use a popsicle stick?"

2. Imaginary props

   e.g., "Without telling us what it is, think of one particular thing or object you could use in three different ways. Show us how you would use it. After you have finished using it three different ways call on us and we will try to guess what objects you were using." Sometimes, after the child has completed his turn, and his object has been guessed, the other children contribute ideas orally on how the object could also be used. Stress is placed on being creatively supportive of each other's ideas.

3. Word cues

Words written on slips of paper are drawn in turn; the child translates the word into pantomime or dance movement. As the other children think they recognize the word cue they join in with the movement in their own ways and within their own framework of understanding. When the action is stopped verbal comparison is made of the meanings the children gave to their movement interpretations. Observations and comments are shared about the different ways used to express the same word-meaning in movement. Movement can then resume with the children's sharing of each other's movement styles. The word cues are usually presented in categories.

e.g., *doing*—chopping, hiding, twisting, carrying, hurrying, touching, dropping, sniffing, bouncing, flying, planting, pushing.

people—old person, mailman, maid, nurse, airplane pilot, cook, policeman, doctor, hunted criminal, fireman, mother, baby.

muscle isolation dances—shoulder dance, head dance, knee dance, hip, hand, elbow, foot, leg, knee, back, finger.

feelings—ashamed, surprised, sad, stuck-up, angry, worried, greedy, jealous, happy, excited, in love, afraid, disgusted.

animals—bee, horse, alligator, lion, snake, spider, elephant, crab, butterfly, worm, monkey, gorilla, mouse.

mime dramas—underwater adventure, a scary time, at the beach, at a bus stop, going on a picnic, climbing a mountain, a visit to the zoo, on a hike outdoors, an afternoon in the park, a baseball game.

a happening story—a siren blowing, red light flashing, thick fog, whistle blowing, fire burning, animal sounds, gun firing, child crying, dream happening, rushing water.

4. Different ways over and under a rope
As a rope is gradually raised or lowered the children use as many different ways as they can to move over or under the rope without touching it.

5. *Idea Box*
Sometimes, a box is kept in which the children put various objects they find or like.
e.g., Leaves, crayon bits, combs, brushes, tiny statues, clothes pins, buttons, pictures, paper clips, rubber discs.
Periodically, an object is taken from the box to *play around* with. The different ideas the children think up about the object can be taken into creative movement, creative storytelling, or creative dramatics.

6. Stories
Sometimes stories are read to the children so they can make up their own endings and/or think about the possible alternative endings which can be used. The stories and the possible endings can be translated into dramatic action, either in part or total.

When feelings are focused on directly, and at a conscious level, children can experiment with different ways feelings can be expressed through movement. The following activities illustrate some of the ways which children can purposefully work with feelings or feeling-tones.

1. Descriptive mime or *dance* movements to a stimulus word indicating a specific feeling.
e.g., The word cue game listed in working with ideas.

2. Descriptive mime, *dance*, or story evolving from a spontaneous sound made by the child reflecting the feeling-tone of that sound.

3. Feeling-tones in music
As music is played, the children respond in their own movement styles to the feeling-quality they *hear* in the music. When the action is finished the children compare their responses with each other, noting differences in responses to the same music. They also *try on* each other's feeling response or movement styles as the music is played again.

4. Stories *danced* to feeling-quality of the music
Turns are taken as individuals, pairs, or several children dance a story they have planned around the feeling-quality in the music. Sometimes the same music is chosen for the whole group; other times the children choose completely different music from one group, or pair, to the other.
When the *danced* story is finished, the children who watched attempt to relate their observations and interpretations of the story to the "dancers." After everyone has had a chance to interpret, the performer(s) describe their own story. When it seems appropriate, children share together some of the movement qualities presented in the stories.

5. Feeling-tones in colors
Lightweight fabrics of different colors are placed around the floor in order of child's color preference; talk about what a specific color "makes you think about"; list ideas on paper; try on some of the ideas in movement.
Can also list ideas about what kinds of feelings there might be reflected in a specific color; experiment and show through movement how one can move to express the feelings listed, either in pairs, groups, or individually.
Continue on from one color fabric to another. The single feeling-action can

be enlarged into pantomime or dramatizations of a story idea woven around the feeling.

6. Baseball game (or alternate sport) in different movement styles: All players work together reflecting a specific feeling in their movement styles as they "play" the game.

e.g., "sad"—the batter waits sadly for the ball to be thrown, the pitcher sadly throws the ball, the batter sadly hits at the ball. If he misses, everyone is sad and says so or makes sounds accordingly. The ball is sadly put back into play. If the ball is hit the batter sadly runs to the base as the pitcher or players sadly go after the ball and try to throw the runner out. Such mood continues throughout the play around the bases until the runner sadly makes a run or is thrown out.

happy—follows the same format as above. The batter is happy when he misses the ball or when he is thrown out. The pitcher is happy when the batter makes a base run or a home run.

e.g., *laughing-angry*—the simultaneous dichotomy of this type of expressive behavior becomes challenging and hilarious. Different combinations of opposite type feelings/sounds demand special awareness of how one uses expressive action. This also touches very closely on the actual reality of mixed communication many people use in less exaggerated fashion in everyday life.

Materials Used in Dance Therapy With Children

Soft materials are used in all three of the above areas for stimulating a variety of safe ac-tivities that are imaginative and self-structuring. Nylon fabrics of different hues, measuring two-and-a-half yards in length, aid in reducing tension and hyperactivity and in relaxing tight muscles. In response to the floating, smooth quality of colorful nylons, children move rhythmically stretching, turning, reaching, and covering themselves in various ways. Their actions seem to reflect a sensuous enjoyment and an aesthetic awareness as the fabrics float and move across their bodies. Paradoxically, the soft fabrics can become a factor in spatial structuring as well. At times, when children feel extremely tense and seem to have a need for containment, being wrapped completely immobile in the full width of the fabric, by either turning when standing or rolling when lying down, will have a relaxing and quieting effect. Without speaking directly to such needs, children will ask for this kind of containment by suggesting familiar activities that have included it in other movement contexts. Nylon fabrics also provide an intermediary focus for children who find it difficult to relate directly to other persons. Spin-arounds, with partners holding opposite ends of the fabric, aid in keeping distance yet staying together. Wrap-up spin-outs allow a moment's closeness with access to quick and immediate freedom from nearness. Imaginative play and imagery occur with the fabric being used as such items as clothing, costumes, bedding, housing, light-shielding to put a color glow in a darkened room. Aggressiveness is accommodated by wrapping a soft yarn ball inside one end of the fabric and throwing it as if it were a comet streaming through space. *Dodge fabric* has aggressive moments of fun and beauty combined when one or several fabrics are loosely wadded into a ball and thrown at a moving human target. The floating open of the fabric(s) while traveling in space sometimes creates unusual beauty. Children also like to lie down and be covered completely using one fabric at a time in layering fashion. As the layers of fabrics

Figure 12.7. Experiencing the spatial structure of soft floating fabric.

Figure 12.9. Experiencing the sensation of directional change in a different way.

Figure 12.8. Soft nylon has a relaxing and quieting effect.

Figure 12.10. Learning trust as the hammock descends.

deepen, children typically comment on the constant change of color and the increasing dimness as the layers thicken.

Soft, stretchy, tubular knit fabrics which are approximately three yards long have soothing, protecting properties. The tubular fabrics make excellent *hammocks* on which to lie and be swung. When persons alternate in lifting ends of the fabric, causing the body to roll from side to side, a special sensation of being moved in space is felt. An interesting sensation of directional change is experienced when running and bouncing forward into a tautly stretched fabric that *gives* and then bounces the person off backwards. Stretch-tube fabrics lend themselves well to non-directed dramatic play and fantasy-action. They become roads, rivers, roofs, *ghosts,*

hooded persons, Roman togas, stuffed sausages, pickles, grass, tunnels. Playing inside stretch-tube fabrics adds further dimension to their use. It is a way for children to shield themselves from direct observation and physical touch contact with other persons while at the same time being able to look out through the fabric and see the persons. When working inside, the fabrics can become an open-ended tunnel to explore, or a closed and safe haven for being swung, rolled, dragged gently around the floor, or for pretending all alone in fantasy-action. Inside the fabrics can also become a place to experiment with making different shapes and forms by bending and extending body parts against the softly resilient material. When lying outside on the fabric, and being swung gently, spontaneous pan-

Figure 12.11. Yarn balls permit safe release of aggressive tensions.

tomimes of *dreams* are easily evoked. These *dreams* touch deeply into children's unconscious urges and needs, and the expressive body action accompanying the dream fantasies allows for safe catharsis and emotional release of tensions reflected in the dream content. The fabrics provide for rocking and swaying when children need comforting and relaxing, without working openly or directly with those needs. *Games* that have been experienced earlier when the children were simply exploring the use of the fabrics can be repeated when the need for comforting arises.

Yarn balls, about six inches in diameter, permit many varieties of throwing activities for imaginative play as well as safe release of aggressive tensions. Imaginative ideation about different ways to throw, jump with, and bat the ball stimulate alternative ways of thinking as well as encourage children to risk expressing their ideas. Warm-up stretches are executed by using different body positions to transfer the ball to the next recipient. One-to-one synchronization of full body action occurs when partners try to support a ball between them with various parts of their bodies while traveling across the room. Yarn balls can be used purposefully aggressively for *bowling*, dodge ball. They can also be kept rolling around the floor by hand-batting vigorously back and forth. More structured and functionally demanding activities are done with rhythmically synchronized toss, catch, and rolling games. Isolations of body parts can be experienced by bouncing the ball off different parts of the body or by contacting the ball with a specific body part before releasing and passing it on to another person. In dramatic play and fantasy-action the balls become various kinds of foods, jewels, rocks, rockets, bombs, and the *equipment* for pretend games of baseball, kickball, touch football, and bowling.

Principles Upon Which Dance Therapy Is Based

With modification, the techniques of dance therapy are applicable to persons of most ages, and with most disabilities, because dance therapy focuses upon qualities of nonverbal communication in everyday life. Marian Chace, one of the major pioneers in the evolution of dance therapy as a profession, influenced persons who studied with her toward acceptance of principles which she felt were basic to dance therapy and common to all forms of therapy. She believed that the dance therapist keeps things simple by leading out from what is happening inside the patient rather than imposing the action from the outside. The therapist allows time for things to happen within the on-going action rather than trying to *do* a lot. Miss Chace recommended that the dance therapist work toward enriching experiences in a nonjudgmental, neutral way, without moralizing. This is best accomplished by working with the patient, rather than *on* him. It is essential that the dance therapist be secure. He must be able to listen and to see what is going on at the verbal level and yet remain aware of subtle nonverbal cues. The therapist should eminate friendliness, yet remain neutral and resist being caught up in the need to be liked by the patient. The disturbed person must be aided in relating to persons who are genuine and truthfully warm.

He needs relationship space that allows him to give back warmth without feeling threatened by the therapist's needs.

Therapeutic Tools

The *therapeutic tools* used by the dance therapist could be thought of as rhythm, touch, verbalization, space, and people. Activities are simply the media for the use of therapeutic tools.

It is the *movement of the patient*, rather than that of the therapist, which is used as a means of establishing the therapeutic relationship. By tuning in and sharing the patient's movements the therapist can say very clearly and quickly that he is *with him*. This allows them to *speak* to each other in movement. The therapist then works toward transcribing the patient's movements into reality-oriented and functional expressions since the patient is unable to do this for himself. The therapist also tries to influence change in the patient's distorted body-image through muscular action.

Basically, it is the rhythmical quality of expressive movement that enables the patient to use body action in safe ways that hurt no one. Open use of aggressive movements has less therapeutic value than rhythmic action which focuses on body awareness. For optimal results expressive movement must be under the patient's conscious rather than unconscious control. Rhythmic action also affords an area for relating that is outside both the patient and the dance therapist. It offers the satisfaction of sharing movement and minimizes destructiveness of action. There is no need felt for the movement to be realized in its destructive form. This leaves the patient free to go on to other things. For the moment, his pathological urges have been released rhythmically, constructively, and safely.

All of therapeutic body movement is geared toward getting in touch with as much of the skin's surface as possible. It is through tactile stimulation and muscular contraction that the patient regains contact with his body surface and comes to understand its boundaries. Direct touch by the therapist is used to reinforce the patient's growing ability to distinquish between himself and others.

Verbalization between the therapist and patient is geared to the meaning of muscular action rather than the feeling-tone behind the action. The patient comes to realize that his movement qualities are reality-based and that he is capable of purposive movement. Verbalization is not for telling the patient what to do, but for helping him to know where he is going and why.

The use of space is important in that it becomes an extension and reflection of the patient's body-image. If a patient is manicy and hyperactive in movement, his own space zone is felt as wide and scattered and as having tremendous force and power. The dance therapist then uses movements far apart from the patient and himself, coming in only tentatively as the patient will allow. The patient already feels that they are *together* even though they are actually far apart. If a patient is frozen or constricted in movement, the space zone is small and constricted. The dance therapist then moves in quite closely, but with care and awareness, because a constricted space is generally a supercharged zone. The dance therapist also uses space to encourage a *coming forward*. Such dance movements can provide safe areas for hostile body action that might have been used out of control. *Going forward* movements can provide safe areas for the withdrawn to find out he can come out and not be hurt, nor will he hurt anybody.

The ultimate goal of the dance therapist is for patients to work in a group. It reduces a one-to-one identification and increases opportunities for the patient to assume responsibility for his own growth rather than staying dependent upon the therapist.

Recommended Activities

1. Obtain a list of members and registered dance therapists from the American Dance Therapy Association, Inc., and invite those residing near your school to serve as guest speakers. Learn about graduate training in dance therapy and standards for registration.
2. Discuss similarities and differences between dance therapy and dance education.
3. Conduct several mini-lessons with children to demonstrate your competence in teaching creative dance. Do not try to conduct dance therapy until you complete advanced training.
4. Demonstrate your competence in teaching folk or square dance to both ambulatory and wheelchair pupils.

Recommended Readings in Dance Education

AAHPER. *Children's Dance.* Washington, D.C.: AAHPER, 1973.

Bruce, Violet R. *Dance and Dance Drama in Education.* London: Pergamon Press, 1965.

Cox, Rosann and Vick, Marie. *A Collection of Dances for Children.* Minneapolis: Burgess Publishing Co., 1970.

Fleming, Gladys. *Creative Rhythmic Movement: Boys' and Girls' Dancing.* Englewood Cliffs, New Jersey: Prentice-Hall, 1976.

Laban, Rudolf. *Modern Educational Dance.* second revised edition. London: MacDonald and Evans, 1963.

Mettler, Barbara. *Materials of Dance as a Creative Art Activity.* Tucson, Arizona: Mettler Studios, 1970.

Murray, Ruth. *Dance in Elementary Education.* third edition. New York: Harper and Row, 1975.

Robins, Ferris, and Robins, Jennet. *Educational Rhythmics for Mentally and Physically Handicapped Children.* New York: Association Press, 1968.

Recommended Readings in Dance Therapy

American Association for Health, Physical Education, and Recreation. *Dance Therapy: Focus on Dance VII.* Washington, D.C.: AAHPER, 1974.

American Dance Therapy Association. *Annual Proceedings.* Published each year. Write to ADTA for cost and titles of back issues still available.

Bartenieff, Irmagard, and Davis, Martha Ann. *Effort-Shape Analysis of Movement: The Unity of Expression and Function.* Bronx, New York: Albert Einstein College of Medicine, 1963.

Bernstein, Penny Lewis. *Theory and Methods in Dance-Movement Therapy.* Dubuque, Iowa: Kendall/Hunt Publishing Company, 1972.

Chace, Marian. Articles in many different periodicals. Write to the American Dance Therapy Association for a bibliography.

CORD. *Workshop in Dance Therapy: Its*

Research Potentials. The Proceedings of a Joint Conference by Research Department of Postgraduate Center for Mental Health, Committee on Research in Dance, and American Dance Therapy Association, November 10, 1968.

Kestenberg, Judith. "The Role of Movement Patterns in Development: 1. Rhythms of Movement," *The Psychoanalytic Quarterly,* Vol. 34, 1965, pp. 1-36. Other articles also in Vol. 34 and 36.

Laban, Rudolf, and Lawrence, F. C. *Effort.* London: MacDonald and Evans, 1947.

Laban, Rudolf. *The Mastery of Movement.* London: MacDonald and Evans, 1960.

Lamb, Warren, and Turner, David. *Management Behavior.* New York: International Universities Press, 1969.

———. *Posture and Gesture.* London: Gerald Duckworth and Co., Ltd., 1965.

Lowen, Alexander. *The Betrayal of the Body.* New York: Macmillan Company, 1967.

North, Marian. *Personality Assessment Through Movement.* London: MacDonald and Evans, 1972.

Rosen, Elizabeth. *Dance in Psychotherapy.* Brooklyn, New York: Dance Horizons, 1974.

Organizations

American Dance Guild, 124-16 84th Rd., Kew Gardens, New York 11415.

American Dance Therapy Association, Suite 216-E, 1000 Century Plaza, Columbia, Maryland 21044.

National Dance Association (NDA), an organization of AAHPER, 1201 Sixteenth Street NW, Washington, D.C. 20036.

Committee on Research in Dance (CORD), Dance Department Education 675D, New York University, 35 West Fourth Street, New York, New York 10003.

Dalcroze School of Music, 161 East 73rd Street, New York, New York 10021.

Dance Notation Bureau, Inc., 8 East 12th Street, New York, New York 10003.

Dance Horizons, 1801 E. 26th Street, Brooklyn, New York 11229.

Aquatics for the Handicapped

Figure 13.0. Though the child is orthopedically handicapped, he is not handicapped in the water.

. . . He might not be able to manage a tricycle, but he had the freedom of a large safe beach where he could run for a mile if he felt inclined. Beach balls eluded him—he could neither throw nor catch—but there was the warm sand to mess with, and the water itself. The big movement of Mike's young life came at three-and-a half, when he learned to swim . . . The beach baby turned into a water rat. By five he could safely swim out of his depth, and by six he not only had a crawl stroke, but was so at home in the water that he literally did not seem to know if he was on it or under it. [1]

Louise Clarke

Thus speaks a mother of her dyslexic son in a poignant account of learning to cope with learning disabilities. At the end of Clarke's book, Mike has graduated from Harvard University with a Doctoral degree; he still cannot "read, write nor talk too good either." But he has persevered in learning to compensate for his weaknesses and to utilize fully his strengths! Like other boys, he longed for athletic success, tried out for teams, failed. . . was especially awkward in baseball and handball. As an adult, he recalls the pleasure derived from swimming and its contribution to the maintenance of some ego strength throughout a childhood characterized by very few successes. Aquatics, perhaps more than any other aspect of the physical education program, appeals to persons with all kinds of conditions. Even those so severely involved as to be bedfast experience satisfaction in water play. The discipline of physical therapy has long recognized the rehabilitative values of exercises executed in water. As early as 1937 Charles Lowman, an orthopedic specialist, published a book on hydrotherapy.[2] Many public schools have Hubbard Tanks where physical therapists work with orthopedically handicapped children.

Therapeutic exercise underwater is especially valuable for the nonambulatory pupil whose body parts lack the strength to overcome the force of gravity. In the pool, the force of gravity is greatly minimized, permitting some range of movement to limbs which have none

when not immersed in water. Children who require crutches and/or braces to walk on land can often ambulate in water.

The methods of teaching the nine regulation swimming strokes to children with physical and mental deficits are similar to those traditionally employed with all beginners. If the primary purpose of swimming in the adapted physical education program were to develop skill, this chapter would be unnecessary. The progression of competencies for earning American Red Cross swimming certificates seems quite adequate. The following pages focus upon adapting swimming instruction to the needs of preschool children and/or any individual whose mastery of aquatic skills appears frozen at the prebeginner level. The content has been tested on children with learning disabilities and/or mental retardation who participate in a year-round aquatic program at the Texas Woman's University.

Over the years three prebeginner swimming certificates have evolved. Initially the levels of competency which the certificates represent were named after fish: minnows, crappies, and dolphins. The children were not as enamoured with these appellations as were the adults who created them. First of all, many of them had never seen real fish, live or dead, and to them the names were meaningless. Some of the pupils did report first-hand knowledge of fish but remembered the unpleasant odor more than the beauty of movement. Said one, "I don't want to be a fish—ugh—they stink." Still another problem arose with respect to self-concept; heavily muscled boys, particularly from economically deprived areas, had no intention of being "sissy minnows" regardless of their dependence upon the teacher in the water.

The three certificates subsequently were

1. Louise Clarke, *Can't Read, Can't Write, Can't Talk Too Good Either* (New York: Walker and Company, 1973), p. 9.
2. Charles L. Lowman, *Techniques of Underwater Gymnastics* (Los Angeles: American Publications, 1937).

designated as Explorer, Advanced Explorer, and Floater in accordance with the levels of competency achieved. These certificates were printed on cards of the same size and shape as the standard Red Cross certificates. Originally they came in different colors, but after the year that one little girl with Down's Syndrome sobbed all through the awards ceremony because her card was not white like that of her boyfriend, it was decided to make the cards uniform in color as well as size, shape, and format.

The motor tasks required for passing each certificate are listed in Table 30. The major achievement at the Explorer level is to release the teacher's hand and perform basic locomotor movement patterns independently at a distance several feet away from the side of the pool. It is not necessary to put the face in the water to earn Explorer status. Many young-sters initially are so terrified of the water that several lessons are required before they will loosen their deathlike grips on the teachers. Many additional lessons pass before enough courage is developed to let go of the side of the pool and walk independently. Nevertheless *all* students have earned the Explorer Certificate, demonstrating as much pride in its possession as do their peers with the regulation Red Cross cards.

The Advanced Explorer denotes two major accomplishments: putting the face in the water and willingness to lift the feet from the pool bottom, thereby assuming a horizontal position with the help of the teacher. At this level also the child begins to experiment with somersaults, standing on his head, walking on his hands, and other stunts which are not based upon the ability to float.

Earning the third and final prebeginner

Table 30 *Beginning Competency Levels of Swimming For Children*

Level I Explorer Movement exploration in the water	Level II Advanced Explorer Movement exploration in the water	Level III Floater Prebeginning swimming
1. Enter and leave water alone 2. Walk across pool holding rail 3. Walk across pool holding teacher's hand 4. Stand alone 5. Walk across pool pushing kickboard 6. Jump or hop several steps alone 7. Walk and do breaststroke arm movements 8. Do various locomotor movements across the pool 9. Blow bubbles through plastic tube 10. Blow ping-pong ball across pool	1. Put face in water 2. Blow bubbles (5 seconds) 3. Touch bottom or toes with hands 4. Retrieve objects from bottom 5. Assume horizontal position with teacher's help 6. Hold onto kickboard pulled by teacher 7. Jump into water without help 8. Take rides in back lying position 9. Change of level—squat to stand; stand to squat 10. Play follow-the-leader type water games 11. Demonstrate bracketing on back with kick	1. Blow bubbles (10 seconds) 2. Bracketing on front with kick 3. Change of position—stand, front lying with support, stand 4. Prone float 5. Change of position—stand, back lying with support, stand 6. Back float 7. Flutter kick using board 8. Jellyfish float 9. Perform breaststroke arm movements 10. Swim one-half width any style 11. Perform at least one stunt like stand or walk on hands, front somersault, back somersault, tub, surface dive

certificate is dependent upon the ability to relax sufficiently to float for several seconds. At this level also, the child usually begins to swim. More often his navigation is under the water than on top, and underwater swimming can be used to fulfill the requirement of one-half width. Long before the pupils learn to swim recognizable strokes they become quite proficient in the basic stunts of synchronized swimming. They develop creative routines to music which are weird combinations of walks, runs, jumps, hops, standing in place and stroking with arms, and regulation synchronized swimming stunts.

The water can be viewed as simply another medium for refining movement patterns and exploring time-space-self relationships. The Texas Woman's University aquatics program is coordinated with lessons in movement exploration conducted in the gymnasium; virtually every activity learned out of water is attempted also in the swimming pool. The movement exploration teaching style (Guided Discovery and Motor Creativity) described in Chapter 3 establishes the framework in which learning occurs. The three most important objectives of the program are (1) to improve self-concept, (2) to increase self-confidence, and (3) to develop courage. Secondary to these goals, the teacher concentrates upon dimensions of body image: (1) identification of body parts; (2) improvement of proprioception; and (3) development of such inner language concepts as bent versus straight, vertical versus horizontal, pike versus tuck; tuck layout versus front layout; and pull phase (application of force) versus recovery phase. As a technique for enhancing self-concept, the child is drilled on the *names* of the stunts and skills he learns to perform. As he acquires a vocabulary which enables him to share his successes with others, he seems to demonstrate increased motivation for undertaking new aquatic adventures. Moreover, this emphasis on vocabulary in the swimming setting reinforces words learned in the classroom and the

Figure 13.1. A one-to-one relationship in the water facilitates learning.

gymnasium, thereby contributing to transfer of learning and reducing development of splinter skills.

Differences Between Movement Exploration and Regular Swimming Instruction

Some of the differences between a movement exploration program in the water and regular swimming instruction are explicit in the following principles for guiding movement explorations.

1. The teacher is in the water with the children rather than on deck. Physical contact between teacher and pupil is based upon the needs of the learner for security and affection. Although independence in the water is the ultimate goal, it is not rushed.
2. The teacher avoids mentioning tasks like putting the face underwater which the pupil interprets as unpleasant. Instead game-like situations are devised which induce the child to attempt the task without conscious realization of what he is doing. The following anecdote demonstrates teaching.

I had been in the water with Charles for about twenty minutes and had had no success with anything I had tried to teach him. I was particularly concerned with getting him to put his entire face and head in the water. I finally decided to make a game out of it, so I borrowed the small inner tube from one of the other instructors. Without any type of explanation I placed the inner tube between Charles and myself and ducked under water and came up with it around my neck. Charles was delighted and asked me to do it again. After repeating it I asked him if he would like to put his head through the inner tube. Without answering my question, he completely submerged his body and came up with the inner tube around his neck. I was more than pleased and had him repeat it five or six times. Then I asked him to submerge without coming up under the inner tube. I received a very blunt "no." He told me he could not put his head under water and he did not wish to try. We continued using the inner tube for the remainder of the hour.

3. As few words as possible are used in teaching. Cue words like up, down, pull, recover, and kick 2-3-4 are substituted for sentences. A well-modulated voice helps convey the meaning of instructions. A *high* voice can be used for up movements and *low* (pitch) voice for down movements. The voice can be loud and forceful during the pull phase and soft and gentle during the recovery phase.

4. Corrections and modifications of movements are generally made by moving the child's limbs through the desired pattern of movement rather than by the explanation-demonstration technique. Some persons refer to this as the *kinesthetic* method of teaching since such input is proprioceptive.

5. Acceptance of the child is shown through frequent mirroring of his movements. Teacher and pupil take turns *following the leader* with precise imitation of postures, arm movements, and kicks.

6. Synchronized swimming, jumping, and diving are introduced much earlier than usual in swimming instruction. Emphasis is upon the combination of stunts and locomotor movements, i.e., creating sequences (routines) and remembering and executing sequences developed by others.

7. Bilateral, unilateral, and crosslateral movement patterns are encouraged in that order, reflecting an understanding of child growth and development. Thus the breast-stroke and the elementary backstroke are the first real swimming strokes to be introduced. The bilateral movements of the breaststroke usually appear, without the benefit of instruction in underwater swimming. Figure 13.2 through Figure 13.5 allow for a comparison of the simplicity of bilateral strokes with the relative complexity of crosslateral strokes.

The bilateral movements of the elementary backstroke are similar to those in angels in the snow and jumping jacks. Land drill is used before the children shower or after they dry and dress to assure transfer of learning. Drill in the water can be facilitated by suspending a hammock from the ceiling, using flotation devices, and lying on a table under the water.

Figures 13.2 and 13.3 show bilateral movements of the arms and legs in underwater swimming, the breaststroke, and the elementary backstroke. Figures 13.4 and 13.5 depict the more difficult crosslateral swimming strokes. Six kicks of each leg are coordinated with every cycle of arm movements. As the right arm pulls, for instance, the right leg kicks *up*, down, *up*. The emphasis in the flutter kick is on the up beat! It is essential that arm strokes and leg kicks be practiced in a horizontal rather than a standing position. Equally important, the teacher should demonstrate new skills in the horizontal position.

No stroke is more difficult to master than the front crawl. Although the rhythm of the flutter kick may come naturally to a few students, it is a nightmare for many others. Land drills to music 3/4 tempo with a strong

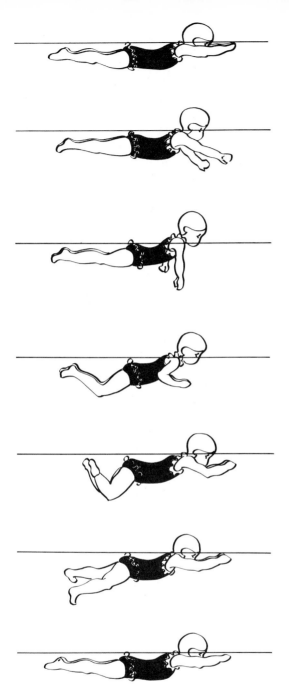

Figure 13.2. Bilateral movements of the arms and legs occur in underwater swimming and the breaststroke.

Figure 13.3. Bilateral movements of the elementary backstroke.

accent on the first beat in every measure may contribute to relaxed, effective kicking in the water; if not, the practice can be justified for its contribution to abdominal strength. Both in land drills and in the water there is a tendency to collaborate with the force of gravity and accentuate the downbeat; this error must be avoided. Devising some kind of contraption twelve to eighteen inches above the floor to be kicked on each upbeat may focus the pupil's attention on the desired accent.

The flutter kick warm-up exercise should begin in the position depicted in Figure 13.6 rather than with both legs on the floor since at no time during the crawl stroke are the legs motionless and in the same plane. With poorly coordinated pupils it is best to leave the arms motionless in the starting position until the rhythm of the kick is mastered. The verbal cues, *right-arm-pull* or *left-arm-pull* can be substituted for *kick-2-3*, even though the arms

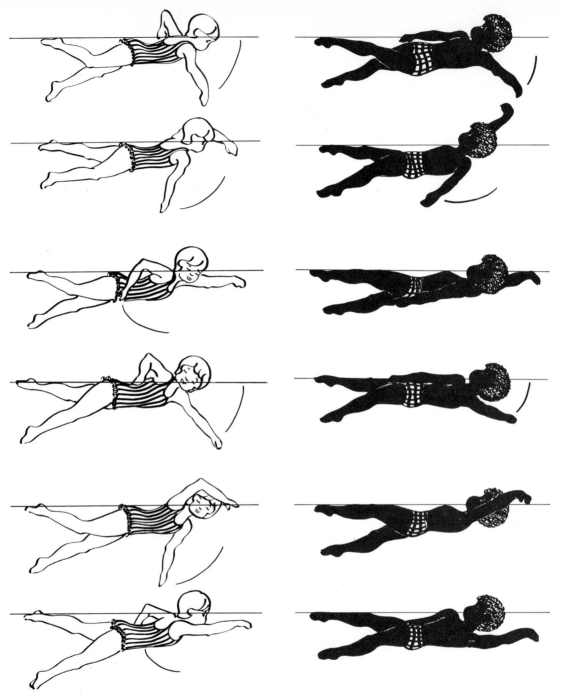

Figure 13.4. Crosslateral movements of the front crawl.

Figure 13.5. Crosslateral movements of the back crawl.

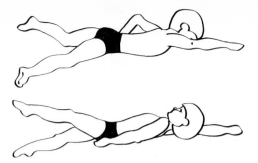

Figure 13.6. Ready position for flutter kick warm-up exercises on floor or bench.

do not move. The first progression for this exercise is lying on the floor; the next progression for this exercise is lying on a bench with arms and legs hanging over.

When a pupil demonstrates no progress in the flutter kick over a period of weeks, it can be safely assumed that the desired movement is not *natural* for him and that an alternate method of kicking should be substituted. In such instances the front crawl can be modified into the *trudgeon stroke* by substituting the scissors kick for the flutter kick.

8. The last difference between movement exploration in the water and regular swimming instruction is flexibility on the part of the teacher in modifying requirements in accordance with individual differences. Testing is planned upon the basis of the strengths of an individual, not pre-established competences which are thought to meet the needs of all beginner swimmers.

The American Red Cross teaches nine basic strokes. The student's ability to perform one or two of these strokes really well is the criterion for success in a program for the handicapped. Which stroke the child chooses makes no difference whatsoever as long as he feels safe in the water and enjoys swimming. One of the purposes of movement exploration is to guide him in the discovery of this stroke for himself.

Activities for the Explorer

Washcloth Games

Each child is supplied with a washcloth, and the swimming pool is compared with the bathtub at home. The teacher's relaxed patter of questions usually elicits the desired exploration of the water.

1. What do you do with a washcloth? Don't tell me; show me!
2. What part do you wash first? Did you wring the cloth out before you started to wash? Don't you wring it out first at home?
3. Did you wash behind your ears? the back of your neck? your elbows? your knees? your ankles? What about the soles of your feet? Are they clean?
4. Do you like to have someone wash your back? If you do, you can find a partner and take turns washing each other's back.
5. Can you play throw and catch with your partner by using the washcloth as a ball?
6. What happens if you miss the catch? Can you pick the washcloth off the bottom of the pool with your toes? With some other part of your body?
7. Let's play steal each other's washcloth. To begin, each of you must fold your washcloth and put it neatly over your shoulder or on top of your head. When I say go, move around stealing as many washcloths as you can but don't forget to protect your own. When I say stop, everyone must have one hand on the railing before I count to ten; then we will determine who is winner.

Sponge Games
Every pupil with a sponge

1. Do you see something at the bottom of the pool? That's correct! There are plates, saucers, bowls, glasses, and cups. Guess what your job is? That's correct! Recover the dishes anyway you wish, wash them with your sponge, and set the table on the

deck. Whoever finishes the most place settings wins.

2. Have you ever scrubbed down walls? Each of you find your very own space on the wall and let's see you scrub! Have you ever washed a car? Let's pretend the wall is a car! What else can we pretend the wall is? Does anyone know how to scrub the floor? Let's see!

3. See this big innertube. Let's use it to shoot baskets with our sponges. Can you make your sponge land inside the innertube?

4. What other target games can we invent with the sponges?

5. Dodge or Catch. This game is played like dodgeball except that the child has the option of dodging or catching. Occasionally someone may get hit full in the face with a wet sponge. Although a sponge cannot hurt, some children feel threatened by this activity; hence, the participants should be volunteers.

All the sponges in the water

1. Who can get his bucket filled with water first? The only method of getting water in the bucket is squeezing out sponges.

   a. Individual game—Who can recover the most sponges, squeeze them out, and toss them back in the water?

   b. Partner game—One pupil remains in the water, recovering sponges, and handing them to his partner on deck who squeezes the sponges and tosses them back into the water. (See Figure 13.7.)

2. Sponges of different colors are floating in the water. Children all have one hand on the pool railing. On the signal, *Go*, they respond to the teacher's question: "Who can recover a blue sponge and put it on the deck first?" A yellow sponge? A pink sponge?

3. Sponges of different shapes or sizes are floating in the water. Same instructions as above.

4. Who can recover two sponges and put one under each of his feet? How many of you

Figure 13.7. A sponge activity for the explorer: who can get their bucket filled with water first?

Figure 13.8. Parachute activities on land can be adapted to water.

are standing on sponges? Can you walk across the pool on the sponges?

Parachute Games

In the water a large sheet of clear plastic makes the best parachute; round table cloths and sheets can also be used. All of the parachute activities played on land can be adapted to the water. "Who can run under the parachute?" invariably gets the face in the water. "Who can climb over the parachute?" leads to taking turns riding on the magic carpet which is pulled through the water by classmates.

Blowing Games

These can be played either in or out of the water; they are important lead-up activities to rhythmic breathing.

1. Each child has a clear plastic tube which is 12 to 18 inches in length. Plastic tubing can be purchased in any hardware store. Who can walk along with your plastic tube in a *vertical* position and blow bubbles in the water? Who can walk along with your plastic tube in a horizontal position and blow bubbles in the water?

2. Who can blow a ping-pong ball across the water? A toy sailboat? A small sponge?

3. On the side of the pool are many balloons which need blowing up. The object is to blow up a balloon while you walk or run across the pool. Who can make the most trips back and forth and thus blow up the most balloons? You may take only one balloon each trip.

4. Inflatable air mattresses and rafts provide ample practice in blowing for several children. Teams of three or four pupils may cooperate in blowing up a mattress with the promise that they may play on it in the water after it has been sufficiently inflated.

5. A yarnball or ping-pong ball is suspended from a string. Each child has one. Who can keep the ball in motion the longest by blowing?

Self-Testing Activities for the Explorer

1. Who can jump forward across the pool? Who can jump backward? Sideward? How many different ways can you jump? Can you carry something heavy as you jump?

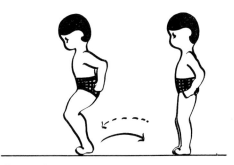

Figure 13.9. Horizontal or long jump.

2. How high can you jump? A pole with flags of various colors provides incentive for progressively increasing the height of the jump. Which flag did you touch when you jumped?

Figure 13.10. Vertical jump and reach.

3. Can you jump over a stick, a scarf, or a rope? In which nursery rhyme does someone jump over a candle stick?

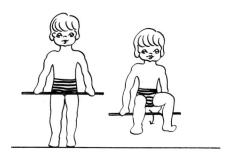

Figure 13.11. Cable jump.

4. Can you greet your toe? Can you hop while holding one foot?

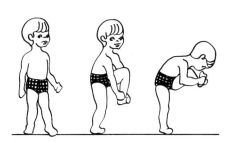

Figure 13.12. Greet the toe.

5. Can you jump up and touch your knees? Can you jump up and touch your toes?

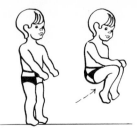

Figure 13.13. Jump and tuck.

6. Stand in the water facing the side of the pool with both hands on deck. How many times can you lift your body up almost out of the water with your arms alone? This is like a push-up on land. Can you lift your body upward and maintain a straight arm support?

Figure 13.14. Straight arm support lean.

7. How many seconds does it take you to run across the pool? How many widths of the pool can you run in three minutes?

Figure 13.15. Aquatic sprint.

8. Can you hang on the pool railing (gutter) and arch your back? Can you do this with the soles of your feet on the wall instead of the floor? Can you do this with only one arm?

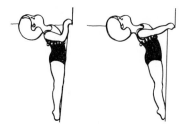

Figure 13.16. Bracketing with back lean.

9. Can you walk a straight line drawn on the floor of the pool? A circular line? A zig-zag line? Can you march on the line? Can you hop on it? Can you do these movements backward? Sideward?

Figure 13.17. Matching locomotor movements to lines and forms.

10. How many different ways can you balance on one foot? Can you do an arabesque? A pirouette?

Figure 13.18. Airplane or single foot balance.

Activities for the Advanced Explorer

The advanced explorer is learning to put his head under water and to change level from up to down and vice versa. He is also experimenting with all of the possible ways to enter the water. He is not yet secure about a horizontal position in the water, but will assume it when the teacher's hand is in contact with some part of his body.

Towel Games

1. Taking rides. When the child trusts the teacher enough to hold his hands and allow the feet to rise from the bottom, thereby assuming a horizontal position in the water, he can be taken on *rides*. These rides can be as dramatic as the child's (or the teacher's) imagination with sound effects for a train, rocket ship, or whatever. The teacher talks to the child continuously, maintaining eye contact, as he pulls him along while walking backward. The next step in the development of trust is to convince the child to hang onto a towel or kickboard while the teacher pulls on the other end. Thus, his rides across the pool continue but his body is progressively farther away from that of the teacher.
2. Individual tug of war. Every two children share one towel, each holding onto one end. A line on the bottom of the pool separates the two children, and the object is to see who can pull the other over the line first. As balance and body control in the water improve, teammates can be added until group tug of war is played. Only one teammate should be added in each progression.
3. Catch the snake. A rope about six feet in length has a towel tied onto the end. The teacher or an agile child pulls the rope around the pool. The object is to see who can *catch the snake* first; the winner then becomes the runner who pulls the snake around the pool.

4. Beater goes round. Children stand in a single circle, facing inward. The *Beater* stands on the outside of the circle, facing counterclockwise and holding a small hand towel (one not big enough to hurt when child is hit with it). A second child is running counterclockwise in front of the *Beater*, trying to avoid being hit by the towel. He can be safe by ducking in front of any player in the circle after he has run around at least one half of the circle. The player whom he ducked in front of must now run to avoid being beaten.
5. Tag with towels on pool bottom as safety rests.
6. Over and Under Relay using towels instead of a ball.

Exploration of Body Shapes Used in Aquatics

The terms tuck, pike, and layout are used in synchronized swimming, diving, and gymnastics. The advanced explorer learns to assume these shapes on land, in shallow water, and in the air. Movement exploration on the trampoline and the springboard in the gymnasium reinforce learning in the pool area. This aspect of aquatic training is designed specifically to improve proprioceptive awareness. The following questions elicit desired responses.

1. In how many different ways can you assume a tuck position on land? In the water? In the air?

Figure 13.19. Tuck positions.

2. In how many different ways can you assume a pike position on land? In the water? In the air?

Figure 13.20. Pike positions.

3. How many ways can you assume a layout position on land? In the water? In the air? Can you do back layouts? Front layouts? Side layouts?

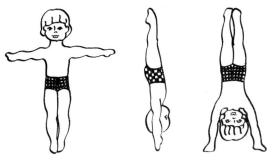

Figure 13.21. Layout positions.

4. In how many ways can you make your body curved on land? In the water? In the air? Can you combine a front layout with a curve? A back layout with a curve? A side layout with a curve?

Figure 13.22. Curved positions.

It is anticipated that early attempts at assuming tuck, pike, and layout positions in the water will result in sinking to the bottom.

Many children accidentally discover floating while concentrating upon body shapes. Those who do not discover floating gain valuable practice in breath control and balance.

Exploration of Ways to Enter the Water

Many children prefer a session of jumping and/or diving to swimming. In the beginning they may wish to have the teacher hold one or both hands and jump with them. Others prefer the teacher to be standing or treading water and awaiting their descent with outstretched arms. Participation in some kind of creative dramatics which demands a jump into the water often subtly evokes the desired response in children who have previously demonstrated fear and reluctance. Themes which have been particularly successful in motivating children to enter the water are (1) playing fireman and sliding down the fire pole; (2) carrying lighted candles through a dark cave or perhaps the ancient Roman catacombs; (3) going on an African safari; (4) imitating Mary Poppins by opening an umbrella in flight; and, of course, (5) emulating spacemen through various trials and tribulations. In response to how many different ways can you enter the water feet-first, children may demonstrate the following:

1. Climb down the ladder. Most efficient method is facing ladder with back to water.
2. Sitting on edge of pool, scoot off into water (a) free style (any way you wish); (b) in tuck position; (c) in pike position; and (d) with one leg straight, one bent.
3. Kneeling or half kneeling, facing water.
4. Kneeling or half kneeling, back to the water.
5. Squatting, facing water.
6. Squatting, back to water.
7. Standing, facing water using: (a) step off; (b) jump and kneel in air before contacting water; (c) jump and tuck in air;

Figure 13.23. Stages in learning to dive from the pool edge can be elicited through movement education challenges.

(d) jump and clap hands; (e) jump and turn; (f) jump and touch toes; (g) hop; (h) leap; (i) arabesque; and (j) pike drop forward (camel walk position).

8. Standing, back to water, using: (a) step-off; (b) jump; (c) hop; and (d) pike drop backward.

In response to how many different ways can you enter the water head-first, children discover the various stages in learning to dive. They may also lie on the side and do a log roll into the water or accidently perform a front somersault.

Self-Testing Activities for the Advanced Explorer

1. Can you jump like a frog under the water?

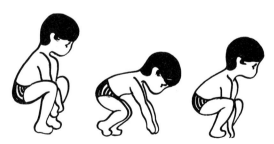

Figure 13.24. Frog jump.

2. Can you squat in water over your head and then jump up and yell *Boo* like a jack-in-the-box?

Figure 13.25. Jack-in-the-box.

3. Can you do a dog walk with your head under water? A lame dog walk?

Figure 13.26. Dog walk when four limbs touch pool bottom; lame dog walk when three limbs touch bottom.

4. Can you do a mule kick in the water?

Figure 13.27. Mule kick.

5. Can you do a seal crawl under the water?

Figure 13.28. Seal walk.

6. Can you do a camel walk under water? This is also called a wicket walk.

Figure 13.29. Camel walk.

7. Can you do an egg sit at the bottom of the pool? Can you do an egg sit near the surface and sink downward?

Figure 13.30. Egg sit followed by V sit.

8. Can you do five bent knee bounces at the bottom of the pool? Pretend you are a ball being dribbled.

Figure 13.31. Human ball bounce.

9. Can you do the coffee grinder stunt at the bottom of the pool?

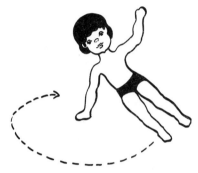

Figure 13.32. Coffee grinder.

10. Can you do a balancing stunt under water with one knee and both hands touching the bottom? Can you lift your arms and do a single knee balance?

Figure 13.33. Knee scale.

Figure 13.34. Bracketing on the front and back.

Bracketing

Bracketing is the term for holding on the gutter (rail) of the pool with one or both hands and allowing the feet to rise from the bottom of the pool so that the body is in a horizontal position.

Retrieving Objects from the Bottom of the Pool

The advanced explorer learns about spatial relationships within a new context as he opens his eyes under water and sees objects *through* the water. In the earliest stages of underwater exploration he may face the teacher, holding both of his hands, as they submerge together. Under water, he may establish eye contact with the teacher, shake hands, and mirror hand and arm movements. Later he can be challenged to retrieve all sorts of things from the bottom. Practice in form, size, weight, and color discrimination can be integrated with the instructions for retrieval of objects.

Activities for the Floater

The floater is comfortable in the water. He can do almost anything but swim a coordinated stroke for 20 yards to qualify for the Red Cross Beginner card. He is probably more competent in underwater swimming than performing strokes near the surface. This is the period during which he masters the following tasks: (1) horizontal to vertical positioning; (2) floating; (3) bobbing; (4) front to back positioning and vice versa; and (5) simple stunts in synchronized swimming.

Horizontal to Vertical Positioning

At this level he demonstrates ease in moving from a horizontal position to a vertical one. The degree of difficulty of this task varies with amount of buoyancy, specific gravity, and absence or paralysis of limbs. Simple sequencing is introduced as depicted in Figure 13.35 through Figure 13.38.

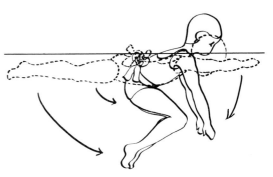

Figure 13.35. Two-part sequence to be practiced in learning change from horizontal to vertical position.

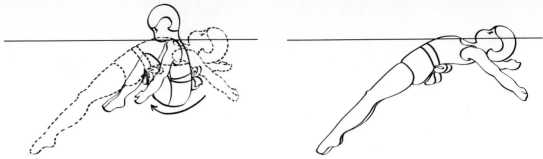

Figure 13.36. Two-part sequence to be practiced in learning to change position from a back layout to a tuck.

Figure 13.37. Back float to tight tub to back float is three-part sequence in learning to change positions.

A   B   C   D   E

Figure 13.38. A five-part sequence in changing position.

Floating

In order to teach floating to persons with varying body builds and/or amputations of one type or another, it is important for the physical educator to have some understanding of the following terms: *buoyancy, specific gravity,* and *center of buoyance* (CB).

Buoyancy is the quality of being able to float. The buoyancy of a human being depends upon the amount of water which each body part is able to displace and the weight of the body part itself. The larger the surface of the body part, the more water it will displace. For instance, the typical woman with wide pelvis and well-rounded buttocks displaces more water than the average man with his characteristic narrow hips and flat buttocks. The lighter the weight of the body part, the less upward

and a marble of the same surface area are force is required to buoy it up. Thus if a cork dropped into water, the cork will float and the marble will sink. Adipose tissue (fat) weighs less than muscle and bone tissue. Thus if two persons of equal surface areas try to float and one individual is fat while the other is heavily muscled, the fat person will be buoyed upward more easily than the person with well-developed musculature. Buoyancy is explained by *Archimedes' principle* which states: a body submerged in a liquid is buoyed up by a force equal to the weight of the displaced liquid.

The *specific gravity* of a human being is its weight compared to the weight of an equal amount of water as shown in this formula:

$$\text{Specific gravity} = \frac{\text{Weight of body}}{\text{Weight of equal amount of water}}$$

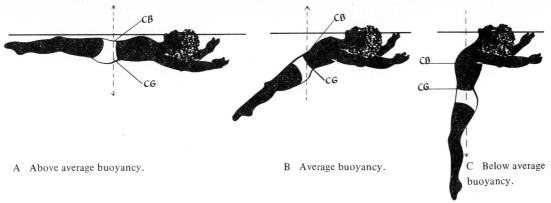

A   Above average buoyancy.   B   Average buoyancy.   C   Below average buoyancy.

Figure 13.39. Effects of buoyancy on floating explain why there are many correct ways.

After full inspiration, the specific gravity of most adult human beings is slightly less than 1. This means that most adults can float with head above the surface of the water when their lungs are filled with air. After exhalation, the specific gravity of most adults is approximately 1.02. Only when the specific gravity is above 1.02 do individuals experience difficulty in floating.

The *center of buoyance* (CB) of a human being in water is similar in function to the center of gravity (CG) when the body is not immersed in fluid. Both are areas where weight is concentrated; both serve as fulcrums about which the body rotates.

The CB, for most persons, is located in the thoracic cavity. The more obese an individual is, the lower his CB is. The CB is defined as the center of gravity of the volume of the displaced water before its displacement. If an object were of uniform density, its CB and CG would coincide; this is not the case with living creatures whether man or fish.

In the water, the body can be likened to a first class lever which, like a see-saw, totters back and forth around its fulcrum (CB) until balance is achieved. Only when the CB and the CG are in the same vertical line can a person float without motion.

It is obvious from Figure 13.39 that there is no one correct way to float. Each person must experiment until he discovers the position in which his CB and CG are aligned vertically. The following hints may help pupils cope with problems of buoyancy.

Below Average Buoyancy

Men, as a whole, have less buoyancy than women. Black students have less buoyancy than white students. Buoyance can be increased by raising the CG and hence the CB. This can be done by extending the arms overhead, by bending the knees so that heels almost touch the buttocks, or by assuming a tuck or jellyfish floating position. It also helps to hyperventilate, keeping the lungs filled with air, and exhaling as seldon as possible.

No attempt should be made to lift the feet and legs and attain a horizontal position since they will only drop downward again, building up enough momentum as they do so to pull the entire body under. Many persons who believe themselves to be *sinkers* could float if they started in the vertical position rather than the horizontal.

Above Average Buoyancy

The obese person experiences many problems of balance for which he must learn to compensate. The alternate arm stroke on the back crawl, for instance, must be performed twice as fast as normal to prevent the body from rolling over. The hips, legs, and feet are often above water level so that no kick is possible.

The most anxiety ridden experience, however, for the obese beginning swimmer is changing position from a horizontal position to a vertical stand. Try as he may, he cannot easily make his legs drop and his shoulders and trunk come forward so that the CG and CB are aligned over the feet.

Amputations

Amputations affect the location of the CG and the CB which in turn affect buoyancy and balance. The loss of a limb causes displacement of the CG and CB to the opposite side. Thus a pupil who has lost a right leg or arm has a tendency to roll to the left where the weight of the body is centered. Most persons with amputations or paralysis of muscles in limbs, whether congenital or acquired, can become excellent swimmers. Extensive movement exploration is recommended to enable each handicapped person to discover for himself the floating position and swimming strokes which best serve his needs. Most pupils with severe orthopedic disabilities seem to prefer swimming on the back. Specifically, the following strokes are suggested:

1. Loss of both legs—back crawl or breaststroke.
2. Loss of one leg—back crawl, elementary backstroke, or sidestroke.
3. Loss of both arms—any kick which can be done on the back. This person has exceptional difficulty in changing from horizontal layout position to a stand.
4. Loss of one arm—sidestroke or swimming on back with legs providing most of the power and the one arm finning.
5. Loss of one leg and one arm—sidestroke with leg on the bottom; arm will create its own effective finning action.

Bobbing

Bobbing is similar to several vertical jumps in place except that all of the power comes from the arms. It can be done in either shallow or deep water, but traditionally is associated with water over the head.

Bobbing consists of two phases. In the *down phase*, both arms are raised simultaneously upward, causing the body to descend. The breath is exhaled. When the feet touch the bottom of the pool, the arm movement ends. The *up phase* is then initiated by both arms pressing simultaneously downward.

Figure 13.40. Down phase in bobbing.

Figure 13.41. Up phase in bobbing.

This action pushes the body upward. The arm movements in bobbing are different from all others the child has encountered. The concept of displacing water, i.e., pushing in the direction opposite from that which you wish to go, should be explained.

Bobbing accomplishes several goals: (1) improves rhythmic breathing; (2) increases vital breathing capacity, i.e., tends to hyperventilate the swimmer; (3) heightens proprioceptive awareness and (4) serves as a warm-up activity. Bobbing is recommended especially for asthmatic children. Variations of bobbing are

1. Progressive bobbing. The down phase is identical to that of bobbing in place. The up phase, however, is modified by using the legs to push the body off of the pool bottom at approximately a 65 degree angle. The arm movement is basically the same. Progressive bobbing is a survival skill in that it can be used as a means of locomotion from the deep end of the pool to the shallow!
2. Bobbing on one leg.
3. Bobbing in a tuck position. Down phase—Arms pull upward, legs extend so that feet touch the bottom. Up phase— Arms press downward, tuck knees to chest so that full tuck is achieved at height of up phase.
4. Seesaw bobbing with a partner. To begin, partners face each other and hold hands. Then a rhythm is established in which one person is up while the other is down as in partner jumping on a trampoline.

Finning and Sculling

After the pupil masters a float, several sessions in movement exploration should focus upon the arms and hands. Such problems as the following can be posed for the back layout, front layout, tuck, and pike positions.

1. In the back layout position, how many different ways can you place your arms?
2. Which positions of the arms make floating easier? More difficult?
3. How many different kinds of movements can you perform with your arms in each position?
4. Which of these movements seem to make you sink? If you do sink, which of these movements can help your body rise to the surface of the water?
5. Which movements of the arms propel the body through the water head first?
6. Which movements of the arms enable you to execute the following changes of position? (a) prone float to stand; (b) prone float to back float; (c) back float to stand; and (d) back float to prone float.
7. If you move only one arm, what happens? Can you propel the body directly to the right by using one arm only? Directly to the left?
8. In what other ways can you propel the body directly to the left? Directly to the right?
9. In how many different ways can you *push* the water away from you? *Pull* the water toward you?

Given sufficient time and encouragement, the pupil eventually discovers finning and sculling for himself. Ideally creative dramatics should be combined with movement exploration so that the child can tell the teacher and/or his peers which emotions are being expressed by particular arm and hand movements. Variations of charades can be played in the water; the low organized game of trades offers opportunities for pantomime; and/or the pupils may *act out* the feeling that a particular musical composition conveys. When *finning* and *sculling* are discovered, the teacher should introduce the names of these movements and explain their usefulness in changing positions in the water. Movement exploration can then focus upon how many different ways the pupil can fin or scull.

Finning

Finning is defined as a series of short pushes with the palms of the hands against the water in the *opposite* direction to the one in which the pupil wishes to move. Each push is followed by a quick bent arm recovery under the surface of the water.

Sculling

There are many different recognized types of *sculling*. In the standard scull the hands are at the hips close to the body. Movement at the shoulder joints is limited to inward and outward rotation of the arms which seem to be initiated by the hands in their execution of tiny figure eight motions close to the surface of the water.

The motion of the hands and wrists consists of an inward and outward phase, each of which is performed with equal force. The palms move toward midline during the inward phase and away from midline during the outward phase so that the water is alternately scooped toward the hips and then pushed away. The thumbs are up during the inward phase and down during the outward phase. If the child does not discover sculling for himself, the movement should be introduced in the classroom and mastered before it is attempted in water. Sculling, for many swimmers, is a difficult pattern to learn through imitation.

Synchronized Swimming

The regulation stunts usually taught in units on synchronized swimming are similar to those performed in tumbling and gymnastics. Executing stunts in the water improves proprioception, enhances body awareness, and provides practice in the imitation of movements. The stunts described on the following

pages can be mastered early in beginning swimming. The primary prerequisites are a feeling of ease in the water, the ability to scull while floating, and a keen sense of where the body is in space. Research at the Texas Woman's University has demonstrated that many slow learners can be taught to execute simple synchronized swimming stunts long before they achieve skill and endurance in regulation strokes.

Figure 13.42. (A) front layout; (B) back layout.

All stunts are begun from either the front layout position or the back layout position as depicted in Figure 13.42. Whereas skilled performers are concerned with the aesthetic appearance of a stunt, the adapted physical educator does not worry about *good form*. The stunts are introduced in a manner similar to other tasks in movement exploration. Very few verbal directions are posed; on some occasions a casual demonstration motivates the pupil to attempt new positions in the water. The stunts which follow are listed in order of difficulty under their respective starting positions. Stunts in which the body is carried in a tuck position are easier than those executed in the pike or layout positions.

Stunts Which Begin in a Back Layout Position

1. *Tub.* Can you change from a back layout position to a tuck position with the thighs perpendicular to the surface of the water? In this position, can you use sculling to revolve the body around in a circle?

2. *Log rolling.* Can you roll the extended body over and over while keeping the legs motionless? This is identical to the stunt by the same name on land.

3. *Back tuck somersault.* Can you perform a backward roll in a tuck position?

4. *Oyster, Clam, or Pike Up.* Can you drop your hips as you simultaneously hyperextend and inwardly rotate the arms at the shoulder joints? When you are touching your toes in a pike position, can you sink to the bottom?

Figure 13.43. Tub.

Figure 13.44. Log roll.

Figure 13.45. Back tuck somersault.

Figure 13.46. Oyster.

5. *Back pike somersault.* Can you assume a pike position with trunk under the water but parallel to the surface? Can you perform a backward roll in this pike position? Which part of this stunt is like the oyster?

6. *Torpedo.* Can you scull with your hands overhead so that your body is propelled in the direction of your feet? Submergence of the head and shoulders is optional.

7. *Back dolphin.* Can you maintain a back layout position as your head leads your body around in a circle under the surface of the water? Can you perform this same stunt with one knee bent?

8. *Single ballet leg.* Can you scull across the pool with one leg perpendicular to the surface of the water and the other leg extended on the surface of the water?

Figure 13.47. Back pike somersault.

Figure 13.48. Torpedo.

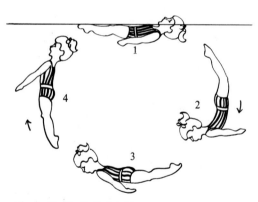

Figure 13.49. Back dolphin.

Figure 13.50. Single ballet leg.

9. *Submarine.* While performing a single ballet leg, can you submerge the entire body up to the ankle of the perpendicular leg and then rise to the surface?

10. *Back walkover.* Can you start a back dolphin but do the *splits* with the legs while they are above the surface of the water? This stunt ends in a front layout.

Stunts Which Begin in a Front Layout Position

1. *Front tuck somersault.* Can you perform a forward roll in a tuck position?

2. *Flying Porpoise.* Can you stand on the bottom, push off, and do a surface dive that looks like a flying porpoise?

Figure 13.51. Submarine.

Figure 13.52. Back walkover.

Figure 13.53. Front tuck somersault.

Figure 13.54. Flying porpoise.

3. *Porpoise.* Can you bend at the waist so that the trunk is almost perpendicular to the bottom while the thighs remain parallel to the water? From this position can you raise both legs until the entire body is vertical and then submerge?

4. *Front pike somersault.* Can you assume a pike position identical to the beginning of a porpoise? From this position can you do a forward roll?

5. *Front walkover.* Can you assume a pike position identical to the beginning of a porpoise? As the legs come out of the water, they do *the splits* so that you finish in a back layout position.

Figure 13.55. Porpoise.

Figure 13.56. Front pike somersault.

Figure 13.57. Front walkover.

Rolling in the Water

Methods of rolling from back to front and vice versa in the water each have names within synchronized swimming circles. These terms are used by the adapted physical educator in his effort to teach children names for the stunts which they can perform, thereby improving their communication skills.

1. *Half Log Roll.* Changing from back to front float or from front to back float.
2. *Log Roll.* Beginning from a back layout position with arms overhead, there are three ways to execute the log roll; (a) reach arm across body; (b) cross one arm over the other; or (c) cross one leg over the other.
3. *Corkscrew.* Log roll from sidestroke posi-

tion to prone float or to same side on which you started. If sidestroke is on the left, a complete roll to the left is executed.

4. *Reverse Corkscrew.* If sidestroke is on the left, a complete roll to the *right* is executed.

5. *Marlin.* (a) Start in *back layout* position, arms in T position, palms down; (b) roll onto right side, moving R arm to sidestroke position and L arm to side for *side layout* position; (c) continue roll onto front layout position, with both arms in T position; (d) roll onto L side, moving L arm to sidestroke position and R arm to side for *side layout* position; and (e) finish in *back layout* position with arms in T position.

Administrative Aspects of an Aquatics Program for the Handicapped

Few teachers of the handicapped have the opportunity to design their own pool, but a community or school committed to serving *all* persons will implement adaptations recommended by a specialist. These may include construction or purchase of the following:

1. Nonskid surface for floors and decks.
2. Handrails in the shower room.
3. Several ways to turn the water off and on in the shower room such as a button on the floor as an alternative for persons who have no use of their arms. Ideally the water in the shower room should turn itself off automatically.
4. Doors into the locker room and the pool wide enough to allow wheelchairs through.
5. Ramps as well as stairsteps; a movable ramp for entrance into the swimming pool; ladders which telescope up and down.
6. Flashing red and green lights at the deep and shallow ends respectively; a metronome or radio playing at the shallow end.

Figure 13.58. Use of chairlift for multiply handicapped. Courtesy of Longview, Washington, YMCA.

7. Floating buoys extended across the pool to warn of deep water; a change in the texture (feel) of the tile along the gutter; the depth of the pool written in braille in the tile every several feet.
8. A horizontal line on the wall which is the same height as the depth of the water below it; this line allows children to compare their heights with the line on the wall to ascertain that the water will not be over their heads if they jump into the pool at a certain point; the line on the wall or the wall itself may be color coded in terms of depth of the water.
9. A large storage cabinet with good ventilation to house the sponges, candles, rubber toys, ping-pong balls, and other accessories to movement exploration not used in ordinary swimming.
10. Hooks on the wall or plans for storage of inner tubes and other flotation devices needed in adapted physical education.

Figure 13.59. Creative teaching uses many props for which storage must be planned.

The temperature of a swimming pool is normally maintained between 78 and 86 degrees. While this temperature is invigorating, it is not geared to the needs of the beginning swimmer who is partially out of the water anytime he is not in a horizontal position; moreover, cold water tends to produce hypertonus and to heighten the spasticity of children with cerebral palsy.

To facilitate relaxation of muscles in the water and to ensure an optimum learning environment, the temperature of water for adapted physical education instruction should be in the low 90°s. Increasing the temperature of the water causes two problems in the management of the pool: (1) the chlorine evaporates in 90° water and (2) the windows in the pool steam up from the evaporated water. Increasing chlorine count is easy enough, but the complaints of the swimmers about the chlorine hurting their eyes appears unavoidable. Sunlamps or infrared lamps built into the ceiling tend to control evaporation.

While the use of flotation devices has been criticized in conjunction with instruction for the nonhandicapped person, they are recommended highly in the adapted physical education setting. Their most important contribution is allowing independence in the water so that the severely involved person does not have to hold onto the teacher for support. In other cases, flotation devices serve as substitutes for missing or paralyzed limbs; they can help immeasurably in assuring a proper head position when the child has poor control of cervical muscles. Cork slabs, styrofoam pieces, and small inflated tubes can be attached to disabled limbs to promote buoyancy.

Swim fins are recommended especially for children with spastic cerebral palsy since they tend to minimize the exaggerated stretch reflex and provide additional power in the kick. Individuals with amputations of upper or lower extremities may use swim fins as substitutes for

The depth of the pool determines, in large part, its expense. The Olympic size pool which provides for progressively deeper water is not recommended for the handicapped, nor for any group of children when instruction is the primary purpose of the pool. There is a definite trend toward building two or three separate pools rather than the multipurpose structure of the past. The instructional pool needs a depth of only 3 1/2 to 4 feet of water. Separate pools are constructed for diving, advanced synchronized swimming, and scuba diving.

Several public schools are now purchasing the porta-pool which can be moved from school to school every several weeks. At the end of the day's instruction, a roof is pulled over the pool and securely locked in lieu of having to provide fencing and other safety measures. Nursery schools and special education units would do well to purchase the aluminum tank type pool sold by Sears and other commercial companies. Such pools are less expensive than trampolines and other pieces of playground apparatus.

limbs. Only by continuous experimentation can the teacher determine the type of flotation device and/or substitute limb which is best for a particular pupil. Considerable creativity is often required in solving problems of where and how to attach such devices to the body.

Health Examination

Written approval of both the physician and the parents should be on file prior to the beginning of swimming instruction. Most physicians prefer to use their own form, but are willing to fill out supplementary information sheets.

Maintenance of close rapport with local physicians is essential to good adapted physical education. A thank you mailed to the physician after receipt of the supplementary sheet contributes to good rapport. Likewise, it is worthwhile to develop a mimeographed sheet ᷂escribing the similarities and differences between swimming in the adapted physical education setting and the regular class. Adaptations such as increased pool temperature, availability of ramps and flotation devices, and individualized or small group instruction should be explained.

Conditions for Which Swimming or Diving Is Contraindicated

Swimming is universally recommended for individuals with all kinds of disabilities with the exception of the following conditions: (1) infectious diseases in the active stage, i.e., the child still has an elevated temperature; (2) chronic ear infections, also the months during which tubes are in the ears; (3) chronic sinusitus; (4) allergies to chlorine or water; (5) skin conditions such as eczema and ringworm; (6) open wounds and sores; (7) osteomyelitis in the active stage; (8) inflammation of joints as in rheumatoid arthritis; (9) severe cardiac conditions; and (10) venereal diseases.

Physicians will sometimes prescribe hydrotherapy for individuals with some of these conditions. Girls who wear internal tampons should be encouraged to participate fully in regularly scheduled instruction during their menstrual periods. Pregnant women generally swim until the sixth or seventh month, depending upon the philosophy of the obstetrician.

Diving may be contraindicated for individuals with arrested hydrocephalus, hemophilia, or anomalies of the face or head which affect normal breathing. Children with spastic cerebral palsy should not be taught to dive unless instruction is requested specifically by the parents and endorsed by the physician.

Time of Day for Swimming Instruction

The practice of waiting one or two hours after eating before engaging in swimming instruction is no longer viewed as valid except in the case of training for competitive swimming. Hence, swimming may be scheduled whenever it is convenient. It is perhaps better to conduct instruction after lunch than immediately before hand when the level of blood sugar characteristically reaches its daily low.

Classroom teachers report that swimming early in the day tends to exert a quieting influence upon hyperactive children. In some schools for the emotionally disturbed, a pupil may request a pass to report to the swimming teacher in lieu of a regularly scheduled class when he feels exceedingly aggravated or in special need of *letting off steam.*

Undressing, Showering, and Dressing

Assisting young children and severely involved individuals with dressing procedures is an integral part of teaching swimming to the handicapped. Extreme care should be given to drying the skin and hair of children with Down's Syndrome since they are especially susceptible to upper respiratory infections.

Moisturizing cream or oil should be applied to dry skin immediately after swimming. The characteristic dry, rough skin of many institutionalized children could be softened by regular applications of cream.

Sample Information Sheet to Be Filled in by Physician

Name _____

Medical Diagnosis _____

Diagnosis in laymen's terms _____

_____

Which part of the body, if any, is involved:

_____ Right arm   _____ Left arm   _____ Neck

_____ Right leg   _____ Left leg   _____ Trunk

Other _____

What specific exercises or movements do you recommend for the involved parts?

_____

Do you recommend learning to float or swim in any particular position?

_____ Front   _____ Right side   _____ Head out of water

_____ Back   _____ Left side   _____ Head used normally in rhythmic breathing

Should any special precautions be taken?

_____ Needs to wear nose clip   _____ Should *not* dive

_____ Needs to wear ear plug   _____ Needs to wear glasses

_____ Should *not* hold breath   _____ Should *not* hyperventilate

_____ Should *not* put head under water

    I recommend that this person participate in regularly scheduled swimming lessons adapted to his special needs as indicated on this sheet.

_____   _____
Date   Name of Physician

If land drill is planned prior to entrance in the water, the preliminary shower should be eliminated. At no time should a child in a wet suit be out of the pool for more than a few seconds.

Teachers must observe their swimmers closely for blueness of lips, teeth chattering, goose bumps, and other evidence of chilling. Children tend to chill more quickly than adults; the thinner the child, the shorter the duration of time in the water which he can endure. In accordance with the principle of in-dividual differences, *all* pupils should not be scheduled for instructional periods of identical lengths. Children in wet suits should *not* be allowed to sit on the edge of the pool with a towel draped about them in hopes that they will magically warm up and return for additional instruction. Anytime the child professes to be too cold to remain in the pool, he should be expected to dry off and dress fully. Activities should be planned for individuals who leave the pool early, and the dressing room should be supervised at all times.

Recommended Activities

1. Work a set number of hours in an aquatics program for children.
2. Find a nonswimmer who is afraid of the water. Take him through the Explorer, Advanced Explorer, and Floater Competency Levels described in Table 30.

   Keep a chronological log in case study style of the teaching techniques used and the learner's responses.
3. Visit your local American Red Cross and YMCA offices and find out about the services they offer the handicapped.

Recommended References

AAHPER. *A Practical Guide for Teaching the Mentally Retarded to Swim.* Washington, D. C.: AAHPER, 1969.

American Red Cross. *Swimming for the Handicapped—Instructor's Manual.* Revised edition. Washington, D. C.: American Red Cross, 1975.

Canadian Red Cross Society. *Manual for Teaching Swimming to the Disabled.* National Office, 95 Wellesley Street E, Toronto 5, Canada.

Lowman, Charles L., and Roen, Susan. *Therapeutic Use of Pools and Tanks.* Philadelphia: W. B. Saunders Co., 1952.

Reynolds, Grace D. ed. *A Swimming Program for the Handicapped.* New York: Association Press, 1973.

Seamons, G. *Swimming for the Blind.* Provo: Brigham Young University, 1966.

United Cerebral Palsy Associations, Inc. *Swimming for the Cerebral Palsied.* Can order from United Cerebral Palsy Associations, Inc., 321 West 44th St., New York, New York 10036.

Organizations

American Red Cross National Headquarters, 17th and D Streets, NW, Washington, D. C. 20006.

National Council of YMCAs, 291 Broadway, New York, New York, 10007.

Part 3
Adapted Physical Education for Special Populations

Behavioral Objectives

After reading Chapters 14 to 26, observing and/or teaching children with the handicapping conditions described, and participating in multidisciplinary staffings, it is anticipated that the reader will be able to:
1. Demonstrate the same breadth of knowledge about each handicapping condition as other specialists involved in educational diagnosis and prescriptive teaching.
2. Understand the reports prepared by other members of the multidisciplinary team and utilize their findings in planning an adapted physical education program for the whole child.
3. Gain the respect of colleagues as a specialist who can knowledgeably present and interpret findings pertaining to physical development and motor behavior of handicapped children.
4. Determine the need for a comprehensive adapted physical education program in a school and/or an entire community; present a written report with statistical documentation to members of the School Board to acquaint them

with the need; and design a proposal for their approval for initiating or expanding an adapted physical education program.

5. Organize and conduct both integrated and separated programs of physical education and recreation for pupils in each disability category.

6. Prepare slide presentations and other public relations materials for orienting parents, administrators, and colleagues to the ongoing program of adapted physical education.

7. Demonstrate awareness of present and past research in adapted physical education and recreation and of available human and documentary resources which may provide additional information about each handicapping condition.

Recommended Readings

Deno, Evelyn. *Mainstreaming: Learning Disabled, Emotionally Disturbed, and Socially Maladjusted Children in Regular Classes.* Reston, Va.: Council for Exceptional Children, 1976.

Mann, Philip H., ed. *Mainstreaming Special Education.* Reston, Va.: Council for Exceptional Children, 1974.

Warfield, Grace J., ed. *Mainstream Currents.* Reston, Va.: Council for Exceptional Children, 1974.

Recommended Activities

In conjunction with each chapter, observe and/or teach one or more persons with the handicapping conditions described. Whenever possible, participate in multidisciplinary staffings or discussions. If persons are not available with whom you can work, read an autobiography or biography.

Recent statistics indicate that there are approximately 75,000,000 children in the United States of which an estimated 7,083,500 are handicapped. Less than one-half of these persons are receiving special education services. Only a small fraction of this one-half is fortunate enough to have any kind of organized physical education instruction. Therapeutic recreation services are practically nonexistent.

In the brief span of time that the handicapped have been served by the public schools, curricular trends have swung in pendulum fashion between segregated separate classes for each disability group and integrated instructional systems which attempt to keep all children in the *mainstream* of education. Since state and federal appropriations for the public schools are invariably broken down into handi-

capping conditions, it is important to consider the physical education needs of special populations. Chapters 14 to 26 present background information on each disability within a multidisciplinary context designed to prepare the adapted physical educator to work cooperatively with other specialists. Whenever possible, opportunities should be created for children with handicapping conditions to participate in regular physical education. This principle demands that good teaching be adapted to the individual needs and interests of all children.

The figures below, representing over 10 percent of all school age children, do not include the many pupils with low fitness and problems of motor awkwardness who should be provided adapted physical education.

Table 31 *Number of Handicapped Children in the United States Listed in Rank Order according to Disabilities*

	Handicapped Children (5-19 Yrs)	Handicapped Children (0-4 Yrs)	Handicapped Children (0-19 Yrs)
Speech Impaired	2,112,600	327,900	2,440,500
Mentally Retarded	1,388,300	309,200	1,697,500
Emotionally Disturbed	1,207,200	180,800	1,388,000
Learning Disabled	603,600	93,700	697,300
Crippled & Other Health Impaired	301,800	46,800	348,600
Hard of Hearing	301,800	46,800	348,600
Visually Impaired	60,400	9,400	69,800
Deaf	45,300	7,000	52,300
Multihandicapped	35,800	5,100	40,900
Totals	6,056,800	1,026,700	7,083,500

Figure 14.0. An alternative to beam walking is a Cratty
floor grid on which every letter of the alphabet and
every number can be found. Here an LD boy leads his
teacher in walking out the number 8.

Thomas Edison, Woodrow Wilson, Winston Churchill, Albert Einstein, Walt Disney, and Mickey Mantle each manifested learning disabilities severe enough to disrupt his early schooling. Each, at one time or another, was labeled a failure because of specific deficits in language or mathematical processes. The discrepancy between estimated intellectual potential and actual academic achievement has long baffled parents and educators.

Numerous terms have been used to describe the underachieving pupil with normal or better intelligence: word-blind, dyslexic, aphasic, brain-injured, neurophrenic. With the recognition in the 1960s that the *whole* child was not handicapped by his specific disability, the terminology switched from adjectives to such prepositional phrases as *with learning disabilities* and *with minimal brain dysfunction*. The founding of the Association for Children with Learning Disabilities (ACLD) in 1964 contributed greatly to the standardization of terminology and the mobilization of efforts directed toward legislation for this group. The purpose of ACLD, as cited in its early literature, revealed a broad definition of learning disabilities: "to advance the education and general well-being of children with adequate intelligence who have learning disabilities arising from perceptual, conceptual, or subtle co-ordinative problems, sometimes accompanied by behavior difficulties."

The year 1968 marks the official recognition of learning disabilities as an educational category with independent funding by the U.S. Office of Education. At this time also the definition of learning disabilities was delimited as follows:

Children with special (specific) learning disabilities exhibit a disorder in one or more of the basic psychological processes involved in understanding or in using spoken or written language. These may be manifested in disorders of listening, thinking, talking, reading, writing, spelling, or arithmetic. They include conditions which have been referred to as perceptual handicaps, brain in-jury, minimal brain dysfunction, dyslexia, developmental aphasias, etc. They do not include learning problems which are due primarily to visual, hearing, or motor handicaps, to mental retardation, emotional disturbance, or to environmental disadvantage.[1]

This definition, although decidedly different from the earlier ACLD concept, is now widely accepted.

Incidence

It is conservatively estimated that 603,600 children between the ages of five and nineteen in the United States have learning disabilities severe enough to warrant special educational services. This represents 1 percent of all children and approximately 10 percent of all handicapped children. Less conservative estimates indicate that one out of every five school children has learning problems of neurological origin which interfere with optimal success in the normal classroom. Unfortunately in some communities the LD label has become an umbrella under which all educational enigmas fall.

The incidence of learning disabilities is far greater among boys than girls. The ratio seems to range from 15 to 1 to 25 to 1.

Characteristics of Children with Learning Disabilities

No two children with learning disabilities exhibit the same constellation of strengths and weaknesses. Yet, in spite of their heterogeneity, LD children display certain behaviors more often than do the normal population. Among these are disordered or hyperkinetic behavior, distractibility, dissociation, perseveration, social imperception, immature

1. "Notes and Working Papers. . .," Education of Handicapped Children (Prepared for the Subcommittee on Education of the Committee on Labor and Public Welfare, United States Congress, Washington, D. C.: U. S. Government Printing Office, 1968), p. 14.

body image, poor spatial orientation, and nonspecific awkwardness or clumsiness.

Hyperkinesis

The hyperactive child manifests disorders of listening, thinking, reading, writing, spelling, or arithmetic primarily because he cannot sit still long enough to complete a task. He is forever wiggling; shuffling his feet, swinging his legs; doodling, pinching, chewing gum, gritting his teeth, and talking to himself or others. He seems never to tire and requires unbelievably little sleep. He has been described as:

being up by 5:05 a.m., into the kitchen by 5:08 a.m., having the pans out of the cupboard by 5:09 a.m., mixing the flour and sugar on the floor by 5:11 a.m., walking through it in bare feet by 5:15 a.m., turning attention to the living room drapes by 5:18 a.m., and inadvertently knocking over a table lamp at 5:20 a.m. This wakens all members of the family who individually and collectively descend on the first-floor scene, and thus begins another day of tension, discipline, and frustration. [2]

Hyperactivity may be worse on some days than others. Classroom teachers have been known to send the child to the playground on such days: "You take him. . . I can't teach him a thing in the classroom." Hyperactive children may display *catastrophic reactions* to unexpected stimuli like a sharp noise, a scary incident in a movie, or a playful jab from a teammate. They tend to fall apart, to sob uncontrollably, to scream, or to display sudden outbursts of anger or physical aggression.

Hyperactivity should not be confused with individual differences in energy, impulse control, and enthusiasm. All toddlers exhibit problems with impulse control. This is evidenced when children of different ages are asked, "How slowly can you draw a line from this point to that point? Or how slowly can you walk across the room? Or how slowly can you do tasks which comprise the Lincoln-Oseretsky tests?" The older the normal child is, the more easily he can slow down his pace and con-

sciously determine the tempo he wishes to maintain. Impulse control may be related to hyperactive behavior, but it is not the same thing.

Hyperactivity is a medical problem. It is usually recognized and referred to a physician long before the child enters school. Most physicians use medication as a last resort in the management of hyperactivity. Nevertheless large numbers of LD youngsters are so uncontrollable that drugs are prescribed: ritalin (methylphenidate), dexedrine, benzedrine, and methedrine, all of which are stimulants. Research has demonstrated that these stimulant drugs slow down the LD child, increase his attention span, and enable him to concentrate on one thing at a time. The use of stimulants in the management of hyperactivity is analogous to the prescription of insulin for the diabetic. Both have deficits in their body chemistry for which drugs must compensate. In the LD child insufficient amounts of serotonin, epinephrine (adrenalin), and norepinephrine which control the activity centers in the brain are circulating in the body. The concentrations of these substances within the body generally change with age, and the deficit normally corrects itself in the middle school or junior high years. Medications cannot correct the physiological deficit; they simply compensate for it until the body chemistry changes of its own accord. Hyperactivity normally ceases to be a problem at about the time of puberty, and medication is stopped. Children do not become addicted to the drugs used in the management of hyperactivity, and there are no withdrawal problems. The main side effects are depressed appetite and sleeplessness.

What educational adaptations must be implemented for the hyperactive child? How do these affect physical education instruction? Numerous approaches have been proposed,

2. William M. Cruickshank, *The Brain-Injured Child in Home, School, and Community* (Syracuse: Syracuse University Press, 1967), p. 34.

several of which are controversial. It is essential, however, that the instructional practices in physical education be consistent with those used by other teachers. If, for instance, the classroom environment is highly structured, then the physical education program must be also.

The concepts of Cruickshank,[3] Strauss, and Lehtinen [4] continue to shape the educational prescriptions of hyperactive children. According to them, a good teaching environment is based upon four principles:

1. Establishment of a highly structured program.
2. Reduction of environmental space.
3. Elimination of irrelevant auditory and visual stimuli.
4. Enhancement of the stimulus value of the instructional materials themselves.

The principle of *structure*, as applied to the physical education setting, requires the establishment of a routine which is repeated day after day and leaves nothing to chance. For instance, the pattern of activities will follow the same sequence each period: sitting on prescribed floor spots while waiting for class to begin; warm-ups always done in the same area and facing the same direction; introduction and practice of new skills; participation in games or dances; return to floor spots and sitting or lying during *warming-down* period of relaxation and discussion. If instructional stations are used, a certain piece of apparatus is always located in the same space and the pupils always mount it from the same direction. Rotation from station to station is always in the same direction, traditionally counterclockwise. Characteristically after warm-ups, each pupil goes to his assigned station to start instruction and rotation always proceeds from this same spot. Identical start, stop, and rotation signals contribute also to structure since the child knows precisely which response is appropriate for each signal.

Moreover, the composition of each squad or team is structured in much the same fashion as are groups for play therapy or psychotherapy. A balance is maintained between the number of hyperactive and sluggish children so that one behavioral extreme tends to neutralize the other. The proportion of aggressors and nonaggressors is weighted as are natural leaders and followers. A genuine attempt, often demanding much trial and error, is made to determine which combination of human beings learn together most efficiently. It must be emphasized that the success of this structure is based upon ease of learning; it is totally unrelated to winning and losing and has little to do with level of skill.

The principle of *space reduction* suggests the use of lane markers and partitions to delimit the vast expanse of play area considered desirable for normal children. Special emphasis must be given to boundaries and the penalties incumbent upon stepping out-of-bounds for LD children. The major value of low organized games may be learnings about boundaries, baselines, and space possession and utilization.

Space reduction necessarily limits the size of the squads which rotate from station to station. Most elementary school children function best in groups of six to eight; LD children often require still smaller groups for optimal learning. It should be remembered that these are the pupils confined to individual cubicles in the classroom. The child who lacks readiness for group activities in the classroom will seldom display success in group games on the playground.

The principle of *extraneous stimuli control* demands the maintenance of a neat, clean, well-ordered play area. No balls or equipment are in sight unless they are required for the

3. Ibid.
4. Alfred A. Strauss and Laura Lehtinen, *Psychopathology and Education of the Brain-Injured Child* (New York: Grune and Stratton, 1947).

game in progress. Cruickshank recommends that wall, floor, and furniture be the same color; that transparent window panes be replaced by opaque glass; and that wooden doors enclose all shelves. Several authorities have challenged the extremity of these measures, but all concur that extraneous visual and auditory stimuli which distract children should be eliminated.

When several squads are each practicing different motor tasks, often on different pieces of apparatus, the attention of the pupil may be diverted by children at other stations. It is not uncommon for the LD child to respond to the attractiveness of another station by roaming about, losing his own squad, forgetting the name of his partner, and becoming generally disoriented. Again partitions to eliminate the extraneous visual stimuli from other stations prevent many such problems. Similar distractions are present when physical education is held out-of-doors: cars in the nearby street, neighborhood animals, leaves rustling on the trees, birds flying overhead, weeds among the grass where the ball is rolling, even the wind and sun. The severely hyperactive pupil should be scheduled only for indoor physical education where environmental variables can be more easily manipulated and controlled.

The principle of *instructional stimulus enhancement,* as applied to the physical education setting, implies the extensive and concentrated use of color to focus and hold the pupil's attention on a particular piece of apparatus, a target, or a ball. Sound may be used similarly. Wall-to-wall mirrors in which the child can see and learn to evaluate his motor performance seem to increase concentration also.

The principles of structure, space reduction, stimuli control, and instructional stimulus enhancement form the basis of a sound physical education program for LD children. Freedom is increased gradually in accordance with the pupil's ability to cope.

Social incentives and extrinsic rewards

Figure 14.1. LD child benefits from visual enforcement afforded by mirrors.

based upon Skinnerian principles of reinforcement for nonhyperactivity are recommended also. For instance, every child who stays within the space boundaries of his station for the allotted time period may be rewarded with a red chip, paper money, or piece of candy just before the whistle blows for rotation to the next station. Stars are pasted on charts for children who stay in line and take their turn at the proper time. Sometimes contracts are made in which pupils specify what they will do in expectation of a certain reward. There is little time for writing out a contract for physical education as is done in the classroom. Therefore, prefabricated contracts of different colors which require only the signatures of teacher and pupil may be readied ahead of time. The child may refuse a contract or select from several which specify varying lengths of concentration on particular activities. Contracts may also give structure to endurance type activities which require walking, running, or swimming certain distances. Reliance upon social incentives and extrinsic rewards is sometimes called *behavior modification.* Numerous books and whole courses are taught on this subject.[5,6]

5. Garth J. Blackman and Adolph Silberman, *Modification of Child Behavior* (Belmont, California: Wadsworth Publishing Company, Inc., 1971).

6. B. F. Skinner, *The Technology of Teaching* (New York: Appleton-Century-Crofts, 1963).

Distractibility

Distractibility is the inability to concentrate attention on any particular object or person in the environment. The pupil is distracted by any movement, sound, color, or smell. He lacks the ability to block out irrelevant stimuli as do normal persons. Admonishing him to *pay attention* is useless. He would if he could. Instead he reacts to:

the grinding of the pencil sharpener, to the colors of dozens of shirts and dresses which surround him, to the movement of the child next to him across the aisle, to an announcement on the intercommunication system, to the leaves on the tree blowing in the wind outside the room, to the movement of the goldfish in the aquarium, to another child who just sneezed, to the teacher's whispers to yet a third child, to the footsteps of a group of children walking past his room in the hall, to the crack at the top of his desk into which his pencil point will just fit, to the American flag hanging in the front of the room, to the Thanksgiving Day decorations on the walls, to dozens and dozens of other unessential things in the room which prevent him from writing his name on the top line! It isn't that he refuses to cooperate with the teacher's request to ''start here.'' It is that he simply cannot refrain from reacting to the unessential stimuli in his environment. This is, we think, the result of a neurological impairment. The difficulty which he experiences in carrying out the simple request of the teacher occurs again and again each day as one learning opportunity after another is presented to him. [7]

Dissociation

Another characteristic of the LD child is *dissociation,* the inability to perceive things as a whole. Dissociation can be social, visual, or auditory. LD children are sometimes criticized for displaying poor judgment when, in fact, they lack the ability to see the whole and hence respond to relatively unimportant details within the whole. The old adage, *He can't see the forest for the trees,* seems appropo.

Visual dissociation is especially a problem in learning to read and write. To form the letter *m*, for instance, a child must be able to bring together three distinct lines:

$$ | \cap \cap \ = \ \cap $$

If the three separate lines are conceptualized but never synthesized into a meaningful whole, the child's *m* may look like this.

$$ \setminus \daleth \daleth $$

Visual dissociation is apparent also in poor performance on pegboards, puzzles, and other assembling tasks. Tests of body image which require the pupil to draw a man or himself often reveal unconnected body parts. The tendency of so many children to touch, stroke, feel, and paw at the teacher has been related to their inability to see whole; tactile contact lends reassurance that the adult is really there. The child's need in this regard can be minimized by the teacher taking the initiative in physical contact, putting an arm around his shoulder, patting him, and reinforcing visual cues.

Auditory dissociation is evidenced when sounds are heard and recognized but cannot be synthesized into a meaningful whole. The child understands individual words but fails to grasp the meaning of the entire sentence. He can follow instructions when given one task at a time but cannot anticipate the outcome. Sometimes, unaware that a task is finished, he continues to wait for the next instruction.

The whole-part-whole teaching methodology with as little verbalization as possible helps to cope with dissociation. The child on the trampoline for the first time, for instance, must get the *feel* of the whole before he cares much about proper use of arms and landing in shoulder-width stride. Beginning instruction in throwing and striking activities should focus upon the target to be hit, not on the stance, grip, backswing, release, and follow through.

LD children characteristically have little faith in forearms, hands, and fingers—the body parts held responsible for awkward handwriting—and generally perform better when

7. William M. Cruickshank, *The Brain-Injured Child in Home, School, and Community* (Syracuse: Syracuse University Press, 1967), p. 33.

not self-conscious about sequential and correct use of such parts.

In the warm-up portion of the period, it seems better to use locomotor activities which demand the integrated working together of the whole body rather than calisthenics that emphasize the movement of parts. Thus runs, hops, jumps, animal walks, log rolls, and tumbling activities are preferable to arm flinging, side bending, toe touching, and head circling.

Practice in getting into different game and dance formations can be used to teach pupils to see themselves as parts of a whole. Creative dance, swimming, and gymnastics in which individuals or partners devise an original stunt or movement sequence and then combine it with those of others reinforce understandings of parts versus wholes. Even a pyramid can be taught as a whole comprised of parts. In movement exploration, children should be helped to combine isolated stunts into routines or set sequences. The teacher is forever challenging, "What two or three movements can you combine to make a whole composition?"

Children who dissociate often experience difficulty with *sequencing*, the ability to remember and/or to put parts together in the correct order. Physical education offers innumerable opportunities for practice in sequencing. Folk and square dance, for instance, are based on the ability to remember and perform sequences of steps in the correct order. Routines on gymnastic apparatus also teach sequencing. Memory of the instructions for a low organized game is still another example.

Perseveration

Perseveration is more apparent in LD children than in peers of the same age. Often interpreted as stubbornness, this is the inability to shift easily from one idea or activity to another. Perseveration is present when a pupil:

1. Continues to grind on and on long after a pencil is sharpened.

2. Continues to bounce the ball after the signal for stopping has been given.
3. Continues to laugh or giggle after everyone else stops.
4. Repeats the same phrase over and over or gets *hung* on one topic of conversation.

Perseveration is the opposite of distractibility, and it is uncanny that the LD child seems to be always at one extreme or the other of the continuum, never in the middle. Perseveration contributes to a behavioral rigidity which is evidenced in games when the pupil refuses to adapt rules or to test a new strategy.

To minimize perseveration, the physical educator should plan a sequence of activities in which each is distinctly different from the other in formation, starting position, basic skills, rules, and strategies. A circle game, for instance, might be followed by a relay in files. In circuit training a station stressing arm and shoulder strength might be followed by one emphasizing jumping activities. Games based upon stop-and-go concepts reinforce the ability to make transitions from one activity to another. Illustrative of these are Red Light, Green Light; Musical Chairs; Cakewalks; Statues; and Squirrels in the Trees.

Social Imperception

Inadequacies of social perception, namely the inability to recognize the meaning and significance of the behavior of others, contribute to poor social adjustment.

An LD child often seems to have difficulty in making and keeping friends of his own age. The problems of hyperactivity, distractibility, dissociation, and perseveration are complicated further by his inability to deal with abstractions and double meanings. He becomes the butt of jokes when he cannot share the multiple meanings of such words as screw, ball, grass, pot, and head. Moreover, much of the humor in our society is abstract and lost on him entirely. Because he fails to comprehend the subtleties of facial expression, tone of voice, and body language, the child does not realize that he is angering, antagonizing, or boring a person until some kind of explosion erupts. Then he retreats with hurt feelings wondering why the other *blew up all of a sudden* or told him *to get out and leave him alone.*

The aspect of physical education perhaps most helpful in remediating social imperception is dance with its inherent concern for body language and nonverbal communication. Games can be devised also to help children learn to cope with imagery and find delight in *make-believe*. The often cruel give-and-take of childhood dramatic play can be cushioned by imposing time and space limitations on such activities. With severely involved children, play should seldom—if ever—be left unstructured. It is far better to delimit the activity with "You may play cowboys and Indians with John and Chris in Room 121 for 20 minutes" than to allow the group interaction to continue indefinitely, ultimately ending with a fight of some kind. In schools which have daily recess, the teacher should specify ahead of time names of persons who have permission to play together, the space on the playground they may occupy, and the equipment they may use. Freedom is given to children with social imperception only in small degrees as they demonstrate increasing ability to cope in social situations.

Immature Body Image

As the normal child matures, he becomes conscious of his own body, internalizes his perceptions, and acquires what is called a *body image*. This, like other acquisitions in the affective domain, is a theoretical construct. It is difficult to define and even harder to measure.

Authorities seem to agree, however, that certain traits comprise an immature body image. Among these are (1) finger agnosia, (2) inability to identify body parts and surfaces,

(3) inability to make right-left discriminations on self and others, (4) difficulty in distinguishing between male and female body types and body proportions, and (5) problems in matching own somatotype and body parts to those of others. These deficits are thought to stem from brain damage, specifically in the nondominant hemisphere which in the average right-handed person is on the right. Lesions here are known to alter recognition of body parts and awareness of corporeal (body) and extracorporeal space.

Of the many body image deficits, finger agnosia has received the most attention.[8] The inability to identify fingers is revealed in self-drawings and finger localization tests. In Benton's test, which has a reliability of .91, the child identifies single fingers which have been tactually stimulated. The task is performed both with the hands visible and hidden from sight. Large numbers of children fail this test and reveal problems in their drawings. The following description of a six-year-old with high average intelligence is typical.

. . . He made the drawing after being instructed to draw a picture of himself and quickly drew all of the figure except the fingers. When he came to the point of wanting to put on fingers, he became confused, looked at the examiner's hands and then at his own mittens in an attempt to adapt them to the situation. Finally, in a mood of desperation, he placed his hand on the paper in the appropriate position and traced around two of his fingers; he repeated this procedure on the other side, thus putting fingers at the end of both arms. From this performance and on the basis of other evidence, we concluded that this boy had a finger agnosia. He was unable, except by highly devious routes, to visualize his own fingers.[9]

Remediation of immature body image problems through physical education involves the use of finger plays, action songs, dances,

8. Arthur L. Benton, *Right-Left Discrimination and Finger Localization* (New York: Hoeber-Harper, 1959).
9. Doris J. Johnson and Helmer R. Myklebust, *Learning Disabilities* (New York: Grune and Stratton, 1967), p. 237.

games, and exercises which refer to body parts. Finger play, sometimes called *handies,* are especially popular with young children.

Opportunities should be provided for children to see themselves in the mirror, on videotape, and in moving pictures. Games should be devised in which older pupils estimate the length and/or the circumference of body parts and then compare their estimations with actual measurements. Activities leading to an understanding of body types should be taught also. Pictures or slides of different body types can be exhibited on the wall and the children taught to recognize a body type similar to their own. The different shapes of faces and dimensions of limbs can be approached in the same manner. Instruction pertaining to body parts can be correlated with a study of grooming, hair styling, clothes selection, postures, and body language.

Movement exploration can reinforce learnings about body parts.

1. Can you bounce the ball with your elbow? Your foot? What other body parts?
2. Can you cross the rope and land on one hand and one foot simultaneously? On both hands simultaneously?
3. Can you hold onto your ankles with your hands and walk? Can you keep your right elbow on your left knee as you walk?
4. Can you grasp the ball with just thumb and index finger? With all your fingers? With your palm?
5. How many activities can you do with your buttocks in contact with the floor? With the front surface of your thigh in contact with the floor?
6. In swimming, how many different body parts can you use in pushing off from the side?

Much research is needed to determine the relationship between participation in certain activities and changes in body image. Conclusive evidence is not available for recommending one kind of program over another.

Poor Spatial Orientation

Closely allied to body image deficits are disturbances in spatial orientation. The LD child is described as *lost in space.* He typically loses his way enroute to a destination and shows confusion when given north-south-east-west and right-left directions. Moreover, he experiences difficulty in estimating distance, height, width, and the other coordinates of space. As a result, he is forever bumping into things and misjudging the space requirements in such tasks as stepping through geometric forms, ducking under a low rope, and squeezing through a narrow opening.

Problems in recognizing and naming right and left body parts may stem from deficits in laterality, visual and auditory perception, or receptive and expressive language. The ability to make right-left discriminations on one's self and to follow instructions using these terms does not normally stabilize until age six or seven. Whereas laterality pertains only to subjective or self-space, right-left discriminations extend to objective or external space. Many normal children are in the upper elementary grades before they can project the directions of right-left from themselves to another person and from object to object. Individuals with learning disabilities, despite special training, seem to experience difficulty with right-left discriminations throughout life.

Problems in crossing the midline relate to the proprioceptive awareness of right and left. This deficit is often revealed in chalkboard activities in which the child draws a horizontal line from his right side to his midline and then switches the chalk to his left hand for continuation of the line. He seems to lack the ability to shift his weight from side to side so that such hand switching is unnecessary. Inadequate follow through and change of weight in sports activities are illustrative of midline problems. The discrepancy between fielding or striking a ball on the preferred side as opposed to the nonpreferred shows that some midline difficulty is normal.

Physical education activities for problems of laterality, right-left discriminations, and crossing the midline are similar in that all pertain to balance and the establishment of cross lateral movement patterns.

Balance beams and boards and the trampoline can be used specifically for this purpose. Sideward beam walking is considered more valuable than other tasks because of the shifting of weight from side to side. For balance beam and trampoline training to contribute toward improved proprioception, movement problems must be posed which necessitate frequent postural adjustments. Unlike regular physical education, training to improve spatial orientation should focus upon movement exploration rather than mastery of traditional gymnastic skills.

Whereas laterality pertains only to self-(subjective) space, directionality is a theoretical construct which refers specifically to external (objective) space. Directionality is the ability to locate oneself in relation to a fixed or moving point outside the body. It develops through the process of perceptual-motor matching and presumes integrity of vision and audition. Directionality is the validation of proprioceptive awareness of right, left; up, down; front, back, side; and other directional concepts with visual, auditory, and tactual feedback and vice versa. Later, the child learns to generalize about the spatial relationships of one external object to another. Reading, for instance, is partially a matter of perceiving spatial relationships between letters, words, and lines. Rotations and reversals of letters are believed to be problems of directionality. Reversals of *b, d, p,* and *q* seem to indicate deficits in proprioceptive awareness of right and left, while reversals of *m, w, n,* and *u* seem to indicate problems with up and down directions. The perceptual-motor match-

ing skills inherent in directionality pertain also to the perception and reproduction of geometric forms in body movement, art activities, and handwriting.

Figure-background constancy is the ability to pick a simple object or figure out of a cluttered, complex background. Symmetrical figures are more easily found than asymmetrical. Deficits in figure-background constancy are either reversals or forced responsiveness. *Reversal* is a situation wherein the background stimuli take precedence over the foreground stimulus. *Forced responsiveness* is an equally strong reaction to all factors in the environment and the inability to select objects from this environment for special attention. This problem is illustrated by the child who responds well in a flashcard drill showing he knows the word, but becomes confused in reading a book because he cannot discriminate the desired word from the others on the page. The problem is apparent in paper-pencil tests or games of embedded figures: Can you find the hidden objects?

On the playground balls and teammates may blend together or float in and out of focus. Confusions pertaining to near-far, front-back, and high-low suggest figure-background problems. These are often confounded further by dissociation since distinguishing a foreground stimulus from background clutter may also entail recognition of a part from its whole.

To minimize such problems, balls, play apparatus, and floor patterns should be brightly colored to contrast with the background. Balance beams and mats should be a different color from the floor. Masking tape figures on walls and floors should utilize reds and blues, colors which have been shown to be children's favorites. Basketball backdrops and goal cages should stand out boldly against less relevant stimuli.

Visual and auditory games which stress the locations of objects and sounds may be directed toward remediation of figure-background problems. Illustrative of these are such

Figure 14.2. Masking tape figures on wall help children with figure-background problems.

Figure 14.3. Following the leader's movements with hollow tubes helps to train both visual and auditory discrimination.

guessing games as I Bet You Can't See What I See, Who's Got My Bone?, Huckleberry Beanstalk, and Hot and Cold. Scavenger hunts also demand the ability to isolate relevant stimuli from the background.

Nonspecific Awkwardness or Clumsiness

The child with learning disabilities is typically uncoordinated and inaccurate in motor responses. There may be a discrepancy as great as four years between motor skills level and chronological age.[10] This, of course, affects peer acceptance and self-concept.

Louise Clarke, the mother of a boy with learning disabilities, devotes several passages to this difficulty in her excellent book.

> There was a new area of incompetence too. Mike's school was very big on athletics. All the men teachers directed at least one sport, and starting in the second grade there was a great deal of talk about who made what team.
> Mike did not make any.
> Mr. Klein, the athletic director, was openly contemptuous, and the best Mike got from any of the male staff was amused tolerance. He wanted very much to make a team, and during vacations he and his father threw balls back and forth, or his father would throw them for him to bat. It was an endless exercise. . . .
> Mike never did get the knack of it. He would miss catches by fractions of inches, but near-misses do not count in games. His batting was so erratic that his father. . . could not field them half the time.[11]

Mike, like most other learning disabled children, seemed to have trouble only in hand-eye coordination and balance. He was an excellent swimmer, winning many ribbons in competitive events from grade school on. Moreover, his strength, cardiovascular endurance, and running speed enabled him to perform well on fitness tests. Having completed a Ph.D. in science at Harvard University in his twenties, Mike recalls his physical education experiences and states:

> My hand-eye coordination was never very good and it still isn't. But I wouldn't tell dyslexics to stay away from sports, just the competitive sports that put a premium on hand-eye coordination, like baseball or handball. Anything where the margin of error is small. Tennis and squash allow for a margin of error. They demand coordination, but you can get away with it; you don't have to hit the ball everytime at dead center of the racquet.[12]

10. William Cruickshank, *The Brain-Injured Child in Home, School, and Community* (Syracuse: Syracuse University Press, 1967), p. 54.

11. Louise Clarke, *Can't Read, Can't Write, Can't Talk Too Good Either* (New York: Walker and Company, 1973), p. 20.

12. Ibid., p. 132

Parents are generally more concerned about awkwardness in fine motor tasks than gross motor. Typically the LD child displays problems in (1) cutting with scissors; (2) handwriting; (3) coping with buttons, snaps, and zippers; (4) tying shoes; (5) using knife, fork, and spoon; (6) lacing and sewing activities; (7) pegboard games; and (8) other tasks demanding manual dexterity. The correlation between fine motor and gross motor activities is low.

Little, if any, evidence exists to show that training in gross motor activities will carry over into manipulative skills and vice versa. *A motor development program therefore should entail practice on the specific skills in which the child is weak. Remediation directed primarily toward the improvement of coordination, however, should not be substituted for a broad comprehensive program of sports, dance, and aquatics.*

Competitive Play and Game Choices

Among the several authorities who question whether LD children can function optimally in integrated physical education programs is Angie Nall, who states:

LD children can easily participate in a daily physical education program of big motor activities if there is a very small group of children, sufficient supervision so that those who need it may have a one-to-one supervision, and if there is no competition in the group. These children cannot take noise and react with negative behavior. It is, therefore, difficult to work with them in a gymnasium. Competition means someone must lose. These children have lost so many times in their lives that one more loss merely compounds the problem. [13]

The game choices of LD children have been studied by Cratty and associates and by Trammell and Sherrill. [14, 15] Both investigations used modifications of the Sutton-Smith Play and Game List. Cratty compared the percentage of children with and without movement problems who indicated a liking for thirty-seven games. His sample of 293 elementary school children

Figure 14.4. The competitive play and game choices of LD children remain an enigma.

ranged in age from five through twelve. He concluded that clumsy children tend to avoid vigorous, active games, particularly those involving direct contact such as football, wrestling, and boxing. He noted also that boys with movement problems seemed to prefer

13. Letter from Angie Nall, Director. Angie Nall School-Hospital, Beaumont, Texas, 1972.

14. Bryant Cratty et. al., *Motor Activities, Motor Ability, and the Education of Children* (Springfield, Illinois: Charles C. Thomas, 1970) pp. 45-85.

15. Carol Trammell, "A Comparison of Expressed Play Interests of Children With Language and/or Learning Disabilities and Normal Children," Unpublished M. A. Study, Texas Woman's University, 1974.

some type of fantasy play in which "pretend" bravery could be evidenced (spaceman, cowboy, cops and robbers). This was not true of boys of the same age representing the normal population.

Trammell and Sherrill used Chi Square values to determine significant differences in the preferences for 120 games, 27 of which were classified as competitive. The subjects were 197 children classified as LD under special education legislative provisions in Texas and 197 children not so classified. The ages ranged from eight through twelve. It was concluded that LD children were more like normal children in game choices than unlike them. Out of 120 games, there were only 18 on which normal and LD boys disagreed enough to yield a significant difference. LD and normal girls were even more alike than the boys. Out of 120 games, there were only 9 in which the two groups disagreed enough to cause a significant difference.

All other differences between LD and normal boys and girls were in the degree to which games were liked or disliked. Particularly significant was the fact that both groups professed to like such competitive games as football, basketball, and baseball.

Organizations and/or Source Materials

1. Academic Therapy Publications, 1539 Fourth Street, San Rafael, California 94901.

2. The Association for Children with Learning Disabilities, 5225 Grace Street (Upper Level), Pittsburgh, Pennsylvania 15236.

3. California Association for Neurologically Handicapped Children, 11291 McNab Street, Garden Grove, California 92641.

4. Institutes for the Achievement of Human Potential (IAHP), 8801 Stenton Avenue, Philadelphia, Pennsylvania 19118. (Central headquarters for Doman-Delacato techniques.)

5. International Reading Association, 6 Tyre Avenue, Newark, Delaware 19711.

6. The Marianne Frostig Center of Educational Therapy, 5981 Venice Blvd., Los Angeles, California 90034.

7. Massachusetts Association for Children with Learning Disabilities, Box 908, 1296 Worcester Road, Framingham, Massachusetts 01701. Publishes newspaper called *Gazette*.

8. New York Association for Brain Injured Children, 305 Broadway, New York, New York 10007.

9. Ontario Association for Children With Learning Disabilities, 88 Eglinton Avenue East, Suite 322, Toronto 315, Ontario, Canada.

10. The Orton Society, Suite 204, 8415 Bellona Land, Townson, Maryland 21204.

11. Quebec Association for Children With Learning Disabilities, 6338 Victoria Ave., Montreal 252, Quebec, Canada.

References

Association for Children With Learning Disabilities. *Selected Papers on Learning Disabilities from Proceedings of Annual Conferences.* San Rafael, California: Academic Therapy Publications.

Arnheim, Daniel, D., and Sinclair, William A. *The Clumsy Child,* St. Louis: C. B. Mosby.

Ayres, A. Gene. *Sensory Integration and Learning Disorders.* Los Angeles: Western Psychological Services, 1972.

Chalfant, James C., and Schefflin, Margaret A. *Central Processing Dysfunctions in Children: A Review of Research.* Bethesda, Maryland: National Institute of Neurological Diseases and Stroke, 1969.

Cruickshank, William M. *The Brain-Injured Child in Home, School, and Community.* Syracuse, New York: Syracuse University Press, 1967.

Frostig, Marianne. *Movement Education: Theory and Practice.* Chicago: Follett Educational Corp., 1970.

Harvat, Robert W. *Physical Education for Children With Perceptual-Motor Learning Disabilities.* Columbus, Ohio: Charles E. Merrill Publishing Company, 1971.

Johnson, Doris J., and Myklebust, Helmer R. *Learning Disabilities.* New York: Grune and Stratton, 1967.

Myers, Patricia I., and Hammill, Donald D. *Methods for Learning Disorders.* New York: John Wiley and Sons, Inc., 1969.

New York Academy of Sciences. *Minimal Brain Dysfunction.* Vol. 205 of *Annals of New York Academy of Sciences,* 1973.

Valett, Robert E. *Programming Learning Disabilities.* Belmont, California: Fearon Publishers, 1969.

Periodicals

Academic Therapy. Published quarterly, 1539 Fourth Street, San Rafael, California 94901.

American Journal of Orthopsychiatry. Published five times a year by the American Orthopsychiatric Association, 1775 Broadway, New York, New York 10019.

Bulletin of the Orton Society. Published annually by the Orton Society, P. O. Box 153, Pomfret, Connecticut.

Children's House. Published bimonthly by Children's House, Inc., P. O. Box 111, Caldwell, New Jersey.

Exceptional Children. Published monthly except for June and August by the Council for Exceptional Children, 1920 Association Drive, Reston, Virginia 22091.

Journal of Learning Disabilities. Published monthly by the Professional Press, 5 North Wabash Avenue, Chicago, Illinois.

Journal of Special Education. Published quarterly by Buttonwood Farms, Inc., 3354 Byberry Road, Philadelphia, Pennsylvania.

The Pointer. Published by the Association for Special Class Teachers and Parents of the Handicapped, Inc., Box 1878, Grass Valley, California.

Rehabilitation Literature. Published monthly by the National Easter Seal Society for Crippled Children and Adults, 2023 West Ogden Avenue, Chicago, Illinois 60612.

The Slow Learning Child. Published three times a year by the University of Queensland.

Teaching Exceptional Children. Published quarterly by the Council for Exceptional Children. 1920 Association Drive, Reston, Virginia 22091.

Deaf and Hearing Impaired

Figure 15.0. The Rome School for the Deaf has their own way of sideline conversation.

The deaf and hearing impaired often excel in physical education. At Gallaudet College in Washington, D.C., the only liberal arts college in the world for the deaf, student interest in athletics is so high that the men engage in eight and the women in five intercollegiate sports. Almost half of the eligible male students are members of one or more of these teams: football, basketball, baseball, soccer, wrestling, swimming, cross-country, track and field. The Gallaudet Modern Dance Group has performed both in Europe and throughout the United States. Says Peter Wisher, founder and director of the group, "The majority of audiences are composed of hearing people, but they soon forget the girls are deaf. They become tremendously involved with the kids, especially during the numbers using abstracted sign language." [1]

Other deaf persons like Penn State halfback Gary Klingensmith [2] and Sam Oates at Hardin-Simmons in Texas have gained recognition as outstanding members of hearing teams. Gary and Sam agree that a deaf athlete must try harder than a hearing one but success is possible if the motto *100 percent all the time* is followed.

The adapted physical educator may choose to work in a school for the deaf or he may wish to integrate one or two deaf or hearing-impaired children with his regular classes. He soon realizes that many children have hearing losses and/or problems of auditory perception.

Understanding the Audiogram

In the multidisciplinary approach to determining the educational needs of children, the physical educator participates in staffings during which an audiologist or speech and hearing specialist discusses the results of various tests. Fig. 15.1 is an audiogram, which presents test results in graph form.

The audiogram provides information about two dimensions of hearing: (1) intensities of

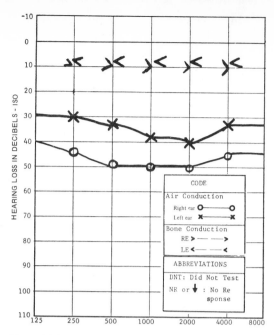

Figure 15.1. Audiogram.

sound as measured by decibels and (2) frequencies of sound, which encompass different pitches. This information is obtained by means of an *audiometer* which can test both for *air-conduction* (AC) and *bone-conduction* (BC). Findings resulting from the AC test are recorded in 0 and X symbols on the audiogram for the right and left ears respectively. Findings resulting from the BC test are recorded in >and <symbols on the audiogram for the right and left ears respectively. When colored lines are used to connect the symbols on the graph, red denotes the right ear and blue or black, the left ear.

Each symbol marks the pupil's hearing level, or threshold, at a different sound frequency. The term *threshold* refers to the minimal level at which the pupil can detect the presence of sound at least 50 percent of the

1. Eleanor Carney, ed., "Beat of a Different Drum," *Gallaudet Today* (Spring, 1971), p. 21.
2. "Star Against Odds," *Family Weekly*, (September 27, 1964), p. 18.

time. When the audiogram is interpreted, findings are given separately for the BC and AC tests. It can be seen on the sample audiogram that this pupil had more or less normal BC hearing ability, but the AC test indicated hearing loss. Specifically, the audiogram is read as follows: at a frequency of 500 Hz, airborne sounds can be heard by the right ear at about 45 decibels and by the left ear at about 30 decibels.

What does this mean to the physical educator? Not much, unless he has some understanding of normal ranges of hearing and different types of hearing losses. The following is intended to enable the physical educator to listen attentively in staffings and to ask pertinent questions. By so doing, the physical educator not only gains the respect of an important member of the multidisciplinary team, but he also gains support for his own efforts.

Attributes of Sound

The attributes of sound are *frequency, intensity,* and *spectrum* or *timbre.* A hearing loss may affect one or all of these.

Frequency is the attribute of a sound wave which gives rise to the subjective perception of *pitch.* The source of sound is always a vibrating mass of some kind: a mass of air, a piano string, the vocal folds. Frequency can be defined as the number of double vibrations or cycles per second (cps). If a sound produces 1000 double vibrations[3] per second, it is said to have a frequency of 1000 cps or Hz. Since 1960, the term *Hertz,* abbreviated Hz, in honor of the famous physicist Heinrich Hertz, has been substituted for cps.

Frequencies are classified as *infrasonic, audible to human ears,* and *ultrasonic.* Most human beings with normal hearing can perceive frequencies from about 20 to 20,000 Hz. It should be noted, however, that the audiogram includes only the frequencies between 125 and 8000 since these are the most important in daily communication.

Three of these frequencies, 500, 1000, and 2000 Hz, are emphasized in relating hearing loss to speech and vice versa. For instance, persons who do not hear frequencies above 2000 Hz have difficulty in recognizing such *high frequency* sounds as the letters *s, z, sh, zh, th* as in think, *th* as in that, *ch* as in chair, *j* as in Joe, *p, b, t, d, f, v,* and *h.* This fact and others about the relative strength of various speech sounds is important to the physical educator who uses games and perceptual-motor activities to develop awareness of the directional differences between *p, b, d,* and *q.* Too often children are thought to have perceptual-motor problems when in reality they are suffering from a hearing loss.

Pitch, defined as the highness or lowness of a sound, depends upon the frequency of vibrations. Teachers try to speak in a low, well-modulated pitch because low frequency sounds are more easily understood than those of high pitch. This fact is important also when physical educators choose a whistle from several different pitches. The teacher who uses musical accompaniment should be aware that the twelve semitones (C, C#, D, D#, E, F, F#, G, G#, A, A#, B) comprising an octave each has a frequency value in Hz. Middle C on the piano, for instance, is 256 Hz. The C for each new pitch, or octave, has twice as many Hz as the previous C as depicted below:

Pitch		Frequency
C4	(Middle C)	256 Hz
C5		512 Hz
C6		1024 Hz
C7		2048 Hz
C8		4096 Hz
C9		8192 Hz

The dance teacher who works with hearing impaired children will wish to learn more about

3. A double vibration or cycle consists of one successive compression and rarefaction. It can be conceptualized also as a complete movement of a pendulum back and forth.

the relationships between pitch and auditory perception.

Intensity is the physical phenomenon which governs the perception of loudness and softness. Specifically, intensity is the amount of physical energy which reaches the hearing mechanism; this energy is dependent upon the amplitude and frequency of each sound wave. The unit of measurement which expresses the intensity of a sound is the *decibel* (db). Normal hearing is established as the zero level in decibels. A sound at 0 level is barely audible. For normal conversation to be heard at a distance from ten to twenty feet, the loudness may vary between thirty-five and sixty-five decibels depending upon the highness of the pitch. This is the normal threshold of hearing for daily living activities. When the intensity of sound ranges above 100 decibels, the sound may become painful. Ninety decibels is the maximum allowable under federal regulations for industrial noise. Noise pollution is one of the greatest health problems confronting communities today. Numerous research studies have shown that the combined sounds of traffic, machinery, and people in highly populated areas often reach levels of intensity which may be causing hearing losses.

Spectrum or *timbre* encompasses the different tonal qualities ranging from pure tone, which has a single frequency, to the complex tones which comprise normal speech sounds. Timbre includes all of the qualities besides highness, lowness, loudness, and softness which enable the listener to differentiate between sounds. Speech sounds, like musical chords, are complex tones made up of several separate sounds or *partials*. The human ear does not normally distinguish the individual tones comprising a speech sound or a piano chord; yet it learns to recognize the distinctive arrangement of partial vibrations which make a *b* or *p* sound. Inability to hear sounds at certain frequencies affects the perception of tonal qualities. It is doubtful that anyone with

normal hearing can be *tone deaf;* yet widespread individual differences exist within abilities to perceive speech sounds. In general, vowels and diphthongs are most easily perceived. Children with mild to moderate hearing losses have the most difficulty in perceiving the following high frequency sounds: *th* as in think, *f, p, d, b, th* as in that, *v, k, g, t, s, z,* and *zh.*

This background is especially important to teachers and parents of LD children. There is increasing evidence that many such children have disorders of auditory perception. Physical educators [4,5] have begun to modify games to give children practice in discriminating vowel sounds and consonant blends. Illustrative of such adapted games are steal the bacon and circle call ball in which players are assigned letter sounds instead of the traditional numbers. For instance, the starting formation for steal the bacon might resemble one of the following patterns:

Team A	Team B		Team A	Team B
a	$\bar{u}$		f	z
e	$\bar{o}$		p	s
i	$\bar{i}$		d	t
o	$\bar{e}$		b	g
u	$\bar{a}$		v	k
Beanbag representing bacon			Beanbag representing bacon	
$\bar{a}$	u		k	v
$\bar{e}$	o		g	b
$\bar{i}$	i		t	d
$\bar{o}$	e		s	p
$\bar{u}$	a		z	f

4. James H. Humphrey and Dorothy D. Sullivan, *Teaching Slow Learners Through Active Games* (Springfield, Illinois: Charles C. Thomas, 1970).

5. Bryant J. Cratty, *Active Learning* (Englewood Cliffs, New Jersey: Prentice-Hall, Inc., 1971).

When the teacher calls out a word like cake, the two children assigned the long *a* sound run to the center and grab for the beanbag. The child who gets it and returns to his baseline without being tagged wins a point for his team, and the game continues with the teacher calling a new word. The use of letter sounds in games instead of numbers opens new horizons for the creative teacher who seeks variety and wishes to develop mental flexibility in his pupils. It is doubtful, however, that these so-called auditory perceptual-motor activities really improve auditory discrimination, i.e., the ability to hear sounds at different frequencies and to recognize the distinctive arrangement of partial vibrations. Physical educators wishing to specialize in perceptual-motor remediation should elect course work in speech and hearing therapy.

Degrees of Hearing Loss

Streng's classification of hearing loss as mild, marginal, moderate, severe, or profound is accepted in most special education settings. [6] In each specificiation of decibel loss, zero is arbitrarily established as normal. Thus a 30 decibel loss means that the child can hear sounds at 30 decibels that the average person can detect at zero on the testing apparatus.

1. *Mild.* The pupil has a 20 to 30 decibel loss in the better ear in frequencies from 500 to 2000. Children in this category do not experience appreciable problems in learning; they may need preferential seating or a place on the front row in the gymnasium. Their speech is usually normal although special help with vocabulary is recommended. Occasionally a young child with the hearing loss approaching 30 decibels will be fitted with a hearing aid, but essentially pupils with mild losses appear so normal that they are seldom identified until the routine hearing test is administered.

2. *Marginal.* The pupil has an overall 30 to 40 decibel loss. He *cannot* hear conversational speech at a distance further than three feet and may miss as much as 50 percent of class instruction if he cannot see the lips of the speaker. If the loss is of high frequency type, he may exhibit a slight speech defect. A hearing aid generally enables him to learn normally.

3. *Moderate.* The pupil has an overall 40 to 60 decibel loss. He can hear *loud* conversation within a three foot range but often misunderstands meanings. For this reason, he may be wrongly labeled as *slow* or a *behavioral problem*. He generally has defective speech, especially with *s, z, sh, ch,* and *j* sounds. His language usage and vocabulary are deficient also. Children with moderate loss often do not hear clearly even with the amplification provided by hearing aids. They require special training in speech reading and are often placed in special education.

4. *Severe.* The pupil who has an overall 60 to 75 decibel loss is considered partially or educationally deaf. Although he retains *residual hearing,* special training is needed in order to learn language. With a hearing aid, he can hear loud noises such as an automobile horn or a dog barking. With amplification, he may also hear words spoken several inches from his ear. If the hearing loss is congenital, he needs special training in order to learn to talk. He can enjoy music, but his pleasure is derived largely from its rhythm.

5. *Profound.* The pupil who has an overall loss greater than 75 decibels is essentially deaf. He cannot hear words even with the amplification of a hearing aid. He may be able to distinguish some noises from others if they are close by. He responds reflexively to loud sounds close to his ears

6. Alice Streng, *et al., Hearing Therapy for Children* (New York: Grune and Stratton, 1958), p. 164.

by turning his head or blinking his eyes, but the sounds themselves are meaningless. A child born deaf must receive specialized help very early in order to learn to speak and communicate with others. He may be fitted with a hearing aid at age two or three to enhance his awareness of loud sounds, thus improving his ability to interpret the environment. The hearing aid does not enable him to discriminate between speech sounds. He responds to music by recognizing the presence or cessation of vibrations.

Children with mild, marginal, and moderate losses are considered hard-of-hearing. Those with severe or profound losses are classified as deaf. Because communication skills are related to the age at which deafness occurs, children are classified further as either *congenitally deaf* or *adventitiously deaf*. The former are born deaf whereas the latter are deafened through illness or accident.

Etiology and Incidence of Hearing Loss

Approximately 62 percent of all severe and profound hearing losses are congenital while the other 38 percent are acquired. The National Foundation estimates that there are over 300,000 children in the United States who were born deaf or with a hearing loss. This condition shares second place in prevalence among the common birth defects: congenital blindness or visual loss, genitourinary malformations, and congenital heart and circulatory disease. Of the hearing losses designated as congenital, some are hereditary; some are idiopathic; and others can be traced to diseases such as German measles (rubella) which the mother contracted during pregnancy. The novel *In This Sign* [7] tells the story of Abel and Janice Ryder, both born deaf. As is often the case, both of their offspring as well as their grandson could hear and speak normally. In most cases congenital deafness seriously impairs language development. Even with ex-

cellent instruction, many deaf infants grow into adulthood unable to speak intelligibly.

Acquired hearing losses vary in severity depending upon the degree of loss and age of onset. Among the many persons with acquired hearing losses are Ludwig van Beethoven, Bernard Baruch, and Thomas Alva Edison. The last twenty-five years of Beethoven's life were spent in almost total deafness. His famous Ninth Symphony, the *Missa Solemnis*, and many of his piano sonatas and string quartets were composed after he became totally deaf. At his last appearance at a public concert, in 1824, Beethoven was completely oblivious to the applause of the audience acclaiming his ninth and final symphony.

It is estimated that between 5-7 percent of all school age children in the United States have auditory disorders. Of these, there are 52,300 deaf and 348,600 hearing-impaired children under age nineteen whose handicap is severe enough to require special educational provisions. [8]

The Deaf-Blind

Persons with combinations of handicaps which prevent their profiting satisfactorily from educational programs provided for the blind or the deaf individual are called *deafblind*. This condition may be acquired through such diseases as rubella, scarlet fever, and meningitis or hereditary. In the latter category, *Usher's syndrome* is the leading causative factor. It is a genetic condition resulting in congenital deafness and a progressive blindness known as retinitis pigmentosa which first appears in the early thirties.

It was not until the widespread rubella epidemic of 1963-1965, however, that large

7. Joanna Greenberg, *In This Sign* (New York: Holt, Rinehart, and Winston, 1970).

8. Estimates of Handicapped Children in the United States Compiled from Multiple Studies of Incidence and from Title VI State Reports. Washington, D. C.: Office of Education for the Handicapped, U. S. Office of Education, 1969.

numbers of children were identified as blind-deaf and receiving inadequate educational services. Estimates revealed that between 2,000 and 2,500 children and 5,000 to 7,000 adults were deaf-blind.

To cope with this problem, the federal government, in 1968, authorized the development of ten (now eleven) regional Deaf-Blind Centers scattered throughout the fifty states. A grant was awarded also to the University of Iowa to develop the *National Institute on Program Development and Training in Recreation for Deaf-Blind Children, Youth, and Adults.* Information on the delivery of recreation and leisure services can be obtained by writing to Dr. John Nesbitt, National Institute on Recreation for the Deaf-Blind, The University of Iowa, Iowa City, Iowa 52242.

The best known of deaf-blind persons is Helen Keller (1880-1968), who was disabled by an illness at nineteen months of age. Helen Keller graduated *Cum Laude* from Radcliffe, mastered five languages, and wrote three books. Her beautifully written biography[9] is among the classics which everyone should read. Less well known is Laura Bridgman[10] (1829-1889), the famous deaf-blind pupil of Samuel Gridley Howe, the founder of Perkins Institution, now located in Watertown, Massachusetts. Laura, who became deaf-blind at age two from scarlet fever, was described by Charles Dickens in his book *American Notes.* Only by reading Dickens's book were Helen Keller's parents in Alabama made aware of the existence of Perkins Institution and the availability of her now famous teacher Anne Sullivan Macy.

Still another deaf-blind person, Robert J. Smithdas, who suffered cerebral spinal meningitis at age five, has gained recognition through the publication of an autobiography[11] and success in his work as a public-relations counselor and lecturer at the Industrial Home for the Blind in Brooklyn, New York. At age thirty-two, after completing a Master of Arts degree at New York University and working at I.H.B. for several years, Smithdas wrote:

Loneliness was continually present in my life after I became deaf and blind. And even now, in adulthood, I find it with me despite all my adjustments to social living. Loneliness is a hunger for increasing human companionship, a need to be part of the activity that I know is constantly going on about me. . . . To share my moments of joy with someone else, to have others sympathize with my failures, appreciate my accomplishments, understand my moods, and value my intelligence—these are the essential conditions that are needed for happiness.

Types of Hearing Loss

The four main types of hearing loss are *conductive, sensori-neural, retriocochlear,* and *central.* These terms supplant the older classification of hearing losses: (1) obstructive or *conductive, sensorineural, retrocochlear,* and acquired hearing losses are of the conductive type, whereas most congenital hearing impairments are of the sensorineural type. Table 32 summarizes the characteristics of these two types. Retrocochlear hearing loss, which results from impairments of the cochlear branch of the auditory nerve, and central hearing loss, implying interference with auditory nerve impulses traveling from the cochlear nuclei in the brain stem to the temporal lobes of the cerebral cortex, will not be discussed since they are relatively rare. Central hearing loss, also known as auditory agnosia, is really a neurological problem rather than a hearing one.

Conductive Hearing Losses

Most acquired hearing losses are of this type. Some dysfunction of the outer or middle ear prevents the vibrations of sound waves from reaching the inner ear. Figure 15.2 depicts the *external ear,* the *middle ear,* and the

9. Helen Keller, *The Story of My Life* (New York: Airmont Publishing Co., Inc., 1965).

10. Edith Fisher Hunter, *Child of the Silent Night* (New York: Dell Publishing Co., 1963).

11. Robert J. Smithdas, *Life at My Fingertips* (New York: Doubleday and Company, Inc., 1958), p. 259.

Table 32 *Comparison of Conductive and Sensorineural Hearing Losses*

Conductive	Sensori-Neural

Dysfunction of outer ear or middle ear
  a. tympanic membrane
  b. ossicles
  c. Eustachian tubes
	Dysfunction of inner ear (labyrinth)
	  a. cochlea
	     organ of Corti
	     basilar membrane
	  b. semicircular canals

Air-conduction loss only	Air-conduction and bone-conduction tests show equal threshold losses.
Results only in partial loss never exceeding 55-60 decibels	Varies from partial to total losses
Tends to have about the same loss of sensitivity for sounds of all frequency. Called a *flat* hearing loss. Largely unaware of noise; benefits by speaker shouting.	Tends to have greater loss of sensitivity for sounds of high frequency than of low. Shouting does not help. Noise is frustrating.
Main problem is amplification of sound; discrimination of speech sounds is normal.	Main problem is discrimination between speech sounds; can usually hear but unable to derive meaning from high frequency sounds.
Hearing aids generally helpful. May hear well over telephone because of bone-conduction of sounds. Speech development and acquisition of language are not impaired seriously.	Hearing aids of limited value. Development of speech, understanding of language structure, and articulation are limited. Mispronounces words with high frequency sounds.
Can hear his own voice through bone-conduction, tends to speak too softly.	Tends to speak with excessive loudness.

inner ear. The *outer ear* consists of three parts: (1) *pinna;* (2) *external auditory meatus,* a cylindrical passageway about one inch long and one-fourth inch in diameter; and (3) the *tympanic membrane.* The external meatus contains wax-producing glands which produce *cerumen* (wax) which protects the eardrum from the penetration of dust and insects.

  External otitis, an inflammation of the outer ear caused by bacteria or fungi, causes temporary loss of hearing. Persons who swim a lot seem more susceptible to this condition than others. It results in swelling and partial closing (stenosis) of the external meatus, severe pain, persistent itching, and a thin watery discharge. Pupils with external otitis should not swim nor should they be allowed in the swimming pool or any other moist area.

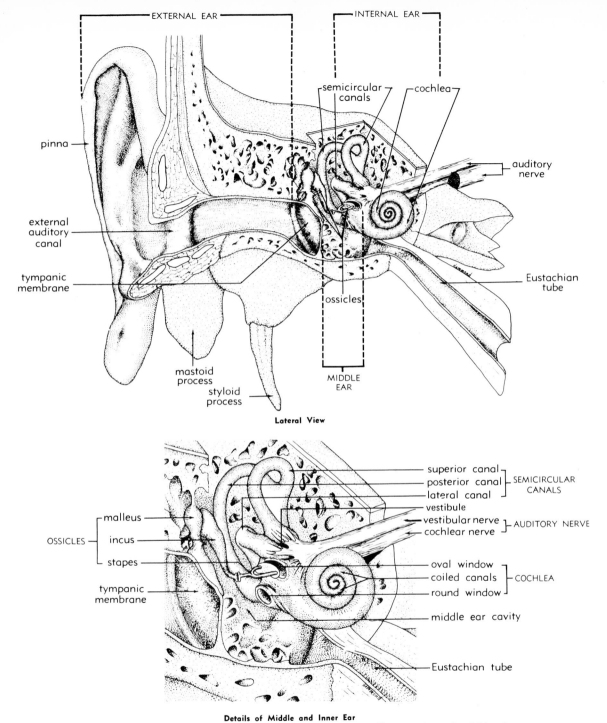

Figure 15.2. Diagram of the human ear.

© Kendall/Hunt Publishing Company

The tympanic membrane constitutes the division between the outer and middle ear. If it is ruptured or unable to vibrate, hearing loss occurs. The membrane may be perforated by objects thrust into the ear. It may be ruptured by extremely loud noises or by a *slap* on the ear which drives air into the external meatus with sufficient force to break through the thin membrane. Most often, however, the tympanic membrane is simply distended by the accumulation of fluid in the middle ear during an infection.

The middle ear, a tiny cavity only one to two cubic centimeters in volume, is where most conductive hearing losses occur. The middle ear is actually an extension of the *nasopharynx* by way of the *Eustachian tube,* and any malfunctioning of this tube affects hearing. Enlarged adenoids around the opening of the tube in the nasopharynx and allergic swelling of the tube cause malfunctioning as does the common cold. The beginning of almost all middle ear infections is the Eustachian tube. Any blockage of the Eustachian tube lowers the air pressure within the middle ear. The resulting unequal pressure on the two sides of the tympanic membrane causes retraction or a sucking inward of the membrane which in turn interferes with the vibration of sound waves. Artificial tubes are often inserted in the young child's ears to allow adequate healing of the middle ear. During the months that these tubes are worn, swimming is contraindicated.

Infection or inflammation of the middle ear, regardless of the cause, is known as *otitis media* and accounts for more conductive hearing losses than any other condition. Chronic inflammation may result in adhesions (very fine tears) between the tympanic membrane and the three tiny bones in the middle ear which in turn prevent the normal transmission of sound waves. Even though the adhesions heal, their scar tissue makes it impossible to regain normal mobility of the ossicles. Active infection in the middle ear is especially dangerous since it may spread backward into the air cells of the mastoid process of the temporal bone, causing *mastoiditis.* Prior to the 1940s, this was one of the most deadly conditions to which children were susceptible. The discovery of antibodies has significantly reduced the number of mastoidectomies once performed as well as the incidence of hearing loss. Chronic otitis media, however, remains a potential killer in that infection in the mastoid area can easily find its way to the meninges of the brain and cause meningitis. Among the many side effects of meningitis is severe sensorineural hearing loss.

Sensorineural and Other Types of Hearing Loss

In order to understand the hearing losses which result from damage to the inner ear, the auditory nerve, and the brain, a brief review of anatomy is necessary. Fig. 15.2 shows that the inner ear can be subdivided into the three *semicircular canals,* the *vestibule,* the *cochlea,* and the *auditory nerve.* The *inner ear,* called a *labyrinth* because of its intricate structure, is divided into the bony labyrinth, or outer hard shell, and the membranous labyrinth which lines the bony portion. Important to both the functions of hearing and balance is the fluid in the inner ear. *Perilymph* fills the space between the bony and membranous labyrinths. *Endolymph* is found inside the membranous labyrinth. Vibrations of the temporal bone cause these fluids to move, thus implementing the transmission of sound by bone conduction. Any change in the position of the head also causes these fluids to move in an effort to preserve balance.

The inner ear governs both the functions of hearing and balance. A hearing loss therefore often affects balance. Specifically, the sensory receptors for sound are within the *Organ of Corti* which is located within the *cochlea* and surrounded by endolymph. The Organ of Corti has been likened to a piano keyboard of 1500 keys, each responding to the pressure of tones of a particular frequency. On one end are the keys receiving tones of a frequency of 16,000 vibrations per second, and at the other end are keys receiving tones of a frequency of only 16 vibrations per second. These keys are really *hair cells* which connect with some 20,000 to 30,000 nerve fibers which form the cochlear branch of the auditory, or VIIIth, cranial nerve. Sound impulses are transmitted to the temporal lobes of the cerebral cortex, the part of the brain which is responsible for the perception and cognition of sounds.

The sensory receptors for balance are located within the *vestibular apparatus*, which consists of the three semicircular canals, the utricle, and the saccule. The vestibular, or labyrinthine, sense enables the body to relate to the gravitational field by detecting changes in both static and dynamic balance. Static balance is governed primarily by changes in head position which are detected by hair cells within the utricle, also called the otolith organ, and perhaps the saccule. Changes in dynamic balance, including the body righting reflexes, are detected by hair cells within the fluid-filled ducts of the semicircular canals. The hair cells within the vestibular apparatus connect with thousands of nerve fibers which form the vestibular branch of the auditory nerve. Sensory impulses reporting changes in position are transmitted to the cerebellum via the vestibulospinal tract. Disorders of balance therefore can be traced more or less to four anatomical sites: (1) the cerebellum, (2) the vestibulospinal tract, (3) the vestibular branch of the auditory nerve, and (4) the inner ear.

Nonconductive hearing losses are more serious than conductive because they interfere with the transmission of sensory impulses to the brain. A hearing aid cannot compensate adequately for such losses, and no cures are known. By far the most common cause of sensorineural hearing loss is normal aging, in which sensitivity for higher frequencies gradually diminishes. Progressive loss of hearing related to aging is callled *presbycusis*. Along with hearing loss, the aged tend to experience a deterioration in balance.

Most deafness has a mixed etiology. Measles, mumps, scarlet fever, diphtheria, whooping cough, influenza, and various viral infections cause conductive impairments through middle ear involvements which in turn toxically affect the sensitive nerve endings in the cochlea. Such drugs as quinine, streptomycin, cinchophen, and the salicylates, when taken in large doses to cure a middle ear infection, may cause severe damage to the nerve endings in the inner ear. Congenital deafness also generally stems from mixed etiology, and infants born deaf often demonstrate problems of balance which do not respond to perceptual-motor training.

Characteristics of the Deaf and Hearing Impaired

Widespread individual differences exist among persons with hearing losses. Only those children who are born with severe or profound losses or who lose their hearing before they develop speech and language are significantly different from their normal peers. The characteristics discussed here apply only to such children.

Socialization

The greatest problems experienced by the deaf are in the social domain, specifically in the acquisition of speech and language. Even with superior training, their vocalizations tend to have a distorted tonal quality. The voice is monotonous, guttural, and highly fluctuating in pitch range. Most persons cannot easily understand what the deaf are trying to say, and communication is often impossible because the listener does not care enough to try to extract meaning from their best efforts at speech. As a result, the deaf suffer almost the same problems as a foreigner whose language is not understood.

The deaf child is likely to be left out of the spontaneous play activities of neighborhood children. The problem is intensified as the low organized games of childhood become increasingly structured and governed by complex rules. Without special help, the deaf child does not grasp the intricacies of such team games as baseball, football, and soccer which are usually acquired in spontaneous play. The rare exception to this generalization occurs when the deaf child exhibits such superior skills that the neighborhood team cannot afford to ignore his potential contributions. These motor skills may have been developed through practice alone, with a parent or sibling, or a special friend; the important point is that they are developed *before* group acceptance occurs rather than in the everyday give-and-take of neighborhood play. For every superior deaf athlete who is accepted by the group, there are hundreds whose motor skills remain average or mediocre. These children may be inordinately lonely. Many withdraw and develop solitary play interests and hobbies. Thus the vicious circle begins. With few or no playmates, there are less opportunities for practicing speech and learning to lip-read. With little practice, the child's speech worsens as does his ability to understand that of others.

The primary purpose of physical education for the deaf in an integrated setting should be *socialization*. When the physical educator welcomes a deaf child into his class, the curriculum for all students must be modified somewhat for a few days or weeks. He must consider: What physical education activities require the least verbal communication for success? In which activities can a *different* child make friends the quickest? Team sports are not the answer. It is extremely important that the deaf child not be integrated onto a hearing team until he is accepted and liked by the team members. They must be willing to give him the ball, to create opportunities for him to score, and to help him understand team signals, the calls of the official, and the suggestions of the coach. The deaf child's motor skills seldom compensate for the inconveniences in team communication which his presence creates. Only when he is genuinely liked and wanted by the team members will his integration on the team be mutually satisfying. The physical educator nor any other adult can rush this process.

The physical educator who agrees to accept a deaf child in his class should be committed to providing individual and dual sports, dance, and aquatics. Swimming, all forms of dance, archery, golf, rifle shooting, bowling, tennis, and badminton are among the many activities which the deaf enjoy most in play with the hearing. In these activities, he can wear his hearing aid and derive maximum social benefits from communication with others. Ideally he can be introduced first to individual sports and dance. Then, as his ability to communicate and make friends grows, he can progress to dual and team sports.

Language

Language functions are classified as *expressive* (speaking and writing), *inner*, (thinking and verbal imagery), and *receptive* (hearing and reading). The deaf child experiences problems with some aspects of each of these functions. His difficulty in learning to speak is often greater than learning to use his residual hearing and/or to read speech. The terms *deaf mute* and *deaf and dumb* are not only repugnant but inaccurate. With good training, most deaf persons can learn to speak although the speech of some will be more intelligible than that of others.

Deaf infants babble normally in infancy, producing the same sounds as others of comparable age. Whereas the child who hears continues to make sounds for his own pleasure as well as to communicate, the child with no auditory sense to reinforce his verbalizations tends to produce fewer and fewer vocal sounds. Normal children, for instance, enjoy growling when doing the bear walk and barking when doing the dog walk. They may talk incessantly to an imaginary playmate. In contrast, the deaf are capable of making sound but seldom do so except to attract attention or to convey a need.

The deaf compensate for their inadequate speech through various modes of nonverbal communication. They use eye contact, facial expressions, and gestures with more success than the normal. The deaf neither derive pleasure from laughing nor *hearing* others laugh; hence, they laugh seldom. Their laughter is characteristically atypical in acoustic quality, inflection, and pitch range. Unlike laughter, crying—although also a vocalization—is essentially normal in the deaf.

The expression of intense emotions in socially acceptable ways is difficult when speech is inadequate. When angered, the deaf person may resort to physical violence. Instead of trying to tell someone to stop annoying him, he is likely to shove or push back. Whereas many persons *work out* problems of grief, insecurity, and misunderstanding by talking to a trusted friend, the deaf find the sharing of emotions difficult. Likewise, the normal channels of individual and group psychotherapy which are basedly largely upon vocalization are denied him. Dance and movement therapy can often meet his needs.

The role which physical education, especially dance, can play in enhancing the development of expressive language is unparalleled. When the physical educator teaches in a school for the deaf, his primary purpose may be instruction in the use of movement as a means of nonverbal expression. Modern dance, synchronized swimming, and free floor exercise in gymnastics offer opportunities for communicating ideas and feelings.

Inner language, that which is used in thinking and *talking to ourselves,* is developed normally in response to hearing certain words and phrases over and over until they acquire meaning. When infants receive no verbal stimuli, either because they are deaf or their parents do not speak, they are forced to develop inner language through visual stimuli. In a study of college youths with normal hearing who were born of deaf parents, it was found that sign language continued to be the language in which they thought even though as adults they could speak several languages. [12]

The deaf person whose inner language is that of signs and gestures has great difficulty in coping with abstractions. Unless the word, idea, or feeling can be conveyed *visually* or *kinesthetically,* the deaf child may be unable to comprehend its meaning until he receives instruction in oral language. Expressive language, or the ability to speak and/or to use signs and gestures for communication, develops only after inner language is established.

Figure 15.3. Abstractions like the dog walk make sense to a deaf child only after he has seen a dog and has a model to emulate.

The slowness with which deaf children develop inner and expressive language skills is often mistaken for mental retardation. The physical educator who works with deaf children must

12. Doris J. Johnson and Helmer R. Myklebust, *Learning Disabilities* (New York: Grune and Stratton, 1967), p. 37.

acquire as much knowledge as possible about nonverbal communication.

The physical educator must ascertain that the learning environment is conducive to the reception of symbolic language. The lighting must be adequate for speech reading, and the person giving instructions must be close enough so that minute movements of his lips and tongue can be perceived. When instruction occurs out-of-doors, care must be taken that the deaf child is not facing the sun as he tries to read lips.

In games like soccer and football which cover many yards of distance, players and teacher should be ever aware that the deaf child cannot read lips from across the field, nor can he hear a whistle. Large hand signals should accompany all verbal instructions and whistle blows. The teacher should position himself so that he is always within the deaf child's view.

Many authorities recommend that hearing aids be removed during physical education. This generalization seems appropriate only for team sports with body contact. In dance, individual, and dual sports there appears to be no reason for removing the hearing aid. It should be remembered, however, that a hearing aid amplifies all noise, not just word sounds. As a result, deaf children may react negatively to prolonged noise and have frequent tension headaches.

Hyperactivity

The deaf child may appear hyperactive. He must move frequently to maintain visual contact with the action. Knowing that he is expected to follow instructions and yet unable to hear them, he feels compelled to watch the teacher's mouth as she moves about the room. Often this is at the expense of completing assigned work at the desk. The deaf child's restlessness often stems from boredom. Unable to hear or comprehend, he may wiggle, shuffle his feet, or grit his teeth. Since he cannot hear,

he is often completely unaware of these disquieting activities. If his pronunciation is poor and sometimes evokes laughter, he may use movement as an attention-getting device rather than risk speaking.

Postures

No studies concerning the relationships between hearing loss and postures have been conducted. Unilateral hearing losses are thought to be a possible cause of abnormal tilts and rotations of the head. The hearing impaired person may show a tendency to lean forward or toward the source of a sound.

In physical education, deaf children should not be expected to enjoy exercises which demand postures in which the body is bent over and the vision limited. There is a tendency, for instance, for the deaf child to keep his head up while touching his toes or performing the various animal walks. In aquatics, for the same reason, many deaf children prefer swimming with the head, or at least the eyes, out of the water. Underwater lights can be used for signaling when deaf children learn regulation strokes and synchronized stunts.

Motor Characteristics

Of the many authorities who have written textbooks on deafness and hearing loss, Helmer R. Myklebust [13] is the only one who has devoted an entire chapter to motor functioning. Since the other writers virtually ignore motor behavior except for brief passages which allude to a shuffling gait and/or balance dysfunctions, Myklebust becomes a primary source to educators concerned with the *whole child*. He has contributed also to the literature on language and learning disabilities [14] and is an authority on disorders of auditory language. Myklebust is Director of the Institute for

13. Helmer R. Myklebust, *The Psychology of Deafness* (New York: Grune and Stratton, 1964).
14. Doris J. Johnson and Helmer R. Myklebust, *Learning Disabilities* (New York: Grune and Stratton, 1967).

Language Disorders at Northwestern University as well as Professor of Audiology in the School of Speech and Professor of Otolaryngology in the School of Medicine.

Myklebust critically reviews the findings of Long (1932), Morsh (1936), and others who have used deaf subjects as only a small part of their research. He refers frequently also to a study conducted by himself in 1946.[15] Experimental evidence concerning the motor characteristics of the deaf comes primarily from research conducted in the 1930s and 1940s. Almost all of the conclusions are now subject to controversy, and many questions need answering. Does lack of auditory experience, resulting in altered perceptual organization, in turn alter the dynamics of motor function? Does congenital deafness cause a change in visuo-motor organization and behavior? Does deafness, with or without semicircular canal dysfunctions, affect proprioception, somasthesis, and tactual motor performance? The need for research in these areas is great. The physical educator should accept the motor characteristics and suggested teaching procedures which follow as hypotheses to be tested rather than as conclusive truths.

Balance

Impairment of balance occurs most frequently when the hearing loss is caused by meningitis. In such cases the destruction is primarily in the semicircular canals rather than in the cerebellum. When deafness and loss of balance are present simultaneously, the convalescent often finds the loss of balance to be the greater problem. In some instances, he must learn to walk again.

Myklebust, Long, and Morsh, in separate studies, each compared deaf and hearing students on several motor tasks. Each investigator found significant differences between their two samples only on balance. Of the six motor abilities measured by the Oseretsky Motor Proficiency Test, the deaf made their lowest scores on general static balance and on speed. Deaf children have also been found inferior on locomotor coordination (dynamic balance) as measured by the Health Rail Walking Test. Furthermore, the meningitic deaf who had known semicircular canal impairment made significantly lower scores on the rail walking test than other deaf children. Berges, a physical education instructor in the Clarke School for the Deaf, Northampton, Massachusetts, notes that participation of deaf children in stunts, tumbling, and apparatus units may have to be limited because of their poor balance and dizziness.[16]

Wisher challenges the many generalizations about the balance ability of the deaf.[17] He states that poor balance, in the sense of total body response, has not been a problem among his students. This may be because his observations have been based on college students rather than the total deaf population. His caution, however, is sound in that widespread individual differences exist among the deaf.

The use of perceptual-motor activities planned specifically to improve balance is controversial. Myklebust states that such training may be ineffective and even unwise since semicircular canal dysfunction is irreversible.[18] No research has been reported which shows that the balance of deaf children can be improved by specific activities. Myklebust does observe that over a long period of time victims of meningitis gradually acquire good balance, apparently through compensatory use of vision

15. Helmer R. Myklebust, "Significance of Etiology in Motor Performance of Deaf Children with Special Reference to Meningitis," *American Journal of Psychology* Vol. 59, No. 2 (April, 1946), p. 249.

16. Shirley Berges, "The Deaf Student in Physical Education," *JOHPER* Vol. 40, No. 3 (March, 1969), p. 69.

17. Peter Wisher, "Dance and the Deaf," *JOHPER* Vol. 40, No. 3 (March, 1969), p. 81.

18. Helmer R. Myklebust, *The Psychology of Deafness* (New York: Grune and Stratton, 1964), p. 200.

Figure 15.4. Deaf children can acquire good balance through compensatory use of vision and kinesthetic cues.

and kinesthetic cues. This occurs naturally rather than through prescribed balance activities.

The physical educator should plan a child's program around his strengths rather than his weaknesses. When balance beam and similar activities are planned for a class, the deaf child should be offered alternative skills to be learned on other pieces of apparatus. He should be allowed but not coerced to try balance boards and beams, stilts, and pogo sticks. A cubicle or closed area should be provided where he can practice these activities away from the staring eyes and comments of classmates. Games and relays performed with the eyes closed or blindfolded are contraindicated for the deaf. Activities should be planned to enhance vision and kinesthesis. All forms of

dance increase body awareness. The increasingly popular Oriental exercise systems and martial arts, karate, kung fu, and Tai Chi contribute to this objective also.

When children, deaf or otherwise, have known balance problems, they should be given special instruction on the kinesiological principles of equilibrium. Movement exploration sessions may be developed around the following themes.

1. Center of gravity. What is it? How do your movements affect it? In what movements can you keep the center of gravity centered over its supporting base? Can your hands be used as a supporting base? What happens when your center of gravity moves in front of the supporting base? In back of it? To the side of it? What activities lower your center of gravity? Raise it?

2. Broad base. How can you adapt different exercises so that the supporting base is larger than normal? In what directions can you enlarge your base, i.e., how many stances can you assume? In which direction should you enlarge your base when throwing? Batting? Serving a volleyball? Shooting baskets?

The child quickly learns to compensate for poor balance by maintaining his body in a mechanically favorable position. He should be allowed to perform exercises in a crouching, kneeling, or sitting position while classmates without balance deficits work from a standing position. An exercise bar or back of a chair provide added support during activities performed on one foot or partially in the air. Because he is more likely to fall than other children, he should be taught the various dance falls and given opportunities to use them in choreography and creative dramatics. His proficiency in the execution of planned falls should carry over into the accidental ones, enabling him to land in mechanically efficient positions and to relax.

Motor Speed

The relationship between deafness, speed, time, and motor behavior is clearly indicated. Myklebust reported that speed was one of the two greatest deficits of deaf children taking the Oseretsky Motor Proficiency Test. Tests timed for speed should not be used in the measurement of intelligence quotients of the deaf. More research is needed before generalizations can be made whether the deaf child is slow in motor tasks because of actual deficits in motor speed or because he does not grasp the concept of performing as fast as he can. Neurologically, there is some evidence that the senses of time and temporalness are dependent upon the same areas of the brain as is auditory perception.

Gait

Persons with severe hearing losses tend to walk with a shuffling gait. This characteristic is not limited to those with semicircular canal deficits; hence, it is assumed that the inability to hear the sounds of movement is the cause rather than brain or ear damage. Some authorities state that the shuffling gait is not readily amenable to training but others suggest intensive work on the heel-to-toe walking pattern. For optimal value this training must begin at the preschool level, and methods of reinforcing the correct walking pattern must be found since the child cannot hear the difference between picking the feet up and dragging them. The heel-to-toe walk can be reinforced visually by practicing walking toward mirrors or by watching a videotape monitor. Visual training, however, tends to result in the habit of watching the feet.

Proprioceptive training, with emphasis upon the difference in the *feel* of walking on heels (dorsiflexion) and on toes (plantarflexion), is recommended. Tap dance offers perhaps the best training of this type. The teacher may tap the rhythm lightly on the child's head so that he can perceive it via bone conduction while moving his feet. Another possibility is positioning the child so that his hand is on the record player, piano, or drum. A system of flashing lights can also be devised to convey rhythmic patterns.

Breathing exercises may be done by the child at home. No evidence exists, however, that breathing exercises contribute to cardiovascular endurance. The activities in Chapter 10 would appear to accomplish the objective of fitness more quickly than breathing exercises which, according to Streng, are often misused. Streng states:

> Deaf children do not need to be taught *how* to breathe, but how to coordinate their breathing with their speech. Sometimes it becomes necessary to teach a child to take in a sufficient amount of breath before he begins to talk, and to practice sentence length-breath with syllable drills, so that he can concentrate on the breath control rather than on the structure of language or on complicated speech patterns.[19]

Since no evidence exists to the contrary, it can be assumed that the deaf are more like the hearing in physical fitness than unlike him. Like most children in our society, the deaf are likely to have low cardiovascular endurance, poor arm and shoulder strength, and poor abdominal strength.

Education for the Deaf

Deaf and hearing impaired children may be educated in residential schools, day schools, and special public school classes for the deaf. Approximately two-thirds of the children with severe and profound hearing losses are educated in residential schools. There is a trend toward integrating partially deaf children with hearing ones. Ziagos describes this integration in physical education as highly successful.[20]

19. Alice Streng, *Hearing Therapy for Children* (New York: Grune and Stratton, 1958), p. 324.

20. Gus Ziagos, "A Survey of Integrated Elementary Physical Education Programs for the Acoustically Handicapped and Hearing Children," Unpublished M. A. study, De Paul University, (1954).

The special educational provisions of the deaf include three approaches to learning communication skills: (1) the manual method which includes finger spelling and signing, (2) the oral method, and (3) the combined or simultaneous method. Most school systems today combine the best of oral and manual methods. It is important that the physical educator demonstrate interest in all aspects of education for the deaf. In many schools which serve the deaf all teachers are expected to complete courses in signing and finger spelling. In other schools which use only the oral method, signing may be prohibited.

Signing can be viewed on several national television stations when church services for the deaf are broadcast in signs. It is used also by the National Theatre of the Deaf, which has toured both Europe and the United States since its establishment in 1967. Most of the company's professional actors are alumnae of Gallaudet College, where both manualism and oralism are used. The National Theatre of the Deaf is housed at the Eugene O'Neill Memorial Theatre Center in Waterford, Connecticut.

General Guidelines for the Physical Educator

The physical educator who works with the deaf should seek orientation concerning whether oral, manual, or combined methods are preferred by his administration. The following guidelines may help him establish rapport with deaf children.

1. Always position yourself where the deaf child can see you.
2. Do not talk nor give directions while writing on the blackboard or facing away from the deaf child.
3. Do not raise your voice when speaking to a person with a hearing aid.

4. When outdoors, position yourself so that you rather than the deaf child face the sun.
5. When a child indicates that he did not understand your instructions, rephrase your sentences, hoping that he can perceive sounds of a different frequency or letters more visible on the mouth than those originally used.
6. Allow children with hearing losses to move freely about the gymnasium in order to be within seeing and hearing range.
7. If your school favors the oral method of teaching, avoid gestures. The child who is accustomed to watching hands forgets to follow the lips.
8. Whether or not you understand a child's attempt to speak, give him some response to reinforce his efforts at the mastery of speech.

Few physical educators have worked with the deaf over an extensive period of time. Myklebust discusses the tremendous need in this area.

An intensive program of remedial physical education seems not only warranted but urgently indicated. In terms of a broad body of knowledge now available, for example, through neurophysiology, such programs could be expected to be most successful if inaugurated in early life during the period of the organism's greatest plasticity. Perhaps the primary deficiency of current physical education programs for deaf children is that they are based more or less exclusively in activities which have been successful with hearing children. The program here implied would be based on the specific needs of deaf children, on those aspects of motor behavior which are influenced significantly by hearing loss. [21]

What kinds of programs will best meet the needs of deaf and hearing-impaired children? Who will meet the challenge?

21. Helmer R. Myklebust, *The Psychology of Deafness* (New York: Grune and Stratton, 1964), p. 200.

Organizations

1. Alexander Graham Bell Association for the Deaf, Inc., 1537 35th Street, N.W., Washington, D. C. 20007.

2. American Instructors of the Deaf, 5034 Wisconsin Avenue, N. W., Washington, D. C. 20016.

3. Council of Organizations Serving the Deaf Inc., (COSD), 4201 Connecticut Avenue N. W., Washington, D. C. 20008.

4. National Association of Hearing and Speech Agencies, 219 18th Street N. W., Washington , D. C. 20006.

5. Chief, Communication Disorders Branch Division of Disability Services, Rehabilitation Services Administration Social and Rehabilitation Service, Department of Health, Education, and Welfare, Washington, D. C. 20202.

References

Berges, Shirley A. "The Deaf Student in Physical Education," JOHPER. Vol. 40, No. 3, (March, 1969).

Birch, Jack. *Hearing Impaired Children in the Mainstream*. Reston, Va.: The Council for Exceptional Children, 1975.

Burns, W. *Noise and Man*. Philadelphia: J.B. Lippincott Company, 1968.

Jerger, J., ed. *Modern Developments in Audiology*. New York: Academic Press, 1973.

Long, J. *Motor Abilities of Deaf Children*. New York: Columbia University, T. C. Contributions to Education #514, 1932.

Morsh, J. *Motor Performance of the Deaf*. Com. Psychological Monograph, #66, 1936.

Myklebust, Helmer R. *The Psychology of Deafness*. New York: Grune and Stratton, 1964.

———. "Significance of Etiology in Motor Performance of Deaf Children with Special References to Meningitis," *American Journal of Psychology*. Vol. 59, No. 2, (April, 1946).

Nesbitt, John, and Howard, Gordon. *Proceedings of the National Institute on Recreation for Deaf-Blind Children, Youth, and Adults*. Iowa City, Iowa: University of Iowa Press, 1975.

Pennella, Lou. "XII World Games for the Deaf," JOHPER. Vol. 45, No. 5, (May, 1974), pp. 12-14.

Robbins, Nan and Stenquist, Gertrude. *The Deaf-Blind "Rubella" Child*. Watertown, Mass.: Perkins School for the Blind, 1967.

Whetnall, E., and Fry, D. B. *The Deaf Child*. London: William Heinemann, 1961.

Wisher, Peter. "Dance and the Deaf," JOPHER, Vol. 40, No. 3 (March, 1969).

Ziagos, Gus. "A Survey of Integrated Elementary Physical Education Programs for the Acoustically Handicapped and Hearing Children." Unpublished M. A. Study, De Paul University, 1954.

Periodicals

The American Annals of the Deaf, first published in 1847, is the oldest educational journal in the United States still in existence. Annual indexes are published every November. It is the official journal of the Conference of Executives of American Schools for the Deaf and the American Instructors of the Deaf.

The Volta Review began publication in 1899 as *The Association Review*. It is the official journal for the Alexander Graham Bell Association of the Deaf.

The Journal of the Acoustical Society of America.
The Journal of Speech and Hearing Research.
The Journal of Auditory Research.
International Audiology.
Gallaudet Today.

Autobiography, Biography, and Fiction

Greenberg, Joanne. *In This Sign.* New York: Holt, Rinehart, and Winston, 1970.

Hunter, Edith Fisher. *Child of the Silent Night.* New York: Dell Publishing Co., 1963.

Keller, Helen. *The Story of My Life.* New York: Airmont Publishing Co., Inc., 1965.

Smithdas, Robert J. *Life at My Fingertips.* New York: Doubleday and Company, Inc., 1958.

Figure 16.0. Charles Buell gives a blind child and his sighted opponent a first lesson in wrestling. (Photo by Steve Edmonds, Ft. Worth Star Telegram.)

Never check the actions of the blind child; follow him, and watch him to prevent any serious accidents, but do not interfere unnecessarily; do not even remove obstacles which he would learn to avoid by tumbling over them a few times. Teach him to jump rope, to swing weights, to raise his body by his arms and to mingle, as far as possible, in the rough sports of the older students, and do not be apprehensive of his safety, and if you see him clambering in the branches of a tree, be sure he is less likely to fall than if he had eyes. Do not too much regard bumps upon the forehead, rough scratches or bloody noses, even these may have their good influences. At the worst, they affect only the bark, and do not injure the system, like the rust of inaction.

Samuel Gridley Howel [1]

Unlike the deaf, the blind and visually impaired in the United States have benefitted from the leadership of persons interested in their physical education from the very beginning. The often quoted statement above comes from Samuel Gridley Howe, the first director of Perkins Institution and Massachusetts Asylum for the Blind, incorporated in 1829 and opened in Boston in 1832. The earliest residential school for the blind in this country, Perkins is known for its training of Anne Sullivan Macy, the teacher of Helen Keller. Perkins is recognized also as the leader in physical education for the blind throughout the nineteenth century.

Prior to 1948, almost all blind children were educated in residential schools. This fact helps to explain why the history of physical education for the blind parallels the growth of residential schools and reflects their leadership. The history of physical education for the blind from 1934-1966 has been recorded by Charles Buell,[2] a versatile physical educator. Buell recently completed a book[3] which includes an annotated bibliography of twenty-three books and eighty-eight articles on physical education, recreation, and camping for the blind. Of this number, Buell himself wrote six books between 1945 and 1973 and twenty-nine articles, the first of which was printed in 1936. Legally blind himself, Buell

holds a Doctoral degree in physical education from the University of California. His enthusiasm, perseverance, and leadership have contributed immeasurably to a growing understanding of the physical capabilities of the blind. No other handicapping condition, with the exception of mental retardation, has such an abundance of literature to guide the physical educator.

Definitions

Visual handicaps are defined in terms of visual acuity as measured by a Snellen chart. The lines of progressively smaller letters are read by a person sitting or standing at a distance of twenty feet from the chart. Sharpness or clearness of vision is designated as 20/20, 20/70, 20/200, 5/200, or some other numerical ratio. The following classifications may appear on a student's school record:

20/200. *Legal blindness.* The ability to see at 20 feet what the normal eye can see at 200 feet. This classification makes the student eligible to receive assistance under state and federal programs.

5/200 to 10/200. *Travel Vision.* The ability to see at five to ten feet what persons with normal vision see at 200 feet.

3/200 to 5/200. *Motion Perception.* The ability to see at three to five feet what the person with normal vision sees at 200 feet. This ability is limited almost entirely to motion.

Less than 3/200. *Light Perception.* The ability to distinguish a strong light at a distance of three feet from the eye but inability to detect movement of a hand at the same distance.

1. Samuel Gridley Howe, *Perkins Report, 1841* (Watertown, Massachusetts: Perkins Institute for the Blind), p. 17.

2. Charles Buell, *Physical Education for Blind Children* (Springfield, Illinois: Charles C Thomas, 1974).

3. Charles Buell, *Physical Education and Recreation for the Visually Handicapped* (Washington, D. C.: AAHPER, 1973).

Lack of Visual Perception. *Total Blindness.* This is the inability to recognize a strong light which is shown directly into the eye.

Since most legally blind persons have some usable vision, these classifications often result in confusion. Buell laughingly describes the disbelief of his colleagues when he uses a pocket magnifier to look up a telephone number in the city directory. "But you are blind," they say. He corrects them by stating that he may be legally blind but he is nevertheless partially sighted. Most persons with 10/200 or better vision, like Buell, prefer reading print over using braille readers. In a study of 14,125 legally blind children registered with the American Printing House of the Blind, Jones[4] found that 76 percent had some *residual vision.* A few of these children could read both print and braille, but the large majority read only print. Books with large type, usually 18 to 24 points, instead of the normal 12 to 14, are available for such children. The traditional classification of visually handicapped children into two categories (the *partially sighted* with vision of 20/70 to 20/200 in the better eye and the *legally blind* with vision of 20/200 in the better eye) is being supplanted by new terminology. It is recommended that persons who cannot read print and must be taught braille be called *blind* and that all others be considered *visually impaired.*

Incidence

Blindness and visual impairment are largely problems of old age. Approximately one-half million persons in the United States are legally blind and countless others have serious visual problems. At least two-thirds of these persons are over sixty-five in age. The statistics concerning visual impairment among school age children vary with the definition used. It is estimated that 60,400 children between ages five and nineteen are visually impaired.[5] This figure represents approximately one-tenth of one percent (or one out of every 1000) of the school age children in this country. The U. S. Office of Education does not break these figures down into the blind versus the visually impaired. It should be noted, however, that visual impairment affects fewer children than any other handicapping condition with the exception of the multihandicapped classification. The most accurate count of children actually being served educationally is the registry of legally blind children with the American Printing House for the Blind. In 1972, this number was 20,048.

Anatomy of the Eye

To understand visual impairments, the physical educator needs more than superficial knowledge about the anatomy of the eye and the physiology of vision. They should also have some knowledge of the six muscles which control the eyeball, of cranial nerves II, III, IV, and VI, and of the part of the brain which controls visual acuity and perception.

Figure 16-1 presents a visual review of anatomy. Table 33 offers brief definitions of the parts of the eyeball.

Body parts can be reviewed by creating games in which their names are used. For instance, in *Steal the Bacon* and *Circle Call Ball* the players can be named sclera, cornea, choroid, ciliary body, instead of being assigned the traditional numbers. The causes of childhood blindness, characteristics of specific conditions, and adaptations required in physical education cannot be understood until the parts of the eye are learned. Certainly these names are equal in importance to the presidents, states, capitols, parts of speech, and other factual material normally covered in elementary school.

4. R. L. Jones, *Blind Children, Degree of Vision, Mode of Reading* (Bulletin 24, Washington, D. C.: U. S. Office of Education, 1961).

5. Planning and Evaluation Staff, Bureau of Education for the Handicapped, U. S. Office of Education, Department of Health, Education, and Welfare, Washington, D. C., (1970).

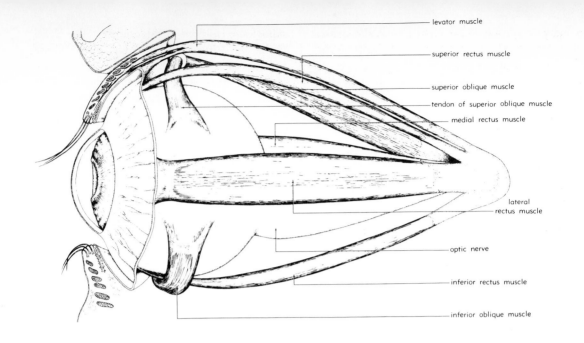

levator muscle

superior rectus muscle

superior oblique muscle

tendon of superior oblique muscle

medial rectus muscle

lateral rectus muscle

optic nerve

inferior rectus muscle

inferior oblique muscle

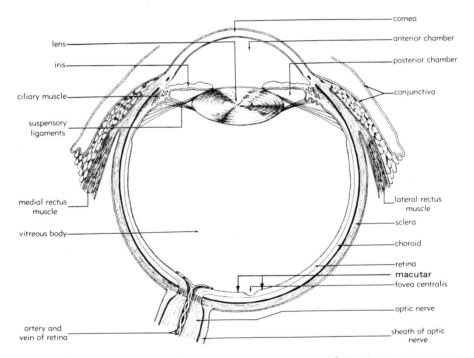

cornea

anterior chamber

posterior chamber

conjunctiva

lens

iris

ciliary muscle

suspensory
ligaments

lateral rectus
muscle

sclera

choroid

retina

macular

fovea centralis

medial rectus
muscle

vitreous body

optic nerve

sheath of optic
nerve

artery and
vein of retina

Figure 16.1. Diagram of the human eye.

© Kendall/Hunt Publishing Company

Table 33 *Outline of Parts of the Eyeball Presented According to Layers*

Outer Fibrous Coat	Middle Vascular Coat (Also called *Uvea*)	Inner Lining
Sclera 　Tough, opaque covering except for small area in front. Envelopes or surrounds eyeball. The white of the eye.	Choroid 　a. Blood vessels 　b. Dark brown pigment which reduces reflection and scattering of light after it has fallen on retina.	Retina—an expansion of optic nerve 　a. Rods—sensory receptors for colorless and twilight vision. 　b. Cones—sensory receptors for color and bright day light vision.
Cornea 　Clear, transparent tissue that completes the sclera anteriorly.	Ciliary Body 　a. Ciliary muscle 　　Origin—sclera near its junction with cornea 　　Insertion—choroid 　　Innervation—3rd cranial nerve 　b. Ciliary processes—fibers that emerge from the muscle and attach to ligaments supporting the lens.	Optic Nerve 　a. Blind spot 　b. Optic chiasm
	Iris (includes the pupil) 　Colored portion of eye. 　A muscular diaphragm with hole (pupil) in middle. 　a. Circular fibers—Cause pupil to constrict in bright light. 　　Innervated by 3rd cranial nerve 　b. Radial fibers—Cause pupil to dilate in dim light.	Lens—Lies just behind iris and pupil. Held in position by ligaments which attach to ciliary body. Divides eyeball into two chambers. 　a. Anterior chamber filled with aqueous fluid 　b. Posterior chamber filled with vitreous fluid.

Causes of Blindness

Most blindness is attributed to birth defects but other causes are reported in percentages as follows:

These statistics are distorted heavily by the incidence of retrolental fibroplasia in premature infants housed in incubators in the 1940s and 1950s and of the rubella epidemics which affected pregnant women in the 1960s. Recent medical advances have almost eradicated these two pathological conditions as causes of blindness in the present decade, but schools will be filled with their victims for years to come.

Prenatal Influence	56.1
Poisonings (Retrolental Fibroplasia)	19.3
Infectious Diseases	7.4
Tumors	5.1
Injuries	4.9
General Diseases	.7
Etiology Unspecified	6.5
Total	100.0

The causes of blindness presented in terms of the part of the eye affected were last intensively studied in 1958-1959.[6] The findings were based upon a sample of 7,757 legally blind children reported by personnel of both residential and day schools in thirty-six states. Listed in order of their incidence, the parts of the eye in which damage or disease results in blindness include:

Retina	40.4
Eyeball in general	24.8
Lens	12.1
Optic nerve, optic pathway, and cortical vision centers	9.5
Uveal tract	
Cornea	
Conjunctiva	
Others	

Birth defects affect several parts of the eye simultaneously. The percentage listed under the eyeball in general appears now to be increasing and that under retina to be decreasing. The following section is designed to introduce the physical educator to terms which appear in children's files. Blind children are generally highly verbal, and it is advisable to allow the pupil to share all that he knows about his particular eye defect, the amount of residual vision, and the precautions to be taken in physical education.

Retina

The *retina*, or inner lining of the eyeball, is an expansion of the optic nerve which contains the sensory receptors for light rays. Specifically rod cells receive stimuli for colorless and twilight vision, and cone cells receive stimuli for color and bright daytime vision.

Three anatomical landmarks are important on the retina: (1) the blind spot or optic disk, (2) the fovea centralis, and (3) the macula lutea or yellow spot. The blind spot, which has no rods and cones, is the point where the optic nerve enters the eyeball. In normal vision, the blind spot is unimportant since the visual fields of the right and left eyes overlap. In a one-eyed person, however, the blind spot could blot out a child at a distance of thirty feet or an automobile at sixty feet. In order to demonstrate the presence of your blind spot, make a poster with a one-half inch square on the left side and a circle of the same size about three inches to the right. Stand a short distance from the poster and close your left eye while focusing on the square with your right eye. Both the square and circle will remain in your field of vision until you walk forward to a distance of about nine inches from the square. At that time the circle will be blotted out by the blind spot. The macula is located at the center of the retina, which is slightly inferior to the blind spot. In normal vision the light rays are focused on the macula by the lens; hence the macula is the area of greatest visual acuity. The fovea centralis is the small depression within the macula opposite the lens. It is the most sensitive part of the retina and has only cone cells.

Conditions of the retina which result in childhood blindness are retrolental fibroplasia (RLF), 33.0 percent; retinal and macular degeneration, 4.4 percent; retinoblastoma, 1.7 percent; and others, such as retinitis and detached retina, 1.3 percent. Retrolental

6. Elizabeth M. Hatfield, "Causes of Blindness in School Children," *The Sight-Saving Review*. Vol. 33, No. 4, (Fall, 1963), pp. 218-233.

fibroplasia, usually listed under poisonings, results from excessive oxygen experienced by premature infants in incubators. Literally it means *fibrous tissue behind the lens* and refers to an inflammatory process of the peripheral retina which eventually results in retinal degeneration and detachment. Most of the blind persons in high school and college today are victims of RLF which raged rampant from 1938 through 1955, causing more blindness than any other single condition in all of modern history. The disease reached its peak in 1952-1953, at which time it accounted for over 50 percent of blindness in all preschool children. While tragic, it should be remembered that its victims could not have survived before the invention of the incubator. Once the cause of RLF was discovered and the mechanics of the incubator refined, the condition became almost nonexistent.

Most of childhood blindness once attributed to RLF is now caused by rubella or German measles during the first trimester of pregnancy. Rubella epidemics recur every six to nine years, leaving thousands of unborn babies deaf, blind, mentally retarded, and/or with heart defects. Since the last major epidemic in 1964-1965, a vaccine has been discovered and licensed. Rubella, like RLF, may soon cease to be a major factor in childhood blindness.

In macular degeneration only central or reading visual acuity is affected. Often the student complains of a lack of regularity of the lines or letters in print and/or of missing letters and words. Macular degeneration may be inherited or result from a gradual interference with nutritional processes. In severe cases it seems to provoke retinal hemorrhage with subsequent involvement of peripheral as well as central vision. Most publicized, however, are the cases of macular burns which result from the unguarded observation of an eclipse of the sun.

Retinoblastoma, referring to a malignant growth or tumor of the retina, is often hereditary. The majority of cases are reported in the preschool years. About one-third of such children have tumors in both eyes although only one is a metastasis. Treatment may be by radiotherapy or enucleation (surgical removal of the eyeball).

Structural Anomalies of the Eyeball

The *eyeballs* rest within the optic orbits of the skull on cushions of fatty tissue which give them resiliency to absorb shocks. Structural abnormalities of the eyeball, which account for approximately one-fourth of blindness in children, include:

1. Multiple anomalies and myopia—5.5 and 4.9 percent respectively.

2. Infantile glaucoma—4.6 percent. Hardening of the eyeball. Other terms used for this condition include:

   a. Buphthalamus—large eyeball; also called ox eye.

   b. Macrophthalmia—abnormally large eyeball, usually resulting from infantile glaucoma.

3. Albinism—4.2 percent of blindness in children. Congenital absence of pigment in the skin, hair, iris, and choroid which is a recessive trait. Called *albinos*, they have platinum blond hair and very fair skin. They generally have myopia, photophobia (sensitivity to light), astigmatism, and nystagmus. Albinos are often objects of misconceptions as evidenced in the book and movie, *God's Little Acre*.

4. Anophthalmos—1.2 percent. Congenital absence of one or both eyes, and microphthalmos, abnormally small eyeball.

   A synonym for microphthalmos is megalophalamus.

5. Coloboma—0.9 percent. From the Greek word meaning mutilation. A congenital

fissure (cleft) of the choroid, iris, or eyelids. Caused by failure of the eye to complete growth in the part affected.

6. Aniridia—0.7 percent. Complete or partial congenital absence or loss of iris.

Other structural anomalies that affect the eyeball, causing the remaining 2.8 percent of blindness, are too rare to be listed separately.

Lens

The *lens* is a transparent colorless body which lies just behind the *iris* and *pupil*. It is biconvex, meaning it has two surfaces, each of which is part of the outer surface of a sphere. Its primary function is to bring the rays of light to a focus on the retina. Defects of the lens not only cause most of the refractive errors but also 12.1 percent of the blindness in children. Of this percentage, congenital cataracts cause 11.5 percent and dislocated lens 0.6 percent. A cataract is an opacity or clouding of the lens. When congenital there appears to be a genetic predisposition. Early surgery often prevents blindness. In *ectopic lentis*, dislocation of the lens, the dislocation is commonly upward.

Optic Nerve, Optic Pathway, and Cortical Visual Centers

About 9.5 percent of blindness in children results from defects in the nervous system rather than in the eye itself. Optic nerve atrophy accounts for 8.6 percent of this blindness.

Structurally, the optic or second cranial nerve is not a true nerve but a fiber tract of the brain which transmits sensory stimuli received by the rods and cones of the retina to the cortical visual center. The pathways traveled by these impulses are illustrated in Figure 16.2. Optic nerve disease is characterized by (1) disturbances in the visual field, (2) loss of visual acuity, and (3) changes in the interior of the

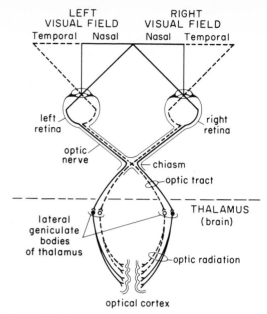

Figure 16.2. Pathways traveled by stimuli to the cortical visual center.

eye involving the retina and/or optic nerve. The *visual field* is the area in which objects can be seen when the head and eyes are stationary. It is divided into a nasal half and a temporal half for each eye.

Destruction of one optic nerve, or the area between the retina and the optic chiasm, results in total blindness of one eye. In contrast, destruction of the visual pathway, which begins at the chiasm and ends in the occipital cortex, causes blindness in only half of the visual field. This phenomenon is readily understood when Figure 16.2 is studied, and it is noted that sensory impulses from the right nasal field cross over at the chiasm and thereafter are carried by the left optic tract. Blindness in half of a visual field is called *hemianopia* or *hemianopsia*. When sight is lost in only a patch of the visual field instead of an entire half or quarter, the blind area is called a *scotoma*. Scotomas are classified as central, paracentral, and peripheral depending upon their location in the visual field. They are commonly associated with multiple sclerosis.

TABLE 34 *Visual Defects Which May Be Caused by Damage to Cranial Nerves*

Cranial Nerve II: Optic Nerve and Tract (Sensory Nerve)	Cranial Nerves III, IV, VI: Oculomotor, Trochlear, Abducens (Innervate Muscles of Eye)
Scotomas—blind or partially blind areas in the visual field	Strabismus or squint (cross eyes)
Amblyopia—poor vision or loss of visual acuity	Diplogia (double vision)
Amaurosis—complete blindness	Tilting of the head to compensate for diplogia

Field defects
  a. Tubular or tunnel vision
  b. Bitemporal hemianopsia
  c. R or L nasal hemianopsia
  d. R or L homonymous hemianopsia
  e. R or L homonymous inferior quadrantanopsia
	Conjugate deviation (both eyes turned to same side)
	
	Nystagmus (rhythmic or undulating movements of eyes)

Other defects
  a. Hemeralopia (day blindness)
  b. Nyctalopia (night blindness)
  c. Color blindness
    Achromatopsia (total)
    Monochromatism (partial)
    Dichromatism (partial)
	Ptosis (lid drop from weakness of superior levator muscle)
	
	Dizziness (often associated with double vision)

Optic agnosia (word blindness)	
Psychic blindness	

Table 34 summarizes the visual defects which result from cranial nerve damage. Only the second cranial nerve is capable of transmitting sensory impulses. Cranial nerves III, IV, and VI, sometimes called the ocular nerves, are motor. Both the sensory and motor nerves of vision are controlled by neurons comprising the occipital cortex.

Whereas optic nerve disease may result in total blindness, disease of the three ocular nerves produces changes in the pupils and disturbances of ocular movements. All three motor nerves are seldom involved simultaneously. Should this occur, the eyeball would become totally immobile, the eyelid would droop, and the pupil would dilate. Despite these disabilities, vision, although somewhat distorted, would be possible if the eyelids were raised.

Uveal Tract

The *uveal tract* is the middle vascular coat of the eyeball which includes the choroid, the ciliary body, and the iris. This middle coat serves to nourish the retina and other intraocular structures and to maintain intraocular pressure. Inflammation of the uveal tract is subdivided into (1) anterior uveitis (iritis and iridocyclitis) and (2) posterior uveitis (choroiditis). Most often the infection has an unknown etiology. *Iridocyclitis* is an inflammation of both the iris and the ciliary body. The eye is red, tender, and bright light is irritating. *Iritis* is inflammation of the iris. The symptoms of both conditions are similar to those of glaucoma except that the diminution of visual acuity is less severe. *Choroiditis,* or inflammation of the choroid, is painless even in its acute stage. The only complaint is loss of visual acuity, and this varies with the size of the lesion. Many persons with scars of healed choroiditis are unaware of ever having an eye infection. Because the uveal tract supplies nourishment for the entire eye, it is affected by diseases in other parts of the ocular system. Uveitis may result from such conditions as keratitis, retinal detachment, intraocular new growth, intraocular hemorrhage, or trauma. A penetration injury or surgery on one eye frequently leads to iridocyclitis in the second eye. Called *sympathetic ophthalmia,* this condition is described in the autobiography of Tomi Keitlen.[7]

Cornea

The cornea, the anterior part of the outer layer of the eyeball, is the clear transparent tissue in front of the lens. Among these defects are

1. Corneal ulcer—infiltration of a certain portion of the cornea, followed by suppuration, loss of substance, and finally opacity of the spot.
2. Keratitis—inflammation of the cornea.
   a. Interstitial—usually caused by transmission of syphilis from mother to unborn child.
   b. Phlyctenular—usually caused by poor nutrition.
3. Leucoma or leukoma—a whitish opacity of the cornea.
4. Pannua—invasion of the cornea by in-

filtration of lymph and formation of new blood vessels.

Conjunctiva

The *conjunctiva* is the mucous membrane which lines the eyelids and covers the front part of the eyeball. Conditions which may affect it are pinkeye or conjunctivitis, trachoma, and ophthalmia neonatorum. Although trachoma is the leading cause of blindness in the world, it is not a problem in the United States. Only ophthalmia neonatorum, an acute inflammation of the conjunctiva in the newborn, causes blindness in this country. Prior to 1897, it caused 31 percent of all blindness in institutions. Its prevalence resulted in state laws requiring a few drops of silver nitrate solution in newborn infants' eyes. Today ophthalmia neonatorum causes only 0.3 percent of blindness, not only because of the mandatory laws but also because it responds well to treatment by penicillin and mycin drugs.

Comparisons of Blind and Partially Sighted

The child who is totally blind has few, if any, restrictions in physical education. Nothing can worsen his vision, and he can participate fully in any physical activity. The child who is gradually losing his visual acuity constitutes a much greater problem. The partially sighted child may fear falling, being hit in the eye by a ball, or other accidents which can rob him of his remaining vision. These fears are generally unfounded.

Often the visually impaired child is pushed to master academic and vocational skills which will be needed in the future. Many local agencies for the blind provide such instruction during summers and after school hours, but few offer opportunities for engaging in physical

7. Tomi Keitlen, *Farewell to Fear* (New York: Avon Book Division, 1960).

recreation and developing lifetime sports skills. Illustrative of the attitudes of many parents is that of the mother of a nine-year-old son who stated,

We just found out that Mike is going blind. We have about a year before he loses the rest of his vision, and we want him to learn to use the braille typewriter and read braille now so that he can keep up with his classmates academically. We plan to keep him in regular classes, and he will be the only blind child in the whole school system. There is so much for him to learn that there just isn't time to give him swimming lessons this summer.

Unless a partially sighted child develops recreational skills that will help him to remain a part of the neighborhood play group, he is likely to become increasingly lonely. No amount of academic success and vocational independence can substitute for the social values derived from informal play. Special instruction should be provided in such activities as swimming, horseback riding, skating, dance, and gymnastics so that the child who is losing his sight can keep up with his classmates socially as well as academically.

The autobiographies of such persons as Harold Krents [8] and Tomi Keitlen emphasize the importance of sports participation in making friends and gaining self-confidence. Krents recalls step by step how his brother taught him to catch a regulation football and to bat a ten-inch playground ball, skills he could have been taught by a physical educator but was not. In high school physical education he was allowed to play touch football with his sighted classmates but admonished to "Keep out of the way." The anecdotes leading to his acquisition of the nickname *Cannonball* make the book well worth reading. Tomi Keitlen describes in detail her first attempts at swimming, golf, horseback riding, fencing, and skiing after becoming totally blind at age thirty-three. [9] In addition to valuable accounts of how such sports can be learned and enjoyed without sight, Keitlen describes the problems of adjusting to blindness. The greatest battle,

she stresses, is to avoid being segregated and labeled as different from sighted persons.

Implications for Physical Education

Although widespread individual differences exist among the blind, certain characteristics appear more often than in the sighted population. Foremost among these are *blindisms*, defined broadly as mannerisms resulting from repression of the innate need to move. The most common blindisms are (1) rocking backward and forward, (2) putting fist or fingers into eyes, (3) waving fingers in front of face, (4) whirling rapidly round and round, and (5) bending the head forward. These same blindisms may be observed among sighted persons with emotional problems or limited opportunities for release of normal tensions. They can be prevented or at least minimized in both the blind and the sighted through the provision of vigorous daily exercise. Other physical characteristics of the blind which have implications for physical education include:

1. Posture is often poor since they have no visual ideal to emulate. The position of the head is a particular problem.
2. Physical growth and maturation are often retarded because of inadequate opportunities to move.
3. There is a definite tendency toward problems of overweight caused by the sedentary quality of life and a paucity of interests.
4. Proprioceptive awareness is frequently poor. There is no evidence that any of the senses are heightened to compensate for loss of vision. Special training is required for optimal development of touch, hearing, taste, smell, and proprioception.

8. Harold Krents, *To Race the Wind* (New York: G. P. Putman's Sons, 1972). Reviewed in *Reader's Digest*, August, 1972.

9. Tomi Keitlen, *Farewell to Fear* (New York: Avon Book Division, 1960), p. 9.

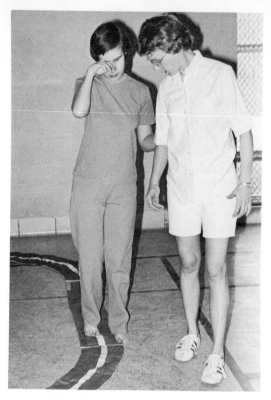

Figure 16.3. Rubbing the eye is a blindism which should be called to the child's attention and extinguished.

Figure 16.4. Special training is required for optimal development of the other senses. (Christian Record Braille Foundation. Photo by Robert L. Sheldon.)

5. Physical fitness is affected by lack of vigorous exercise. When running and throwing activities are used as measures of fitness, the blind child is at a particular disadvantage. He tends to be equal to sighted children in such events as pull ups, push ups, sit ups, arm hang, and standing long jump. Norms based upon the administration of the AAHPER fitness test to blind children appear in Buell's book. [10]

6. Like other physically unfit children, blind pupils tend to fatigue easily.

7. Blind pupils are often highly verbal, giving the appearance of being tense and high strung. It should be remembered that lulls in conversation and periods of quiet are tolerated less easily by the blind than the sighted because of their inability to perceive the many nonverbal cues by which others communicate.

8. Blind persons often seem insensitive to the needs of others, primarily because they cannot modify their behavior in response to facial expressions, gestures, subtle exchanges of eye contact among group members, and other nonverbal cues taken for granted in the sighted world.

9. Whereas the sighted show more expression with age, the face of the blind person may become increasingly mobile

10. Charles E. Buell, *Physical Education and Recreation for the Visually Handicapped* (Washington, D. C.: AAHPER, 1973), pp. 26-30.

and expressionless. Games and creative dramatics should be designed to teach facial expressions appropriate to different emotions and settings.

10. Although blind children may excel in folk and square dance, they experience difficulty with modern dance and spontaneous creative movement. Since they have never seen gestures and movements of others, the communication aspects of dance are hard to teach. The concept of good form in gymnastics, diving, and other sports lacks meaning when different motor performances cannot be compared visually.

11. Partially sighted persons often profess to see more than they actually do. The desire for normalcy is strong, and the child may even convince himself that he sees more than he does. Many partially sighted persons, although legally blind, are very sensitive about being called *blind*.

12. Blind persons who adapt successfully to the environment seem particularly skilled in memorization. The physical educator should reinforce this strength by calling upon the blind child to review instructions given in previous lessons.

Haptic Perception

Perhaps more than any other disability group, blind children need extensive experiences in creative dance and spontaneous movement. The traditional visually oriented instructional approach should be adapted to the predominantly haptic perception of most blind children. Creativity in movement is elicited in blind children through discussions of muscular sensations, kinesthetic experiences, touch impressions, and cognitive considerations of the self rather than the environment as the central reference point. The blind haptic child is subjective rather than objective in his choreography. He tends to invest movement with feeling rather than to concentrate upon such visual outcomes as good form, proper space relationships, and group composition. No experimental research concerning methods of teaching creative dance to the blind has been reported. Lowenfeld's suggestions for developing creativity in the blind through sculpture and painting can be adapted by the dance teacher.[11] Distinctly different methods of teaching should be used with predominantly haptic and visual perceptual types.

When planning movement exploration activities for the blind, the physical educator must realize that space is interpreted unconventionally by haptic minded persons. Whereas the visually oriented child perceives distant objects as smaller than those at close proximity, the blind child does not differentiate between foreground and background. The size of objects is not determined by nearness and farness but rather by their emotional significance to the child attempting to imagine what something might look like. The blind child experiences difficulty in conceptualizing boundaries. Having no visual field to restrict him, his space is as large as his imagination. He tends, however, to think in parts rather than wholes since realistic conceptualization is limited to the amount of surface he can touch at any given time. In order to familiarize himself with the gymnasium, he may move from one piece of apparatus to another, feel the walls, discover windows and doors, and creep on the floor, but never is he completely certain what the unified whole feels or looks like. Three dimensional models, similar to doll houses should be made available of the gymnasium, swimming pool, playground, campsite, and other areas of space. Miniature figures can be arranged on the simulated playground to acquaint him with playing positions, rules, and strategies. Dolls can be used also to teach him spatial relation-

11. Viktor Lowenfeld, *Creative and Mental Growth* (New York: The Macmillan Company, 1952), pp. 231-265.

ships between dancers in a group composition, cheerleaders in a pep squad demonstration, and swimmers in the assigned lanes of a meet. Unless small dolls with movable joints are taken through such movements as forward rolls, cartwheels, and skin the snake on a parallel bar, the blind child has no way of conceptualizing the whole prior to attempting a new activity.

Spatial Awareness

Cratty makes the following observations about the body image of blind children.

1. Among populations of blind children, who have normal IQ's and who are free from emotional and motor problems, are children as proficient as sighted youngsters of a similar age in the verbal identification of body parts, the left-right dimensions of their bodies and similar judgments.
2. Among populations of blind children whose mean IQ's are below normal (i.e., 80), their deficiencies in body image, as identified by verbal tests, are similar to those that would be expected in populations of sighted youngsters with similar IQ's.
3. Clinical experience has taught us that through training, the verbal identification of body parts may be significantly improved in both blind children and in children with vision.
4. The body image of blind children may be reliably measured. [12]

Other topics included in Cratty's book are manual identification of objects, the orientation to stable and moving sounds, spatial orientation, the improvement of movement efficiency, complex spatial orientation, and mobility training. Cratty, among others, emphasizes that the blind child needs special training in recognizing the right-left dimensions of objects which are facing him. Not

capable of seeing, he has never received a mirror image and hence the concept of someone facing him is especially difficult. The art products of the blind reveal that they conceptualize another person's body from behind rather than reversing the features as would occur normally.

The blind child must be provided with opportunities for learning about his own body parts as well as those of animals and other human beings. This can be accomplished, at least partially, by tactual inspection. Three dimensional figures must be available to teach similarities and differences between ectomorph, mesomorph, and endomorph builds; stereotypes of male and female physical characteristics; and appearances of various postural deviations. Movement exploration based upon modifications of the dog walk, seal crawl, mule kick, et cetera is meaningless unless the blind child can feel, smell, hear, and perhaps taste (lick) the animal about to be imitated. Tactual inspection of persons, animals, and objects is called *brailling*; thus the child may say he *brailled* a dog before doing the dog walk.

Other activities which will help the blind child to organize and learn about space include

1. Practice walking a straight line. All sightless persons tend to veer about 1.25 inches per step or walk a spiral-shaped pathway when attempting to traverse a straight line. The ten-year-old, however, should not veer more than ten feet when attempting to walk forward for fifty feet nor more than thirty feet when moving forward 150 feet.
2. Practice facing sounds or following instructions to make quarter, half, three-quarter, and full turns. Blind adults tend to turn too much (100-105 degrees). Full turns are the most difficult with the

12. Bryant J. Cratty, *Movement and Spatial Awareness in Blind Children and Youth* (Springfield, Illinois: Charles C. Thomas, 1971), p. 24.

average person moving only 320-325 degrees.

3. Practice reproducing the exact distance and pathway just taken with a partner.

4. Take a short walk with a partner and practice finding the way back to the starting point alone.

5. Outside, where the rays of the sun can be felt, practice facing north, south, east, west. Relate these to goal cages and the direction of play in various games.

6. Practice determining whether the walking surface is uphill or downhill or tilted to the left or right; relate this to the principles of stability and efficient movement.

7. Practice walking different floor patterns. Originate novel patterns and then try to reproduce the same movement.

These and many other space explorations offer fun and excitement for sighted youngsters who are blindfolded as well as for the blind child in their classroom. It should be remembered, however, that the blindfolded child is at a greater disadvantage than the sightless youngster who has had several years to cope with spatial problems.

Trust and Courage

The blind child and his blindfolded friends should be provided with a *guidewire* stretched from one end of the playfield or gymnasium to another which will enable them to meet such challenges as "Run as fast as you can," "Roller skate as fast as you can," or "Ride a tricycle or bicycle as fast as you can." The children can hold on to a short rope looped around the guidewire or follow the guidewire with their fingers. Window sash cord stretched at hip height is probably best for this purpose. A knot at the far end of the rope warns the runner of the finish line. Residential schools for the blind erect permanent guidelines on their tracks. It is possible, of course, for a blind child to improve his running efficiency or

Figure 16.5. A blind child and sighted partner practice running the length of the gymnasium.

master a new locomotor skill by grasping the elbow or holding the hand of a sighted partner, but the ultimate goal should always be self-confidence in independent travel.

Sound Usage in Locomotion and Sports

Blind children can be grouped with LD children who have auditory perception deficits for special training in recognizing and following sounds. A continuous sound is better than intermittent ones. Whenever possible, the sound source should be placed in front of the pupil so that he is moving directly toward it. The next best position is behind the child so that he can proceed in a straight line away from it. Most difficult to perceive and follow are sounds to the side of a person or those moving parallel to his intended line of travel. A progression from simple through difficult must be developed so that children can learn to capitalize on all kinds of sounds. When the pupil can cope with a single sound source, he must be exposed to several simultaneous

Figure 16.6. Balloons attached to the target enable the blind child to hear a bull's eye.

5. Recognize, in archery, the sound of a balloon bursting which has been hit by an arrow or of an arrow penetrating a target made of a sound producing material.
6. Recognize the difference between the center of the trampoline and its outer areas by the sound of a ball attached to its undersurface.
7. Walk a nature trail or participate in a treasure hunt by following sounds from several tape cassettes located about the area.
8. Follow a voice or bell as he swims and dives in an open area.
9. Perceive the rhythm of a long rope alternately touching the ground and turning in the air so that he knows when to run under and can learn to jump the rope.

Mobility Training in Physical Education

Units on orientation, travel, and locomotion are included in a comprehensive physical education program for blind children. Many children are overprotected prior to entering school and hence need immediate help in adjusting to travel within the school environment. Illustrative of objectives for young children are the following ones devised by Charles C. Young, physical educator and principal at the Texas School for the Blind at Austin.

1. Select a partner and take a short, safe, and enjoyable walk on the campus under the direction of the teacher.
2. Be able to give a general description of the campus.
3. Show evidence of using sounds, landmarks, smells, and wind currents as aids in traveling alone.
4. Walk with good posture free from all tics.
5. Be able to go from cottage to gymnasium, athletic field, and hospital unassisted.

The physical educator must also orient young blind children to the use of playground

sounds with instructions to pick out and follow only the relevant one.

He must develop such competences as the following:

1. Discriminate between the bouncing of a small rubber ball for playing jacks, a tennis ball, a basketball, and a cageball.
2. Judge the height of the rebound of a basketball from its sound and thus be able to catch a ball bounced by himself or another.
3. Perceive the direction of a ground ball and thus be able to field or kick one being rolled toward his left, right, or center.
4. Discriminate, in bowling, the difference between sounds of a ball rolling down the gutter as opposed to the lane; the difference also between one bowling pin versus several falling.

equipment. Bells may be attached to the supporting chains of swings to warn children of the danger. Blind children often excel in climbing and hanging feats. Unable to see their distance from the ground, they seem fearless in the conquer of great heights and enjoy the wonder and praise of their sighted classmates. Illustrative objectives for a unit on the use of playground equipment are

1. Demonstrate how to play safely on all equipment.
2. Tell safety rules and reasons for each.
3. Display a cooperative attitude and express a willingness to learn.
4. Walk a hand ladder.
5. Pump self (sitting) while swinging.
6. Climb to top of both 8 and 14 foot slide alone and slide down feet first.
7. Perpetuate tilted merry-go-round by swinging out on downside and leaning in on upside.
8. Play simple games on the jungle gym.
9. Use seesaw safely for a short period with a companion.

Adaptations of Equipment and Facilities

Teachers and parents of visually impaired children should write to the American Foundation for the Blind for catalogs of special equipment which can be ordered. Each year improvements are made in sound-source balls and audible goal locators which facilitate the teaching of ball skills. Electronic balls with beepers are gradually replacing balls with bells. They should be painted orange or yellow for the partially sighted. In most elementary school activities beanbags with bells sewn inside are preferred over balls which are harder to recover.

Outside softball diamonds should have wide asphalt paths from base to base and from the pitcher's mound to the catcher. Inside, guidewires can be constructed from base to base. Boundaries for various games are

Figure 16.7. Electronic balls with beepers make basketball a possibility.

marked by a change in floor or ground surfaces which can be perceived by the soles of the feet. Tumbling mats, for instance, can be placed around the outside periphery of the playing area to mark its dimensions.

Braille can be used on the swimming pool walls to designate the changing heights of the water. It can be used also on gymnasium floors and walls as aids in determining the colors, shapes, and sizes of targets.

Portable aluminum bowling rails, nine feet long and three feet high, are available through the American Foundation for the Blind. These rails are easily assembled and broken down for transportation to different bowling alleys.

For the most part, however, equipment does not need to be adapted to the special needs of the blind. The play area should be quiet enough to facilitate sound utilization and well lighted to enhance use of residual vision.

Patterns of General Education

Since World War II, there has been a steady increase in the number of blind and visually impaired children who remain at home and receive special training through the public schools. The public school physical educator will find that only about one out of four visually handicapped children is totally blind or has light perception. Occasionally a child who is legally blind is not called to his attention and remains unnoticed in a large class. If limitations are not imposed upon him, the partially sighted youngster often has learned to compensate well enough to engage in the regular physical education program. In contrast, over half of the children served in residential schools are totally blind. The other half have vision ranging from the ability to see hand movements up to 20/200 acuity. A growing number of children in residential schools are multihandicapped. Yet, for the most part, state schools for the blind have outstanding physical education and athletic programs.

Residential Schools

Buell offers comprehensive coverage of physical education and athletics in residential schools. [13] Activities he recommends most highly are wrestling, tumbling, gymnastics, bowling, swimming, weight training, judo, relays, dance, roller skating, ice skating, shuffleboard, horseback riding, tandem cycling, hiking, camping, fishing, rowing, water skiing, and surfing. Little or no adaptation in these sports must be made in order for the blind to participate with the sighted. Ball handling activities and team sports are de-emphasized.

Wrestling seems to be the only sport in which the blind can compete with the sighted on a comparatively equal basis. About four-fifths of the schools for the blind have interscholastic wrestling teams, and many blind pupils excel over their sighted opponents in

state and national events. Track and field, bowling, and swimming are next in popularity among the interscholastic sports although competition is limited largely to other schools for the blind. A number of athletic associations have been formed to govern competitive events sponsored by the residential schools. Buell points out that many of the excellent physical educators in residential schools are partially sighted. According to him, only 20/200 vision is necessary to conduct the physical education program.

Public Schools

Two out of three visually handicapped students in public schools are not being offered programs of vigorous physical activity. This statistic stems, not from lack of physical ability among the blind, but from the unconcern and/or ignorance of the sighted. Two patterns of special instruction prevail in the public schools: (1) the resource room and (2) the self-contained classroom. In the former, the blind child spends most of the day in the regular classroom with his sighted peers. He goes to the resource room which is staffed either by an itinerant or fulltime special education teacher primarily for assistance in learning Braille. In this setting the physical education specialist often is not informed that a blind child is enrolled in the school. Well meaning teachers and parents assume that he cannot participate in regular physical education and tend to schedule this time for special help in the resource room. When given the opportunity, however, the blind child can learn physical activities as readily as other subjects.

Less desirable because it segregates the blind from their neighborhood friends is the self-contained classroom in one school within the system to which blind children from all

13. Charles E. Buell, *Physical Education for Blind Children* (Springfield, Illinois: Charles C. Thomas, 1966), p. 56-1000.

parts of the city are transported. Opportunities for association with sighted children are limited to the cafeteria, auditorium, library, and sometimes the playground. If activities are not planned, however, to help the pupils in the self-contained classroom to become acquainted with sighted children, the resulting isolation and loneliness may be greater than in totally segregated facilities.

In which activities can a group of ten or more blind children be integrated with sighted children? Is such integration feasible in the physical education class? In the afterschool recreational program? The physical educator assigned to a school with a self-contained classroom of blind children will often be allowed to decide the nature and scope of their physical education program. He may ignore their existence, leaving the direction of their motor development to the special educator, or he may teach the group segregated from or integrated with sighted pupils. Physical education with sighted classmates seems to be the best pattern. Except for ball handling activities, the blind child can participate with few adaptations. His success, in large part, depends upon the ability of the physical educator to give precise verbal instructions. Like any other child, he strives to fulfill the expectations of his teacher. Falls, scratches, and bruises should be disregarded as much as possible and the blind person allowed the dignity of recovering without oversolicitous help. Physical assistance should not be given unless requested. In tandem walking, for instance, the blind child should hold onto the upper arm of his sighted partner, not vice versa. The sighted person, of course, bears the responsibility for making his presence known and should state his name when initiating a verbal exchange rather than assuming the infallibility of the other's auditory memory.

When activities are practiced in small groups, the leader should ascertain that the blind pupil knows the names of his classmates, the approximate space allocated to each, his place in the order of rotation if turns are being taken, and the direction of movement. Sight is not required for success on the trampoline, parallel bars, and other pieces of apparatus; for tumbling, free exercise, and dance; for weight lifting, fitness activities, swimming; nor for many sports.

Figure 16.8. Blind persons can enjoy many sports with their sighted friends.

Camps for the Blind

Each summer special camps are held coast-to-coast for visually handicapped boys and girls. Several of the illustrations in this chapter show that blind children in the camp setting can experience the same activities that their sighted friends enjoy. National Camps for Blind Children, Box 6097, Lincoln, Nebraska 68506, should be contacted for further information.

Organizations

1. American Blind Bowling Association, Box 306, Louisville, Kentucky 40201.
2. American Foundation for the Blind, 15 W. 16th Street, New York, New York 10011.
3. American Printing House for the Blind, 1839 Frankfort Avenue, Louisville, Kentucky 40206.
4. Association for the Education of the Visually Handicapped, 1604 Spruce Street, Philadelphia, Pennsylvania 19103.
5. National Foundation of the Blind, Inc., 1908 Q Street, N. W., Washington, D. C. 20009.
6. National Society for the Prevention of Blindness, 79 Madison Avenue, New York, New York 10016.
7. Royal Institute for the Blind, 224 Great Portland Street, London, W.1, England.
8. Seeing Eye, Inc., Morristown, New Jersey 07960.

References

Buell, Charles E. *Physical Education and Recreation for the Visually Handicapped*. Washington, D. C.: AAHPER, 1974.

———. *Physical Education for Blind Children*. Springfield, Illinois: Charles C Thomas, 1966.

Cratty, Bryant J. *Movement and Spatial Awareness in Blind Children and Youth*. Springfield, Illinois: Charles C Thomas, 1971.

Hatlen, P. H. "Physical Education for the Visually Handicapped," *International Journal for the Education of the Blind*. Vol. 17, (October, 1967), pp. 17-21.

Jackson, C. R. S. *The Eye in General Practice*. Sixth edition. Baltimore: The Williams and Wilkins Company, 1972.

Johnson, P. R. "Physical Education for Blind Children in Public Schools," *New Outlook for the Blind*. Vol. 63, (November, 1969), pp. 264-271.

Kratz, Laura E. *Movement Without Sight*. Palo Alto: Peek Publications, 1973.

Lefkowitz, L. J. "Evaluating Physical Education Programs," *New Outlook for the Blind*. Vol. 56, (April, 1962), pp. 137-139.

Lowenfeld, Berthold. *Our Blind Children*. Springfield, Illinois: Charles C Thomas, 1971.

———. *The Visually Handicapped Child in School*. New York: The John Day Company, 1973.

Martin, G. *Mainstreaming: Mainstreaming*. Reston, Va.: Council for Exceptional Children, 1976.

Periodicals

New Outlook for the Blind published by the American Foundation for the Blind.

Bulletin for Physical Educators of the Blind published by the Association for the Education of the Visually Handicapped (AEVH).

Education of the Visually Handicapped, formerly published as the *International Journal for the Education of the Blind* by the AEVH.

Sight Saving Review published by the National Society for the Prevention of Blindness.

17 Asthma, Cystic Fibrosis, and Other Respiratory Problems

Figure 17.0. The asthmatic child experiences difficulty blowing up balloons.

Table 35 *Phenomena of Normal Breathing*

Inhalation	Exhalation
1. Bronchial tubes widen.	1. Bronchial tubes narrow.
2. Diaphragm contracts and descends. Contraction of the diaphragm pulls down on the central tendon, and up on the sternum and ribs, thereby increasing vertical diameter of thorax.	2. Diaphragm ascends as a result of its elastic recoil action when it relaxes.
3. Abdominal muscles relax (return to normal length).	3. Abdominal muscles shorten, particularly in forced exhalation.
4. Upper ribs are elevated.	4. Ribs are depressed.
5. Thoracic spine extends.	5. Thoracic spine tends to flex.

the bronchioles results in increasing shortness of breath. Wheezing is caused by the movement of the air in and out of the constricted bronchial tubes and in and through the accumulated mucus. During this stage the pattern of breathing is markedly altered. The problem appears to be taking insufficient air whereas, in reality, the expiratory phase is most difficult.

A brief look at normal respiration helps to explain the extreme difficulty with exhalation during an asthmatic attack. During both inspiration and expiration in asthma, more and more muscular effort is needed to move air through the constricted passageways. Because of the difficulty and prolongation of the expiratory phase, normal deflation of the lungs cannot occur before the next inhalation begins. The lungs therefore remain in a state of maximum expansion. Because of the growing oxygen deficit, the child tries to take in more and more air, thereby compounding the problem of exhalation.

Normally the discomfort during this stage is intense. Since the child cannot inhale sufficient air in a lying position, he sits or paces until medication takes effect. While suppositories and inhalators bring more-or-less im-

mediate relief, most medications taken by mouth require several minutes. Intellectually, the asthmatic may be well aware of the need to relax and control himself but the ability to do so in the absence of oxygen is lessened. The tenser he becomes, the more difficult it is to exhale. As the medication begins to dilate the bronchioles, the attack subsides, usually with much coughing and spitting of phlegm.

If the treatment does not prove effective, severe bronchial obstruction results in so little passage of air that the child becomes cyanotic and may die if emergency measures are not taken. Breathing during this stage may become inaudible, wheezing may cease, and the fatigued respiratory center in the medulla may no longer function normally. An asthmatic attack seldom progresses this far. If it does, the child should be rushed to the nearest hospital.

Incidence

In the United States asthma is the leading chronic disease in the age group below eighteen. Approximately five million Americans suffer from asthma, most of whom are under age fifteen. The incidence of asthma is slightly higher among boys than girls. Many children seem to *grow out of* asthma during puberty;

thus, the greatest concentration of asthmatic children is in elementary school.

Children with asthma tend to be multiply handicapped in that they frequently suffer also from hayfever, various allergies, sinus trouble, and upper respiratory infections. They are prone also to weight problems, often exhibiting the low fitness syndrome stemming from inadequate physical activity.

In the past asthma has been considered troublesome but essentially benign. Few attacks were lethal. The mortality rate now appears to be rising steadily. Last year over 7,000 deaths in the United States were caused by asthma. Atmospheric pollution is a potent factor in the increasing mortality rate, and persons with severe asthma are advised to avoid heavy exercise on days when air pollution is heavy. No substantial epidemiological data are available, however, which compare death rates from asthma in regions with and without pollution.

The rising mortality seems to be related to excessive sedation and overdoses of various bronchodilator drugs. Whereas the aerosol bronchodilators carried by many asthmatics stop attacks, overreliance on the aerosol spray may result in serious abnormalities in the blood gases. *Hypoxemia,* or insufficient oxygenation of the blood, makes the asthmatic extremely vulnerable to slight changes in the status of the bronchial airways. The use of morphine, phenobarbital, and other sedatives is contraindicated.

The physical educator should know that most of the bronchodilating drugs prescribed for asthmatics do tend to cause hypoxemia which, in turn, explains why children with asthma are frequently restless, agitated, and/or depressed. The drugs appear to cause *a high* somewhat similar to that associated with diet pills. As the *high* levels off between pills, the child's behavior may change. Severe depression may follow the withdrawal of some drugs such as the corticosteroids which are used in the management of asthma. Unless the side effects of drugs are understood, the asthmatic pupil himself may be distressed by his predisposition toward crying, nervous jitters, and other problems which arise in relation to drug management. The incidence of attempted suicides among adolescent asthmatics warrants study.

Causes of Asthma

Multiple factors interact to produce the symptoms of asthma. The tendency to develop allergic sensitivities is clearly inheritable. Persons with asthma may manufacture a special type of antibody which has been termed reaginic, homocytotrophic, skin sensitizing, or immunuglobulin E (IgE). These antibodies, called *reagins,* are responsible for positive skin tests. Although allergies to specific pollens, molds, foods, and animals frequently are present, asthma is no longer considered fundamentally an allergic disease.

The etiology of asthma has now been traced to deficient homeostatic function at the cellular level, specifically an abnormality in the beta adrenergic receptors. This relates to the normal sympathetic nervous system balance between the functioning of nerve fibers which release epinephrine (adrenalin) and those which liberate acetylcholine. Any alteration of this balance is believed to cause changes in the tonus of the bronchial tube linings. The resulting deficient homeostasis increases irritability of the bronchii to all kinds of stimuli.

Within the broad spectrum of individual differences, asthmatics may be hypersensitive to cigarette smoke, alcohol, changes in weather, changes in body temperature, air pollutants, and other stimuli too numerous to name. Because infection affects homeostasis, it is a major precipitator of bronchial constriction and other asthmatic symptoms.

Excitement, fear, and other emotions which stimulate the production of adrenalin

Most of us take breathing for granted. We squeeze air out of our lungs 20,000 times a day and seldom think about the phenomenon of respiration. Yet respiratory diseases are the fastest rising causes of death in the United States. This chapter is about persons who struggle to breathe. They may have *asthma, chronic bronchitis, emphysema,* or *cystic fibrosis.* The symptoms are similar in all four conditions, and exercise is vital for the maintenance of respiratory fitness.

Breathing exercises, postural drainage, games for improving exhalation, and other activities are discussed under asthma since this condition most often confronts the physical educator. It is estimated that almost half of the chronic diseases suffered by children under age seventeen are respiratory in nature. Asthma, hayfever, and other allergies account for 32.8 percent of all chronic diseases in this age group. Bronchitis, sinusitis, and related conditions cause 15.1 percent. Cystic fibrosis is included in this chapter because 90 percent of its victims die from chronic lung disorders, and the physical activities for these children are the same as those for asthma. Emphysema is primarily a disease of middle and old age, but its origins can often be traced to asthma and chronic bronchitis in earlier years. Over a million persons in this country lead restricted lives because of emphysema. The fastest growing cause of total disability in the United States, it is surpassed only by heart disease.

Asthma

Asthma and respiratory infections account for 25 percent of the illnesses in the United States. Perhaps no other health problem is more troublesome to the physical educator. Should the asthmatic child engage in strenuous exercise? What limits, if any, should be placed upon him in the physical education setting? How should notes from parents requesting excuse from physical activity for their asthmatic offspring be handled? It is imperative that physical educators understand asthma, the pros and cons of exercise, and other aspects of treatment which may affect motor performance.

Asthma is a lung condition which is characterized by spasms of the bronchial tubes, swelling of their linings, and excessive secretion of mucus, all of which cause coughing, wheezing, dyspnea (breathing difficulty), and a feeling of constriction in the chest. Attacks may last a few minutes or several days or weeks. The severity of an asthmatic condition is described as follows: (1) *spasmodic,* if attacks occur with long intervals of freedom in between symptoms; (2) *continuous,* when daily wheezing is present; (3) *intractable,* when all symptoms are continuous; and (4) *status asthmaticus,* when treatment brings little or no relief.

Since exercise may precipitate asthma, the physical educator should be cognizant of the symptoms characteristic of the three stages through which an attack progresses: (1) *coughing* (2) *dyspnea,* and (3) *severe bronchial obstruction.* Treatment should begin before the onset of the third stage.

Sneezing and/or a hacking, nonproductive cough constitute the first warnings of an impending attack. In this stage the bronchial tubes are responding to the irritation of an *allergen* by secreting mucus which accumulates and obstructs the passage of air. The coughing is caused by the reflex action of the smooth, involuntary muscles of the bronchioles in an attempt to remove the accumulating mucus. Cessation of exercise at this point may prevent the appearance of other symptoms. If the allergen is dust, a household animal, ragweed, or some substance which can be shut out or removed, the coughing and sneezing will gradually lessen.

If the coughing continues, the linings of the bronchioles swell, thus narrowing the air passages. The diminished flow of air through

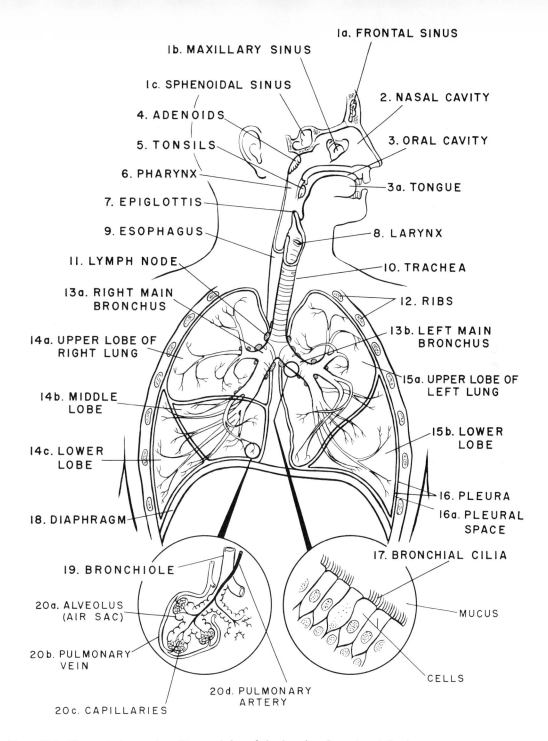

Figure 17.1. The respiratory system. (By permission of the American Lung Association.)

Labels:
- 1a. FRONTAL SINUS
- 1b. MAXILLARY SINUS
- 1c. SPHENOIDAL SINUS
- 2. NASAL CAVITY
- 3. ORAL CAVITY
- 3a. TONGUE
- 4. ADENOIDS
- 5. TONSILS
- 6. PHARYNX
- 7. EPIGLOTTIS
- 8. LARYNX
- 9. ESOPHAGUS
- 10. TRACHEA
- 11. LYMPH NODE
- 12. RIBS
- 13a. RIGHT MAIN BRONCHUS
- 13b. LEFT MAIN BRONCHUS
- 14a. UPPER LOBE OF RIGHT LUNG
- 14b. MIDDLE LOBE
- 14c. LOWER LOBE
- 15a. UPPER LOBE OF LEFT LUNG
- 15b. LOWER LOBE
- 16. PLEURA
- 16a. PLEURAL SPACE
- 17. BRONCHIAL CILIA
- 18. DIAPHRAGM
- 19. BRONCHIOLE
- 20a. ALVEOLUS (AIR SAC)
- 20b. PULMONARY VEIN
- 20c. CAPILLARIES
- 20d. PULMONARY ARTERY
- MUCUS
- CELLS

affect homeostasis which, in turn, may cause asthma. Belief in the unity of mind and body negates the idea that asthma can be entirely psychological or physiological in origin. Clearly, it is both.

Perhaps nothing upsets an asthmatic more than the implication that his attacks are psychosomatic. Yet this may be partially true. Emotional stress does lead to physiological changes which resemble asthmatic symptoms and/or render the tissues more sensitive to allergens. Research shows that asthmatics tend to be introspective, ultrasensitive to criticism, eager to please, and generally submissive. They have been known to worry themselves into an attack over an impending test, a conflict in interpersonal relations, or an especially demanding social obligation.

The psychological phenomenon known as a *reaction formation* is common among asthmatics. In order to prove their worth to others, they tend to establish unrealistically high levels of aspiration and then totally exhaust themselves in all-out effort to accomplish such goals. When it appears that they cannot live up to their own or the perceived expectations of others, an asthmatic attack is a way of saving face. "I could have made the deadline if I hadn't gotten sick!" "I would have won the match if I hadn't started wheezing." The physical educator will find many asthmatic children eager to play, despite parental restrictions, and unwilling to withdraw from a game even when they evidence asthmatic symptoms. Many do not impose limitations upon themselves, refusing to accept the inevitability of an attack. Like all children, they want to be *normal.* The following memories of asthmatic adults lend some insight into the phenomenon of reaction formation.

I can remember going out to play with the kids in the neighborhood. I never thought about my asthma. I was highly competitive. . . loved to run. . . had to win. The asthma never came while I was playing. Oh, maybe a little wheezing, but I ignored that. But invariably in the middle of the night, after an usually hard day of play, I would awake gasping. . . terrified. . . unable to breathe.

Of course, this roused up the whole family and we were all exhausted the next day.

My parents used to find me sitting and holding a neighborhood cat. . . stroking and loving it. My nose would be running and my eyes half swollen and filled with tears. It wasn't any special cat, just any animal I could find. They wouldn't let me have a pet at home because I was so allergic to them. The first thing I did after college was to buy a cat and start taking weekly injections to build up tolerance. I still take pills.

I never took a test in high school that I didn't stay up all night beforehand studying. By the time everyone else woke up, I'd have diarrhea, stomach cramps, a headache. . . and be literally convinced I didn't know enough to make an A. But I always made it to school. If I accidently fell asleep or something prevented me from learning the material, I'd wake up with asthma and be in bed for a week. The whole time I was in bed I'd worry about not taking the test and this would make me sicker. Then my mouth and nose would break out with fever blisters, and I would be too ashamed of my appearance to return to school until it healed. I'd catch up on my studies and make A's on the next round of tests. I always felt like the teachers wouldn't like me if I didn't make A's.

The reaction formation in the asthmatic creates a vicious circle in which stress precipitates coughing, wheezing, and dyspnea. The inability to breathe, particularly in a young child, results in helplessness, frustration, and anxiety which, in turn, intensifies the asthmatic problem. He wants his parents to awaken and keep him company during an attack, yet he experiences considerable emotional conflict about such dependency. Should an attack occur in the physical education class, he likewise has mixed feelings. He wants attention and an offer of help; yet he dislikes himself for seeking solicitousness. The more he worries about what others think, the worse the asthma becomes. Once an attack begins, the asthmatic cannot will it to stop. Nor can he *consciously* bring on an attack. The interplay of physiological and psychological etiological factors in asthma is so enigmatic that they remain little understood.

Implications for Physical Education

In 1970, the Committee on Children with Handicaps of the American Academy of Pediatrics issued a formal statement on the asthmatic child and his participation in physical education. It states:

Both physical and mental activities are useful to asthmatic children. The majority of asthmatic children can participate in physical activities at school and in athletics with minimal difficulty, providing the asthma is under satisfactory control. Overfatigue and emotional upheaval in competitive athletic contests appear to be predisposing factors in precipitating asthma attacks in some instances. This may depend to some extent on the duration and the severity of the disease. As a general rule, every effort should be made to minimize restrictions and to invoke them only when the condition of the child makes it necessary. [1]

The committee recommended that any decision to modify the regular physical education program should be shared cooperatively by physician, child, parents, and physical educator. Before a group conference for this purpose is called, the physical educator should take the initiative in acquainting the physician with the nature and scope of the physical education activities. Without such orientation, many pediatricians do not have adequate background to evaluate specific sports, dance, and aquatics activities as strenuous, moderate, or mild. Nor will they know that the physical educator has special training in adapting activities to the needs of the asthmatic.

Problems characteristic of some asthmatic children which can be remediated through adapted physical education include an inefficient pattern of breathing, poor circulorespiratory endurance, excessive nervous ten-

sion, and postural defects. Work on these specific problems should supplement participation in the regular physical education program.

Inefficient Pattern of Breathing

Breathing exercises may: (1) improve efficiency of expiratory phase; (2) decrease activity in the upper part of the chest; (3) teach diaphragmatic breathing; (4) relax spasmodically contracted muscles; and (5) increase flexibility of intercostals, pectorals, scaleni, and trapezius. Asthmatic children must be taught the kinesiology of respiration. They should understand the difference between costal and diaphragmatic breathing and be able to feel the muscles of inspiration and forced expiration. The asthmatic typically overworks his upper chest, using the intercostal muscles more than the diaphragm. The diaphragm is a dome-shaped structure which separates the thoracic and abdominal cavities. The top of the dome, called the central tendon, is the part of the diaphragm that descends during inspiration and ascends during expiration. Surrounding the central tendon are the muscle fibers which attach the diaphragm to the circumference of the thoracic outlet. The diaphragm should be the principal muscle of inspiration. In normal quiet breathing it should be the only respiratory muscle in action.

Diaphragmatic breathing is sometimes called abdominal breathing since the abdomen can be seen alternately protruding in inhalation and flattening in exhalation. In normal expiration no muscle contraction is required. Exhalation depends, in large part, upon the ability of the diaphragm to relax and be car-

1. Committee on Children with Handicaps, "The Asthmatic Child and His Participation in Sports and Physical Education," *Pediatrics*, Vol. 45, No. 1, Part I (January, 1970), p. 150.

ried upward by its elastic recoil action. The phrenic nerve which innervates the diaphragm is extremely susceptible to nervous tension. Hence any coughing, wheezing, or anxiety producing conditions increase the tonus of the diaphragm which in turn tenses the pectorals, the three scaleni, and the trapezius. The result is distension of the chest similar to that felt when the breath is held for a long time. The discomfort of the distension cannot be relieved because the fully contracted diaphragm cannot relax and ascend, thereby helping to push air out of the thoracic cavity. In normal respiration the diaphragm may move from one to seven centimeters; during an asthmatic attack it may move up and down only a fraction of a centimeter or not at all. As an asthmatic relies more and more upon costal breathing, he gradually loses the flexibility of his lower chest muscles.

Screening Tests

Information which should be obtained about the asthmatic child before beginning a program of breathing exercises includes: (1) age; (2) type of asthma; (3) season during which asthma is most severe; (4) number of attacks during each of the previous three months; (5) specific allergens or conditions which seem to precipitate asthma; (6) specific dosage of tablets or number of times inhalators and/or suppositories have been used during the last ten days; and (7) a measure of pulmonary efficiency. The two tests used most often to measure pulmonary efficiency are the FEV_1 (Forced Expiratory Volume for One Second) and the MBC (Maximal Breathing Capacity). Both require laboratory apparatus such as a spirometer or respirometer.

To determine MBC the child is asked to breathe as hard and fast as possible into a hose for a certain number of seconds. The volume of the expired air is collected and measured. The MBC is the number of liters of air per minute the child can move when breathing as deeply

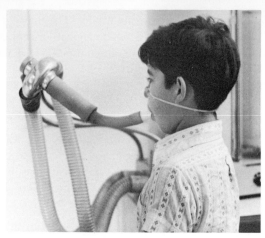

Figure 17.2. Child exhales into spirometer as test of pulmonary efficiency.

and rapidly as possible. Normal values on the MBC range from 43 to 155 liters for males and 41 to 123 liters for females. Kazemi[2] recommends that the MBC be used as a screening test to determine degree of severity of asthma. Asthmatics have lower MBC values than individuals free of lung disease. Gaensler and Wright[3] state that the MBC correlates more highly with dyspnea than any other test.

The FEV_1 is the number of cubic centimeters of air forcefully exhaled in the first second after a deep inspiration. Normal FEV_1 values range from 500 to 4,500 cubic centimeters for boys and from 350 to 3,400 cubic centimeters for girls. Any disease which causes bronchial obstruction and resistance in the airways reduces FEV_1. Asthmatics whose FEV_1 or MBC measure are significantly lower than normal values should be excluded from research studies which investigate the relationship between exercise and pulmonary efficiency.

2. Homayoun Kazemi, "Pulmonary-Function Tests," *Journal of the American Medical Association,* Vol. 206 (December 2, 1968), pp. 2302-2304.

3. Edward A. Gaensler and George W. Wright, "Evaluation of Respiratory Impairment," *Archives of Environmental Health* Vol. 12 (February, 1966), pp. 149-189.

Breathing Exercises

Special physical education for severe asthmatics should begin daily with a few minutes of breathing exercises. Suggestions for teaching these exercises include:

1. Provide each child with his own exercise mat, waste paper container, and box of tissues.

2. Encourage the children to blow their noses and attempt to cough up phlegm. Many asthmatics are embarrassed by the noise of their nose-blowing and hence acquire the habit of sniffing.

3. Emphasize a short inspiration through the nose and long expiration through gently pursed lips, making a whistling or hissing noise. This is called *pursed lip breathing*. Try timing the expiration phase with a stop watch or metronome. Expiration should be at least twice as long as inspiration.

4. Ascertain that older girls are not wearing girdles and that all belts are removed and restrictive clothing loosened. Emphasize that during exhalation the abdomen must sink in order for the diaphragm to rise in the chest.

5. Concur with children that in the beginning the exercises do make them feel worse. Warn them ahead of time to expect coughing and wheezing during the first few seconds of diaphragmatic breathing.

6. Establish behavioral objectives to serve as motivation. Illustrative objectives might be:
   a. MBC increased by certain percent.
   b. FEV_1 increased by certain percent.
   c. Chest expansion at the fourth rib increased by a certain number of inches.
   d. Abdominal expansion increased by a certain number of inches.
   e. Complete control over the full range of diaphragmatic breathing.
   f. The ability to dissociate costal from diaphragmatic breathing.

Fein and Cox recommend the following twelve breathing exercises for asthmatics: [4]

1. *Diaphragmatic Breathing Exercise—Lying.* The position is on the back with the knees bent, feet on bed, completely relaxed. The hands are placed on the abdomen on the lower ribs.

   The exercise consists of three parts: breathing out slowly making the chest as small as possible and tightening the abdominal muscles, relaxing the abdominal muscles and breathing in quickly through the nose, and then breathing out quickly through the nose and mouth, again tightening the abdominal muscles.

Figure 17.3. Phase one of diaphragmatic breathing exercise.

Figure 17.4. Phase two of diaphragmatic breathing exercise.

4. Bernard T. Fein and Eugenia P. Cox, "The Technique of Respiratory and Physical Exercise in the Treatment of Bronchial Asthma," *Annals of Allergy,* Vol. 13, (July-August, 1955), pp. 378-383. Reprinted by permission.

2. *Side Expansion Breathing Exercise.* The position is on the back with the head and shoulders resting on pillows with the hands placed on the lower ribs and the knees bent.

The exercise consists of three parts: breathing out slowly making the chest as small as possible and tightening the abdominal muscles, relaxing the abdominal muscles and breathing in quickly through the nose, and then breathing out quickly through the nose and mouth, again tightening the abdominal muscles.

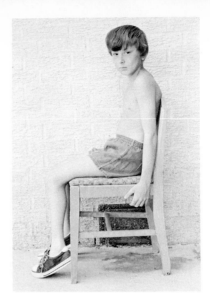

Figure 17.7. Phase one of diaphragmatic breathing exercise.

Figure 17.5. Phase one of side expansion breathing exercise.

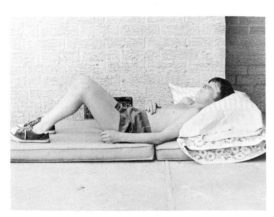

Figure 17.6. Phase two of side expansion breathing exercise.

3. *Diaphragmatic Breathing Exercise—Sitting.* The position is sitting with the back resting against a chair, completely relaxed. The patient breathes out slowly, sinking in the chest and tightening the abdominal muscles, then relaxing the abdominal muscles while breathing through the nose.

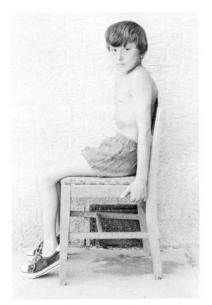

Figure 17.8. Phase two of diaphragmatic breathing exercise.

4. *Side Expansion Breathing Exercise with Belt for Pressure.* The position is sitting in a chair with back supported. A wide belt is placed around the lower ribs above the waist. The crossed ends of the belt are grasped by the

patient. Breathing is started by blowing out slowly and allowing the chest to become smaller. When all the air is out, the ribs are squeezed a little by tightening the belt. The lower ribs are then expanded against the belt easing up the pressure at the end, as the patient quietly breathes through the nose.

5. *Elbow Circling Exercise.* The position is sitting in a chair, leaning forward with the back straight. The fingertips are placed on the shoulders, elbows are bent and out to the side, in line with the shoulders. There is a circling of the elbows up, back, and down; the four circles are performed, then relaxation.

Figure 17.9. Phase one of side expansion exercise with belt for pressure.

Figure 17.11. Phase one of elbow circling exercise.

Figure 17.10. Phase two of side expansion exercise with belt for pressure.

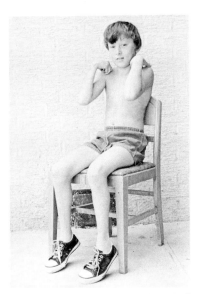

Figure 17.12. Phase two of elbow circling exercise.

6. *Forward Bending Exercise.* The position is sitting with the feet apart and arms relaxed at the sides. The patient breathes out slowly as he bends forward, first the head, then the shoulders, until the head almost touches the knees. The abdominal muscles are tight. The body is gradually raised, by first pushing the lower back against the chair, then the middle and upper back, shoulders, neck, and head, breathing in as the upper back is straightened, and relaxing the abdominal muscles, keeping the back and head erect. Small breaths should be taken, expanding the lower ribs and relaxing the abdominal muscles.

7. *Relaxing Exercise.* The position is sitting in a chair. Leaning forward, the patient presses the back of the head, neck, arms, and shoulders to the count of two. Then he relaxes, dropping the head and arms and allowing the back to round out to the count of four.

Figure 17.15. Phase one of relaxing exercise.

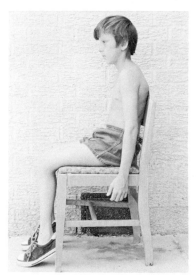

Figure 17.13. Phase one of forward bending exercise.

Figure 17.14. Phase two of forward bending exercise.

Figure 17.16. Phase two of relaxing exercise.

8. *Abdominal Muscle Exercise.* The position is lying on back with knees bent and feet on the bed, keeping the arms and the shoulders relaxed. The right knee is slowly raised to the chest while breathing out and tightening the abdominal muscles. The patient should then pause in breathing, lowering the right knee; then breathe in, relax the abdominal muscles, and gently expand the lower ribs only. This is repeated for the left knee, and repeated again bringing both knees to the chest.

Figure 17.17. Phase one of abdominal muscle exercise.

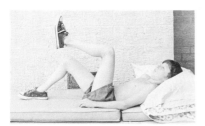

Figure 17.18. Phase two of abdominal muscle exercise.

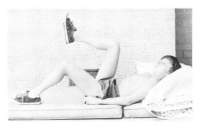

Figure 17.19. Phase three of abdominal muscle exercise.

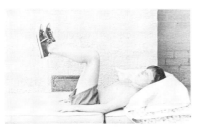

Figure 17.20. Phase four of abdominal muscle exercise.

9. *Side Bending Exercise.* The position is sitting with the feet apart with the right arm relaxed at the side and the left hand placed over the sides of the right middle ribs. While breathing out, the patient bends the head and shoulders to the right and presses the hand against the side, bending the head and shoulders to the left slightly while breathing in, and swelling the right lower ribs as much as possible to the right. This part of the exercise is done quicker than the first part. After six bends to the right, a change is made to the left and six more bends are made.

Figure 17.21. Phase one of side bending exercise.

Figure 17.22. Phase two of side bending exercise.

Asthma, Cystic Fibrosis, and Other Respiratory Problems **361**

10. *Trunk Turning Exercise.* The position is sitting with the feet apart and the hands on the knees. The back is kept straight without leaning forward. The twisting is done from the waist up. The patient turns the body and flings the left arm sharply to the left, turning the trunk as far as possible, so that the left shoulder is back, the right forward, and the head turned to look at the palm of the hand. After relaxing he should turn back to the starting position, and repeat, turning to the right.

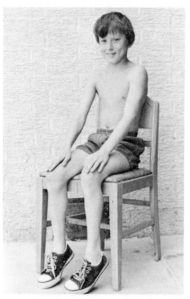

Figure 17.23. Phase one of trunk turning exercise.

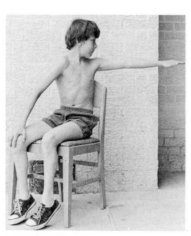

Figure 17.24. Phase two of trunk turning exercise.

11. *Forward Bending Exercise.* The position is standing with the back, shoulders, and head against a wall and the feet about six inches from the baseboard. The patient breathes out as he bends down slowly, dropping first the head, then the shoulders, the upper back, and finally, the lower back. The arms are hung limply and the abdominal muscles are tight. Then he must straighten up, keeping the abdominal muscles tight, and flatten the lower back against the wall, relaxing the abdominal muscles to breathe in as he straightens the rest of the back gradually. He must hold the upper back and head against the wall and breathe out quickly by tightening the abdominal muscles, forcing the low back against the wall. A small breath is taken before repeating the exercise.

Figure 17.25. Phase one of forward bending exercise.

Figure 17.26. Phase two of forward bending exercise.

Figure 17.27. Phase three of forward bending exercise.

12. *Side Bending Rotation Exercise.* The position is standing with the feet apart. The arms are brought above the head as the patient breathes in. Then he bends slowly to the left as far as possible while breathing out, letting the arms bend loosely at the elbows. While bending, the body is twisted so the arms are fully carried outside of the left foot, while continuing to breathe out. The body is raised upright, with the arms overhead as he breathes in. The exercise is repeated to the right.

Figure 17.28. Phase one of side bending rotation exercise.

Figure 17.29. Phase two of side bending rotation exercise.

Figure 17.30. Phase three of side bending rotation exercise.

Games to Improve Expiration

In ordinary expiration, no muscles are used. In vigorous exhalation, the following muscles contract: internal and external obliques, transversus abdominis, transversus thoracis, serratus posterior inferior, and posterior portions of the intercostals. Since the abdominal muscles participate vigorously in laughing, coughing, panting, and singing, games based upon these activities can be developed.

Games Using Abdominal Muscles

1. *Laugh-In.* Circle formation with *it* in center. *It* tosses a handkerchief high into the air. Everyone laughs as loudly as possible as it floats downward but no laugh must be heard after the handkerchief contacts the floor. Anyone breaking this rule becomes the new *it.* For variation, pupils can cough instead of laughing.

2. *Laugh Marathon.* Each pupil has a tape recorder. The object is to see who can make the longest playing tape of continuous laughing.

3. *Guess Who's Laughing.* All pupils are blindfolded. One, who is designated as *it,* laughs continuously until classmates guess who is laughing.

4. *Red Light, Green Light Laughing.* This game is played according to traditional rules except laughing accompanies the running or is substituted for it.

All games designed to improve exhalation should be played in erect standing or running postures since the spine and pelvis must be stabilized by the lumbar extensors in order for the abdominal muscles to contract maximally.

Blowing Activities

Blowing activities are especially valuable in emphasizing the importance of reducing residual air in the lungs. Learning to play wind instruments is recommended strongly. Swimming offers a recreational setting for stressing correct exhalation. Games found to be especially popular follow:

1. *Snowflakes*
   Equipment: A one-inch square of tissue paper for each child.
   Procedure: Two teams with each child having one piece of paper. Each participant attempts to keep the paper above the floor after the whistle is blown. When the paper touches the floor the participant is disqualified. The winner is the team in which a player keeps the tissue in the air for the longest time.

2. *Ping Pong Relay*
   Equipment: One ping pong ball for each team.
   Procedure: Two teams with one-half of the players of each team behind lines fifty feet apart. A player blows the ping pong ball across the floor to his team member who blows the ball back to the starting line. The relay continues until each player has blown the ball. The team which finishes first is the winner.

3. *Under the Bridge*
   Equipment: One ping pong ball for each team.
   Procedure: Teams with players standing in single file with legs spread. The last player in the file blows the ball forward between the legs of his team members with additional blowing provided by the other players to move the ball quickly to the front. If the ball rolls outside the legs of the players, the last player must retrieve the ball and blow it again. When the ball reaches the front, the first player in the file picks up the ball, runs to the end of the file, and blows the ball forward again. The team finishing first is the winner.

4. *Balloon Relay*
   Equipment: One balloon for each player. One chair for each team placed on a line ninety-five feet from the starting line.
   Procedure: Children on the teams line up in single file behind the starting line.

Upon the signal to start, the first player of each team runs to the opposite line, blows up his balloon, places it on the chair, and sits on the balloon until it breaks. He then returns to the starting line and tags the next player, who procedes in the same manner.

5. *Blow Out the Candle*
   Equipment: A candle is placed on the floor between every two children.
   Procedure: Opponents lie on the floor on opposite sides eight feet from the candle. Players attempt to blow out the candle from the greatest distance possible. The child who blows out the candle at the greatest distance is the winner.

6. *Ping Pong Croquet*
   Equipment: Ping pong balls and hoops made of milk cartons taped to the floor.
   Procedure: Each player crawls and blows the ping pong ball through the series of hoops, positioned on the floor in the same manner as in a game of croquet. The ball must be moved and controlled entirely by blowing. The hands may not touch the ball at any time. The players who finish first are the winners. Several playing areas may be provided to accommodate more players.

7. *Self-Competition in Candle Blowing*
   Equipment: Movable candle behind a yardstick placed opposite the mouth.
   Procedure: Child attempts to blow out lighted candle set at gradually lengthened distances on the yardstick.

8. *Self-Competition in Bottle Blowing*
   Equipment: Two half-gallon bottles, half filled with water and connected with three rubber hoses and two glass pipes. See Figure 17.31.
   Procedure: Child attempts to blow water from one bottle to another, first from sitting position and then standing position.

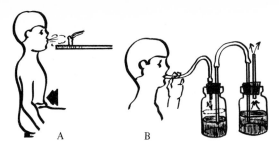

Figure 17.31. Blowing exercises: (A) self-competition in candle blowing and (B) self-competition in bottle blowing.

Other Activities

The activities described in Chapter 10 are recommended especially for the asthmatic child. Franklin[5] offers a complete set of lesson plans for progressively increasing the respiratory fitness of asthmatic children. On the twentieth day of an experimental conditioning program, her subjects completed 200 jumping jacks, 42 push-ups, 65 sit-ups, 31 laps around a gymnasium 110 X 90 feet in size, jumped the rope continuously for five minutes, did wind sprints for five minutes, jogged ten minutes, and played a game of basketball. When motivated, asthmatic children appear capable of achieving the same levels of circulorespiratory fitness as their nonasthmatic friends.

The relaxation activities described in Chapter 11 should be incorporated into the daily physical education regime for the asthmatic child. In many instances psychotherapy should be available along with the training in relaxation.

Posture Problems

In chronic asthma, permanent deformities of the chest may result—kyphosis, barrel chest, pigeon chest, and Harrison's sulcus. These defects can be traced to an actual

5. Janice Franklin, "An Experimental Study of Physical Conditioning for Asthmatic Children," Unpublished M. A. Thesis, Texas Woman's University (1971), p. 122.

shortening of the muscle fibers of the diaphragm and intercostals. When maintained in the lowered position characteristic of inspiration, the diaphragm affects the position and function of the viscera which are pushed against the abdominal wall. The asthmatic typically experiences difficulty in flattening the abdomen which, along with the chest, may become permanently distended. Until the pattern of breathing is corrected, abdominal exercises will not prove beneficial.

Postural Drainage

Postural drainage is a quiet activity in which the child lies in various positions which enable gravity to help the cough drain the bronchial tree of accumulated mucus. The bronchodilator is used prior to assuming ten different positions. The teacher, therapist, or parent taps the child's upper torso with his fingers as depicted in Figure 17.32. Each of these positions is designed to drain a specific area of the bronchial tree; hence the benefit

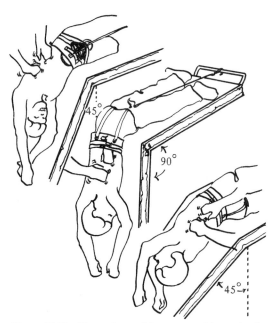

Figure 17.32. Illustrative positions assumed in postural drainage.

derived from the position depends upon the amount of congestion present. Not all positions are required each session.

Intermittent Positive Pressure Breathing (IPPB)

In IPPB, the student covers his nose and mouth with a mask which is attached to a machine which forces a measured amount of oxygen through his lungs under a controlled level of pressure. Bronchodilators and other kinds of medication can be put in the positive pressure machine. IPPB may be prescribed on a daily basis or used only in times of pulmonary crises.

IPPB is believed to produce a lowered alveolar PCO_2, decreased outward filtration of plasma from the pulmonary capillary membrane, decreased residual volume, increased intrapulmonary mixing, more uniform aeration, increased cough efficiency, and decreased bronchial resistance.

Modification of Rules and Instructional Environment

Since so many asthmatic children are sensitive to pollens and dust, physical education should be conducted indoors at least during the seasons of peak incidence of attacks. Ideally the room should be air conditioned and entirely dust free. The humidity should be maintained as low as possible.

Changes in weather, particularly dampness, predispose children to attacks. Alterations in body temperature, specifically becoming overheated, seem to cause wheezing. A cold, wet towel on the forehead and/or the back of the neck between activities will help to maintain uniform body temperature.

When the chalkboard is in use, the asthmatic should be stationed as far away from it as possible. Nylon covered, allergen-free mats containing foam rubber as filler are recommended.

Whereas all children become thirsty during vigorous physical activity, they are generally encouraged to wait until the end of the period to get a drink of water. In contrast, forcing fluids is an essential part of the total exercise program for the asthmatic. As tissues become drier during exercise, the mucus thickens and is more difficult to cough up. More than three or four consecutive coughs should be avoided since coughing itself dries out the mucus membranes. The only means of thinning this mucus is through fluids taken by mouth or intervenously. Four or five quarts of water a day are recommended. Cold drinks are contraindicated since they may cause spasms of the bronchial tubes; hence hot drinks and fluids at room temperature are recommended. The physical educator should ascertain that fluids are taken periodically throughout the exercise session.

Antihistamines are not desirable for asthmatics because they tend to dry out the mucus in the airway. If, because of hayfever or other allergies, the asthmatic is taking antihistamines, it is even more important that fluid intake be increased.

Occasionally childhood asthma cannot be managed efficiently in the school and home environment. In such instances, the child is typically referred to such treatment centers as CARIH, the Children's Asthma Research Institute and Hospital, in Denver, Colorado. CARIH is the largest hospital in the western hemisphere which treats asthmatic children and the only center whose staff conducts research exclusively on asthma and allergic diseases.

Chronic Obstructive Pulmonary Diseases

Chronic obstructive pulmonary diseases (COPD) including chronic bronchitis and pulmonary emphysema, now constitute the fastest growing chronic disease problem in America. The death rate has doubled every five years over the past twenty years.

Chronic bronchitis is defined as a recurrent cough characterized by excessive mucus secretion in the bronchii. The three stages are (1) *simple*, in which the chief characteristic is mucoid expectoration, (2) *mucopurulent*, in which the sputum is intermittently or continuously filled with pus because of active infection, and (3) *obstruction*, in which there is narrowing of the airways in addition to expectoration. This is the stage at which the complications of emphysema and/or heart failure occur. The three stages may merge one into the other and span a period of twenty or more years.

Pulmonary emphysema is a destruction of the walls of the alveoli of the lungs. This destruction results in overdistention of the air sacs and loss of lung elasticity. Emphysema is a Greek word which means literally to inflate or puff up. Like the asthmatic, the person with emphysema has difficulty expelling air. Whereas the normal person breathes fourteen times a minute, the emphysematous person may breathe twenty to thirty times a minute and still not get enough oxygen into the bloodstream. The characteristic high carbon dioxide level in the blood causes sluggishness and irritability. The heart tries to compensate for lack of oxygen by pumping harder, and possible heart failure becomes an additional hazard.

Emphysema is more common among men than women. Over 10 percent of the middle-aged and elderly population in America is believed to suffer with emphysema. The specific etiology is still under study, but smoking and air pollution are considered the most potent causal factors.

Patients with COPD tend to restrict their activities more and more because of their fear of wheezing and dyspnea. This inactivity results in muscle deterioration, increased shortness of breath, and increasing inactivity—a vicious cycle! The activities recommended for the asthmatic child are suitable also for individuals with bronchitis and emphysema.

Cystic Fibrosis

Cystic fibrosis, a childhood disease which was not recognized as a separate entity from bronchiopneumonia until 1936, is included in this chapter because 90 percent of its victims die from chronic lung disorders. The physical education program for a child with cystic fibrosis is similar to that of asthmatic students.

It is estimated that one child in every 1,000 is born with cystic fibrosis. The cause of the disease is unknown, but research strongly suggests transmission through a recessive gene. There are approximately ten million carriers of this gene in the United States. If two carriers happen to bear offspring, there is a one-in-four chance that their infant will have cystic fibrosis and a two-in-four chance that he will be a carrier.

Cystic fibrosis accounts for almost all of the deaths in childhood from chronic nontuberculosis pulmonary disease. Although the life span of cystic fibrosis patients is increasing, over 60 percent of the children still succumb before age ten and 80 percent before age twenty.

The child with cystic fibrosis looks and acts essentially normal. In most cases, no one, save the parents and physician, are aware of the disease until the final stage. No cure is known, and treatment revolves around prevention and/or control of pulmonary infection, maintenance of proper nutrition, and prevention of abnormal salt loss. Research shows that many cystics perform well above average in tests of muscle power, endurance, and agility despite moderately severe respiratory disease as judged by clinical and chest x-ray scoring. [6]

The primary disorder in cystic fibrosis is the abnormal secretion of the membranes which line the internal organs. Normal mucus is thin, slippery, and clear. In cystic fibrosis the mucus is thick and sticky, creating two major problems. First, it clogs the bronchial tubes, interferring with breathing, and lodges in the branches of the windpipe, acting as an obstruction. The resulting symptoms resemble those in asthma, bronchitis, and emphysema. Second, it plugs up the pancreatic ducts, preventing digestive enzymes from reaching the small intestine and causing malnutrition. Commercially prepared pancreatic extracts must be taken to substitute for the enzymes no longer present in the digestive tract. In some severe cases the intestinal tract is obstructed completely by an accumulation of the thick, putty-like material. The sweat glands also produce an unusually salty sweat. Excessive loss of sodium chloride in perspiration is an ever present danger. Many sufferers take salt tablets regularly as part of their general management program.

In addition to regular breathing exercises, the cystic fibrosis child undergoes daily aerosol therapy. A nebulizer or inhalator may be used to relieve broncho spasms. At night and during naps, the child sleeps under a mist tent which helps to liquify mucus and clear the respiratory tract.

6. Caryl W. Darby, A. G. F. Davidson, and I. D. Desai, "Muscular Performance in Cystic Fibrosis Patients and Its Relation to Vitamin E," *Archives of Disease in Childhood,* Vol. 48, No. 1 (January, 1973), pp. 72-75.

Organizations

1. The Allergy Foundation of America, 801 Second Avenue, New York, New York 10017
2. American Lung Association, 1740 Broadway, New York, New York 10019. Formerly The National Tuberculosis and Respiratory Disease Association. Remains responsible for Christmas Seals.
3. American Thoracic Society is the medical section of the American Lung Association. Same address as above.
4. National Center for Chronic Disease Con-

trol, United States Public Health Service, 4040 N. Fairfax Drive, Arlington, Virginia 22203.

5. National Cystic Fibrosis Research Foundation, 3379 Peach Tree Road, N. E., Atlanta, Georgia 30326.

References

Caplin, Irvin. *The Allergic Asthmatic.* Springfield, Illinois: Charles C. Thomas, 1968.

Hirt, Michael L. *Psychological and Allergic Aspects of Asthma.* Springfield, Illinois: Charles C. Thomas, 1965.

Kendig, Edwin L., ed. *Disorders of the Respiratory Tract in Children.* New York: W. B. Saunders, 1967.

Jackson, Vicki, *Asthma: A Comprehensive Approach Through Exercises,* edited by C. Sherrill. Dallas: American Lung Assoc., 1975.

McGovern, John P., and Knight, James A. *Allergy and Human Emotions.* Springfield, Illinois: Charles C. Thomas Publisher, 1967.

Robbins, Jacob John. *Asthma is Curable.* New York: Exposition Press, 1965.

Rowe, Albert Holmes. *Bronchial Asthma: Its Diagnosis and Treatment.* Springfield, Illinois: Charles C. Thomas, 1963.

Speer, Fredric. *The Allergic Child.* Evanston, Illinois: Harper and Row Publishers, 1963.

Theses and Dissertations

Claverie, Elsa, "Changes in Pulmonary Efficiency and Working Capacity of Asthmatic and Non-Asthmatic Children in the Swimming Program," (Unpublished Master's Thesis, Texas Woman's University, 1971).

Franklin, Janice Carrie. "An Experimental Study of Physical Conditioning for Asthmatic Children," (Unpublished Master's Thesis, Texas Woman's University, 1971).

Periodicals

American Review of Respiratory Disease. Official Jounal of the American Thoracic Society. Formerly *The American Review of Tuberculosis and Pulmonary Diseases.* Published monthly by the American Lung Association, 1740 Broadway, New York, New York 10019.

Annals of Allergy. Official Journal of the American College of Allergists. Published monthly by the American College of Allergists, 2100 Dain Tower, Minneapolis, Minnesota 55402.

British Journal of Diseases of the Chest. Published quarterly by Bailliere Tindall, 7 and 8 Henrietta Street, London, WC28-QE.

Bulletin. Published ten times a year by the American Lung Association, 1740 Broadway, New York, New York 10019.

Clinical Notes on Respiratory Disease. Published quarterly by the American Thoracic Society at 1740 Broadway, New York, New York 10019.

Chest.

International Archives of Allergy and Applied Immunology.

Journal of Allergy.

Review of Allergy.

Thorax.

The Ear, Eye, Nose, and Throat Monthly.

The Journal of Asthma Research.

18 Crippled and Other Health Impaired

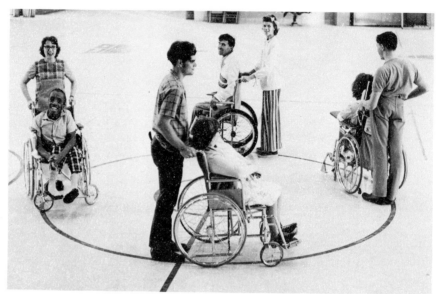

Figure 18.0. Wheelchair square dance.

The handicapped child has a right:

1. To as vigorous a body as human skill can give him.
2. To an education so adapted to his handicap that he can be economically independent and have the chance for the fullest life of which he is capable.
3. To be brought up and educated by those who understand the nature of the burden he has to bear and who consider it a privilege to help him bear it.
4. To grow up in a world which does not set him apart, which looks at him, not with scorn or pity or ridicule—but which welcomes him, exactly as it welcomes every child, which offers him identical privileges and identical responsibilities.
5. To a life on which his handicap casts no shadow but which is full day by day with those things which make it worthwhile, with comradeship, love, work, play, laughter, and tears—a life in which these things bring continually increasing growth, richness, release of energies, joy in achievement.*

*White House Conference on Child Health and Protection, Committee on Physically and Mentally Handicapped, *The Handicapped Child* (New York: D. Appleton-Century Company, 1933), p. 3.

. . . But I, that am not shaped for sportive tricks,
Nor made to court an amorous looking-glass;
I, that am rudely stamp'd, and want love's majesty
To strut before a wanton ambling nymph;
I, that am curtail'd of this fair proportion,
Cheated of feature by dissembling nature,
Deform'd, unfinish'd, sent before my time
Into this breathing world, scarce half made up,
And that so lamely and unfashionable
That dogs bark at me as I halt by them;
Why, I, in this weak piping time of peace,
Have no delight to pass away the time,
Unless to spy my shadow in the sun,
And descant on mine own deformity;

King Richard III [1]

This quotation from Shakespeare offers some insight into the problems of body image and self-concept experienced by the handicapped. In a society which holds physical attractiveness in high esteem, the orthopedically different person is confronted with unattainable goals. He can be taught that beauty comes from within. This truism does not, however, alleviate loneliness, nor the teasing to which the ugly or awkward child is subjected.

Much of the harassment experienced by such children occurs during free play. It could be minimized if supervised physical education were provided and nonhandicapped children were taught acceptance of individual differences. It is ironic indeed that high level athletes equate their abilities with those of other competitors through carefully structured systems of handicaps in golf, bowling, and other sports, whereas pupils in physical education are treated as though individual differences do not exist.

In elementary school physical education, *why* must

> . . . a basket or a goal score the same number of points for each child regardless of his height, weight, and motor coordination?
> . . . all children cover the same distance in a relay?

> . . . all children stand on the same starting line?
> . . . all children have the same number of safeties in tag games?
> . . . the same number of serves in volleyball, tennis, and badminton?
> . . . the same number of strikes in softball and baseball?
> . . . the same tempo of music in folk dance?

Children should be taught to sit down together, appraise individual and team strengths and weaknesses, and devise systems of handicaps which give everyone a fair chance at winning. The presence of one physically handicapped child in a classroom can lead to new insights in the utilization of human resources and the implementation of democratic beliefs. By adult standards, children are cruel in their honest assessment of potentials and their uninhibited curiosity about physical defects. This openness is balanced by an uncanny sense of fair play and concern for one another's welfare. The first principle in integrating a physically different child into the normal group is to guide the pupils in the solution of their own problem: How can we change the game so that everyone can play an approximately equal amount of time, experience challenge, and have fun? The problem solving should not focus exclusively upon the integration of one child but the wise utilization of the diversified talents of each group member.

Terminology

Persons using prostheses, wearing braces, maneuvering wheelchairs, or ambulating with the aid of crutches or canes bear many labels: crippled, disabled, impaired, or handicapped.

---

1. William Aldis Wright, Ed., *The Complete Works of William Shakespeare* (The Cambridge Edition Text, Philadelphia: The Blakiston Company, 1944), p. 113.

Each has his personal preference as to what he wishes to be called and should be asked. Some authors assign slightly different meanings to each term, but this practice seems merely to be playing with words. The Bureau of Education for the Handicapped, Department of Health, Education, and Welfare, Washington, D. C., recognizes a category designed *Crippled and Other Health Impaired.* In this chapter, the term *crippled* will be used interchangeably with related labels to denote a person of normal intelligence who has been deprived in part or in full of the use of his limbs and whose condition is more or less static and incurable. Cerebral palsy and other neurological disorders are excluded from this chapter because of the frequency with which they form part of a multihandicapping condition. The crippled are further described as ambulatory and nonambulatory depending upon their independence in locomotor activities. Particular orthopedic handicaps are described as congenital and/or chronic or as acquired and/or acute.

Congenital and/or chronic conditions are birth defects. When abnormalities of structure or function are apparent at birth, they are called congenital. When they appear later in life, but are genetically caused, they are termed chronic. The etiology of birth defects is often unknown. It is estimated that 20 percent are hereditary, 20 percent are environmental in the sense that viral, parasitic, or bacterial infections of the pregnant mother affected the fetus, and 60 percent result from an interaction of hereditary and environmental factors.

Acquired and/or acute conditions are those which arise from trauma, disease, or disorders of growth and development. Trauma encompasses conditions stemming from motor-vehicle accidents, falls, fires, firearms, and explosives. Each year accidents injure, disable, and cripple approximately 10 million persons of whom 40,000 to 50,000 are children. Almost one-half of these crippling accidents occur in the home, with *falls* causing the most injuries

among the total population and *fires* resulting in the most among persons ages one through forty-four. Disease, as a cause of orthopedic handicaps, includes cancer, diabetes, poliomyelitis, osteomyelitis, and many others. Disorders of growth and development, sometimes called the *osteochondroses,* may occur in over fifty anatomical sites.

Many orthopedic deformities are not handicaps in the sense that movements are restricted. Children learn quickly to compensate for the inconvenience of a deformed or absent foot or arm. At the elementary school level such children, if so inclined, can achieve considerable success in athletic activities . Many participate in Little League baseball and Pee Wee football, deriving most of their childhood satisfactions through sports. Unfortunately, as they progress to the middle grades and competition for a position on the team increases, the deformity influences speed and accuracy just enough to prevent selection. The adolescent with a deformity usually contents himself with intramurals or warming the bench as a member of the B interscholastic team. He may gradually lose interest or channel his energies into such compensatory activities as athletic trainer, team manager, sportswriter, photographer, broadcaster, scorekeeper, or official. Regardless of his role, inclusion on out-of-town trips, practice sessions, and extracurricular activities meets social and emotional needs more fully than that of substitutes.

Congenital Defects

The four most common congenital orthopedic defects in order of their frequency of occurrence are *club foot; cleft lip* and/or *cleft palate; spina bifida* and/or *hydrocephalus;* and *congenital dislocation of the hip.* The need for adapted physical education depends upon the extent to which the condition was corrected in infancy and early childhood. Bracing, casting, and surgical techniques have advanced so much that the casual observer often cannot detect birth defects. Conceivably, the psychological effects of spending months in casts and braces, of hospitals and surgery at so young an age, and the oversolicitous attitudes of parents and siblings leave the child more handicapped than the original defect. Certainly the life experiences of such pupils have been grossly different from those of normal children, and mild emotional disturbances, feelings of inferiority, and overcompensation are fairly common. It is recommended that all prospective teachers read *Of Human Bondage*,[2] the semiautobiographical novel of the effects of a club foot on normal growth and development, by W. Somerset Maugham, as an introduction to this chapter.

Club Foot

Talipes equinovarus, or congenital club foot, is the most common of all orthopedic defects with an incidence of one out of approximately 700 births. *Talipes* comes from two Latin words, *talus* meaning ankle or heel and *pes* meaning foot. *Equinovarus* is an adjective specifying a position in which the entire foot is inverted, the heel is drawn up, and the forefoot is adducted. This forces the child to walk on the outer border of his foot which in turn may lead to the formation of a bursa over the cuboid and proximal end of the fifth metatarsal bone. Although bracing, casting, and surgery may correct club foot, the child reverts to supinated walking when especially tired or upon first awakening.

Figure 18.1 depicts the club foot of a preadolescent boy who has undergone several operations and spent months in casts and braces. He is an enthusiastic athlete and in the starting line-up of his Little League baseball team. His slight limp is noticeably worse during cold winter days and rainy seasons when he can hardly walk the first hour or so after

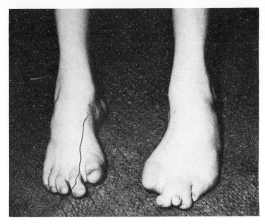

Figure 18.1. Surgically corrected feet of preadolescent boy with talipes.

awakening. As the day wears on, his gait becomes almost normal, enabling him to run fast enough to hold his own in athletic feats with peers.

Talipes equinovarus varies in degrees of severity. Changes in the tendons and ligaments result mostly from contractures. The Achilles and tibial tendons are always shortened, causing a tendency to walk on the toes or forefoot. Bony changes occur chiefly in the talus, calcaneus, navicular, and cuboid. Tibial torsion is usually present.

Several other types of talipes are recognized.

Talipes cavus—hollow foot or arch so high as to be crippling.

Talipes calcaneus—contracture of foot in dorsiflexed position.

Talipes equinus—contracture of foot in plantar-flexed position.

Talipes varus—contracture of foot with toes and sole of foot turned inward.

Talipes valgus—contracture of foot with toes and sole of foot turned outward.

Just as the most common form, *talipes equinovarus*, is a combination of two types, so

2. W. Somerset Maugham, *Of Human Bondage* (New York: Doubleday and Company, Inc., 1915).

any two types can coexist as calcaneovarus, calcaneovalgus, or equinovalgus.

Metatarsus varus is a frequent congenital defect similar to club foot except that only the forefoot or metatarsal area is affected. The treatment for talipes and metatarsus varus is similar, beginning preferably within the first two weeks of life. Corrective plaster casts are applied to the foot and ankle and often extended to a long leg cast which holds the knee in right angle flexion. Such casts are changed at intervals from three to fourteen days to provide a gradual correction of the deformity; the final cast may be left on several weeks. The weight of a cast prevents normal mobility of the infant and may delay the accomplishment of such motor tasks as rolling over, standing alone, and walking.

The *Denis-Browne splint,* an alternate corrective procedure, is a flexible aluminum crossbar which extends horizontally between the abducted legs with one foot taped to either end. When shoes are substituted for the adhesive strapping to hold the feet on the bar in correct position, the child may become adept in creeping and develop tremendous strength in hip and thigh muscles from kicking with the added weight. The Denis-Browne splint does not permit standing or walking. Long after the child with a club foot enters school, he may be wearing the Denis-Browne splint in bed each night.

Children who have undergone casting and splinting for club foot are generally required to wear *corrective shoes*. Extremely expensive, these shoes are often unattractive high top leather shoes with many laces. Many children, sensitive about this prescription, refuse to wear their corrective shoes as they grow older. Or they may ask to wear tennis shoes, at least in physical education, in order to be like their friends. Permission should be tactfully denied unless written instructions from the physician indicate that the child need not wear his corrective shoes during physical education.

Cleft Lip and/or Cleft Palate

Cleft lip afflicts about one in every 1,000 infants, approximately 70 percent of whom also have cleft palate. These defects are now commonly corrected by plastic surgery in infancy. With the exception of speech therapy, no adaptation in normal educational placement and daily activities is needed.

Spina Bifida and/or Hydrocephalus

Spina bifida occurs once in every 1,000 births, but a large percentage of the infants die within the first year. The survivors are generally multiply handicapped with hydrocephalus and mental retardation coexisting. Yet many of these children attend public school and participate in physical education. The National Foundation estimates that there are 60,000 children under age twenty with spina bifida and/or hydrocephalus.

The three most common types of spina bifida in order of their severity are (1) *occulta* (2) *meningoceles,* and (3) *myeloceles.* All are developmental defects of unknown etiology in which one or more vertebral arches failed to close *in utero.* Usually they occur in the lumbar region.

Figure 18.2. Child with arrested hydrocephalus enjoys ring toss (Denton State School).

Spina Bifida Occulta

The child with this condition generally requires no special adaptations in physical education. In its mildest form this is no more than an abnormal hair growth, mole, or dimple (sometimes called a sinus) in the skin or a split spinous process. Often it remains undetected.

Occasionally spina bifida occulta is characterized by abnormalities of the spinal cord or its meninges (protective coverings) which give rise to deviations in posture and muscle tone. Muscle weakness may lead to deformities of the hips, legs, and feet. Sphincter control may be affected also with increased or prolonged incidence of the child wetting his pants. Hydrocephalus is not a common involvement.

Spina Bifida Meningocele

The least common of the three types, the meningocele is a sacular protrusion of the meninges of the spinal cord. The spinal cord and nerve roots remain in normal position, but some of the cerebrospinal fluid is displaced into the sac. Usually no treatment is needed for meningocele except removal of the sac. Should any paralysis, urinary and bowel incontinence, or loss of sensation be present, it is permanent and cannot be lessened.

Spina Bifida Myelocele

For simplicity myeloceles, meningomyeloceles, myelomeningoceles, and syringomyeloceles are all grouped together under this heading. All of these terms refer to sacular protrusions of the meninges which include nerve tissue as well as cerbrospinal fluid. These sacs are often called tumors.

Whenever possible a myelocele is closed surgically within forty-eight hours after birth. Unfortunately this surgery is done only at special centers throughout the country, and often the infant dies or is severely paralyzed before an operation can be arranged. The surgical separation of nerve tissue from skin is difficult, and many infants die of spinal meningitis in spite of the best surgical assistance.

Hydrocephalus is a common complication which is sometimes corrected surgically. In this case, it is called arrested hydrocephalus.

Few children born with myeloceles survive until adulthood. They do, however, attend public schools or receive some physical education or therapy in residential facilities. Those whose condition is not complicated by multiple handicaps can become excellent swimmers by reliance upon strong arm strokes. Typically they are limited out of the water by long leg and back braces, crutches, or wheelchairs. Almost always there is some paralysis below the waist as well as urinary and bowel incontinence.

The adapted physical educator should request information from the parents in the application and removal of long leg and back braces since the child is certain to need bathroom facilities at one time or another. Sometimes a teacher-aide takes care of these problems. Unless the physician advises otherwise, the braces should be removed for rest periods, training in relaxation, and passive range of motion exercises.

Children with myeloceles can enjoy all the physical education activities possible from a wheelchair. Those in long leg braces have been known to complete the 600 yard walk-run and to master simple sport skills like dribbling and basketball shooting. In addition to activities which stress socialization, *range of motion exercises* must be performed daily to prevent contractures of the hip flexors and outward rotators, the knee flexors, and the plantar flexors and inverters of the feet.

Congenital Dislocation of the Hip

Congenital dislocation of the hip encompasses various degrees of *dysplasia*, or abnormal development, of the acetabulum and/

or head of the femur. This same condition appears also in certain blood lines of German Shepherds. In humans it is more common among girls than boys and usually occurs in one hip rather than both. Its incidence is approximately one to three per thousand births.

The terms *subluxation* and *luxation* are synonyms for dislocation, describing the position of the femoral head in relation to a shallow, dysplasic acetabulum. In subluxation the femur is only partially displaced whereas in luxation the femoral head is completely dislocated above the acetabulum rim. These aberrations often are not recognized until the child begins to walk. Nonsurgical treatment involves repositioning, traction, and casting. In the majority of cases in which the child is above age three, surgical reduction (repositioning) is used. After age six, more complicated operative procedures such as osteotomy and arthroplasty are applied.

Reference to congenital hip dislocation on a child's record usually means that he has undergone long periods of hospitalization and immobilization in splints or casts extending from waist to toes. Generally, he has had fewer opportunities to learn social and motor skills through informal play than his normal peers. As in other congenital anomalies, any problems he manifests are more likely to be psychological than physical.

Other birth defects with which the physical educator must cope include *congenital amputation, arthrogryposis, dwarfism, osteochondrodystrophy, nonnutritional rickets,* and *osteogenesis imperfecta.* In most instances, these conditions appear in persons of normal intelligence who prefer to participate in regular physical education with their classmates.

Congenital Amputations

Occasionally a child is born with one limb or a part of the arm or leg bones missing. These skeletal anomalies, known as *congenital*

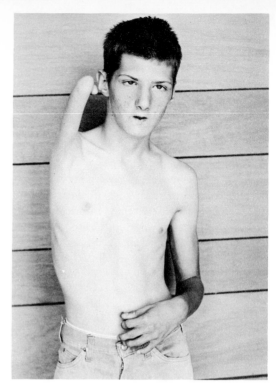

Figure 18.3. Congenital amputations have little effect on physical education potential.

amputations, are often associated with the thalidomide babies born after World War II.

Great strides have been made in the prosthetic devices used to enable such children to lead nearly normal lives. They are fitted with prostheses in the toddler stage, and various agencies assist with the expense of replacing the devices each time they are outgrown.

Arthrogryposis

Approximately 500 infants with *arthrogryposis* are born in the United States each year. In this condition, several joints are fixed rigidly at birth and, therefore, are referred to as *multiple congenital contractures.*

Figures 18.4 and 18.5 depict two boys, ages seven and eleven, from the same school system who have arthrogryposis. Although both boys have some limb involvement, their

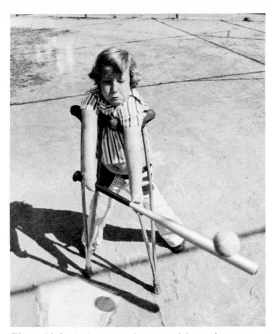

Figure 18.4. Arthrogryposis, overweight, and poor fitness combine to make batting a real chore for this eleven-year-old.

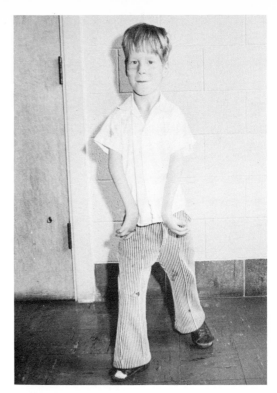

Figure 18.5. Lively seven-year-old with arthrogryposis demonstrates his best posture.

greatest handicap is the fixed medial rotation of the shoulder joints. Both have normal intelligence as is almost always the case in arthrogryposis. Until recently the older boy walked without the use of crutches. His present reliance on them is believed to be somewhat psychosomatic although the literature does state that a deterioration of articular surfaces does occur with age.

In most cases, the lower extremities are more involved than the upper. Characteristics include fixed lateral rotation of the legs at the hip joint accompanied by flexion and abduction contractures, flexion contractures at the knee joint, and fixed medial rotation at the shoulder joint. The arms of the boy in Figure 18.4 show the characteristic increase of subcutaneous fat and loss of skin flexion creases which result in a tubular appearance sometimes described as *wooden and doll-like*. Despite the awkwardness of joint positions and mechanics, no pain is felt and the child is free to engage in any activities.

Figure 18.6. Medial rotation at the shoulder joints complicate fine muscle coordination.

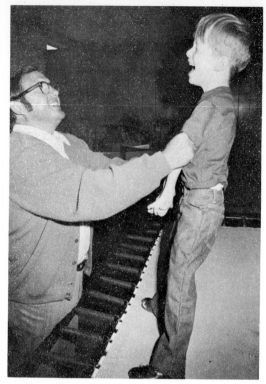

Figure 18.7. A male teacher to guide trampoline activities and share in the joy of growing up.

Dwarfism

Dwarfism is defined as retarded physical growth which is more than three standard deviations from the mean for the age group. Contrary to popular opinion, most growth retardation in children is not the result of an endocrine disturbance. Steiner reports over 100 syndromes characterized by either abnormal shortness or dwarfism, many of which are congenital.[3]

The dwarf most often seen in physical education classes is a victim of a congenital skeletal anomaly called *achondroplasia*. The etiology is autosomal dominant although older paternal age may be a factor in fresh mutations. The achondroplasic dwarf, unlike most others, almost always has normal or better intelligence and does well academically. He can participate in an unrestricted physical education program with only occasional problems because of his disproportionately short limbs. One dwarf in a university body mechanics class could do everything assigned except for the backward roll. Like other achondroplasic dwarfs, she had a relatively normal trunk and head with disproportionately short arms and legs. Extension of the elbows was limited, and the characteristic protrusion of abdominal and gluteal regions with marked lumbar lordosis was present. Her gait was typically waddling, but the musculature was good and sexual development normal.

Osteodystrophy or Osteochondrodystrophy

Also called *Morquio's disease,* this inborn error of mucopolysaccharide metabolism results in progressive spinal deformity with kyphosis and sometimes scoliosis. Skeletal malformation is not evidenced until several months after birth, but becomes increasingly severe with age. The lower rib cage flares out by eighteen months, and severe knock knees are present by age three or four. Other characteristics include muscular weakness and poor joint support, flat foot, joint hypermotility, and waddling gait caused by the genu valgum. There is no treatment.

Genu valgum makes running activities difficult or impossible and affects balance adversely. Carefully developed strength exercises should contribute to improvement of joint support.

Osteogenesis Imperfecta

This inherited condition in which the bones are abnormally soft and brittle is transmitted by a dominant mutant gene. The more severely

3. Matthew K. Steiner, *Clinical Approach to Endocrine Problems in Children* (Saint Louis: The C. V. Mosby Co., 1970), p. 135.

involved infants may die early in life. Those who live sustain many fractures each year. A heavy touch, slight fall, or even attempts to stand or walk can cause fractures throughout the bony framework. Many such children are unable to walk. Pillows are kept around both sides of the bed as well as at the head and feet. Heavy books and toys are not allowed.

If the child survives the first few years, or has the later appearing condition *osteogenesis imperfecta tarda,* the fractures gradually become fewer in number, he begins to ambulate, and he can enroll in public school. The book *Give Every Day a Chance*[4] describes such a child who now drives her own car, attends college, and seems well on her way to a normal life.

The child who approaches normalcy in other areas continues to require a highly adapted physical education program which is limited to gentle range of motion exercises, preferably to music, in the aquatic or gymnasium setting. Although the diagnosis of *osteogenesis imperfecta* is assigned only to severe cases, many children seem to have a propensity for broken bones. Physical educators must take softness of bones into consideration in developing the physical education prescriptions for children.

Rickets

Many forms of *rickets* exist: (1) nutritional, (2) vitamin-resistant rickets, (3) the Fanconi syndrome, and (4) renal (glomerular) rickets. Of these, the nutritional type is almost extinct in the United States. The other types result from inborn errors of metabolism and/or congenital renal (kidney) impairment.

The characteristic skeletal changes include bone softening, curvature of long bones, deformities of chest, enlarged epiphyses, and retarded skeletal growth. Vitamin D in massive dosages helps to correct bone changes but does not restore the serum phosphate to a normal level. In renal rickets, the underlying kidney condition must be treated also. More severe than the other types, renal rickets may result in dwarfism, coxa vara, genu valgum, and valgus deformities of the feet.

In physical education, weight bearing activities which might aggravate postural deviations should be avoided. Since sunlight promotes the synthesis of vitamin D in the body, rest periods and quiet exercises should be conducted out-of-doors whenever possible.

Crippling Conditions Caused by Trauma

Trauma can be *elective* as in the case of bone surgery or *accidental* as in burns, fractures, dislocations, sprains, crush injuries, bruises and contusions, and various kinds of wounds. Burns are discussed in detail in this chapter because they are the number one cause of crippling under the broad category of trauma. The other types of musculoskeletal injuries are studied intensively by the physical educator in courses on first aid, health emergency care, and athletic injuries. The prospective adapted physical educator, although sometimes not interested in athletics *per se,* can learn much by serving as the assistant to the university athletic trainer.

Thermal Injuries

Approximately 300,000 Americans annually suffer disfiguring injuries from fires. Another 12,000 die each year. The mortality rate is greatest among persons under age five and over age sixty-five. No other type of accident permanently affects as many school-age children.

During past decades, children with more than 60 percent of their skin destroyed seldom survived. Now, increasing numbers of individuals are returning to society scarred and horribly disfigured. What kind of physical education should be provided for the young child

4. Beverly Plummer, *Give Every Day A Chance* (New York: G. P. Putman's Sons, 1970).

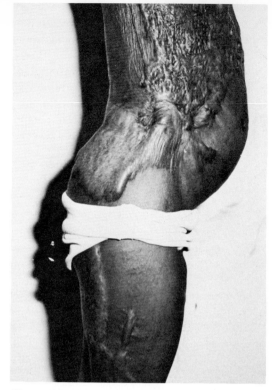

Figure 18.8. Hypertrophic scarring of healed burn on lateral aspect of trunk two years after burn occurred.

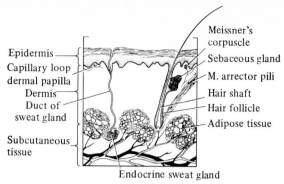

Figure 18.9. Cross section of skin layers.

eyebrows or eye lashes, and scar tissue covers the face. In spite of their hideous appearance, they generally have no restrictions in physical education. As more and more such children are kept alive, physical educators must become increasingly adept at coping with all aspects of thermal injuries. Some knowledge of the child's months of hospitalization and treatment will contribute to better understanding of his playground behavior.

Evaluation of Thermal Injuries

Thermal injury is evaluated in terms of the extent and depth of burn. The extent is determined by the total body surface area involved. The depth or degree of burn falls into three categories. The first degree burn is fiery red and sensitive to touch. It involves only the epidermis and is not serious unless combined with other categories.

Partial thickness injuries (second degree), which destroy the cutaneous (dermis) layer of the skin, usually result from scald or flash burns. Touch elicits severe pain because of the exposed nerve endings. There may or may not be blister formation, and varing degrees of blanching and redness are present.

Full thickness burns (third degree) involve the whole of the integument, epidermis, dermis, and subcutaneous layers. Burns of this nature are anesthetic. Pressure blanching is

with extensive scar tissue? How can the physical educator help such children find social acceptance? What are the effects of disfiguring thermal injuries upon self-concept?

Nature and Causes of Thermal Injury

Thermal injury is the alteration of the integument, the skin, and its underlying structures by fire, chemicals, electricity, or prolonged contact with extreme degrees of hot or cold liquids.

Children who have sustained disfiguring thermal injuries, upon entering school, frequently recognize for the first time that they are deviates from the *normal*. They have been known to describe themselves as monsters. Typically they have no hair on scalp, no absent, and cutaneous tissue is nonpliable. The affected area is dry and white, tending to look and feel like a piece of leather. Little or no pain is present because nerve endings are destroyed. Flame and high temperature explosions most frequently produce full thickness burns.

Course of Burn Treatment

Partial and full thickness burns require prolonged hospitalization which is usually divided into four treatment phases. The first is to attain physiologic homeostasis (body systems in equilibrium). This phase is succeeded by a period during which the burned individual is subject to varying degrees of infection. During the second phase the painful and tedious procedure of removing necrotic or dead tissue from the burn wound is endured. Once removal of necrotic tissue is accomplished, the individual with full thickness burns begins the lengthy ordeal of multiple trips to surgery for final debridement of the burn wound and autografting (skin for individual) of the open areas. The desired effect of grafting is to cover the burn wound with viable skin. The last phase is rehabilitation which may extend from a month to five or more years. The burn victim is released from the hospital early in this phase. He returns to outpatient clinics on a periodic basis for observation of the healed wounds and for corrective exercises.

Nature of Burn Disabilities and Corrective Measures

Scar tissue and contractures are inevitable outcomes. Wound coverage is attained by the growth of scar tissue from the periphery to the center of the wound. As wound coverage is achieved, a *hypertrophic scar* is formed by the increased volume and thickness of the collagen fibers. Reddened, elevated masses of tissue over the healed area (called nodular) are characteristic of hypertrophic scar tissue.

Thick scar tissue forming contractures across joints limits range of motion, causes scoliosis of the spine, and shortens underlying muscles. The severity of hypertrophic scarring and scar contracture may be decreased by early splinting, pressure, and therapeutic exercise. As the scar ages, it becomes less responsive to corrective measures. Surgery is often required to reduce contractures which could have been prevented by daily range of motion exercises. Some full thickness burns result in amputation of fingers, toes, or entire limbs. The course of scar maturation is of primary importance in providing corrective therapy. Since scar tissue is most responsive to therapy in its early stages, the physician carefully observes for beginning signs of scar hypertrophy, firmness, and nonpliability.

Jobsts, elastic supports made to fit a specified portion of the body, may be prescribed as a means of reducing scar hypertrophy. The purpose of the jobst is to apply constant pressure to the healed areas which are presenting signs of thickening scar tissue. The elastic supports achieve the best results when worn twenty-four hours daily. Therefore, as the child is returned to the classroom, he is expected to wear these supports under his clothing.

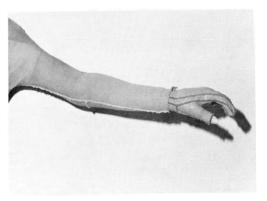

Figure 18.10. Jobsts elastic support jackets applied to arm and hand.

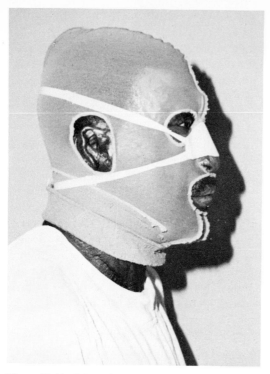

Figure 18.11. Jobsts elastic face mask and isoprene splint applied to the junction of the nose and cheek.

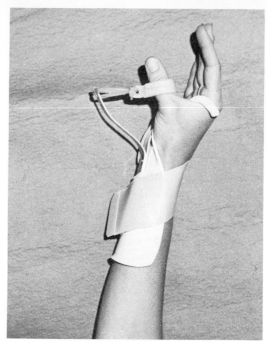

Figure 18.12. Isoprene hand splint abducting thumb may be worn long after burn victim returns to regular physical education. (Parkland Memorial Hospital in Dallas, Occupational Therapy Department.)

Isoprene splints or *braces* may be applied to areas where the jobsts do not provide adequate pressure to the scar tissue. The elastic face mask does not apply significant pressure to the junction of the nose and cheek which frequently fills with scars (Figure 18.11). The isoprene splints require frequent removal for cleansing of the splint and application of lotion to prevent skin dryness. There are various types of hand splints for abduction of the thumb which a child may be required to wear during his daily activities. The pupil wearing such splints should be encouraged to use the hands normally in physical education activities. He should be given no restrictions and hence encouraged to increase pain tolerance. The physical educator may need to assist him in proper cleaning and reapplication of the splint after vigorous exercise.

Other Implications for Physical Education

Several years of rehabilitation are required for the severely burned child. He must not be excused from physical education because he is wearing jobsts, braces, or splints. Each pupil must learn the tolerance of his new skin tissue to such elements as direct sunlight and chlorine in freshwater pools. He must expose himself for a progressively longer period each day. The physical educator may wish to confer with a specialist in thermal injuries.

The young tissue of healed burns is delicate. It quickly becomes dry when exposed to sunlight for an extended period of time. Full thickness burns have a tendency to dry and irritate easily because of the absence or impairment of sweat ducts, hair follicles, and sebaceous glands. Scar tissue causes atrophy, destruction, or displacement of the ducts and glands in the integument. Pruritus (itching) occurs with drying and irritation of healed burn wounds. Frequent applications of a lanolin lotion are recommended.

Indoor physical education is preferable to activities in the direct sunlight. Since contractures are a major problem, emphasis should be upon flexibility or range of motion exercises. Dance and aquatic activities are recommended especially.

Acquired Amputations

ps. 454

Of the various disabilities which can result from trauma and disease, the elective amputation is the most dramatic. Not only does the child suffer anxieties about no longer being *whole,* but efficient use of prosthetic devices demands much effort.

The etiologies of acquired amputations in children in order of incidence are trauma, cancer, infection, and vascular conditions like gangrene. Under trauma, the leading causes of amputation are farm and power tool accidents, vehicular accidents, and gunshot explosions. Most of these occur in the age group from twelve through twenty-one. Children who lose limbs because of malignancy are also primarily within this age group.

Since 1964, immediate postsurgical prosthetic fitting has gradually become the trend. In most cases, prostheses are fitted in less than thirty days after the amputation. This practice offers several advantages. First, particularly in a person with cancer, a prosthesis and early ambulation contributes to a positive psychological outlook. Second, amputation stumps in children do not usually shrink and there is

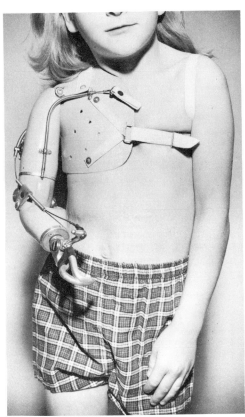
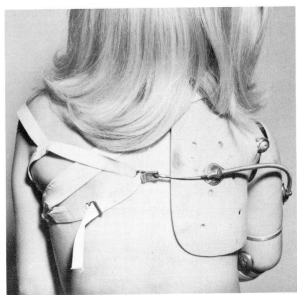

Figure 18.13. Front and rear views of a prosthesis from *The Child With an Acquired Amputation,* publication ISBN 0-309-02047-6, Subcommittee on Child Prosthetic Problems, Division of Engineering, National Academy of Sciences—National Research Council, Washington, D. C., 1972.

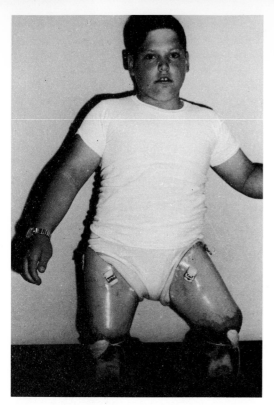

Figure 18.14. What kind of physical education would be provided *for the bilateral amputee*? Photo from *The Child With an Acquired Amputation,* publication ISBN 0-309-02047-6, Subcommittee on Child Prosthetic Problems, Division of Engineering, National Academy of Sciences, National Research Council, Washington, D. C., 1972.

no physical reason for delaying fitting. Third, phantom pain has become almost nonexistant because of improved surgical techniques. Fourth, edema (swelling) is best controlled and wound healing facilitated by an immediate postsurgical socket.

In modern hospital settings the child is provided training in use of his prosthesis by physical therapists and occupational therapists. Ideally this training includes exposure to playground equipment and recreational activities. If the amputee does not appear secure in class activities utilizing gymnastic and playground equipment, the adapted physical educator may need to supplement the hospital training. This means, of course, that his professional preparation should include some work in an orthopedic unit of a hospital, a crippled children's camp, or a special education classroom comprised of physically handicapped pupils. He should be able to touch a child's stump, discuss stump hygiene, and assist the amputee, if needed, in putting on the prosthetic device.

Authorities agree that children with properly fitted prostheses should engage in regular physical education.[5] The only adaptations recommended pertain to dressing and shower rules. Girls and boys should be allowed to wear long pants or the type of clothing in which they feel most comfortable. Shower rules should be waived. The amputee who is sensitive about changing clothes in the locker room should be allowed a place of his own and classmates encouraged to give him the desired privacy.

The general attitude among physicians is that an amputee can do anthing if the prosthesis is well fitted. Epps and Vaughn state:

Athletic activity is possible for the amputee and there are numerous examples of those who have competed successfully in many sports—both as amateurs and as professionals. When strenuous activities are planned, it is recommended that the limb maker check the limb to make certain that the anticipated hard use can be tolerated. Special exercises are given to help the amputee acquire the balance, coordination, and ability to run rapidly that are prerequisites for sports. [6]

Balance is probably the one aspect of motor performance which gives the amputee the most trouble. The unilateral lower limb amputee should be taught to use his sound limb for kicking balls as the prosthetic limb maintains the weight of the body. In ascending stairs, he should lead with the sound limb; in descend-

5. Yoshio Setoguchi, "School and the Child Amputee" in *The Child with an Acquired Amputation* (Washington, D. C.: National Academy of Sciences, 1972), p. 67.

6. Charles H. Epps, Jr. and Helen H. Vaughn. "Training the Child With an Acquired Lower-Limb Amputation" in *The Child With An Acquired Amputation* (Washington, D. C.: National Academy of Sciences, 1972), p. 129.

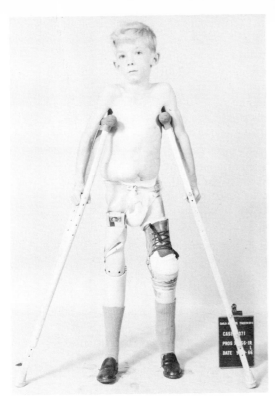

Figure 18.15. The bilateral above-knee amputee may require months of physical rehabilitation. From *The Child With an Acquired Amputation,* publication ISBN 0-309-02047-6, Subcommittee on Child Prosthetic Problems—Division of Engineering, National Academy of Sciences—National Research Council, Washington, D. C., 1972.

ing, he should lead with the prosthesis in the stable extended position. The bilateral above-knee amputee has more difficulty with steps and often requires a railing and crutch. He typically climbs and descends stairs in a sideward manner. The unilateral upper-limb amputee finds that the weight of a bowling ball or tennis racquet in its descent throws him off balance because his prosthetic arm may not compensate in accordance with the principle of opposition. This problem, at least in bowling, can be overcome by developing a scissors step, crossing the leg on the good arm side over the other, and taking the weight of the ball in stride.

Amputees swim without their prostheses. Fins may be strapped to the arm or leg stumps as needed. For water skiing and/or activities in salt water an old pair of artificial legs are used since salt water may cause the new ones to crack.

In addition to guiding the amputee in sports, dance, and aquatic activities, the physical educator should recognize any gait deviations which may develop and refer the pupil back to the physical therapist and/or the prosthetist. Most gait deviations result from problems with the alignment or fit of the prosthesis. Deviations to watch for include: rotation of the foot at heel strike, unequal timing, side walking base, abducted gait, excessive heel rise, instability of the knee, excessive knee flexion, hyperextension of the knee, terminal impact noise, excessive piston action, foot slap, and rotation of the foot with continuing whip. Deviations caused by instability and weakness of the hip joint or by contractures include lateral bending of the trunk, circumduction, and excessive forward bending of the trunk.

Crippling Conditions Caused by Bone Infections

The only types of bone infection which are prevalent in the Western Hemisphere are *osteomyelitis, tuberculous infection,* and *syphilitic metaphysitis.* Osteomyelitis is caused by staphylococcus, streptococcus, or pneumococcus organisms. Tuberculous infection of bone, which is rare except in the vertebral bodies or in association with tuberculous infection of joints, is caused by tubercle bacilli. Syphilitic infection, also uncommon in the United States, may appear early in life with congenital syphilis or as a late manifestation of acquired syphilis.

Of these, *osteomyelitis* is frequently a childhood disease. Even with the best medical treatment, it may result in permanent crippling. The bones most often affected are the tibia, femur, and humerus. The symptoms are similar to those of an infected wound: (1) pain and tenderness, particularly near the end of the bone in the metaphyseal region; (2) heat felt through the overlying skin; (3) overlying soft tissues feel hard (indurated), and (4) neighboring joints may be distended with clear fluid. Generally a good range of joint movement is retained although the child begins to limp from the acute pain. Pus forms and finds its way to the surface of the bone where it forms a *subperiosteal abscess.* If treatment is not begun, the abscess eventually works its way outward, causing a *sinus* (hole) in the skin over the affected bone from which pus is discharged continuously or intermittently. This sinus is covered with a dressing which must be changed several times daily.

Although only a single limb is typically affected and the child appears otherwise healthy and energetic, *the physical educator should remember that exercise is always contraindicated when any kind of infection is active in the body.* The medical treatment is rest and intensive antibiotic therapy often accompanied by surgery to scrape the infected bone and evacuate the pus.

In its early stages osteomyelitis is described as *acute.* If the infection persists or reoccurs periodically, it is called *chronic.* Since chronic osteomyelitis may linger on for years, the physical educator should confer with the physician about the nature of an adapted program.

Crippling Conditions Caused by the Osteochondroses

The adapted physical educator working with junior high or middle school youngsters is confronted with a high incidence of *osteochondroses* or growth plate disorders. Such diagnoses as *Perthes disease, Osgood-Schlatter disease, Kohler's disease, Calve's disease,* and *Scheuermann's disease* all fall within this category and demand adaptations in physical education.

An osteochondrosis is an abnormality of an *epiphysis* (growth plate) in which normal growth or ossification is disturbed. The etiology is generally unknown, although trauma is sometimes suspected. The terms osteochondrosis, osteochondritis juvenilis, apophysitis, and growth plate disorders are all used interchangeably.

A brief review of the growth and development of bones contributes to an understanding of the osteochondroses. Skeletal growth in the fetus consists of the transformation of hyaline cartilage and fibrous membrane into bone by the processes of endochondral and intramembranosus ossification. This transformation is not complete at the time of birth. Throughout childhood cartilage is slowly being replaced by bone. Moreover, existing bone continues to grow in diameter and length until adult skeletal dimensions are reached.

The growth plate is the structure responsible for longitudinal growth of the immature bone which has the following identifiable parts:

(1) *Diaphysis*—a primary center of ossification in the embryo; the shaft of the long bone in the child.
(2) *Metaphysis*—the end of the diaphysis which constitutes the most recently formed bone.
(3) *Bony epiphyses*—secondary centers of ossification at the ends of long bones. In the immature skeleton these are pieces of bone separated from the end of the bone by cartilage. In adulthood the epiphyses fuse with the diaphysis.
(4) *Apophysis*—a bony projection without an independent center of ossification.

The growth plate, a cartilaginous disc between the epiphysis and the metaphysis, traditionally has been designated the *epiphyseal plate.* Newer sources, however, refer to the *growth plate* or *metaphyseal growth plate* since the metaphysis, not the epiphysis, contributes to new growth. Rang[7] describes in detail the architecture of the growth plate as well as

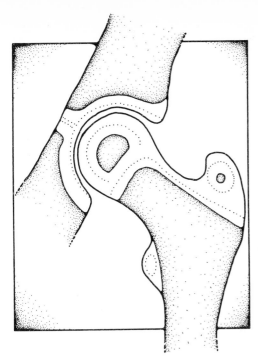

Figure 18.16. Growth cartilage at the hip joint where Perthes Disease occurs. The line of dots represents germinal cells. They are laying down cartilage which is later replaced by bone.

its blood supply which provides the nutrients for normal ossification of the diaphysis toward the epiphysis. Sometime before age twenty-five, at a date which is specific for each bone, the metaphyseal cartilage ceases to proliferate and closure takes place between the diaphysis and the epiphysis. Normally this closure occurs from one to three years earlier in girls than in boys.

Disorders of the growth plate include premature closure, delayed closure, and interruption in the growth process. Stature is considered the best guide of growth plate activity, although skeletal maturity itself is generally determined by x-rays of the carpal bones. Bone growth and subsequent closure are affected by heredity, diet, hormones, general health status, and trauma. Ill health and malnutrition generally delay skeletal maturity while trauma affects a single growth plate closure. Obese

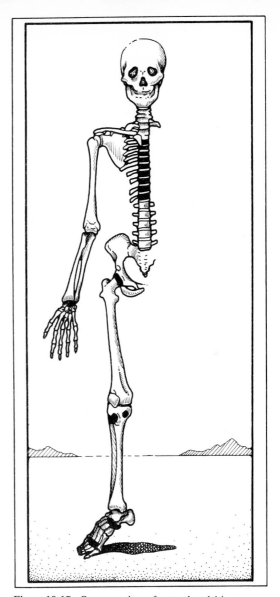

Figure 18.17. Common sites of osteochondritis.

children are particularly susceptible to disorders of the growth plate.

The most common sites of growth plate disorders, as depicted in Figure 18.17 include those listed on page 388.

7. Mercer Rang, *The Growth Plate and Its Disorders* (Baltimore: The Williams and Wilkens Company, 1969), p. 11.

Bony Part Affected	Name of Disorder
1. Tibial tuberosity	Osgood-Schlatter
2. Calcaneal apophysis	Sever
3. Vertebral epiphyses	Scheuermann
4. Capital femoral epiphysis	Perthes (Legg-Calve-Perthes)
5. Tibia, proximal epiphysis	Blount
6. Tarsal, navicular	Kohler
7. Secondary patellar center	Sinding-Larson
8. Iliac crest	Buchman

Over 71 percent of the osteochondroses are found at the first four sites. Although not statistically the most common, *Perthes disease* is the most important of the osteochondroses because massive destruction of the femoral head may occur if weight-bearing activities are not forbidden.

The pathology in all of the osteochondroses is similar. For unknown reasons, cells within the bony center of the epiphysis undergo partial *necrosis* (death), probably from interference with the blood supply. The *necrotic* tissue is removed by special cells called osteoclasts, and the bony center is temporarily softened and liable to deformation of shape which may become permanent. In time, new healthy bone cells replace the dead tissue, and the bone texture returns to normal.

This cycle of changes may take as long as two years, during which time the youngster must be kept off of the affected limb. Enforcing the rule of no weight bearing on an athletic child is not easy since he experiences no symptoms of illness and only occasional pain in the involved area. The primary danger in osteochondroses is not in the present, but rather is the deformity, limp, and predisposition to arthritis which may occur if rules are not followed.

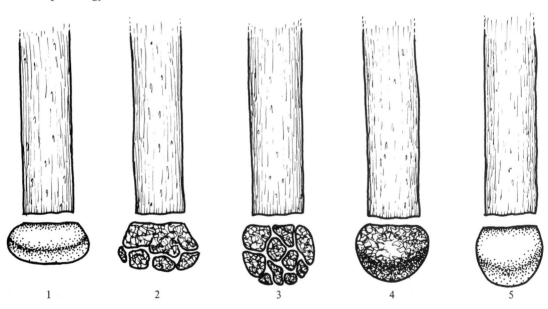

1   2   3   4   5

Figure 18.18. The cycle of changes in osteochondritis; (1) normal epiphysis before onset; (2) the bony nucleus undergoes necrosis, loses its normal texture, and becomes granular; (3) the bone becomes fragmented; (4) if subjected to pressure the softened epiphysis is flattened; (5) normal bone texture restored, but deformity persists. The cycle occupies about two years.

Physical Education for Nonambulatory Pupils

In which physical education activities can pupils using prostheses, wearing braces, maneuvering wheelchairs, and ambulating with the aid of crutches or canes succeed? Chapter 7 focuses upon the appraisal of locomotor activities. Many children with crippling conditions can engage in games and sports with few adaptations. Almost all can enjoy swimming and dance activities.

Appraisal of the nonlocomotor movement capabilities of persons restricted to wheel chairs lends insight into program planning. The answers to the following questions can be derived from movement exploration in a dance or aquatic setting.

(1) What body parts can he bend and straighten? What *combination* of body parts can he bend and straighten? When performed rhythmically, bending and straightening become swinging.

(2) What body parts can he stretch? In which directions can he stretch?

(3) What body parts can he twist? What *combination* of body parts can he twist? Can he twist at different rates of speed? Can he combine twists with other basic movements?

(4) What body parts can he circle? What *combination* of body parts can he circle?

(5) Can he rock forward in the wheelchair and bend over to recover an object on the floor? If lying or curled up on a mat, can he rock backward and forward? Can his rocking movement provide impetus for changing positions? For instance, when sitting on a mat, can he rock over to a hands and knees creeping position?

(6) Does he have enough arm strength to lift and replace the body in the wheelchair in a bouncing action? Can he relax and bounce on a mattress, a trampoline, or a moon walk?

(7) What body parts can he shake? What combination of body parts? Can he shake rhythm instruments?

(8) Can he sway from side to side? Can he sway back and forth while hanging onto a rope or maintaining contact with a piece of apparatus?

(9) Can he push objects away from the body? Does he have the potential to succeed in games based upon pushing skills like box hockey and shuffleboard? Can he maneuver a scooter board? A tricycle? A wagon? Can he walk while holding onto or pushing his wheelchair in front of him? Can he push off from the side of the swimming pool? Can some part of his body push off from a mat?

(10) Can he pull objects toward him? In which directions can he pull? Can he use a hand-over-hand motion to pull himself along a rope, bar, or ladder? Can he manipulate weighted pulleys?

(11) Can he change levels? For instance, can he move from a lying position to a sitting, squatting, or kneeling position or vice versa? How does he get from a bed, sofa, chair, or toilet to his wheelchair and vice versa?

(12) Can he demonstrate safe techniques for falling? When he loses his balance, in which direction does he usually fall?

Having appraised the student's vocabulary of nonlocomotor movements, the physical educator is challenged to adapt and/or create sports, dance, and aquatics activities which will enrich life in a wheelchair. Information on wheelchair sports is presented in Chapter 3. The organizations listed at the end of this chapter should be contacted for specific recommendations.

Figure 18.19. Fishing is a lifetime sport which should be included in the Adapted Physical Education Curriculum. (Courtesy of the National Society for Crippled Children and Adults, Inc.)

Figure 18.20. Tossing beanbags with a string attached to simplify retrieval (Denton State School).

Other Health Impaired Conditions

Among the many other health impaired conditions which may require adapted physical education are *kidney and urinary tract dis-*

orders, blood disorders, and *obesity.* Each of these necessitates individualized planning as well as understanding of concomitant social and emotional problems.

Kidney and Urinary Tract Disorders

Approximately 3 percent of American school children have some history of a kidney or urinary tract disorder. Moreover, urinary-genital malformations account for 300,000 of the common birth defects in the United States, sharing second place in prevalence with congenital blindness and congenital deafness. Only mental retardation afflicts more newborn infants. Vigorous exercise is contraindicated when kidney infection is present, and the physician often excuses the child from physical education because no one has oriented him to the possibilities of an adapted program.

The child suffering from chronic or acute nephritis or nephrosis will probably be in and out of the hospital many times. Each time he returns to school the physical educator must be aware that his exercise level is low because he has beeen confined to a hospital room without appreciable exercise. Most physicians concur that children with kidney and urinary tract disease need moderate exercise. They are adamant, however, that such children should not be subjected to physical fitness tests nor to actual physical stress of any kind.

Hemophilia

The term *hemophilia* encompasses at least eight different bleeding disorders that are caused by the lack of any one of ten different clotting factors in the blood. Although only one in 10,000 persons is afflicted in the United States, the physical educator who has one hemophiliac child is likely to have several since it is an inherited disorder. Historically it has been said to appear only in males and to be transmitted through females. Recently, however, a type of hemophilia in women has been identified.

Contrary to popular belief, outward bleeding from a wound does not cripple most hemophiliacs. Rather it is internal bleeding. A stubbed toe, a bumped elbow, a violent sneeze, or a gentle tag game can be fatal. Each causes bleeding beneath the surface of the skin which is manifested by discoloration, swelling, and other characteristics of a hematoma. The hemophiliac child tends to have many black and blue spots, swollen joints, and considerable limitation of movement. Minor internal bleeding may be present much of the time. When internal bleeding appears extensive, he is rushed to the hospital for transfusions.

Over a period of years, repeated hemorrhages into joints, if untreated, result in hemophilic arthritis. To minimize joint bleeding, the afflicted body part is frequently splinted. Pain is severe, and the hemophiliac may avoid complete extension. This tendency, of course, results in such orthopedic complications as contractures. The hemophiliac child should be allowed to engage in regular physical education and expected to establish his own limitations. As in so many other handicaps, the problems of peer group acceptance, parental overprotection, and social isolation are more intense than the unpredictable episodes of bleeding that halt the usual routine of life. Swimming, creative dance, rhythmic exercises on heavily padded mats, and such individual sports as fishing, shuffleboard, and pool offer much satisfaction. Catching activities generally are contraindicated.

Sickle-Cell Disease

Although discovered by physician James Herrick in 1910, *sickle-cell disease* did not receive widespread attention until the early 1970s. At that time, one out of every 400 black Americans was believed to have the disorder.

Sickle-cell disease is an inherited blood disorder which takes its name from the sickle-shape form the red blood cells assume when the oxygen content of the blood is low. Persons

with the disease are anemic, suffer crises of severe pain, are prone to infection and often have slow healing ulcers of the skin, especially around the ankles. Many do not live to adulthood.

Regular exercise should not be curtailed, but tests and activities of cardiovascular endurance are contraindicated. Under intense exercise stress, particularly at altitudes above 10,000 feet where the oxygen content of the air is decreased, the sickle-cell victim may collapse. He should also avoid becoming overheated since the normal evaporation of perspiration cools the skin and may precipitate an attack.

The disease develops at the time of conception, but symptoms do not usually appear until the child is six months or older. The first symptoms are pallor, poor appetite, early fatigue, and complaints of pain in the back, abdomen, and the extremities. The child may not evidence sickle-cell anemia until he catches a cold or has an attack of tonsillitis; then he reacts worse than the normal child.

The course of the disease is marked by a sequence of physiological crises and complications which can be recognized, predicted, and treated, but not prevented. The crisis results from spasms in the key blood vessels. The child experiences agonizing pain in certain muscles and joints, particularly those of the rib cage. He may run a high fever. Some crises are severe enough to require hospitalization. As the child grows older and learns his limitations, his attacks become less frequent.

Obesity

Obesity is an orthopedic handicap. Often more crippling than the loss or disability of body parts, obesity affects 10 to 15 percent of the school-age children in the United States. Moreover, one out of four girls and one out of five boys will be at least 10 percent overweight by the time they reach twenty years of age.

Figure 18.21. Obesity is an orthopedic handicap. (Photo by Fonda Johnstone.)

In the elementary grades the classroom teacher periodically records the height and weight of each child. Later the physical education specialist assumes responsibility for the classification of students into height-weight categories and the referral of the obese to their family physician. What criterion should be used in making decisions as to whom should be referred?

Most teachers use reference tables based upon desirable body weights for certain combinations of age, sex, and height factors. All such tables are subject to controversy. Children who are 10 to 20 percent above their desired weight are considered *overweight*. Persons over 20 percent of their desired weight are *obese,* and those over 50 percent of their desired weight are *super-obese.* This decision-making process is a screening technique since the clinical diagnosis of obesity is based upon many variables not considered in height-weight tables. Clinical judgment takes into account somatotypes, distribution of fat, muscle development, and sexual maturation as well as actual weight, height, age, and sex. No clinical tool for measuring obesity or estimating total body fat, not even the popular skin-fold thickness caliper measurements, is a reliable substitute for the physician's clinical judgment.

Causes of Obesity

Obesity in childhood can be endocrine or nonendocrine in origin. Endocrine obesity can be divided into several clinical subtypes.

1. Cerebral-hypothalamic obesity including Frohlich's Syndrome, Pseudo-Frohlich's Syndrome, and Laurence-Moon-Biedl Syndrome. In all of these syndromes the genitalia are markedly undeveloped, and the weight is concentrated about the breasts, hips, and abdomen.
2. Pituitary obesity, generally designated as Cushing's Syndrome. *Hirsutism,* or excessive hair growth, occurs in about 25 percent of the cases. Other characteristics are menstrual irregularities, acne, irregular fat distribution with adipose tissue concentrated around the breasts and abdomen, a ruddy, moon-shaped face, and a *buffalo hump.*
3. Thyroid obesity, including cretinism, juvenile hypothyroidism, and myxedema. These clinical types are often puffy and myxedematous (swelling of tissues) but not actually fat.
4. Adrenocortical obesity, including combinations of Cushing's Syndrome with disorders stemming from overstimulation of the adrenal cortex, the outer-covering of the adrenal glands which are imbedded in the perirenal fat above each kidney. Hypersecretion of the cortex in childhood causes sexual precocity, i.e., the early

development of secondary sexual characteristics.

5. Iatrogenic obesity, a clinical term which designates obesity which develops as a result of long-term administration of cortisone and other adrenocortical steroids for control of chronic asthma, allergies, rheumatoid arthritis, nephrosis, or leukemia. In addition to cushingoid obesity, long-term reliance on steroids may also cause growth retardation, osteoporosis, and hypertension.

Less than 10 percent of the cases of childhood obesity can be ascribed to one of these five clinical types. It is customary, however, for a physician to rule out endocrine disorders before delving into other possible causes of obesity.

Nonendocrine causes of obesity include (1) habits of overeating in relation to energy output, (2) familial and genetic patterns, (3) environmental influences, (4) metabolic sluggishness, and (5) psychogenic effects. Obesity is seldom traced to a single cause. The interaction between hereditary and environmental factors, complicated by a vicious circle of emotional problems stemming from and contributing to fatness, must be explored skillfully.

Familial patterns of fat distribution are often apparent. Fat may be centralized or localized about the hips, thighs, breasts, chest, or abdomen. Before planning weight reduction regimes, it is advisable to obtain information about the total body weights and patterns of fat distribution of parents, grandparents, and siblings. Even with stringent dieting, it is difficult to change the prominence of such body parts as hips and buttocks which may be genetically predisposed to heavy padding. Children should be helped to understand that losses in weight do not necessarily slim down desired body parts. Body build is determined by the bony skeleton, not by adipose tissue. Goal setting must be realistic.

Studies show that in families with parents of normal weight, only 8 to 9 percent of the children are obese. When one parent is obese, 40 percent of the children are likewise. When both parents are obese, this percentage doubles. Eating patterns learned early in childhood and passed down from generation to generation seem to be as much a factor as genetic predisposition. The leisure time attitudes, interests, and practices of family and neighborhood also affect the balance between food intake and energy expenditure. Some ethnic and cultural values also contribute to obesity: (1) a fat baby is a healthy one; (2) the amount of food on the table is indicative of economic status; (3) it is impolite to refuse a dessert or a second helping; (4) a good hostess always has something in the pantry or refrigerator; (5) new neighbors should be welcomed with gifts of food; and (6) desserts, rather than fruits and less fattening foods, are traditionally the proper refreshments for social functions.

The physical educator who wishes to introduce a weight reduction program into his school must be conscious of working, not only with the *whole* child, but with his entire family and ethnic group. Perhaps the most successful weight reduction classes are part of the extracurricular program organized so as to include both parents and children.

Whether curricular or extracurricular, weight reduction programs should be engaged in voluntarily and supported by sympathetic counseling. The approach must be nonthreatening and nonchastising. Fat children often have emotional problems which perpetuate habits of overeating. Many psychologists believe that eating is a form of oral gratification to which persons unconsciously regress when they feel unloved or insecure. Such persons tend to nibble continuously, not because they are hungry, but to meet hidden needs and drives. The fat child must be reassured that he is loved and accepted for what he is. This is difficult when one realizes that the child does not easily separate the self from the body. Criticism of excessive body weight is often internalized as criticism of self. Many obese persons have built up elaborate defense mechanisms in order to preserve ego strength. It should not be assumed that they will be receptive to offers to help with weight loss, nor that they will admit openly to dissatisfaction with their bodies.

Management of Obesity

Long-term management of obesity has been likened to that of alcoholism and drug abuse. The problem can be solved temporarily but never cured. Of the many persons who make rapid and large weight losses, only 10 percent achieve lifetime weight control. Steiner states in this regard:

Obesity is more preventable than curable, particularly if the weight gain starts early in life and becomes excessive or progressive beyond adolescence. In our experience most early and excessive weight gainers remain obese into adulthood. Out of 200 children who were obese under the age of 9 years, 74 percent of the boys and 70 percent of the girls remained obese at age 18 years regardless of the type of diet or medication used to manage the obesity. [8]

Mayer reports a number of studies in which patients were subjected to vigorously controlled weight reduction programs.[9] Although temporary success was usually achieved, most of the obese persons regained the lost pounds within a period of three years. Clearly only the symptoms of obesity are being treated in most management programs, and the underlying causes of weight gain have not been eliminated.

Implications for Physical Education

The obese child can often be helped by a combination of diet control, exercise, drugs, and psychiatric therapy. One therapeutic approach without the others is generally futile and serves only to disappoint the pupil. Hence, the physical educator must work as part of a team which never loses sight of the *whole* child nor his role in the family setting.

The goal of most weight reduction programs is to achieve a new balance between food intake and energy output. A pound of body weight is the equivalent of 3,500 calories. In order to lose an average of two pounds a week over a long duration of time, the dieter must take in 1,000 less calories a day. This deficit can be created partially through exercise as demonstrated by the following list.

The Caloric Cost of Various Activities

Activity	Caloric Cost	
	Minute	Hour
Walking slowly (2.6 mph)	1.92	115
Walking moderately fast (3.75 mph)	3.58	215
Walking very fast (5.3 mph)	9.42	565
Running	13.33-21.67	800-1,300
Swimming } depending on	5 -16.67	300-1,000
Rowing } speed	16.67-21.67	1,000-1,300
Cycling	2.5 -10	150- 600

8. Matthew M. Steiner, *Clinical Approach to Endocrine Problems in Childhood* (St. Louis: The C. V. Mosby Company, 1970), p. 23.

9. Jean Mayer, *Overweight: Causes, Cost, and Control* (Englewood Cliffs, New Jersey: Prentice-Hall, Inc., 1968).

The exact caloric count for an activity depends upon body weight, but these approximations give an idea of the caloric loss which can be expected through exercise. The well proportioned physical educator often does not realize how unpleasant vigorous exercise can be for the obese. A consideration of the physical characteristics of the obese pupil leads to realistic program planning.

1. Distended abdomen. This results in anatomical differences in the position of the stomach and the length of the intestinal tract, thereby affecting vital processes. It also creates excessive pressure on the diaphragm which leads to difficulty in breathing and the consequent accumulation of carbon dioxide which helps to explain patterns of drowsiness. The distended abdomen makes forward bending exercises difficult or impossible.

2. Mobility of rolls of fat. The bobbing up and down of breasts, abdomen, and other areas where excessive fat is deposited is uncomfortable and often painful during locomotor activities.

3. Excessive perspiration. Layers of fat serve as insulation, and the obese person more quickly becomes hot and sweaty than the nonobese.

4. Galling between the thighs and other skin areas which rub together. After perspiration begins continued locomotion causes painful galling or chafing somewhat similar to an abrasion. Such areas heal slowly because of continuous irritation and sometimes become inflamed.

5. Postural faults. Obese children are particularly vulnerable to knock knees, pronation, flat feet, sagging abdomen, drooped shoulders, and round back. These postural deviations all affect mechanical efficiency in even simple locomotor activities.

6. Skeletal immaturity. The growth centers in the long bones of obese adolescents are particularly susceptible to injury, either from cumulative daily gravitational stress or sudden traumas from such strenuous or heavy activities as contact sports, weight lifting, and pyramid building.

7. Edema. Obese persons seem to retain fluids more readily than nonobese. This causes swelling of ankles, breasts, and wrists, particularly during the menstrual period.

8. Broad base in locomotor activities. The combination of knock knees, tendency toward galling between thighs, and pronation result in a slow, awkward gait with feet often shoulder width apart.

9. Fear of falling. Added weight makes falling from heights both painful and dangerous.

10. Excessive buoyancy in water. The inability to keep most of the body submerged makes the mastery of regulation swimming strokes difficult.

The truly obese child finds any exercise more vigorous than walking almost impossible. Physicians recommend that a 1,200 calorie regimen designed to cause a weight reduction of approximately two pounds a week be supplemented by a daily walk of at least one mile. Physical education for the obese pupil should be scheduled immediately after lunch and offer sufficient time for the completion of a mile long walk. A pedometer fastened to the pupil's belt enhances record keeping.

In a weight reduction program the primary purpose of the physical educator is to change attitudes toward exercise and to develop habits of regular daily activity which will endure beyond the program itself. What will make walking pleasurable? An opportunity to socialize with a friend, the chance to take a dog for an outing, the freedom to walk to an agreed upon destination across town? Many individual sports—golf, archery, the discus and javelin throws, horseshoes, and croquet—are walking activities in which the obese can find success. Any throwing or striking activity in which balls or projectiles must be repeatedly recovered can be adapted into games with motivational point systems. Often times the walk to a community bowling alley or batting range is more valuable in terms of caloric expenditure than the sport itself. Some obese children have developed such power in batting that their slowness in getting to base is not a real handicap. In some schools the obese pupil is given his turn at bat, and a friend runs the bases for him.

The need for socialization through play is the same for obese children as others with crippling conditions. Walking and exercising done in conjunction with a special weight reduction program should not substitute for physical education activities with his peers even though his participation may be limited to score keeping or umpiring. Others must learn to accept him as he is just as they would an amputee.

Like other orthopedically handicapped pupils, the obese child should be allowed privacy in dressing and showering if it is requested. Regulation gymnasium costumes may be impossible to find, and long pants may be more appropriate than shorts.

The heavier a child is, the more important it is that certain activities be avoided. These include tasks which involve lifting his own weight as chinning and rope climbing and those which entail lifting external weights as weight training, serving as the base of a pyramid, and couple tumbling stunts. The sympathetic teacher can devise many adaptations to draw the pupil into the group and foster the development of favorable attitudes toward fitness.

The use of successive contracts, specifying specific goals and rewards after the loss of each five or ten pounds, has been found an effective motivational technique in weight reduction. [10] The pupil is free at all times to revise his contract and allow himself more food and less exercise, but few take advantage of this option. This contract is a means of involving the child in his own decision making, yet reinforcing his successes.

10. Michael Dinoff, Henry C. Rickard, and John Colwick, "Weight Reduction Through Successive Contracts," *American Journal of Orthopsychiatry,* Vol. 42, No. 1 (January, 1972), p. 110.

Organizations

1. American Corrective Therapy Association, Inc., 1265 Cherry Road, Memphis, Tennessee 38117.

2. American Occupational Therapy Association, Inc., 6000 Executive Boulevard, Rockville, Maryland 20852.

3. American Physical Therapy Association, 1156 15th Street, N.W., Washington, D. C. 20005.

4. The National Easter Seal Society for Crippled Children and Adults, 2023 West Ogden Avenue, Chicago, Illinois 60612. Publishes *Rehabilitation Literature.*

5. The National Foundation—March of Dimes, 800 2nd Avenue, New York, New York 10017.

6. National Rehabilitation Association, 1522 K Street, N.W., Washington, D. C. 20005.

7. National Paraplegia Foundation, 333 N. Michigan Avenue, Chicago, Illinois 60601.

8. International Medical Society of Paraplegia, E. & S. Livingstone, 43-45 Annandale Street, Edinburgh EH7 4AT. Publishes journal *Paraplegia,* which includes many articles on sports and exercise.

9. National Wheelchair Athletic Association (NWAA), 40-24 62nd Street, Woodside, New York 11377.

10. National Wheelchair Basketball Association (NWBA), 110 Seaton Bldg., University of Kentucky, Lexington, Kentucky 40506.

11. American Wheelchair Bowling Association, 2635 Northeast 19th Street, Pompano Beach, Florida 33062.

12. Paralyzed Veterans of America, 7315 Wisconsin Avenue, Suite 301-W, Washington, D. C. 20014.

13. American College of Sports Medicine, 1440 Monroe Street, Madison, Wisconsin 53706. Publishes journal *Medicine and Science in Sports.*

References

Adams, Ronald C., et al. *Games, Sports, and Exercises for the Physically Handicapped.* Philadelphia: Lea & Febiger, 1976.

Anderson, William. *Teaching the Physically Handicapped to Swim.* London: Faber and Faber, 1968. (Distributed in U. S. by Transatlantic Arts, Inc., North Village Green, Levittown, New York 11756.

Bauer, Joseph J. *Riding for Rehabilitation: A Guide for Handicapped Riders and Their Instructors.* Toronto, Ontario, Canada: Canadian Stage and Arts Publications Limited (49 Wellington Street East), 1972.

Covalt, Nila Kirkpatrick. *Bed Exercises for Convalescent Patients.* Springfield, Illinois: Charles C Thomas, 1968.

Cratty, Bryant J. *Developmental Games for Physically Handicapped Children.* Palo Alto, California: Peek Publications, 1969.

Dibner, Susan, and Dibner, Andrew. *Integration or Segregation for the Physically Handicapped Child.* Springfield, Illinois.: Charles C Thomas, 1973.

Pomeroy, Janet. *Recreation for the Physically Handicapped.* New York: The MacMillan Company, 1964.

Figure 19.0. A protective helmet is necessary for many children with convulsive disorders.

Van Gogh, de Maupassant, Dostoevski, Flaubert, da Vinci, Caesar, Alexander, Lord Byron, Mohammed, Mendelssohn, Handel, Swinburne, Paganini, Socrates, Buddha, Napoleon, and Saint Paul all had *convulsive disorders*. Manifested in seizures or fits of some kind, most convulsive disorders are epileptic in nature. Because of the social stigma associated with the word *epilepsy*, many physicians and parents are reluctant to use it, substituting instead the newer term convulsive disorders and prescribing anticonvulsive drugs. In medical circles where reference to *epilepsy* is still often made, the condition is no longer considered a disease but rather an upset in the electrical rhythm of the brain which causes seizures.

Approximately two million persons in the United States have epilepsy. This is roughly one out of every 150 to 200 persons. Most of these individuals are on medications which are almost 100 percent effective in preventing seizures. They live completely normal lives, and friends seldom know about their condition. The ages of onset of the first seizure helps to explain why so many physical educators must cope with this problem. Twenty percent of all epileptics have their first seizure before age ten; these are usually children with known or suspected neurological damage which results in multiple handicaps. Cerebral palsy, mental retardation, and learning disabilities often are complicated by convulsive disorders. Thirty percent of the epileptics have their first seizure in the second decade, while 20 percent convulse initially in the third decade. The final 30 percent have their first seizure after age forty.

Seizures seldom, if ever, occur while a child is engaging in vigorous physical activity. In the cool-down period immediately after a game, usually in the locker room, a number of *first* seizures occur. No one knows why. Up to that point the pupil has been completely *normal*,

and nothing in his medical history explains the sudden onset of a convulsive disorder. Since more first seizures appear in the adolescent years than any other decade, it is understandable why the physical educator should become involved in helping the pupil to make necessary social and medical adjustments.

The social problems in epilepsy are greater than the medical ones. The student regaining consciousness after a first seizure does not remember anything that happened. He is self-conscious and embarassed about being stared at by a cluster of classmates. Who wouldn't be? Adolescence in our culture is a time of particular sensitivity, and most teenage epileptics confess that their greatest hang-up is what their friends think. On the other hand, the peer group which has witnessed the seizure has undergone a terrifying, traumatic experience. It is probably the first seizure they have seen, and they are eager to talk about it and share perceptions. Individual responses are as variable as human beings themselves, but many persons are reluctant to continue dating or even socializing with an epileptic. Parents too exert pressure, not wanting their child to marry an epileptic. Some states still have legislation that epileptics cannot marry and/or have children. Driver's licenses, if issued, have restrictions. Employment opportunities are reduced, and insurability under workmen's compensation is a problem.

Phenobarbital and dilantin, the drugs used most often in controlling *grand mal seizures*, were not introduced until 1912 and 1938 respectively. Perhaps new generations will be increasingly free of prejudice. Today it is relatively rare for a person to have seizures in public. Teachers who work with children from low income families see many seizures, almost always caused because a prescription is not filled on time. Often the problem is carelessness or ignorance rather than lack of money. When taken regularly according to directions, modern medications are almost completely effective in preventing seizures.

The period of time required to determine correct dosages varies with individuals. Hence the first few months after an initial seizure may be especially troublesome, with too little medication resulting in seizures and too much causing drowsiness and other side effects. During this time the pupil may have many absences from school with the subsequent problems of lowered grades and inability to keep up with social activities. Once the correct dosage is decided upon, the medical problem is essentially eliminated.

Physical educators who work in residential facilities for the mentally retarded know that seizures are fairly common occurrences among the institutionalized population. It is estimated that approximately one-third of institutionalized retardates have convulsive disorders. Whether these individuals fail to take their medications or simply respond less well to treatment is not known. It is not uncommon to see a seizure a day.

Types of Seizures

Five types of seizures account for most epilepsy: (1) *grand mal*, (2) *Jacksonian*, (3) *petit mal*, (4) *psychomotor*, and (5) *mixed*. The term *status epilepticus* encompasses all kinds of seizures and refers specifically to a condition in which one seizure occurs after another with no recovery period in between. If these do not respond to drugs and continue for several days, death may result. A description of each type of seizure follows.

Grand Mal

The most dramatic and easily recognized of the seizures, the grand mal has four characteristic stages.

1. *Aura.* This is a warning or premonition of the attack which is always the same for a particular person. An aura may be a cer-

tain smell, flashing of lights, vague feeling of apprehension, a sinking feeling in the abdomen, or a feeling of extraordinary rapture. Only about 50 percent of the persons have auras.

2. *Tonic phase. Tonic* means constant, referring to the continuous contraction of muscles. The person straightens out, utters a cry, and loses consciousness. If there is a tonic contraction of respiratory muscles, the person becomes cyanotic. Fortunately this phase seldom lasts more than thirty seconds.

3. *Clonic phase.* Clonic refers to intermittent contraction and relaxation of muscles. The clonic phase persists from a few seconds up to two or three minutes. The tongue may be bitten as the jaws work up and down. The sphincters around the rectum and urinary tract relax causing the person to urinate or pass fecal material into his clothing.

4. *Sleep or coma phase.* After a period of brief consciousness or semiconsciousness during which the person complains of being very tired, he lapses into a sleep which lasts from one to several hours. Upon awakening, he is at one extreme or another: either very clear, or dazed and confused. Usually there is no memory of the seizure.

Jacksonian

Sometimes considered a variation of the grand mal type, the Jacksonian seizure resembles the latter except that it does not have an aura or a tonic phase. The clonic contraction begins in one part of the body, usually a hand or foot, and from that point spreads up the limb until all of the muscles of the involved part are intermittently contracting and relaxing. The Jacksonian seizure may affect all of the body or only a part. Jacksonian and grand mal types account for about 51 percent of all seizures.

Petit Mal

Accounting for about 8 percent of all epilepsy, the petit mal does not cause a loss of consciousness. Its symptoms are so subtle that the inexperienced observer seldom notices the seizure. There is an impairment of consciousness, never more than thirty seconds, in which the child seems dazed. His eyes may roll upward. If talking at the time, there is a momentary silence after which he continues where he left off with no loss of unity in thought. Petit mal seizures are rare before age three and often disappear after puberty. They are more common in girls than in boys.

Psychomotor Attacks

Most misunderstood by teachers and parents are psychomotor attacks. These are unexplainable short term changes in behavior which the pupil later does not remember. One child may have temper tantrums, suddenly exploding for no reason, hitting another student, provoking a fight, or throwing things about the room. Another may have spells involving incoherent chatter, repetition of meaningless phrases, and inability to answer simple questions. Still another has episodes of sleep walking or awakens the family at night with hysterical unexplainable sobbing. Psychomotor attacks may also be confused with daydreaming or not paying attention in class.

Psychomotor epilepsy gained nationwide publicity during the 1964 trial of Jack Ruby, the assassinator of President Kennedy's assassin. Only about 5 percent of all epilepsy is psychomotor in origin, but persons with this type perhaps suffer the most for their condition is seldom properly diagnosed. Their aberrant behaviors are misinterpreted as discipline problems, and punishment is given out for deeds the pupil cannot remember.

Mixed Types

About 35 to 40 percent of epilepsy is a combination of two or more types. This classification usually refers to the combination of grand mal and petit mal.

The etiology of epilepsy falls within two broad classifications: (1) idiopathic (genetic or endogenous) and (2) acquired (symptomatic or exogenous). *Idiopathic* means the cause is unknown, and 80 percent of all epilepsy remains unexplainable. There appears to be a genetic predisposition toward epilepsy, but this is subject to controversy. In general, the epileptic parent has one chance in forty of giving birth to an epileptic child. The incidence is increased if both parents are epileptic. Acquired epilepsy can be traced directly to birth injuries, brain tumors, anoxia, lead poisoning, cerebral abscesses, and penetrating injuries to the brain.

Factors Which Aggravate Seizures in Known Epileptics

1. Changes in alkalinity of the blood. These changes are very subtle and minute.
   a. High alkalosis favors seizures.
   b. High acidity inhibits seizures.
   Diet therapy is used frequently. Acid-producing diets, high in fat content, such as cream, butter, eggs, and meat, have successfully produced a quieting effect. This kind of diet is called a *ketogenic diet* (high in fat). The ability of the epileptic to metabolize fat is disturbed as in diabetes; they can metabolize fat down to ketone bodies (acidosis) but have difficulty with further metabolism to CO_2 and H_2O. The accumulation of acid products in the blood as a result of exercise is believed to help prevent seizures.
2. Alcoholic beverages. An excessive intake lowers threshold.
3. In women, menstrual periods. Many girls and women have seizures only around their periods. Edema aggravates the onset of seizures. One of the side effects of ovarian (esterogenic) hormones is to encourage retention of salt (sodium) in the

body. This retention of sodium binds water within the tissue, obvious through the swelling of breasts, nasal membranes, ankles, fingers, and possibly even a gain in weight.

4. Psychogenic stimulus. Anger, fright, bad news, and other high stress factors may precipitate seizures.

5. Hyperventilation, or overbreathing, precipitates petit mal attacks. Holding the breath as long as possible as in distance underwater swimming is a common form of hyperventilation which is contraindicated for epileptics. Breath holding lowers the carbon dioxide content of the blood which normally acts as a stimulant for the respiratory center in the brain. Some forms of hyperventilation, like voluntary forced breathing exercises, increase the alkalosis of the blood, thereby lowering the seizure threshold. Bobbing in swimming, blowing a wind instrument, and singing may cause hyperventilation. Dizziness and/or feeling faint are warning signals.

6. Chronic recurrent head trauma such as might occur in boxing or soccer (when the ball is given impetus with the head). This factor is controversial in that some physicians report that their patients have participated regularly with no ill effects in boxing, soccer, and other sports in which the head repeatedly was subjected to blows.

Treatment of Epilepsy

Treatment divides itself into two phases: surgical and medical. Surgery can eliminate seizures in about 35 percent of the cases in which the cause is known. Primarily this involves removal of growths creating pressure in the brain. Medical treatment is multifaceted revolving around the use of anticonvulsive

Figure 19.1. The epileptic child can participate fully in physical education.

drugs and adherence to a healthful daily living regime.

Implications for Physical Education

In 1968, the Committee on Children With Handicaps of the American Medical Association issued a formal statement on the epileptic child and competitive school athletics.[1] This group recommended that epileptic children participate fully in physical education ac-

1. American Medical Association, "The Epileptic Child and Competitive School Athletics," *Pediatrics,* Vol. 42, No. 4 (October, 1968), p. 700.

tivities. Three restrictions were discussed: (1) underwater swimming in which the breath is held for long periods, (2) body contact sports in which head injuries might occur, and (3) activities in gymnastics and diving which involve heights from which a fall could be dangerous. The sports which might be contraindicated were boxing, tackle football, ice hockey, diving, soccer, rugby, and lacrosse. The report was careful to emphasize, however, that the decision should be made on an individual basis and all epileptic children in a school system should never be banned from a particular activity simply because they are epileptic.

Livingston, a physician at Johns Hopkins Hospital, took issue with the conservative AMA statement, pointing out that the emotional disturbances of boys excluded from the sports of their peers were more difficult to handle than medical problems. He allows his patients to participate in all sports but diving, prohibiting it not because of the possibility of head injuries but because of the obvious complications associated with a seizure underwater. Livingston states:

Over the past 33 years I have observed at least 15,000 young children with epilepsy, many of whom have been under my personal care during their entire scholastic careers. Hundreds of these patients have played tackle football, some have participated in boxing, lacrosse, wrestling, and other physical activities which render the participant prone to head injuries. I am not cognizant of a single instance of recurrence of epileptic seizures related to head injury in any of these athletes.[2]

The normal epileptic child whose seizures are under control is no different from his peers. He needs good supervision when enrolled in beginning swimming, but so do all children! Likewise, he needs a gymnastics teacher who is competent in spotting techniques. Again, this does not make him different from his peers who also need a good spotter when they undertake activities on the high balance beam, parallel bars, and trampoline. Most importantly, the epileptic child needs the acceptance and belonging that team membership assures.

2. Samuel Livingston, "Letter to the Editor," *Journal of American Medical Association,* Vol. 207, No. 10 (March, 1969), p. 1917.

Organizations

1. National Epilepsy League, Inc., 116 South Michigan Avenue, Chicago, Illinois 60603 or 203 North Wabash Avenue, Room 2200, Chicago, Illinois 60601.

2. Epilepsy Foundation of America, 1820 L Street, N.W., Suite 406, Washington, D.C. 20036.

References

Bagley, Christopher. *The Social Psychology of the Epileptic Child.* Coral Gables, Florida: University of Miami Press, 1971.

Baird, Henry W. *The Child With Convulsions.* New York: Grune and Stratton, 1972.

Boshes, Louis D., and Gibbs, Fredric A. *Epilepsy Handbook.* Second Edition, Springfield, Illinois: Charles C. Thomas, 1972.

Livingston, Samuel. *Comprehensive Management of Epilepsy in Infancy, Childhood, and Adolescence.* Springfield, Illinois: Charles C Thomas, 1972.

Epilepsia. Journal of the International League Against Epilepsy. Published quarterly. Subscriptions should be sent to Elsevier Scientific Publishing Company, P.O. Box 330, Amsterdam C, The Netherlands.

Horizon. A newsletter published by the National Epilepsy League, Inc.

National Spokesman. A newsletter published by the Epilepsy Foundation of America.

Cerebral Palsy

Figure 20.0. A teacher establishes rapport with a
five-year-old spastic cerebral palsied child before
crutches are thrown aside and movement exploration
on the Lind Climber is begun.

Cerebral palsy is a group of neuro-muscular conditions caused by damage to the motor areas of the brain. About 90 percent of such brain damage occurs before and during birth. Anoxia, infection, and injury to the brain during childhood account for the other 10 percent. Over 550,000 persons in the United States have been diagnosed as cerebral palsied, one-third of whom are under twenty-one years of age. The condition is more common among the white race than the black, among males than females, and among the first born. The incidence is 3.5 cases per 1,000 births. Cerebral palsy, to most persons, implies moderate to severe motor involvement. Mild cases often are not identified, but the careful observer of movement will note that many awkward children display characteristics described in this chapter.

The first description of cerebral palsy can be traced back to 1862 when W. J. Little, an English orthopedic surgeon, published a report on sixty-three children. For many years, the condition was known as Little's Disease. In the 1930s the name changed to *spastic paralysis.* The writings of Carlson, Phelps, Fay, Perlstein, and others in the 1940s led to the widespread use of the term *cerebral palsy,* encompassing several distinctly different motor disturbances which stem from brain damage. Recently much of the literature on cerebral palsy has appeared under such broad titles as brain damage, organic brain disorders, and hyperkinetic behavior.

Multiple Handicaps

Almost all cerebral palsied persons have multiple handicaps. Approximately 50 to 60 percent are mentally retarded. Cruickshank reports a study involving 992 cerebral palsied children in which 49 percent had intelligence quotients between 0 and 60; 22.5 percent, between 70 and 89 ; 21.9 percent, between 90 and 109; and 6.6 percent, over 109.[1] Difficulties of speech and voluntary motion, however, make a valid evaluation of intellectual functioning impossible.

It is estimated that 55 to 60 percent have visual defects. *Strabismus,* the inability to focus both eyes simultaneously on the same object, is the most common problem, not a surprising fact when one remembers that eye focus requires the coordinated action of six muscles of the eyeball. Imbalances in strength cause squinting, loss of binocular vision, and inefficiencies in depth perception, pattern discrimination, and figure background detection.

Between 5 and 8 percent have hearing loss. Among cerebral palsied children born with *kernicterus,* a yellow jaundice condition, the incidence is almost 80 percent.

Approximately one-third have seizures at some time in their lives. This fact, coupled with their poor coordination, explains why so many wear padded helmets. Frequent seizures present hazards of falling, interfere with learning, and may lead to additional brain damage.

Lack of concentration, hyperexcitability, perseveration, distractibility, emotional lability, conceptual rigidity, hyperactivity, and motor awkwardness are *soft* signs of organic brain injury. They are called *soft* because they cannot be substantiated neurologically. Nevertheless these characteristics often result in a vicious circle of underachievement, misbehavior, lowered self-esteem, and lack of motivation. *Emotional overlay* is said to be present when the soft signs and/or self, parent, and sibling attitudes seem to evoke emotional disturbances.

Approximately 85 percent of the cerebral palsied over age seven are below age level in

1. William M. Cruickshank, ed., *Psychology of Exceptional Children and Youth* (Englewood Cliffs, New Jersey: Prentice-Hall Inc., 1965), p. 345.

reading, and 93 percent are below age level in arithmetic. The causes of academic under-achievement are multiple. Expressive, receptive, and global aphasias contribute to many of their difficulties.

Almost all cerebral palsied children need speech therapy. The incidence of actual speech defects varies from 30 to 75 percent, with about half able to improve with training. Most frustrating is the characteristic delay of speech development in youngsters with extensive left cerebral hemisphere damage. Many never learn to talk although they can make noises of various kinds.

Classification According to Extremities Involved

Despite the dismal picture painted above, the *whole child* often is not motorically involved. The following terms are used in cerebral palsy as well as in orthopedic conditions.

1. *Paraplegia.* Involvement of the lower extremities only.
2. *Hemiplegia.* Involvement of the entire right side or left side.
3. *Triplegia.* Involvement of three extremities, usually both legs and one arm.
4. *Quadriplegia.* Involvement of all four extremities.

Classification According to Types of Cerebral Palsy

Six neuromuscular classifications are recommended by the American Academy for Cerebral Palsy: (1) *spasticity,* (2) *athetosis,* (3) *rigidity,* (4) *tremor,* (5) *ataxia,* and (6) *mixed.* The specific motor impairment indicates the anatomic localization of the brain injury. For instance, when there is spasticity, the lesion is usually in the cerebral cortex.

Athetosis, rigidity, and tremors are caused by pathology in the basal nuclei, whereas ataxia is a sign of cerebellar damage.

Spasticity

Approximately 66 percent of the diagnosed cases of cerebral palsy are spastic. *Spasticity is characterized by exaggerated stretch reflexes, a marked decrement in ability to perform precise movements, and increased hypertonicity.*

The exaggerated stretch reflex is responsible for the jerky movements of the spastic. It is caused by the failure of antagonistic muscles to relax when the prime movers initiate an action which opposes gravity. The antagonists resist any stretching by an explosive recoil sort of action which is sometimes called the *clonus phenomenon.* When the arm reaches forward or upward, for instance, it is often jerked back toward starting position by the antagonists. Likewise, when the spastic strives to maintain good posture with head, neck, and spinal column in extension, he is frustrated by the antagonists which contract reflexly and result in undesired flexion postures.

Physical Characteristics of the Spastic

The spastic is less normal in appearance than persons with other types of cerebral palsy. Assuming that all parts of the body are involved, the following characteristics may be observed.

Head and Neck. There is a tendency toward flexion with frequent changes of head position probably caused by visual disturbances. Strabismus is almost always present.

Shoulder Joint. The hypertonicity of the shoulder joint adductors draws the arm in toward the midline of the body. Reaching movements, as in the overarm recovery in the front crawl, may be severely limited. The muscles require very slow or static stretching

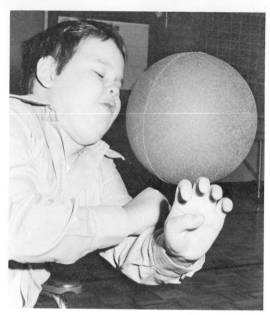

Figure 20.1. The fisted hand is characteristic of spastic cerebral palsy.

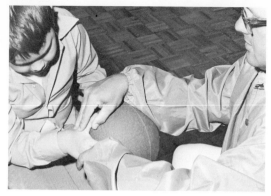

Figure 20.2. Pressing against the sides of a large ball stretches the finger flexors.

exercises. Activities should be devised in which the arms remain elevated such as walking while holding on to a rope strung overhead. Hanging from stall bars may be helpful.

Forearm. The forearm is maintained in pronation. To counterbalance this tendency, exercises should be executed in a supinated position. Turning door knobs, using keys, and manipulating a screwdriver are illustrative supination activities.

Wrist and Fingers. The hand is typically held in a fist. The flexors are hypertonic, and there is a tendency toward permanent shortening. A *wrist drop* is often present. Games should be devised which demand simultaneous *extension* of the fingers and the wrists. Hyperextension of the wrist, however, is contraindicated because it elicits the palmar grasp reflex as explained on page 413. In ball activities the teacher must be ever watchful that the pupil does not throw, catch, or volley with a fisted hand. Pressing against the sides of a large ball held with both hands stretches the finger flexors. Likewise

pressing with an open palm against the wall, the floor, or someone's hands is desirable. Stunts such as the wheelbarrow, creeping, head stands, and animal walks which take part or all of the body weight on the hands are recommended. Pressing downward on clay, flour dough, mud, or sand to engrave palm and fingerprints accomplishes the same goal.

Hip Joint. The flexors, inward rotators, and adductors at the hip joint are excessively tight. The hypertonic adductors pull the thighs toward midline causing the advancing leg to cross slightly in front of the other in a scissors gait. The overly strong inward rotators explain the tendency to walk pigeon-toed. Children who toe inward and hold the forearm in pronation should be suspected of mild cerebral palsy whether or not the condition has been diagnosed. Activities involving hip adduction like rope climbing are contraindicated. Nor should CP children be allowed to toe inward even in movement exploration activities. Yoga and other slow or static stretching exercises for the tight muscles are recommended. Those performed in a wide-stride sitting position with thighs rotated outward are particularly helpful.

Knee Joint. The hamstrings, which cause flexion at the knee joint, are often so tight that long leg braces are required to prevent severe flexion contractures. Occasionally a *tendon transplant* alleviates the problem. In this surgery the tendon which normally crosses over the posterior knee joint to insert on the tibial condyles is transplanted to the distal end of the femur. When the hamstrings no longer cross the knee joint, they cannot initiate flexion there. Approximately six to eight weeks after the surgery, the child is free of postoperative pain and can walk without abnormal knee flexion. In milder cases, where surgery is not indicated, daily exercises from a long sitting or long lying position help to stretch the hamstrings.

Ankle Joint. The hypertonic gastrocnemius and soleus and tight Achilles tendon contribute to the tendency to walk on the toes. Activities which emphasize plantar flexion, or pointing the toes, are therefore contraindicated. Corrective shoes and/or short leg braces are used to hold down the heels and assure the heel-to-toe transfer of weight. Dorsiflexion exercises which stretch the Achilles tendon are recommended. Walking up an inclined box, landing properly on the trampoline, and the kicking steps employed in La Raspa are among the activities which maintain the feet in dorsiflexion.

Balance. Cerebral brain damage in itself does not cause balance problems as lesions in other parts of the brain might. The spastic tends to fall often, however, because the scissors gait utilizes a narrow base for ambulation. Contractures at the hip, knee, and ankle joints throw the body out of alignment and lessen its stability. Walking on the toes leads to frequent falls in a forward direction. Anticonvulsive medications may affect balance adversely. Most young CP children are several years behind their peers in such activities as walking a narrow balance beam, standing with the body weight supported on one foot, hopping, and skipping. Beam walking should be attempted first on wide benches and/or boards. Barres, like those in ballet studios, are helpful in the maintenance of balance during standing exercises. Where barres are not available, the pupil may hold onto the back of a chair for support. Even parallel bars are used by physical therapists in teaching the standing and walking balance prerequisite for ambulation.

Breath Control. The muscles of respiration are often affected. This makes teaching rhythmic breathing almost impossible. Many such children prefer back strokes. The breathing activities described in the chapter on asthma are recommended.

Hypertonus is greatest in the flexors of the upper extremities and the extensors of the lower extremities. Contractures occur in these muscles if range of motion exercises are not performed daily. A contracture is a shortening or distortion of a muscle or group of muscles caused by prolonged hypertonicity and/or contraction against weak or flaccid muscles.

The ambulatory child appears always to be tense. Not only does he exhibit hypertonus, but his entire body seems to respond in exaggerated fashion to even the slightest stimulation—noise, a light touch on the shoulder, the temperature of the air or water. His learning environment should be structured so as to minimize external stimuli; his teacher speaks in a low, well-modulated voice; and the pupil is sheltered from emotionally charged events which may increase hyperexcitability. Physical education for the spastic child should stress relaxation and *slowing down* activities. Competitive games focus upon *who can go the slowest* rather than the traditional striving for speed. Hand signals, a flicker of the lights, or a drum beat are substituted for the high shrill of the whistle.

Athetosis

From 20 to 30 percent of the cerebral palsied have some degree of athetosis manifested in continuous *overflow* movement of involved body parts. The motion is slow, wormlike, involuntary, uncontrollable, unpredictable, and purposeless. The muscles of the fingers and wrists are affected most often, rendering handwriting and similar coordinations almost impossible. Facial expression, eating, and speaking are major problems. The head is usually drawn back, but may roll unpredictably from side to side; the tongue may protrude, and saliva drool down the chin. This lack of head control results in problems of visual pursuit and focus. Some athetoid children cannot move their eyes unless they simultaneously move the head.

The athetoid child who has enough muscle control to stand usually exhibits lordosis. To compensate for this postural problem, he may hold his arms and shoulders forward. His legs are hyperextended, and he leads with his abdomen as short, stiff steps are taken. He falls backward more often than forward.

Many athetoids lack the muscle control to stand, creep, or lift the head from a prone lying position. A common locomotor pattern, particularly among young children, is executed from a supine position. The back of the head and legs provide impetus to slide the body along the floor. The arms are generally useless. Rolf Thomassen, famous artist and writer from Norway, indicates that this was his earliest method of locomotion. It was not until he began losing the hair on his scalp from *walking on his head* that his father constructed a chair with wheels. In a beautiful autobiography written by a pencil held between his teeth, Rolf shares his feelings about a lifetime of sitting:

But although I can rightly deem myself lucky in getting this chair, it has been like a prison cell to me, and however brilliant my father's invention was, and however much love and ingenuity he put into the work when he made it, I have always felt like an eagle in a cage sitting in this chair. . . Later my father rebuilt it so that the seat could be removed, and I could then stand in the chair frame. Gradually I learned to walk about a little in it. . . But the years went by, and I sat for so long in my chair that the tendons under my knees gradually contracted so

that I was unable to stretch out my legs. Because of this I was, unfortunately, unable to walk in an erect position, but had to pull myself along with my legs while I sat. In this way I walk in my chair to this day. [2]

Thomassen's statement eloquently attests to the need for regular daily exercise. Flexion contractures of the hamstrings are common to anyone forced to spend long periods sitting. Although many games can be played from a wheelchair, none fulfill the objectives of preventing contracture deformities, maintaining strength, and increasing range of motion.

Warm-ups are not needed by the athetoid whose muscle contractions keep him in a state of never-ending readiness. Instead the emphasis should be upon relaxation and tension reduction. It is generally believed that athetosis ceases during sleep. During waking hours, the ever present overflow of movements fluctuates with the level of stress. Often the harder the child tries to relax, the more troublesome his movements become.

Hellebrandt[3,4] and her colleagues report cinematographical and electromyographic research in which a fifty-year-old athetoid woman was taught bowling, tennis, and golf. The woman's chief problems were difficulty in walking and in the use of the hands. Bowling with a ten pound ball was executed from a sitting position. To develop sufficient strength for bowling, the number of throws attempted was increased each day until 100 throws in a single practice session no longer produced undue fatigue. The less affected of the two arms was used in bowling, and it was found that involuntary motions did not distort the throwing pattern. Throwing the bowling ball

2. Rolf Thomassen, *Beyond Today* (Minneapolis: Augsburg Publishing House, 1953), pp. 26-28.
3. Frances A. Hellebrandt, Joan C. Waterland, and C. Etta Walters, "The Influence of Athetoid Cerebral Palsy on the Execution of Sports Skills: Bowling," *Physical Therapy Review,* Vol. 41 (February, 1961), pp. 106-113.
4. Frances Hellebrandt and Joan C. Waterland, "The Influence of Athetoid Cerebral Palsy on the Execution of Sports Skills: Tennis and Golf," *Physical Therapy Review,* Vol. 41 (April, 1961), pp. 257-262.

seemed to suppress all overt manifestations of athetosis on the same side.

The forehand drive in tennis and the drive in golf were executed from a standing position. As in bowling, swinging the sports implements suppressed all overt manifestations of athetosis in the body parts directly involved in the motor task. The application of force was surprisingly smooth. The movement abnormalities included prominence of tonic neck reflexes, exaggerated postural adjustments, and problems with balance before the stroke was initiated and during its follow-through. The findings of the two studies led the Wisconsin researchers to conclude that moderately involved athetoid persons can learn individual sports which demand accuracy in aiming and swinging. More research of this nature is needed. Most writings, in contrast to those of Hellebrandt, still state that tasks requiring aiming and steadiness are contraindicated for the athetoid. Voluntary relaxation, meticulously controlled movement, and the avoidance of stress constitute the traditional guidelines for planning physical education for athetoid children.

Ataxia

Disorders of balance and proprioception constitute the major problems for approximately 8 percent of the cerebral palsied. Ataxia is a widely used word which denotes poor motor coordination stemming from vestibular and kinesthetic inadequacies. Thus *ataxia* can be alcoholic, autonomic, cerebellar, choreic, or hysterical. Ataxic cerebral palsy is believed to originate from cerebellar damage, and probably many more persons have ataxia than are diagnosed. If motor awkwardness and problems of balance are not inherited from parents, it can be assumed that mild ataxia is present.

Ataxic cerebral palsy is usually not detected until the toddler begins to walk. The child appears normal except for a somewhat awkward gait. In mild cases, he is simply labelled *clumsy* and resigns himself to C's in physical education and the occasional embarrassment of missing a step or upsetting a dinner glass. With concentrated effort, he may become good in a particular sport and make the varsity team. Nevertheless he is acutely aware that he must practice twice as hard as most of his friends. Seldom is he able to expend the time and energy required to maintain his athletic skills over a period of years.

In more severe cases of ataxia, such as those seen frequently among LD children, the pupil may seem lost in space. His defective proprioceptive sense gives him inadequate information about his center of gravity, his postures, and his relationships to the objects about him. When he reaches for an object, he is inclined to overshoot his mark. When climbing stairs or stepping over an obstacle, he tends to lift his feet too high. In ducking under and/or between obstacles he misjudges the distance. He bumps into things, knocks them over, and seems to stumble over his own feet. He may walk and run fairly well on level ground, but on an uneven surface or downhill grade fails to make the necessary postural adjustments to avoid loss of balance.

Rigidity

Rigidity in cerebral palsy is associated with severe mental retardation. Approximately 4 percent of all cerebral palsy falls within this category. Brain damage causes rigidity in both the contracting muscles and their antagonists, but most strongly affects the antagonists. The result is a tendency toward diminished rather than abnormal motion. It is manifested as a generalized inelasticity or stiffness. Because the stretch reflex is decreased or absent, hyperextension of body parts occurs.

In extreme cases, the child lies helpless in an opisthotonic or *wind swept* position as depicted in Figure 20.3. The cervical, thoracic, and lumbar spine is hyperextended, and the

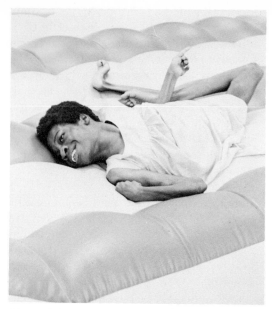

Figure 20.3. The opisthotonic or wind swept position caused by severe muscle rigidity.

Figure 20.4. Boy with severe rigidity enjoys scooter activities.

hypertonicity of affected muscles makes moving body parts difficult.

Rigidity is subdivided into two types: (1) leadpipe and (2) cogwheel. When muscles resist completely all attempts to move a limb, the condition is labelled *leadpipe rigidity*. When muscles respond to attempts to move a body part by releasing and stretching momen-

tarily before offering resistance, the *cogwheel phenomenon* is present. Rigidity is not always associated with cerebral palsy and mental retardation. It is a symptom of Parkinson's Disease and other syndromes caused by damage to the basal ganglia and/or the cerebellum.

Tremors

Tremors are involuntary vibrating movements which are usually regular and rhythmic. They account for about 2 percent of cerebral palsy. When caused by cerebellar damage, the tremor is accentuated by voluntary movement, increasing in severity as the body part approaches the end of the movement. This type of tremor is called intentional, action, or terminal. It occurs more often in the arms than in the legs. When caused by damage to the basal ganglia, the tremor decreases in severity and/or disappears during sleep and certain motor tasks which require concentration. This type of tremor is called nonintentional, rest, or passive. It mostly affects the cranial and digital muscles.

In their most severe form tremors produce a condition of *dystonia*. In its generic sense, dystonia refers to abnormally heightened or lessened states of muscle tone. Cooper[5] devotes 160 pages with beautiful illustrations to this syndrome which produces fixed bony deformities of a totally disabling nature. Inversion deformities, which are among the first to appear, make ambulation difficult or impossible. Torsion spasms of the spine produce lordosis, scoliosis, and torticollis. Rigidity often accompanies tremors. A surgical procedure called a *cryothalamectomy* can relieve the symptoms of dystonia providing the patient

5. Irving Spencer Cooper, *Involuntary Movement Disorders* (New York: Hoeber Medical Division, Harper & Row), 1969, pp. 131-291.

does not exhibit spasticity, mental retardation, and other signs of widespread cerebral pathology.

Mixed Type

Most persons with cerebral palsy exhibit symptoms of several types. Spasticity and athetosis almost always coexist with some body parts more involved spastically than others.

The child is classified into one of the five types according to the symptoms which seem to predominate. When no one type predominates, the cerebral palsy is designated as mixed. This category is used infrequently. Persons classified as having mixed cerebral palsy are usually severely involved and multiply handicapped.

Evolution of Basic Reflex Patterns

In order to understand the motor behavior of CP children, the teacher should learn about evolutional reflexes which explain many bizarre involuntary movements. An evolutional reflex is inborn, normally persists a set number of weeks, gradually lessens in strength, and then disappears altogether. In the CP infant the evolutionary reflexes disappear more slowly than is normal. Some of these reflexes are clinical signs used in the diagnosis of certain motor dysfunctions.

Palmar Grasp Reflex

The palmar grasp reflex normally disappears by the fourth month when it is replaced by voluntary grasping and releasing. It is elicited by pressing an object into an infant's palm or hyperextending his wrist. Throughout his life the CP person finds grasping easy and releasing difficult. The grasp reflex explains the fisted hand which may lead to flexion contractures of the fingers and wrist. The physical educator therefore emphasizes throwing activities (release) rather than catching (grasp). He avoids activities which hyperextend the CP child's wrists since hyperextension elicits the grasp reflex.

Tonic Neck Reflexes

Muscle tone is regulated in all human beings to some extent by movements of the head and neck. In CP children the reflex mechanism which controls the distribution and amount of muscle tone is defective in inhibitory functions, causing hypertonus and exaggerated head and neck movements. Figure 20.5, illustrates symmetrical tonic reflexes which may be observed in normal infants. These reflexes occur in standing and ambulatory postures as well as in lying.

The tonic neck reflex (TNR) and asymmetrical tonic neck reflex (ATNR) normally disappear between the fourth and sixth

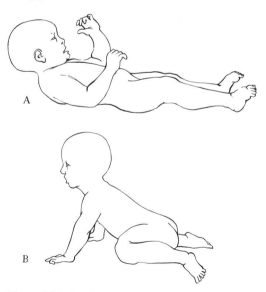

Figure 20.5. Tonic neck reflexes. (A) flexion symmetrical tonic reflex and (B) extension symmetric tonic reflex.

Figure 20.6. Abnormal asymmetrical tonic neck reflex is often evidenced in trampoline jumps of children with mild brain damage.

months. Early research stated unequivocally that retention of the TNR after six months of age was a sign of brain dysfunction. Recent research tends to show that the TNR can be elicited in normal persons. The controversy serves to reinforce belief in individual differences. It is possible that many persons considered *normal* do have mild brain damage which explains the presence of the TNR under particular conditions.

Symmetrical Tonic Neck Responses

Flexion of the neck results in increased hypertonus and/or flexion of the arms and upper trunk and extension of the legs and lower trunk.

Extension or hypertension of the neck results in increased hypertonus and/or extension of the arms and upper trunk and flexion of the

legs and lower trunk. This helps explain the difficulty young children have in maintaining knee joint extension during the bear walk and inchworm stunts.

Asymmetrical Tonic Neck Reflex

Rotation or lateral flexion (tilt) of the head results in increased hypertonus and/or extension of the limbs on the face side and flexion of the limbs on the nonface side. This is sometimes called the Fencer's *en garde* position. The ATNR, although normal, may be exaggerated in babies with brain damage. The following anecdote by a young mother in psychotherapy shows how the exaggerated ATNR can create problems from the very beginning.

My son hates me. He has to be bottle fed. In the hospital everytime I turned his head toward my breast to take nourishment, he thrust his arm out against my sore bosoms, hyperextended his neck, opened his mouth, and lost the nipple. He rejected me from the first time I ever fed him, and he still pushes me away when I try to hold him.

Of course, this young mother did not know anything about the ATNR, nor do many teachers who attempt to hold and cuddle certain children and wonder why they are rebuffed.

Moro or Startle Reflex

The Moro reflex, which normally disappears between the fourth and seventh months, is elicited by noise, jarring the surface on which an infant is lying, tapping the abdomen, or making a supporting position seem insecure. In the first half of the Moro reflex, the infant stiffens, spreads his arms apart, and throws out his legs. The fingers extend but the thumb and index finger remain in a *C* position.

In second half of Moro reflex, the arms and legs come back together in an *embracing* motion. Such an action enables a baby to grab hold of the mother's body for protection. Nor-

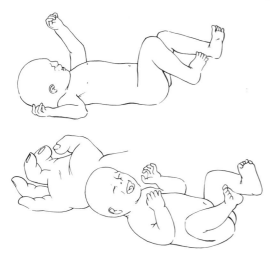

Figure 20.7. Moro or startle reflex.

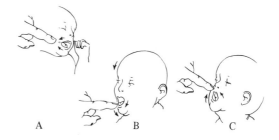

Figure 20.8. Rooting and sucking reflexes. (A) stroking the corner of the mouth and moving the finger toward the cheek causes the head, mouth, and tongue to move in the direction of the stimulus; (B) stroking the lower lip in the direction of the chin causes a downward movement of the tongue, lower lip, and head; (C) stroking the upper lip in the direction of the nose causes elevation of the upper lip and tongue and hyperextension of the neck.

mally all that remains of this response by the seventh month is a weak body jerk accompanied by blinking. The CP person, however, continues to overreact to noise throughout his lifetime. He repeatedly throws out and retracts his arms under environmental conditions of excitement, stress, and unexpected noises.

Rooting and Sucking Reflexes

Normally, when an infant's cheek is stroked, his head turns to the side being stroked. Stroking the lips causes the normal child to suck. When a baby is born without this reflex or with a weak one, he tends to regurgitate food and drool. Some drooling is normal between the third and ninth months. Should it be excessive or persist as it does in some types of cerebral palsy, this indicates presence of either too much or too little of the reflexes.

Physical education often involves activities in which the head and mouth are in contact with a tumbling mat or other surface. Such contact elicits rooting and sucking reflexes in some CP children. This, in turn, initiates reverse peristalsis and food is regurgitated or saliva appears. Activities should be planned so that the mouth is *not* in contact with surfaces.

Babinski Reflex

The Babinski reflex normally disappears between the fourth and eighteenth months. It is positive, or present, when the big toe extends upward in response to stimulation of the sole of the foot. Normally the Babinski reflex is replaced by the plantar reflex which causes the toes to curl when the sole of the foot is stimulated.

Implications of Evolutional Reflexes for Physical Education

The physical educator should not subject CP children to activities which elicit evolutional reflexes and/or encourage their persistence. Reflexes are *involuntary* and cannot be consciously stopped or controlled. The more self-conscious and embarrassed a child becomes about a reflex, the more exaggerated it is likely to be. Obviously he should not be admonished for involuntary movements.

The physical educator who supplements his training with courses in physical therapy learns techniques for minimizing evolutional reflexes and/or for using them to elicit desired movement patterns. For instance, clenching an

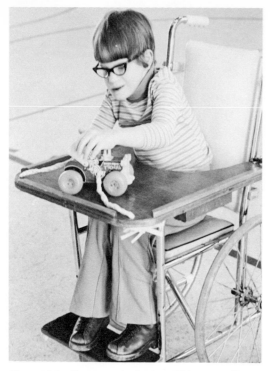

Figure 20.9. Young cerebral palsy children are often nonambulatory.

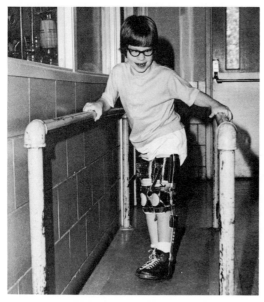

Figure 20.10. Long leg braces offer new opportunities for movement exploration.

object in the fist can be used to increase muscle tone throughout the body. Turning the head to the left facilitates flexion of the right arm and right leg. The physical therapy systems of such authorities as Crothers, Deaver, Fay, Brunnstrom, Bobath, Kabat, Knott, and Rood should be investigated by persons who work daily with CP pupils. Perhaps the best single reference concerning these systems is the Proceedings [6] of a conference held at the Northwestern University Medical School in Chicago in 1966. The resulting volume presents excellent illustrations of several systems and thorough critiques.

Illustrative Case Studies of Children Attending Public Schools

Few persons have studied the physical education needs and interests of CP children. Spragens,[7] however, offers case studies of eleven such children which may serve as guides to the reader in collecting data and writing similar case studies. Abstracts of some of the cases follow.

Case CD: Athetosis

CD is an average size boy of thirteen. As he sits in his wheelchair, the uncontrolled motions of arms and head at once tell of his severe CP condition. One also notices his large, drooling mouth and halting speech. He wears glasses, long leg braces, and weighted shoes. Weighted crutches are used for walking. CD is in the sixth grade, attends the intermediate special education class, and receives daily physical therapy.

6. *American Journal of Physical Medicine,* Volume 46, No. 1, February, 1967, Published bimonthly by the Williams and Wilkins Company, Baltimore, Maryland 21202.

7. Jane Spragens, "A Study of the Physical Education Needs and Interests of a Selected Group of Orthopedically Handicapped Children With Recommendations for Planning and Conducting Physical Activities," Unpublished Master of Arts Study, Texas Woman's University, 1964.

Medical Report—CD was born with athetosis. He has undergone bilateral transplants of the hamstring muscles which reduced the equinus in foot position and modified the scissoring in walking. CD has extremely poor use of his arms and hands, with the left hand more severely involved than the right. His abdominal and back musculature is fair. CD has a dorsal round back and contractures of the hip flexors.

Therapy includes passive exercises; gait training with braces and crutches and with braces alone; and balance training in standing and walking. The physician recommended: (1) gait training out of braces with emphasis upon a high steppage gait to improve knee flexion and ankle dorsiflexion; (2) aggressive quadriceps stretching in the prone extended position; and (3) knee flexion reciprocating exercises.

Psychological status— Although it is difficult to assess the intellectual potential of a severely involved CP child, he is rated as a slow learner. CD's scores on standard achievement tests are one and two grades lower than his grade placement. His teacher expressed the opinion that poor vision, resulting from the incoordination of eye muscles, is a large contributing factor.

CD is the younger of two children and the only one at home since his sister recently married. In the neighborhood he plays with a group of about five boys and girls of mixed ages. CD's father is the regional executive of a voluntary health agency and his mother is a full-time homemaker. CD is a member of a bowling group for handicapped children which meets once a week throughout the year.

Physical education experience—CD spends most of his day in a wheelchair, but he can stand and walk slowly with his hips and knees partially flexed. His arm muscles are strong but involved with much involuntary movement. He is able to stoop slightly but cannot jump or skip. CD can throw or strike with very poor control and can kick when in a sitting position. His balance is poor while standing.

He must be held upright by a belt when using his crutches or walking between the parallel bars at school. At home, where there are rugs to fall on, he walks without this extra assistance. In therapy sessions he has done as many as 100 sit-ups.

CD receives no physical education in school, although he sometimes observes the regular sixth grade physical education classes. For the past six summers he has attended the Soroptimist Camp for crippled children, where he enjoys swimming. CD has participated also in swimming through the city recreation program. During the past year he was a regular member of a bowling group for crippled children. Since CD is well accepted socially, he should be scheduled to participate in regular physical education. Instruction should include safe and relaxed ways to fall, creative dance activities, and active throwing games in which bean or yarn bags are substituted for balls. With constant athetoid movements of the hands and arms, beanbags are much easier to handle than balls.

HI: Mild Spasticity

HI, a boy of about average size for his thirteen years, has moderate left spastic hemiplegia caused by trauma. It results in limited use of his left hand and a mild limp. He is a full-time member of one of the regular sixth grade classes, but comes daily to the special education wing of the school for physical therapy.

Medical report—HI had a blood clot on the brain at about five years of age. When it was surgically removed, a nerve connection was severed, causing the paralysis of the left extremities. HI is expecting a transplant of the tibialis anterior and tibialis posterior muscles to be inserted into the third cuneiform bone so that they can function as dorsiflexors of the foot.

The therapist reported the following physical characteristics: (1) left medial plantar fascia moderately tight; (2) left heel cord moderately tight; (3) left supinators moderately tight; (4) gross arm movements good; (5) left hand and fingers poor. Therapy includes active and assistive exercises, muscle education, and gait training with brace. HI wears a short double upright brace on his left leg. His muscle training is achieved through the use of weights, pulleys, and swinging rings for arm and hand development.

Psychological status—HI is classified within the average intelligence range. He is the middle child of three with sisters aged fifteen and eight. The father is a consulting engineer and his mother a full-time homemaker. In the neighborhood HI plays with a group of about seven boys of mixed ages. At home he is active and energetic, but overcritical of others. He tends to be quarrelsome and resents correction. He converses easily with strangers but remains distant.

Physical education experience—Although a shorter left leg forces HI to limp, he moves quickly. His running, however, is slower than that of the average boy of his age. When running backward, as in fielding a softball, he is awkward. He can squat, jump, and skip with average ability. His right arm provides the principal means of support when hanging from the rings, although he uses the left arm to some degree. He throws well, easily clearing the distance from center field to home plate. Because of the power in the right arm, he can bat, but he needs coaching to turn his batting stance to the left in order not to foul continually to the right. He angers easily, however, when corrected by classmates. HI's mother asserts that he is extremely competitive and seeks to excel in physical activity. At five years of age his skill at throwing the football won him tremendous praise. The boys with whom he now plays tease him about what he cannot do, which tends to anger him. The family is planning golf lessons for him, since they feel that this is a sport in which he might excel.

His past physical education experience includes participation with a regular class at school and active play in a neighborhood group. He has taken swimming lessons at the Young Men's Christian Association for two winters and attended the Lion's Club for crippled children last summer. His mother states that he becomes engrossed in all kinds of ball games, riding his bicycle, and playing chess, but when summer comes, swimming is his main concern. Since HI's major interest is active sports, he needs to discover activities other than swimming in which he can excel. His poor social relationships may stem partly from the realization that he cannot compete on an equal basis in team sports. He should be introduced to such one-arm sports as tennis, badminton, and bowling in which his disability is minimized. With proper instruction he can learn to compensate for his handicaps in team sports. The golf lessons sound promising.

AB: Athetosis and Spasticity

AB is a quiet, slender thirteen-year-old girl who moves about school in a wheelchair. A member of the intermediate special education class with sixth grade placement, she receives a half hour of physical therapy daily.

Medical report—AB has had cerebral palsy since birth. Contractures are present in the internal rotators and adductors of the hips, the knee flexors, and the ankle dorsiflexors. At age nine, AB was able to walk in braces from her car to the schoolroom. Inactivity and irregular therapy, however, resulted in severe contractures which now confine her to a wheelchair. She is presently involved in a program of active and passive exercises and is building arm strength through the use of weights and pulleys.

Psychological status—Intellectually AB ranks in the slow learner category with scores approximately three years below her grade placement.

Physical education experience—AB has engaged in no school physical education this year. At some previous time she attended the Soroptimist Camp for crippled children, where she participated in swimming and camping out. AB's only locomotion is by wheelchair. She has normal upper extremity flexibility but the athetoid movements affect motor coordination. Scoliosis is present, but does not appear to limit forward, backward, and sideward trunk movements. AB can throw, strike, or bat with poor control. Her sitting balance is satisfactory, but she cannot stand even with braces because of contractures at knees and hips. She can kick a large ball with fair skill from a seated position. AB could be asked to bring some of her records and help initiate a program of rhythmic activities. Folk and square dances could be learned by pairing ambulatory and wheelchair persons as partners. Successful, enjoyable experiences in physical education might help AB to regain a sense of purpose. She needs success in order to convince herself and others of her own worth.

Organizations

1. United Cerebral Palsy Associations, Inc., 66 East 34th Street, New York, New York 10016; or 50 West 57th Street, New York, New York 10019.

2. American Academy for Cerebral Palsy, University Hospital School, Iowa City, Iowa 52240. Founding members of the American Academy for Cerebral Palsy include many of the persons cited in this chapter: Carlson, Crothers, Deaver, Hohman, Perlstein, and Phelps. The Academy's main publication is *The Journal of Developmental Medicine and Child Neurology.*

3. National Committee for Multi-Handicapped Children, 339 14th Street, Niagra Falls, New York 14303.

4. National Society for Crippled Children and Adults, Inc., 2023 W. Ogden Ave., Chicago, Illinois 60612.

References

Cooper, Irving. *Involuntary Movement Disorders.* New York: Hoeber Medical Division, Harper and Row, 1969.

Finnie, Nancie R. *Handling the Young Cerebral Palsied Child at Home.* New York: Dutton, 1970.

Gillette, Harriet E. *Systems of Therapy in Cerebral Palsy.* Springfield, Illinois: Charles C Thomas, 1969.

Hellmuth, Jerome, ed. *Exceptional Infant.* Seattle, Washington: Special Child Publications, 1967.

Rusk, Howard A. *Rehabilitation Medicine.* St. Louis: C. V. Mosby Co., 1972.

Wolf, James M. *The Results of Treatment in Cerebral Palsy.* Springfield, Illinois: Charles C Thomas, 1969.

Periodicals

Developmental Medicine and Child Neurology. Published bimonthly by the Spastics International Medical Publications, 20-22 Mortimer St., London, W. I. Subscription details for North America are available from J. B. Lippincott Co., East Washington Square, Philadelphia, Pa. 19105.

Archives of Physical Medicine and Rehabilitation. Official Journal of American Congress of Rehabilitation Medicine and American Academy of Physical Medicine and Rehabilitation. Published monthly.

30 N. Michigan Ave., Chicago, Illinois 60602.

Current Problems in Pediatrics. Published monthly by Year Book Medical Publishers, Inc., 35 East Wacker Drive, Chicago, Illinois 60601.

UCP Crusader. Published bimonthly by the United Cerebral Palsy Associations, Inc.

Journal of Developmental Disabilities. Published quarterly. P.O. Box 8470, Gentilly Station, New Orleans, Louisiana 70182.

Autobiography, Biography, and Fiction

Ayrault, Evelyn West. *Take One Step.* Garden City, New York: Doubleday and Co., 1963.

Brown, Christy. *My Left Foot.* With a foreward and epilogue by Dr. Robert Collis, New York: Simon and Schuster, 1955.

Carlson, Earl Reinhold. *Born That Way.* New York: John Day Co., 1941.

Hoopes, G. Gertrude. *Out of the Running.* Springfield, Illinois: Charles C Thomas, 1939.

Jurgensen, Barbara. *Leaping Upon the Mountains.* Minneapolis: Augsburg Publications, 1960.

Killilea, Marie. *Karen.* Englewood Cliffs, New Jersey: Prentice-Hall, 1952.

Killilea, Marie. *Wren.* New York: Dodd, Mead and Co., 1954.

McKee, John D. *Two Legs to Stand On.* New York: Appleton-Century-Crofts, 1958.

Miers, Earl Schenck. *The Trouble Bush.* New York: Rand McNally, 1966.

Segal, Marilyn M. *Run Away, Little Girl.* New York: Random House, 1966.

Smoot, Gerald D. *I'm Handicapped for Life: The Story of an 18 year-old's Fight Against Cerebral Palsy.* New York: Vantage Press, 1958.

Thomassen, Rolf. *Beyond Today.* Minneapolis: Augsburg Publishing House, 1953.

21 Conditions That Result in Muscular Weakness

Figure 21.0. Box hockey is enjoyed by man with muscular dystrophy.

Many conditions have the same symptoms as cerebral palsy: (1) *muscular dystrophy;* (2) *muscular atrophy;* (3) *inflammatory diseases affecting motor behavior;* (4) *demyelinating diseases;* (5) *metabolic disorders of the nervous system;* and (6) *involuntary movement disorders.* The problem of contractures is universal whenever muscles weaken. Since the onset of muscular weakness is often slow and insidious, the physical educator may be the first to recognize deviations from normal strength and flexibility. No other teacher has the necessary background for recognizing movement abnormalities, nor does the average parent. It is important therefore that the physical educator be ever conscious of his role in screening for musculoskeletal problems, conferring with parents, and suggesting referrals to physicians.

Terminology

Widespread confusion exists concerning the difference between *dystrophy* and *atrophy.* Both words stem from the Greek *trophe,* meaning nourishment, and *trephein,* meaning to nourish. The difference in the two conditions, therefore, must be ascribed to their prefixes. The Greek prefix *a* means *without;* hence *atrophy* is defined as a wasting away because of nutritional deficits caused by disuse, disease, spinal cord injury, or interference with the nerve or blood supply. The Greek prefixes *hyp, hyph,* and *hypo,* all meaning *under* are used interchangeably with *a.* Thus atrophy and hypotrophy can be considered synonyms. The adjectives *atonic* and *hypotonic* describe the absence or decreased amount of tonus in atrophied muscles. The adjective *hypertonic* refers to the opposite extreme, that of excessive or more than normal tonus.

The Greek prefix *dys* means bad, painful, or difficult. Thus dystrophy is defined as a pro-gressive weakening of the muscle. A dystrophic muscle does not necessarily change in size; it may, however, atrophy or hypertrophy. The term *dystrophy* is applied almost always to the disease known as muscular dystrophy. In contrast, *atrophy* has multiple uses, referring to any body part which becomes progressively smaller as it *wastes away.*

Prior to reading this chapter, it is recommended that the anatomy of muscle tissue and the physiology of muscular contraction and relaxation be reviewed. Since so many muscular conditions are hereditary in nature, the unit may be enriched by a study of genetics and/or an outside speaker on this subject.

Muscular Dystrophy

The muscular dystrophies are a group of genetically determined diseases in which progressive muscular weakness can be attributed to pathological, biochemical, and electrical changes which occur in the muscle fibers. The specific causes of these changes remain unknown. Several different diseases have been identified since 1850, many of which are rare. The three muscular dystrophies having the highest incidence are Duchenne, Facioscapulohumeral, and Juvenile. Approximately 250,000 persons in the United States suffer from the muscular dystrophies. Of this number, 50,000 are presently confined to a wheelchair or bed. Most of the sufferers fall between the ages of three and thirteen and attend public school. Of these, few will reach adolescence and almost all will die before maturity. Specifically, one out of every 500 children in our schools will get or has muscular dystrophy. Boys are affected five or six times more often than girls.

Muscular dystrophy in itself is not fatal but the secondary complications of immobilization heighten the effects of respiratory disorders and heart disease. With the weakening of respiratory muscles and the reduction in vital capacity, the child may succumb to a simple respiratory infection. Dystrophic changes in cardiac muscles increase susceptibility to heart disease. The dilemma confronting the physical educator is how to increase and/or maintain cardiovascular fitness when muscle weakness makes running and other endurance type activities increasingly difficult. Breathing exercises and games are recommended.

Duchenne Muscular Dystrophy

The Duchenne type of muscular dystrophy is the most common and most severe. Its onset is usually before age three but symptoms may appear as late as ages ten or eleven. The victims are almost always boys. It is caused by a sex-linked trait which is transmitted through females to males. The sister of an affected male has a 50 percent chance of being a carrier and will pass the defective gene on to 50 percent of her sons. Muscular dystrophied victims themselves seldom live long enough to marry. Characteristics of Duchenne muscular dystrophy include:

1. Awkward side-to-side waddling gait.
2. Difficulty in running, tricycling, climbing stairs, and rising from chairs.
3. Tendency to fall frequently.
4. Peculiar way of rising from a fall. From a supine lying position, the child turns onto his face, puts hands and feet on the floor, and then climbs up his legs with his hands. This means of rising is called the *Gowers' sign.*
5. Lordosis.
6. Hypertrophy of calf muscles and occasionally of deltoid, infraspinatus, and lateral quadriceps.

This hypertrophy (sometimes called pseudohypertrophy) occurs when quantities of fat and connective tissue replace degenerating muscle fibers which progressively become smaller, fragment, and then disappear. The hypertrophy gives the mistaken impression of extremely well-developed healthy musculature. In actuality the muscles are quite weak.

The initial areas of muscular weakness, however, are the gluteals, abdominals, erector spinae of the back, and anterior tibials. The first three of these explain the characteristic lordosis and difficulty in rising while the last explains the frequent falls. Weakness of the anterior tibials results in a foot drop (pes equinovarus) which causes the child to trip over his own feet. Within seven to ten years after the initial onset of symptoms, contractures begin to form in the ankle, knee, and hip joints. Contractures of the Achilles' tendons force the child to walk on his toes and increase still further the incidence of falling. Between ages ten to fifteen most dystrophic children lose the capacity to walk, progressively spending more and more time in the wheelchair and/or bed. This enforced inactivity leads to severe distortions of the chest wall and kyphoscoliosis.

Facio-Scapular-Humeral Type

This is the commonest form of muscular dystrophy in adults. It affects both sexes equally. Symptoms generally do not appear until adolescence and often are not recognized until adulthood. The prognosis is good compared with that of the other dystrophies, and the sufferer lives until normal old age. The disease may arrest itself at any stage. Characteristics include:

1. Progressive weakness of the shoulder muscles beginning with the trapezius and pectoralis major and sequentially involving the biceps, triceps, deltoid, and erector spinae.
2. Progressive weakness of the muscles of the face, causing drooping cheeks, pouting lips, and the inability to close the eyes completely. The face takes on an im-

mobile quality since muscles lack the strength to express emotion.

3. Hip and thigh muscles are affected less often. When involvement does occur, it is manifested by a waddling side-to-side gait and the tendency to fall easily.

Juvenile or Limb Girdle Type

The juvenile type may occur at any time from age ten or after. The onset, however, is usually the second decade. Both sexes are affected equally. The earliest symptom is usually in raising the arms above shoulder level or awkwardness in climbing stairs. Weakness manifests itself initially in either the shoulder girdle muscles or the hip and thigh muscles, but eventually both the upper and lower extremities are involved. The muscle degeneration progresses slowly but relentlessly, and the life expectancy is shortened considerably. Death comes from respiratory or cardiac involvement or other secondary problems stemming from years of confinement to wheelchair or bed.

Implications for Physical Education

In the public schools, the physical educator most often encounters Duchenne multiple dystrophy. Until confined to a wheelchair, these children are entirely normal and should participate in regular physical education. They may fatigue more easily than their classmates, but specialists concur that they should be allowed to play as hard as they wish. Normal fatigue from vigorous physical activity is intrinsically good, and the dystrophic child should be withdrawn from a game only when he appears totally exhausted. Should this occur, several *normal* children who are also showing signs of exhaustion should be excused with him. At no time should the dystrophied child be sitting alone on the sidelines! It is hoped that full participation in games and athletics while the disease is in the early stages will enable the child to form close friends who will stick by him as he becomes increasingly helpless. It is imperative, therefore, that the dystrophied child and his friends receive instruction in some sedentary recreational activities which will carry over into his wheelchair years. Rifle shooting, dart throwing, archery, bowling, fishing, and other masculine-oriented individual sports are recommended. The parents may wish to build a rifle or archery range in their basement or backyard to attract neighborhood boys in for a visit as well as to provide recreation for their son. Unusual pets as snakes, skunks, and raccoons also have a way of attracting preadolescent boys. Swimming is recommended with emphasis upon developing powerful arm strokes to substitute for the increasing loss of strength in the legs.

The dystrophied child is learning to adjust to life in a wheelchair just when his peers are experiencing the joys of Little League baseball and other competitive sports. He is easily forgotten unless helped to develop skills like score keeping and umpiring which keep him a valued member of the group. The physical educator should not wait until crippling sets in to build such skills but should begin in the early grades to shape the dystrophied child's image, congratulating him on good visual acuity, knowledge of the rules, his decision-making skills, and other competencies requisite to score keeping and umpiring. Dystrophied children tend to have lowered motivation for achievement, a withdrawal of interests from the environment, emotional immaturity, and a low frustration tolerance. These traits are not surprising when one considers that the child suspects his prognosis, no matter how carefully guarded is the early impending death. Why should he study? Why should he consider different careers? Why should he care about dieting and personal appearance? Who wants to date him? The emphasis in his academic studies, physical education, and social learnings must be upon the present for he does not have a tomorrow.

Stages of Functional Ability

Daily exercise is believed to slow the incapacitating aspects of the disease. As long as the child is helped to stand upright a few minutes each day and to walk short distances, contractures do not appear. Once confined to the wheelchair, fitness seems to deteriorate rapidly. Stretching exercises become imperative at this point as do the breathing activities described in Chapter 17.

Eight stages of disability are delineated by the Muscular Dystrophy Associations of America, Inc. The fourth stage is the critical point at which the student can no longer push himself erect from a sitting position. He can, however, still walk if he is helped into a standing position. The tendency to push persons in the fourth stage into a wheelchair or bed existence creates a life of inactivity which hastens cardiorespiratory degeneration. The eight stages are

1. Ambulates with mild waddling gait and lordosis. Elevation activities adequate (climbs stairs and curbs without assistance).
2. Ambulates with moderate waddling gait and lordosis. Elevation activities deficient (needs support for curbs and stairs).
3. Ambulates with moderately severe waddling gait and lordosis. Cannot negotiate curbs or stairs, but can achieve erect posture from standard-height chair.
4. Ambulates with severe waddling gait and lordosis. Unable to rise from a standard-height chair.
5. Wheelchair independence. Good posture in the chair; can perform all activities of daily living from chair.
6. Wheelchair with dependence. Can roll

chair but needs assistance in bed and wheelchair activities.
7. Wheelchair with dependence and back support. Can roll the chair only a short distance, needs back support for good chair position.
8. Bed patient. Can do no activities of daily living without maximum assistance. [1]

Even in stage eight some time each day is planned for standing upright by use of a tilt table or appropriate braces. The child should attend regular public school and engage in adapted physical education as long as possible with emphasis upon the social values of individual and small group games, dance, and aquatics. In the later stages he may attend school only a small part of each day. Since he is not being educated for a future, he should be allowed to engage in those school activities which give the most pleasure and allow the greatest socialization. The following illustrative case study describes a child in the early stages of muscular dystrophy.

Case RS: Duchenne Muscular Dystrophy [2]

RS's walk is characterized by a marked lordosis, with weight carried on the balls of the feet, arms slightly abducted for balance, and head held erect. RS is nine years old and a member of a third grade section in the regular wing of the school. He comes to the special education wing daily for mathematics and for physical therapy.

Medical Report—There is hypertrophy of the

1. Reprinted with permission from the Muscular Dystrophy Associations of America, Inc., 27th Floor, 810 Seventh Ave., New York, New York.

2. Jane Spragens, "A Study of the Physical Education Needs and Interests of a Selected Group of Orthopedically Handicapped Children With Recommendations for Planning and Conducting Physical Activities," Unpublished Master of Arts Study, Texas Woman's University, 1964.

calf muscles, some shoulder involvement, winged scapulae, and a quadriceps weakness in addition to the hypertrophy of the gastroc-soleus group. The school physician has recommended a program of active exercise, muscle education, gait training, and hydrotherapy. RS has therapy sessions five days per week for thirty minutes each day with a group of three other boys. Four of these sessions are held in the pool and the other in individual activity.

Psychological and Social Status—Intellectually RS ranks in the average group. In the classroom RS is sometimes a leader and sometimes a follower. When working with others he seems to resent correction. His general temperament is outgoing and his emotional outlook quite healthy. When faced with a frustrating situation, however, he angers easily, saying, "I can't," or quits trying.

RS is the second of three boys in his family. His brothers are twenty-two and three years old. The father is a building contractor and the mother a homemaker.

Physical Education Experience—RS's mobility is adequate for daily activities. He can walk and run though somewhat more slowly than most of the boys in his class. He runs holding his head erect and swinging each leg out to the side as he moves it forward. He cannot squat or stoop well because of the difficulty of recovery from these positions. Arm movements are practically normal. He throws, catches, and bats with average skill and enjoys hanging and swinging in the flying rings. His kicking is limited because of only fair balance. In kickball a teammate kicks for him, and RS does his own running. He plays in the infield when his team is on the defense. School records indicate that RS participates in regular physical education classes. RS's mother indicates that she thought he needed more physical exercise. His teacher believes that he is carrying as full a schedule as is desirable for a child with progressive muscular dystrophy. While his program should be as active as possible, RS

should also be developing sedentary recreational interests for the future.

Muscular Dystrophy Association of America

Abbreviated MDAA, this association was founded in 1950. Now chapter affiliates exist in every major city. In the past two decades, since popular television and movie star Jerry Lewis has begun conducting annual telethons to raise money for MD, the disease has become widely known. The organization extends services also to persons with such related disorders as myositis, amyotrophic lateral sclerosis, peroneal muscular atrophy, infantile spinal muscular atrophy, benign congenital hypotonia, juvenile spinal muscular atrophy, and spinal muscular atrophy of adults.

Muscular Atrophy

Conditions of progressive muscular atrophy include the Werdnig-Hoffman Disease, Oppenheim's Disease, Thomsen's Disease, and Charcot-Marie-Tooth Disease. These conditions are sometimes confused with muscular dystrophy but are much less common. The implications for physical education are similar to those already stated. The muscular atrophies are all neurological disorders in which the lower motor neuron cell bodies degenerate, thus failing to transmit impulses through the motor nerve fibers which ordinarily innervate the muscles. Lesions of the lower motor neurons result in the following characteristics:

1. *Paralysis.* Always flaccid and hypotonic, the extent of paralysis depends upon the number of cell bodies destroyed.
2. *Atrophy.* The degree depends upon the number of cell bodies destroyed.
3. *Fasciculations.* These are irregular fine or coarse twitchings of parts of muscles, appearing irregularly and unassociated with movement of the affected muscle at

the joint. They can be seen with the naked eye. They are not usually present in acute disease of the anterior horn cells as in poliomyelitis.

4. *Fibrillations.* These are similar to fasciculations but cannot be seen through the skin. They are recorded electromyographically.
5. *Loss of reflexes* occurring because of interruption of the reflex arc.
6. *Absence of sensory disturbances.*

Inflammatory Diseases

Poliomyelitis and *polymyositis* are two conditions which produce muscle weakness. In poliomyelitis the inflammation affects the motor cells in the spinal cord which, in turn, affects the muscles whereas in polymyositis the inflammation occurs in the muscle tissue itself. The Greek prefix *polio* means gray and refers to the fact that nerve cell bodies are gray matter. The Greek prefix *poly* means many and refers to the fact that many muscles are inflamed simultaneously.

Poliomyelitis

In 1915-1917, 1944, and again in 1952 major epidemics of poliomyelitis left thousands of persons paralyzed. The most famous of these was Franklin D. Roosevelt who, in 1938, organized the National Foundation for Infantile Paralysis and the memorable March of Dimes campaigns. Until the late 1950s when the Salk vaccine was introduced, polio was the leading crippler of children in the United States. Now most of these victims have graduated from high school or college, and the physical educator seldom sees the residual paralysis left by polio.

Polio is caused by a virus which attacks the motor cells in the anterior horn of the spinal cord. Three stages are detectable in the course of the disease: (1) *acute,* which lasts a week to ten days, and is characterized by sore throat, fever, nausea, vomiting, and muscle stiffness; (2) *convalescent,* which lasts anywhere from a few weeks to several months, during which muscles improve in function or return to normal depending upon the extent of damage, and (3) *chronic,* which begins about eighteen months after the onset of the disease and continues for years. Tendon transplants and arthrodesis are common during the chronic stage. Approximately 6 percent of the persons who contract polio die, 14 percent have severe paralysis, 30 percent suffer mild after effects, and 50 percent recover completely.

Polymyositis

The inflammation of several muscles simultaneously may occur in either children or adults. In children it is less common than muscular dystrophy, but in adults the incidence is about equal. Of unknown etiology, polymyositis affects twice as many females as males. Persons with acute polymyositis develop high fever, severe muscular weakness, and muscular pain. They may die in a few days or months. Persons with the chronic form manifest a slow progresssive weakening of the muscles with symptoms similar to those of muscular dystrophy. ACTH and the corticosteroids have greatly improved the treatment, management, and prognosis.

Demyelinating Diseases

Myelin is the thick innermost covering of nerve fibers which gives nerves their white color.

Demyelination, the disintegration of the myelin covers, occurs in such diseases as multiple sclerosis and amyotrophic lateral sclerosis (ALS). Lou Gehrig, the New York Yankees baseball player, was a victim of ALS.

Multiple Sclerosis

Approximately 500,000 persons in the United States have *multiple sclerosis,* a progressive neurological disorder which ends in total incapacitation and death. Its name is derived from the Greek word *sklerosis* which means hardening and refers to the scar tissue which replaces the disintegrating myelin. The resulting lesions throughout the white matter of the brain and spinal cord vary from the size of a pinpoint to more than 1 centimeter in diameter. The cause of the demyelination is unknown.

Since multiple sclerosis characteristically affects persons between the ages of twenty and forty, the college physical educator may be called upon for counsel. Early symptoms of demyelination include numbness, general weakness, partial or incomplete paralysis, staggering, slurring of speech, and double vision. The disease is characterized by periods of relative incapacitation followed capriciously by periods of remission.

The following description of multiple sclerosis over an eight year period was written by Sherry Rogers, who was stricken with MS while a junior physical education major in college.

Now with the diagnosis starts the story of the most demanding years of my life. The pain I experienced was tremendous. It was more localized now. It was mostly on my right side and the lower part of my back, especially the sciatic nerve of my right leg.

After about a month of getting one or two bottles of ACTH intervenously every day, I could see some improvement. Then the physician started me on cold showers to stimulate my circulation. All of this and my prayers worked for me. Physical therapy, mainly to exercise my legs, was given me also. I had not moved much of my body for about a year, and the therapy was designed to stimulate the muscles. I continued to progressively get better control of myself.

Then blindness, seeing only a narrow vision of light, appeared, lasting for about three weeks. Seeing double lasted for about another month. Then my vision progressively got better until it seems normal at present except that I now need glasses to read or do any close work.

I went to Gonzales Warm Springs for a short time, where I lost my voice for a while. I was told that the only thing to do for my disease was to rest

and walk very much. Because of this, I rest each day for about an hour or more. I walk some distance each day depending upon how I feel.

The effects of multiple sclerosis on me can best be described as weakening. There are days when I need crutches to walk and other days when I feel fine and can walk without any assistance. The muscle groups affected the most were all of the voluntary muscles of my right side. The most noticeable to me has been my right hand, which feels like it is asleep all of the time. I again was fortunate because I am left handed. Endurance was the most noticeable change in fitness. I have to rest after any strenuous exercise. My strength is about one-fourth of what it used to be before I was stricken. My posture has been very much affected. I bend forward from my waist some days when I stand. This is more apparent on some days than others depending upon my strength. I was paralyzed for about a year. Gradually I improved until now I walk almost normally.

My handwriting is not as legible as it was, and there are times when MS recurs slightly and affects portions of my right side. This sometimes lasts for days but always returns to what is now normal for me.

In spite of my handicap, I returned to college and received my Bachelor of Science degree in physical education in the spring of 1972 and was presented the most representative woman physical education major award from Delta Psi Kappa. All of this has impressed upon me the fact that the bodies of men are truly temples of God and should be cared for as such. If there is one thing I could tell you it is that nothing is certain in this life and it is not to be taken for granted. Make certain that you live to the fullest because you never know what the future holds for you. [3]

The value of exercise for persons with multiple sclerosis has not been proven. Some physicians feel that exercise is contraindicated and others recommend complete bed rest. Most seem to believe, however, that bed rest leads to secondary complications and hence advocate breathing exercises, gait retraining, gross coordination activities, stretching exercises, and hydrotherapy.

Swimming is recommended. Therapeutic exercises such as walking between two parallel bars are easier in water than on land. The am-

3. Sherry Rogers, RR3, Box 83C, Victoria, Texas 77901.

bulatory patient may sit in a large whirlpool and perform such movements as hip flexion, hip abduction, knee flexion, knee extension, ankle dorsiflexion, ankle eversion, and trunk flexion. The Hubbard tank should be used for nonambulatory patients. In each setting the water temperature should not exceed body temperature (92° to 96°F) since fatigue occurs sooner in warm water than moderate.

The stationary bicycle is recommended. Gait retraining itself may involve the following progression: (1) standing, (2) walking between two parallel bars, (3) walker, (4) quad canes, and (5) a regular cane. Full-length mirrors are used whenever possible. Of all the locomotor activities, ascending stairs is perhaps the most difficult because of the characteristic quadriceps weakness and impairment of balance. Standing in front of stall bars and slowly touching each rung with the toes, while lifting the foot as high as possible, is an ameliorative exercise.

In the most advanced stages of multiple sclerosis, loss of bladder or bowel control occurs as well as difficulties of speech and swallowing. Progressively severe intention tremors interfere with writing, using eating utensils, and motor tasks.

The prognosis for multiple sclerosis varies. Many patients have long periods of remission during which their lives are essentially normal. James Rodger,[4] fifty-two years old when he wrote his autobiography, describes the progress of his MS over twenty years. It was not until the thirteenth year after initial diagnosis that he was confined to a wheelchair. His schedule in a rest home at that time included:

5:30—Rise
6:30—Mass
7:15—Breakfast
8:30—Passive exercises
9:00—Whirlpool every other day
10:00—Rest
11:00—Dinner—Freetime
2:00—Resistive exercises
3:00—Stand in specially designed appliance
4:00—Rest
5:00—Supper
6:00—10:30 Recreation

Rodger makes the following statement about his exercise program:

So far I have had over 600 whirlpools for which I am grateful because they relax me and reduce the spasticity in my legs. I can't enjoy the Resistive Exercise though. They are killing, really, especially when they involve my right arm and leg. As for the standing—it gives me a thrill to be able to stand for one hour each day—even if I am secured to a standing table.

Parkinsonism

The group of syndromes which are characterized by rigidity, tremor, and/or bradykinesia (extreme slowness of movement) is known as Parkinsonism. Once considered a specific disease, Parkinsonism is now used as a broad category which encompasses involuntary movement disorders of a progressively degenerative nature. Among the most common varieties of Parkinsonism are (1) idiopathic paralysis agitans, called Parkinson's Disease, (2) post-encephalitic Parkinsonism, and (3) arteriosclerotic Parkinsonism. The idiopathic variety which appears in middle age derives its name from James Parkinson who wrote the first monograph on this disease in 1817. By the 1920s various forms of encephalitis, including the influenza epidemic of 1918, were associated with the onset of rigidity, tremor, and/or bradykinesia. In 1929 an arteriosclerotic Parkinsonism was described. In each of these syndromes the site of the lesion is the basal ganglia although the specific etiologies vary. The physical educator should be able to recognize and cope with the following Parkinsonian characteristics: (1) rigidity; (2) gait abnormalities; and (3) postural tremors.

4. James Rodger, *The Silent One* (Breckenridge, North Dakota: St. Frances Home, 1965), p. 53.

Rigidity

Rigidity, or the sensation of muscle stiffness, is the most common abnormality in Parkinsonism. Like spasticity, it is characterized by hypertonus or chronic shortening of muscles. It is differentiated from spasticity, however, by the absence of clonus, deep muscle reflexes, and a pathological plantar response.

The onset of Parkinsonian rigidity is enigmatic and slow. The loss of normal arm swinging movements in ambulation is an early sign. As rigidity progresses, the flexor muscles become more hypertonic than the extensor muscles. The result is a *flexor posture* which resembles a modified fetal position. When the facial muscles are affected by rigidity, the face takes on a staring, masklike, expressionless characteristic. In addition to producing a flexion posture, rigidity compromises balance. Whereas the normal person automatically makes many postural adjustments which prevent falling, the person with rigidity cannot move fast enough to make such adjustments. Moreover, once he falls, he lacks the flexibility to rise of his own volition.

As rigidity progresses, all voluntary movements become increasingly difficult. It becomes impossible to execute simultaneously two motor tasks like speaking on the telephone and taking notes. Yet under periods of extreme stress, as in automobile accidents, persons with Parkinsonism have been known to move normally for a few minutes before returning to an immobile state. Likewise they often respond normally to a ball thrown unexpectedly toward them, either catching it or raising an arm to protect themselves from being hit. The major problem is the initiation of voluntary movements. In advanced stages, the patient must concentrate totally upon movements normally taken for granted: rising from a chair, walking across the room, or turning a doorknob. This absorption with daily living activities and resulting lack of awareness of persons and things give the impression of a growing mental impairment. In reality, however, the intellectual processes remain intact.

Gait Abnormalities

Gait abnormalities in Parkinsonism are attributed primarily to rigidity and to abnormal labyrinthine righting reflexes. The earliest deviation from a normal walking pattern is the tendency to drag one leg and/or to scuff the toes of one foot. This abnormality is caused by the rigidity of the flexors and the failure of the antagonists to be stretched fully which in turn results in shortened steps. The person who walks with tiny steps is said to have the gait known as *marche a petits pas*.

As rigidity increases and the flexors become progressively shorter, the center of gravity shifts forward, causing the head and chest to lead in walking. To compensate for this abnormal flexion posture, the velocity of the tiny steps increases until the person is actually running. This is called a *festinating gait* or *festination*. It is characteristic of advanced Parkinsonism. Interestingly enough, festination makes it easier to climb stairs than to walk on a normal terrain. *Retropulsion* is another gait abnormality in advanced Parkinsonism. It is the tendency to fall backward or sideward and/or to take a short series of backward steps. Retropulsion occurs most often when a person is trying to stand still or to rise from a chair.

Postural Tremors

In its early stages this tremor often begins with the rhythmic beating of a singe finger. Over the years the tremor increases in intensity, spreading to involve the more proximal parts of the extremities. First one side of the body is involved and then the other. In its severest manifestations, the tremor may spread to head, neck, face, and chin. In a state of absolute rest, as in sleep, the Parkinsonian tremor disappears. During waking hours, it is constantly present in about one-third and ceases on voluntary motion in the other two-thirds of the victims. The Parkinsonian tremor, which occurs in antagonistic muscles, is increased by emotional duress, pain, psychologic trauma, and illness. It has a rhythm of 4 to 8 per second and can be recorded electromyographically.

Prognosis

At this time, no cure is known for Parkinsonism. Persons with symptoms of rigidity, tremors, and/or bradykinesia should be kept physically active as long as possible with special emphasis given to gait retraining, neuromuscular relaxation, and gentle stretching exercises. Massage, passive motion exercises, and hydrotherapy help to relieve rigidity. Swimming, rhythmic spontaneous dance movements, and such exercise systems as yoga and Tai Chi are recommended.

In recent years the prognosis has been improved greatly. The major breakthrough occurred in 1960 when it was observed that the brains of persons dying of Parkinsonism had grossly reduced amounts of *dopamine* and *5-hydroxytryptamine* in the striatum. This led to the use of a drug called *L-dopa* which has had miraclelike results in alleviating the problems of Parkinsonism. L-dopa, like many drugs, has numerous side effects, some of which are manifested in movement and hence should be understood by the physical educator. Barbeau, et al., list forty-seven dyskinesias induced by L-dopa.[5] Moreover L-dopa seems to provoke agitation, restlessness, and impulsive, aggressive behavior on the part of about 25 percent of its users.

Few physical educators have reported working with persons debilitated by the conditions described in this chapter. Medical references extol the efficacy of physical therapy and ignore the possible values of a comprehensive program of physical education and recreation. The resulting paucity of published materials reflects the great need for physical educators to seek out crippled children and adults whose lives are devoid of play. The handicapped themselves tend to believe that the social values of physical education far outweigh other benefits. In *Stigma: The Experience of Disability,* written by twelve persons with muscular dystrophy, polio, and other disabilities, the essential loneliness of the handicapped child is emphasized.[6] No amount of physical therapy can substitute for adapted physical education and a caring teacher who creates opportunities for integrating the handicapped into the recreational activities of their peers.

5. A. Barbeau et al., "A Proposed Classification of Dopa-Induced Dyskinesias," *L—Dopa and Parkinsonism* (Philadelphia: F. A. Davis Company, 1970), pp. 118-121.

6. Paul Hunt, ed., *Stigma—The Experience of Disability* (London: Geoffrey Chapman, 1966).

Organizations

1. Muscular Dystrophy Association of America, Inc., 27th Floor, 810 Seventh Ave., New York, New York or 1790 Broadway, New York, New York 10019.
2. National Multiple Sclerosis Society, 257 Park Avenue South, New York, New York 10010.
3. National Institute of Neurological Diseases and Blindness (NINDB), U. S. Public Health Service.

References

Cooper, Irving. *Involuntary Movement Disorders*. New York: Hoeber, 1969.

Dubpwotz, Victor. *The Floppy Infant: Amyotonia Congenita*. London: Spastics International Medical Publication in association with Heinemann, 1969.

Ducroquet, Robert. *Walking and Limping—A Study of Normal and Pathological Walking*. Philadelphia: Lippincott, 1968.

McAlpine, Douglas. *Multiple Sclerosis: A Reappraisal*. 2nd. ed. Baltimore: Williams and Wilkins, 1972.

Millar, J. H. D. *Multiple Sclerosis, a Disease Acquired in Childhood*. Springfield, Illinois: Charles C Thomas, 1971.

Rose, Augustus. *Mechanisms of Demyelination*. New York: Blakiston Division, McGraw-Hill, 1963.

Salter, Robert. *Textbook of Disorders and Injuries of the Musculo-Skeletal System*. Baltimore: Williams and Wilkins, 1970.

Swaiman, Kenneth, and Wright, Francis. *Neuromuscular Diseases of Infancy and Childhood*. Springfield, Illinois: Charles C Thomas, 1970.

Vinken, P. J., and Bruyn, G. W., eds. *Multiple Sclerosis and Other Demyelinating Diseases*. New York: American Elsevier Publishing Co., 1970.

Autobiography, Biography, and Fiction

Bourke-White, Margaret. *Portrait of Myself*. New York: Simon and Schuster, 1963.

Greenblatt, M. H. *Multiple Sclerosis and Me*. Springfield, Illinois: Charles C Thomas, 1972.

Hunt, Paul, ed. *Stigma: The Experience of Disability*. London: Geoffrey Chapman, 1966.

Jonez, Hinton D. *My Fight to Conquer Multiple Sclerosis*. New York: Julian Messner, 1952.

Neville, Joan. *So Briefly My Son*. London: Hutchinson and Co., 1962.

Rodger, James. *The Silent One*. Breckenridge, North Dakota: St. Francis Home, 1965.

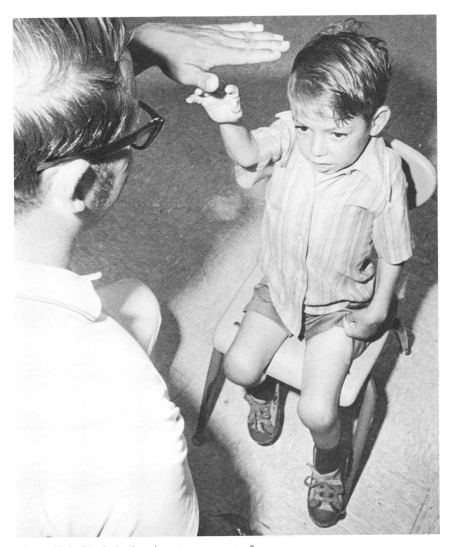

Figure 22.0. Physical education stresses range of motion exercises for the arthritic child.

Over twelve million Americans suffer from some form of arthritis and other rheumatic diseases. The terms *rheumatism* and *arthritis* are sometimes used synonymously, but technically they are separate entities. Rheumatism refers to a whole group of disorders affecting muscles and joints. It includes all forms of arthritis, myositis, myalgia, bursitis, fibromyositis, and other conditions characterized by soreness, stiffness and pain in joints and associated structures. Arthritis means, literally, inflammation of the joints. Rheumatoid arthritis is also completely different from rheumatic fever although a side effect of the latter.

Over 100 causes of joint inflammation have been identified, but the majority of cases fall within seven major categories: (1) rheumatoid arthritis; (2) degenerative joint disease (osteo-arthritis); (3) nonarticular rheumatism, including those of psychogenic origin; (4) arthritis resulting from known infectious agents; (5) arthritis resulting from fractures, torn ligaments, and abnormal joint stresses and/or traumas; (6) arthritis resulting from rheumatic fever; and (7) gout. The first three of these seven categories account for two-thirds of all arthritis. Rheumatoid arthritis, which affects 30 to 40 percent of all cases, may strike at any age. Degenerative joint disease, which accounts for 25 to 30 percent, is a natural outcome of aging. Nonarticular rheumatism, which afflicts 10 to 20 percent of the cases, is primarily an adult problem of psychogenic origin. It appears in the wake of an unusually stressful situation with which the person is coping poorly.

Not only is rheumatoid arthritis the nation's number one crippler, but it is the type which is found most often in school age children. Approximately 30,000 children and adolescents in the United States suffer from rheumatic arthritis, with 16,000 a year requiring medical care. This discussion is limited, therefore, to rheumatoid arthritis as it may affect students enrolled in school physical education.

Juvenile Rheumatoid Arthritis

The average age of onset is six years, with two peaks of incidence occurring between ages two and four and between ages eight and eleven. Rheumatoid arthritis affects three to five times as many girls as boys. The specific etiology is generally unknown. Because young children seldom complain of pain, a slight limp is often the only manifestation of the disease.

Mode of Onset
The onset of juvenile rheumatoid arthritis is capricious, sometimes affecting only one joint (monarticular disease) and other times involving several joints (polyarthritis). In about

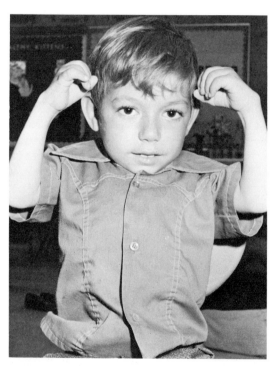

Figure 22.1. Arthritic pupil demonstrating his best upward reach.

30 percent of the initial episodes, only one joint, usually the knee, is involved but within a few weeks or months many more joints may swell. The onset of arthritis may be sudden, characterized by severe pain, or progressive with symptoms appearing almost imperceptibly over a long period of time. In the latter situation, joint pain is not a major problem.

Rheumatic arthritis may be *systemic*, affecting the entire body, or *peripheral*, affecting only the joints. When the disease is systemic, the joint inflammation is accompanied by such symptoms as fever, rash, malaise, pallor, enlargement of lymph nodes, enlargement of liver and/or spleen, and pericarditis. Systemic rheumatic arthritis in children is known as *Still's Disease,* deriving its name from George F. Still, a London physician who first described the condition in 1896.

Description of Inflamed Joints

Examination of affected joints reveals the following characteristics: (1) swelling, (2) heat, (3) redness, (4) tenderness, (5) limitation of motion, (6) crepitation (sounds when joints are moved), and (7) muscular atrophy. Tenderness to palpation is common, while the presence of pain is variable. Acute episodes of intense pain have been known to last from one or two days to several weeks, but generally pain occurs only with motion or not at all.

Knee—The knee is involved more often than other joints, causing a slight limp as the child walks. The characteristic swelling gives the appearance of knock-knees. The quadriceps femoris muscle group is the first to atrophy since swelling makes extension difficult or impossible. Knee flexion deteriorates from its normal range of 120 degrees to 80 or 90 degrees. Flexion contracture usually develops.

Ankle—Involvement of the ankle joint results in a ducklike, flat-footed gait similar to that of the toddler. Muscles of the lower leg tend to atrophy, and the Achilles tendon becomes excessively tight. Limitation of motion and pain occur most often in dorsiflexion.

Foot—Swelling within the joints of the foot makes wearing shoes uncomfortable. Characteristic arthritic defects are pronation, flat-foot, valgus of the calcaneous, and a cock-up position of the metatarsal phalangeal joints. Later manifestations are muscular rigidity because of flattening of the longitudinal arch, peroneal muscular spasm resulting from talonavicular joint involvement, and a flattening of the entire posterior foot. The cock-up toe position may eventually lead to a cavus deformity.

Wrist—Extension is limited by a combination of synovial involvement, tenosynovitis of associated tendon sheaths, muscular atrophy, and weakness. A common late manifestation is *ankylosis*. This is an abnormal union of bones whose surfaces come into contact because the interjacent cartilages have been destroyed. In ankylosis of the wrist, the carpals fuse, the joint space within the wrist is reduced, and cystic changes occur within the bones themselves. Swelling and tenderness characterize the radial side of the wrist.

Hand—Normal grip strength is lessened by the combination of muscular atrophy, contracture, and pain on motion. The interosseus, thenar, and hypothenar muscle groups all tend to atrophy. Flexion contractures occur primarily in the proximal interphalangeal joints.

Shoulder—Atrophy of the deltoid muscle, a shoulder drop, and/or deformities in the head and neck of the humerus are characteristic. Limitation of abduction is greater than that of flexion and extension.

Elbow—Swelling is most noticeable on the extensor surface, medial and lateral to the olecranon. Functional limitation of movement occurs rather quickly followed in severe cases by ankylosis.

Hip—Over one-third of the children favor an affected extremity. All ranges of movement are limited, but the flexion contracture is most troublesome. The gluteal muscles tend to atrophy. Fibrous ankylosis is a later manifestation. Osteoporosis and degenerative changes in the acetabulum sometimes occur. Observations of the following traits suggests that arthritis of the hip joint is present: (1) limp in which the pelvis tilts away from the involved hip because of weakness in the hip abductors (2) positive Frendelenburg test (see Chapter 10); (3) reduction in the posterior swing of the thigh during walking; (4) presence of lordosis; and (5) inequality of leg length. The child may require crutches during the period of acute inflammation.

Spinal Column—Juvenile rheumatoid arthritis tends to limit motion in the cervical spine. There may be spasms of the upper trapezius muscle and local tenderness along the spine. The thoracic and lumbar spine are seldom involved. In young males a form of rheumatoid arthritis, classified as *rheumatoid spondylitis,* affects the posterior intervertebral articulations, causing pain and stiffness in the back. This condition is also called *Marie-Strumpell Disease* in recognition of two independent investigators who described it in 1897-1898. It usually originates in the sacroiliac joints and extends upward, causing a trunk flexion deformity which resembles kyphosis. Sequentially the vertebral bodies atrophy, the longitudinal ligaments become calcified, the pectoral muscles shorten, and the rib cage is compressed and rigid, causing deep breathing to be difficult. Hyperextension braces are often prescribed for victims of Marie-Strumpell Disease.

Course of the Disease and Prognosis

In spite of enlargement of the liver and spleen, pericarditis, and other side effects, rheumatoid arthritis is rarely fatal. It does cause severe crippling in about 25 percent of

Figure 22.2. Permanent crippling in arthritis is decreased by daily physical exercise.

the cases and mild to moderate crippling in 30 percent. Complete functional recovery is reported in from 30.1 to 77.4 percent of the samples studied by nine different physicians.[1]

The physical educator is likely to see the child only when his disease is in remission. It is important, however, to understand the wide spectrum of disease patterns which may occur. When the disease affects the entire body, the period of acute illness lasts from one week to several months. During this time the child may be confined to home with his education guided by an itinerant teacher; he requires frequent rest periods and daily physical therapy treatments. When significant reduction of joint swelling is evident and other symptoms disappear, the disease is said to be in partial or total remission. Unfortunately periods of remission are interspersed with weeks of acute illness and maximum joint involvement; the course of the disease continues in this way for an unpredictable duration. About one-half of the sufferers are afflicted with recurrences of joint swelling for an average period of three years. For the other half, the active periods alternate with remissions for a much longer duration. Permanent crippling is decreased by daily physical exercise.

1. Earl J. Brewer, Jr., *Juvenile Rheumatoid Arthritis* (Philadelphia: W. B. Saunders, 1970), p. 44.

Therapeutic Exercise

The purposes of therapeutic exercise for the child with rheumatoid arthritis are (1) relief of pain and spasm, (2) prevention of flexion contractures and other deformities, (3) maintenance of normal ranges of motion for each joint, and (4) maintenance of strength, particularly in the extensor muscles. *Daily exercise* is perhaps more important in rheumatoid arthritis than any other disability. It must begin as soon as the acute inflammation starts to subside. At this time, even gentle passive movement may be painful, but every day of inactivity increases joint stiffness and the probability of permanent deformity. The physical educator and/or physical therapist should work with the parents in establishing a home exercise program. In addition, the child should participate in a school physical education program adapted to his needs.

Nature of the Exercise

The deformities which develop in rheumatoid arthritis bear out the following kinesiological facts: (1) flexors are stronger than extensors; (2) adductors are stronger than abductors; and (3) external rotators and supinators are stronger than internal rotators and pronators. It is essential, therefore, that the physical educator plan exercise sequences which will strengthen the extensors, the abductors, the internal rotators, and the pronators. Most authorities agree that all flexion exercises are contraindicated. The activities of daily living provide adequate flexion, and there is no danger that the joints will stiffen in inflexion.

Figure 22.4. First half of log roll demands all out effort.

Figure 22.5. Execution of log roll shows characteristic flexion.

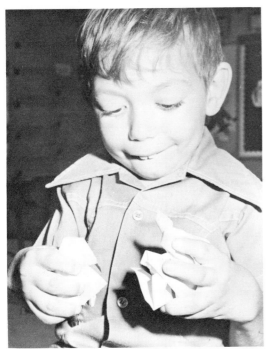

Figure 22.3. Swollen fingers and hands require special attention.

In the early stages of remission most of the exercises should be performed in a lying position to minimize the pull of gravity. When exercise tolerance is built up sufficiently, activities in a sitting position can be initiated. Riding a bicycle or tricycle affords a means of transportation as well as good exercise. Sitting for long periods of time, however, is contraindicated since it results in stiffness. The child may need guidance also in correct placement of the fingers in rising from a chair or bed. Flexing the fingers and pressing on the back of them should not be permitted since it increases both flexion and ulnar deviation. Another practice which should be eliminated is sitting with the arms crossed over the chest. Neither should he be allowed to rub aching joints.

Some children such as the eight-year-old boy depicted in Figure 22.6 are left so crippled that they cannot walk. Those who can ambulate usually require some kind of gait reeducation with emphasis upon the heel-to-toe transfer of weight and the maintenance of good posture. Severe foot deformitites make the selection of flat-heeled shoes with ample toe room especially important. The gait of the severely involved arthritic child is slow and halting. He has difficulty ascending and descending steps. Any accidental bumping or pushing in the hallway or while standing in lines is especially painful. Older pupils who change rooms should be released from each class early so that they can get to the next location before the bustle of activity begins. Occasionally their schedule of courses must be adjusted so that all classrooms are on the same floor and/or in close proximity.

Occasionally the physician may prescribe mild, moist heat as a preliminary to exercise. This is accomplished by immersing the extremities in warm (92 to 102°) or hot (102 to 110°) water or by using compresses for a period of twenty to thirty minutes. Heat should not be applied longer than thirty minutes.

Figure 22.6. Cortisone and other drugs used in arthritis tend to inhibit normal growth. This eight-year-old boy is so crippled that he uses a tricycle in lieu of walking.

Range of Motion

The physical educator should know the normal range of motion in degrees for each joint and be proficient in the use of the goniometer. The number of degrees through which each body part can move is recorded and serves as an index against which progess can be measured. Each body part, even the individual fingers and toes, should be taken through its full range of motion two or three times daily.

Physical Education

The following activities are contraindicated because of their trauma to the joints:

1. All jumping activities, including jump rope and trampoline work.

2. Activities in which falls might be frequent as roller skating, skiing, and gymnastics.
3. Contact sports, particularly football, soccer, and volleyball.
4. Hopping, leaping, and movement exploration activities in which the body leaves the floor.
5. Diving
6. Horseback riding.

During periods of remission the child who can participate in an activity *without pain* should be allowed, but not forced, to do so. Because of his weeks and/or months of enforced rest during acute attacks, his circulorespiratory endurance is likely to be subaverage. Hence he will need more frequent rest periods than his peers.

Swimming and creative or modern dance are among the best physical education activities. The front crawl and other strokes which emphasize extension are especially recommended. Water must be maintained at as warm a temperature as is feasible for other swimmers. Creative dance also stresses extension in its many stretching techniques and affords opportunities for learning to relate to others. Group choreography and performance can provide as many of these positive experiences as the team sports which are denied arthritic youngsters. Quiet recreational games include croquet, ring or ball tossing, miniature golf, horseshoes, shuffleboard, and pool. Throwing activities are better than striking and catching ones.

Other Factors

Cortisone and its derivatives (steroids) appear to be the most effective medications at this time. Unfortunately one of their major side effects is the inhibition of normal growth, causing the child to look several years younger than he really is. Alterations in body growth occur as the direct result of severe rheumatoid arthritis. This stunting of growth, coupled with the overprotection of parents, may contribute to serious problems in peer adjustment.

Changes in weather are known to correlate with arthritic flare-ups. Attacks seem to occur most often prior to cold rain or snowfall.

Morning stiffness is characteristic of the arthritic child as well as of the adult. It may be so severe that the child cannot rise from the bed alone.

Any prolonged inactivity such as an afternoon nap or simply sitting in the classroom for an hour results in a return of this stiffness. It can be relieved by a few minutes of moving about and/or a warm bath.

Organizations

1. The Arthritis Foundation, 1212 Avenue of the Americas, New York, New York 10036. Publishes *Bulletin on the Rheumatic Diseases*.

References

Brewer, Earl J. *Juvenile Rheumatoid Arthritis.* Philadelphia: W. B. Saunders, 1970.

Covalt, Nila Kirkpatrick. *Bed Exercise for Convalescent Patients.* Springfield, Illinois: Charles C Thomas, 1968.

Hollander, J. L. *Arthritis and Allied Conditions.* 7th edition. Philadelphia: Lea and Febiger, 1966.

Lowman, Edward W. *Arthritis, General Principles, Physical Medicine, Rehabilitation.* Boston: Little, 1959.

Talbott, J. H., and Ferrandis, R. M. *Collagen Diseases.* New York: Grune and Stratton, 1956.

Periodicals

Annals of the Rheumatic Diseases. A Journal of Clinical Rheumatic and Connective Tissue Research. Published by the Arthritis and Rheumatism Council for Research in Great Britain and the Common Wealth, B.M.A. House, Tavistock Square, London WC1H 9JR.

Arthritis and Rheumatism. Official Journal of the American Rheumatism Association Section of The Arthritis Foundation, 1212 Avenue of the Americas, New York, New York 10036. Published by the Medical Department, Harper and Row.

Bulletin On the Rheumatic Diseases. Published by The Arthritis Foundation, 1212 Avenue of the Americas, New York, New York 10036.

Figure 23.0. Many sports activities are appropriate for the pupil with cardiovascular problems.

Table 36 *Cardiovascular Disorders and Percentage of Deaths*

Disorder	Percentage of all cardiovascular deaths
Coronary artery disease	56
Stroke	20
Hypertension	7
Myocardial degeneration	5
General arteriosclerosis	4
Rheumatic fever	2
Other cardiovascular diseases	5

Over 20 million Americans of all ages have some form of cardiovascular disease. Moreover, the incidence of death from cardiovascular disease in the United States is higher than in any other country in the world. Specifically, coronary artery disease in the United States accounts for 16 percent of all deaths between ages twenty-five and thirty-five; 33 percent between ages thirty-five and forty-five; 45 percent between ages forty-five and fifty-five; 53 percent between fifty-five and sixty-five, and 70 percent of all deaths in persons over sixty-five years of age. Table 36 shows the percentage of deaths caused by the various cardiovascular disorders.

Congenital Heart Malformations

Out of every thousand infants born alive, from one to five have a congenital defect of the heart. Approximately 40 percent of these babies die during the first year. Those who live may require several heart operations before school age is reached. Characteristically they are short of breath, inhaling 60-100 times a minute instead of the normal rate of 30-40 for this age. Everything, including feeding, is an effort. Severely affected cardiac children demand many adaptations. Children with small ventricular septal defects and the milder forms of pulmonary stenosis can lead essentially normal lives with no corrective measures. The names of the various conditions are formidable, and the physical educator should be able to distinguish the benign forms from the more severe. A listing of congenital defects and the frequency with which they occur lends insight into those with which the physical educator should be most comfortable.

Incidence of Congenital Heart Defects

One-half of all congenital heart defects are caused by three conditions:

Ventricular septal defect	22 percent
Patent ductus arteriosus	17 percent
Tetralogy of Fallot	11 percent

Of the remaining half, 32 percent are caused by five conditions:

Transposition of the great vessels	8 percent
Atrial septal defect	7 percent
Pulmonary stenosis	7 percent
Coarctation of the aorta	6 percent
Aortic and subaortic stenosis	4 percent

Other rather rare conditions are tricuspid atresia, total anomalous pulmonary venous return, endocardial fibroelastosis, and truncus arteriosus. It is important to note, however, that no two children with the same defects are alike. The probable effectiveness of heart surgery and/or medication and the type of exercise prescription for each child must be evaluated individually.

Review of Terms

A brief review of the anatomy of the heart and the physiology of normal blood circulation enhances understanding of the medical terms used in relation to congenital heart defects. This review is afforded by Figure 23.1 and by Table 37. The definitions of terms on page 444 will help also.

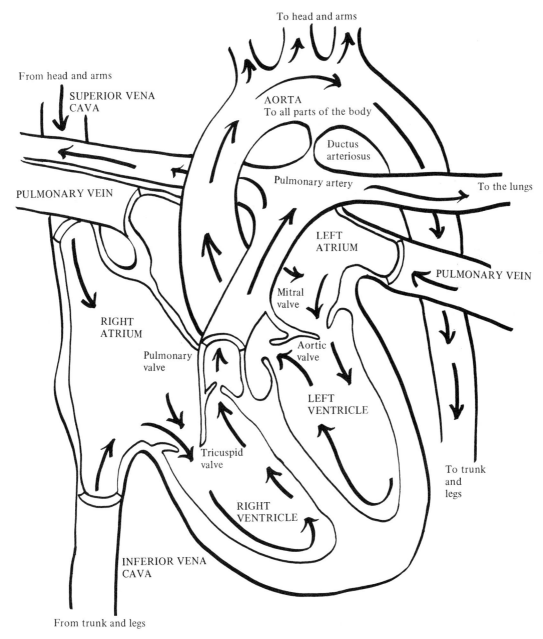

To head and arms

From head and arms

SUPERIOR VENA CAVA

AORTA
To all parts of the body

Ductus arteriosus

Pulmonary artery

To the lungs

PULMONARY VEIN

LEFT ATRIUM

PULMONARY VEIN

RIGHT ATRIUM

Mitral valve

Pulmonary valve

Aortic valve

LEFT VENTRICLE

Tricuspid valve

To trunk and legs

RIGHT VENTRICLE

INFERIOR VENA CAVA

From trunk and legs

Figure 23.1. The normal heart. Adapted from diagram in "If Your Child has a Congenital Heart Defect," © American Heart Association, 1960. Reprinted with permission.

Table 37 *Review of Blood Flow in Pulmonary and Systemic Circulation*

Pulmonary Circulation

Collecting Chamber for Blue Blood	Valve	Pumping Chamber	Valve	Artery	Circulation	Venus Return	Collecting Chamber for Pink Blood
Right Atrium	Tricuspid	Right Ventricle	Pulmonary	Pulmonary	Lungs	Pulmonary Veins	Left Atrium

Systemic Circulation

Collecting Chamber for Pink Blood	Valve	Pumping Chamber	Valve	Artery	Circulation	Venus Return	Collecting Chamber for Blue Blood
Left Atrium	Mitral	Left Ventricle	Aortic	Aorta	Total Body	From head and arms via superior vena cava From trunk and legs via inferior vena cava	Right Atrium

Septal Refers to septum, meaning a dividing wall between two chambers. In the heart there are an atrial septum and a ventricular septum.

Patent From the Latin word patens, meaning wide open or accessible.

Ductus arteriosus A tubelike passageway in the fetus between the aorta and the main pulmonary artery.

Tetralogy A group or series of four.

Great vessels Aorta and pulmonary artery.

Stenosis Constriction or narrowing of a passageway.

Coarctation Tightening or shriveling of the walls of a vessel; compression.

Atresia Pathological closure of a normal anatomical opening; or a congenital absence.

Shunt A hole in the septum between the atria or the ventricles which permits blood from the systemic circulation to mix with that of the pulmonary circulation of vice versa.

Cyanosis Blueness resulting from deficiency of oxygen in blood.

Description of Congenital Heart Defects

Ventricular Septal Defect

Small openings (holes) in the septum often close spontaneously during the first or second year of life. Many small and even medium sized openings which do not close are harmless and can be ignored completely. Some shunting occurs in any septal defect. The severity of the problem depends upon the effect which the shunt has on pulmonary circulation and the extent that the amount of oxygen normally circulated throughout the body is decreased.

Ventricular septal defects can now be repaired in open heart surgery with a mortality risk of less than 5 percent. The surgeon may either suture the sides of the defect together or insert a plastic patch over the hole.

Patent Ductus Arteriosus

The ductus is a normal part of circulation before birth. While in the uterus, the fetus does not use his lungs; therefore the blood flows directly from the pulmonary artery into the aorta. Normally, after birth, this passageway closes and eventually shrivels into a thin cord of fibrous tissue. When this closure does not occur or is incomplete, the condition is called *patent ductus arteriosus.* Often there are no symptoms, and the defect is discovered only by accident in a routine physical examination in later life. When a patent ductus is undiscovered or purposely not subjected to surgical correction, the possibility of heart failure remains a risk. The surgery for patent ductus is relatively simple.

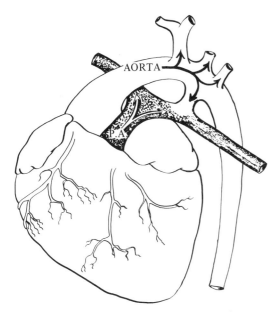

Figure 23.2. Patent ductus arteriosus. Adapted from "If Your Child has a Congenital Heart Defect," © American Heart Association, 1960. Reprinted with permission.

Tetralogy of Fallot

This combination of four abnormalities is the most common of the congenital heart defects which produce cyanotic or *blue babies.* The abnormalities are (1) ventricular septal defect; (2) pulmonary stenosis; (3) enlarged right ventricle; and (4) an abnormal positioning of the root of the aorta so that it *overrides* both the right and left ventricles. These abnormalities cause interrelated malfunctioning which results in cyanosis. The overriding of the aorta allows some blood from the right ventricle to escape through the aorta rather than traveling its normal course through the pulmonary artery. The pulmonary stenosis causes the pressure in the right ventricle to become higher than that in the left ventricle. This, in turn, forces the ventricular septal defect to become a right to left shunt with *unoxygenated* blood from the right ventricle forced through the left ventricle and circulated throughout the body. The unoxygenated blood is bluish in color. If enough of it mixes with the pink blood in the systemic circulation, the infant becomes cyanotic.

Tetralogy of Fallot can be corrected through surgical repair, but the mortality rate is still 5 to 25 percent. Whenever possible, corrective surgery is not undertaken until the child is four or older.

Transposition of the Great Vessels

This defect occurs when the roots of the aorta and the pulmonary artery are switched so that they arise from the wrong ventricles. As a result, the blue deoxygenated blood which should be going to the lungs via the pulmonary artery is circulating throughout the body while pink, oxygenated blood circulates repeatedly in the pulmonary system. This phenomenon would result in death were it not for the multiple defects which usually accompany it. When the great vessels are transposed, a septal defect or patent ductus which permits mixing of pulmonary and systemic bloods are life

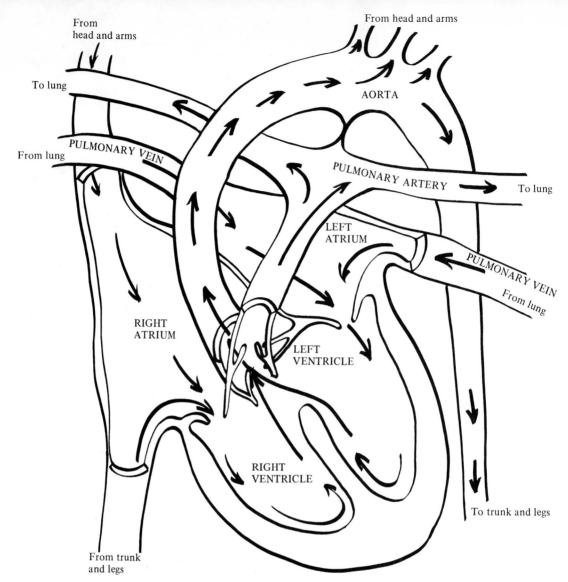

From head and arms

To lung

PULMONARY VEIN

From lung

From head and arms

AORTA

PULMONARY ARTERY

To lung

LEFT ATRIUM

PULMONARY VEIN

From lung

RIGHT ATRIUM

LEFT VENTRICLE

RIGHT VENTRICLE

To trunk and legs

From trunk and legs

Figure 23.3. Tetralogy of fallot. Adapted from "If Your Child has a Congenital Heart Defect," © American Heart Association, 1960. Reprinted with permission.

savers. Although tremendous progress is being made, transposition of the great vessels constitutes one of the surgeon's greatest challenges.

Atrial Septic Defect

The severity of this condition depends upon the size and position of the hole(s). In most in-

stances, the shunting will be from left to right, resulting in an enlargement of both chambers on the right side. An excessive volume of blood flows through the lungs, increasing susceptibility to upper respiratory infections. The condition seldom needs surgery unless a valve abnormality is involved. The surgery carries little risk.

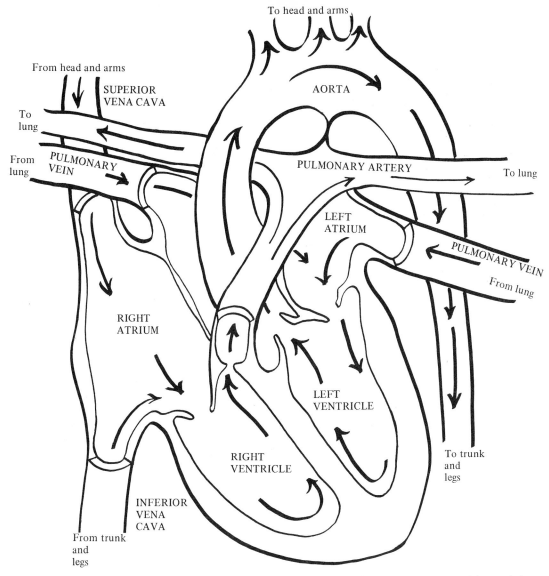

Figure 23.4. Pulmonary stenosis. Adapted from "If Your Child has a Congenital Heart Defect," © American Heart Association, 1960. Reprinted with permission.

Stenosis and Coarctation

Both of these terms refer to a narrowing or constriction of a valve or the area near it, resulting in decreased flow of blood. This congenital narrowing is relatively frequent in the pulmonary and aortic valves. If the constriction is great, the muscle wall of the affected ventricle hypertrophies as it repeatedly exerts the extra effort required to push the blood through the valve. Pulmonary stenosis leads to right heart failure with the increased pressure backing up into the veins of the body. Edema is a side effect. Aortic stenosis leads to left heart failure with the pressure building up in the left atrium and the lungs. Insufficient blood is pumped to the brain and other vital

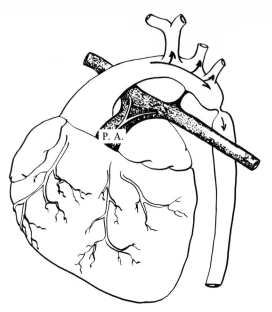

P. A.

Figure 23.5. Coarctation of the Aorta. Adapted from "If Your Child has a Congenital Heart Defect," © American Heart Association, 1960. Reprinted with permission.

organs of the body including the heart itself. Symptoms of severe aortic stenosis are breathing difficulty, chest pain, and fainting.

Heart Surgery

Of the thirty to forty thousand infants born with heart defects each year, it is estimated that 75 to 80 percent can be helped by surgery. Ideally this surgery is undertaken before age six so that the child can start school with a normal or near-normal heart and few exercise restrictions. In the case of the blue baby, however, surgery may be done during the first few weeks of life.

Surgery may take the form of either closed or open heart operations. In both cases, the incision in the chest is large, and special postoperative exercises are recommended for rehabilitation of the involved muscles. *Atelectasis,* a condition in which the air sacs or alveoli in the lungs collapse, is one of the postoperative

dangers that prescribed breathing exercises prevent. Atelectasis results in the accumulation of mucus in the bronchials and other symptoms discussed in Chapter 17. The activities suggested for persons with respiratory disorders are appropriate for the postoperative heart patient.

Once the congenital defect has been corrected by surgery, the chances are good that the child will have no exercise restrictions. Many participate in strenuous high level competitive sports. The pupil should be allowed the freedom to decide how hard to play since his sensations are usually a reliable guide to exercise tolerance. The psychological problems stemming from parental overprotection and preoperative anxieties and fears are generally greater than residual physiological limitations.

Rheumatic Fever

Approximately two-thirds of the heart disease found in children is caused by rheumatic fever. About 500,000 youths between ages five and nineteen have rheumatic heart disease. Moreover it is the number one cause of death in the United States for persons in this age range. Rheumatic fever and rheumatic heart disease are separate entities. Out of every 100 persons with a streptococcus infection, approximately one to three will develop rheumatic fever. Of the youngsters who have rheumatic fever, only half will develop rheumatic heart disease.

Rheumatic fever is a chronic inflammation caused by an allergic reaction to the antibodies which the body produces to fight streptococcus bacteria. The reaction results in the formation of millions of *Aschoff bodies* in the joints, lungs, tissues under the skin, the brain, and the heart. Masses of these microscopic inflammatory bodies seem to form and heal at random, with new areas becoming inflamed as fast as old ones heal. Scar tissue remains when the Aschoff bodies heal. Only when the scar tissue laid down in the heart is extensive does heart disease occur in conjunction with rheumatic fever. Often the clinical signs of heart disease are transient, disappearing entirely within a few years.

In recent years, there has been a tendency to overdiagnose rheumatic fever. To combat this problem the American Heart Association has derived five criteria for use in making a valid diagnosis. At least one of the following criteria, along with laboratory evidence based upon a throat culture, must be present to confirm a diagnosis of rheumatic fever.

1. *Arthritis* manifested in tenderness, swelling, heat, and redness in one or more joints. Aching of joints without these symptoms is not indicative of rheumatic fever.

2. *Infection of Heart Muscle* often diagnosed by the presence of heart murmurs. It is cautioned, however, that about 60 percent of all children have benign heart murmurs. Three types of inflammation may occur:
   a. *Myocarditis.* Inflammation of the wall of the heart often resulting in enlargement of the heart. When the acute phase of the inflammation is over, the heart usually returns to its normal size and frequently recovers completely.
   b. *Pericarditis.* Inflammation of the outer lining of the heart.
   c. *Endocarditis.* Inflammation of the valves and/or the inner lining of the heart. This is the most dangerous side effect in that the scar tissue left by the Aschoff bodies causes the valves to become either *stenotic* or *regurgitant.* The mitral and aortic valves are affected most frequently. Regurgitant valves cause the condition popularly known as *leakage of the heart* in that they permit blood to leak into the chamber it has just left. Stenosis, or narrowing of the valves, often does not

occur until several years after the first attack.

3. *Chorea* also known as St. Vitus Dance. Rheumatic inflammation of a part of the brain which results in tics, motor awkwardness, and tremors. It should be noted that chorea is caused by numerous other factors besides rheumatic fever.

4. *Skin Rash.* May appear only from twenty-four to forty-eight hours.

5. *Subcutaneous nodules.* Seen only in more severe cases of rheumatic fever, these are nontender, hard lumps which may appear over the elbows, knees, shins, backs of the forearms, or wrists.

In the past, the main form of treatment was strict bed rest for two or three months followed by a six-to-nine-month period of convalescence in which activity was limited. Walker[1] states that the judicious use of steroids now enables pupils to get up in a few days and return to school in two or three weeks. He indicates that no activity restrictions other than exclusion from competitive sports for two or three months are necessary. The introduction of exercise early in the therapeutic regime, even when severe heart damage is suspected, is recommended to avoid the physical and psychological problems of prolonged invalidism.

Once a child has had rheumatic fever, he is increasingly susceptible to recurrences of inflammation. Each new attack brings the possibility of permanent heart damage. Since the initial flare-up of rheumatic fever often does not injure the heart, prevention of subsequent attacks is all important. This is accomplished through daily ingestion of penicillin tablets or monthly intramuscular injections over a period of years. Streptococcus never becomes resistant to penicillin, so the dosage remains essentially the same as the child grows into

---

1. Colin H. M. Walker, "Rheumatic Fever," in *The Human Heart* (St. Louis: The C. V. Mosby Company, 1971), p.48.

adulthood. The age at which the daily medication can cease is controversial, ranging between twenty to forty, but there is agreement that the individual should be free of all rheumatic symptoms for at least five years.

Individuals who have had valvular heart disease of any kind are urged to take large doses of appropriate antibodies before dental work or surgery regardless of their age. Adults who have had rheumatic heart disease are especially susceptible to pericarditis, myocarditis, and endocarditis throughout their lifetimes. Because of the amount of bacteria normally present in the mouth, dental work poses a particular threat.

Implications for Physical Education

Every child who has had rheumatic fever is different. Half of them never develop heart disease and hence have no activity restrictions. The other half vary tremendously with respect to degree and duration of disability. Many children have grown up believing that they have heart disease only to learn in adulthood that physicians can no longer detect symptoms of cardiac imperfection. As a whole, persons with cardiovascular problems probably impose more restrictions on themselves than need be.

No child who is able to walk to school and/or a distance of a block or so should be excused from physical education. In severe cases, his physical education may be limited only to walking and relaxation exercises but some type of regular activity is essential to *total* rehabilitation. The physical education program for a pupil with a history of rheumatic heart disease is similar to the progressive reconditioning plan followed by the middle-aged after a coronary attack. If, however, there is severe valvular involvement, physical exercise will contribute little to improved cardiovascular function. Whereas exercise is almost always emphasized in the rehabilitation of an adult after a heart attack, it may be con-

traindicated in children whose hearts are pumping against the narrowed aortic valve or leaking mitral valve so characteristic of rheumatic fever heart disease. In such cases, the primary objective of physical education is to develop interest and skill in such lifetime sports as fishing, archery, and leisurely hikes. No attempt is made to work on cardiovascular fitness through exercise. In rheumatic heart disease, as in other cardiovascular conditions, the work tolerance of each pupil must be determined individually. The classifications denoting severity of disability and the general guidelines for planning exercise are applicable to all kinds of heart disease.

Guidelines for Planning Activity

1. The individualized physical education program for a student with cardiac involvement should be developed in a multidisciplinary setting. Physician, parents, classroom teacher, physical education specialist, and pupil should all provide input.
2. Activities described in Chapter 11 on relaxation and reduction of hyperactivity should be taught as well as breathing exercises and games.
3. If the pupil already knows how to swim and relaxes easily in water, aquatic activities are excellent since the water minimizes the pull of gravity on the body. In contrast, perhaps no activity is more demanding than swimming the width of the pool when one is a beginner!
4. In order to determine the appropriate amount of exercise, the pulse rate should be taken before and after a new sequence is tried. The pulse rate rises normally during the exercise, but it should return to resting rate in no more than three minutes after cessation of movement. If it does not, the sequence should be made easier before the next attempt.

5. Exercises performed in a back lying position are the least demanding of all activities. Each student should be encouraged to establish his own cadence rather than conforming to the pace set by a teacher. He should also assume increasing responsibility for the number of repetitions and duration of rest periods.

6. The Guided Discovery and Motor Creativity Teaching Styles can be used to facilitate a growing understanding of the body and an appreciation of abilities and limitations.

7. Guidance in establishing a realistic level of aspiration for various activities should be provided. Emphasis should be upon competition against self rather than others. Recreational activities which encourage competition against self should be taught; the student should be introduced to community facilities where these are conducted.

Organizations

1. American Heart Association, Inc., 7320 Greenville Ave., Dallas, Texas 75231.

2. National Foundation—Birth Defects, 800 Second Avenue, New York, New York 10017.

3. The Aerobics Center, 12100 Preston Road, Dallas, Texas 75230.

References

American College of Sports Medicine, ed. *Guidelines for Graded Exercise Testing and Exercise Prescription.* Philadelphia: Lea & Febiger, 1975.

American Heart Association. *If Your Child Has A Congenital Heart Defect.* New York: American Heart Association, 1970.

Billig, Donal. *The Management of Neonates and Infants with Congenital Heart Disease.* New York: Grune and Stratton, 1973.

Conn, Hadley, ed. *Cardiac and Vascular Diseases.* Philadelphia: Lea & Febiger, 1971.

Cooper, Kenneth. *Aerobics.* New York: M. Evans and Company, Inc., 1968.

Fletcher, Gerald F., and Cantwell, John D. *Exercise and Coronary Heart Disease.* Springfield, Illinois: Charles C Thomas, 1974.

Jokl, Ernst. *Heart and Sport.* Springfield, Illinois: Charles C. Thomas, 1964.

Nadas, Alexander, and Fyler, Donald C. *Pediatric Cardiology.* 3rd edition. Philadelphia: Saunders, 1972.

Ross, John and O'Rourke, Robert. *Understanding the Heart and Its Diseases.* New York: McGraw Hill Book Co., 1976.

Zohman, Lenore, and Tobis, Jerome. *Cardiac Rehabilitation.* New York: Grune and Stratton, 1970.

American Heart Journal. An international publication for the study of circulation, published monthly by The C. V. Mosby Company, 11830 Westline Industrial Drive, St. Louis, Mo., 63141.

The American Journal of Cardiology. The Official Journal of the American College of Cardiology. Published monthly except September by the Magazine Division, Dun. Donnelley Publishing Corporation, 666 Fifth Avenue, New York, New York 10019.

Atherosclerosis. International Journal for Research and Investigation on Atherosclerosis and Related Diseases. Published by Elsevier Scientific Publishing Co., Amsterdam.

British Heart Journal. A monthly journal of cardiology published in association with the British Cardiac Association, Editor, B. M. A. House, Tavistock Square, London WC1H 9JR.

Current Concepts of Cerebrovascular Disease: Stroke. Newsletter published by the American Heart Association, Inc., 7320 Greenville Ave., Dallas, Texas 75231.

24 Diabetes

Figure 24.0. Diabetic children can achieve high levels
of skills and fitness.

A metabolic disturbance resulting in insufficient insulin in the bloodstream, diabetes mellitus affects approximately eight million persons[1] in the United States. It is the second most frequent cause of blindness and the most common cause of irreversible blindness. Diabetes now ranks eighth in the causes of death in this country. It occurs most frequently in persons over forty, bringing with it such severe complications as renal diseases, cardiovascular disease, blindness, and amputations.

According to the American Diabetes Association, for every 10,000 persons in the community there will be one diabetic under age twenty, ten diabetics between ages twenty and forty, 100 diabetics between ages fifty and sixty, and 1,000 diabetics over age sixty. Females are more likely to have diabetes than males, and there seems to be a direct relationship between obesity and the onset of diabetes in middle age. All ethnic groups are affected, but the highest incidence occurs among Jewish persons.

Only fifty years ago a diagnosis of diabetes mellitus meant sure death within a few years. Now the average child diabetic lives to about age forty. Persons afflicted with diabetes in middle age have a life expectancy of about one-third less than the general population. Although the discovery of insulin in 1921 by Canadians Banting and Best completely transformed the outlook for diabetes sufferers, further medical progress has been slow. The cause of diabetes is still unknown. The major factors in the treatment of diabetes continue to be diet, insulin, and exercise.

Exercise

Regular exercise is tremendously important in the control of diabetes. The rationale for this lies in the fact that exercise helps to burn sugar, thereby influencing the amount of sugar that the body will use or tolerate. A daily consistent exercise plan not only lessens the insulin requirement for a diabetic but also can be used to help with weight reduction. With the exception of his physician, perhaps no one is more important to the diabetic than his physical education teacher. Positive attitudes toward vigorous physical activity must be developed early. Lifetime sports must be taught and the use of community recreation resources encouraged.

Insulin dosage is dependent upon amount of exercise and degree of strenuousness. It is recommended that the standard insulin dose be decreased 5 to 10 percent for any exercise beyond that included in the daily regime. For this reason, consistency and regularity in exercise procedures are more important for the diabetic than other children. Until the pupil learns to regulate his insulin intake in accordance with exercise demands, he should not be subjected to tests of physical fitness which call for all out effort on a particular day. Instead his score must be based upon average performance over several class sessions in which the duration and/or intensity of the exercise is increased very slowly.

Types of Diabetes

Traditionally diabetes has been classified into two types: (1) juvenile and (2) adult or maturity-onset. Approximately 85 percent of the known diabetics fall in the latter classification. Synonyms for these categories are as follows:

Juvenile	Adult
Ketoacidosis-prone	Ketoacidosis-resistant
Insulin-dependent	Noninsulin-dependent

Individuals who develop diabetes before the age of twenty generally have the juvenile

1. Of these, three million are under treatment.

type. Such persons almost always require insulin whereas individuals in the other category rely primarily upon diet therapy and oral hypoglycemic drugs. Little or no insulin is manufactured by the pancreas of the juvenile sufferer who may go rather quickly into diabetic coma which can result in death if not treated adequately. In contrast, adult diabetes is less dramatic. The pancreas is capable of manufacturing some insulin even though the amount is insufficient for body needs.

Terms which the physical educator may see on the diabetic pupil's medical record include:

Latent or *prediabetes*—A child of two diabetic parents; an identical twin of a diabetic; any person genetically predisposed to diabetes before the onset of symptoms.

Brittle diabetes—A condition in which blood and sugar urine fluctuate widely in spite of adherence to a regular healthful regimen; the severity of this condition is intensified by even a mild illness.

Bronzed diabetes—A condition accompanied by iron deposits in the pancreas, liver, and skin.

Pancreatic diabetes—A condition resulting from partial or total removal of the pancreas because of cancer or chronic infection. As much as 35 to 40 units of insulin a day may be required.

Hepatic diabetes—A condition resulting from severe liver disease in which the blood sugar is elevated.

Diagnosis of Diabetes

The most common symptoms of diabetes are constant thirst, frequent urination, extreme hunger, drowsiness and fatigue, dryness of mouth, lips, and skin, visual disorders, rapid weight loss, itching of the genitals, and skin problems which do not heal readily. Urine tests are used for screening, but the blood glucose tolerance test is the most accurate diagnostic technique. These tests, of course, are administered initially by the physician.

Once the condition is diagnosed, the diabetic is expected to test his urine one or more times daily. In severe diabetes, urine tests may be prescribed as often as four times a day: (1) morning, before breakfast; (2) noon, before lunch; (3) afternoon, before supper; and (4) bedtime, around 9 p.m. In mild cases controlled by diet alone, diabetics usually test their urine daily before breakfast and occasionally before other meals.

The purpose of the urine test is to ascertain the amount of sugar in the urine. A negative test, or one in which no sugar is apparent, is desired. The physical educator should be sensitive enough to associate fluctuations in a pupil's moods with the disheartening experience of an occasional positive urine test. It is important also in terms of body image and self-concept that urine and urination be assigned positive connotations. Counseling should be provided for youngsters who have been taught that certain bodily functions and/or parts are dirty or bad. Allowing a diabetic pupil to perform urine tests on his classmates in a lecture-demonstration setting may lead to increased understandings among peers.

Treatment

Good diabetic control is based upon proper diet, exercise, and insulin. The diet for diabetics should be kept constant. The number of units of insulin self-administered with a syringe is then based entirely upon amount of exercise. One milligram of standard U. S. P. insulin contains 23 units. The average diabetic child requires approximately 20-30 units of insulin on a day filled with normal physical activity. If he plans to engage in an interscholastic athletic event, a dance recital, or any exceptionally strenuous activity, the pupil should cut his morning insulin dose by 10 to 15 percent. Otherwise he may experience an insulin reaction or have to gorge himself with candy bars to prevent such a reaction. If, on the other hand, he plans to spend the day watching television or reading a book, he should increase his insulin 5 to 10 percent. Otherwise, he may go into an insulin coma.

The diabetic diet should be characterized by (1) regularity of food intake from day to day; (2) regularity in mealtime; (3) exclusion of refined sugars; and (4) mild to moderate restriction of carbohydrates. If the diabetic is forced to skip a meal, his insulin dosage must be reduced.

Since most diabetics tend to be overweight, the diet is generally low in calories. Food exchanges are figured with precision, and emphasis is placed upon weight control. To maintain the blood sugar at a constant level, five or six small meals daily are recommended in lieu of the traditional large meals.

Since insulin injections are made to parts of the body not generally exposed to public view, the physical educator may be the only teacher aware of the condition. With the growing incidence of drug abuse, the physical educator's role in the locker room and shower area takes on greater responsibility. He alone may see the sites of injections and be forced to investigate whether the pupil is diabetic or taking illegal drugs. The physical educator is also in a position to evaluate the inevitable growth of scar tissue and to comment upon changing the site of injections. Insulin may be injected into the buttocks, upper arms, outer sides of thighs, and lower part of the abdomen. The site of injection should be changed frequently to minimize the breakdown of tissue.

Insulin Reaction

Insulin reaction, or shock, may be caused by delaying or skipping meals, overexercising, or accidentally injecting too much insulin. Each of these practices can result in *hypo-*

glycemia or low blood sugar which in turn can lead to convulsions similar to epileptic seizures or unconsciousness. Early symptoms of insulin shock include: (1) shakiness or trembling, (2) nervousness, (3) nausea, (4) headache, (5) fatigue, (6) excessive perspiration, and (7) hunger. If these symptoms are recognized in time, the reaction can be prevented by drinking fruit juice or carbonated drinks or by eating candy, corn syrup, or honey. Many diabetics carry Lifesavers for such occasions.

Characteristics of insulin shock include: (1) sluggish thinking, (2) muscle weakness, (3) drowsiness, (4) blurred or double vision, (5) unconsciousness and/or convulsions. Occasionally a person in insulin shock is mistakenly charged with alcoholic intoxication. If the person is conscious, eating something with sugar should end the reaction. If not, he should receive an injection of *glucagon* which will cause the liver to break down liver glycogen and release free glucose into the bloodstream. A coach taking students on an overnight trip may wish to require that a diabetic bring along glucagon as an emergency precaution.

William F. Talbert, who has been a diabetic since age ten, tells of having an insulin reaction during a finals tennis match with Pancho Gonzalez, then the amateur champion.

I took the first set from the fiery Californian but lost the next two. In the fourth set my game collapsed completely as I double-faulted, sprayed shots wildly out of court and stumbled about. My old doubles partner, Gar Mulloy, rushed out on the court after I had lost three games in succession to Pancho.

"Drink this, Willie," Gar commanded. He put a glass of sugared water into my hand and I downed it greedily. It was the answer. Gar had realized that I was losing control of my functions and going into insulin reaction through rapid burning of sugar. In a reversal of form that baffled Pancho and the gallery, I took twelve of the next fourteen games to win the match and the Southampton trophy. [2]

2. William F. Talbert, "Double Challenge for a Champion," *World Health* (February-March 1971), p. 27.

Another description of an insulin reaction comes from the parents of a six-year-old boy:

I found him sobbing on the edge of his bed at five in the morning. I thought he was having a nightmare. He couldn't tell me what was wrong. He lay looking at his hands like someone on an LSD trip finding minuscule meanings in the texture of his skin. Then I noticed that he was unsteady when he went for a drink of water, and I knew. It was insulin reaction.

We were frantic—preparing orange juice, jelly on bread, cookies, ice cream—but he cried more hysterically and pushed away the food. We tried to force him; he fell and bumped his head. We panicked. We felt the insulin reaction was too far gone. We injected glucagon—a hormone that rapidly raises the blood sugar level.

In a few minutes his head was clear and he began to eat some of the sweets. But none of us was ever the same again. [3]

Since insulin reaction can occur anytime that a diabetic engages in physical activity more strenuous than he anticipated in his injection, it is imperative that the physical educator be able to recognize symptoms and give immediate treatment. It should be emphasized that *overexercising* is not the problem. Rather it is the inability to judge ahead of time the amount of insulin needed for the forthcoming exertion. Diabetics should engage in all activities in the regular physical education program. They can participate also, without restrictions, in all interscholastic competitive athletics.

Coma or Ketoacidosis

Less common, but more severe in possible consequences, is the diabetic coma, more properly called *ketoacidosis.* This is caused by an increase in acids (ketone bodies) resulting from too rapid a breakdown of fat in the bloodstream. Before the discovery of insulin, ketoacidosis ended in death for most diabetic children and many adults. It can still result in death, and any diabetic in coma should be rushed to the hospital. There the coma is treated with large doses of insulin and intravenous fluids to reduce the characteristic dehydration.

Warning symptoms of an impending diabetic coma include extreme thirst, loss of appetite, nausea, vomiting, abdominal pain, leg cramps, nervousness, and dimness or blurring of vision. Diabetics sometimes are temporarily blinded by a coma. In cases of *diabetic retinopathy* (disease of the retina characterized by hemorrhages within the eye), a coma may eventually bring irreversible blindness. Hence many diabetics must live with the fear of an unexpected coma from which they will emerge totally blind. Once the diabetic lapses into unconsciousness, the following signs are present: labored breathing, rapid pulse, lowered blood pressure, fruity odor to breath, dry skin, and flushed face.

Some of the causes of diabetic coma are (1) insufficient insulin, (2) neglecting to take injection, (3) onset of infection or mild illness, (4) diarrhea, vomiting, and mild stomach upsets, (5) overeating or excessive drinking of alcoholic beverages; and (6) emotional stress. Pregnancy also must be a time of extra precaution. Essentially any deviation from *regular* eating, sleeping, and exercise patterns holds some danger. Even a mild cold complicates a diabetic's metabolism. Insulin needs may be increased by as much as one-third when the individual runs a fever.

Diabetic Camps

Over fifty summer camps in the United States and Canada exist specifically for diabetic children. A list of these camps, as well as general information about diabetes, can be obtained through the American Diabetic Association.

3. Ned Brandt, "Your Son Has Diabetes," *Today's Health* (June 1973), p. 36.

The psychological effects of a special summer camp on 110 diabetic children were studied in 1972.[4] At the end of camp both boys and girls showed significant increases in self-esteem as measured by the Coopersmith Test of Self-Esteem and decreases in anxiety as measured by the Children's Manifest Anxiety Test.

4. Ronald K. McCraw and Luther B. Travis, "Psychological Effects of a Special Summer Camp on Juvenile Diabetics," *Diabetes: The Journal of the American Diabetic Association* (April, 1973), pp. 275-278.

Organizations

1. American Diabetic Association, 1 East 45th Street, New York, New York 10017.

References

Boshell, Buris R. *The Diabetic At Work and Play.* Springfield, Illinois: Charles C Thomas, 1971.

Caird, Francis. *Diabetes and the Eye.* Oxford, Edinburgh: Blackwell Scientific, 1969.

Pedersen, Jorgen. *The Pregnant Diabetic and Her Newborn.* Copenhagen: Munksgaard, 1967.

Sussman, Darl E., ed. *Juvenile-Type Diabetes and Its Complications.* Springfield, Illinois: Charles C Thomas, 1971.

Traisman, Howard Senn. *Management of Juvenile Diabetes Mellitus.* 2nd edition. St. Louis: The C. V. Mosby Co., 1971.

Warren, Shields. *The Pathology of Diabetes Mellitus.* 4th edition. Philadelphia: Lea & Febiger, 1966.

Periodicals

Diabetes: The Journal of the American Diabetes Association. Published every month by the Association at 18 East 48th Street, New York, New York 10017.

Diabetes In the News. A newspaper published by Ames Company, Division Miles Laboratories, Inc., Elkhart, Indiana 46514. Address for subscriptions: 3553 W. Peterson Avenue, Chicago, Illinois 60659.

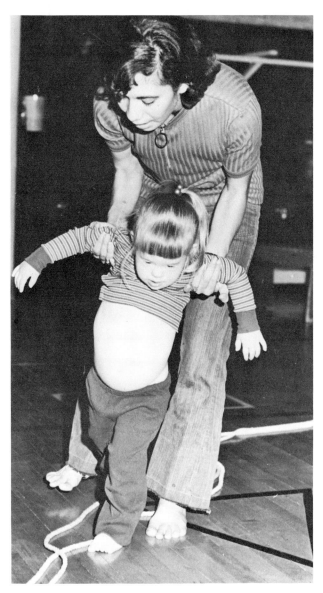

Figure 25.0. Child with Down's Syndrome learns through guided movement exploration.

Mental retardation refers to significantly subaverage general intellectual functioning existing concurrently with deficits in adaptive behavior, and manifested during the developmental period. The three parts of this definition warrant analysis.

Subaverage general intellectual functioning refers to performance which is two or more standard deviations below average on a standardized intelligence test. On the Stanford-Binet and the Wechsler scales, the two most widely used intelligence tests, this represents I.Q.'s of 68 and 70 respectively. Because of the many inaccuracies in intelligence testing, a

Table 38   *Levels of Adaptive Behavior Used in Classification of Mental Retardation*[1]

	Pre-School Age 0-5 Maturation and Development	School Age 6-21 Training and Education	Adult Age 21 and Over Social and Vocational Adequacy
Level I Mild	Can develop social and communication skills; minimal retardation in sensorimotor areas; often not distinguished from normal until later age.	Can learn academic skills up to approximately sixth grade level by late teens. Can be guided toward social conformity. "Educable"	Can usually achieve social and vocational skills adequate to minimum self-support but may need guidance and assistance when under unusual social or economic stress.
Level II Moderate	Can talk or learn to communicate; poor social awareness; fair motor development; profits from training in self-help; can be managed with moderate supervision.	Can profit from training in social and occupational skills; unlikely to progress beyond second grade level in academic subjects; may learn to travel alone in familiar places.	May achieve self-maintenance in unskilled or semi-skilled work under sheltered conditions; needs supervision and guidance when under mild social or economic stress.
Level III Severe	Poor motor development; speech is minimal; generally unable to profit from training in self-help; little or no communication skills.	Can talk or learn to communicate; can be trained in elemental health habits; profits from systematic habit training.	May contribute partially to self-maintenance under complete supervision; can develop self-protection skills to a minimal useful level in controlled environment.
Level IV Profound	Gross retardation; minimal capacity for functioning in sensorimotor areas; needs nursing care.	Some motor development present; may respond to minimum or limited training in self-help.	Some motor and speech development; may achieve very limited self-care; needs nursing care.

1. *The Problem of Mental Retardation.* U.S. Department of Health, Education, and Welfare, Office of the Secretary, Secretary's Committee on Mental Retardation, Washington, D.C., Government Printing Office, 1969.

diagnosis of mental retardation is never made on subaverage intellectual functioning alone.

Deficits in adaptive behavior refer to problems of maturation, learning, and/or social adjustment which result in the individual's failure to meet standards of personal independence and social responsibility expected of his age and cultural group. Adaptive behavior is measured by such standardized instruments as the Vineland Social Maturity Scale, the Gesell Developmental Schedules, and scales similar to that depicted in Table 38.

Adaptive behavior is becoming increasingly important as a criterion for mental retardation and for educational classification. Discrepancies between adaptive behavior and measures of intellectual functioning have led to such terms as the "Six-Hour Retarded Child," used to designate the child who performs normally except during the six hours each day that he is in school. [2]

Developmental period, the third part of the definition, specifies that the subaverage intellectual functioning and deficits in adaptive behavior are severe enough that they are identified within the first eighteen years of life.

Approximately 6.1 million Americans meet these criteria and are regarded as mentally retarded. Table 39 presents a breakdown by age and level of retardation.

Where Are the Mentally Retarded?

In the average community, for every 1,000 school-age children there are approximately 25 mildly retarded, 4 moderately retarded, and 1 severely or profoundly retarded. The incidence of mild retardation varies with socioeconomic and cultural levels. Poverty areas have roughly twice as many as middle-class neighborhoods. The incidence of severely and profoundly retarded is remarkably stable for all income groups. Most mildly and moderately retarded children live at home and attend public schools. The quality of their physical education instruction varies widely, reflecting the

2. President's Committee on Mental Retardation, *The Six-Hour Retarded Child*. (Washington, D. C.: Government Printing Office), p. 197.

Table 39 *Estimates of Retardation by Age and Level—1970*[3]

1970 Census	All Ages	Under 21 Yrs.	21 Yrs. and above
General Population	203.3 million	80.5 million	122.7 million
3% General Population	6.1 million	2.4 million	3.7 million
The Retarded Population			
Profound (I.Q. 0-20) About 1 1/2%	92 thousand	36 thousand	56 thousand
Severe (I.Q. 20-35) About 3 1/2%	214 thousand	84 thousand	130 thousand
Moderate (I.Q. 36-52) About 6%	366 thousand	144 thousand	222 thousand
Mild (I.Q. 53+) about 89%	5.4 million	2.1 million	3.3 million+

3. The President's Committee on Mental Retardation, "Facts on Mental Retardation," (Washington, D.C.: PCMR, 1970).

philosophy of administrators and school board and the initiative of their teachers.

Less than 10 percent of all retarded persons are institutionalized. Generalizations about institutionalized populations are:

1. Most of the residents have I.Q.'s under 35. This reflects the nationwide trend toward providing institutional care only for persons who cannot be integrated back into the community.
2. The medical classifications are primarily *unknown causes and prenatal influence.* The clinical type which occurs most frequently is Down's Syndrome.
3. Approximately one-third to one-fourth of the residents have convulsive disorders.
4. Over one-third of the residents have obvious motor dysfunctions. Most prevalent of these is spasticity.
5. Approximately one-third to one-fourth are multihandicapped by sensory impairment. Visual deficits occur with the greatest frequency.

It is obvious that physical education and recreation program planning in residential facilities and public schools serve vastly different groups. The range of individual differences among the retarded is probably far greater than among the so-called 'normal.'

Medical Classifications and Etiologies

The American Association on Mental Deficiency (AAMD) recognizes ten medical classifications of mental retardation.[4] Within several of these classifications are *clinical types* such as Down's Syndrome, microcephalus, and hydrocephalus in which the person has certain anatomical, physiognomical, or pathological features which permit easy identification. Most retarded persons, however, cannot be distinguished from the normal population on the basis of physical appearance. Nor is the cause of their retardation known. Hence the AAMD classifications for the great majority of retarded persons are

Other Conditions and Environmental Influences.

1. *Other Conditions.* Includes cases in which there is (a) no evidence of a physical cause or structural defect, (b) no history of subnormal functioning in parents and siblings, and (c) no evidence of an associated psychosocial factor.
2. *Environmental Influences.* Includes retardation resulting from neglect, sensory deprivation, severe deficits of special senses, and other indications of adverse environmental conditions.
3. *Chromosomal Abnormality.* Includes all kinds of physical aberrations, most common of which is mongolism (Down's Syndrome), which ranks fourth as a cause of mental retardation among institutionalized populations. Approximately 10 percent of such populations have Down's Syndrome.
4. *Unknown Prenatal Influence.* Includes:
   (a) Cerebral malformation including the partial or complete absence of a part of the brain (anencephaly)
   (b) Craniofacial anomalies of unknown origin, including microcephalus, Cornelia de Lange Syndrome, Apert's Syndrome, Laurence-Moon-Biedl Syndrome, and different kinds of craniostenosis
   (c) Status dysraphicus, including various kinds of spina bifida and other disorders related to faulty closure of the neural tube
   (d) Hydrocephalus
   (e) Other.

Approximately 17 percent of the retardation in institutionalized populations is attributed to congenital cerebral defects, unknown prenatal influences, and primary cranial anomalies.

4. Herbert J. Grossman, ed., *Manual on Terminology and Classification in Mental Retardation* (Washington, D. C.: American Association on Mental Deficiency, 1973), pp. 49-68.

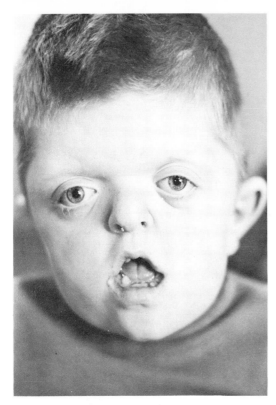

Figure 25.1. Apert's Syndrome—illustrative of cerebral malformation of unknown prenatal influence. Characteristics are craniostenosis (premature closure of cranial sutures), bulging of eyes, and defective formation of facial bones. Severity of mental retardation varies.

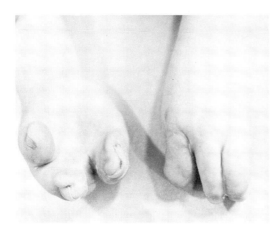

Figure 25.2. Ball handling activities must be adapted to hands of child with Apert's Syndrome.

Figure 25.3. Toddler with Cornelia de Lange Syndrome.

5. *Gestational Disorders.* Includes low birth weight (2,500 gm or 5 pounds, 8 ounces), premature birth, and postmature birth (exceeding normal time by seven days).

6. *Trauma or Physical Agents.* Includes injuries to the brain before, during, or after birth. *Anoxia* or *hypoxia* (insufficient oxygen) may result in brain injury as a side effect of poisoning, shock, convulsions, and severe anemia.

7. *Infection and Intoxication.*
   (a) Prenatal and maternal infections which affect the child in utero as rubella (German measles) and syphilis.

Figure 25.4. Microcephalic adults may exhibit wide range of individual differences.

(b) Postnatal cerebral infections, i.e., encephalitis.

(c) Cerebral damage caused by toxic agents (drugs, poisons, maternal disorders like diabetes and malnutrition).

8. *Metabolism or Nutrition.* Includes disorders caused by metabolic, nutritional, endocrine, or growth dysfunctions. Listed in order of their incidence among institutionalized retarded populations are the following:

(a) Unspecified

(b) Phenylketonuria (PKU)

(c) Hypothyroidism (Cretinism)

(d) Galactosemia

9. *Postnatal Gross Brain Disease.* Includes neoplasms and hereditary conditons in which there are combined lesions of the skin and nervous system. Although rare, the following physical characteristics are easily identified in a visit to any state residential facility.

(a) Cafe-au-lait spots on the skin named because their color is that of *coffee with cream.* These are particularly symptomatic of *neurofibromatosis* (von Recklinghausen's disease).

(b) Port wine stain on face and/or scalp symptomatic of *Sturge-Weber-Dimitri's* disease. The port wine stain is caused by an *angioma* (a growth comprised of dilated blood vessels).

(c) Butterfly-shaped rash extending from cheeks to forehead, head, and neck with nodules varying in size from a pinhead to a pea. This rash is evident in *tuberous sclerosis,* a condition characterized by nodules throughout the central nervous system and tumors of various organs.

10. *Following Psychiatric Disorder.* Includes retardation following psychosis or other psychiatric disorder when there is no evidence of cerebral pathology.

Physical education programming is affected, not only by medical classifications, but also by levels of retardation. The term *retarded* should never be used without specifying the level as mild, moderate, severe, or profound since individual differences within this special population are far greater than those within the normal. It should be emphasized also that *mildly retarded persons are more like the normal in motor performance than like the lower level of retardation.* Since 89 percent of all retardation falls within the mild classification, most retarded pupils can participate successfully in regular physical education and athletics. Programming for pupils with mild retardation is, therefore, primarily a matter of facilitating attitudinal changes among regular educators and normal peers. In contrast, the provision of movement experiences for lower level retarded children demands an understanding of realistic expectations for motor performance at each combination of age and level. The following pages suggest ideas for programming the average child within each level. Individual differences should be kept in mind, and each pupil encouraged to achieve optimally. With good physical education, particularly in early childhood, retarded persons in the future may accomplish motor feats as yet undreamed of.

Physical Education for the Mildly Retarded

Kirk[5] and other special educators concur that in height, weight, and motor coordination most mildly mentally retarded children approximate their normal peers. All elementary school pupils should receive daily physical education instruction which is broken down into small, sequential progressions designed to

5. Samuel A. Kirk, *Educating Exceptional Children.* 2nd ed. (Boston: Houghton Mifflin Company, 1972), p. 195.

Figure 25.5. The mildly retarded can excel in athletics.

insure success. It is recommended, therefore, that children with mild retardation be integrated as early as possible into the regular physical education and athletic program. When any pupil, whether retarded or normal, deviates more than two standard deviations from the mean on fitness or skill tests, he should receive adapted physical education instruction in addition to the regularly scheduled program.

Approximately 80 percent of the mildly retarded population marry and rear children. Almost all of them find employment, usually in blue collar jobs which demand high levels of fitness. Their jobs, like those of millions of Americans, allow for a growing abundance of leisure time. It is estimated that the average work week by the year 2000 will drop to thirty hours or less and that three day weekends will be the rule rather than the exception. These facts may make good physical education instruction for the mildly retarded more important than for his academically capable peers who are more likely to hold desk jobs demanding little fitness and to use their leisure time in reading and other intellectually oriented tasks.

In addition to regular physical education, the high level retardate must be introduced to community recreation facilities and helped to earn money to take advantage of bowling al-

leys, golf driving ranges, skating rinks, and swimming pools. Habits of using such facilities should be well established before graduation. He must be guided also in the selection of lifetime sports suited to his body build, motor coordination, and level of fitness. The acquisition of skills in lifetime sports should be a high priority.

Because he is likely to be deficit in verbal communication, he should be provided with socially acceptable means for nonverbal expression of creativity, frustration, anger, hostility, and elation. He can be taught to sublimate emotions into physical activity—dance, jogging, shadow boxing, riflery, or golf. Repeated failure experiences in life and in school may leave him with a low frustration tolerance. Striking, hitting, and kicking sports activities offer alternatives to drug and alcohol abuse, overeating, and other acts harmful to himself or others. The child must be taught that sports and dance activities can be mood modifiers.

About the same percentage of high level retarded can achieve success in team sport competition as normal children. They play by regulation rules and derive all of the values associated with athletics. Leisure counseling should help graduating students find opportunities for continued team sport participation within the community recreation structure and/or make the transition to individual sports which are available.

Physical Education for the Moderately Retarded

Children within the 36-52 I.Q. range are found in residential facilities, public school special education classes, public or private preschools, sheltered workshops, and comprehensive community day care centers. Their physical education needs are entirely different from mildly retarded and normal children. In planning physical education activities for lower level retardates, social or mental age is more important than chronological age. Social age is determined by adaptive behavior. Mental age, as used in special education literature, is generally based upon Stanford-Binet I.Q. scores. [6]

Depending upon his chronological age and I.Q., *the moderately retarded child has a mental age between 2 and 7 years.* Several principles of program planning are based upon social or mental and/or chronological age: (1) In order of their importance, social maturity, mental age, and chronological age are the criteria for the selection of games and recreational activities; (2) the younger the children, the smaller the chronological age range of the instructional group should be; (3) the lower the intelligence, the greater the chronological age range of the instructional group may be; and (4) orthopedically handicapped children seem to adjust best with children of lower chronological age but similar mental age.

Estimates of the highest possible level of adaptive behavior functioning (social maturity) for the moderately retarded child by the AAMD lend insight into the kinds of instruction which are appropriate for each chronological and mental age. Chapter 7, Locomotor Movement Patterns and Related Skills, should be referred to for teaching progressions.

Moderate Retardation, CA 3-9 (MA 2-5)

With a mental age somewhere between 2-5 years, this child is making his first attempts at locomotor movements. Generally after age 3 (chronologically), he learns to walk alone, run, negotiate stairs, and to pass an object to another. Between ages six to nine, he may learn to jump and later to balance on one foot briefly. Often, he needs to hold on to a bar, chair, or rope when attempting balance activities. He may climb up and down stairs but does not alternate feet. He can throw a ball or beanbag but lacks the hand-eye readiness for catching.

Essentially this child functions motorically and socially like a preschooler. He seems to profit most from a movement exploration approach using simple homemade apparatus. He is responsive to adults but tends to ignore peers except for brief altercations about sharing. The best teaching occurs on a one-to-one ratio with the teacher verbally motivating and manually helping the child to discover ways his body can move. Few words are needed, and the important verbal cues and phrases of praise are repeated over and over. Hand clapping, hugs, and gestures help to reinforce verbal praise. Swimming instruction, i.e., movement exploration in the water, should be begun. The child is not yet ready for organized games and does not understand formations.

Moderate Retardation CA 9-12 (MA 3-5)

Between ages 9-12, he may learn to hop, gallop, and then to skip. He learns to ascend a short flight of stairs, alternating feet, without support, before he masters descending tasks of the same nature. He appears to grasp the concept of throwing an object at a target, sometimes achieving success in hitting it. He makes his first fairly successful attempts at climbing trees and jungle gyms and at riding a tricycle.

He begins to interact with other children in simple make believe play as *House* and *Hospital*. His play interests are similar to his mental age which ranges from 3 to 5 years.

He should be introduced to his first low organized games. Flying Dutchman, Musical Chairs, and Catch My Tail are examples of activities which have proven appropriate for this group. In Flying Dutchman, a line of children holding hands is walked in any direction. When the verbal cue, *Flying Dutchman* is called out by the teacher, the children drop hands and run back to a mat which has been

6. Lewis M. Terman and Maud A. Merrill, *Stanford-Binet Intelligence Scale, Manual for the Third Revision, Form L-M.* (Boston: Houghton Mifflin Company, 1960), pp. 257-295.

preestablished as home base. Musical chairs can be played without modification, but the children may need help in finding their chairs. In Catch My Tail one corner of a scarf is tucked into the back of the belt of one child who runs about the room with the others trying to grab hold of the scarf.

Examples of games not usually successful are Chicken, Come Home, Cat and Rat, Dodge Ball, and relays. In Chicken, Come Home and similar activities, the children cannot remember which role they are playing or which direction to run. Only a few of the students seem to understand the concepts of tagging, dodging, and catching. In Cat and Rat there seems to be no idea about who is chasing whom, that one should get away, or that the circle should either help or hinder the players. In Dodge Ball they fail to grasp the idea of the game and wander away from the circle. These children can be forced through the motions of a relay but have no idea of its purpose, nor of winning and losing, nor of belonging to a team.

Moderate Retardation CA 12-15 (MA 3-7)

Between ages 12-15, the moderately retarded child may master the locomotor movements generally practiced in the primary grades: run, hop, gallop, skip and simple dance steps. He learns to go up and down stairs, alternating feet, without hesitation. He is partially successful in jump rope activities and may learn to use skates and a sled. His consistency in throwing and hitting a target improves, but he still lacks readiness for catching activities.

He begins to participate spontaneously in group activities and seems to enjoy simple low organized games. *His physical education needs are similar to those of children in the primary grades but he is socially mature enough to react negatively to baby games. Names of games and stunts must sometimes be changed to assure their acceptance.* In his striving to be like other persons his age, he demonstrates interest in the popular team sports and social dance. He can be introduced to the concepts of competition but tends to be frozen at the *I* stage of development.

Moderate Retardation CA 15 and over (MA 4-7)

Sometime between middle and late adolescence, his motor behavior stabilizes. Although his mental age falls between 4-7 years, his social and recreational interests approximate those of the average young teenager. The moderately retarded child performs better in individual events like track, swimming, and gymnastics than in team sports. He enjoys social dance and keeps abreast of new fad steps.

Down's Syndrome

About one out of every 600 or 700 children—15,000 per year—is born with Down's Syndrome (Mongolism). *In public school classes for moderately retarded pupils, they make up 30 to 40 percent of the students.* In state residential facilities, they comprise approximately 10 percent of the population. Because they closely resemble each other in facial features and body structure, children with Down's Syndrome are recognized more easily than any other clinical type. Their characteristics and special needs should be understood by the physical educator.

Almost nothing was known about this syndrome until 1959, when it was demonstrated that these children have 47 chromosomes in each cell rather than the normal 46. The extra chromosome is in the twenty-first chromosomal pair; thus the term *trisomy 21* is often used. Since 1959, three distinct types of Down's Syndrome have been discovered: (1) the standard trisomy, (2) translocation, and (3) mosaicism. The cause of this chromosomal abnormality is still unknown. A high risk exists in those parents carrying chromosomal defects themselves; those exposed to

Figure 25.6. Most Down's Syndrome children are moderately retarded.

istics which follow as hypotheses to be tested rather than as accepted facts.

From an anatomic point of view, newborn infants with Down's Syndrome are unfinished. All of the systems in the body show gross deficiencies in growth and development. Not only is the physical growth abnormally slow, but it ceases altogether at an early age, thereby resulting in stunted growth or dwarfism. Few persons with Down's Syndrome ever exceed a height of five feet. In addition to dwarfed stature and short broad hands and feet, he is recognized by almond shaped, slanting eyes which are often close-set and strabismic, a flattening of the bridge of the nose, and a large tongue which protrudes frequently from the abnormally small mouth. Protrusion of the tongue is probably due to the smallness of the oral cavity rather than the size of the tongue. This latter characteristic is a definite health problem in that it induces mouth breathing and contributes to susceptibility to upper respiratory infections. The skin lacks elasticity, hangs loosely, and tends to be rough. Hair is straight, fine and sparse. With regard to dental health, persons with Down's Syndrome are known to have small teeth in abnormal and maloccluded alignment.

Congenital heart disorders are common. Benda states specifically, "More than sixty percent of our patients reveal a heart murmur and evidence of septum defect." The circulatory system is immature with arteries remaining narrow and thin and the vascular tree having fewer branches than normal. It is interesting to note that a large percentage have "systolic heart murmur" written on their school records, but no medical restrictions on physical activity are generally stated. For legal protection, it is recommended that the physical educator be particularly cautious in working with this group and insistent upon having current health clearance forms on file.

genetically damaging agents such as virus, repeated x-rays or chemical exposure; or those of advanced maternal age. At age 25, a woman has a risk of one in 1,000 of bearing an infant with Down's Syndrome; at age 35, a risk of one in 250; at age 40, a risk of one in 100; and at age 45, a risk of one in 50. It is believed that genetic counseling and prenatal screening will all but eliminate chromosomal abnormalities in the next few decades.

Children with Down's Syndrome are so different from other retarded individuals that physical educators must study their characteristics separately. Clemens E. Benda, Director of Research and Clinical Psychiatry at Walter F. Fernald State School in Waltham, Massachusetts, is recognized as the foremost authority on this clinical type.[7] The dearth of research studies, which exist, however, require replication and expansion. It is hoped that physical educators will consider the character-

7. Clemens E. Benda, *The Child With Mongolism.* (New York: Grune and Stratton, 1960).

Figure 25.7. Child with Down's Syndrome learns to catch. (Courtesy of Recreation Center for the Handicapped, Inc., in San Francisco.)

Figure 25.8. The joy of success. (Courtesy of Recreation Center for the Handicapped, Inc., in San Francisco.)

Newborn infants with Down's Syndrome, like most severely neurologically involved babies, exhibit an extreme degree of muscular hypotonia; this fact has led to the coinage of the term *floppy babies*. The muscular flabbiness decreases with age, but never completely disappears. The abdomen of the adolescent and the adult generally protrudes like that of a small child. Almost 90 percent have umbilical hernias in early childhood, but the condition often corrects itself. This finding suggests that abdominal exercises be selected and administered with extreme care. Straight-leg lifts and holds and timed consecutive sit-ups are contraindicated. Other postural and/or or-

thopedic problems commonly associated with Down's Syndrome are dorsolumbar kyphosis, dislocated hips, funnel shaped or pigeon breasted chest, and club feet.

The lax ligaments and apparent looseness of the joints lead some authors to describe persons with Down's Syndrome as "double-jointed." The characteristic structural weakness of ligaments perhaps affects the function of the foot most. Many children have badly pronated feet. Others, whose ligaments are too weak to support the longitudinal arch, become flat-footed as their body weight becomes increasingly heavier. Daily foot exercises are recommended in an effort to ward off these problems. Seefeldt[8] reports hyperextensible joints in 88 percent of a sample. He believes that the retarded ossification of bone tissue and the consequent overabundance of cartilage explains this hyperextensibility. These facts seem to suggest that children with Down's Syndrome may excel in dance and gymnastics activities which demand high degrees of flexibility.

Assessment of the differences in tactual, spatial, and kinesthetic skills of familial, brain damaged, and Down's Syndrome children have shown the latter to be the most perceptually handicapped.[9] Persons with Down's Syndrome are especially deficient on nonvisual tasks which require the interpretation of tactual, kinesthetic sensations. Benda states also that they are poorest in tactile and fine motor discriminations and highest on visual tasks. Vision, however, is often impaired by strabismus, myopia, and astigmatism. Auditory discrimination has received little attention, but research shows that most can hum a tune correctly in note and time. Most are able also to perform folk and square dances in time to the music.

Balance is one of the perceptual-motor abilities in which persons with Down's Syndrome are most deficient. In this area, they tend to perform one to three years behind other persons with the same level of retardation.

Cratty[10] reported that approximately seventy-five percent of the children with Down's Syndrome he tested could not balance on one foot for more than a few seconds and most could not maintain balance at all with eyes closed. In general, basic movements are awkward. The gait is conspicuously infantile until about age six. Many walk with a broad base through life. According to Cratty, children with Down's Syndrome show severe impairment in perceptual-motor functioning when they attempt to perform accuracy tasks such as hopping or jumping prescribed floor patterns. Only about fifty percent can jump with both feet simultaneously one or more

Figure 25.9. Preadolescent with Down's Syndrome exhibits balance deficits.

times. Only about one-fourth can hop on one foot and/or jump backwards.

Persons with Down's Syndrome show marked variability in learning capacities. Generally speaking, the large majority, whether institutionalized or not, fall into the moderately retarded category. Recent observa-

8. Vernal Dennis Seefeldt, "A Longitudinal Study of Physical Growth and Development in Down's Syndrome," Unpublished PhD. Study, University of Wisconsin, 1966.

9. Robert M. Knight, Joseph A. Hyman, and Marius A. Wozny, "Psychomotor Abilities of Familial, Brain Damaged, and Mongoloid Retarded Children," *American Journal of Mental Deficiency* Vol. 70, No. 3 (November, 1965), p. 457.

10. Bryant J. Cratty, *Developmental Sequences of Perceptual-Motor Tasks* (Freeport, New York: Educational Activities, Inc., 1967), p. 5.

tions, however, have revealed that those who remain in their natural home settings often have an I.Q. of 60 or 70 and function at a higher level than others. Characterized by a good memory, many can acquire a large vocabulary, read at the primary level, and learn to spell well. Seagoe[11] tells the story of a boy with Down's Syndrome who read at the seventh-grade level and kept a daily diary using Spanish as well as English over a period of years. Children with Down's Syndrome often give the impression of knowing more than they do because of their astounding gift of mimicry. This trait may be simply a manifestation of their protracted infancy, since normal children between two and four characteristically imitate those around them.

The I.Q. of children with Down's Syndrome tends to drop slowly during early adolescence so that many initially are enrolled in the highest level special education classes and later are transferred to lower groups. During puberty marked changes in the intellectual status may occur; they may become less attentive, slower, and more difficult to teach than before. The cause of such deterioration is unknown.

The social maturity of persons with Down's Syndrome is consistently greater than their mental ages would lead one to expect. Affectionate, relaxed individuals with friendly dispositions, they adapt easily to institutional life. They are described as mannerly, responsible, cooperative, scrupulous, cheerful, and gregarious. Although usually cooperative, persons with Down's Syndrome may exhibit extreme stubbornness. They seem to like routine and may resist strongly any changes in the daily school schedule, in their diet, or in sharing toys. This trait, similar to perseveration and conceptual rigidity in the brain damaged, makes the person with Down's Syndrome seem similar to the normal two-year-old who is frozen at the "No" stage. Stubbornness appears to be a CNS deficit and should be dealt with accordingly rather than punished.

Physical Education for the Severely and Profoundly Retarded

Children whose I.Q.'s fall below 35 are totally dependent. Usually institutionalized in early childhood, they are likely to remain in a residential facility throughout their life span. Physical growth and development are so slow that these youngsters function as infants during their first six or seven years. They are confined to cradles and playpens and only with patient, persevering training are they taught purposive movement. The highest level severely retarded child seldom learns to walk alone steadily before age six. The highest level profoundly retarded may not do so until age nine or so. The average performance is much below this estimate, and some profoundly retarded persons never become ambulatory.

These are the children who do not play spontaneously. Even after some locomotor skills are mastered, they may lie or sit for hours, perseveratively rocking back and forth, and giving little evidence of environmental awareness. IRUC, in 1974, disseminated the first bibliography pertaining specifically to programming for individuals with I.Q.'s under 35.[12] Drawing from many sources, this chapter breaks physical education for the low level retarded person into the following areas: (1) sensory-motor training; (2) basic movement performance; and (3) fitness, rhythms, and games.

Sensory-Motor Training

Sensory-motor training is the earliest form of physical education provided for most severely and profoundly retarded children. It generally aims at improving four areas of behavior: (1) level of awareness, (2) movement, (3) manipulation of environment, and (4) posture and locomotion. Table 40 summarizes techniques of sensory-motor training.

11. May V. Seagoe, *Yesterday Was Tuesday, All Day and All Night* (Boston: Little, Brown, and Co., 1964).

12. IRUC, *Physical and Recreational Programming for Severely and Profoundly Mentally Retarded Individuals* (Washington, D. C.: AAHPER, 1974).

Table 40   *Techniques of Sensory-Motor Training*

Goal	Senses Stimulated	Therapy Activity	Equipment
Raising Level of Awareness	1. Tactility	1. Toweling, brushing, icing, stroking, tapping, contact with textures	1. Towels, brushes (light), ice bags, sensitive hand reflex hammer
	2. Kinesthesia	2. Applying restraints as "K contrasts" for short periods, promoting body awareness by cuddling and holding tightly	2. Sand bags, splint jackets, strong gentle arms
	3. Vision	3. Following flashlight, hanging ball, colored toys	3. Flashlight, ball hanging from ceiling, gay blocks, balls, dolls
	4. Audition	4. Calling name of child, naming objects used, nearby persons and actions, shaking ball, rattle, presenting music and commands	4. Wrist and ankle balls, Noisemakers, Tape recorders, Nursery rhymes and records with varying loudness, pitch and tempo
	5. Taste	5. Exposing child to extreme tastes	5. Sweet, sour, bitter, salt substances (honey, lemon, alum, salt)
	6. Olfaction	6. Exposing child to extreme odors	6. Pungent substances (coffee, cinnamon, vinegar)
	7. Temperature	7. Exposing child to extreme temperatures	7. Two basins with warm and cold water
	8. Sensory Integration	8. Mirror play	8. Full length mirror
Improving Movement	Kinesthesia	1. Rolling	1. Mat with rough, smooth, hard, soft surfaces (fine screening, plank, sponge rubber)

Table 40   *Techniques of Sensory-Motor Training—Continued*

Goal	Senses Stimulated	Therapy Activity	Equipment
		2. Rocking	2. Rocking chairs and horses, large beach balls
		3. Bouncing	3. Air mattress, trampoline, jump-up seat
		4. Swinging	4. Hammocks, suspended seats
		5. "Channeling" hyper-activity through specific movements of limbs	
Improving Manipulation	Sensory-Motor Integration	1. Reaching	1. Toys with various textures, colors, and sound, water play, sticky clay, sand, finger paint, punching balls
		2. Grasping	2. Same as 1
		3. Holding	3. Same as 1
		4. Throwing	4. Small balls
		5. Responding to social cues	5. Balls, praise, food treats, affection
		6. Developing relationship to one person	6. Individual therapist
Developing Posture and Locomotion	Sensory-Motor Integration	1. Lifting head while prone	1. Chest support
		2. Sitting	2. Rubber tube
		3. Crawling	3. Crawler, crawl in path
		4. Standing	4. Standing tables, human support
		5. Riding tricycle	5. Tricycle with or without seat support and feet straps
		6. Walking	6. Parallel bars, human support, pushing weighted cart
		7. Stair climbing	7. Practice stairs

13. Ruth C. Webb, "Sensory-Motor Training of the Profoundy Retarded," *American Journal of Mental Deficiency* Vol. 74 (Seieder, 1969), p. 287.

Level of Awareness—Activities are designed to help children recognize pleasant and unpleasant stimuli, to remember past exposures to them, and to exercise discrimination in anticipating or avoiding future contacts. Specifically, avoidance reactions (crying or turning away) are evoked in response to uncomfortably hot and cold water, vigorous toweling of skin, restraints as splint jacket or weights on legs, taps from a rubber hammer, and extreme tastes as alum or lemon. Approach reactions (smiling or turning toward a visual or auditory stimulus) are encouraged in response to bell ringing, music, a human voice, and various colorful objects. Response to cuddling by drawing closer is another important approach reaction. Children are drilled also on such discriminatory reactions as responding to name, obeying simple verbal and/or gesture commands, and turning toward objects as they are named. All responses at this level are nonverbal since the child has not yet acquired speech.

Movement—As the child becomes increasingly aware of sensory stimuli, he must be trained to make progressively more adequate motor adjustments. Externally imposed motion promotes discriminatory reactions as the child learns the difference between movement and no movement. At first all purposive movement must be initiated by the teacher who carries, rocks, rolls, bounces, and swings the child. Eventually the child begins to offer active assistance when the limbs are manipulated or the body moved. As independent movement is achieved he is led through the following teaching progression: (1) roll to side, (2) roll from front to back, (3) roll completely over, (4) roll in a barrel, (5) roll over such obstacles as firm pillows and inner tubes, (6) rock on a rocking chair or horse, (7) bounce on a bed, jump-up seat, or trampoline, and (8) swing in a hammock or suspended seat. These activities are continued until sufficient muscle strength is developed to allow sitting and standing without external support.

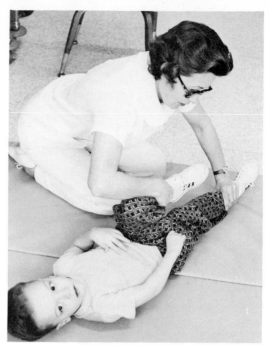

Figure 25.10. Externally imposed movement helps children learn the difference between movement and no movement.

Manipulation of Environment—Whereas the normal infant reaches for objects, grasps and plays with them, and eventually learns to get attention by throwing them on the floor, the severely or profoundly retarded child will evidence these behaviors only after training. Manipulation of environment implies lessons in reaching, grasping, releasing, throwing, holding, passing from hand to hand, rubbing, squeezing, tasting, pounding, shaking, taking apart, and reassembling. It also includes socialization experiences, beginning with response to mirror image and extending to communication with others through sounds, gestures, or words. Self-help skills are emphasized, and the child is taught to manipulate eating utensils, to assist in dressing himself, and to cooperate in bathing and toilet activities. The practice of these tasks can be made into games, and the child's work becomes inseparable from play.

Posture and Locomotion—Training begins with lifting the head while in different lying positions. Motivational devices like the smell of a food treat or the sound of a bell are often required to elicit a head lifting response, particularly from a prone position. Children who lack the muscular strength to sit without support are strapped into correct sitting position for a few minutes each day. Various kinds of apparatus on wheels or rollers facilitate the first attempt at creeping, standing, and walking. The teacher must repeatedly manipulate the limbs through the desired movement patterns in an attempt to elicit kinesthetic and vestibular feedback which enables the child to remember and reproduce particular movements. For optimal results, this work should be done in front of a mirror to facilitate visuo-motor integration. Sound effects should be used also to reinforce positive attempts.

Basic Movement Performance

Severely and profoundly retarded persons may spend their lifetimes acquiring basic locomotor movements. It is doubtful that running, jumping, and other motor skills can be taught except on a one-to-one basis with the teacher repeatedly moving limbs through desired movement patterns. A review of Chapter 7 will help with the development of a sequential progression for teaching motor patterns normally acquired during ages 1-6.

Several residential facilities use the following Basic Movement Performance Profile (BMPP) as the basis for curriculum planning.

Assessment Instrument—Basic Movement Performance Profile
Items Listed in Order of Difficulty for Profoundly
Retarded Residents at the Denton State School

BASIC MOVEMENT PERFORMANCE PROFILE

SCORE SHEET: Perfect score is 80.

Name: _____ School: _____

Age: _____ Sex: _____ Date: _____

Mental Retardation Classification: _____ Total Score: _____

Circle appropriate basic movement response _____

1. Walking
   0—makes no attempt at walking
   1—walks while being pulled
   2—walks with toe-heel placement
   3—walks with shuffle
   4—walks with heel-toe placement and opposite arm-foot swing

2. Pushing (wheelchair)
   0—makes no attempt to push wheelchair
   1—makes some attempt to push wheelchair
   2—pushes wheelchair once with arms only
   3—pushes wheelchair with continuous motion for 10 ft.
   4—pushes wheelchair carrying adult occupant continuously for 10 ft.

3. Ascending Stairs (up 4 stair steps)
   0—makes no attempt to walk up stairs
   1—steps up one step with assistance
   2—walks up 4 steps with assistance
   3—walks up 4 steps; two feet on each step
   4—walks up 4 steps; alternating one foot on each step

4. Descending Stairs (down 4 stair steps)
   0—makes no attempt to walk down stairs
   1—steps down one step with assistance
   2—walks down 4 steps with assistance
   3—walks down 4 steps, two feet on each step
   4—walks down 4 steps, alternating one foot on each step

5. Climbing (4 rungs; 1st choice, ladder of slide, 2nd choice, step ladder)
   0—makes no attempt to climb ladder
   1—climbs at least one rung with assistance
   2—climbs 4 rungs with assistance
   3—climbs 4 rungs, two feet on each rung
   4—climbs 4 rungs, alternating one foot on each rung

6. Carrying (folded folding chair)
   0—makes no attempt to lift chair from floor
   1—attempts but not able to lift chair from floor
   2—lifts chair from floor
   3—carries chair by dragging on the floor
   4—carries chair 10 ft.

7. Pulling (wheelchair)
   0—makes no attempt to pull wheelchair
   1—makes some attempt to pull wheelchair
   2—pulls wheelchair once with arms only
   3—pulls wheelchair with continuous motion for 10 ft.
   4—pulls wheelchair carrying adult occupant continuously for 10 ft.

8. Running
   0—makes no attempt to run
   1—takes long walking steps while being pulled
   2—takes running steps while being pulled
   3—jogs (using toe or flat of foot)
   4—runs for 25 yds., with both feet off the ground when body weight shifts from the rear to front foot

9. Catching (bean bag tossed from 5 ft. away)
   0—makes no attempt to catch bean bag
   1—holds both arms out to catch bean bag

2—catches bean bag fewer than 5 of 10 attempts
3—catches bean bag at least 5 of 10 attempts
4—catches bean bag at least 8 of 10 attempts

10. Creeping
    0—makes no attempt to creep
    1—will assume hands and knees position
    2—creeps with a shuffle
    3—creeps alternating hands and knees
    4—creeps in a crosslateral pattern with head up

11. Jumping Down (two foot take-off and landing from 18 in. folding chair)
    0—makes no attempt
    1—steps down from chair with assistance
    2—steps down from chair
    3—jumps off chair with two foot take-off and landing with assistance
    4—jumps off chair with two foot take-off and landing while maintaining balance

12. Throwing (overhand softball, 3 attempts)
    0—makes no attempt to throw
    1—grasps ball and releases in attempt to throw
    2—throws or tosses ball a few feet in any direction
    3—throws ball at least 15 ft. in air in intended direction
    4—throws ball at least 30 ft. in the air in intended direction

13. Hitting (volleyball with plastic bat)
    0—makes no attempt to hit ball
    1—hits stationary ball fewer than 3 of 5 attempts
    2—hits stationary ball at least 3 of 5 attempts
    3—hits ball rolled from 15 ft. away fewer than 3 of 5 attempts
    4—hits ball rolled from 15 ft. away at least 3 of 5 attempts

14. Forward Roll
    0—makes no attempt to do forward roll
    1—puts hands and head on mat

2—puts hands and head on mat and pushes with feet and/or knees in an attempt to do roll

3—performs roll but tucks shoulder and rolls to side

4—performs forward roll

15. Kicking (soccer ball)
   0—makes no attempt to kick stationary ball
   1—pushes stationary ball with foot in attempt to kick it
   2—kicks stationary ball several feet in any direction
   3—kicks stationary ball several feet in intended direction
   4—kicks ball rolled from 15 ft. away in direction of roller

16. Dynamic Balance (4 in. beam with shoes on)
   0—makes no attempt to stand on beam
   1—stands on beam with assistance
   2—walks at least 5 steps with assistance
   3—walks at least 5 ft. without stepping off beam
   4—walks at least 10 ft. without stepping off beam

17. Hanging (2 hands on horizontal bar)
   0—makes no attempt to grasp bar
   1—makes some attempt to hang from bar
   2—hangs from bar with assistance
   3—hangs from bar for at least 5 seconds
   4—hangs from bar for at least 10 seconds

18. Dodging (a large cage ball rolled from 15 ft. away)
   0—makes no attempt to dodge ball
   1—holds up hands or foot to stop ball
   2—turns body to avoid ball
   3—dodges ball at least 5 of 10 attempts
   4—dodges ball at least 8 of 10 attempts

19. Static Balance (standing on one foot with shoes on)
   0—makes no attempt to stand on one foot
   1—makes some attempt to stand on one foot

2—stands on one foot with assistance

3—stands on one foot for at least 5 seconds

4—stands on one foot for at least 5 seconds with 5 lbs. weight in the same hand as elevated foot

20. Jumping (standing long jump, 3 attempts)
   0—makes no attempt to jump
   1—jumps with a one-foot stepping motion
   2—jumps from crouch with two foot take-off and landing at least 1 ft.
   3—jumps from crouch with two foot take-off and landing at least 2 ft.
   4—jumps from crouch with two foot take-off and landing at least 3 ft.

First developed by Fait [14] and colleagues at the Mansfield Training School, the BMPP has been revised and standardized by Ness [15] at the Denton State School. It has a reliability coefficient of .94, derived by the test-retest method using sixty profoundly retarded adults.

Profoundly retarded residents at the Denton State School scored from 25-65 on the BMPP. The only tasks which 90 percent of the residents could perform without training were walking and pushing a wheelchair. The next easiest were walking up and down stair steps. Catching was easier than throwing, a finding contradictory of normal early childhood development. The most difficult tasks, on which none of the residents scored a 4, were walking ten feet on a four-inch walking board, hanging from a horizontal bar, dodging a cage ball, standing on one foot, and long jumping. After the administration of the BMPP, individualized physical education prescriptions should be devised to help each resident develop the basic movement patterns he lacks.

14. Hollis F. Fait, *Special Physical Education* (Philadelphia: W. B. Saunders, 1972), pp. 208-209

15. Richard Ness, "The Standardization of the Basic Movement Performance Profile for Profoundly Retarded Institutionalized Residents," Unpublished PhD., North Texas State University, Denton, Texas, 1974.

Fitness, Rhythms, and Games

The mastery of skills beyond running and jumping is probably less important than the maintenance of a minimum level of fitness. Far too many severely and profoundly involved persons spend so much time sitting that their muscles tighten and contort trunks and limbs into unusable shapes. But how do you motivate such persons to run or even walk sufficient distances to develop minimal circulovascular endurance? How do you persuade them to do a repeated number of sit-ups, toe touches, or arm circles? How can you obtain valid test scores on persons who cannot grasp concepts of time, distance, speed, force, and number? This writer has not found any objective fitness test which works with persons having I.Q.'s of 35 and under. Many of the retardates can perform some of the items commonly used on fitness tests but their failure to comprehend instructions makes evaluation of maximal or even submaximal performance impossible. Much research is needed on the severely and profoundly retarded.

The teacher of these persons must possess abundant energy and a high level of fitness. The child will generally run only as long as the teacher runs with him; this is true of most other exercises. If there is no model to imitate, the child will not respond to movement instructions—possibly because he cannot remember even simple exercises without visual stimuli.

By adolescence, a few (but not many) can begin to enjoy simple games and dance activities as Drop the Handkerchief; Duck, Duck, Goose; Musical Chairs; and Did You Ever See a Lassie? Most severely and profoundly retarded children continue to respond best on a one-to-one basis. Ball handling (rolling, bouncing, chasing, and retrieving), water play, and repetitive activities such as block stacking and bead stringing are effective. Interesting music with a strong beat generally elicits rhythmic movement which bears some resemblance to social dance. Frozen at the *I* stage, the severely and profoundly retarded prefer to dance without partners and seldom relate to others on the dance floor.

Background music seems also to improve response to exercise sessions, and some experiments have shown that the retarded can be conditioned to perform a certain exercise each time the same melody is heard. Most training centers provide for 5 to 10 minutes of exercise at regularly scheduled times each day, so that the children respond appropriately as they do to meal, bath, and bed time. For best results, exactly the same exercises to the same music should be executed daily at the designated times. The lower level retardate is not bored by repetition. On the contrary, it provides him with security and a sense of well-being.

Initial exercise training demands the calculated use of as much sensory stimuli as possible. For instance, each time the music begins visual stimuli in the form of videotapes or slides can be used to remind the students of the correct response. In the early stages of training, the teacher is unable to provide such stimulus through demonstration since he and the aides must move the children manually through the expected actions and personally reward every cooperative effort. The association of color with certain exercise positions seems helpful when slides are used, i.e., the demonstrator wears red for standing exercises, blue for sitting exercises, pink for prone lying, and green for supine lying. The olfactory sense is appealed to by burning a certain incense or scented candle only for exercise sessions or by using an aerosol spray with a pleasant odor. Verbal commands are limited to one or two word cues like *down, up, down, up.*

Operant conditioning or *shaping* is used to reinforce learning through the immediate rewarding of each correct response. The reward is generally eatable like M & M candy or cereal but may be a hug, pat, or words of praise. In operant conditioning, one teacher is needed for each child as illustrated in the following example of a fifth lesson on the toe touch exercise.

Teacher: Turns on music and flips slide projector on to automatic. Red slides begin to show.

Child: Rises from chair and stands on specified floor marking.

Teacher: Puts M & M in his open mouth and says "Good Boy."

Child: Makes slight forward motion as though he intends to touch toes.

Teacher: Puts M & M in mouth and says "Good Boy;" manually pushes him down to the correct position.

Child: Fingers touch floor at end of down phase.

Teacher: Puts M & M in mouth and says "Good Boy."

Child: Extends to starting position.

Teacher: Puts M & M in mouth and says "Good Boy." Turns off music and slide projector. Allows child to wander off. Then repeats entire sequence.

As conditioned responses grow stronger, fewer M & M's are given so that eventually only one reward is required at the completion of the toe touch. Later the child may progress to a series of eight toe touches before the reward is received. The success of operant conditioning depends upon the teacher's ability to break an exercise down into a sequence of very small tasks and his consistency in rewarding each success. The initial tasks must be so simple that success in inevitable. For instance, rising from a chair might be broken down into the following tasks, each of which is rewarded separately: (1) puts one or both feet on floor; (2) bends forward slightly; (3) positions hands on arm rest for balance; (4) lifts buttocks from chair; (5) takes weight on one or both feet; (6) lifts head; (7) extends trunk and (8) extends knees. In accordance with the principle of individual differences, the type of reward may vary with each child. Ultimately, however,

it is hoped that verbal praise, a smile, or head nod can be substituted for the more tangible rewards. In some instances, the pleasure of the activity itself will be remembered and serve as motivation in subsequent stimulus-response situations.

While a one-to-one ratio is desirable with the lower level retardate, most residential facilities have too few staff members to implement such a program. Barbara Ross, a recreation therapist at the Denton State School, wrote the following four descriptions of group activities, comparing the responses of profoundly retarded and severely retarded males. Activities for the two groups were conducted separately. The sizes of the profoundly retarded and severely retarded groups were thirty and twenty-five respectively. Two or three therapists work together in handling groups of this size.

The Special Olympics Program

In some communities, Special Olympics is synonymous with physical education for the mentally retarded. It is a year-round program of sports training which ideally involves some athletic competition for all children ages eight and over regardless of how low their skill may be. The Special Olympics dream was conceived and implemented by the Joseph P. Kennedy, Jr. Foundation after national surveys in the mid 1960s revealed that less than 25 percent of the retarded school age population in the United States was receiving physical education instruction. The motivating force behind the dream was the initiation of physical education and athletic programs for the retarded where none existed and the expansion of opportunities in on-going programs.

Positive successful experiences in sport are believed to contribute to improved self-concept and to carry over into the classroom, the home, and the sheltered workshop. Hence Special Olympics are organized so that every child can be a winner. Awards are given for participation as well as for excellence among peers. Meets are arranged to give competitors the feeling of being an athlete rather than a retarded child. The Special Olympics Oath, repeated before engaging in competition, reinforces this feeling:

Let me win
But if I cannot win
Let me be brave in the attempt.

Daily physical education instruction is the most important aspect of Special Olympics. Ideally the program culminates each spring in local and state meets where youngsters have an opportunity to exhibit the skills which they have been practicing all year. For many children, the meet represents a first time to win an award, to have a picture in the newspaper, to receive recognition at a school assembly, and to have parents and neighbors observe.

Responses of Profoundly Retarded Males Ages 10-32 (MA 0-2)	Responses of Severely Retarded Males Ages 14-20 (MA 2-5)

Beanbag Activities

Tasks: Free play, carry on head, step and hop over one bag, toss beanbag into container, toss beanbag to instructor.

This group preferred to chew or eat the beanbags. The free play consisted primarily of releasing the bag as soon as it was placed into the hand. The students were manually manipulated through each movement on a one-to-one basis. The shape of the beanbag appeared to make little difference, but occasionally a student would reach for a certain color. Pleasure was derived mainly from attention of the teacher rather than the activity itself.

The majority of severely retarded boys were more creative with the beanbags than the profoundly retarded group. There was less tendency to chew the bag and a better concept of throwing. Free play consisted of the students bringing the bag to the teacher to play with them on a one-to-one basis. Several observed the demonstrations and attempted to imitate the teacher. Coordination was more highly developed than in the other group, but much manual assistance was required in the foot work.

Rope and Yarn Activities

Tasks: Hop on one or both legs; hop over rope; use vertical and horizontal space; crouch down and stretch tall with rope in hand; curl up on floor and stretch long; grip rope and follow instructor.

The profoundly retarded group did not follow instructions. Individuals were manipulated through the movements by two instructors. Curling and crouching were accepted far more readily than stretching. Walking out floor patterns seemed to be simply a matter of follow the leader with no real awareness of the patterns.

The severely retarded group copied demonstrations, often adapting them to their own abilities. Although most attempted to hop, there was little success. This group had some concept of what was beneath their feet and enjoyed being led through and around objects. They preferred to hold the instructor's hand rather than a rope.

Cage Ball Activities

Tasks: Roll ball to students on a one-to-one basis; small group activities in a circle—sit and kick ball to each other, sit and push ball to each other; repeat from a standing position.

The ball appeared to be irritating to a number of the profoundly retarded children. They turned away from it or attempted to push it away. Others grinned as they pushed it away indicating that they recognized the teacher's pleasure at their correct response. A few attempted to tease the teacher by pushing the ball the opposite way and watching the teacher for a reaction. None of the students used their feet to kick the ball without constant reminders. The students remained in the circle but did not interact with their peers. Essentially the activity was a one-to-one exchange with the teacher.

The severely retarded children performed the activities with little effort. Their attention span, however, was short. The teacher had to repeatedly call out names to get responses to the ball and to close gaps in the circular formation. The group appeared to grasp the concept of the circle and playmates but preferred to roll the ball to the teacher rather than their peers. Compared to other daily lessons, the cage ball activities were especially successful.

Universal Gym and Mat Activities

Tasks: Press weights with legs: push and pull weights with arms; sit up on inclined board; log roll; forward roll; creeping activities on mat.

On a one-to-one basis, approximately half of the profoundly retarded group would perform what was requested to some degree. They enjoyed raising the weights and letting them drop with a loud bang. The noise appeared to be exciting to them and the center of the entire activity. The heights and weights of the adult students made mat work extremely fatiguing for the instructors. Many of the students were so large that they could not be safely manipulated by the two instructors. Four of the thirty pupils could do the mat activities. The group was too large for implementation of goals.

With a few exceptions, all of the severely retarded children learned to perform simple presses and pulls on the universal gym. These students also enjoyed making loud noises with the weights but would lower them slowly and quietly when under the direct surveillance of the instructor. About half of the twenty-five pupils performed all of the mat activities with the teacher's help. Others attempted the activities only after repeated urging. Most of the pupils expressed more fear and distress than enjoyment of the mat activities.

Nine sports have been designated as official Special Olympics events: (1) track and field, (2) swimming, (3) gymnastics, (4) bowling, (5) volleyball, (6) basketball, (7) floor hockey, (8) diving, and (9) ice skating. New sports may become Special Olympics official sports as they gain widespread acceptance and meet the criteria established for the health and safety of the participants. Also at all levels of Special Olympics, other sports are practiced as well as other recreational activities so that the participants have a broad range of activities to choose from and can find one or more to suit their individual abilities and preferences. Demonstration clinics are held at the games, sometimes led by well-known athletes, to teach the children new skills in sports such as football, gymnastics, basketball, etc.

Because there is a great range of athletic ability among the retarded, competition takes place in five divisions based upon ability as well as age and sex. Emphasis, even in state and national competition, is upon including children with low skill. Thus, in the bottom classification, Division V, at most of the state meets all of the contestants could be beaten by almost all normal children. In the Special Olympics they emerge as winners with almost everyone receiving some kind of medal or ribbon. In contrast, about 90 percent of the Division I competitors could compete satisfactorily against most normal children. Data from recent International Games indicate that approximately 10 percent of the Division I athletes might be potential medal winners in Junior Olympic Competition for normal children.

The range of abilities encompassed by each division is left to the discretion of local meet directors rather than predetermined by national norms. Assignment to a division is based upon actual performance in an event as recorded on the entry form by the coach or teacher. This requirement demands that all children be tested beforehand in the events they wish to enter. Current scores, times, and distances should be available for each child on such events as the following: track and field—50-yard dash, overarm softball throw, long jump, 220-yard run, high jump; swimming—25-yard freestyle, 50-yard freestyle, 25-yard backstroke; gymnastics—balance beam, free exercise, and tumbling. Special educators as well as physical educators should know how to assess performance in these activities. Only after the scores of all pupils have been submitted to the meet director does he determine who belongs in Divisions I, II, III, IV, and V under each age group. Competition within each division is separate for boys and girls.

Special Olympics competition is conducted for eight age groups as follows:

8 to 9 years	16 to 17 years
10 to 11 years	18 to 19 years
12 to 13 years	20 to 29 years
14 to 15 years	30 years and older

The veterans' category, 30 years and older, permits the retarded to enjoy sports programs throughout adulthood.

The pageantry and color of Special Olympics are as exciting to many children as the sports events. The opening ceremonies of a meet may include such highlights as the lighting of a Special Olympic torch, a parade of the athletes and/or of a band and local dignitaries, the raising of the American flag and the Special Olympic flag, a release of doves or balloons, the Special Olympic oath repeated in unison, and group warm-up exercises led by a visiting professional athlete. The closing ceremony is equally impressive with a final parade of the athletes, extinguishing of the Special Olympic flame, lowering of flags, and friendship songs. Most state meets are organized so as to provide competitors with an overnight experience. Special educational events include sports clinics and the opportunity to meet famous athletes and government figures.

Special educators and physical educators must work cooperatively to make the year-round Special Olympics program a success. Information on establishing, developing and becoming involved in such a program can be obtained by writing to the state director or Mrs. Eunice Kennedy Shriver, Special Olympics, Inc., Joseph P. Kennedy, Jr. Foundation, 1701 K Street, N. W., Suite 205, Washington, D. C. 20006. (A brochure and list of state directors is available from the Kennedy Foundation upon request.)

Physical Fitness Testing

The need for special fitness tests for the mentally retarded is substantiated by research. Retarded children and youth may lag several years behind normal children in the development of physical fitness. Although this lag is attributable more to inequalities in physical education programs than to innate inferior-

ities, there appears to be ample justification for separate test batteries and norms for the retarded and the normal. Among the special fitness tests for the mentally retarded which have gained widespread acceptance are the AAHPER-Kennedy Foundation battery and the Fait Physical Fitness battery. Both batteries include a 300-yard run-walk, a bent arm hang, and a 50- or 25-yard dash. In other respects they are different.

AAHPER-Kennedy Foundation Special Fitness Test

With the exception that three of its seven items have been modified for the retarded, this test is identical to the AAHPER Youth Fitness Test. Norms have been established for mildly retarded boys and girls ages eight through eighteen. A major strength of this battery appears to be the availability of awards at three levels of achievement. The AAHPER Special Silver and Gold Emblems for children who achieve standards on any five of the seven items can be ordered from AAHPER Headquarters. The Kennedy Foundation CHAMP

Figure 25.11. Classroom flags and parades of athletes contribute to the pageantry of Special Olympics.

Award for boys and girls who achieve standards on all seven test items and engage in at least thirty hours of physical activity is available without charge from the Joseph P. Kennedy, Jr. Foundation. Progress certificates for physically limited children offer additional motivation. The teacher interested in establishing a special fitness program should order the test manual and official record forms from AAHPER Headquarters.

Fait Physical Fitness Battery for Mentally Retarded Children

Fait's rationale for developing a test battery specifically for the mentally retarded is the high correlation which exists between intelligence quotient and certain fitness tasks. His research shows that the intelligence factor often influences the score on a fitness test as much or more than the physical fitness factor which the test is purported to measure. The six items comprising the Fait battery each have a very low correlation with intelligence. They are:

1. 300 Yard Run-Walk (Purports to measure cardio-respiratory endurance). Identical with item on AAHPER-Kennedy Foundation Special Test.
2. Bent Arm Hang (Purports to measure static muscular endurance of the arm and shoulder girdle). Identical with item on AAHPER-Kennedy Foundation Special Test with two exceptions. The bridge of the nose is used as an anchoring point rather than under the chin or at the forehead and a reverse grip (palms toward face) is used rather than the harder overhand grasp.
3. Stork Stand with Eyes Closed (Purports to measure ability to maintain static balance). The child places both hands on hips, lifts one leg, and places the foot on the inside of the knee of the weight-bearing leg. The score is the number of seconds this position is maintained with eyes closed.
4. Fleishman's Twenty Second Leg Lift Test (Purports to measure dynamic muscular endurance of the leg flexors and the abdominal muscles). The child assumes a supine lying position with hands clasped behind neck. Two aides are required, one to hold the child's elbows to the mat and one who provides a target by extending his arm for the child's toes to touch at the peak of the straight leg lift. The score is the number of leg lifts completed in twenty seconds. This item is not valid for retarded children unless the two aides are used.
5. Squat Thrusts Without Stand (Purports to measure a specific type of agility). The starting position is a squat with feet and palms of hands on floor. At no time during the test does the child rise to a stand. On the signal, "Go," the child transfers the weight to his hands and thrusts the legs straight out behind him. Then he returns his legs to the original position. One-half point is awarded for each thrust-out and thrust-in. The time limit is twenty seconds.
6. Twenty-five Yard Run (Purports to measure the speed of running short distances). The test is structured so that the child actually runs thirty yards although he is timed only on the first twenty-five. This adaptation is necessary because retarded children often do not understand that they should not slow down as they approach the finish line. The use of two finish lines helps to prevent this problem.

Fait has established a low, average, and good score for each test item for boys and girls in three age groups: 9-12 years; 13-16 years; and 17-20 years. These are presented in Table 41.

Table 41 *Fait Physical Fitness Test Battery for Mentally Retarded Children*

25 Yard Run

Boys (Score in seconds)

Age	Trainable Low	Av.	Good	Educable Low	Av.	Good
9-12	7	6	5.2	6.2	5.2	4.4
13-16	6.5	5.5	4.7	5.4	4.7	4.2
17-20	6	5	4.2	5.1	4.4	3.9
Girls						
9-12	7.4	6.3	5.3	5.8	5.4	5.2
13-16	6.7	5.6	4.7	6.1	5.2	4.3
17-20	7.3	6.1	5.1	6.4	5.4	4.7

Bent Arm Hang

Boys (Score in seconds)

Trainable Low	Av.	Good	Educable Low	Av.	Good	Age
2	10	16	3	19	33	9-12
11.2	22	30.2	5	25	43	13-16
23	23	31	8	30	50	17-20
						Girls
2	8	12	3	9	13	9-12
4	14	22	5	15	23	13-16
3	9	13	4	12	18	17-20

Leg Lift

Boys

Age	Trainable Low	Av.	Good	Educable Low	Av.	Good
9-12	6	9	12	7	10	13
13-16	6	9	12	8	11	14
17-20	7	10	13	8	11	14
Girls						
9-12	6	10	14	6	10	14
13-16	7	11	15	7	11	15
17-20	6	10	14	6	10	14

Stork Stand

Boys (Score in seconds)

Trainable Low	Av.	Good	Educable Low	Av.	Good	Age
3	4.4	5.8	4	5	6	9-12
3.1	4.5	5.9	5	6	7	13-16
3.2	4.6	6	5	10	15	17-20
						Girls
2.2	3.2	4.2	2.5	3.5	4.5	9-12
5.1	6.1	7.1	8.6	9.6	10.6	13-16
4.9	5.9	6.9	5.2	6.2	7.2	17-20

Thrust

Boys

Age	Trainable Low	Av.	Good	Educable Low	Av.	Good
9-12	4	8	10	6	12	14
13-16	4	8	10	8	14	16
17-20	5	9	11	8	14	16
Girls						
9-12	4	8	10	5	9	11
13-16	4	8	10	8	12	14
17-20	5	9	11	5		11

300 Yard Run-Walk

Boys (Score in seconds)

Age	Trainable Low	Av.	Good	Educable Low	Av.	Good
9-12	145	115	95	105	80	60
13-16	111	86	66	95	75	55
17-20	104	79	59	74	59	39
Girls						
9-12	198	148	108	143	113	83
13-16	158	108	65	125	91	61
17-20	159	107	66	142	102	71

Hollis F. Fait, *Special Physical Education* (Philadelphia: W.B. Saunders Co., 1972), pp. 392-393.

Figure 25.12. Preparation for squat thrust.

Figure 25.14. The completion of squat thrust.

Figure 25.13. The thrust.

Organizations

American Association on Mental Deficiency (AAMD), 5201 Connecticut Avenue N. W., Washington, D. C. 20015.

The Council for Exceptional Children, 1920 Association Drive, Reston, Virginia 22091.

Canadian Association for Retarded Children, 149 Alcorn Avenue, Toronto 7, Ontario, Canada.

Joseph P. Kennedy, Jr. Foundation, 1701 K Street NW, Suite 205, Washington, D. C. 20006.

National Association for Retarded Citizens, 2709 Avenue E East, Arlington, Texas 76011. (Formerly the National Association for Retarded Children)

President's Committee on Mental Retardation, Washington, D. C. 20201.

References

American Association for Health, Physical Education, and Recreation. *The Best of Challenge.* Vol. I. Washington, D. C.: AAHPER, 1971.

————. *The Best of Challenge.* Vol. II. Washington, D. C.: AAHPER, 1974.

————. *A Practical Guide for Teaching the Mentally Retarded to Swim.* Washington, D. C.: AAHPER, 1969.

————. *Special Olympics Instructional Manual—from Beginners to Champions.* Washington, D. C.: AAHPER, 1972.

American Association on Mental Deficiency. *Manual on Terminology and Classification in Mental Retardation.* 1973 revision edited by Herbert J. Grossman. Washington, D. C.: AAMD, 1973.

Beter, Thais, and Cragin, Wesley E. *The Mentally Retarded Child and His Motor Behavior: Practical Diagnosis and Movement Experiences.* Springfield, Illinois: Charles C Thomas, 1972.

Birch, Jack. *Mainstreaming: Educable Mentally Retarded in Regular Classes.* Reston, Virginia: Council for Exceptional Children, 1974.

Carlson, Bernice Wells, and Ginglend, David R. *Recreation for Retarded Teenagers and Young Adults.* Nashville, Tennessee: Abington Press, 1968.

Cratty, Bryant. *Motor Activity and the Education of Retardates.* 2nd ed. Philadelphia: Lea & Febiger, 1974.

Davis, Patricia. *Teaching Physical Education to Mentally Retarded Children.* Minneapolis, Minnesota: T. S. Denison & Company, Inc., 1968.

Drowatzky, John N. *Physical Education for the Mentally Retarded.* Philadelphia: Lea & Febiger, 1971.

Hackett, Layne C. *Movement Exploration and Games for the Mentally Retarded.* Palo Alto, California: Peek Publications, 1970.

Humphrey, James H., and Sullivan, Dorothy D. *Teaching Slow Learners Through Active Games.* Springfield, Illinois: Charles C Thomas, 1970.

Moran, Joan, and Kalakian, Leonard. *Movement Experiences for the Mentally Retarded or Emotionally Disturbed Child.* Minneapolis, Minnesota: Burgess Publishing Co., 1974.

Rarick, G. Lawrence; Dobbins, D. Allan; and Broadhead, Geoffrey, D. *The Motor Domain and its Correlates in Educationally Handicapped Children.* Englewood Cliffs, New Jersey: Prentice Hall, Inc., 1976.

Robinson, Christopher M.; Harrison, Julie; and Gridley, Joseph. *Physical Activity in the Education of Slow-Learning Children.* London: Edward Arnold Publishers, 1970.

Taylor, Z. Ann, and Sherrill, Claudine. *A Health Centered Core Curriculum for Educationally Handicapped Children.* Palo Alto, California: Peek Publications, 1969.

Periodicals

American Journal of Mental Deficiency. Published bimonthly by the American Association on Mental Deficiency. Editorial Office, Box 503, Peabody College, Nashville, Tennessee 37203.

Education and Training of the Mentally Retarded Child. Published quarterly by the Council for Exceptional Children.

Mental Retardation. Published bimonthly by the American Association on Mental Deficiency. A quarterly by the same name is published by the Canadian Association for Retarded Children.

Mental Retardation Abstracts. Published quarterly by the U. S. Department of Health, Education, and Welfare, Social and Rehabilitation Service, Division of Mental Retardation, U. S. Government Printing House.

Mental Retardation News. A newsletter published monthly except July and August by the National Association for Retarded Citizens.

PCMR Message. Published monthly by the President's Committee on Mental Retardation.

Autobiography, Biography, and Fiction

Abraham, Willard. *Barbara: A Prologue.* New York: Rinehart and Co., 1958.

Gant, Sophia. *One of Those.* New York: Pageant Press, 1957.

Hunt, Douglas. *The World of Nigel Hunt: The Diary of a Mongoloid Youth.* New York: Garrett Publications, 1967.

Keyes, Daniel. *Flowers for Algernon.* New York: Harcourt, Brace and World, 1966.

Lee, Carvel. *Tender Tyrant.* Minneapolis: Augsburg Publishing House, 1961.

Lukens, Kathleen, and Panter, Carol. *Thursday's Child Has Far To Go.* Englewood Cliffs, New Jersey: Prentice-Hall, Inc., 1969.

Murray, Dorothy Garst. *This Is Stevie's Story.* Nashville, Tennessee: Abingdon Press, 1967.

Patterson, Katheryn. *No Time For Tears.* Chicago: Johnson Publications Co., 1965.

26 Emotional Disturbance, Mental Illness, and Behavioral Disorders

Figure 26.0. The emotionally disturbed child must be taught how to channel aggression.

The monkey bars, crisscrossing up and down, forward and backward, intrigued him. There was no question that his jiggler pointed in their direction. But what if he got caught in the middle of all that iron? What if he couldn't get out?

He walked over cautiously and touched the closest bar. It was cold. A sinister chill ran through him. But the jiggler pointed in that direction again. This time he touched a bar warmed by the sun. This felt different, more inviting, but he was still afraid. It looked like a wonderful toy to climb over and swing from. And it looked like an awful monster that could tangle you up, crush you, and kill you. [1]

The playground can be terrifying to a child as depicted so well by Rubin, a practicing psychiatrist in Brooklyn, whose book should be read by all teachers interested in childhood schizophrenia. In the passage above, he describes Jordi, an eight-year-old boy with a diagnosis of schizophrenic reaction-type: mixed, undifferentiated, chronic. Like most emotionally disturbed children today, Jordi lives at home and attends a day school. Jordi is afraid of almost everything and carries a jiggler (a doorknob tied to a string) for security. Only when he learns to play stoop ball does he give up the jiggler. Later it is his skill in stoop ball which gives him enough confidence to respond affirmatively to an invitation to participate in a handball game—one of his first efforts to relate to the peer group.

Incidence

It is conservatively estimated that approximately 2 percent of the school age population is so severely emotionally disturbed that special education provisions are required. This includes about 1,207,200 pupils between ages five and nineteen. Another 10-15 percent need psychiatric help to function optimally.

Many teenagers have emotional problems severe enough to commit suicide; frequently these are not recognized until too late. Suicide ranks third as the leading cause of death in the fifteen to twenty-four age bracket. Statistics for all age groups combined reveal that over 25,000 suicides occur each year. Approximately two million persons in this country have made one or more attempts at suicide.

Delinquency, a legal term reserved for youngsters whose behavior results in arrest and court action, is another manifestation of emotional problems. The crime rate among young persons has increased steadily during the past decade. It is estimated that youthful offenders account for 61 percent of all auto thefts, 54 percent of larcenies, 55 percent of burglaries, and 33 percent of robberies. Long before their initial arrest many delinquents are described by classroom teachers as defiant, impertinent, uncooperative, irritable, bullying, attention seeking, negative, and restless. Other delinquents are seen as shy, lacking in self-confidence, hypersensitive, fearful, and excessively anxious.

The diagnosis of mental illness in childhood is difficult, and most psychiatrists prefer not to attach a label. For this reason, the large majority of children with behavior disorders are enrolled in regular classrooms with normal children. Kirk[2] concludes from a review of several survey studies that the prevalence of behavior disorders in the school population ranges from 2 to 22 percent, depending upon the criterion of behavior disorders used. The ratio of boys to girls is approximately four to one.

Behavior Disorders of Childhood and Adolescence

The American Psychiatric Association[3] recognizes seven categories of behavior disorders which do not approximate the se-

1. Theodore Isaac Rubin, *Jordi, Lisa, and David* (New York: The Macmillan Company, 1962), p. 42, by permission of the author.

2. Samuel A. Kirk, *Educating Exceptional Children* (Boston: Houghton Mifflin Company, 1972), p. 416.

3. American Psychiatric Association, *Diagnostic and Statistical Manual of Mental Disorders* (Washington, D. C.: The Association, 1968), pp. 50-51.

riousness of psychoses, neuroses, and personality disorders but nevertheless are stable, internalized, and resistant to treatment.

1. Hyperkinetic reaction characterized by short attention span, distractibility, restlessness, and overactivity.
2. Withdrawing reaction characterized by shyness, sensitivity, detachment, seclusiveness, and general inability to form close interpersonal relationships.
3. Overanxious reaction characterized by chronic anxiety, unrealistic fears, sleeplessness, and nightmares.
4. Runaway reaction characterized by escape from threatening situations by running away from home.
5. Unsocialized aggressive reaction characterized by hostility, quarrelsomeness, destructiveness, temper tantrums, and other forms of aggressiveness.
6. Group delinquent reaction characterized by the acquisition of the values and behavior of a delinquent peer group with whom they steal, skip school, and get into trouble.
7. Other reactions which do not fall into the fixed six categories but which are more serious than transient situational disturbances and less serious than psychoses, neuroses, and personality disorders.

Most special educators use the term *behavior disorders* rather than emotional or mental illness. In 1962 the Council on Exceptional Children formed the Council for Children with Behavioral Disorders (CCBD).

Sports, dance, and aquatics are often viewed as vehicles for the amelioration of behavior disorders. Team membership can be made meaningful enough that a youngster will curb unsocialized behaviors. The physical educator soon learns to help aggressive children express their hostility in socially acceptable ways: punching a bag, jumping, leaping, throwing, pushing, and pulling. Offensive strokes like the smash and skills like

Figure 26.1. Tetherball is a group activity in which hostility can be released in socially acceptable ways.

the volleyball spike can be practiced when tension is especially great. It sometimes helps to paint faces on the balls and punching bags. The teacher can join in stomping empty food cans, paper cups turned upside down, and balloons. The making of noise itself relieves tension. It is important that children learn that it is acceptable to take out aggressions on things, but never on persons or animals. Thus, boxing or wrestling against other children is contraindicated for some emotionally disturbed children who have not yet mastered control of their emotions. Aggressive children often can be developed into good squad leaders. Always they demand special attention—a personal "Hello, John" at the *first* of the period and the frequent use of their names throughout the class instruction.

More difficult to cope with are withdrawing and overanxious reactions. Most authorities concur that children should not be forced to participate in activities which they fear or intensely dislike. Swimming, tumbling, and apparatus seem to evoke withdrawal reactions more often than other physical education activities. In normal children these fears gradually subside when it becomes obvious that the peer group is having fun. Coaxing, cajoling, and reasoning accomplish little other than giving the child the extra attention he may be seeking. In the case of actual behavior disorders, psychotherapy and other specialized techniques are generally needed. The physical educator should work cooperatively with the school psychologist in strengthening the child's self-confidence and feelings of worth.

Mental Illness

The nomenclature of mental illness is established by the American Psychiatric Association.[4] In addition to the behavior disorders of childhood and adolescence, the physical educator should have some knowledge of neuroses, psychoses, and personality or character disorders. Almost all persons in our society have some neuroses, the term given to relatively benign personality disturbances. These include anxiety, phobias, obsessive ideas, compulsive rituals, excessive depression reactions, chronic fatigue (neurasthenia), depersonalization, and hypochondriases. Any neurotic problem tends to create a split in the unity of the personality and to reduce its contact with reality. Neuroses do not, however, cause serious personality disorganization. Any withdrawal or evasion of reality should receive the physical educator's attention. The neurotic tends to ignore reality while the psychotic denies it. Between these two extremes lies a broad range of schizoid states in which the degree of emotional detachment and personality split becomes progressively severe. Persons are not diagnosed as having psychoses until their mental functioning is so impaired that they can no longer meet the ordinary demands of life.

Of the many psychoses, schizophrenia is by far the most common. Half of all mental patients are schizophrenic. Moreover, one out of every 100 persons in the world suffers from schizophrenia at some time or another. In the United States, more than a quarter of all hospital beds are filled with patients who have it. The estimates of childhood schizophrenia range from 100,000 to half a million. There are approximately 4,000 psychotic children in state hospitals, close to 2,500 in residential treatment and day care centers, and at least 3,000 schizophrenic children in day care clinics. All of them require help in learning to play.

Affective disorders are the second most common group of psychoses. Persons with these disorders lose contact with their environment because of either extreme depression or elation (mania). Manic-depressive illnesses typically are marked by severe mood swings and a tendency to remission and reoccurrence.

Personality or character disorders is the official term for deeply ingrained maladaptive behavior patterns. Alcoholism, drug dependence, and socially unacceptable sexual behavior fall into this broad category as do most of the personality problems which lead to social and economic inadequacies. Movies such as *The Bad Seed* and *To Catch a Butterfly* depict personality disorders as do many of Eugene O'Neil's plays.

General Characteristics of Schizophrenic Disorders

Schizophrenic disorders are defined broadly as abnormal behavior patterns involving varying degrees of personality disorganization with less than adequate contact with reality. While there are important differences between the many types of schizophrenic disorders, the primary symptoms common to all can be thought of as "splits." The first of these is a "split of affect," referring to the lack of integration between thoughts and feelings. Whereas a normal individual feels sadness

4. American Psychiatric Association, *Diagnostic and Statistical Manual of Mental Disorders* (Washington, D. C.: The Association, 1968).

when he thinks of something sad, the schizophrenic person may present a cold or apathetic appearance. When a close relative dies, for example, the schizophrenic may appear happy and laugh. Such peculiar emotional responses on the part of the patient may be attributed to a split between the emotional and the intellectual facets.

A second symptom is the "split of associations." The schizophrenic's process of reasoning may differ considerably from that of the normal individual. Inherent in the thought patterns of a normal individual are associations which link together ideas in a sensible and logical order. In contrast, the thoughts of the schizophrenic may be isolated units with no logical association. Thought X may be isolated from Thought Y which, in turn, may be isolated from Thought Z. When confronted with a question such as "What have you been doing today?", the schizophrenic may respond with an irrelevant answer such as, "My father is a general."

A third symptom is the "split of attention," pertaining to the inability to focus the mind upon one subject. The attention of a schizophrenic patient may be directed toward several things simultaneously with the result that he is unable to concentrate adequately on a particular activity.

A fourth symptom concerns the sense of reality. The schizophrenic usually views himself and the world as a single unit. The idea that individuals are talking about him or that they are looking at him is a frequent delusion. As his contact with reality diminishes, the schizophrenic retreats from the real world and creates his own. This make-believe world is comprised of ways of thinking, acting, and speaking which are significant to the patient but incomprehensible to the normal individual.

The onset of schizophrenia is often slow. The individual experiences feelings of loneliness and depression which, in turn, may lead to withdrawal and complete seclusion. The thoughts of these individuals are described as bizarre, regressed, or deteriorated. Hallucinations and delusions commonly occur. The speech of the schizophrenic may be rambling, lacking in spontaneity, evasive, stylized, or incoherent. Neologisms, or words devised by the patient which have personal meaning and significance, and echolalia, or the repetition of words and phrases spoken by others, may be present.

As a group, schizophrenics tend to show disturbances in neuromuscular coordinations. Their movements are often inaccurate and awkward with extremely slow reaction time. Especially noticeable among chronic, hospitalized patients are their poor postures, lethargy, low fitness, and paucity of ideas in creative dance and/or spontaneous movement.

Specific Characteristics of Schizophrenic Disorders

Although common symptoms of schizophrenia exist, the schizophrenic disorders may be differentiated from one another by special characteristics.

Schizophrenia Catatonic. In this type of schizophrenia, a defense mechanism of denial is utilized. A catatonic patient attempts to deny loss of reality, lack of concentration, and disintegration of the ego by becoming either overactive in an attempt to push the world away or by withdrawing into himself. The denial of the outside world by withdrawing is the stupor phase of catatonia whereas denial by pushing the world away is the excited phase.

The classic descriptions of catatonic schizophrenia usually focus upon the stupor phase which includes a combination of mutism, rigidity, and *cerea flexibility,* or waxy flexibility, of the limbs. During the stupor phase, the catatonic may appear to be more out of contact with his surroundings than he actually is. He characteristically does not respond to environmental stimuli. Patients who have experienced catatonic stupor have later described the events which took place about them but confessed that they felt unable to respond in a meaningful manner.

The motor symptoms of catatonia are observed more readily than other symptoms. The patient may sit or stand in one position for hours; during this period he appears not to understand anything which is said to him and he refuses to talk. Occasionally symbolic movements, posturing, stereotyped gestures, and fixed attitudes may occur.

Schizophrenia Paranoid. The defense mechanism of projection, in which the patient transfers to the outside world something taking place within himself, is the main characteristic of the paranoid schizophrenic. When the schizophrenic paranoid individual begins to lose contact with reality and subsequently becomes unable to repress internal feelings and impulses, he becomes terrified. As a result, he projects unconscious thoughts and feelings onto someone else and then directs them back to himself. In the early stages of paranoia, the patient appears evasive, suspicious of others, and hostile. Delusions at the onset of the illness may involve religious ideas and feelings of exaggerated self-importance and grandeur. These delusions and hallucinations may be deceptively plausible or ridiculously bizarre. Persecutory ideas in which the patient is convinced that various forces are in operation against him dominate the characterization of the schizophrenic paranoid. Illustrative of this type of schizophrenia is Tony in *This Stranger My Son* and Deborah in *I Never Promised You a Rose Garden*. It is interesting that the main characters in both of these semiautobiographical books attributed their final breakdowns to stressful summer camp experiences.

Schizophrenia Hebephrenic. Hebephrenia, derived from the Greek word meaning *youthful mind*, utilizes primarily the defense mech-

anism of regression. By means of this defense mechanism, the patient may revert to a time when his world was secure. This type of patient illustrates a severe disintegration in personality. The readily distinguishable symptoms include inappropriate laughter and giggling, silly and childish behavior, facial grimaces, and bizarre language. In addition, a wide range of mannerisms, gestures, posturings, and attitudes may be present.

Lisa, the young adolescent who talks in rhymes in *Lisa and David,*[5] exemplifies the hebephrenic type. Her behavior at age thirteen is described as:

She hopped around the room, first on one foot, then on the other. On her left foot she always said, "sow," and on her right foot, "cow." She sat down on the floor each time she said, "They sat, they sat." But in seconds she was up again—hopping around the room, and in a loud, clear, high-pitched voice, saying, "A cow, a cow; a sow, a sow— black, black, black, black, black, black, black, black." Her voice changed. She was shrieking now. Then she sat down, held her head with her hands, and moved it up and back, moaning softly, "Dark, dark, dark, dark, dark—so, so, so, so dark."

The nonsense phrases repeated over and over by the hebephrenic are called word salads. While a phrase may hold little meaning for the listener, the utterer may be driven by a definite perseverative thought. One patient kept babbling, "One and one equals three." The therapist, in accordance with institutional philosophy, continuously challenged this falsehood with "That doesn't make sense; one and one are two." After months of therapy, the patient finally explained, "One man and one woman make a baby which makes three."

Schizophrenia Undifferentiated. The category of schizophrenia undifferentiated includes those cases whose exact nature cannot be determined or classified readily into any of the accepted categories. When a condition occurs in which a combination or an overlapping of symptoms exists, a diagnosis of schizophrenia

5. Theodore Isaac Rubin, *Lisa and David* (New York: The Macmillan Company, 1961).

undifferentiated is made. This condition has two phases, acute and chronic. A diagnosis of schizophrenia acute undifferentiated is made when the symptoms appear suddenly and disappear in a brief period of time. This category is utilized when the psychiatrist is unable to understand the patient, when the progress of the disease is unknown, or when the nature of the patient's defense mechanisms cannot be discerned. Jordi, the boy described in the opening passage of this chapter, illustrates this type.

Techniques for Working with Schizophrenic Children

Wolman[6] cites four principles which guide work with schizophrenic children: (1) graded reversal of deterioration, (2) constructive progress; (3) education toward reality; and (4) directive guidance. Under the first principle, he emphasizes: *We do not remove, take apart, or take away whatever neurotic defenses the schizophrenic child possesses. We build upon what we find.* It is essential that the child not feel disapproval and not be criticized for acting like a baby. The growth process is likened to the normal child's transition from a nipple to a cup. The nipple is not taken away, but the cup is made as attractive as possible. For a while, the child uses both and gradually he rejects the nipple. The principle of constructive progress implies the addition of new, more mature, and tempting elements to life. Since the schizophrenic child is afraid of growing up, he must be lured and/or bribed into accepting adolescence and adulthood.

Since schizophrenic children typically are trying to escape reality through withdrawal, no therapeutic procedure is more important than reality testing. This necessitates acquainting the child with the physical and social environment and shifting his attention from the inner world of fantasy toward the real world of happenings. Physical education, since the nor-

Figure 26.2. Helping the disturbed child to cope with fear.

mal child's world centers about play, is tremendously important in this process. When the child tries to attribute monsterlike qualities to playground apparatus or magical powers to a jiggler or ball, as Jordi does in the opening paragraph, the physical educator must convince him of the true nature of the things about him. It is wrong to *play along* with the fantasy of an emotionally disturbed child. Likewise, the educator should not *play along* with hallucinations nor ask questions pertaining to them, thereby appearing to be interested. Recommended responses to hallucinations are: "You know that is not true" or "That doesn't make sense."

Directive guidance, the fourth principle, emphasizes the importance of telling the child the difference between right and wrong rather than hoping he will learn for himself in a laissez faire environment. The schizophrenic child, to become whole, must become a well-adjusted adult in a *given* society. He must believe in the value of rules and laws and be

6. Benjamin B. Wolman, *Children Without Childhood* (New York: Grune and Stratton, 1970), pp. 194-196.

capable of accepting the power figures in our society: umpires, policemen, teachers, and administrators. Helping the child to understand the structure of games and the importance of rules and penalties in facilitating good play is often a first step toward wellness.

Schizophrenic children do not respond well to firm discipline as do neurotic and normal children. They are terrified by external power, both real and imagined. Wolman[7] states:

A schizophrenic child becomes more paranoid when treated with firmness. He considers it proof of his paranoid ideas. But a loving, soothing attitude of a familiar, affectionate adult will bring him back to normal behavior.

Whereas normal children may feel hostile to authority figures, they can do so without acting out and without excessive guilt. In schizophrenic children even small bits of criticism may elicit destructive behavior. The physical educator should understand that hostility is basically a protective reaction of the organism to danger. The schizophrenic feels much more endangered by criticism and/or even helpful suggestions than can be imagined. Yet he must be given firm limits. An important part of his reality testing is the growing knowledge that there are adults who do not get angry when he misbehaves. The physical educator must combine friendliness and warmth with consistent enforcement of limits. Should a temper tantrum occur, it is better not to try to talk over the noise. A child driven by panic or rage is out of contact with reality and reasoning will not help. Sometimes there is no alternative but physical restraint in stopping aggressive behavior.

The following suggestions may help the teacher in working with schizophrenic and/or overly aggressive children.

1. Avoid conflict with the child which might cause temper tantrums. Overlook minor transgressions. Each temper tantrum is a step backward.
2. If the child becomes aggressive, try to distract him. Get him interested in some new toy or game.
3. Should a child strike or bite you, do not become ruffled or angry. In a cool, calculated manner, say something like "Ouch, that hurt! What in the world did I do to cause you to bite me?"
4. Do not show fear or confusion about the child's behavior. Schizophrenics tend to be extrasensitive to the feelings of teachers and may use such information to manipulate the adult. Never say, for instance, "I just don't understand you" or "I don't know what to do with you."
5. Do not use threats of physical violence or abandonment. Do not punish the child, since punishment reinforces paranoid beliefs.
6. Reward good behavior and structure the situation so as to avoid bad behavior.
7. Create situations for learning to relate socially to others in individual and dual sports before pushing the child into the complex human relationships of team sport strategy.
8. Structure play groups and/or class squads very carefully, ascertaining that a balance is maintained between the number of aggressive and passive children. The school psychologist may help the physical educator with this endeavor.

Techniques for Working with Depressed Children and Adolescents

Extreme depression can characterize any age group. Depressive symptoms are present in approximately 40 percent of the adolescent suicide attempts. The incidence of suicide is rising among young children as well as teenagers where it is already the third leading cause of death in this country.

7. Benjamin B. Wolman, *Children Without Childhood* (New York: Grune and Stratton, 1970), p. 20.

The depressed child typically reveals social withdrawal, loss of initiative, a decrease in appetite, and difficulty in sleeping. He generally has a self-depreciating attitude, believing that he is bad and wishing to punish himself. Suicide, truancy, self-destructive behaviors like head banging and disobedience may all be behavioral equivalents of depression.

More than anything else, depressed persons need to be kept active. Yet they often refuse to participate in physical activity. They have no desire to learn new skills since life is not worth living and they intend to kill themselves anyway. Some depressed persons will sit for days, crying and thinking of methods of suicide. Whereas most of us are inclined to sympathize with anyone who cries, it is best to display a rough, noncommittal exterior. For instance, the patient may be asked, "Do you play golf?" The typical response is a self-depreciating, "I'm not any good" or "I'm not good enough to play with so-and-so." Instead of trying to build up his ego, as a teacher might do with a well person, it is best to agree with a statement like "That's probably true!" In other words, the teacher should mirror or restate the patient's thoughts rather than contradicting him. Psychologists concur that praise and compliments serve only to make the truly depressed person feel more unworthy. They feel guilty when others say good things about them and/or are nice to them.

Severe depression is often treated by electric shock therapy (EST) and antidepressant medications. The teacher or therapist cooperates with the psychiatric staff by maintaining a full schedule of physical activities for the depressed patient who generally follows instructions although he will not engage in recreational activities voluntarily. One of his greatest problems is learning to recognize and cope with the anger which he turns inward toward himself, thereby causing the state of depression. If he can be made angry by an external force and helped to express this anger outwardly instead of repressing it, a major goal is accomplished. Situations must be devised to make him angry enough to risk standing up for himself, a first step back to self-respect and self-love. In one institution this was accomplished by awaking five severely depressed patients before dawn and insisting that they were scheduled for a 6 a.m. swimming class. Without breakfast, they were ushered into an ice cold outdoor pool and told they must stay in the water. In addition to these unpleasantries, the therapist scolded and ridiculed them. Typically the depressed person submits to such a program, but if the unpleasantries are intense enough, there may be mild protests. When these are autocratically ignored, real anger can sometimes be evoked. Whatever techniques are used, the teacher or therapist must work closely with the psychiatric staff.

Each depressed person is uniquely different from others, and no single approach can be recommended. Physical education and recreation personnel should remember, however, that their primary role is to engage the patient in activity, not to listen to sad stories and self-criticism. Other staff members are employed specifically to listen and conduct verbal therapy.

Autism

Whereas severely disturbed older children are described as psychotic or schizophrenic, young children with aberrant behavior are often called *autistic.* Used in psychiatry to mean withdrawn and self-absorbed, *autism* comes from the Greek word *autos,* meaning self. Kanner,[8] in 1943, was the first person to describe autistic children as a group. Since then, a growing body of literature has resulted in much controversy. The causes of autism remain unknown, and the values of various therapeutic techniques are highly speculative.

8. L. Kanner, "Autistic Disturbances of Affective Contact," *Nervous Child* (April, 1943), pp. 217-250.

In most cases autistic behavior is diagnosed between ages two and five, and some kind of therapy is begun. Children may be autistic from birth, but few parents recognize symptoms until age two or so. Autistic children typically remain frozen at an infantile stage of emotional and intellectual development or regress back to the primitive personality structure of toddlers. The common denominator in all infantile autism is the inability to relate to people. When picked up, they do not cuddle nor do they seem to respond to the human voice and facial expression.

Characteristics of autism are

1. Withdrawal from, or failure to become involved with, people.
2. Muteness or inability to use speech for communication.
3. Unusual bodily movements and peculiar mannerisms.
4. Abnormal response to one or more types of sensory stimuli, usually sound.
5. Pathological resistance to change manifested by observance of rituals, excessive preoccupation with certain objects without regard for their accepted functions, and emotional outbursts when sameness of environment is threatened.
6. Apparent intellectual retardation.

More often than not, the autistic child—at least in the early years of diagnosis—does not speak. Nor does he allow the teacher to establish eye contact. Indeed he gives no evidence of recognizing the presence of another human being. Physical education consists mostly of the teacher following the child about the play area in a vain attempt to establish some kind of rapport. This one-to-one activity may persist for many months before the child begins to relate to the teacher.

Bettelheim and others emphasize that the major objective in working with autistic children is to provide an environment of potentially positive valence in which nothing is forced on the child.[9] For years he has functioned mechanically; as the child begins to consciously act, he must be reassured that it is he alone who has power over his own behavior: eating, moving the bowels, playing, or talking. This helps to explain why often his first positive acts are the reverse of the teacher's wishes. Illustrative of this is the large number of autistic children who give up toilet training in their first steps toward wellness. To do even this, they must receive encouragement—but not too much lest they feel pushed. The role of the teacher in such cases is to subtly encourage the child into defiance.

Some physical educators, accustomed to praising children for positive acts, may find such approaches difficult to implement. The importance of seeking further training in psychology cannot be overemphasized. The autistic child is fragile, and his progress can be inhibited months because one unknowledgeable staff member scolds him for dirtying his pants or expresses too much enthusiasm over a small achievement.

Aberrant motor behavior displayed by autistic children includes rocking, head rolling and banging, and tapping or twiddling with the fingers. These acts often constitute the sum total of the autistic child's experience, his maximum ability for dealing with reality. Thus it is important that the teacher not interfere. Bettelheim recommends that, however difficult a symptom is to accept, the worker must communicate his respect for the child's means of coping with the world. Whenever possible, he seeks to help the child improve on these spontaneous idiosyncracies rather than drop them. For instance, a child who twiddles only his fingers may be encouraged to twiddle objects.

While the schizophrenic may have a distorted body image, the autistic child has never formed an intrapsychic representation of

9. Bruno Bettelheim, *The Empty Fortress* (New York: The Macmillan Co., 1967), p. 93.

his own body. Kalish [10] emphasizes the importance of helping him form a body image through movement therapy which utilizes rhythms, vocalizations, and body actions on a primitive sensory-motor level. The progress of an autistic child is very slow. Kalish, for instance, describes sessions with a child over a period of three years. Several months of this time were spent simply in establishing rapport and building trust. Initially the five-year-old tolerated little or no physical contact. She hovered in one corner of the room and occupied herself with perseverative head movements. Occasionally she would burst out of her corner, jump up and down three or four times in a stylized ritual, and then return to the corner. Never did she stray more than a few feet from this spot. Kalish [11] describes her method of establishing contact as follows:

My first approach to her was to make use of the diagonal spatial path from the opposite corner of the room. Moving tentatively and in an indirect line, but toward Laura, I tried to incorporate her finger and hand rhythms into my feet and body movements. I did not venture past "her" side of the center of the room. Taking my cues from her, I would suddenly jump up and down, using her timing and return to the corner.

For many sessions, she gave only a fleeting glance, but as she seemed to get "used" to my presence, her glance was more sustained looking, at a distance. I moved closer to her corner, then back to my own, until now we shared all the space in the room, sometimes together and sometimes separately.

Approximately two years later, after sessions were increased to three or four times a week, Laura was willing to sit on the therapist's lap and able to concentrate on movement patterns in a mirror. She was still unable to imitate movements but was making definite progress toward this end. One of the most significant changes was her interest in the mirror. It seemed as though Laura was discovering her body for the first time.

Adler, [12] another dance therapist, has developed a beautiful 29 minute film depicting work with an autistic child. Adler, like Kalish, is concerned with helping the autistic child establish self-identity. Her philosophy is summarized in the following paragraph: [13]

I am impressed with the simplicity of Ronald Laing's statement: "the sense of identity requires the existence of another by whom one is known." But of course, the difficulty is—How to know another and How to let another know you. My premise, at this point, is, if the other is a severely disturbed child, my "meness" can only be effective in developing her identity if it is genuinely reflective of what she knows best—her tiny, perseverative intensely physical world. Therefore, at this time, in my own evolution, I am deeply invested in providing an opportunity for a disturbed child to BE—to BE herself literally, with all of her "bizarre" and "crazy" mannerisms and expressions. I begin there, by reflecting her world, primarily on a body level. I try to "speak" her language by moving with her, as she moves in space. In the beginning, there is much direct imitation, which by definition, means delayed response on my part. However, as she permits my presence, and as the trust develops, I find that the one-sidedness falls away and a more mutual dialogue begins to creep into being; we become synchronous.

Movement or dance therapy appears the best way to work with autistic children who characteristically are mute or severely retarded in language development. Even after learning to talk, they stubbornly reverse pronouns to avoid using "I." A typical verbal exchange might be: Teacher: "Do you want to jump on the trampoline?" Child: "You want to jump," meaning "I want to jump." The physical edu-

10. Beth Kalish, "Body Movement Therapy for Autistic Children," *American Dance Therapy Association Proceedings* (Third Annual Conference, Baltimore: ADTA, 1968), p. 51.

11. Beth Kalish, "Body Movement Therapy for Autistic Children" *American Dance Therapy Association Proceedings* (Third Annual Conference, Baltimore: ADTA, 1968), p. 56.

12. The film "Looking At Me" can be rented through University of California Extension Media Center, 2223 Fulton Street, Berkeley, California 94720.

13. Janet Adler, "The Study of An Autistic Child," *American Dance Therapy Association Proceedings* (Third Annual Conference, Baltimore: ADTA, 1968), p. 43.

cator should not try to correct this speech pattern. The avoidance of "I" is believed to be either a denial of selfhood or an absence of awareness of self, while the substitution of "you" shows some awareness of the selfhood of others. Autistic children, like normal two-year-olds, also avoid the word *yes*, responding negatively to both invitations and commands whether they mean it or not.

Theories vary as to whether autistic children do not relate to human beings or simply do so negatively. Characteristically the persons they treat as nonexistent feel rejected and find it difficult to work with autistic children over a period of months. Objectives which might be accomplished through physical education activities remain largely unexplored.

Coping Techniques for Normal and Handicapped Persons

This chapter has dealt sequentially with the behavior disorders of childhood, various forms of mental illness, and the developmental deficit of autism. It is important that every physical educator play his part in the early detection of emotional problems and the prevention of mental illness. The handicapped child has more problems to cope with than his nonhandicapped peers. Reality may be unacceptable or even intolerable. O'Gorman [14] suggests that there are four ways of coping with an unwanted reality situation: (1) the child may seek to alter or influence the situation by appropriate action—fleeing, fighting, enduring, manipulating; (2) he may try to prevent this and similar unwanted situations by insisting on sameness in all aspects of his environment, his people, or toys, or space; (3) he may try to make reality acceptable by distortion, fantasy, delusion, or hallucination; and (4) he withdraws, living as far as possible within himself, ignoring or failing to respond to sensory stimuli or to make emotional relationships. The physical educator must be

aware of the coping techniques of his pupils and know the persons in the school system qualified to offer psychological help.

The following review of commonly used defense mechanisms serves to increase awareness that *all behavior* is caused. A limited use of defense mechanisms is good and may contribute to good mental health. When applied too frequently, however, defense mechanisms become signals that help is needed.

1. *Compensation* is a mechanism whereby failings in one area are offset by real or imagined successes in another. The poorly skilled child may compensate for his awkwardness by becoming the best reader in the class. Persons who are aggressive and domineering may be compensating for feelings of inadequacy.

2. *Fantasy* is the use of daydreaming, play acting, and related activities to escape situations that are unpleasant, frustrating, or boring. The handicapped child may, for instance, fantasize that he will grow up to be a professional athlete or ballet dancer.

3. *Fixation* is the cessation of personality development. Adult methods of coping with frustration and controlling emotions are never learned, and the person continues to function as a child in certain situations. Overdependence on the mother is a form of fixation.

4. *Identification* is a mechanism whereby a person associates himself with another individual, usually someone whom he admires and/or idealizes. In childhood and adolescence, it is often akin to hero worship. Some persons tend to identify with underdogs.

5. *Projection* is a mechanism for shifting responsibility and/or blame for an act or thought to someone else. "The Devil made me do it" is a humorous attempt at

14. Gerald O'Gorman, *The Nature of Childhood Autism* (New York: Appleton-Century-Crofts, 1970), p. 24.

projection. Attributing problems to minority groups in a scapegoating manner is projection as is blaming the teacher for a failing grade.

6. *Rationalization* involves making excuses and/or thinking up plausible reasons for behavior rather than revealing the true cause. It is unconscious and tends to relieve persons of guilt, depression, and other negative feelings about an act. The college student with low average intelligence may rationalize that he did not study sufficiently when he receives a C grade rather than accept his inability to perform better.

7. *Reaction-formation* is exemplified when a person exhibits behavior exactly the opposite of socially unacceptable or disturbing inner feelings. The overaggressive boy may, for instance, fear that he is a sissy or weakling. The overly friendly or protective person may, in actuality, feel hostile toward the object of his attention. The asthmatic child may persist in doing the things which cause his allergies.

8. *Regression* is a return to the past, usually a more infantile manner of coping such as crying or refusal to make decisions. Temper tantrums, tattling or blaming others, and playing make-believe can all be modes of regression.

9. *Repression* is the subconscious attempt to hide a problem. It is a means of forgetting pain, guilt, shame, and other feelings of anxiety. Unfortunately repressed thought and feelings are often brought to surface by incidents similar to those which caused the original feelings.

10. *Sublimation* is the mechanism whereby sex drives and other primitive impulses or feelings which cannot be realized at the moment are channeled into socially acceptable activities.

11. *Substitution* is a form of compensation in which one goal, success, or outcome is accepted in place of a less attainable one. The handicapped child may accept the role of team manager in lieu of a place on the varsity lineup.

12. *Suppression* is the conscious effort to dismiss undesirable thoughts and impulses from the mind. A person might, for instance, suppress suicidal thoughts, the desire to hurt someone, or a wish to get even.

Organizations

1. National Society for Autistic Children (NSAC), 169 Tampa Avenue, Albany, New York 12208
2. American Psychological Association, 1200 17th Street N.W., Washington, D. C. 20036
3. American Schizophrenia Foundation, Box 160, Ann Arbor, Michigan 48107.

References

American Psychiatric Association. *Diagnostic and Statistical Manual of Mental Disorders.* Third edition. Washington, D. C.: The Association, 1968.

Kugelmass, I. Newton. *The Autistic Child.* Springfield, Illinois: Charles C Thomas, 1970.

O'Gorman, Gerald. *The Nature of Childhood Autism.* Second edition. New York: Appleton-Century-Crofts, 1970.

Wolman, Benjamin B. *Children Without Childhood.* New York: Grune and Stratton, 1970.

Periodicals

Journals printed by the American Psychological Association include:

1. *American Psychologist* (monthly)
2. *Contemporary Psychology* (monthly)
3. *Journal of Abnormal Psychology* (bimonthly)
4. *Journal of Applied Psychology* (bimonthly)
5. *Journal of Comparative and Physiological Psychology* (bimonthly)
6. *Journal of Consulting and Clinical Psychology* (bimonthly)
7. *Journal of Educational Psychology* (bimonthly)
8. *Journal of Experimental Psychology* (monthly)
9. *Journal of Personality and Social Psychology* (monthly)
10. *Psychological Abstracts* (monthly)
11. *Psychological Bulletin* (monthly)
12. *Psychological Review* (bimonthly)
13. *Developmental Psychology* (bimonthly)

Rehabilitation Counseling Bulletin. Published quarterly by the American Rehabilitation Counseling Association, 1607 New Hampshire Avenue, N.W., Washington, D. C. 20009.

Schizophrenia. Published quarterly by the American Schizophrenia Foundation, Box 160, Ann Arbor, Michigan 48107.

Mental Hygiene. Published quarterly by The National Association for Mental Health, Inc., Suite 1300, 10 Columbus Circle, New York, New York 10019.

Crime and Delinquency. Published quarterly by National Council on Crime and Delinquency, 44 East 23rd Street, New York, New York 10010.

American Dance Therapy Association Newsletter. Published by the ADTA and edited by Mrs. Penny Bernstein, 310 North Lang Avenue, Pittsburgh, Pennsylvania 15208.

Devereux Dial. Published monthly except for July and August by The Devereux Foundation, Devon, Pennsylvania.

Therapeutic Recreation Journal. Published quarterly by the National Therapeutic Recreation Society, 1601 North Kent Street, Arlington, Virginia 22209.

Name Index

Subject Index

general, 66, 68, 159, 160, 270, 274, 304, 324, 409, 470
static, 75, 149, 150, 167, 319, 323
tests, 162, 167, 169, 177, 178
Ball handling, 70, 166, 175, 176, 190, 191, 197, 254, 256, 305, 344, 345, 410, 411, 476, 480, 481
Barrel chest, 102
Beevor sign, 106
Behavior disorders, 490-92
Behavior modification, 299, 396, 478, 479
Bicycling, 222, 429, 438
Bill of Rights, Handicapped, 370
Binocular coordination, 197, 201
Binocular fusion, 201
Biofeedback, 229
Biographies, 315, 328, 338, 339, 420, 429, 432, 488
Birth defects, 113, 117, 334, 372-79, 442-51, 462
Blind and visually impaired, 330-48
characteristics, 338-43
diagnostic background information, 330-38
education, 339-46
general, 46, 289, 293, 454, 457
history, 21
instructional patterns, 346-47
Blindisms, 339, 340
Blue baby, 445
Body awareness, 227, 230, 251-57, 271-72, 277, 302, 472, 473, 474
Body image, 77, 83, 84, 302-3, 342-43
Body mechanics, 15, 50, 233
Body types, 77, 82, 83. See somatotypes
Bone-conduction losses, 310, 315-18
Bowlegs (genu varum), 111, 112
Braces, 93, 98, 109, 373, 382, 391, 408, 409, 416, 418
Brailling, 342, 345
Brain-injured, 233-35, 296-308, 406
Breathing patterns, 228, 325, 350-52, 402, 409, 425, 468
Bronchitis, 350, 367
Bunion (hallux valgus), 118
Buphthalamus, 335
Bureau of Education for the Handicapped, 20, 27
Burns, 372, 379-83

Callus, 117, 118
Caloric cost, 394, 456
Camps, 347, 457, 458
Cardiovascular disease, 222, 287, 425, 441-52, 454

Cardiovascular endurance, 208, 213, 214, 215, 216, 217, 218, 219, 220, 221, 222, 223, 224
CARIH (Children's Asthma Research Institute and Hospital), 367
Case studies
cerebral palsy, 416-19
multiple sclerosis, 428
muscular dystrophy, 425-26
Casts, 98, 373, 374, 376
Cataracts, 336
Catastrophic reaction, 397
Catatonia, 493, 494
Center of buoyancy, 277-78
Center of gravity, 132, 324
Central processing, 204, 205, 336-37
Cerea flexibility, 493
Cerebral Palsy, 405-20
case studies, 416-19
characteristics, 406-13
education, 415-19
general, 73, 131, 286, 287, 289
reflexes, 413-15
Chorea, 449
Choroiditis, 338
Chronic Obstructive Pulmonary Diseases (COPD), 350, 367, 368
Ciliary muscles, 198, 199, 202, 332, 333, 337
Circuit training, 218-20
Cleft lip (cleft palate), 372, 374
Clonus, 400, 407, 430
Club foot, 117, 372, 373, 374, 469. See talipes
Coloboma, 335
Color blindness, 337
Coma, 457
Communication process, 158, 465
Congenital hip dislocation, 372, 375, 376
Conjunctiva (pink eye), 338
Convergence, 202, 203
Convulsions, 456, 462
Convulsive disorders, 398-404
aggravating factors, 401-2
education, 402-3
types of seizures, 400-1
Coordination
bilateral, 155, 162
eye-hand, 162, 225
general, 163, 164, 225, 302, 305, 493
Coping techniques, 500-1
Cornea, 332, 333, 338
Cornelia de Lange syndrome, 462, 463
Corrective physical education, 14, 15, 17
Corrective shoes, 374

Macular degeneration, 334, 335
Mainstreaming (integration), 21, 25, 30, 57, 292, 293, 325, 327, 339, 346-47, 348, 379, 397, 403, 464, 465, 487
Manualism, 309, 326
Marsden ball, 194
Martian canals, 159
Mastoiditis, 318
Meningitis, 315, 318, 323
Mental illness, 389-502
Mental retardation, 459-88
  AC/FMR Standards, 28
  general, 32, 51, 131, 132, 148, 202
  levels, 460-62
  medical classifications, 462-64
  mild, 464-65
  moderate, 33, 465-71
  profound, 471-81
  severe, 471-81
  Special Olympics, 8, 27, 41, 42, 43, 482-83
  tests, 176, 484-86
Metatarsalgia, 117
Metatarsus varus, 374
Microcephalus, 463
Midline problems, 303-4
Mild retardation, 464-65
Mobility training, 344, 345
Moderate retardation, 465-71
Mongolism (Down's syndrome), 148, 149, 176, 262, 462, 467-71
Morquio's disease, 378
Morton's toe, 117
Mosaicism, 467
Mosher exercise, 105
Motor characteristics, 305-6, 322-25, 339-43, 395-96, 402-3, 407-11, 423, 425, 427, 431, 435-39, 466-70, 477, 493, 498
Movement education, 122
Movement elements, 240-43
Movement exploration
  in water, 262, 269-74, 279, 281-84
  on land, 239, 240, 241, 242, 243, 247, 249, 251-56, 303
Movement patterns
  ascending and descending stairs, 133-36, 385, 423, 438
  bobbing, 278-79
  crawling, 125, 389
  creeping, 123, 125, 389
  finning, 279-80
  floating, 275-78
  galloping, 150, 242
  hopping, 137, 148, 149, 172, 242, 470
  hurdling, 136, 137
  jumping, 4, 125, 137, 139-48, 171, 173, 175, 176, 223, 225, 242, 272, 273, 279, 470
  kicking, 264-67
  leaping, 136, 137, 150, 169, 177, 178, 242
  rolling, 121, 125, 145, 147, 281, 284, 285, 474
  running, 132-34, 221-23, 242, 270
  sculling, 279-80
  skipping, 150, 242
  sliding, 150
  swimming, 260-84
  walking, 126, 127, 130, 150, 175, 177, 221-23, 273-75, 323, 325, 342-44, 470
Multidisciplinary, 155, 194, 291, 293
Multiple sclerosis, 131, 336, 427-29
Muscular atrophy, 425, 426
Muscular dystrophy, 422-26
Myelin, 427
Myopia, 200, 335, 470

NART, 25
National Foundation for Progressive Relaxation, 236
Nearsightedness, 200, 335, 470
Nerves, cranial, 198, 332, 336, 337
Neurofibromatosis, 464
Neuromuscular tension, 228, 229, 240
Nonambulatory, 389
Nonverbal communication, 242, 243, 246-54, 256-57, 320-22
Normalization, 25
Novels, 49, 261, 305, 314, 328, 335, 371, 373, 379, 420, 432, 488
NTRS, 25, 27, 502
Nystagmus, 335, 337

Obesity, 83, 100, 387, 391-96
Object constancy, 156, 205
Obstacle courses, 224
Occlusion, 202, 203
Ocular
  control, 162
  fixation, 194
  muscles, 198, 201, 202
  pursuits, 162, 194, 206
  tracking, 194, 202, 203
Oculo-Rotor, 195, 197
Operant conditioning (shaping), 478, 479
Ophthalmia, 338
Ophthalmologist, 194
Optic nerve disease, 336, 337
Optometrist, 194, 195
Oralism, 326

Organizations
  aquatics, 289
  arthritis, 439
  blindness, 348
  Cerebral Palsy, 419
  crippled, 396-97
  dance, 279, 502
  deaf, 327
  diabetes, 458
  Easter Seal, 396
  epilepsy, 403
  heart, 451
  learning disabilities, 307
  mental illness, 502
  mental retardation, 487
  muscular conditions, 431
  respiratory disorders, 368-69
  therapies, 496, 502
  wheelchair, 397
Orthopedically handicapped, 370-90
  amputations, 383-85
  bone infections, 385-86
  congenital defects, 372-79
  nonambulatory, 389
  osteochondroses, 386-88
  thermal injuries, 379-83
Orthoptic training, 202, 203
Osgood-Schlatter, 388
Osteochondroses, 372, 386-88
Osteodystrophy, 378
Osteogenesis Imperfecta, 378, 379
Osteomyelitis, 385, 386
Other health impaired
  asthma, 390-96
  hemophilia, 390-91
  kidney disorders, 390
  obesity, 391-406
  Sickle-cell disease, 391
  urinary disorders, 390
Overload principle, 213, 214

Papillomas, 118
Paralysis, 131, 427
Paranoia, 494
Paraplegic, 40, 103, 407
Parkinson's disease, 132, 429-31
Patent ductus arteriosus, 442, 445
PEPI, 30-31
Perception
  auditory, 66, 157
  definition, 155
  haptic, 157, 158, 159
  kinesthetic, 157, 160, 161
  proprioception, 159, 160

  tactile, 157, 159
  vestibular, 157, 160
  visual, 156-57
Perceptual-Motor
  screening, 181-82
  testing, 164-81, 205
  theory, 155-64
  training, 182-91
Perceptual-motor match, 162
Periodicals
  arthritis, 440
  asthma, 379
  blindness, 348
  cardiovascular, 451
  crippled, 396, 420
  deafness, 327-28
  diabetes, 458
  epilepsy, 404
  learning disabilities, 308
  mental illness, 502
  mental retardation, 488
Perkins Institute, 315, 330
Perseveration, 229, 301, 471
Perthes disease, 89, 386-88
Pes cavus (hollow foot), 117
Pes planus, 115, 116, 479
Phenylketonuria (PKU), 464
Phi phenomenon, 157
Photophobia, 335
Physical education
  criteria (classification), 71, 72
  definition, 30
  elementary, 49
  instructional patterns, 57
  objectives, 30-31
  relationship to perceptual-motor training, 182
  scope, 31, 49
Physically handicapped, 370-90
  amputations, 383-85
  bone infections, 385-86
  congenital defects, 372-79
  general, 38, 131, 215, 222, 260, 278, 287
  history, 22, 26
  nonambulatory, 389
  osteochondroses, 386-88
  thermal injuries, 379-83
Physical therapy, 14, 15, 26
Pigeon chest, 103, 469
Plantar warts, 118
Poliomyelitis, 26, 27, 98, 427
Polymyositis, 427
Postural drainage, 366
Postures
  adults, 86, 93, 96, 97, 99, 100, 111

anatomical reference points, 80
early childhood, 79, 84, 101, 102, 104
elementary, 101, 322
examination, 69, 79, 81
grid, 79
obese, 395
photography, 79, 80, 84, 86, 93, 96, 97, 99,
    100, 101, 104, 111
screening, 78, 79
Postures, imitation of, 162, 166
Pott's disease, 87, 88
Practice (mass, distributed), 72
Pranayanas, 232
Presbycusis, 319
Presbyopia, 198
Prescription
    formations, 184
    general, 20, 25, 64-76
    interval training prescription, 215-18
Principles
    dance therapy, 256-57
    extraneous stimuli control, 298, 299
    general teaching, 74
        instructional stimulus enhancement, 299
    normalization, 25
    opposition, 70, 91, 123
    overload, 213
    reciprocal innervation, 85
    reducing hyperactivity, 234-35, 298-99
    reinforcement, 299, 496
    space reduction, 298
    specificity, 225
    structure, 32, 74, 298, 496
    teaching emotionally disturbed, 495
    warm-ups, 224-25
Profound retardation, 471-81
Programming
    accountability, 10-11
    generic, 21
    model, 5-6
    problems, 6-7
    size, 5, 7, 72
Progressive approximation, 171
Progressive Resistance Exercises (PRE), 214, 215
Pronated feet, 114, 116-17, 479
Proprioception, 66, 159, 160
Prostheses, 383-85
Psychiatric disorders, 464, 492-500
Public Law, 28, 94-149

Reaction formation, 354, 355, 501
Recreation, 43-47
Reflexes, 407, 413, 414, 415, 416, 427
Refraction, 197, 199, 202, 203

Relaxation, 227-36, 370, 409, 411
Respiratory system, 451
Retina, 334-35, 457
Retinal inhibition, 157
Retinoblastoma, 335
Retrocochlear hearing, 315, 318, 319
Retrolental Fibroplasia, 334
Retropulsion, 431
Rheumatic fever, 442, 448-51
Rheumatism, 434
Rheumatoid arthritis, 434-39
Rhythm, 66, 244, 245, 246, 257, 470, 478
Rickets, 102, 103, 379
Rigidity, 411, 430, 431
Round shoulders, 75, 83, 86, 99-102
Rubella, 314, 327, 335, 463

Saccadic movements, 198
Scheuermann's disease, 89, 388
Schizophrenia, 492-96
Scissors gait, 131, 409
Scoliosis, 93, 94, 95, 96, 97, 98, 99
Scotoma, 336, 337
Scout's pace, 222, 223
Screening
    auditory, 310, 311
    basic movement, 475-80
    fitness, 208-10, 484-86
    nonambulatory strengths, 389
    perceptual motor, 181-82
    posture, 78-79
    pulmonary efficiency, 356
    visual, 155, 203, 204, 330, 334
Seizures, 399-404, 406, 462
Self operations control, 230
Self-testing
    in water, 269-76, 282-84
    on land, 179-84
Sensorineural hearing, 315-19
Sensory-motor training, 471-75
Sequencing, 301
Severe retardation, 471-81
Shapes, 183-88, 271-72
Shaping
    in dance, 241
    in mental retardation, 478
Shoulder height, 98, 99, 101
Sickle-cell disease, 391
Sight, 194
Signing, 309, 326
Sit-ups, 6, 18, 208
Skin, 118, 380, 468
Snellen Chart, 194
Social imperception, 301, 319-20, 339-40

scanning, 203, 204
   tracking, 168, 188-91, 194, 203, 204

Warm-ups, 224, 225, 301, 410
Water play, 159
Weight lifting, 214, 215
Weight reduction, 394-96
Werdnig-Hoffman disease, 426
Wheelchair, 40, 41, 215, 222, 397
Winged scapulae, 101, 102

Yoga, 232, 233